ABRAHAM ON TRIAL

ABRAHAM

ON TRIAL

THE SOCIAL LEGACY
OF BIBLICAL MYTH

Carol Delaney

PRINCETON UNIVERSITY PRESS · PRINCETON, NEW JERSEY

Library of Congress Cataloging-in-Publication Data

Delaney, Carol Lowery, 1940–
Abraham on trial : the social legacy of biblical myth / Carol Delaney.
p.   cm.
Includes bibliographical references and index.
ISBN 0-691-05985-3 (hardcover : alk. paper)
1. Isaac (Biblical patriarch)—Sacrifice.   2. Child sacrifice—
Religious aspects—Comparative studies.   3. Abraham (Biblical patriarch)
4. Bible. O.T. Genesis XXII, 1–19—Criticism, interpretation, etc.—
History.   5. Koran. Surat al-Ṣāffāt—Criticism, interpretation,
etc.—History.   6. Fatherhood—Religious aspects—Comparative studies.
7. Gender.   8. Ishmael (Biblical figure).   I. Title.
BS1238.S24D44   1998
222'.11068—dc21   98-12174

"The Story of Abraham" by Alicia Ostriker, which originally appeared
in 5 A.M. 2, no. 3 (1990), is reprinted with the permission of the author;
"Sarah's Choice" by Eleanor Wilmer, which originally appeared in Sarah's Choice,
The Phoenix Poets Series (Chicago: University of Chicago press, 1989),
pp. 21–24, is reprinted with the permission of the author.

Frontispiece and part title pages: Detail of a Rembrandt etching of
Abraham and Isaac, from a private collection.

This book has been composed in Sabon

http://pup.princeton.edu

Printed in the United States of America

1   3   5   7   9   10   8   6   4   2

To MY MOTHER,

MY DAUGHTER, AND

MY GRANDSON

and to all those without whose care

and protection none of us

would be here

To see what the writer makes

of Abraham is often to see most clearly

what the writer is trying to say.

S. SANDMEL, 1956:29

Contents

Illustrations

Acknowledgments

BECAUSE of the wide range this book traverses, I have relied upon numerous people for help in finding my way in different discourses and reference systems. First, I wish to thank members of the family and all the participants in the California trial—the attorneys, the judge, the psychiatrist, the translator, and the jurors. John Sullivan, a friend and a public defender in California, shared information and expertise and read drafts of the trial chapter. When she was a student at Harvard Law School, Megan Muir, now a Seattle attorney, discussed legal material with me and researched important documents in the law school library. When I was daunted by writing something so different from my usual subjects, Marcia Yudkin helped me over a writer's block. Paul Rock, professor of criminology at the London School of Economics, was an excellent critic of the trial chapter. His own work on trials and courts so closely paralleled my own that I felt less alone.

Without leave from Stanford and a research fellowship at Harvard Divinity School in 1992–93 the research for the chapters on archaeology and religious commentary would have taken much longer. I am exceedingly grateful for the opportunity to return to a place where I had studied (1973–76) and worked as assistant director of the Center for the Study of World Religions (1985–87) and where I knew the library well. The faculty, students, and staff were, as usual, interested, stimulating, and helpful. I especially thank Professor JoAnn Hackett for generously sharing her knowledge of the ancient Near East, for numerous references, and for informative, delightful discussions.

Several former graduate students at Harvard Divinity School need special note. Denise Buell, now assistant professor at Williams College, helped enormously with her mastery of Hebrew, Greek, and Latin and her deep knowledge of Judaism and Christianity during what is called the "intertestamental" period. Similar thanks are owed to Gene McAfee, a tutor at Lowell House, Harvard. Larry Wills, a professor at the Episcopal Divinity School, shared his enthusiasm and knowledge of Greek and early Christian society. The other research associates—Rosalind Shaw, Tal

Ilan, Hyun-kyung Chung, and Stephanie Jamison—provided stimulating discussions and conviviality during a long, cold, and lonely winter.

Tal Ilan showed me how to negotiate the labyrinthine system of rabbinic reference. Later, Howard Eilberg-Schwartz, formerly assistant professor of Jewish studies at Stanford, read a draft and corrected some dates and misrepresentations. Bob Gregg, the dean of Memorial Church at Stanford University and an expert on early Christianity, read a draft of the Christian chapter and encouraged my nonapologetic critique. The Muslim chapter was helpfully commented on by Gordon Newby, Bill Beeman, Saba Mahmood, and a number of respondents at the meetings of the American Academy of Religion, 1995, where I presented a summary.

Diane Jonte-Pace of Santa Clara University, whose expertise is in the field of psychoanalysis and religion, graciously read the Freud chapters. I also received comments and suggestions from Judith Van Herik, professor of religious studies at Penn State, who has, herself, written eloquently about Freud, femininity, and faith. Graduate students in my seminar, "Religion," helped me clarify my critique of Freud, and Bill Maurer, now assistant professor at the University of California, Irvine, helped me see that one chapter should become two.

I am also indebted to Sandra Razieli, who, during her fieldwork in Jerusalem, alerted me to some uses of the Abraham story and took the photograph of the Dome of the Rock; to Shari Seider, whose work among Orthodox Jews in Argentina provided insightful discussions about Judaism and nationalism; and to Stefan Helmreich who helped me think about the title and chapter headings. In the last stages, I benefited greatly from the comments of the reviewers, Bill Beeman, Jorunn Buckley, Gillian Feeley-Harnik, and Gordon Newby, who kindly revealed themselves to me, enabling us to discuss further their proposed revisions. Mary Murrell, my editor at Princeton, suffered through the whole process, providing inspiration, incisive criticism, and numerous clippings and references. Marsha Kunin did a superb job of copyediting the final manuscript. I have tried to accommodate their suggestions, but the mind truly does have a mind of its own and I could not always find the proper place for them. There is much that has been left out—otherwise the manuscript could easily have grown to a book for each chapter.

A fellowship at the Center for Advanced Study in the Behavioral Sciences (1996–97), partly funded by a grant from the Andrew W. Mellon Foundation, allowed me time to complete the book, which had languished due to a heavy teaching load. The interest and enthusiasm of the other fellows provided the fuel to get on with it and get it done. I am especially grateful to those who read and commented on drafts of chapters: Gillian Feeley-Harnik, Martin Green, Susan Okin, Paul Rock, and the Family and Children group. I wish also to thank several members of the Center staff: Patrick Goebel, the computer wizard, taught me how to operate my new computer and was there when I or it got stuck; Kathleen Much edited the penultimate draft; and Virginia MacDonald helped with some of the word processing.

Finally, I wish to thank my daughter, Elizabeth Quaratiello, who is, herself, a gifted writer and editor. Her reading of an early draft helped with the subsequent ones. She also contributed by giving birth to her first child, my first grandchild. During the hard work of writing, they were a most delightful distraction and helped me keep some needed perspective. Stephen poignantly kept in front of me the insanity of a system that has made a virtue out of the willingness to sacrifice a child.

ABRAHAM ON TRIAL

1. And it came to pass after these things, that God did tempt Abraham, and said unto him, Abraham: and he said, Behold here I am.

2. And he said, Take now thy son, thine only son Isaac, whom thou lovest, and get thee into the land of Moriah; and offer him there for a burnt offering upon one of the mountains which I will tell thee of.

3. And Abraham rose up early in the morning, and saddled his ass, and took two of his young men with him, and Isaac his son, and clave the wood for the burnt offering, and rose up, and went unto the place of which God had told him.

4. Then on the third day Abraham lifted up his eyes, and saw the place afar off.

5. And Abraham said unto his young men, Abide ye here with the ass; and I and the lad will go yonder and worship, and come again to you.

6. And Abraham took the wood of the burnt offering, and laid it upon Isaac his son; and he took the fire in his hand, and a knife; and they went both of them together.

7. And Isaac spake unto Abraham his father, and said, My father: and he said, here am I, my son. And he said, Behold the fire and the wood: but where is the lamb for a burnt offering?

8. And Abraham said, My son, God will provide himself a lamb for a burnt offering: so they went both of them together.

9. And they came to the place which God had told him of; and Abraham built an altar there, and laid the wood in order, and bound Isaac his son, and laid him on the altar upon the wood.

10. And Abraham stretched forth his hand, and took the knife to slay his son.

11. And the angel of the Lord called unto him out of heaven, and said, Abraham, Abraham: and he said, Here am I.

12. And he said, Lay not thine hand upon the lad, neither do thou anything unto him: for now I know that thou fearest God, seeing thou hast not withheld thy son, thine only son from me.

13. And Abraham lifted up his eyes, and looked, and behold behind him a ram caught in a thicket by his horns: and Abraham went and took the ram, and offered him up for a burnt offering in the stead of his son.

14. And Abraham called the name of that place Jehovah jireh: as it is said to this day, In the mount of the Lord it shall be seen.

15. And the angel of the Lord called unto Abraham out of heaven a second time;

16. And said, By myself have I sworn, saith the Lord, for because thou has done this thing and has not withheld thy son, thine only son:

17. That in blessing I will bless thee, and in multiplying I will multiply thy seed

as the stars of heaven, and as the sand which is upon the seashore; and thy seed shall possess the gate of his enemies;

18. And in thy seed shall all the nations of the earth be blessed because thou has obeyed my voice.

19. So Abraham returned unto his young men, and they rose up and went together to Beersheba; and Abraham dwelt at Beersheba.

20. And it came to pass after these things, that it was told Abraham, saying, Behold, Milcah, she hath also born children unto thy brother Nahor;

21. Huz his firstborn, and Buz his brother, and Kemuel the father of Aram,

22. And Chesed, and Hazor, and Pildash, and Jidlaph, and Bethuel.

23. And Bethuel begat Rebekah: these eight Milcah did bear to Nahor, Abraham's brother.

24. And his concubine, whose name was Reumah, she bare also Tebah, and Gaham, and Thahash, and Maachah.

Introduction

IN THE BEGINNING of the last decade of the twentieth century, in that most modern of places, California, a tragedy of Biblical proportions unfolded with the morning newspaper:

Father Sacrificed Child. God Told Him To.

So accustomed are we to horrendous tales of domestic violence that this headline might seem only a bizarre twist on the ordinary. People who read about the incident over their morning coffee noted it, registered a reaction, and turned the page, muttering, "The man must be crazy." In this way, the man was defined, the deed was labeled, and the whole thing could be put out of mind. A year later, when Cristos Valenti came to trial, only one of the jurors remembered the newspaper story.[1]

Yet once upon a time, God asked another father to sacrifice his child. For *his* willingness to obey God's command, Abraham became the model of faith at the foundation of the three monotheistic (Abrahamic) religions: Judaism, Christianity, and Islam.[2] His story has been inscribed on the hearts and minds of billions of people for millennia. Even today, Abraham's devotion is revered and his example extolled in countless sermons and in the secular media. With that cultural model readily available, it is not so surprising that Cristos Valenti felt he must obey God's command. Yet for his willingness to comply with God's request, Cristos Valenti was brought to trial.

This book puts the Abraham story on trial. The contemporary case, to be discussed in chapter 2, helps bring the Abraham story emotionally closer and raises several issues that recur throughout the book. But it could not raise the most important question, the question that motivated this book and the years of research that have gone into it: Why is the willingness to sacrifice one's child *the* quintessential model of faith, why not the passionate protection of the child? What would be the shape of our society had *that* been the supreme model of faith and commitment? By critically examining the Abraham story, I think we can catch a glimpse.

If it is true, as Shalom Spiegel suggests, that the "story of Abraham renews itself in every time of crisis" (Spiegel, 1969, back cover), then the time has come to take another look. The crisis of society today is about values, about the very values that, I think, are epitomized by the Abraham story—not just faith and sacrifice, but also the nature of authority; the basis and structure of the family, its gender definitions and roles; and which children, under what circumstances, shall be deemed acceptable and be provided for. My purpose is not to reinvigorate these values but to challenge them at their foundation.

The story of Abraham, some will say, is just a story about something that happened (or might have happened) long ago. They feel it has little to do with their lives or their faith, and thus they do not usually imagine that it has any bearing on contemporary life. What they forget is that the story of Abraham, like that of Jesus, was powerful enough to change the course of human history.[3] It is clear that the story of Abraham is not just one story among others; it is "central to the nervous system of Judaism and Christianity" (Goldin in Spiegel, 1969:xvii). It is also central to Islam. Insofar as it has shaped the three religious traditions, their ethical values, and their views of social relations, it has shaped the realities we live by. Even if we are not believers, any of us raised in a culture influenced by Judaism, Christianity, or Islam has been affected by the values, attitudes, and structures exemplified by the story.

My interpretation of the Abraham story attempts to uncover the set of assumptions that make the story possible; it is a way to get behind the story. Traditional exegeses proceed out from the story, and move quickly to conventional contexts for interpretation, namely sacrifice and faith, contexts that predetermine possible lines of interpretation. For example, if the story is viewed in the context of the theories and meanings of sacrifice, then the questions put to it will be how and in what ways does it conform to, deviate from, or shed light on known sacrificial practices? Related, surely, is whether the story represents the end of the supposed practice of child sacrifice and the institution of animal sacrifice. But even if child sacrifice was practiced in the ancient Near East, a discussion of which will occupy chapters 3 and 4, such interpretations fail to recognize that Abraham is revered not for putting an end to the practice but for his willingness to go through with it. *That* is what establishes him as the father of faith. *That* is what I find so terrifying. The story is not about substitution, symbolic or otherwise, but about a new morality; it represents not the end of the practice of child sacrifice but the beginning of a new order.

Interpretations that focus on Abraham's faith argue that to demonstrate his absolute, unswerving faith he had to be willing to sacrifice the thing he loved most in the world—the son he waited so long to have, the very child his God had promised. The paradoxical aspect reveals, to some, the mystery of God and the power of faith; one must simply make a leap of faith and believe.[4] I am suspicious of these types of interpretations and think there is another, less mysterious question that, perhaps because it is so simple, has been overlooked.

Neither religious commentators nor lawyers in the contemporary trial asked the question that has nagged me: what allowed Abraham (and Cristos) to assume the child was *his* to sacrifice? At first blush, the question seems meaningless. God asked him. But could or would the all-knowing God ask only one parent for the child, knowing that a child belongs to both mother and father or, perhaps, to neither? The story, however, conveys the impression that the child belonged to Abraham in a way he did not belong to Sarah.[5]

The focus on fatherhood pervades Genesis; one need only think of all the *begats* and the emphasis on the patrilineage, to realize that this is the case. But if so, on what basis were children attributed to their fathers? To say that the child belongs to the father because of patriarchy, a usual response, explains nothing, because *patriarchy* means the power of fathers; such an answer is circular and only defers the question. What we need to ask is: what is it about fathers or fatherhood that conveys such power?

My interpretation turns on the meaning of paternity and shows how the definition and assumptions about paternity made it possible for Abraham (and perhaps Cristos) to think that the child was his to sacrifice. The meanings are integral to the story; it does not make sense without them. Moreover, the same meanings have been carried over and reinforced by ancient as well as modern, religious as well as secular, interpretations; the meanings have been assumed, not examined. Drawing on anthropological studies of kinship and gender, I argue that neither the role nor the power of the father is a given in nature and the order of things, but that both are intimately connected to a particular *theory* of procreation, a theory that is, in turn, connected to a cosmological/metaphysical system.

Paternity has not meant just the recognition of a biological relationship between a man and a specific child, nor the social role built on that recognition; paternity has meant *the primary, creative, engendering* role. In the Bible (and in the popular imagination) it is symbolized by the word "seed." Identity, whether of plant or of person, is imagined as a matter of seed; in human terms it is bequeathed by the father. The soul, also, was imagined as transmitted via seed. The child belongs to the father because it *is* his seed. Women, in contrast, have been imagined as the nurturing medium in which the seed is planted rather than as co-creators; they foster its growth and bring it forth, but do not provide its essential identity. The very notion of paternity, therefore, already embodies *author*ity and power and provides the rationale for a particular constellation of the family and the structure of relations within it. This notion of paternity is integral to the story of Abraham, for it is all about his "seed."

The seemingly simple word *seed* is anything but simple or neutral. By evoking associations with agriculture and the natural world, the image naturalizes a structure of power relations as it also conceals it (see Yanagisako and Delaney, 1995). Represented as seed and soil, male and female roles have been differentially valued and hierarchically ordered. This theory of procreation, common to both the ancient Hebrews and the ancient Greeks, has been the dominant folk theory in the West for millennia, shaping popular images and sentiments of gender.[6]

From today's perspective, this theory of procreation is obviously erroneous. Today we believe that both male and female contribute the same kind of thing to the identity of a child, namely genes, and that each contributes half the genetic endowment, half the seed, so to speak. Women, of course, contribute much more—by way of nurture to the fetus in utero, by giving birth, and often by providing additional nurture and care during its early life—but women are still popularly associated only with the nurturing, not the creative aspects. The modern, biogenetic understanding of reproduction is relatively recent, known only to certain of the world's peoples, and it tends to be confined explicitly to biomedical discourses. Yet notions of paternity and maternity were culturally constructed long before the development of biology and genetics, and these older notions are still being perpetuated by popular images and sentiments about gender and by the social arrangements, especially the family, that continue to affect the way men and women are thought about.

The meanings of paternity and maternity were not originally based on biological theory, and they do not simply change in response to changes in biological theory. They are rooted far deeper and their extent is far wider than the discourse and domain of reproduction; ultimately they are rooted in a cosmological system, in this case the monotheistic world view that is elaborated somewhat differently in Judaism, Christianity, and Islam. The foundational story of Abraham is central to these belief systems as well as to the societies influenced, and the social arrangements legitimated, by them.

For believers, the story has a central place both theologically and ritually in each of the religions. Jews recite Genesis 22 annually at the new year services of Rosh Hashanah; it is also included as part of the daily morning prayers of the devout. Christians think the story prefigures the Crucifixion, when God the Father sacrificed his only begotten son; a recitation of Genesis 22 is traditionally part of the services during Easter week. Muhammad's mission was to recall the people to the one true religion given in the beginning to Abraham. Each year Muslims dramatically reenact the event on the most sacred day of the Muslim calendar—the Feast of the Sacrifice—that occurs at the end of the rituals of the *Hajj*. On that day, whether in Mecca or at home, each male head of household sacrifices a ram (or substitute) in place of the intended child. And every male child can imagine that, but for the grace of God, there might he be. Told year after year, generation after generation, the story has continued to make an impact on the minds and emotions of people who are, as promised, countless "as the stars of heaven and as the sand which is upon the seashore" (Gen. 22:17).

The Abraham story overflows the boundaries of religious communities. As one of the most common religious themes depicted in painting and also well represented in literature, sculpture, and music, it has become part of the cultural mainstream. In the space of two weeks in November 1992, just when I was beginning work on this book, the story was the subject of (1) an art exhibit in Berkeley, California; (2) a sermon delivered by a minister in Little Rock Arkansas, and directed at Bill Clinton, who was sitting in the first pew the Sunday after his election to the presidency; and (3) a *Peanuts* cartoon just before Thanksgiving.

As a way of protesting the Vietnam war, Bob Dylan wrote a song ("Highway 61 Revisited") that imagined Abraham questioning God's order. Perhaps he was aware of the practice of using the story of Abraham to legitimate war, as was Wilfred Owen in his famous poem against the "fathers" sending the "sons" off to World War I. Leonard Cohen wrote a song called "The Sacrifice of Isaac." When George Segal was commissioned to make a sculpture commemorating the deaths of the students at Kent State, he chose the theme of Abraham and Isaac. And when Kent State rejected it on the grounds that it was too inflammatory, Princeton University bought it and placed it near the chapel on campus (see fig. 1). The story was the subtext of President Carter's book about the Middle East, *The Blood of Abraham*; more recently of a novel, *The Sacrifice of Isaac*, by Neil Gordon, about the ambivalent legacy of the Holocaust; as well as of Woody Allen's film *Crimes and Misdemeanors*.[7] On Easter Sunday and Monday 1994, in the midst of my writing, a miniseries entitled *Abraham* was shown on television. I mention each of these uses of the story—and there are many more—primarily to make the point that the story is very much alive in contemporary American culture.

I approach the story of Abraham as an anthropologist viewing it not purely as a religious text but also as a cultural text, for no matter how divinely inspired it may have been, it is an artifact of human culture. My goal, however, is not to recover the particular time and place of Abraham. The story was transmitted orally and edited repeatedly for hundreds of years before it ever reached its canonical form; therefore "any interpretation which substantively depends on relating the text to an historical

FIG. 1. Sculpture by George Segal, *Abraham and Isaac*.
Princeton University. Photo by author.

context must itself be forever tentative and hypothetical" (Moberly, 1988:312). At the same time, I do not mean to imply that it can be totally taken out of its context, for the opposite hermeneutical tendency often assumes that it is, therefore, timeless and represents "the human condition" or universal human psychology. That approach is equally misleading.

Regardless of its provenance, the story does not merely reflect a particular culture and society; it also incorporates a vision of society, indeed, a vision of the cosmos that has animated numerous cultures over considerable time. To connect it only to a particular time and locale would be to lose sight of that fact. Too often we forget the way that events themselves are transformed in relation to mythic structures of interpretation (see Mintz, 1984; McNeill, 1986; Sahlins, 1981; Samuel and Thompson, 1990). People continue to derive their identity, orient their lives, and interpret the meaning of life from the patterns first charted by the story.

> Scriptures are not only a record of the past but a prophecy, a foreshadowing and foretelling of what will come to pass. And if that is the case, text and personal experience are not two autonomous domains. On the contrary, they are reciprocally enlightening; even as the immediate event helps to make the age-old sacred text intelligible, so in turn the text reveals the fundamental significance of the recent event or experience. (Goldin in Spiegel, 1969:xvi)

Religious myth has social implications; conversely social events (are made to) speak to religious themes. In this way is woven the moral fabric that helps people make sense of their lives. We can never recapture the living quality of the culture of the biblical writers, but we can investigate their vision of the world and its legacy. We can ask about the role of the Abraham story in that vision. And we can ask if this vision is one we wish to perpetuate.

GUIDE TO READERS

First a caveat and then a *brief* on how the book will proceed. Although questions I put to the material are contemporary, this does not mean that I expect people who lived thousands of years ago to have had the same ideas we do, or to have acted according to values we cherish. Quite the contrary. New questions can expose assumptions of the past, and can show that those assumptions were not naturally given or inevitable, but part of a culturally constituted universe. By asking new questions of well-known stories, stories that we continue to tell ourselves and, perhaps more important, our children, we may gain new insight into their meanings. Such questioning does, however, make some people nervous. Directed to foundational stories, the questions are felt by some as if they are threats to the foundations of a house, for they begin to unsettle the edifice built upon it. But for those of us concerned with dismantling patriarchy, it is important to understand the power of this most patriarchal of stories.

Using anthropological and historical methods, I scrutinize material from several disciplines: archaeology, biblical and religious studies, and psychoanalysis. Each begins from different premises—different assumptions are made, different questions are asked, and different styles of interpretation prevail. Because of these differences it is not easy to move from one to the other; the distinctions are important and their blurring too often leads to distortions, errors, and anachronisms. For this reason, the material from each discipline is treated in a separate section—each focusing on the questions, subjects, arguments, and evidence that characterize it; each section also tends to partake of the discursive style of that discipline. Despite the differences, I demonstrate that the same assumptions about gender, kinship, and procreation pervade them all. These assumptions form the backdrop for interpretations; they are the things that go without saying; they underlie and unite a seeming variety of interpretations and contemporary social practices. By turning our attention to these assumptions, we begin to glimpse the outlines of a powerful myth we live by—its destructive legacy as well as the possibilities for constructive change.

The chapters are not meant to form an argument built up layer upon layer; instead they should be imagined as different facets of the same basic argument. Each has a different slant; each adds light to the cumulative power of the whole. Chapter 1 is the case for the prosecution. It outlines my argument: (a) it discusses the relevance of anthropology, the importance of the study of kinship and origin myths; (b) it elaborates the notion that paternity and maternity are cultural constructions rather than reflections of natural roles; and (c) it discusses the power of language and what happens when we try to change it. After the first chapter, the reader may move to any of the subsequent chapters. Chapter 2 is an account of the trial in California of Cristos Valenti, who sacrificed his child because God told him to do so. His story is not the same as that of Abraham if for no other reason than that Cristos had the model of Abraham before him. It is not so much because one is secular and the other sacred or because, in Cristo's case, the child was killed whereas Abraham's God intervened in time; Cristos Valenti's story unfolds within a context already shaped by the values inherent in the Abraham story. His rationale depends on these values and his defense rests on them. The emotional power of Valenti's story helps to focus a number of moral issues, but it never challenges the model on which it is based: Abraham is never put on trial.

The second section (chapters 3 and 4) addresses the common belief that the story is meant to mitigate a more ancient practice of child sacrifice by the substitution of a ram. I discuss the evolutionary assumptions embedded in such views and the archaeological evidence for and against the practice. Like the archaeological evidence, the evidence in the Bible is generally considered later both narratively and chronologically than the Abraham story. Although the sacrifice of children may have occurred at some time in the circum-Mediterranean world, the Abraham story cannot be seen as the mitigation of such a practice. In addition, I question whether the story should even be interpreted in the context of theories of sacrifice.

The third section (chapters 5 through 7) is devoted to exegeses of the meaning and place of the story in each of the three religious traditions and to the kinds of debates that have arisen in each. In an attempt to preserve the integrity of each tradition, each will be treated separately. At the same time, I undermine the religious "defenses" by showing that all of them rest on similar assumptions about paternity and gender that, in turn, are integral to the theological meaning.

Psychoanalytic theory has also grappled with the relationship between gender, kinship, and religion. In the fourth section (chapters 8 and 9) I challenge Freud's theory of the Oedipus complex as foundational not only for individual psychology but also for society as a whole, that is, as the foundation story wherein "religion, morals, society and art converge" (Freud, SE 13:156). Why did Freud focus only on the son's desires and acts without considering those of the father? In the Oedipus story, why did he ignore Laius's homicidal impulse? In *Moses and Monotheism*, why did Freud fabricate a story of the symbolic "sons" killing the "father" rather than using the story *in* the biblical text of the father willing to kill the son? His proposal of Oedipus as the myth we live by eclipsed that of Abraham; Freud's blindness allowed the story of Abraham and its values to persist unchecked.

Finally, in chapter 10, I briefly discuss how the story of Abraham has bequeathed a moral legacy in which we have been taught not to question the authority of "fathers," even though, in the process, we betray children. Contemporary examples illustrate the ways in which the sacrifice and betrayal of children has been institutionalized. One can point to the dreadful conditions in which most children in the world are living. Children are abused at the hands of their parents, most frequently fathers or their surrogates, and by priests—the very "fathers" who stand in for God and whose mission it is to protect children. One can also include war and point out that "children" are sent off to fight old men's battles and that the U.S. military budget vastly exceeds that of welfare. The recent welfare debate itself shows how the "fathers" (of state) exercised their power to determine the fate of a whole generation of children.

The story of Abraham is not causative in any direct sense. But because it exemplifies and legitimates a hierarchical structure of authority, a specific form of family, definitions of gender, and the value of obedience that are simultaneously the fountainhead of faith and the bedrock of society, it has created an environment that has made it seem sacrilegious to question these issues.

As Abraham takes the knife to slay his son, God calls out: "Because thou hast done this thing, and hast *not* withheld thy son, thine only son: I will bless thee, and I will multiply thy seed as the stars of heaven and as the sand upon the seashore, and thy seed shall possess the gate of his enemies. And in thy seed shall all the nations of the earth be blessed, because thou hast obeyed my voice" (Gen. 22:16–19).[8]

Like that knife eternally poised in mid-air, several questions should be held in the mind of the reader. Why is the willingness to sacrifice the child the model of faith? What is the function of obedience? Why so little attention to the betrayal of the child? Whose voice counts? Like another sacrificed by his father, did Abraham's son cry out at the critical moment: "Father, father, why hast thou forsaken me?" Why have we eulogized their submission?

This book puts on trial the story often referred to as "Abraham's trial"—a reference both to God's testing of him and his own suffering. The question before us is whether we should perpetuate the story and the lessons it has taught. In the next chapter I present my general argument. In the following sections, evidence from several very different perspectives is brought forth. Attend to the kinds of questions that have been asked, and to the silences. Consider whether and how well the evidence supports my argument. You the reader must consider the verdict.

PART ONE

Abraham on Trial

CHAPTER ONE

Abraham on Trial: Case for
the Prosecution

FOR CULTURES influenced by Judaism, Christianity, and Islam, Abraham is symbolically the first patriarch. As Abram, his name meant something like "exalted father" or "the father is exalted," and as Abraham, it meant "father of nations." His story begins what are aptly called the "patriarchal narratives." What better place, then, to begin an investigation of patriarchy?

Although feminists have long been concerned with patriarchy, no feminist theorist, as of this writing, has focused directly on Abraham.[1] Some feminist interpreters of the Bible have included the story of Abraham along with those of other biblical figures as if it were merely one story among others. A few have skirted it in their discussions of Sarah, Abraham's wife, or Hagar, her handmaid, his concubine (e.g., Teubal, 1984, 1990; Trible, 1984), but all have failed to recognize the centrality and the social weight of the story in Genesis 22.

The desire of some feminist interpreters to resurrect the voices of ancient women is important as no expression of their feelings exists in the text. Indeed, that is where I began. Although the Abraham story has bothered me since childhood, I began a serious investigation of it only after becoming a mother. It was easy then to imagine how Sarah might have felt when she discovered that her child was missing and learned what had happened. Imagining her reaction, however, could only register her pathos and her exclusion; it could not directly challenge the story, for, given the way the text is constructed, she can only react. I wanted to know why the story was constructed that way. I wanted to know why the foundational story is centered on a father, his son, and a male-imaged god. Is their gender merely accidental, or is it precisely the point?

When I told people I intended to analyze the story in terms of gender, most did not understand what that could mean. "But it is not about women," some said, as if only women have gender. "The story of Abraham," others countered, "is about religion, about spirituality. What can it possibly have to do with gender?" Gender may seem irrelevant to those concerned with drawing out the spiritual message of the story, which, they further presume, could be addressed to anyone. But does the story have the same meaning for women, or is it inextricably entangled with meanings of masculinity, particularly fatherhood?

Gender *is* precisely the point. The religious content cannot be separated from notions of gender and notions of generativity, especially paternity. The importance of paternity has been missed by most scholars because they have misunderstood what it means; they have assumed that it means merely the recognition of the biological relationship between a man and a given child.[2] That is not so surprising—most people in the West assume that kin terms *mean* the biological relations that are established through sexual reproduction.

Rather than reflecting natural facts, the meanings of father and mother, paternity and maternity emerge relative to a *theory* of procreation. In this theory, the male role is construed as the creative one: he is the one who "begets" and by means of his "seed" imparts the life-giving essence that defines a child. The female role is to nurture the seed-child implanted in her and to give birth. I have elsewhere (Delaney, 1986, 1991) called this a *monogenetic* theory, as the *principle* of creation comes from only one source. Symbolically, it is the human analogue of divine, monotheistic creation. The life-giving abilities attributed to men allied them with God, and women became associated with what was created by God, namely the Earth.

The power to create life implies the concomitant power to destroy. God both creates and destroys; if he chooses, he has the right to destroy what he has created. Indeed, that is a pervasive threat in Genesis and in the Hebrew Bible more generally, as well as in the Qur'an. Men, with the help of God, were thought to bestow life; analogously they were also given power over it. That is what the story of Abraham enacts. God speaks to Abraham, Abraham speaks to Isaac. He does not tell Sarah where he is going or what he is about to do; he does not need to. Isaac is his, Isaac is Abraham's seed. The transaction is between Abraham and God on the one side and between Abraham and Isaac on the other. The story is about the deal these three struck: by relinquishing some of his power to God, Abraham received it back a thousandfold. When he submits to God's will, God's will flows through him and becomes identical with his; male authority is invested with sacred power.[3]

God is symbolically masculine, imagined foremost as Creator; his divinity could easily be imagined as a denaturalized and reified male-paternal generativity.[4] In the natural world that he created, that creativity is channeled through males and becomes part of the definition of masculinity. The religious aspects of the story lend an aura that naturalizes patriarchal power; it is seen as part of the natural order, an order that is, however, ordained by God. In other words, patriarchy is not just a secular social order, but an order at once sacred and secular, a point often missed in numerous social analyses, including feminist ones, that have focused on economics and/or politics and relegated religion to a peripheral or residual category. Regardless of the religious identities or affiliations of the analysts, there is a tendency to see religion as a reflex of social-structural arrangements or as a personal choice having to do primarily with one's spiritual concerns. There are, of course, notable exceptions, for instance the tradition beginning with Weber.

Gender is clearly not a peripheral or subsidiary aspect of the story, or of theology more generally, but an integral part of the theological meaning, and vice versa. Expressing the opinion of many who are opposed to female ordination, Michael Novak, a contemporary Catholic thinker and editor of the journal *Crisis*, says, "sex differentiation is not simply a trivial detail, to be discarded or altered without concern for consequences; it is essential to the story of salvation. Fundamental. Foundational" (Novak, 1993:29). Recent unprecedented changes in reproduction, such as chemical birth control and new reproductive technologies, not to mention surrogacy and legalized abortion, have begun to erode traditional meanings of gender and family. These changes strike at the heart of religious authority and portend the erosion of theological meanings and structures. It is no wonder that these are the issues at the center of contemporary religious and social debate.

This threat to religious authority is a crisis unlike any other. In the past the story of Abraham was offered to encourage people to keep the faith of Abraham; today the crisis seems to be about that kind of faith and about the values that are integral to the story: a particular definition of family and "family values," gender definitions and roles that derive from an outmoded theory of procreation, and a hierarchical social order that stresses authority and obedience. The struggle is between those who believe that the traditional definitions and values should be upheld at all costs and those, like myself, who feel that they are part of the problem. Today, both liberals and conservatives who speak about the "social crisis" focus on the breakdown of religious values as well as on the so-called breakdown of the family. Furthermore, they often imply that it is father-absence rather than the lack of emotional and financial support (as well as day care, health care, education, and opportunities) for the mothers that is the cause of juvenile crime, teenage pregnancy, drugs, and gangs. Such politicians and social scientists reinforce gender (as well as racial and class) stereotypes when they imply that "mothers can't control the kids," as if only fathers can instill moral values, demand respect, and provide appropriate discipline. Rather than accept that the "family as we know it" is not (and perhaps never really was) the norm, they call for a reinvigoration of the supposedly natural and traditional family. Instead of thinking of creative ways for helping people raise and support their/ our children, they impose impossible demands on those who do not conform. At such a juncture, it is useful to return to the foundation story, not to ascertain its truth or falsity (as if that were possible) but to better grasp what it presupposes and implies.

ORIGIN MYTHS

When anthropologists study other cultures they usually include a study of the foundational stories or origin myths of that culture, for a myth "is a sacred narrative explaining how the world and man came to be in their present form" (Dundes, 1984:1). Anthropologists look to origin myths to learn something about a people's conception of the world, of nature, of time and history, of male and female, of social organization, within which the identity of a specific group is situated. And given such conceptions, they ask what kinds of values and attitudes are implied by such a vision. In other words, anthropologists, at least since Malinowski, have tended to assume that "an intimate connection exists between the word, ethos, and sacred tales of a people on the one hand, and their ritual acts, moral deeds, their social organization and even their practical activities on the other" (Malinowski, 1954:96). Yet they do not apply this wisdom to their own culture. Fewer than a handful have turned their attention to Genesis, the preeminent origin myth of Western culture, to consider its structuring function.[5] Ironically, just at the time when a number of "master narratives" are being challenged, the religious narrative remains relatively untouched.[6]

Myths of origin may not point to "real, true" historical origins, but they are important *representations* of origins: they provide a framework within which people situate and interpret their lives; they affect people's identity and orientation in that world; and most important, they provide answers to the questions "Who are we? Where do we come from? Where are we going?" Jews, Christians, and Muslims have been able to say, "We are the children of Abraham."

For centuries, however, these children have been fighting over the patrimony, both theologically and in everyday life. Who is the true "seed" of Abraham and who will inherit the promises? That biblical myth still affects social life was tragically illustrated by the massacre in Hebron on 25 February 1994 at the Cave of the Patriarchs, allegedly the tomb of Abraham. The area continues to be one of the most fought-over places in

Israel. I often think that if these "children" would just look up from their battles, they might see that their common father is the source not just of their unity but also of their strife.

THE STORY OF ABRAHAM

Regardless of whether he ever lived, Abraham is considered the person through whom a new conception of the divine entered human society. According to tradition, the new conception was not just of a new god or gods, but of the one and only God. Although that conception entered history at a particular time, it was projected back to the beginning; a vision not just of the way things are but of the way things always had been, a picture "of the way things in sheer actuality are" (Geertz, 1973: 89). There could be no stories about struggles between the gods for preeminence, as in some of the neighboring Near Eastern traditions; the new conception of God rendered them senseless. There could be only a story of recognition, that is, of acknowledging and submitting to the one true God. Abraham is imagined as the vehicle for revealing God's splendor to the world.[7]

Although the Bible begins with Creation, the narrative of Western cultural origins begins with Abraham. The creation of the world, of humans, of plants and animals, of language and its dispersion, and the Great Flood—that is, events of supposedly universal significance—take only eleven of the fifty chapters in Genesis. "The break between Primeval History and the story of the Patriarchs is sharper than is immediately apparent" (Speiser, 1964:liii). The primeval history has many parallels with material from other ancient Near Eastern cultures, for example, the order of Creation, and the stories of Cain and Abel and of the Flood.[8] But the story of Abraham is unique. It is with Abraham that Jewish, Christian, and Muslim religious traditions have their beginnings; it is the center of gravity, the pivotal story. A number of scholars believe that the Biblical editors borrowed much of the primeval material from their Near Eastern neighbors, reinterpreted it according to their guiding vision of the one and only God, and used it as a frame for the patriarchal narratives that begin with Abraham.

Abraham's story begins when he first obeys the call from God to "Go forth from your country and your kindred and your father's house to the land that I will show you" (Gen. 12:1). During his migration he is subjected to a number of tests or trials of faith.[9] One of them concerns the covenant God made with Abraham (Gen. 17), the sign of which is engraved on male flesh: circumcision. "The last trial," the one that established him as the father of faith, was the one in which he was instructed: "Take your son, your only son Isaac, whom you love, and go to the land of Moriah, and offer him there as a burnt offering upon one of the mountains of which I shall tell you" (Gen. 22:2). Abraham had so much faith in his God that he was willing to sacrifice his son when that God commanded.

That is the story at the foundation of the three monotheistic religions. The story is performative, for it is Abraham's action that gave shape and substantive reality to the God to whom the action was directed.[10] Abraham's action established his faith as well as the traditions of faith it set in motion. But the meaning and explanation of the act has been the subject of considerable debate for millennia. At the same time only certain kinds of questions have been asked, and certain voices given expression. For example, if Abraham had wanted to prove his devotion and obedience, why didn't he offer to sacrifice himself? Speaking for him, some people assume that, of course, he would have been willing to sacrifice himself in order to save his son. However, if he had been willing to go that far (and that is purely conjecture on their part), why didn't he do *anything* to save his son? Why didn't he argue with God as he did when Ishmael was to be banished, or as he did to try to save Sodom and Gomorrah from destruction? Instead, he was silent.

Continuing the line of this argument, some go on to say that if Abraham had sacrificed himself, it would not have been the ultimate sacrifice, for he had to sacrifice the thing he loved the most. Yet it is one thing to relinquish something one values or to do without it; it is quite another to extinguish the life of a human being. The former sense of sacrifice is illustrated by the story of the two women (1 Kings 3:16–28), each of whom claimed the same infant as her own. Solomon judged that the one willing to relinquish the child, rather than letting it be divided in two, was the real mother. The primary value was the protection, not the possession, of the child. The sacrifice is the mother's; she protects the child even as she lets him go. Although this story illustrates a model of love and sacrifice different from that in the Abraham story, it has not been used to challenge it. Significantly, *it is not the foundational story.*[11] The conflation and rationalization by commentators of the different meanings of sacrifice obscures important implications and is, for me, the proverbial slippery slope.

A far more important question is never, or rarely, asked: *Is Isaac his to sacrifice?* What gives Abraham the right to take Isaac? To sacrifice him without consulting Sarah? (Or, in the Muslim version, Hagar?) Why is she excluded from this most important communication from God? One must ask either (a) why would God have asked only Abraham, or (b) what were the assumptions of the biblical writers about paternal rights that allowed them to portray the story this way, that allowed them to ignore the mother? Such questions must have seemed beside the point;

one does not question God. Commentaries begin with God's command. They take it at face value and do not see the exclusion of Sarah (or Hagar) as problematic.[12] Although theologians routinely give voice to Abraham (and even to God) in their interpretations, the voices of the mother and child have been muted. The mother and child have little place in the discourse, as the focus is on God and Abraham. As we shall see, mother and child also had little place in the modern courtroom. We need to think not only of the processes of their exclusion but also of the implications such processes have for interpretations. In this case it blinded subsequent interpreters from asking what allowed the biblical writers to portray the story as if Abraham had an unquestioned right to take the child.

If the child was thought to belong to Abraham in a way that he did not belong to Sarah or Hagar, then we need to know the reason. Those who pass off the question as reflecting patriarchy imply that patriarchy is self-explanatory and assume that patriarchal organization was already established and was/is separable from the beliefs that construct and support it; they overlook the possibility that patriarchy is conceptually and institutionally established on the basis of certain meanings and practices. The very word *patriarchy* includes a notion of father and so, too, does Abraham's name. That fathers are exalted is not a bad *description* of patriarchy, but we need to go further and ask *why*.

We need to ask why fatherhood is so important. Much of Abraham's story is taken up with his desire to have a son; only a son will fulfill God's promise that he would be a "father of nations." But why a son rather than a daughter? And why is the father exalted above the mother? When I asked myself these questions, gender and generativity began to seem central to the story, and terms that I had taken for granted, namely *father* and *mother*, began to seem less transparent. Instead, I became aware that the terms relate to and derive from the way procreation is understood, that is, to a specific *theory* of procreation. I had to ask what theory of procreation is embedded in the Abraham story, and what were the culturally perceived roles of male and female in the process. These questions, normally passed over by traditional as well as feminist scholarship, marked the turning point in my research.

THE RELEVANCE OF THE ANTHROPOLOGICAL
STUDY OF KINSHIP

My questions pushed me in the direction of anthropology, which had been involved with issues of procreation, kinship, and religion since its inception in the nineteenth century. Indeed, type of kinship system and type of religion were often seen to go hand-in-hand and arrayed in evolutionary sequence (e.g., Bachofen, 1861; Durkheim, 1915; Morgan, 1870, 1877; Engels, 1884). Like these early anthropological theorists, I, too, believe there are integral connections between kinship, procreation, gender, and religion, but unlike them, I do not imagine the different integrations as stages on an evolutionary ladder. Instead, I imagine them as different cultural systems. The differences in our theoretical stances involve different assumptions about kinship and the nature of language. As I have dealt with these issues at greater length elsewhere (Delaney, 1986, 1991) I will not elaborate them here. Kinship theory is an extraordinarily complex topic and what follows is admittedly an oversimplification.

The traditional patriarchal family, according to these nineteenth-century theorists, was the bedrock of society; it was the real, true, and proper form because it was ordained by the Bible. But the biblical basis was being undermined from within and without. The idea that the Bible was a pastiche of stories from various times and places, pieced together by a few editors, cast doubt on the idea that it was the direct, literal word of God. Archaeological discoveries revealed ancient, sophisticated civilizations not mentioned in the Bible, and anthropological discoveries of contemporary "primitives" who had different notions of kinship, family, and religion raised questions about the basis of their own family systems. From another angle, women were challenging the system by demanding rights in marriage and the right to divorce. All these considerations prompted the theorists to seek a *natural* foundation for the family. As they did so, however, they incorporated a number of biblical assumptions about family and kinship into their theories.[13]

They became obsessed with origins—of family, marriage, religion, and the human species itself.[14] They thought an investigation of origins (where or what they had come from) would provide some insight into who they were and what they had become. Like them, I, too, am concerned with origins, but unlike them I am concerned with people's *representations* of their origins, not for information these might "really" provide about the past, but about what they can reveal about the present—the concepts and values that underpin a people's view of themselves and their world.

Debates in the nineteenth century raged over whether human society was always patriarchally organized (as the Bible portrays it) or whether it had gone through various stages of cultural evolution beginning with primitive promiscuity or a matriarchal order and then simply switching to patriarchy with the "discovery" of paternity.[15] Like their predecessors, most people today, if they think about it at all, probably assume that these are the only alternatives. Behind this assumption, however, is a prior one: that kinship is always and everywhere rooted in the natural facts of procreation. Most people today, like the theorists of the nineteenth century (e.g., Bachofen, Durkheim, Engels, Freud, Marx, Morgan, and Smith), tend to assume that kin terms reflect biological relations and that, at the very least, the mother is always known. This idea fostered theoretical speculations that the original organization of society was matriarchal.[16] For some of these theorists, the so-called "discovery" of paternity marked a great leap forward in human cultural evolution. Peoples who had achieved it were therefore considered intellectually superior. The family, as depicted in the Bible, could then be viewed as an advance over what they construed as primitive forms of social organization.

> The progress from the maternal to the paternal conception of man forms the most important turning point in the history of the relation between the sexes. The mother's connection with a child is based on a material relationship, it is accessible to sense perception and remains always a *natural* truth. But the father as begetter presents an entirely different aspect. The triumph of paternity brings with it the liberation of the spirit from the manifestations of nature. . . . Maternity pertains to the physical side of man, the only thing he shares with the animals: whereas the paternal-spiritual principle belongs to him alone. . . . Triumphant paternity partakes of the heavenly light, while childbearing motherhood is bound up with the earth that bears all things. (Bachofen, [1861]1973:109–10)

Similar ideas, perhaps without the same flair, can be found in the work of thinkers such as Morgan, Marx, Engels, and Freud. Morgan was an American lawyer who initiated the anthropological study of kinship after coming into contact with the Iroquois in upper New York state. He soon became aware that they had a kinship system quite at variance from the one with which he was familiar. In order to make sense of the discrepancy, he began an exhaustive study first of other Native American peoples and then, by means of questionnaires sent out with missionaries and explorers, of numerous peoples around the world. He learned that there is a great variety of kinship terminology systems. The variety is not just a matter of different languages; the terms are structually different—they do not always refer to the same sets of people. The explanation of these differences became the basis of the anthropological study of kinship; but to this day there is no consensus among anthropologists about the basis of kinship.[17]

Because Morgan assumed that his own (English) kin terms, such as *mother, father, son, daughter, aunt,* and *uncle* represented the true and accurate outflow of the streams of blood (Morgan, 1871:486), Morgan called kinship systems of this type *descriptive.* When he and other theorists came across peoples who had very different sets of kin terms, they were thrown into a quandary. Especially puzzling were what Morgan called *classificatory* systems, in which one term was used to classify a number of people, for example, one term for all the women in the generation above me. Because of his assumption that kinship was necessarily about blood relations produced by heterosexual intercourse and legitimated by marriage, he leaped to several interrelated but erroneous conclusions. Either these others must be practicing different forms of marriage that implied they did not understand the real, true facts of procreation (namely paternity, as maternity was assumed to be self-evident) and thus could be stashed on a lower rung of the evolutionary ladder, or that the terms had survived from a prior time when people lacked that knowledge.[18]

Morgan's work had a great impact on Marx and Engels, for whom the so-called discovery of paternity marked "the world historical defeat of the female sex" (Engels, [1884]1972:120). As we shall see in chapter 8, Freud believed that the "discovery" of paternity was a great intellectual and cultural advance, and he, too, associated the achievement with males. The associations between fatherhood and the spiritual realm and between motherhood and nature have hardly disappeared, but it is clear, in the quotation from Bachofen, that paternity has meant far more than merely a recognition of a biological relationship.

THE MEANING OF PATERNITY (AND MATERNITY)

The discovery of peoples who seemed to get along quite well without a concept of paternity sparked a protracted debate referred to as the Virgin Birth debate after the title of a pivotal paper by Edmund Leach (1967).[19] In that paper, he equated the Christian doctrine of the Virgin Birth with beliefs of the Trobriand Islanders (and others) that pregnancy occurred because of actions by spirits rather than as the occasional but necessary outcome of heterosexual intercourse. I have taken issue (Delaney, 1986) with his assumption that these beliefs are equivalent, primarily because the Trobriand women (a) were hardly virgins, and (b) did not consider their conceptions unique events in world history, as the Virgin Birth is considered by believing Christians. Instead, their notions of conception described the normal everyday way the process was assumed to occur. The debate over these issues represents deep and continuing divisions in anthropology, the social sciences, and Western thought more generally. The issue concerns theories about the nature of language (whether it is reflective or constitutive of reality) and whether there is one form or multiple forms of knowledge and truth (see Rosaldo, 1989).

Of course, sense perception tells us that babies come from the bodies of women. But sense perception tells us nothing about the meaning of that observation, nor does it tell us about how a baby is thought to be related to the woman out of whose body it comes. To know that, we need to know what people say about what babies are made of and who or what contributes to their coming into being. In some places babies are considered reincarnations of gods or spirits, and the "mother" is imagined as merely the incubator for the baby, who comes from a god, a spirit, or an ancestor; in these cases, there is, according to Ashley-Montagu (1937) a physical relationship but not a biological one. It is not, therefore, a natural conclusion to assume that all peoples believe that the woman who bears a child is biologically related to it, for that demands, as a prior condition, a theory of biology.

The main point I wish to make here is that not even *mother* is self-evident. All that one can assert is that a child comes out of the body of a specific woman. *Mother* is a term relative to a specific theory of procreation; although we have presumed there is a biological connection between mother and child, we have imagined that connection differently from the one through the father, namely that the mother is the nurturer of the seed implanted by the father, the primary agent. Genetic theory has hardly eroded these popular images. As the meanings of *mother* are today being fragmented and challenged by new reproductive technologies and surrogacy, we might learn something from these "primitive" others.

What about paternity? Is it only the recognition that heterosexual intercourse is/was necessary for pregnancy to occur? That is what most people assume. They do not imagine that there can be a number of conceptual possibilities for the male role—all of which have been documented ethnographically in a variety of societies. For example:

1. In Trobriand (and Australian aboriginal) society the male may merely open the passage for a fetus/child to come by other means—in which case intercourse is necessary for pregnancy to occur but does not imply any notion of biological relatedness—and in some instances, sexual intercourse is expendable.

2. Again, in the Trobriands and elsewhere, repeated intercourse can be imagined as the act whereby the male feeds, or provides the nurture for, the fetus.[20]

3. In China and some African societies, the male contributes a particular substance such as bones.

4. Or in the folk theory of our own society, the male is imagined as the primary, engendering, creative agent.

Only the last is what has been meant by paternity. It is tempting to add something like "in Abrahamic societies" or "in the West." But that would completely miss the point I am trying to make. It is not that "paternity" is some kind of Platonic idea that each culture can fill in as it pleases, but that there is no way to think about it outside of this construction.[21] Because the contemporary meaning of paternity in the West is often reduced to its purely physiological or genetic sense, we lose sight that its wider meaning, illustrated by so many phrases, images, and laws, has constructed the male role as the life-giving role. It is this ability that symbolically allies men with divine creativity.

What has been so difficult for most Westerners to grasp is that the lack of a concept of paternity does not mean there is no role for the male in relation to a woman and the children she bears. It does mean that their roles and relationships are conceptualized differently, and that means that gender and procreation are also conceptualized differently. Conceptually, we have linked together physiological difference, sexual intercourse, pregnancy, and kinship, and the social consequences thought to result from them, such as marriage and the provisioning of the domestic group, because we think they go together naturally. These connections do not necessarily obtain elsewhere.

In Trobriand society, for example, they are constructed differently. All the men in the generation above my own would be called *tama*, but that does not mean they are all my fathers. There is no concept *father*. Nevertheless, a man will do a considerable amount of child care and express deep affection toward a child of the woman he lives with without the idea that it *belongs* to him, without the idea that it is his "flesh and blood." He feeds the child and helps to shape it, but the child is a reincarnation of a matrilineal ancestor. The child, whether male or female, is constituted from matrilineal flesh and blood as well as spirit (see Malinowski, 1929; Weiner, 1976, 1978; Montagu, 1983); the child belongs to, and inherits from, the matrilineal clan. In societies influenced by the monotheistic traditions, a person's soul is thought to be given by God, but through men. Children belong to their fathers and inherit their names, status, and property from their fathers.

To his credit, Malinowski, who brought the celebrated case of the Trobrianders to public attention, tried to show the *conceptual* basis of paternity. He said "the term 'father,' as I use it here, must be taken not as having the various legal, moral and biological implications that it holds for us, but in a sense entirely specific to the society with which we are dealing" (Malinowski, [1929]1982:4). He also recognized the intimate connection between the notion of paternity and Christianity: "The whole Christian morality . . . is strongly associated with the institution of a patrilineal and patriarchal family, with the father as *progenitor* and master of the household" (ibid., 159, emphasis added). Furthermore, "a religion whose dogmatic essence is based on the sacredness of the father to son relationship, and whose morals stand or fall by a strong patriarchal fam-

ily, must obviously proceed by confirming the paternal relation, by showing that it has a *natural* foundation" (ibid., emphasis added).

Yet Malinowski did not take his insights to their logical conclusion to
point out that there are not different meanings of the terms or concepts
mother and *father*, instead there are different concepts of the male and
female roles in the process of procreation and child rearing; clearly, if a
spirit, god, or totem is thought to be involved, the roles are not limited to
just male and female. The number and description of procreative roles are
imagined differently in each culture and in each are linked to more general beliefs about coming-into-being.

Although Malinowski recognized that the Trobrianders had a different
system, he believed there was a true doctrine of procreation. He confessed
that in order to test the firmness of their beliefs he became "aggressively
an advocate of the *truer* physiological doctrine of procreation" (ibid.:
158 emphasis added). Fortunately, Malinowski, unlike most other theorists, was quite explicit about what he meant by that. He "advanced the
embryological view of the simile of a *seed* being planted in the *soil* and the
plant growing out of the *seed*" (Malinowski, [1948]1954:223, emphasis
added). The natives were understandably curious and "asked whether
that was the white man's way of doing it" (ibid.).

Malinowski, unwittingly perhaps, had presented the millennia-old
Western folk theory of procreation. From our perspective framed by the
science of genetics, it is just as erroneous as the theory he was trying to
refute. To reiterate, *maternity* and *paternity*, *mother* and *father* do not
merely reflect biological relationships, they are concepts that derive their
meaning from cultural understandings about the process of coming-into-
being at both human and cosmological levels. It should be obvious that
these cultural understandings vary. This brings us back to Genesis.

GENESIS AND GENDER

Although it may never be possible to know exactly what the theory of
procreation was in Abraham's time, or at the time of the Biblical editors,
there are clues in the text. In Genesis, especially, there are numerous references to *seed*, whether of plants, humans, or Abraham. For example,
in reference to plants: "the herb yielding seed and the fruit tree yielding fruit after his kind, whose seed is in itself" (Gen. 1:11); or to humans:
"let us make our father drink wine, and we will lie with him that we
may preserve the seed of our father" (Gen. 19:32); or to Abraham: "All
the land which thou seest, to thee will I give it and to thy seed forever"
(Gen. 14:15).

The emphasis on seed can be immediately grasped, especially if one has a Hebrew, Greek, Latin, or King James version of the Bible, for the word (*zera*, *sperma*, *semine*, *seed*, respectively) occurs many more times in Genesis than elsewhere. The Revised Standard Version (RSV) of the Bible, in an attempt to use nonsexist language, translates *seed* as children or progeny. Although the ancient writers may also have meant children or progeny, children were, nevertheless, imagined as the product of seed and only men had seed.[22] This issue raises serious questions about efforts to make the biblical text contemporary and relevant. Attempts to make the language more inclusive may make some women feel more comfortable, but they simultaneously conceal the reasons for their exclusion in the first place. My position here is very close to that described by the Swedish biblical scholar Anders Hultgård, who wrote, "By projecting the modern image of a genderless and sublimated God back into the biblical times, it becomes possible to reinterpret a massively patriarchal body of text in more 'favorable' directions. This appears to me to be but an attempt to save the Bible as the canon of church and synagogue" (Hultgård, 1991: 35). Salvage attempts to change the language imply that gender had nothing to do with the theological concepts or spiritual message.

Implicit in the linguistic changes are assumptions both about language and about the meaning or message of the text. Those arguing for the inclusive changes appear to be saying that the real, underlying meaning has nothing to do with gender, that words such as *seed* are merely accidents of history. They might also be implying that the gendered meanings embodied in *seed* can be extended to women without changing the entire system of beliefs, practices, and institutional structure. Something similar is going on among those who think the image of God the *Father* is accidental, not integral, to the concept; some suggest replacing it with "Mother/Father God." It seems to me that this would further reify and reinforce the very meanings that are under question. In contrast are those who believe that meaning is not separable from the words in which it is expressed; words, they argue, do not reflect meaning but construct it.[23] God, or at least the ancient Hebrews, clearly had a constructivist understanding of language—after all, God created with the word. From a constructivist stance, the language of procreation creates the way it is thought about and the roles that men and women (and possibly God) play in it. It is not so easy to dismiss a theory of procreation as merely bad biology and assume that everything else can remain the same. Instead, one becomes aware of how deeply implicated are notions of procreation in gender definitions and theological conceptions.

Religious people and biblical commentators have long discussed *who* is the seed of Abraham, but they have not thought to examine *what* is seed. As we shall see in chapter 6, they have focused on which group (Jews, Christians, or Muslims) is meant. Because they have not even noticed the gendered aspects of the concept of *seed*, they have totally missed the social and theological implications embedded in the belief that only men produce seed. In order to address this issue, we must get a more contextualized understanding of seed and its implications.

Genesis is preoccupied with the interrelated notions of seed, paternity, and patriliny: who begat whom. Only men produce seed and only men have the power to transmit the line. The line was conceptually eternal if each man had a son; thus the focus on fathers and their sons. The language of seed conveys an image of women as the material in which the seed is planted; like the earth, they provide the nurture that builds up the physical body. Not surprisingly, women were and are defined in terms of barrenness or fertility, words that are also applied to soil. The issue of barrenness is emphasized more in Genesis than elsewhere in the Bible; Sarah, Abraham's wife, is the first woman to whom the term *barren* is applied. Men's procreative ability is defined in terms of potency—the power to bring things into being. This power symbolically, at least, allies men with God; *Yahweh*, linguistically, appears to come from a root that means the power to call into being (a son), to create (Cross, 1973:66). The sign of God's covenant with Abraham, circumcision, was carved on the organ felt to be the fountain of generativity, the vehicle for the transmission of seed.

These images of seed are not confined only to the ancient past but continue up to the present day. They are deeply ingrained, even unconscious. A most graphic representation of this belief appeared in *Time* magazine (15 August 1994) in an article about the biological basis of gender. The illustration portrayed a man sowing seed—which looked like tiny sperm—into the ground; there was no comparable image of woman or of ova, instead the idea conveyed is that women are like the undifferentiated soil. When we use the word *inseminate* we convey, however subliminally, that the male put the seed in; and this concept is implicit in the phrase "she's having his baby." This belief was horribly illustrated by the statements in the 1990s of Muslim Bosnian women who had been raped by Serbian soldiers: they said they did not want to have a *Serbian* baby. The horror of the rape is compounded by their assumption that the child's identity is bestowed by the man. In an episode of a popular television show, a woman learns that it is not her fault she has not become pregnant. She says to her husband: "You're the one who couldn't get the seed planted."[24] David Koresh, the Waco cult leader, like Elijah Muhammad, seemed to have had little difficulty convincing a number of women and girls to carry his divine seed. The night of the tragedy, Koresh's ex-wife was interviewed on television and said: "He thought he was God. His children were God's seed. How could they die? He believes they will be resurrected and will come back to repopulate the earth."

Nor is this language confined only to the context of procreation. We speak of seminal ideas and pregnant thoughts. A seminal idea is creative and, as several people have told me, "starts a whole new line of thinking"; a pregnant one is merely potential. Women may have seminal ideas, but the language implies that creative thinking is masculine in character. The controversial Korean feminist theologian, Hyun-kyung Chung, told me that Christian missionaries to her country imagine themselves planting the seminal word in the barren soil, figuring her country not only as female but also as empty, as having nothing of its own to contribute. And a seminary is that place where the divine word is implanted and nurtured.

Seed has been used theologically. Indeed, procreative imagery for conceptualizing the divine has been used for over two millennia.[25] Seed is the essence of the father, and his child is of the same essence. Because the seed "belongs" to the man, so too does the child belong to him in a way it does not belong to the mother. In addition to being of the same essence as the father, a male child additionally has the ability to reproduce that essence. Father and son *are* one. This is the Christian definition of God. In this theory of procreation I have outlined, mother and child are not one, they are not of the same essence, the same seed, even though they are literally of one and the same body for the period of pregnancy. In this theory of procreation, women cannot provide the image for God. Jesus was known by the term *Monogenes*, which meant "only begotten, begotten of the father." Mary provided the physical body, but she was not co-Creator.

In Genesis, the awareness of the identity between father and son is related to the issue of succession. But rather than a struggle among the gods over succession, as occurs in some other ancient Near Eastern texts, the issue is worked out through humans: who shall be chosen to carry on the divinely ordained line? The fact that the male child possesses the same generative power as the father, and will grow up to take the place of the father, also raises the issue of authority. An ethic of obedience would help to keep sons in line. Abraham's obedience to God is the model for the son's obedience to the father.

Devora Steinmetz, a Jewish theologian who has written a book about fathers and sons in Genesis, claims that "the son represents (for the father) both the ultimate promise and the ultimate threat, immortality and death" (Steinmetz, 1991:29). Neither she nor anyone else makes the same kind of argument about mothers and daughters, reinforcing the idea that they are not considered related in the same way as fathers and sons. She goes on to say that "Isaac can serve as the substitute for Abraham's act of self-dedication to God because he is in essence identical with Abraham."

But only, of course, within a specific *theory* of procreation in which a man identifies with his seed.

The Canadian psychologist David Bakan has also seen a connnection between paternity and the story of the near-sacrifice of Isaac. The Bible, especially Genesis, represents for him the crisis precipitated by the discovery of paternity. "The essence of Judaism and Christianity," he asserts, "is the management of an infanticidal impulse" provoked by that discovery, "and a *binding* on the father against acting out the impulse" (Bakan, 1974:208, emphasis added). He sees in the *Akedah* (the term used by Jews for the story of the "binding" of Isaac) redemptive possibilities—the symbolic substitution is a means to mitigate and control these tendencies. But it seems to me that the substitution also perpetuates the idea that the child is the *appropriate* sacrifice.

Both Steinmetz and Bakan believe these social consequences follow naturally upon the "discovery" of paternity, which they see as true and inevitable. Neither of them understands that paternity is not merely the *discovery* of a physiological relation of a man to a specific child, but the *construction*, indeed the invention, of that relationship. If paternity were merely the recognition of a biological relationship, then similar issues would presumably confront mothers.

Steinmetz and Bakan, like so many others, assume that paternity means merely the recognition that sexual intercourse is necessary for pregnancy, a recognition that they presume automatically implies that the male has a physiological relation to the child.[26] They misunderstand the meaning and implications of paternity, for they never consider that there are a number of other conceptual possibilities for the male role. They never considered that it is a notion constructed in relation to an entire system of the world, not just the "discovery" of a biological relationship. Nor did they understand that the female role of *mother* is *simultaneously* constructed and relative to the notion of *father*. The female capacity to bring forth children would have a different meaning if conceptualized in the absence of the male role, or if the male role were imagined as secondary. In the theory I have been discussing, the female role has been understood as secondary, receptive, and nurturing; it associates women with nature, with what was created *by* God. God has no female partner in the monotheistic religions, instead Nature (the Creation) is symbolically female. Nature is in a dependent, subordinate position to God; so too have women been imagined in relation to men.

Gender, I believe, must be situated and understood within this wider cosmological framework. In the "monogenetic theory" of procreation, the principle of creation is symbolically masculine. Projected onto the cosmic plane, it came to be felt as inherent in the structure of the universe. Monogenesis and monotheism are, I suggest, two aspects of the same symbolic universe manifested somewhat differently in Judaism, Christianity, and Islam, and each is inherently, not accidentally, patriarchal.

At the center is the story of Abraham. So too is gender and generativity. Although gender may have something to do with procreation, procreation is not just about sex, biology, and the natural. Instead, procreation has been imagined as the vehicle for channeling divine creativity to earth. And ever since Abraham, it is men who embody the power to do so. That is the basis of patriarchy.[27] These beliefs form the common ground of assumptions over which a variety of interpretations tread, yet few have taken the opportunity to look at what is directly beneath their feet.

From here, the reader may dig into the two chapters that present the archaeological and biblical evidence for and against the practice of child sacrifice in the ancient Near East, or leap ahead to the section devoted to religious interpretations. The following chapter, in contrast, presents the quandary in which a contemporary court found itself when confronted by a modern version of the story. In that trial, just as in the original and its voluminous commentary, the child disappears. The focus of concern and center of gravity is on the father and on the strange conjunction of insanity and faith. Cristos Valenti never admitted to murder; he claimed that what he did was a sacrifice ordained by God. That was his explanation, his excuse. In that sense the story of Abraham served as his alibi.

CHAPTER TWO

Abraham as Alibi? A Trial in California

THE EVENING was just passing into darkness, the first stars were becoming visible. Cristos Valenti took his youngest child, his most beloved child, with him in his truck. He often took her with him to visit friends and she liked to accompany him. They drove to the place he had been directed to—to the place in the park where all the trees are. They got out of the truck. He took her hand and together they walked into the park. It was dark and quiet. She held on to his hand more tightly. "Don't be afraid," he said, trying to allay her fears. "We are going to meet God." "I don't know anyone named God." "You will meet him soon," was the answer and they walked on in silence. When they arrived at the place God had appointed, her father told her to lie down on the grass. "Start praying the Our Father, Our Father who art in Heaven," he said as he took the knife and took her life.

He sat next to her body and prayed for several minutes. When he looked up, he saw her star shining brightly in the night sky; he saw two stars moving closer together. He knew then he had fulfilled her destiny, he knew he had done the right thing. He picked her up and took her home. When his oldest daughter opened the door she saw her father holding the child, like a *pieta.* "Call the police," he said. "I have given her to God."

This is a true story. It happened on 6 January 1990, in California.[1] The above statement was taken from the verbatim report given to the police that evening. The same story was repeated when the case came to trial more than a year later. I attended the trial and have interviewed the participants—the jurors, the judge, the district attorney, the public defender, the psychiatrists, the minister, and members of the family. Except for a story in the newspapers the day after the event, it did not appear in the media again.

As soon as I saw the newspaper headline, I knew I had to follow the case. I had long been interested in the story of Abraham,[2] and I thought the case might provide a new perspective on the biblical story that it, superficially at least, so closely resembled. This chapter examines the issues as they emerged in the courtroom, in the living rooms of the jurors and the family, in the judge's chambers, in the psychiatrist's office, and in the church.[3]

The mystery lies in the radical disjunction between the horrible nature of the deed and its supposed religious motivations. How could one make sense of it? That was the job of both the district attorney and the public defender assigned to the case. They conducted their own investigations, trying to put together pieces of the puzzle that baffled family and friends, as well as the legal system. They talked to members of the family and neighbors, they searched the defendant's medical records, they interviewed the minister of the family's church—all for some clues to the mystery. Unlike a typical murder mystery, the body was present and its identity known; the perpetrator was also known, and the weapon was surrendered. About these basic facts, there was no doubt or difference of opinion. For the attorneys, this was the first time in their careers that both sides agreed on the basic facts, but the stories they would tell to connect these facts would be quite different.

The disjunction between the deed and its religious motivation raises the issue of how a secular court can deal with such a case. Whether it was murder or sacrifice can hardly be decided in court, as sacrifice is not a category recognized by the law. Today, the law circumscribes the intervention of religion in secular affairs, but this obscures its origin. We have forgotten, according to legal scholar Harold Berman, that "without the fear of purgatory and the hope of the Last Judgment, the Western legal tradition could not have come into being" (Berman, 1983:558).

In contemporary America, the word *sacrifice* means giving up things, doing without; alternatively, it is thought of as something only pagans, witches, satanists, or primitives do.[4] The only permissible religious sacrifice is a symbolic one, the Eucharist, celebrated in the Catholic, and some Protestent, churches. Whether it is a sacrifice or merely a commemoration of the Last Supper is a sectarian debate that has become more vigorous recently because of the issue of women's ordination (as, traditionally, only men could perform blood sacrifices).

Given the secular nature of American society and the supposed separation of religion and state, sacrifice was not a possible plea; the deliberate killing of a child could only be called murder; the deed was already defined.[5] The legal question could only be, what kind of murder. Was it murder in the first or second degree, or could it be considered manslaughter, even though it was clearly not accidental? Was there malice involved? Was it the result of insanity? Several jurors thought that such an act was crazy by definition; they didn't need a psychiatrist to tell them that.

Day after day we sat in the room watching Cristos Valenti. We became familiar with the visible details of his person, and these became signs for much more. Every morning, before the court was called to order, we witnessed a touching scene. Very discreetly, a clean shirt was passed from the family to Cristos's lawyer, and a soiled one made the reverse transit. His self-presentation was clean as well as serene. He sat very still throughout the proceedings and did not fidget. More than one juror commented on his very white, soft hands. "His hands were so white, I could hardly keep my eyes off them."[6] Another juror noted: "They give me the creeps. How could such baby soft hands have done what they did?"

We became more than observers, however; we became unwitting participants in the unfolding drama. "It felt like you became a witness to a crime, and you wish you hadn't seen it," said one of the jurors. In a time and space separated from everyday life, the ritual was more like a morality play, observed one of the psychiatrists. And each of us had a role to play.[7] The essential characters were the judge, the attorneys, the jurors, and, of course, the defendant; the supporting cast consisted of the court stenographer, the bailiff, and the translator. These participants were on the other side of the rail, separating them from the observers. Although all these people are unique individuals, I refer to them only by the roles they played, that is, *juror, judge*, and so on. I do, however, distinguish between the attorneys and the sex of the jurors, when relevant. In order to preserve the anonymity of family members and jurors, I do not use their names, nor do I make up names, which would add unnecessary clutter. In this telling of the story, their views, but not their identities, are important.

The audience was meager. In addition to Cristos's father and mother, who came every day, and a changing number of his siblings, there was only the minister from an evangelical Baptist church that Cristos had recently been attending, and me. Occasionally, a friend of one of the attorneys dropped in for a brief period. It was an intimate group. One could not disappear in the crowd. As the days wore on, the feeling that we were all in it together intensified.

Because of the intimacy of the place and the size of the group, I quickly became known to everyone. During the recesses, the family, the jurors, and I were all in the hall together. As the judge commented, "We try to protect jurors from outside influences in court, and then out in the hall they get them all." Jurors could not discuss the case with me, but when I asked if they would be willing to talk with me when it was over, all but one consented.

VOICES

They wanted the story told; they wanted their voices to reach beyond the jury room; this may be why they were happy to talk with me. I have had the benefit of hearing these voices, all these different opinions, about what happened and why. The story I tell, however, is my version, my interpretation. I include their voices, but ultimately I am the one choosing; there is no way around it. Nevertheless, my interests do not totally affect the telling. Nor would the issue of veracity have been solved by a verbatim account of the proceedings, which would have filled more than a thousand pages, and would not have included my observations or those of the participants; the quality of voice and facial expression; my interviews; or the initial written reports made by the public defender, the police, and the psychiatrist.[8] I am also a witness, if not to the deed, to its retelling and evaluation in a court of law. The collective burden, the desire to tell it, weighs on me.

Jurors felt strongly that because they would be making a decision that would affect a man's life, they ought to be able to ask questions. They could not, and the judge told them that they "must not make any independent investigation of the facts of the law or consider or discuss facts as to which there is no evidence. This means, for example, that you must not on your own visit the scene, conduct experiments, or consult reference works or persons for additional information." Their job, the judge instructed them, was to "determine the facts from the evidence received in the trial and not from any other source. A fact means something that is proved directly or circumstantially by the evidence. Second, whether or not you agree with the law, you must apply the law that I state to you, to the facts, as you determine them, and in this way arrive at your verdict." Witnesses, too, are held to the questions asked; they cannot just give their own story. This became most poignant, as we shall see, when Cristos's wife, the mother of the child, took the stand.

The question of voice takes on a whole new meaning in this case because it turns on whether one particular voice, namely God's, can actually speak. Because Cristos heard voices, especially the voice of God, the plea of insanity was entered. Hearing voices is taken as a sign of insanity. Do we believe that? What if it *was* the voice of God? Do we allow for the possibility? If not, why not? Is there any way to tell? Did Cristos gain a voice by allowing God to speak through him?[9] What did Cristos want to say? The question of voice became pertinent with regard to the motive for the crime. "How could you *want* to kill your child unless you're mental?" asked Cristos. "I did not want to kill her, I loved her." He loved her so much that sometimes his other children complained. And she, in turn, adored him. This was not a child who irritated him or angered him. "Whenever he'd be working around the house, she was with him all the time. He liked her very much. . . . He was a nice man, really, with the children," said one of his closest neighbors.

No one in their right mind would want to kill their child, but if you do kill your child, that, according to Cristos, does not necessarily mean you are either evil or insane. Yet those are the only alternatives the legal system acknowledges. "How can you say no to God? Everything is his. We all belong to Him. It was an order directly to me from God; God asked me for her. You can't back out. I had no choice. The master of the universe commanded it. He could end all this in the next microsecond. You don't say no to God."

We cannot easily dismiss these words as those of a crazy man since similar sentiments appear with some frequency in the news and from the pulpit. "When the Father tells you to do something, you don't argue with Him. . . . You don't need to know why," (Rev. Brian Cox from his church in Truro, Virginia, quoted in *The Nation*, August 1991). I don't know whether Cristos heard similar things from his minister, but it is not out of the question. This rhetoric, applied to contemporary issues, is becoming common and acceptable. Anti-abortionists have claimed that God tells them to obstruct a particular clinic. David Koresh claimed an inside line to God and on 3 March 1993, he informed the police that he was not ready to come out of the compound because, "God is telling me to wait." Further along the continuum, Presidents Reagan and Bush occasionally said that God guided them in certain decisions. And recently, Patrick Buchanan, a Republican candidate for president of the United States, claimed to "have God's own word on how America can be healed again," (*San Francisco Examiner*, 10 September 1995). What is harder to understand is why so few challenge them on the extraordinary arrogance of their claims.

We all hear voices—usually negative ones. But most of us attribute them to our own conscience, our own thoughts and fears internalized, perhaps, from figures of authority—the superego, according to Freud. Voices like these can be destructive; they can paralyze one's thoughts and one's actions. Normally, however, we can distinguish between these kinds of voices and the kind that Cristos heard. When we "hear" voices, they are in our heads, they are silent—whereas Cristos experienced the voice he heard as sound, as seeming to come from outside himself. The psychiatrists called Cristo's experience an *auditory hallucination*.

In court, one of the psychiatrists gave a minilecture explaining two fairly common kinds of auditory hallucinations: (1) those that deprecate, that call one bad names; and (2) those that give commands, that tell one to do something. Cristos heard the latter, but he had also heard the former in other contexts.

God had spoken to Cristos before, but on January 6, late in the afternoon, God's voice was clear when He told him to offer one of the children, the "little one," the one Cristos loved most. Cristos was outside painting the house, and he nearly fell off the ladder. According to his cousin, Cristos first began hearing voices about five months before the day of the event. Cristos could not quite make out what they said, and it hurt him to try to think about it. His cousin said, "he saw things, he heard voices, people telling him to do things; they took over his mind. He saw a little white light when he was alone and then God would talk to him. Once, when God was speaking to him, he fell down and got somewhat delirious. He was scared and we took him to the hospital." At the hospital, he underwent psychiatric observation, but the doctors, with their tests, could discover nothing wrong with him.

Sometime before Christmas, he heard the voices again. This time he was in church. Cristos responded audibly, "I don't belong here. I am Judas. I am Judas." He went out into the street speaking incoherently and shaking his fist at the sky. The next moment, he was on his knees praying the "Our Father." Later, he went to visit his sister-in-law, begging her forgiveness. "But you have done nothing wrong," she said. Again he was taken to the hospital for observation; again he was released. The doctors could find nothing specifically wrong with him, but he may not have received a complete evaluation, because he was poor, without health insurance, the father of six, and temporarily out of work.

All members of the family and a number of friends and neighbors described him as a happy person, often playing with this child, singing when he got a bit drunk. He was not a mean man and never hit the children. After hearing the voices, he became withdrawn, morose. "He seemed to be trying to fight something in his mind and was afraid he would have to give in."

SEARCH FOR AUTHORITY

One psychiatrist said that, when someone begins to deteriorate mentally, he or she often searches for some authority: the church, the pope, some kind of higher power. Cristos had given up drinking about eight months prior to the event and had been going to Alcoholics Anonymous (hereafter AA). The philosophy of AA includes the admission of one's guilt, and step 3 of the program encourages members to surrender themselves to a higher power. A juror who had some familiarity with AA felt that part of its method (and cure) was to try to shift a person's dependence on alcohol to a dependence on AA or on God. Perhaps this became somewhat blurred in Cristos's mind. It would have been interesting to know what was said at the meetings he attended, yet no one from AA was called as a witness. Nor was his wife's statement that "he had been sentenced to death at AA," followed up on. She did not mean that someone was going to kill him, but that if he kept drinking he would surely die. But he may have taken it literally, as a judgment on his life. Regardless, this judgment must have had some effect on his state of mind. Several doctors concurred that withdrawal would not have caused him to hear voices; one even said that alcohol may have masked his psychotic symptoms. Perhaps the abstinence enabled him to see his life more clearly, and he felt guilty about his inability to live up to his own and his culture's ideals of masculinity. It is difficult to know for sure, but his feelings of guilt seemed to be strong.

Cristos had long been a reader of the Bible, and his wife said he had quite a bit of knowledge and wisdom about it. Yet he had been brought up in the Catholic Church, which discourages individual interpretations of the Bible and individual relations with God. Revelation and authority are mediated through an intensely institutional, bureaucratic, and hierarchical system from the pope down to the local parish priest. According to his wife, Cristos had found God, in a new sense, at AA. And at about the same time, he began going to what he called a "Pentecostal" church. Although the minister of the church would not characterize it quite that way, it clearly had charismatic, evangelical aspects. It was the minister of that church who attended the trial, not the family's Catholic priest.

On Christmas Eve, the little one, the one he would kill a few days later, was a star in the Christmas pageant. Maybe Cristos wanted to make her one forever. That seemed to be behind his thinking, because that was the reason he gave the police: "God needed her, to put her in a star."

On the fateful day, January 6, Epiphany, the night the wise men saw the star showing the way to Jesus' birthplace, that is what he did. The day began like any other—some of the older children went to school or work; he puttered around the house and had lunch with the little girl. Off and on he read the Bible. No one knows precisely which stories he had been reading. At one point he remarked to his wife that Gabriel was telling someone to make a sacrifice. In the afternoon he went outside to paint the doors. That is when the voice came; he knew then that he must sacrifice one of the children. He tried to allude to the topic, in a fairly general way, to test his wife's feelings on the subject. She said, "That's crazy, you must be misunderstanding. God is not bad, he wouldn't ask for a child. There used to be animal sacrifices, but not humans." "But I saw it in the Bible, to make a sacrifice. . . ." Her abrupt dismissal silenced him. He stopped talking about it.

He had dinner with the family and made a special Jell-O that the "little one" had asked for. Then he read to her from the Bible, explaining the pictures. The others who were at home went in to watch TV half-heartedly, and they soon dozed off. Some of the jurors wondered how Mary, the mother of the child, could possibly have fallen asleep given the discussions earlier in the day. They felt that she was at least partly to blame for what happened. They did not know that she cleaned houses every day and was exhausted. It was just after she dozed off that Cristos took the child with him in his truck.

On two occasions, outside of court and in his office, I spoke with one of the psychiatrists for several hours. In court, he gave his medical opinion: the voices were auditory hallucinations. In his office, I was able to ask a question that he was not asked in court: "Do you think God can talk to people?" to which he responded, "A lot of people make that claim, but, for me, the evidence for the existence of God is marginal. The claim that God can speak directly to people presupposes a worldview in which God most certainly exists. If there is doubt on that score, then it follows that there must be doubt about whether or not he speaks to mortals."

Not all people are so logical, however, and many people hold contradictory beliefs. There are also plenty of people who go to church, but do not really ever think about what they mean by God and do not puzzle over the philosophical issue of the existence of God. They take it for granted as one of those things that goes without saying. Those who make claims about God publicly are not usually asked to give an argument for the existence of God.

Most people are not trained to think through an ethical issue or to work out their own position on it. It is hard work, as the jurors discovered. Thrown together in a small room, twelve strangers—males and females of different ages and from diverse socioeconomic, educational, ethnic, and religious backgrounds and life experiences—were sequestered until they were able to reach a verdict.[10] They had to thrash out their views of what had happened and, given that, come to an agreement on the verdict. But in order to reach a decision they had to expose their most personal moral beliefs to the scrutiny and judgment of the others. "Emotionally, we had to take off our clothes and get naked," said one.

Several times they almost came to blows. Another commented, "It is a good thing they don't allow murder weapons in the jury room, I thought J was going to kill S." It became apparent that making a decision was neither obvious nor easy. None of them was really prepared for the experience. "This was a lot more than we bargained for, but I realized it was no free ride, no mental free ride." Although the deliberations were difficult, most of the jurors felt, in the end, that their service had been worthwhile and extremely educational. Differences of opinion, they soon realized, were not easily resolved by reason alone, because they entailed different values, different notions of what a person is, of what motivates people, and even of what kind of world we live in. They talked about God and religion, about voices and authority, about fatherhood, mother-hood, sacrifice, love, and family—not to mention about crime and pun-ishment. Most of us rarely have a chance to spend hours talking about such topics, stating our opinions, trying to back them up, and trying to convince others to adopt our point of view.

Certain voices began to dominate, but they were not always male. One woman said she was impressed by the men: "They were quite emotional and that was wonderful to see. They didn't dominate, at least not in a raised-voice kind of way, maybe in length of time." But others felt that certain men did raise their voices, and even the bailiff heard them.

One of the more assertive jurors, who called himself an agnostic, told me, "If there is a God, then yes, I guess he could speak directly to people, but I don't think it happens on a regular basis on this planet." An equally assertive woman said: "Very few chosen people have experienced that—I don't think even a priest or the pope—you have to be an extra special person. People like that Oral Roberts who say, "If I don't make a million dollars, I'll die,' are using it [the idea that God speaks to them] just to make money." She had her own system for classifying religions: "There are Catholics, Evangelicals (well, Episcopalians), Jews, Greeks, Protes-tants, and Lutherans—they're religions. But the Baptists—the Bakkers and the Swaggarts—they're just out to make money."

Another woman felt quite strongly that she had been given personal direction by God. At a critical time in her life she searched for some guid-ance and, in her hour of need, God did come. "God can speak to people sometimes; I get premonitions about things, like a flash." One of the men agreed, "Yes, it's possible, why not? But that doesn't mean I think God is necessarily a Being—like you or me—but something else, something bigger." He was convinced that Cristos believed God had spoken to him. But another man was adamant in his belief that God, whether or not he exists, cannot speak to people. "People use it as an excuse, it makes them feel better to have God on their side. It made Cristos feel easier about killing his child, if it was God who told him to."

One of the alternate jurors was a nurse. She said that some of her elderly and dying patients had auditory hallucinations, but not one of them had ever said that God spoke to them. And "you would think that might be just the time." Instead, they have said things like, "I am at peace," "I feel close to my Maker." For her, a patient's claim that God spoke to him or her would indicate mental illness. And she added, "When one is under the influence of mental illness, it doesn't much matter whether the voice is God's or the devil's." That was the position of most of the jurors, but one or two said it would make a difference. "If Cristos thought it was the devil, I would have thought him a wicked man, but since it was God's voice, it makes him kind of holy."[11] On the other hand, she said, "God wouldn't ask such craziness. If God had asked me to do such a thing, I would have said: why me? what's so special about me? why do I have to prove something?"

She would have argued with God and would have resisted. In the biblical story, Abraham argued with God about trying to spare the few good men of Sodom and Gomorrah. Yet when it came to his own beloved son, he never murmured, never argued. He acquiesced without a word. So, too, did Cristos. According to the psychiatrist, "There was not even a question, no conflict in mind; it only became so later under questioning."

Another of the women said that her first impulse would have been to protect the child, even though she does not have one. She went on to describe a situation in which she was in charge of her younger siblings. They had all gone to a movie and on the way home five men tried to get in the car. When she saw her little sister sleeping in the back seat, she "stepped on the pedal and took off, leaving two bodies on the ground. . . . [T]he impulse was so strong to protect the children that if I hit them [the men] then I hit them." They were not killed. "The whole idea that God would ask for a child to be sacrificed is simply nuts." She had thought Abraham was first told to sacrifice the lamb, and so she had wondered why he took his child instead. She thought Cristos was as confused as Abraham, but in the course of the trial she realized that she had had the story mixed up and wondered whether that was what she had been taught in Catholic Sunday School. "But if Cristos heard the voice of the devil, I would have thought he belonged to a cult." She and a couple of the others first thought maybe he did belong to some kind of Satanic cult. "Occasionally you hear such things about cults, that supposedly human sacrifice is performed." She also confided that when the other jurors heard that I was an anthropologist some of them thought I must be interested in ritual sacrifice. Others thought I was observing interpersonal dynamics among the jurors. On such slender threads of evidence, we weave elaborate stories.

Connecting what Cristos did with ritual sacrifice is a common enough conceptual move; it is the same move that scholars of the Bible make when interpreting the story of Abraham. Yet a ritual sacrifice would, by its very nature, be a regular, even if rare, occurrence, for that is what *ritual* means. Cristos was following a pattern established by Abraham, but ritual sacrifice is not an appropriate arena for interpreting the Abraham story, although it is just where most interpretive efforts have focused. It is also important to remember that the most important sacrifice in the Christian world was a one-time event and, therefore, hardly ritual.

What has been ritualized, instead, is the symbolic repetition, or the memory, of that event.

Cristos claimed that his deed, too, was unique and in response to a direct command from God. It was not about following a ritual but about following orders—from God. For him, clearly, the voice mattered. Not so for many of the jurors. For them, it was just a voice. It made no difference whether the voice was God's or the devil's.

The judge, however, thought differently. Although this was his first murder case and his first insanity case, he had seen lots of people who claimed to have had communications from all kinds of voices. "Just go take a look at the LPS roster."[12] Speaking with him in his chambers a few weeks after the trial, I was impressed by his open mind and his willingness to tolerate ambiguity. He said, "Throughout human history there have been phenomena that are not easily explained in our common framework of explanation." He cited the belief in beings from outer space as an example. "In the 1950s there were all kinds of reports of flying saucers. Most people don't believe it happens, but a few wonder." He left open a space for that wonder, that uncertainty—a good quality in a judge, I thought. The more I thought about it, the more I thought Cristos Valenti had been well served by the justice system. He had had an excellent public defender, whom a number of the jurors thought was an expensive private lawyer. Cristos had also had a thoughtful psychiatrist and an open-minded judge. The judge told me that I had witnessed an excellent trial, meaning that all had played their parts to perfection and that the procedure had been smoothly accomplished. "You don't see many like that," he said.

He took a long time pondering whether it would make a difference if the voice had been from the devil, not from God. Finally he said, "Yes, it does make a difference. There is something more sympathetic about a person who says it is God, not the devil, who is telling him what to do. It casts the perpetrator in a better light. . . . But it is a two-edged sword because if you do evil at the command of God, it almost seems hypocritical. It is easier to understand if evil things are done at the command of evil. Then there is not such a contradiction, not such a paradox." It was just that paradox that exercised Kierkegaard in *Fear and Trembling*, his book on the story of Abraham. When I asked the judge about the story of Abraham, he said he could not help but make the connection, the parallel was so strong. "But," he said, his association with it "goes back more than forty years. I thought it was gruesome at the time and found it very difficult as a child, in Sunday School."

Neither the prosecutor nor the public defender called Cristos's minister to the stand. He might have provided valuable information about Cristos's character, religious involvement, and background; he might have been able to recall the contexts in which he had discussed the Abraham story and/or sacrifice. When I interviewed him at his church, he told me that he did not think Cristos was insane, even though he claimed to hear voices. He had trusted Cristos to drive the church's school bus. The minister also said that God had not told Cristos to do it, that another voice had. "He was driving toward the park—right over there," he pointed. "He heard another voice that said: take the child back to her mother. He was going to turn around, but too many cars came along and he couldn't. He was going to obey that voice, but then the other voice said: take her, take her." How the minister knew all this, he did not say.

The minister is the only one who gave any indication that Cristos struggled between good and evil, between the voice of God and the voice of the devil. But which is which? In both Jewish midrash and Muslim legend, to be dealt with in chapters 5 and 7 the voice of ethical reason is expressed by the figure of the devil, who says to Abraham something like: "How could you possibly think of killing your precious son? This is the son God said would make you the father of many nations." The point of both midrash and legend is that the devil is trying to tempt Abraham away from his duty to God by arousing his compassion for his son. Abraham's duty was to follow God's command. But in the twentieth century, the minister felt that the voice telling Cristos to do the deed could not possibly have been God's.

The minister's view was made clear in the next sentence: "If he'd turned around, then it would have been like the Abraham story." In other words, Cristos's story would have (should have) had the same ending. Stories, for the minister, were models, if followed exactly. What he failed to recognize was that it was not Abraham who averted the sacrifice, but God. Cristos, too, was following a command from God, not the biblical model, and his God did not tell him to stop.

During the autumn prior to the fateful event, the church's Bible study group had studied Genesis 22. The minister could not remember whether Cristos had been there, but other members of the family were. The minister read to me some of the Christian commentary he had used in the group, some of which construes Abraham's sacrifice as a trial run for the Crucifixion. "Abraham laid the wood on Isaac as the cross was put on Jesus." The minister connected this to Noah getting wood for the Ark and went on to explain that the word for "*tar pitch*, that which sealed Noah's ark, is also the word for the blood of Jesus protecting us from the evil of the world, the outside."

There was a huge, crudely constructed wooden cross in the vestibule of the church. I asked him about it. He was obviously pleased; he had made it. "We used that at Easter time; a child was fastened to it throughout the service. People were very moved." In physically representing the Crucifixion, the central act of Christianity, the sacrifice that atoned for sins, he had made it present and visible. (Recall, too, that Genesis 22 is recited during the services of Easter week.) Returning to Cristos, the minister said, "God has no need for sacrifices any more. Jesus is the sacrifice. In Old Testament times animal sacrifices were made. However, a lot of it was simply due to the fact that all meat that was to be eaten had to be brought to the altar to be sacrificed. People don't know that," he said. But he went on to talk of other sacrifices that were performed to cleanse people so that they could enter into the presence of the Lord. "But now, those who love Jesus are saved. They do not need to make sacrifices, they need to love God." How? He then alluded to Gospel passages (Matt. 10:37; Luke 14:26) that say, in effect: If you love your wife, mother, daughter, son more than me, you are not worthy of my love. These Gospel passages have always disturbed me. The message is the same as the one in the story of Abraham. The love of God takes precedence and is often represented as conflicting with love of family. But why shouldn't love of God be shown *through* caring relationships with family and fellows?

Why should the minister or anyone else assume that God always wants the same thing? Nevertheless, the most common response was that Cristos would have been following God's orders if he had followed the Abraham story more exactly. How do they know? How can they presume to know the mind of God?

Cristos seemed to believe that he was following God's orders, that he was being obedient to God. That is why he felt he had done the right thing, even though it conflicted with human law and ethical norms. "He was a man at peace with himself and his Maker," was the impression of the police who questioned him the night of the event. He surely gave that impression in court. He scarcely moved throughout the long, grueling hours of the trial; his facial expression did not change, and he kept his hands folded on the table.

The psychiatrist said that Catholics of his generation, and he included himself as well as Cristos, were brought up by nuns, priests, and parents who stressed obedience. "You were taught that the ultimate expression of goodness was to do what parents, father, cardinal, pope wanted. If you do what you are told you will always be saved; that was the important message."

Several jurors corroborated this view. One woman said she had divorced the Catholic Church when she was eleven, and that leaving the church was as difficult as leaving a marriage. But the church had betrayed her. She had gone to Catholic school and church. She had missed mass a couple of times and went to the priest to confess. But, instead of absolving her, he raged at her, "You don't deserve to be in Catholic school," and told her to get a transfer to public school. "I said I was sorry, but he didn't forgive me. I realized then I had a choice: either I am damned forever, this is not my church, or, if I remained, I would go crazy." She decided that it was not her church and left it; that difficult decision caused psychological pain that is still with her thirty years later. "It takes a lot of work to undo the harmful stuff; it's scary because it pervades everything. A lot of it you are just not aware of until something happens. You are not always being tested on a day-to-day basis." But when her test came, she resisted, she did not acquiesce.

A nun to whom she confided this incident did even more damage. "I trusted her but she screwed up my mind even more than the priest because she said: I want you to forget everything that happened; pretend it never happened and don't tell anyone." The nun wanted her to deny what had happened as well as her feelings about it; the nun did not support her. "I still didn't get absolution and I felt like a sinner; it meant eternal damnation." That event had a major impact on her life; after that she couldn't trust nuns or priests. "That was a crazy thing to do to a young child." She decided that *her* God would not be like that. She came to the conclusion that God does not make these rules, that men do. "All my life it was inculcated in me to uphold men and their values." She was betrayed by the very people she'd been brought up to trust, who represented authority as well as love. But in her hour of need, they had betrayed her.

It was precisely on the dictum of obedience to a higher authority that Cristos Valenti made his defense. He knew it was against human morality, but how could you not obey God, "the Boss of everything?" That was the position the public defender argued. He also argued that Cristos's belief in a higher power overrode malice, a necessary condition for murder in the first degree.

Trial by Jury[13]

There is religious precedent for a jury of twelve, and that is the number in modern American jury trials.[14] The jury selected for Cristos's trial consisted of six men, six women, and two alternates, both of whom were women. All but one of the women, including the alternates, had been raised Catholic, and the one exception had often gone to mass with her Catholic friends. Most of them were not, at the time of the trial, practicing Catholics. The religious background of the men was more varied; only one was Catholic. One, born in Europe, claimed he had been brought up without any religious training because his father was so against it. "Religion is what caused my father to emigrate to the United States." Another man, who was an avowed agnostic, said his wife calls him a heathen. One was Baptist, and two were Methodist.

Fourteen people with such different backgrounds, such varied histories and life experiences were brought together as peers not only of each other but also of the accused. The notion of a trial by peers begins with the Magna Carta, but surprisingly, the U.S. Constitution mentions only a trial by an impartial jury. According to the judge's instructions, this means, "You must not be influenced by pity for a defendant or by prejudice against him. You must not be biased against the defendant because he has been arrested for this offense, charged with a crime and brought to trial. You must not be influenced by mere sentiment, conjecture, sympathy, passion, prejudice, public opinion, or public feeling." Yet it seems unreasonable, contrary to human nature, even perverse, to ask jurors to suppress their human feelings.

This view of rationality and objectivity has been revered in Western tradition as a whole, not only in its legal tradition.[15] As we shall see in chapter 5, Abraham is revered because he suppressed his compassion for his son and was willing to kill him in order to do God's will. The ability to suppress human feeling is also the quality desired in jurors. But isn't human compassion more appropriate?

The popular belief that one should be tried by one's peers—consisting, at least partially, of people of the same ethnicity, race, sex, religion, and class—may make more sense than the norm of impartiality. Popular sentiment recognizes that these cultural issues do make a difference. According to the American Heritage Dictionary, "A peer is one who has equal standing with another as in rank, class, or age." Although a trial of peers may seem more just than a trial by an impartial jury, can there ever really be a jury of peers at a murder trial?

The most significant impediment is the obvious power discrepancy. The decision of the jury affects the life of the defendant, whereas the latter has no power over them—so they can hardly be considered peers in power or rank. One juror felt it was inequitable that the jurors all spoke English well, whereas Cristos needed an interpreter. Three of the jurors, however, were from the same ethnic group and spoke the language he did. Although one of the jurors was retired, none of the others was unemployed, as the defendant had been for some time. The incomes of the working jurors ranged from about thirty thousand dollars to a high of ninety thousand. Clearly, they were not peers in class or income. All the jurors had more education than the defendant. All but one of the jurors had children. The defendant was forty-seven; the ages of the jurors ranged from thirty-four to sixty-nine but most were in their late forties or early fifties. The religious background of the defendant was well represented among the jurors.

The closest peer was a man who was the same age and of the same ethnic group, had been brought up Catholic, had been in jail for domestic violence, and had been a drinker, like the defendant. "I've been there," he said. He had to use up his vacation time in order to be on the jury. Others missed several weeks of work, without pay. The court paid only five dollars a day—hardly enough to cover transportation and lunch. Some jurors' employers absorbed the costs. But the burden of fulfilling their civic duty fell, not surprisingly, on the very people who could least afford it.

When the jurors were given a brief description of the case, only one recalled having seen it in the newspaper more than a year earlier. Although four of them had been jurors in civil cases, none had ever sat on a murder trial. "Most of us didn't know what it meant to be a juror. I got some pamphlets and read up on it," one of the men told me, when I interviewed him after the trial. One of the women, who had recently moved to the area and was taking a self-imposed extended break from work, was happy she had the time to fully throw herself into the trial and to be able to give it her undivided attention. Not all of them were as diligent or took it so seriously. One woman admitted that she had almost faked an excuse to get out of jury duty because it was going to interrupt her professional life. But in the middle of the jury selection, she decided it was an opportunity to see the workings of the court and the mechanics of the law.[16] She also felt that destiny was involved, because her birthday fell on the same day that the murder was committed. Another juror turned forty-seven the day the jury was selected. Several other jurors mentioned personal connections to dates, names, or places associated with the case. Was this a tacit acknowledgement that they, too, believed in some external power moving their fate?

Most admitted that they were pretty naive and had little idea about what would be demanded of them intellectually and emotionally. They went into the trial thinking of themselves as observers called upon to make a rational decision based on evidence and facts. They did not expect that the trial would have a powerful emotional effect that would change their lives.[17] "It was an extraordinary learning experience compressed into the space of a couple of weeks." Although some of the explanations by the lawyers and psychiatrists were like lectures, the jurors were especially referring to how much they learned about themselves and about human nature.

All but two of the jurors knew the story of Abraham and were aware of the parallels. One of the men said, "You remember what you are taught, and it affects the way you think." Another of the men told me that it was after he had heard the Abraham story (the sacrifice part) that he stopped being religious. He also told me that children usually hear this story when they are very young, as he did, in Sunday School or in catechism class, before they are really able to understand or question it. In that way it becomes part of their cultural and psychological landscape. And I thought that this might be related to the widespread assumption that because the story takes place in the mists of time, it has no present effect. I wondered also about the way one's own early history can become intertwined with what one is taught about the early history of the (human) race. A few of the jurors, nevertheless, felt uncomfortable when Abraham was mentioned in court. Religion had its place—in church—and the two do not mix. The importation of a Biblical story into the courtroom seemed to muddy the distinctions, confound the categories.[18] Regardless of whether the Abraham story directly affected their decision, their views and feelings about religion were very much a part of their deliberations.

Framing a Trial

A trial is framed in a number of ways—spatially, temporally, procedur-ally—and the frame determines, to a large extent, what can take place; it allocates power, classifies people, and determines who has the right to speak and when, and what kinds of speech and action are legitimate.

This California courtroom was relatively new. It was paneled in fine pale oak, was well lit, and had comfortable padded seats arranged in rows along either side of a center aisle—like church. Several jurors and other participants remarked that the structure of the room and the ritual reminded them very much of church. A juror remarked, "there is no in-cense, no communion, but it is male dominated, the judge has his own altar, and they could be speaking Latin because it is a language all their own" (see also Nicholls, 1993). They would be interested to know that, traditionally, courthouses *were* built to look like churches. The translator was reminded of church by the judge on his high altar, the jury off to the side like a choir, and the chancel rail separating the legitimate partici-pants from the congregation. For me, it was more the sepulchral, hushed atmosphere and the way the process was set apart from ordinary life—in a kind of sacred space and time—that made me think of church.[19]

As soon as I entered, another analogy struck me. Which side should I sit on? Was it like a wedding, where you sit on either the bride's side or the groom's? Would it make a difference? The side I chose would be obvi-ous to all, as there were so few of us. I sat on the side of the family, mostly to be less conspicuous. Did others think, therefore, that I was sympathetic to the accused? The jurors didn't make that assumption, but the family did, and that, no doubt, made them more open in talking with me. I realized only later how quickly and unwittingly a course can be shaped.

COURT PROCEDURE

Court proceedings, as any viewer of Court TV is aware, are highly ritualized, very much like church ritual.[20] A trial occurs in a special place and time; there is a definite beginning and end to each day of hearings and to the trial as a whole. There is a precise order to the proceedings, and each person, from the judge to the bailiff, has a role to play. The language is highly stylized, as is the behavior and order of deference. Yet, as Rosaldo reminds us, it is important to remember that "rituals serve as vehicles for processes that occur both before and after the period of their performance" (Rosaldo, 1989:20), that is, by the structures and values that operate outside the specific ritual event.

The jury filed in past the railing that separates the official area from the spectators, and they took their seats on the right-hand side. The bailiff said, "Please rise," and we all stood up. I almost expected to hear processional music. The judge, in flowing black robes, entered through a private door and took his place on the bench. I learned later, when I interviewed him, that the door through which he entered led to "secret" corridors and offices, his chambers and those of the other judges—that is, to a whole area of the court normally invisible and inaccessible to an outsider. The term *bench* is hardly accurate, as it describes a very high, raised platform not unlike an altar, where, according to the jurors, the judge seemed to be performing his own rituals, which seemed to be attuned more to his private computer and phone than to the trial. "Perhaps the danger that unregulated contact with the public may profane the sacred aura of judges helps to explain why, even in secular republics, they retain more of the trappings of traditional authority than any other branch of the government" (Scott, 1990:13). The judge, wrapped in his black robes, sat up there alone with the symbols of his power behind him—the U.S. and California flags, and the seal of the state.

We were told to be seated. Then the judge summarized what was about to happen. "*The People v. Cristos Valenti*, accused of murder, a felony, number 187 of the penal code. He killed X, a human being, with a knife (exhibit A), and has entered a plea of not guilty by reason of insanity." We learned that there would be two phases to the trial. The first phase, the guilt phase, would determine the kind of crime he had committed—whether, for example, it was murder in the first degree or manslaughter. The second phase would determine whether he was insane at the time the crime was committed. The second phase was more critical because whatever was decided during the first could be mitigated by insanity.

The judge told the jurors the procedure: there would be opening statements by the attorneys; then, in the guilt phase, evidence would be presented by the attorney for the state. The defense would then present its evidence, and the prosecuting attorney (the district attorney) would have an opportunity for rebuttal. Finally, each would make a closing argument. In the insanity phase the burden was on the defense.

> Jurors are to determine the facts developed by evidence and come to a verdict. In considering the facts think about what weight to give them, about the credibility of the witnesses—standards here are the manner or demeanor, character of testimony, extent of ability to recollect and communicate, character of witness, veracity, interest, bias, prejudice, and contradictions, and to distinguish between correct evidence and circumstantial evidence. Attorneys' statements are not evidence. It is not your job to determine the law; the judge will instruct on the law and about the rules of evidence and the conduct of the trial. It is better not to take notes.[21]

THE GUILT PHASE: WAS IT MURDER OR SACRIFICE?

After summarizing the story and events of 6 January 1990, the prosecutor concluded his opening remarks, saying: "Cristos Valenti planned and executed the plan knowing it was wrong and had the disapproval of the family; he made a choice, a deadly choice. There is only one conclusion. Cristos Valenti killed his daughter; it is a case of murder in the first degree."

The job of the defense was more difficult. The crime is heinous and most of us are repulsed when we hear of it. People said things like: "The guy should be hanged or at least be put away for five hundred years. There is no reason to keep this person around; I would have gone for the death penalty." The grand jury, meeting before the trial, had determined that the death penalty was not an option in this case.

The public defender told the jury that a "trial is a struggle between two directors over who controls the script." The essential facts were known and agreed upon, but each attorney constructed a somewhat different story to explain them. For the district attorney the "script begins and ends on January 6th," whereas for the public defender, that day was placed in a wider context that included not just the extenuating circumstances and the events leading up to the killing, but also the ancient biblical story of Abraham.

The attorneys may struggle over the script, but its parameters are quite narrowly drawn. Given the way a trial is framed, certain things are not and cannot be considered. I felt that there was something very similar between the structure of the trial and the structure of the biblical story. What neither of the attorneys included, or could include, was the mother's story. Her feelings, her loss, her betrayal were irrelevant. She was permitted to focus only on the deed and on her husband. Her story had no place in the trial; even less was there a place for the dead child. No one spoke *for* her. The district attorney argues the State's case, the public defender defends the accused; no one, including the mother, was permitted to argue for the child. According to criminologist Paul Rock, "Victims have no standing in law" (Rock, 1993:169ff.); it is the State that is the metaphysical victim, which is why the case is mounted as *The People v. Cristos Valenti*.

The public defender began by denying that it was a clear-cut case of first degree murder. According to him, there was no malice—a rather archaic word, but crucial, as the definition of first degree murder must include evidence of "malice aforethought."

Murder in the second degree is "also the unlawful killing of a human being with malice aforethought when there is manifested an intention unlawfully to kill a human being but the evidence is insufficient to establish deliberation and premeditation" (CALJIC 8.30 of the Penal Code 187). Where there is doubt about whether the murder is first or second degree "you must give the defendant the benefit of that doubt and return a verdict fixing the murder as of the second degree" (CALJIC 8.71). Murder and manslaughter are distinguished by the idea that murder *requires* malice, whereas manslaughter does not.

Voluntary manslaughter is an intentional killing without malice aforethought. There is no malice "if the killing occurred upon a sudden quarrel or heat of passion or in the honest but unreasonable belief in the necessity to defend oneself against imminent peril to life or great bodily harm" (CALJIC 8.40).[22] Finally, a killing is unlawful if it is neither justifiable nor excusable. The specific definitions vary somewhat from state to state, and the judge said that there is some debate about definitions of degree of homicide in the appellate court. He also informed me that the Supreme Court was considering several cases in order to clarify the definition of manslaughter. A more uniform but detailed classification of homicide would be useful, as none of them seemed to quite fit the case at hand.

The public defender went on to say that murder in the first or second degree and manslaughter are all *intentional* killings. He digressed somewhat to give a brief history of the reasons for the distinction. When California became a state in 1850, laws about crimes and punishments were passed, but by 1856 they were already not working very well. People recognized that there were different kinds of killings, that there are different degrees of blameworthiness or moral culpability when a crime is committed in the heat of passion or as the result of premeditated deliberation.[23] He stressed that *deliberate* does not mean on purpose, that that is what *intention* is meant to cover.

> Here *deliberate* means that there were deliberations about the pros and cons of an action, as you will deliberate in coming to your decision. There is no dispute that this was an intentional killing, but of what kind? Is this a case of cold-blooded murder or an almost unspeakable tragedy that befell a family and a man who loved his daughter and a daughter who loved her Daddy? Was it the result of a tragic mental illness or a cold blooded execution? What has the ring of truth to it?

This was the only time Cristos was seen looking directly at the jury—and it tore at the heart. Several people had tears in their eyes.

The pivotal difference between murder and manslaughter is malice. And it was difficult to see malice in this case. The defense attorney painted a picture of Cristos as a quiet, respectful, unassuming, and religious man who went to mass. Not native-born, he struggled to make a living and bring up his family of six children (five girls and one boy). With his own efforts he had built a small but tidy house. He did a lot of carpentry, had added another room to the house, and continued to improve it and keep it in good repair. He worked as a carpenter but had been laid off about eight months before the event. He tried to eke out a living repairing tires in his backyard until neighbors complained of the noise. They described him as a good husband and a good father who never struck or spanked the children. Several of his children were called to the witness stand. They had not seen him since the event. Despite their tears and anger at him, they all testified that he "was a good father, was always there, did a lot of family things, was not strict and didn't hit them."

He did, however, go out drinking with the guys, as was customary among his peers. Although his drinking created some domestic discord, he didn't turn mean when drunk, but happy. He used to sing along with the band that occasionally played in one of the local bars. His drinking buddies, a couple of whom took the witness stand, said that he was law abiding, believed in the police, gave good advice, and did not hassle women. One of them revealed that his nickname was *Christ*, and his sister later confirmed this.[24]

In 1981 (ten years earlier) he ran into an old friend who had stopped drinking and found God. Cristos was impressed and went with him to his church; he, too, gave up drinking for more than a year. Then he had a relapse and continued to drink on and off until about six months before the killing. But just before he quit again he got involved in a bar fight, sustained head injuries, and was taken to the hospital. Doctors could find nothing wrong with him but superficial trauma. He was also arrested for driving under the influence, and the judge ordered him to AA. This was about 5 to 6 months before January 6. The public defender recounted a number of strange events that occurred during the fall—the two hospitalizations, his bizarre behavior in church and outside, and especially the fact that he heard voices.

The act Cristos committed, according to the public defender, was not a malicious killing, but the result of severe mental illness. The jury did not buy it, at least not in this phase of the trial. Fairly quickly, they returned a verdict of murder in the first degree. The public defender was stunned; he had thought manslaughter would be the obvious choice because there had been no malice. Their verdict, however, seemed to reflect the jury's feelings about the heinous character of the deed, rather than the intentions of the defendant. That marked the end of the first phase, but the trial was not over. This was not the final verdict.

THE INSANITY DEFENSE

We had a one-week recess before the second phase, the insanity phase, began. The task of the public defender was now much more difficult; he had to convince the jury that his client was insane at the time he committed the crime. He was insane, according to the public defender, because he heard the voice of God, he obeyed God's order, and he made a sacrifice. Curiously, the argument turned on Cristos's unwavering belief that what he had done was a sacrifice. He had to be proved insane *because* of his religious beliefs. How did Cristos know the voice was God's? But, so too, how did Abraham? If we think Cristos was insane because he heard God speaking to him, why, then, don't we think Abraham was insane? Conversely, if we believe Abraham heard the voice of God, why don't we believe Cristos? Complicating these issues are the more basic questions: do we think God can speak to humans, and, ultimately, do we believe there is a God?

The public defender seemed to believe Cristos; he gave a very moving and convincing performance. He told us that Cristos Valenti "believed absolutely that God commanded that he make a sacrifice. Like Abraham, he didn't tell his wife; he felt he had no choice. Since the master of the universe commanded it, it could not be wrong. God had ordained this act, yet Cristos knew it was against the law and that it would upset his family. Like Abraham, he knew he had to sacrifice the one he loved the most; it was his destiny and hers. She would become a star—God had a plan for her." When Cristos was asked: "What God, the God of what religion, told you to do it?" he said, "The God of all of them, and none of them," a theologically correct and sophisticated answer.

When Cristos was asked whether he would do it again, if God asked him, he answered yes. Since he had nothing to gain by that answer and everything to lose, his answer was evidence for both the psychiatrist and the public defender that he was not feigning mental illness. They felt that it demonstrated the severity of his mental illness, as well as the sincerity of his defense.

A long verbatim account of the testimony Cristos gave to the police the night of the event was entered into the record. It had been videotaped, and we watched portions of it in the courtroom. We were thrown back in time to the night of the event, brought emotionally closer to it. The purpose of the questioning was to test Cristos's basic level of functioning. Questions were asked about vital statistics—age, date and place of birth, address, phone number, social security number, license number, things that seemed so trivial in proportion to the magnitude of the event. More relevant perhaps were the names, ages, and dates of birth of his children and his own siblings. But since he was one of ten children, that was quite a task, especially because most of them also had children (his nieces and nephews), and he was asked about them as well. The entire process was long and monotonous. I doubt many so-called sane people could have responded as well as Cristos; indeed, some jurors were surprised that a person could be labeled insane and still function so well. The district attorney had picked up on this and had argued that, because Cristos functioned quite well, he must be sane and that, therefore, the act was first degree murder. And it *was* difficult to see him as insane—he seemed normal with regard to everyday functions. Even in regard to the sacrifice, he presented his case and his reasons in a calm, clear way. He clearly believed that God had told him to do it. *That* is what was considered insane; the psychiatrist said he suffered from a religious delusion.

At one point, near the beginning of the questioning, the police asked the following series of questions.

POLICE: How many children do you have?
CRISTOS: Well, I have five left.
POLICE: How many in total?
CRISTOS: There were six, five are left.
POLICE: How were there six?
CRISTOS: Don't you know why I'm here?

He must have begun to wonder just who was crazy. Although there were some questions he couldn't answer because he didn't know or couldn't remember, throughout the entire process, he never referred to what he had done as anything but an offering, a gift to God, a sacrifice in accordance with God's command.

But why that child? Why didn't he sacrifice his son, his only son? That would have followed biblical precedent. Perhaps that question is like asking, as did a juror, "Why didn't he stay his hand, like Abraham?" But Abraham did not stay his hand, God did. Maybe this time God decided not to; perhaps this time he needed more proof of obedience, of love. Although the Bible emphasizes sons, especially firstborn sons, in the one case in which a daughter is involved (Judg. 11), she is sacrificed.[25]

According to his son, who visited him in jail soon after the event, Cristos was in the backyard painting when God asked him for a sacrifice. "He was confused by God's request and went inside to read the bible about sacrifices. . . . God told him to sacrifice the person he loved the most . . . and that was when he knew it would be the little one. . . . He said he couldn't sacrifice himself. He did not feel guilty about her. When God came into his life," said his son, "he followed God's orders."

THE LAW

The court-appointed psychologist questioned Cristos about the law.

> PSYCHOLOGIST: Why are laws necessary?
> CRISTOS: Laws are for everybody because there's a lot of trouble around out there.
> PSYCHOLOGIST: Thou shalt not kill, what about that law?
> CRISTOS: That's God's commandment.
> PSYCHOLOGIST: Did you break that law?
> CRISTOS: Yes and no. I did break it because the Bible says that, but I didn't break it because God told me to.

Which is the law? That which is written or that which is given by the Giver of Law? What is the ultimate authority—tradition or conscience, a mediated relation with God or a personal one? This is no simple question: it is at the heart of the Catholic-Protestant split. Cristos embodied that split in his own life, as he left the Catholic Church and moved to a charismatic, Pentecostal Church.

The debate about written versus higher law enters into interpretations of the Abraham story. Abraham was before the law, before the written code given to Moses, so he could be said to be above the law, a law unto himself, abiding by the law given directly by God. He had a special relationship with God; he is one of the few people in the Bible with whom God speaks. As we shall see in chapter 6, Luther argued that Abraham was justified by faith alone. Since his personal relationship with God was unmediated by law or tradition, Abraham has been imagined as a quintessentially Protestant figure! God singles him out for his mission. Yet it is precisely the fact that Cristos had a special, singular relationship with God that today marks him, not as the friend of God, as Abraham was known, but as a psychotic.

The claim to a higher law is also a recognition that temporal, secular state law is made by humans and therefore fallible. The claim to a higher law is a claim of transcendence over human authority. Yet notions of God, regardless of whether he exists, are also humanly constructed, though this rarely enters into the arguments. In a secular court of law, there can be no higher law. Conscientious objectors claim to follow a law higher than secular, civil law; they claim to follow their consciences. But it could also be argued that they are actually following biblical law, specifically the Mosaic commandment not to kill, which is in conflict with the power of the state to command killing in war.

The claim to be following a higher law has, of course, been used by a number of people and groups in addition to conscientious objectors.[26] Yet even if we accept Cristos's claim that he was following a higher law, one that allowed him to abrogate human and even biblical law, there is still a question that has not been asked. What made him think he had the right to take the child? This may seem a nonquestion, because he claims God told him, that he acted on God's authority. And we have a whole tradition spanning at least two thousand years that tells us that everything belongs to God and He can do what He wants. This is what Cristos said throughout. But if there had been no model, he could not have made such a claim. This is when my own feeling about Cristos began to change. Even though Cristos was not physically elsewhere when the crime was committed, his mind was. He was preoccupied by notions of biblical sacrifice, and he understood his motivations and the deed in that sacred context. In that sense, the story of Abraham served as an alibi, an excuse.

The ideas that inspired his action did not begin with him. He was following in Abraham's footsteps, in the tradition that Abraham initiated. Cristos inherited a venerable tradition in which sacrifice, or the willingness to sacrifice, is central. Even though Judaism teaches that, with Abraham, God put an end to human sacrifice, and Christianity teaches that the sacrificial death of Jesus atoned for all time the sin of the world, the tradition has also taught that you must love God more than money, fame, and even your family, and that, if called upon, you must be willing to sacrifice what you most love.[27] That idea is at the heart of Judaism, Christianity, and Islam. It is the standard of faith. And it is that standard, that model, that I am calling into question.

Taking a person's life is quite different from relinquishing something precious, yet both can be defined as sacrifice. The conflation is dangerous, but it is traditionally promoted in interpretations of the Abraham story. In the modern courtroom, a sacrificial killing is not a legitimate option. Although Abraham did not, in the end, sacrifice Isaac, he did not question the legitimacy of the demand. He did not ask, "By what right can one sacrifice the life of another?"

What made Cristos Valenti assume he was an instrument of God's will in this case? The child was not *his* to sacrifice. Despite the fact that in his belief system everyone belongs to God, in the human world, the child also belongs as much to the mother as to the father if, indeed, it belongs to anyone. Yet paternal privilege is deeply rooted in the Bible and in our culture.[28] Like Abraham, Cristos did not think he had to get permission from the mother; he assumed he had a right to take the child by himself. The assumption is built into the story. It is so much a part of it that commentators have not felt it was worth mentioning.

WHAT THE STRUCTURE EXCLUDES

Where is the mother; where was Sarah or Hagar? The most dramatic moment of the trial came when the district attorney called Cristos's wife, Mary, the mother of their child, to the stand. She was a handsome, tastefully dressed woman who carried herself with dignity. The jurors were clearly impressed. She was shy about her ability to speak English and had requested an interpreter. That added to the drama, or at least to the tension, for the drama never really materialized, despite the poignancy of her testimony. She was never really allowed to give her story, to tell her feelings, so focused were the questioning and cross-examination on the event and her husband.[29] "There was so much I wanted to say at the trial, but my feelings were trapped inside me," she said later.

Mary wanted to give some expression to her anguish and her sorrow; she felt that her feelings should be considered, but they were not. She told me she wanted to cry out: "How could you [Cristos] have done this? Why? Why? Why?" She wanted some answer to the mystery, something that would help to ease her emotional unrest. Her emotional turmoil contrasted sharply with her husband's calmness, and this reveals the craziness of conventional associations regarding the irrational versus the rational. She wanted the court to know of the effects of his deed on her and the children, and about their nightmares. It was her daughter, the child she had carried in her womb, given birth to, and suckled. What about the effect of that loss on *her* life and on that of the other children? When I spoke with her some time after the trial, she told me she wished she had never gone to the court. "I was very confused after the trial."

The court seemed to ignore her claims or interests in the child. Her rights as well as her perceptions were silenced by the very structure of the court and the trial. She expected to be able to present her side and to have her feelings vindicated, but instead she had to focus on the deed and on her husband.[30] The procedure focuses on the deed, the specific event. The jury is instructed to focus on what is said, not on what is left unsaid. Mary could not ask any questions, she could not make her claims. She was as peripheral in the court as in the event and as Sarah was in the Abraham story. There was no room for her; it was not her story. Had she shown undue emotion, her testimony would have been discredited, "just like a woman." But isn't it more perverse to think she should have been calm, rational "just like a man" under these circumstances? Yet that is the expected and respected courtroom behavior; she had been well groomed by the lawyer.

We learned that she had been married to Cristos for twenty-six years and had given birth to nine children, of whom six lived and now only five remained. Enough tragedy for one woman. She had wanted to stop having children when she was twenty-nine, but he persisted. The little one was born when she was forty. We learned her version of the fateful day and what happened when she woke up from her nap and found them missing. "I felt desperate and ran out into the street screaming. I begged God that nothing had happened to my little girl. I woke up our daughter and together we took the car and went searching for the truck. . . . I drove through red lights. . . . I don't know why the police didn't stop me." When she got to the place where AA met, all was dark; no one was there. She went to her mother-in-law's house, and her sister-in-law went out with her to look for Cristos. When she finally returned home she saw the street closed off by police cars, lights flashing, and yellow tape surrounding the house. She swooned. "I knew something had happened to the baby; I thought she hurt herself, that there had been an accident. I never imagined what had happened."

The police would not let her into the house. They told her the baby had been hurt. They took her to the hospital, but only for a minute before they whisked her off to the police station. I felt that this was cruel and barbaric. She did not get to see her daughter or to stay with her. My shock at their insensitivity seemed to give her permission to register again her anger and her grief. With tears in her eyes and halting breath, she said: "I never saw her until the funeral parlor, and then I couldn't believe it was she, it was so unreal."

From the police station, the son that had accompanied her called the hospital. When he burst out crying, she knew something dreadful had happened. "She didn't make it, she died," he said. Repeating it in court, she also cried.

With such swiftness that we gasped, the questions switched to the mundane, as if to brush these emotions aside, as if to say they do not belong in the court of law, they are irrelevant to the case at hand. It affected me and the jurors as exceedingly cruel, and it did not work to the advantage of the district attorney. When I talked to him later, he realized that in this story, as in the biblical one, the child is left out. No one is an advocate for the child. "No one thought about her; we dismissed her, she [was] dead." He became pensive for some time.

From the emotions tearing at her heart, Mary was asked to think back to a time before the event. Then surprising news: Cristos had wanted to get out of his obligations to support the family. He did not want a divorce, only to be relieved of his responsibility for the children. We learned that he had driven their car through the fence around the yard and run into the house waving a piece of paper and demanding that she sign it. "He said he no longer wanted any responsibility, that I and the daughters could cope. I asked him, 'What about the baby? She's our own, you have to help her along. How can you say you don't want any responsibility? Ever since the first child you already had responsibility.' "[31]

"If you don't do it, I'll knock the house down," he threatened. "Give me time to get the children out," she said, without signing the paper. They went to a neighbor's house, but he didn't do anything further. So there *was* an ulterior motive, maybe. The district attorney brought it up and then dropped this tantalizing bit of evidence. The public defender changed the subject. Why didn't the district attorney press this? When I talked to the lawyers, both said something to the effect that lots of people threaten divorce, but don't really mean it. "There is not enough to go on." I am not so sure. He had no job, his unemployment compensation was about to run out; the pressure was mounting. Because the other children were mostly grown up, he may have viewed the little one as holding him back or holding him to his responsibility. Yet, if that had been the motive, Mary said she would feel even worse. "That is no reason to kill a child, that is not enough of a reason."

He could have just walked away, as so many fathers do, but he was probably not prepared to do that. His family and his familiarity with the area were supports for him. Without intellectual, psychological, or financial resources, where would he go? He may have felt trapped. The resolution he chose may have been the desperate act of a desperate man. The desperation may have pushed him over the edge. Who knows? Perhaps it does not matter, as he began to hear voices.

The whole trial is focused on him; he is the center of attention. The wife and child are excluded from consideration by the presumptions of law and the structure of court procedure. One is silenced by death and no one speaks for her. Her death should have been present in the courtroom, instead it was all but ignored. The mother was used merely as a witness, an accessory, not to the crime but to the main story, which centered on him.

The child is invisible and the mother's story has no legal weight; so, too, is her suffering ignored. After the "accident," which is how Mary refers to the killing of her daughter, her son slept in the same room with her to calm and protect her. It has taken a toll on all of them, especially the oldest girl (who was twenty-five at the time). She was the one, in addition to Cristos, who looked after the "little one." "She has no confidence in men, she doesn't want to get married, she just wants to be with her mother, but I don't want that to happen." Mary understands her daughter's desire yet hopes that she will be able to move on with her life. But she has no money to pay for the psychiatric help she needs for herself and her children. She is also responsible for her husband's hospital bills, and her house may be taken away. These affronts add to what she has suffered.[32] With one blow, Mary lost her husband and her daughter, and she is not compensated. No wonder she feels as if she is the accused.

DELIBERATION

The end of the trial approached. All the witnesses had been called and the experts had given their opinions. The attorneys had a last chance to persuade the jury of their version of the facts. The district attorney asked them to focus on January 6th, whereas the public defender asked again whether it was "a cold blooded murder or an almost unspeakable tragedy as a result of mental illness? What has the ring of truth to it?" Everything turned, of course, on the legal understanding of insanity. That was not a word used by the psychiatrists, who preferred the term *mental illness*. Most of the jurors had the common image of an insane person as out of control, not in touch with reality. Yet here they were confronted with a man who looked normal, who sat still and didn't fidget or roll his eyes or drool. His answers seemed rational.

According to police testimony, witnesses, and even the psychiatrists, Cristos was a man who was able to function quite well; he could plan normal everyday activities and carry them out. It was difficult to square that with insanity. The jury was to decide about the day on which the event occurred, so it was irrelevant that he seemed sane now. Still they wanted some empirical evidence that he was not sane; it would have made their task easier. The public defender used their expectations to his advantage, to prepare them for the district attorney's position: "Even though the psychiatrists and psychologist agreed that he had a mental illness, the district attorney will say when you hear the legal definition of insanity, you will find him sane."

The legal definition of *insanity* is not the same as the definition of *mental illness*, of which there are a number of different kinds. The judge instructed them: "A person is legally insane when by reason of mental disease or mental defect he was incapable of knowing or understanding the nature and quality of his act *or* incapable of distinguishing right from wrong at the time of the commission of the crime. The defendant has the burden of proving his legal insanity at the time of the commission of the crime by a preponderance of the evidence" (CALJIC 4). This is a clear statement of the M'Naughten rule, over which there has been some debate.[33] At issue is whether one needs both "prongs" of the definition or only one to judge a person insane—it is a case of either/or, or both/and. The judge further explained that a moral wrong is one that is in violation of general standards of morality.

During the deliberations, the one question the jury asked the judge to clarify was whether both prongs or only one was necessary to consider Cristos insane. The judge wrote: "In order to find the defendant sane, you must find that at the time of the commission of the crime he was capable of distinguishing between legal right and wrong with respect to the act, *and* you must find he was capable of distinguishing between moral right and wrong with respect to the act." The judge was following the ruling in Skinner.

Cristos Valenti clearly knew he had committed a legal wrong, otherwise he would not have asked his daughter to call the police. He also said as much in the first interview with the police. But with regard to moral wrong, the ground was murky. He knew that what he had done went against the general standard of morality and even against the biblical commandment "Thou shall not kill." He told the psychologist, "Well, you could look at it as wrong because it is against the commandment, but I saw it as doing what God wanted me to do. He calls the shots, if it's a toss between what is said in the Bible and what God tells me, I do what God says." Thus he was actually capable of *distinguishing* between moral right and wrong, if distinguishing is the salient term. What made this side of the scale more difficult was, of course, his belief that because God had commanded it, it could not be morally wrong.

If the jury found him sane, would they also be saying that God could be ignored? An insanity verdict, ironically, allows for belief in God and the possibility that they, the jurors, could not be the ultimate judges. Perhaps a verdict of not guilty by reason of insanity is our way of showing mercy. "The defence of insanity was, properly understood, only a way of extending mercy to some whose sickness led us to wish to forgive them their acts—that was all: a means of extending mercy when we sympathised with what would otherwise be a crime" (Morris, 1992:113).[34]

"He had no remorse at the time, but felt calm. He must have thought, I am returning her to God, maker of the universe, he'll put her on a star. He wasn't thinking, when I stab her, she will be dead." The public defender made the further point that if Cristos had not been insane at the time, he could not and would not have done it. "How could he? He loved her." He showed no anger, no hostility, no vengefulness during all of the questioning.

The psychiatrist said Cristos's mental illness was not as severe as some he had seen, but it was as debilitating. He said he had talked with other people who had murdered their children, siblings, parents, but in those cases "the quality of evil was unredeemed by insanity."

The district attorney then asked whether the psychiatrist would have a different opinion if Cristos belonged to a religious cult in which sacrifice was acceptable practice. "Then he wouldn't be crazy."

JUDGMENT

"Judging is nothing less than the wielding of power over life and
death through language."[35]

The jury got the case at noon on Thursday. They deliberated all that afternoon and returned again on Friday. I arrived at the courthouse at 11 A.M.; the jury was still sequestered. Cristos's family (mother, father, siblings) were all there. So, too, was the minister, who sat off by himself. I talked with one of Cristos's sisters. She said that the family, meaning their family of origin, did not like the minister. "He performed the funeral. We are all Catholic, but he did the funeral." Nor did she like the idea that he would report to Mary about their testimony and their behavior. The sister also told me that she had seen a change in Cristos over the fall. They had been very close, but he had become more distant. He used to sing and tell jokes, but he had become morose. "He used to come over to our parents' house and just sit without talking." That was when she told me that he was sometimes called Christ.

While we were sitting there, the jurors came out for a break. Their faces revealed the stress. Gone was the lightness and conviviality of the group. They went their separate ways to the toilet, or stood alone. They had to pass the family. How did that affect them? They did not talk with me. Some faces were dark with what appeared to be suppressed rage or maybe just frustration. It appeared they were struggling, not just with a decision but with each other. Later I learned that three of them had walked into the jury room and declared, "Obviously he is insane, there is not much to discuss." Even if some jurors agreed with them, such a preemptory move was sure to anger other jurors. The judge's instructions made it clear that their behavior was inappropriate. At lunchtime it was evident they were still struggling. I learned later that by that time a few more had gone over to the side of insanity, several were straddling the fence, and at least two were adamant that Cristos was sane and therefore guilty of murder.

By the afternoon break their faces seemed calmer, some rapprochement had been effected, they were approaching a resolution—but what would it be? Their decision turned on the M'Naughten rule, the only issue they asked the judge to restate. At 4:50 we were called back into the courtroom. The jury had reached a decision. They seemed relaxed. But the tension mounted. Would they affirm the verdict of murder in the first degree reached in the first phase of the trial, or would they cancel that out by deciding that the defendant was insane at the time of the killing?

It was Friday, it was almost five o'clock. The public defender announced that he could not stay afterward to talk with the jury, as was his normal custom, because he had to pick up his four-year-old daughter. Their faces registered this information—that all this time he had been defending a man who had killed his four-year-old daughter.

The foreperson of the jury (a woman) handed a piece of paper to the bailiff who handed it to the female clerk who handed it to the judge, who slowly and carefully unfolded it and silently read it. Then he handed it back down to the clerk. She stood up and began slowly: "The State of California, . . . Section . . ." and finally just before we might explode with tension, she said: "The jury finds the defendant, Cristos Valenti, was insane on the day of January 6, 1990."

Verdict, But No Conclusion

When the judge rephrased it and announced to the court that Cristos Valenti was thereby acquitted of murder, the jury was noticeably shocked. Somehow the word *acquitted* had not entered their minds as they struggled with the question of insanity. Many of them told me later that when they heard that word, they felt betrayed. They had assumed he would be put away for a long time and now they were not sure. Even though he was acquitted, he was not free to walk out of the courtroom; he would be assigned to a mental hospital instead of a jail. Just to be sure, several of the jurors decided to attend the hearing when the decision about his placement would be made. Nevertheless, with this verdict and this kind of placement, he will be eligible for release every six months.

The verdict of "not guilty by reason of insanity" may be a way of showing mercy, but in this case, anyway, and however much below the surface, it was also a way of affirming paternal power (*patria potestas*), a man's right to determine the fate of his child unilaterally, that is, without consulting the mother. He was never asked: by what right did you take the child without discussing it with her mother? And the question never came up in court. It was a crime of omission on two counts.

The trial was over. The family cried, I cried, the public defender cried. The district attorney was noticeably angry and stalked out, agreeing along the way to meet with jurors outside the courthouse. It would be closed in a few minutes. As the jurors filed out, one of them asked me about the nature of my project, for he had made a bet with another juror. When I told him it was about religion and the Abraham story, he said he had lost. He had thought I was there observing interactions among the jurors.

The trial was over but people's lives go on. More than a year after the trial, two years after the killing, I met with Mary again. I didn't know it, but it was the eve of what would have been her daughter's sixth birthday. Mary had just come from the cemetery, where she had laid flowers. She told me about the continuing effects of the "accident." She and the children continue to have nightmares, and they are terrified that if Cristos is released from the mental hospital, he will come back and kill again. Their story and their lives are private and they bear the consequences alone.

EPILOGUE

As one part of my research on Abraham, I attended a meeting of a small Jewish study group at Stanford University on the day scheduled for a discussion of Genesis 22. The group consisted of a rabbi, some students, and a few professional people from the area. By extraordinary coincidence it was the morning after the conclusion of the trial, a coincidence that made my participation more than academic. I had wanted to know how contemporary Jews were interpreting the story; now I also wanted to know how they would react to the story of the trial.

We were not allowed to take notes, because the use of pencils or pens is forbidden to Jews on the Sabbath.[36] Commentaries were distributed to each member of the group; a few were in Hebrew; most were in English or English translated from the Spanish, French, or German. Each participant, in turn, read the commentary he or she was assigned; by the end of the meeting we were able to perceive something of the whole through the different facets revealed in each text. Although each commentary was a Jewish interpretation, and strictly within Jewish tradition, each had a slightly different light to shine on the story.

At the end of the meeting, I asked them how they would respond if they heard about a similar story occurring today; and I told them about the trial I had just witnessed. The majority opinion was, "God would not ask us to do something contrary to Scripture." They thought the man had gotten it all wrong, that he must be crazy. The rabbi, however, raised the question I had in mind: "How can you presume to know the mind of God?" The first response is bound by tradition and is within the law; the other could be considered more theologically based, and in the spirit of Abraham, who was before, and therefore above, the law.

PART TWO

Archaeological and

Biblical Evidence

CHAPTER THREE

Child Sacrifice: Practice
or Symbol?

ONE of the most common attempts to interpret Genesis 22 is as an injunction against the practice of child sacrifice. This interpretation was given to me by lay people, by a number of ministers, and by a highly educated rabbi in a very sophisticated congregation. This kind of response finds support in numerous religious and scholarly publications. For example, the popular *Interpreter's Bible* states that the "story of the proposed sacrifice of Isaac would not have been told except to discourage a custom which already existed" (Interpreter's Bible, 1952, 1:1009). The *Encyclopedia Judaica* says the following: "The original intent of the narrative has been understood by the critics either as an etiological legend explaining why the custom of child sacrifice was modified in a certain sanctuary by the substitution of a ram (Gunkel) or as a protest against human sacrifice" (Encyclopedia Judaica, 2:480–81).

Despite the commonality of this type of interpretation, there are historical, anthropological, and theological reasons why such interpretations are untenable. Because it is so common, it is necessary to challenge it before moving ahead. This chapter focuses on the archaeological-historical evidence for and against the practice of child sacrifice in the ancient Near East and chapter 4 will take up the passages in the Bible that have been thought to refer to such a practice. Regardless of whether the practice ever existed in that part of the world, the evidence used to support these assumptions points to a period later than the story of Abraham, and thus may have little relevance for the Abraham story. Unlike most other theorists, I don't think sacrifice—whether human or animal, ritual practice or theoretical discourse—is the most appropriate context for the interpretation of the story. Just because (animal) sacrifice as a ritual practice became important in the Israelite cult and is discussed in later books of

the Pentateuch, it does not mean it is the appropriate context for the interpretation of the Abraham story, especially since there is so little mention
of sacrifice prior to the Abraham story, and no mention of the practice of
child sacrifice. *Sacrifice* is an important category of religious analysis and
is applicable to a fairly wide range of societies including that of the ancient Israelites. Although it may be appropriate for interpreting animal
sacrifices that were a central part of the cultic practice, it is an enormous
leap to suggest that they were a substitution for ritual child sacrifice, and
even more so to suggest that this is the background of the Abraham story.
Even if incidents of child sacrifice did occur, the notion of ritual child
sacrifice as a religious obligation and unitary phenomenon is, I believe, a
concoction of biblical scholars who constructed it from various fragments and allusions. It seems similar to the construction of "totemism"
among anthropologists who, from supposed beliefs about the soul among
Australian aborigines and from bits and pieces of their ritual practices,
fabricated "totemism" as a specific *religion* relative to a specific rung of
the social evolutionary ladder. But it does not and did not ever exist in
fact.[1] I am not presumptuous enough to assert that child sacrifice never
existed, although I am dubious that it was ever a cultic ritual. If it existed
in the Near East, I believe it was late, sporadic, and symbolic of patriarchal power. But let us turn to the interpretations.

PROBLEMS WITH THE ETIOLOGICAL EXPLANATION

The etiological explanation assumes that human (or child) sacrifice had
been practiced before Abraham's time. There is, of course, no mention of
it in Genesis before the story of Abraham and, except for that story, it is
not mentioned again in Genesis. If the Abraham story was meant to pro-
hibit the practice, one would think the biblical writers would have portrayed it as common. Instead, the preceding stories are about sexual relations and sexual transgressions. In subsequent books of the Bible the
theme of sexuality often occurs in relation to other supposed references to
the sacrifice of children; this association has not received the attention it
warrants and will be taken up in chapter 4. Finally, if the story was meant
to demonstrate that child sacrifice was "modified" by the substitution of
a lamb, it implies that child sacrifice preceded animal sacrifice.

Yet the story itself shows that animal sacrifice was presupposed. In the
most poignant sentence in the whole story, Isaac asks Abraham: "Father,
Behold the fire and the wood: but where is the lamb for the burnt offering?" Isaac, anyway, knew that the expected sacrifice was an animal.
Nevertheless, even animal sacrifice is rarely mentioned before Genesis 22;
there is the precedent of Abel's offering (Gen. 4:4), and though sacrifice

may have been the intention, it is not specifically mentioned. The only clear mention of an animal sacrifice before Genesis 22 is that offered by Noah in thanksgiving for the safe delivery of the Ark unto dry land (Gen. 8:20).[2]

Far more important, an etiological tale seems unlikely as the foundation story of three world religions. The etiological interpretation diminishes the theological importance of the story. A prohibition against child sacrifice, if that is what it was, is merely negative, rather than a positive constitution of the new faith. "The Akedah in its final form is not an attempt to combat existing practice, but is itself the product of a religious attitude" (Sarna, 1966:162). That religious attitude understands the story as a unique event and a "test of faith." Religious interpretations will be the subject of chapters 5 through 7.

EVOLUTIONARY ASSUMPTIONS

Etiological explanations generally incorporate assumptions about cultural evolution that are untenable. The notion that animal sacrifice substitutes for, or modifies, the practice of human sacrifice reflects just such an evolutionary bias—that is, an assumption that the more ancient the group, the more barbaric it was, and that, obviously, the most barbaric must have practiced human sacrifice.[3] Shalom Spiegel, for all the merits of *The Last Trial*, his fine book on this story, perpetuates such a view. "The ancients can accept the rigors of sacrifice as they offer up their first born to the gods. . . . It is only inch by inch that laws were mellowed and humanized. [In the story of Abraham is the] remembrance of the transition to animal from human sacrifice—a religious and moral achievement which in folk memory was associated with Abraham's name, the father of the new faith" (Spiegel, 1969:63–4). This statement implies that the ancients were not quite human, that human sacrifice preceded that of animal sacrifice, and that the religion of Abraham is, therefore, a moral and cultural advance. That is, of course, what we have been taught to believe.

Yet human sacrifice, when it is found, is found not in primitive or pastoral societies but in urban, highly sophisticated, and civilized ones. My use of *civilized*, in this context, does not mean morally advanced, or the preordained goal of cultural evolution; I mean merely to indicate a society characterized by certain complex forms of social organization, artistic and, often, literary achievement, as well as religious institutions involving temples and priests. This was not part of the culture generally ascribed to Abraham, which is portrayed as seminomadic, pastoral, and tribally organized.[4] Of course, whether Abraham lived at all is an open question; he may have been a real person, an eponymous ancestor of a particular group, a legendary, mythic hero, or a fictional character. Regardless, there is no indication in the biblical narrative that child sacrifice was practiced before or at the time of Abraham. All allusions to the practice occur not only after Abraham but after the patriarchal narratives, that is, much later in the narrative of the Israelites.

HISTORICAL ISSUES

The use of material occurring later in the biblical story (e.g., Exodus, Leviticus, Judges, Ezekiel) for explaining narratively earlier material is therefore already ideological for it incorporates theoretical assumptions that are not often articulated explicitly. It is not that I necessarily object to these interpretations, but the presuppositions need to be stated. In this case, such usage assumes that the narrative chronology can be dispensed with. Simply put, the problem is this: is the text a historical document and does it reflect or refer to historical traditions? If so, how? Or is it meant primarily to be an inspirational, even allegorical, story? These basic assumptions need not be mutually exclusive, for even allegorical stories reflect assumptions about what is considered "natural," the things that "go without saying." Nevertheless, they do affect the way one approaches the text. Different assumptions engender different projects and different modes of interpretation. To paraphrase Sandmel, the way one thinks about the story of Abraham indicates how one thinks about the biblical text.

Most scholars today assume the historicity of the text but debate the history that it reflects. Do the patriarchal narratives reflect authentic traditions of an early period, or are they retrojections that thinly disguise the preoccupations at the time the biblical texts were gathered together? The latter, of course, depends upon an acceptance of the documentary hypothesis, a theory first developed in the eighteenth century, that the Bible is composed of different strands from different places and times. Although "fundamentalists" and some others reject the documentary hypothesis, it is, today, a common assumption among biblical scholars and an increasing number of lay people. They no longer believe that the Pentateuch or Torah (the first five books of the Hebrew Bible—those that are most relevant for this discussion) is a seamless story that was composed by, or revealed to, Moses as had been the accepted tradition for generations.

The "documents" from which the Bible is thought to be composed are, in the documentary hypothesis, assumed to represent the various strands that have been detected in the text. These have been labeled E, J, P, and

D, and they are thought to have been woven together and edited by R. J refers to the Yahwist strand which means that the term for God in the text is *Yahweh* (sometimes translated as *Jehovah*).[5] J is generally conceded to be the oldest strand, written during the time of the Monarchy, sometime in the tenth to ninth century B.C., though Friedman (1987:87) makes J and E roughly contemporaneous.[6] In any case, that does not mean that the traditions recorded in J are necessarily older than those in E (Wenham, 1980). In the E strand the term used for God is *Elohim*, a plural form of *El*, a common Canaanite word for god. All of Genesis 22 except for a few lines is usually attributed to E. P stands for Priestly and is so named because the concerns of which the P strand treats are those of a priestly caste; D stands for Deuteronomy and is felt to have been written by someone close to the court of King Josiah. R is for Redactor(s), that is, for the editors who put the whole thing together into the text we have received.

Although the biblical text does not always form a seamless coherent story (for example, there are two different versions of the creation of humans), nevertheless, it is assumed that the editor(s) have spliced the various strands together according to some kind of guiding frame. The detective work that has gone into unraveling the different sources is fascinating but a different kind of study (see Friedman, 1987, for one of the best and most readable accounts). Most scholars assume there has been an enormous amount of splicing, but they do not really tell us just how they think the process actually occurred.

The questions to be asked about the story in Genesis 22 are: (1) Does it reflect or echo an ancient barbaric practice that the substitution is meant to supersede? This is, as we have seen, the common etiological, evolutionary position. (2) Or does it reflect contemporary practices projected backwards and, if so, are the practices those of vile others or of their fellow countrymen? (3) Does the Abraham story possibly represent the first introduction of the *idea* of child sacrifice—an idea later put into practice by some people? Surely, it has been a very powerful idea in the history of religious thought, particularly in Judaism, Christianity, and Islam.

Exegesis over the past hundred years or so has vacillated among several positions: (a) that the stories are literally true and describe the origins of the Israelites, (b) that, properly interpreted, they can provide a glimpse into these early origins, or (c) following Wellhausen, that the stories of the patriarchs "reflected the times of the later writers and not an older period in Israel's history" (Van Seters, 1975:7).

Biblical archaeology, though not confined to any of these positions, is, nevertheless, the result of acting on the belief that the stories incorporate or point to real events of real people in real places. Biblical archaeologists

were perhaps inspired by Schliemann's discovery of Troy and its trea-
sures. Schliemann openly admitted that his discovery was the outcome of
pursuing his belief that the Greek myths reflected real events and places,
albeit transformed and dramatized.[7] Some scholars harbored similar beliefs about the biblical text and began, in earnest, to explore the Holy
Land archaeologically.[8] Rather than "artifical creations of Israelite
scribes of the Divided Monarchy or tales told by imaginative rhapsodists
around Israelite campfires during the centuries following their occupation
of the country . . . archaeological discoveries of the past generation have
. . . [provided] the rapid accumulation of data supporting the substantial
historicity of patriarchal traditions" (Albright, 1950:3). Eventually, these
were dated by a number of scholars to sometime between the early and
middle second millenium (e.g., Albright, 1950; Bright, 1959; Glueck,
1955; Wright, 1960).

In 1975 John Van Seters challenged the view that the "patriarchal traditions" must belong to the second millenium and proposed the startling
idea that they referred to the period of the Exile, that is around 600 B.C.
Other scholars are more cautious and recognize that even though one
does not need to accept a second millenium date, one is not forced to
accept such a late date. A return to an early date for the patriarchal narratives has, however, been proposed by a number of British scholars (Millard and Wiseman, 1980). Regardless of when the stories were written
down, they argue that the stories contain authentic traditions from the
early second millenium (Wenham, 1980; Wiseman, 1980) and specifically to the Middle Bronze I period, circa 2000–1800 B.C. (Bimson,
1980).[9]

An important theoretical issue that is not well addressed in any of the
commentaries is a discussion and rationale of what historical material the
story *must* reflect. An old story can be recast in new garb as is so often
done in opera and film, for example. We need more information about
the criteria by which these scholars have determined what aspects or
items are essential and what are substitutable. Debates about the dating
of the patriarchal narratives will undoubtedly continue for some time, yet
regardless of their outcome, if such there can ever be, there is little or no
evidence to support an attribution of the practice of child sacrifice to an
early date or to the area from which Abraham is said to come. Because
this is such an important issue, it is important to consider the evidence.

THE EVIDENCE

Evidence for the practice of child sacrifice has been based on either physical, archaeological remains or epigraphical material, written material
explicitly referring to the practice. Mythological material is often in-

cluded, uncritically, in the latter category. Freewheeling comparisons from different times, places, and cultural traditions can only indicate that such a practice is possible; they can hardly be used as evidence that it did occur at one time in the land of Israel. Such comparisons might provide insight into evaluating a possible occurrence, but, clearly, the most reliable evidence would be from cultures that are related temporally and geographically.

Most scholars discuss the story of Abraham in relation to Israel; a few have also given attention to Mesopotamia and the cultural background whence Abraham allegedly migrated with his father.[10] Fewer have focused on Haran (alternatively Harran), the town they are said to have migrated to and dwelled in for a long time before Abraham left for the land of Canaan. Although there is no evidence for the practice of child sacrifice in Haran, it is here that Abraham's new faith emerged. Haran was strategically located and could very well have been the cauldron in which new ideas were forged.

Haran

Haran is a real place located in upper Mesopotamia in the Balikh valley off a tributary of the Euphrates. Today Haran, also known by its Turkish name, *Altın Başak* (Golden Wheat), is a small village in eastern Turkey very near the Syrian border. Extrabiblical references to Haran have been found in Cappadocian texts from the twentieth and nineteenth centuries B.C., and from the Mari texts of the eighteenth century B.C. Although there has been speculation about whether contemporary Haran is the same place as ancient Haran, most scholars now believe it is, making it one of the oldest continuously inhabited places in the Near East. Because it is still occupied, archaeological excavation has been confined primarily to the upper, Islamic levels, although a few exploratory soundings have revealed very early material evidence of habitation.[11]

Haran was a major stopping place on the trade routes connecting East and West, from Iran (perhaps even India) and Mesopotamia to Anatolia (and perhaps on to Greece), and North and South, from the Black Sea to Syria-Palestine (and perhaps into Egypt). In this ancient melting pot, stories, beliefs, and customs—not only relating to heroes and gods but also to kinship, affiliation, gender, and procreation—would have been exchanged along with goods, and these would have been carried home again with the traders. Recent scholarship has noted the similarity between the Akedah and some stories in early Vedic literature (Shulman, 1993; also Turner to Delaney, 1975, discussing work by Ramanujan). A conclusion would be that the Akedah must, therefore, reflect universal human psychology or a stage in its development.

Anthropologists are suspicious of such claims. Even though themes similar to the Akedah may be present in the myths of several contiguous cultures stretching from India to Greece, they are surely not universal. The myths of a father killing his son often have something to do with the male sexual organ (castration or circumcision), as well as struggles over succession; one can imagine that beliefs about masculinity-paternity spread across this area and were absorbed differently in different cultures depending on the circumstances.

Rather than taking sexuality, gender, and procreation for granted, we need to ask: what notions of the person (male and female), of affiliation (kinship), and of procreation are embedded in the texts, and in what ways are they similar across these varied cultures? Because Western scholars tend to believe that kinship is natural and biological, we have often tended to assume equivalence between ancient terms and our own, and to project our own meanings back onto ancient peoples. Biblical (and literary) scholars would do well to familiarize themselves with the anthropological literature on kinship. The problem with assessing ancient terms is compounded because there is hardly any corroborating sociological material.[12]

Some scholars of the Bible have speculated on the relevance of Hurrian custom and belief for patriarchal narratives. The Hurrians, a non-Semitic people, settled in the area around Haran at the end of the third millenium B.C. and "may have been responsible for the sudden emergence of high urban civilization in that region" (Foster, 1989:143). Hurrian marriage and adoption contracts, such as those found at Nuzi (a site in what is now Iraq), indicate a kinship system different from that found in the Bible, incorporating, therefore, different notions of affiliation, descent, and procreation. Speiser (1963, 1964:92) thought they revealed a kind of "fratriarchal system" that conforms to a certain kind of matrilineal system, and Jay (1992:94–111), possibly influenced by Smith (1903), attempted to show that remnants of a matrilineal descent system exist in the biblical text.[13] Children may be distinguished by their mothers in a polygynous society, but that hardly denies the overarching patriarchal, patrilineal structure. It is quite possible that the biblical stories were a response to another type of kinship system, and incorporated some elements of it, but that does not mean that the system was matrilineal, even less that it was matriarchal. (For problems with this concept, see chapter 1.) Because most of these theorists tend to assume that kinship is, self-evidently, about biology and blood relations, they also assume that notions of affiliation, descent, and inheritance must follow the flow of either patrilineal or matrilineal blood.

Although an explicit connection between Haran and Ur is made in Genesis, it does not disclose the religious connection between them.

FIG. 2. Beehive-domed houses in Haran, allegedly Abraham's home,
now a village in southeastern Turkey. Photo by author.

Archaeologically informed historians have suggested that temples to the
same deities existed in both places, even though the specific deities may
have changed over time. For example, Haran was, allegedly, the site of a
temple to the moon god Sin, apparently the "daughter" of the "mother"
temple in Ur (Parrot, 1968).[14]

Regardless of the enigmatic points of interest regarding Haran's past,
it is a pivotal place in the story of Abraham. Although Haran is, today, a
dusty village of beehive-domed houses (see fig. 2) not far from the Turkish
city of Urfa, the inhabitants are quite aware of its religious and archaeological significance. Stories and traditions about the figure of Abraham are found in both Jewish and Muslim texts and have become part of
the folklore there (see chapters 5 and 7). The area is now considered pro-
pitious for those seeking relief from problems associated with barrenness,
pregnancy, and childbirth.

Mesopotamia

Without specifying a date for Abraham, Philo of Alexandria, one of the
earliest commentators writing on the story of Abraham, notes in his *De
Abrahamo* that "in Babylonia and Mesopotamia and with the nations of

the Chaldeans with whom he was brought up and lived the greater part of his life the custom of child slaughter does not obtain" (Philo of Alexandria, [20 B.C.–A.D. 50] 1959, vol. 6:93). His opinion is supported by a number of twentieth century scholars who have investigated this topic (de Vaux, 1961; Mosca, 1975; Cartun, 1975; and Day, 1989). Roland de Vaux, for example, notes that "the theory of human sacrifice is scarcely tenable for Oriental cultures other than of Israel, but it has been asserted that even Israel practiced it" (Vaux, 1961:442), and he concludes that it was introduced into Israel quite late. The Akkadian words that have been translated as *sacrifice*, he contends, referred to libations—of water, beer, and wine—or to a meal that included all kinds of food but without any mention of blood (ibid.: 433). Furthermore, he claims that the ritual use and meaning of blood was minimal or nonexistent. He does note possible evidence for an offering in times of danger but claims that not even animal sacrifice took place; instead a substitution made of a reed-and-mud model of an animal was offered and then destroyed (ibid.:434).

Some people assume that the royal tombs at Ur, uncovered in the excavations by Leonard Woolley between 1922 and 1934, which contained the remains of several royal personages and their retinues, were clear indication that human sacrifice was practiced. The "standard interpretation now is that these were not human sacrifices but funeral gifts for the departed" (Cartun, 1975:18; see also Vaux, 1961:441). That distinction may be stretching the point; nevertheless, there was no evidence of violence.[15] "The search for corroborative evidence from Mesopotamian texts has so far turned up only blind alleys, as far as human sacrifice is concerned" (Cartun, 1975:18; cf. Mosca, 1975; Day, 1989).

Although the scholarly consensus appears to be that human sacrifice was not practiced in Mesopotamia, Green (1975) claims that it was and even distinguishes between northern Mesopotamia where he claims residential sacrifice was performed, and southern Mesopotamia where he believes human sacrifice was practiced as part of a temple cult. Residential sacrifice refers to the idea that children were sacrificed at the construction of a house, and it is true that skeletons of children have been found in the foundations of houses. Without additional evidence, it is difficult to ascertain whether these were actually child sacrifices or merely burials after the fact. With respect to a temple cult, the evidence he marshals is primarily glyphic: seal stones that portray "shackled individuals conducted by guards and put to death in the presence of seated deities" (Green, 1975: 192). Whether this represented the execution of criminals, prisoners of war, or sacrificial victims is, again, difficult to assess without textual evidence. But texts are problematic, as they do not necessarily reflect reality; just as often they construct a vision of it, and they are especially unreliable when referring to the practices of a "repugnant other."[16]

Even if one considers these events—whether the extraordinary burial of an entire royal retinue, or the execution of prisoners—human sacrifice, they are quite different from ritual sacrifice of children, especially of the firstborn son. Yet it is these alleged practices that are most relevant to the Hebrew Bible, in general, and to Genesis 22, in particular.

Canaan

When we turn to Canaan, the evidence for child sacrifice is hardly more substantive. The popular image of lascivious, barbaric, and child-sacrificing Canaanites has been abstracted from the Bible itself and embellished over the centuries by believing Jews and Christians. Ironically, the identity of Canaan appears to evaporate on closer scrutiny. Often, it is assumed to be the name that refers to the land of Palestine before the establishment of Israel. Others associate it more specifically with Ugarit (also known as Ras Shamra) and the Ugaritic texts found there. Ugarit was apparently a city in the early second millenium with its golden period in the Late Bronze Age (1350–1150 B.C.). There *is* a Ugaritic myth about the god El killing his son, a myth that appears to have analogies to a Hurrian myth about Kumarbi and to the Greek myths about Uranus, Kronos, and Zeus. In each of these the theme of succession is strong—the son is seen as a threat to the father or an oracle says as much. The theme of paternity and authority is quite clear in these stories, but they are not so much concerned with religious concepts and practices related to sacrifice.

Canaanite is also used to refer to a set of languages that includes Hebrew, Moabite, Ammonite, Phoenician, and Edomite, among others, but Ugaritic is not a Canaanite language![17] The Phoenicians apparently did call themselves Canaanites, and Phoenicia became a named place about the same time as Israel, around 1000 B.C. Phoenicia established a colony in Carthage, a city on the coast of North Africa, and it is from Carthage that most of the supposed archaeological evidence for child sacrifice comes.

Carthage

Although Carthage was founded sometime around 750 B.C., the archaeological "evidence" relating to child sacrifice occurs later, with most of it concentrated from 400–146 B.C., the year Carthage was destroyed. Therefore this material is, by any account, much later than the Abraham story. Excavations of Carthage have unearthed hundreds of urns filled with the charred bones of small children and small animals, such as lambs, as well as amulets, beads, and perhaps toys. Projecting from the density of the material excavated to date, Stager and Wolff "estimate that as many as 20,000 urns may have been deposited there between 400 and 200 B.C." (Stager and Wolff, 1984:32, see also Stager, 1982:158). They note that in the later period the percentage of infant bones versus animal bones actually increases, which overturns, for them, the evolutionary argument in which animal sacrifice is supposed to replace that of human sacrifice.

The human bones are those from stillborn or newborn babies, and they state that it is very difficult to distinguish between the two. If they are the former, the burial could not possibly be considered the result of sacrifice, as the baby would have been born dead. If not stillborn, it is still possible that the baby died within the first few days of life. The neonate bones, however, were often found together with those of a somewhat older child (one to four years old).[18] Stager and Wolff assumed that they must have come from the same family, "since this range is the natural birth interval that can be expected in families not practicing prenatal forms of birth control" (ibid.: 49). Nevertheless, they give no reason for assuming that these families were not practicing birth control, nor any convincing reason why the children must have been from the same family. Clearly they were unaware of the substantial scholarly literature on premodern knowledge and forms of contraception (e.g., Noonan, 1965; Musallam, 1983; and Riddle, 1992). And they quickly discounted the possibility "that disease or some other disaster would have affected only the two youngest children" (Stager and Wolff, 1984:39), without considering that the most dangerous period (because of disease, accident, or lack of care) for children is from birth to about four years. Instead, they interpret the finds as follows: if the child who was the intended sacrifice died before the sacrifice occurred, the parents would offer the next oldest child (ibid.:49).

Stager may be right that these urns and bones are the remains of a grisly practice of child sacrifice, but the evidence is not unequivocal.[19] His interpretation has, in part, been affected by classical references to the practice, some of which explicitly cite Carthage. All of these references can be found in the six-page appendix compiled by Day (1989).

Classical References

The earliest classical reference is supposedly a fragment of Sophocles' *Andromeda* (fifth century B.C.), which states: "There is amongst the barbarians a law which from olden times prescribes the offering of a human sacrifice to Kronos" (Day, 1989:87). Other authors often cited are: (1) Diodorus Siculus, who wrote in the first century B.C. but refers to instances of child sacrifice, also offered to Kronos, that are supposed to have taken place in Carthage in 406 B.C.; (2) Tertullian, a Church Father who lived sometime between A.D. 160 and 225 in Carthage, also refers to the practice of child sacrifice in earlier times (curiously, however, he notes that "between murder and sacrifice by parents—oh! the difference is great!" [*Apology* 2–4, cited in Stager and Wolff, 1984:33]);[20] and (3) Philo of Byblos, who wrote in the first century but allegedly quotes a much earlier Phoenician scribe Sanchuniathon (also cited as Sakkunyaton[21]) but is nevertheless preserved only in Eusebius's *Preparation for the Gospel* composed in the fourth and fifth centuries. Uranus, reports Eusebius, had several sons, including one Elus who is also Kronos whom he tried to destroy; Kronos, however, waylays his father and emasculates him. "But on the occurrence of a pestilence and mortality Kronos *offers his only begotten son as a whole burnt offering* to his father Uranus, and *circumcises* himself, compelling his allies (the Eloim) to do the same" (Eusebius, 1903:29, emphasis added). Whether the parallel to the biblical story was original or Eusebius's doing, the interrelated themes of sacrifice and circumcision are not difficult to miss. The question remains, however, as to whether the theme is about sacrifice or about the power and authority of fatherhood.

The references, in any case, occur over a period of about eight hundred years; none of them is an eyewitness account and only one (Sophocles') is contemporary with the events of which they write. The reports appear to be so similar that it is also possible that rather than being multiple accounts, as they are often presumed to be, each writer—or at least several of them—simply transmitted, and perhaps embellished, the same story. Then the question arises as to whether it was simply a story, or whether it refers to something that really happened and, if so, whether it ever became a ritual practice. Nevertheless, Stager believes that "even if we dismiss the classical literary evidence for child sacrifice as ancient slanders spread by foreign antagonists who wanted to discredit the Carthaginians, the growing body of archaeological and epigraphic evidence, provided by the Carthaginians themselves, strongly suggests that the classical and biblical writers knew what they were talking about" (Stager, 1984:38). He means, not just the burial urns, but also inscriptions on stelae that have to do with vows, and he cites a recurrent phrase "Life for life, blood for blood, a lamb as a substitute" (Stager and Wolff, 1984:40), which, according to Weinfeld, is "reminiscent of the biblical talio formula" (Weinfeld, 1972:135). Stager and Wolff assert that there can "be little doubt that the burnt animal burials at Carthage are animal substitutes for child sacrifices" (Stager and Wolff, 1984:40). But why should we not interpret the passage and the sacrifice as a propitiation, made with the *hope* that the child will live?

Day (1989:8, n.23) cites a similar but more extended inscription taken from Eissfeldt that comes from Algeria and is dated circa A.D. 200. "Prosperity and salvation! To the holy lord Saturn a great nocturnal sacrifice—breath for breath, blood for blood, life for life, for the salvation of Concessa—on account of a vision and a vow Felix and Diodora have offered a sacrifice *molchomor* with willing hearts, a lamb as substitute" (Eissfeldt, 1935:3–4). Levenson goes even further, stating that the vow "suggests that the daughter had become ill. Presumably, the parents, crediting Saturn with her recovery, wished to present him with an equivalent of the child who, had she died, would have become his" (Levenson, 1993:23). Let me suggest an alternative: there is no reason to suspect that the child had been ill; her parents may have offered a sacrifice so that the god would not take their daughter. Perhaps they had a vision that she would become ill if they did not perform the sacrifice.

This alternative interpretation was suggested to me in 1975 by an encounter in Urfa, a city close to Haran in eastern Turkey, where stories and practices related to Abraham still abound. There I met a pregnant woman who told me she had been unable to conceive for a long time. A few years earlier she had made a sacrifice (of a lamb or sheep) at a shrine dedicated to Abraham, where such offerings are thought to be especially effective. After that sacrifice she had become pregnant, but the child died. When I met her, she had come to make another sacrifice, with the hope that the child she was pregnant with would live.[22] In other words, it is possible to read the ancient inscriptions not as references to substitute sacrifices, not as animals in place of children, but as propitiatory sacrifices, requests for a healthy child.[23] I am not arguing for one interpretation over the other, but I am suggesting that there is more than one way to read the current evidence.

The Carthaginian material is often used to illuminate biblical references regardless of the fact that, even if such a practice existed, it was hundreds of years later than the biblical stories and perhaps as much as a millennium later than the story of Abraham. We should also consider how biblical references have conditioned our interpretations of the material from Carthage. Because of the cultural similarity between the Phoenician and Punic worlds, it has been assumed that similar rites must have been practiced in the "mother" country, Phoenicia, or more popularly, Canaan, and from there infiltrated Israel.[24] (But perhaps it was the reverse.)

The assumption of the existence of human/child sacrifice in Canaan has been derived primarily from the Bible and not from any explicit evidence, either archaeological or historical, from ancient Canaan. There are mythological fragments that include a story of the father-god El killing his son. El was a common word for God among the "Canaanites"; it was associated with the north and, in the plural form *elohim*, it is the word used for God by the patriarchs. *Yahweh*, in contrast, is the name used for God from the Mosaic and southern traditions.

Frank Cross, the eminent Harvard biblical scholar, thinks that the Canaanite El is best characterized by the word *patriarch*. Sitting at the head of the assembly of the gods, he is judge, lawmaker, creator, king, and father. El did not come by his position easily; there were many struggles for succession, similar to those fought by Kronos and Zeus in Greek mythology. The struggle was for patriarchal authority (Cross, 1973:43). The myths of Kronos, Zeus, and El are what he calls *succession myths*.

Cross sees an echo of the succession motif in the story of Abraham, but the struggles (between the gods) have been excluded. In the Bible, God was there from the beginning; he created the world and established his order. Although Genesis is not about the succession of the gods, it is all about succession: about which son will inherit, about who is the proper heir and transmitter of the sacred line. The struggle has been transferred from gods to men. In the story of Abraham, the issue of the succession concerns Ishmael versus Isaac. The story is not ostensibly about the father's jealousy of the son, as is the case in the Greek and Canaanite myths, but it is about obedience; the beloved son is the obedient son. The story concerns the issue of paternal authority and power. There is a problem comparing myth with biblical story, for the latter claims to be, and many people believe it is, the story of real, historical people and practices, whereas myth concerns the antics of the gods; and though these may reflect human practice, they may be purely imaginative.

The heritage in which the Canaanites have been constructed as "the repugnant other" obscures the fact that ethnically, linguistically, socially, and, no doubt, religiously, they were close relatives of the Israelites. According to Vaux (1961:438) "Canaanite sacrifices do not seem to be materially different from those which were offered to Yahweh," but they do appear to contrast with those of other neighboring peoples. That "which distinguishes Israelite and Canaanite rituals from those of other Semitic peoples is that, when an animal is sacrificed, the victim or at least part of it, is burnt upon an altar" (ibid.:440). Because the practice of human/ child sacrifice is often assumed for the Canaanites, the question arises as to whether it was also practiced in Israel. The idea that it may have been practiced in Israel touches some very sensitive nerves. This may explain the circuitous route from the periphery to the center—from other cultures to Israelite culture—that scholarship on this issue has taken.

Israel

It is becoming more and more difficult to maintain the view that the Abraham story reflects, and thus is a survivor of, an even more ancient practice by barbaric others, as Frank Moore Cross implied when he saw in Genesis 22 an echo of the human sacrifice supposedly made to Kronos (El) and the myth whereby El sacrificed his own children (Cross, 1973:26). Instead, some scholars are beginning to conclude that the practice was centered in the land of Israel itself (Mosca, 1975; Green, 1975; Day, 1989; Levenson, 1993) and that the story of Abraham and the "sacrifice" of Isaac was constructed in a context where child sacrifice was being practiced either by the Canaanites or the Israelites, or by both. These scholars focus on biblical passages that imply sacrifice to Molech or those that stress the idea that the firstborn belongs to Yahweh. These alleged practices, often used in the interpretation of the Abraham story, are the subject of the next chapter.

CHAPTER FOUR

Child Sacrifice in the Bible

IN THE BIBLE there is textual evi-
casional sacrifice of children. The story of the sacrifice of
ghter in fulfillment of a vow (Judg. 11), often compared
story of Agamemnon's sacrifice of Iphigenia, is the most
are a number of other cases, but whether they should be
ntinuum with the Abraham story is questionable.[1] They
at human sacrifice was a possibility, but can they be used
t such a practice was widespread during the time of Abra-
ham? First, these stories are very much later in the biblical narrative than
the story of Abraham. Second, in each case the child *was* sacrificed,
whereas in Genesis 22 it is not. Third, the sacrifices differ in motivation.
More important, however, these stories are not foundational, as is the
story of Abraham.

In general, the debates about the practice of child sacrifice in Israel
have focused on passages regarding: (a) the worship of Molech, (b) the
dedication of the firstborn, and (c) the relevance of circumcision. Sexuality in the service of procreation is prominent in these contexts, especially
as it relates to issues of legitimacy, yet it is hardly ever taken into account.
I suggest that it is the *theory* of procreation that relates and illuminates
these seemingly unrelated issues.

Once the male is imagined as creator/author of a child, the question
arises as to which child belongs to which man. A man's anxiety would be
most severe over the firstborn, because the woman may have been pregnant when he married her or had sex with her. The anxiety is also greatest regarding a son, because in this theory of procreation, only a son is
imagined as able to pass down the lineage via his seed. The emphasis on
making sure that the line passes to the "right" son is hard to miss in
Genesis. Insecurity over paternity might help to explain the ambivalence
over the firstborn; it would be expedient to pass over the firstborn son or,
conceivably, to sacrifice him. Before resuming this discussion, let us turn
to the issue of Molech.

SACRIFICES TO MOLECH

The ambiguity of passages, such as the following, have given rise to considerable debate. "And thou shalt not let any of thy seed pass through the fire to Molech, neither shall thou profane the name of thy God" (Lev. 18:21; see also Lev. 20:2, 3, 4, 5; 2 Kings 23:10; Jer. 32:35). Although the term *Molech* appears only eight times in the Hebrew Bible, five of them are in the Holiness Code of Leviticus—that is, Leviticus 17–26 (Mosca, 1975:121–2). Debates have ranged around several questions: (1) is Molech a deity or a kind of sacrifice? (2) if he is a deity, is he Canaanite or Israelite and, most important perhaps, (3) does passing through the fire mean a purification ritual or a burnt offering? That is, does it refer to child sacrifice?[2]

"Until 1935 it was universally believed that when the Old Testament speaks of Molech it is referring to a god. Scholars certainly differed on the question of the identity of the god and the nature of his cult, but there was nevertheless unanimous agreement that a god was intended" (Day, 1989: 4). In 1935 Eissfeldt threw a wrench into the works by proposing that the word (*molek*) was a "term for a type of sacrifice, just as *mlk* (*molk*) in Punic is a sacrificial term" (ibid.). Day, a lecturer on the Old Testament at Oxford, challenges this view and has reverted to the older view. He asserts, that although it is true that *molk* is a sacrificial term in Punic texts, there is little reason to assume that it means the same thing in Hebrew texts (cf. Weinfeld, 1972, 1978; Smith, 1975). Nor does he believe that the Israelites merely misunderstood the term and personified it.[3] In a short, concise, and scholarly book, Day claims, instead, that Molech *was* a god and that he was an Israelite god. Molech, for Day, was an underground deity whose abode was crevices and underground caves in the valley of Hinnom, not far from the center of the Israelite cult in Jerusalem. The worship of Molech, he believes, included the sacrifice of children at the *tophet*—a word that is taken to mean the place, perhaps a kind of pyre—on which they were burned (see Day, 1989:24ff., for discussion of various attempts to translate the word). In the Bible, *tophet* is used only in relation to the valley of Hinnom, not elsewhere. Even if this deity and the practices associated with him had been taken over from the Canaanites, Day believes that the cult was part of Israelite religious practice. In other words, he implies that there were (at least) two major deities—Yahweh and Molech—that were the focus of human devotion. The Molech cult may not have been official, but he claims it was popular among some of the people, especially among the ruling class, who turned to it in attempts to avert disaster (ibid.:62).

Day differs from scholars who "have concluded that, although Molech may have been a foreign god in origin, those who worshipped him equated him with Yahweh" (ibid.:65, see note 121). Some people accept this equation because of the (rare) associations of Yahweh with human sacrifice (such as Genesis 22) and because of the dedication of the first-born (see below), both of which, Day argues, are not the same as the sacrifices of children supposedly offered to Molech. He thinks it highly unlikely that people confused the two, partly because Yahweh is not mentioned in connection with the *tophet*s in the valley of Hinnom. He alerted me to the very interesting and thought-provoking suggestion that *Gehenna*, the term for Hell in Jewish literature, is derived from the Aramaic name for Hinnom. Gehenna is usually associated with fire and "the only fires that are certainly attested in connection with the valley of Hinnom are those associated with the sacrifices offered to the god Molech" (ibid.: 53). Without too much imagination, one can see how the *tophet* may have developed into the popular notion of Hell, as the underworld, with the devil (formerly, Molech) presiding over the fires.

Despite the protests in the Hebrew Bible against the cult of Molech, Day thinks the people did not see their worship of Molech as incompatible with the worship of Yahweh, nor did it necessarily imply their faithlessness (ibid.:68–9). They simply had different kinds of worship for different purposes, even though both may have involved child sacrifice. The sacrifices to Molech, Day claims, were children—both sons and daughters—and therefore should not be associated or equated with the dedication of the firstborn, who were always sons. He thinks these were different rites, established by different religious motivations, and that they should not be conflated (cf. Weinfeld, 1972).

Levenson, a professor of Jewish Studies at Harvard Divinity School, disagrees. He traces what he purports is the transformation of child sacrifice in Judaism and Christianity, and sees the types of sacrifice above, as well as a number of others (e.g., Jephthah's daughter; Mesha), as part of the same continuum. Not only does he place these biblical examples on a continuum, he assumes a comparative method: "without reference to ancient myths associated with child sacrifice, certain biblical narratives about the origins and character of the people of Israel and of the Church cannot be properly understood" (Levenson, 1993:37). Because his book is likely to receive a fair amount of attention among scholars, it is important to point out some of the flaws in his principal assumptions.

That similar practices can have very different motivations and meanings was made very clear by one of the foremost anthropologists in this century, Franz Boas, and it is a point that most anthropologists learn at the beginning of their studies. Rather than comparing all these various myths and fragments, we need to explore the function the story has in the Bible and in the religious traditions of Judaism, Christianity, and Islam.

Levenson's argument is basically psychological, for in order to make his argument, he must assume psychological continuity, even fixity, over time and geographical area, perhaps even a universal human psychology. But if one assumes a basic human psychology, as Freud and his followers do, how then does one explain the diversity of myths and practices? The mediating, even constitutive, role of culture is disregarded in Levenson's analysis, just as it is in Freud's. Levenson does not consider the interrelations between a culture's myths and stories and its people's psychology; that is, rather than assuming that myths, stories, and practices reflect universal human psychological needs and desires, one could assume that these needs and desires are themselves shaped by a culture's stories and myths. As Mary Douglas succinctly put it: "Psychological explanations cannot of their nature account for what is culturally distinctive" (Douglas, 1966:121). Not only does Levenson assume a certain fixity in human psychology but, as we shall see, he takes for granted that the meanings of gender are stable and self-evident.

He collapses Molech worship, the sacrifice of Jephthah's daughter in honor of a vow, Mesha's killing of his son to avert defeat, and Abraham's intention to sacrifice Isaac into a more general theme that he calls "the death and resurrection of the beloved son." Immediately, problems emerge: there is a difference between a daughter and a son, between a "beloved son" and a firstborn son (Isaac, after all, was not the firstborn son of Abraham), between an actual sacrifice of a child and an animal substituted for one, and between a sacrifice to fulfill a prior vow and the motivation of Abraham. In addition, in a chapter entitled "YHWH vs. Molech," Levenson speaks very little about Molech but suggests that, "to understand the nature and extent of the cult of Molech," we must turn to the "largest body of data on the grisly practice" (Levenson, 1993:20), namely to Carthage. Not only is he taking the contested material at Carthage as fact and repeating all the usual anachronisms, but he is assimilating the practice of offering *children* to Molech with the notion of the sacrifice of the firstborn son as it appears in the Bible (e.g., Exod. 13.2; 22:29–30). He does recognize some of the difficulties, but he says, nevertheless: "Lest the two practices be too sharply disengaged, however, the obvious point should be restated: both involve child sacrifice, and both seem to have had some frequency in ancient Israel" (ibid.:18). It is not at all clear to me what relevance material from Carthage, even if it is true, has for Israel. Levenson argues backward, both temporally and in significance, from Carthage to Israel, rather than beginning with what is clearly the most important story, the foundation story, of the three Abrahamic religions—the Abraham story. He further undermines the significance of this story when he refers to it as "the wrenching *little* narrative that is the aqedah" (ibid.:23, emphasis mine).

This *little* narrative, unlike any of the others, was, or at least is considered to be, a turning point in the world's orientation. But rather than beginning with that and moving out, Levenson collects bits and pieces of information and rituals from various places in an attempt to support his claim for the common motif or theme. Problems with creating such a typology—namely, who is creating the theme and the typology and for what purposes—have been noted ever since Frazer's *Golden Bough*. Even if we were to accept Levenson's typology, only one of the three explicit biblical examples he gives comes close to that theme—the one found in Genesis 22—and even there, the construal as death and resurrection is really stretching the point.

MOLECH AND SEXUALITY

A more fruitful approach, at least regarding "sacrifices" to Molech, might begin with the recognition that the biblical injunctions against this practice are in the midst of a discussion of sexual behavior. Much of the Holiness code and all the references to Molech are preceded or followed by discussions of who may engage in what kind of sexual practices with whom. Giving one's seed to Molech is analogous to playing the whore/harlot with Molech (Lev. 20:5), and immediately after this passage there is a discussion of adultery and other profane unions. Two scholars, according to Day, have supposed "that it was the children of sacred prostitutes who were offered up to Molech" (Day, 1989:23). Others, notably Weinfeld (1972:142; 1978:412), not so literal-minded, have noted the association between sacrifice and prohibited sexual behavior, but such suggestions have been ridiculed by Smith (1975:478).

Day, however, thinks the sexual context of the prohibitions is important and suggests that it is precisely because "the Molech cult is thought of metaphorically as an adulterous one *vis à vis* Yahweh" (Day, 1989: 23). He notes that "the ease with which the Old Testament slips from speaking of literal adultery to spiritual adultery is well known (cf. Jer. 3.1, 2, 6, 8–9)" (ibid.); that is, each context illuminates and reinforces the meaning of the other. Although Day recognizes the sexual context and connotations, he does not recognize the assumptions about, and implications for, gender that are embedded in these allusions. The warning, "do not give any of your seed to Molech," is addressed, at least figuratively, to men, whereas "whoring after other gods" implies promiscuous behavior on the part of women.[4] At issue is the fate of "seed." It is as wrong for men to give it away to whores or to Molech as it is for women to play the whore and bring alien seed into the pure community. In either case, the purity of God's chosen is sullied; the message was meant to keep the lines pure, and that demanded something of both men and women. The injunctions were also used figuratively. Israel was sometimes imagined as the "bride" of God; if "she" went whoring after other gods, "her" stain would have to be scrubbed out by, in today's vernacular, ethnic cleansing. Sexuality and gender are used for conceptualizing theological ideas and spiritual relations, but it is sexuality and gender as constructed in relation to a particular theory of procreation, as is made clear in the following passage: "The ultimate purpose of biblical genealogies was to establish the superior strain of the line through which the biblical way of life was transmitted from generation to generation. In other words, *the integrity of the mission was to be safeguarded in transmission, the purity of the content protected by the quality of the container*" (Speiser, 1964: 93–4 emphasis added). In Speiser's interpretation, the male is construed as the transmitter of the valuable content, the female is figured as the container. The pivot, of course, is Abraham, because it is through his seed that the pure line really begins. This issue, cast in a different light, is, I believe, intimately related to the issue of the "sacrifice of the first born." None of the interpreters have considered the sexual and gendered components.

Sacrifice or Dedication of the Firstborn Son?

The presence of child sacrifice in Israel is also deduced from biblical passages such as: "Sanctify unto me all the first-born, whatsoever openeth the womb among the children of Israel, both of man and of beast. It is mine." (Exod. 13:2) This and other passages like it have sometimes been interpreted as indications that perhaps children were once sacrificed, presumably to Yahweh himself.

Although the passage does not specify sons, that is the way it is usually interpreted. Clearly, not all firstborn children are sons. Conceivably a woman could have several daughters before a son; does that mean they were not counted? The word used, *bekhor*, is a masculine noun and could conceivably be inclusive of gender in the way that *man* has functioned in English, or it could be more like the Turkish *çocuk*, which means both child and son; *kız* is the Turkish word for girl or daughter.[5] *Bekhor*, however, has traditionally been understood to be gender specific, to mean firstborn males. I have no argument with traditional interpretations that assume, I believe correctly, that the referent was sons; but interpreters have not been explicit about *why* it is sons who are considered the appropriate sacrifice, and why firstborn sons.

Interpretations often assume that "because of his favored status, the first born is considered the most desirable sacrifice to the deity where human sacrifice was practiced" (*Encyclopedia Judaica*, 1971:1306). They do not say why the firstborn is the favored status, nor consider that its status may have become elevated *because* of sacrifice. One cannot simply assume that the firstborn was already favored—that is exactly what needs to be proved.

Curiously, Freud suggested that the favored position was that of the youngest son, and that it was natural because "protected by his mother's love, [he] could profit by his father's advancing years and replace him after his death" (Freud, 1939:103). Levenson suggests that *beloved son* is meant symbolically rather than literally, but he still presumes a status that reflects the concepts and significance of primogeniture. He is distinguished from other interpreters only by the idea that the status can be assigned at the discretion of the father (Levenson, 1993:69). Because "primogeniture is a persistent and widespread institution whose legal, social and religious features were reflected in the norms of ancient Israelite society" (*Encyclopedia Judaica*, 1979:1306), it is assumed to have been the norm in Abraham's society.

Regardless of which son, neither Freud nor Levenson nor any of the other interpreters considers the question: Why sons? What is it about sons that makes them special? It is far too easy to say simply that sons are valuable in a patriarchal society; one needs to ask why.[6] And one also needs to make explicit one's assumptions about the foundations of patriarchal society, that is, whether one assumes it is a natural formation or the result of specific concepts, practices, and institutions. Even if there was a tendency toward male dominance, patriarchy is an ideology in which the notion of *father* is integral. It may be true that the principle of primogeniture *became* the norm in Israelite society, but there seems no justification for assuming that was the case in Abraham's society. Any perceptive reader of Genesis recognizes that *all* of the firstborn sons are passed over, whether for blessing, favor, or inheritance, beginning with Cain (see Delaney, 1977; Syren, 1993). Levenson may be right that this is not simply a matter of God favoring or choosing the younger over the elder, but that does not mean he is right in concluding that God "*reversed* the order of the two and assigned the one he favored the status of the first born" (Levenson, 1993:69, emphasis added).

If one believes that the documents are humanly constructed, it is not a question of *God choosing* but of the motives of the writers for showing that God passed over the firstborn. Levenson does not consider that. Instead, he reads into the patriarchal stories motives that derive from the law/lore of a later (at least later narrative) time. His prior assumption is that the status of the firstborn is of greater importance, even if of less fixity—that is, he gives the father the power to *assign* that status (ibid., 1993:69). Because he does not question the concept of paternity and its integral relation to a *theory* of procreation, he does not consider the possibility that some of the textual ambiguity and ambivalence about the firstborn son might represent a conflict with other notions of procreation, or might be related to a transitional period during which notions of paternity and its implications were being socially assimilated. That is, he does not consider the possibility that the story of Abraham represents the establishment of the *concept* of paternity and its powerful implications. In that case, then, the passing over of the firstborn, as well as the favoring of the second or younger, could be seen as representing two sides of the same thing, representing the insecurity a man might have over the paternity of a particular child. A more nuanced reading can be found in Syren's *The Forsaken First-Born: a Study of a Recurrent Motif in the Patriarchal Narratives* (1993), which Levenson does not cite. Syren argues, basically, that the patriarchs stand in for God, their choices really signal God's choice of who is deemed appropriate heir. He thinks the motif highlights the whole idea of divine election. He still does not address the issue of gender: why fathers and sons?

In connection with the sacrifice of the firstborn son, the following biblical passage is often cited: "Thou shalt not delay to offer the first of thy fruits and of thy liquors: the first born of thy sons shalt thou give unto me. Likewise shalt thou do with thine oxen and with thy sheep; seven days it shall be with his dam; on the eighth day thou shalt give it to me." (Exod. 22:29). I want to explore several issues in relation to this passage: (1) the analogy established between fruits and liquors (assumed to be the press from grapes) on the one side, and sons and animals on the other, (2) the equivalence of the animal and human offering, and (3) the significance of the eighth day.

FRUITS AND SEEDS

Regarding the equation between fruit offerings and animal offerings, the allusion to the story of Cain and Abel is hard to miss. In that story, Cain offered the fruits of the soil and Abel the firstling of the flock; without any reason given, God is shown to prefer the animal offering over the fruits. The different valuation has often been thought to represent the "conflict between the pastoral and the agricultural ways of life" (Speiser, 1964:31; see also Pritchard, 1950; and Wolkstein and Kramer, 1983; but for an opposing opinion see Sarna, 1966:28).[7] Exegesis has also focused on what is assumed to be the paltry quality of Cain's offering in comparison with Abel's. One presentation seems to be more an offering, the other a sacrifice; one involves gifts from one's abundance, the other involves the destruction of life; one is a gift from the soil, the other of blood.

The conflation between these different types of offerings may conceal a theological/political agenda. We must consider the possible motivations of the ancients as well as of the modern expositors who have usually placed offerings of grain, animals, and humans along a sacrificial continuum in which the differences lie in their unequal value rather than in different motivations and conceptual systems. Fruit, cereals, and the soil have often been associated with women and with devotion to female figures (Kraemer, 1988; DuBois, 1988), whereas blood sacrifice is primarily associated with patriliny (Jay, 1992),[8] yet here and in other passages a conflation has been made between fruit and seed and child, as, for example in Micah's question: "With what shall I approach the Lord, Do homage to God on high? Shall I give my first-born for my transgression? The *fruit* of my body for my sins?" (Mic. 6:6–7). Clearly the man is imagining the child as the fruit of *his* body, the fruit of his seed (cf. discussion between Weinfeld and Smith cited above). Might the conflation between fruit and seed be an attempt to co-opt, encompass, and thereby appear to supersede, not a different means of subsistence, but a different socioreligious system, just as, later, Christianity rhetorically attempts to do with Judaism?

Human and Animal

In the Exodus passage we are discussing (Exod. 22:29, and in the earlier one [Exod. 13:2]), the human offering (sacrifice?) is named first; the animal offering (sacrifice?) is not a substitute for the son, nor the son for the animal: they are presented as analogous and both are required.[9] In Exodus, more explicit references to the killing of the firstborn are found, but they are not ritual sacrifices; instead, they are a sign of God's punishment. They occur in relation to what God did to the firstborn of the Egyptians: "At midnight, the Lord smote all the first born in the land of Egypt, from the first born of Pharaoh who sat on his throne to the first of the captive who was in the dungeon, and all the first born of the cattle" (Exod. 12:29). This was God's punishment meted out to Pharaoh because, although Pharaoh had witnessed the power of Moses' God, he refused to submit. His heart had hardened, and so God punished him by killing all the firstborn Egyptian males—both human and beast.[10] Yet it was not just Pharaoh who suffered. So, too, did all the innocent firstborn of other Egyptians, as well as their animals. Israel was sometimes conceptualized as God's firstborn son (e.g., Exod. 4:22–3), and when "he" was not being a proper son, showing proper respect for his "father," there were threats of punishment and destruction, similar to those meted out to the Egyptians.

In Exodus 13:13 and 13:15, however, there is a shift: "And every first-ling of an ass thou shalt redeem with a lamb; and if though wilt not redeem it, then thou shalt break his neck: and all the firstborn of man among thy children shalt thou redeem" (Exod. 13:13). This does not say the firstborn is redeemed with a lamb; instead the passage is followed by a reference to the exodus: "the Lord slew all the firstborn in the land of Egypt, both the firstborn of man, and the firstborn of beast: *therefore* I sacrifice to the Lord all that openeth the matrix, being males; but all the firstborn of my children I redeem" (Exod. 13:15). The Israelite God does not oppose the killing of children in general, but only the killing of certain ones. This passage implies that the redemption of the firstborn of Israel came on the backs of the slaughter of the innocent children of Egypt.

Circumcision, Sacrifice, and the Eighth Day

Let us look again at the passage above: why is the eighth day the one on which the offerings should be made, rather than, say, the fourth or the sixteenth or the thirtieth? The traditional explanation is that the eighth day is significant because it is, in Jewish tradition, the day on which circumcision is performed. The traditional explanation analogizing circumcision with sacrifice merely begs the question, however, for we need to ask why circumcision is performed on the eighth day and, more to the point, why circumcision?

Circumcision

The practice of circumcision was instituted with Abraham. It was the sign of the covenant God made with Abraham, a promise—engraved on the flesh of the male sexual organ—that he would be a father of nations.

> And I will make thee exceedingly fruitful, and I will make nations of thee, and kings shall come out of thee. And I will establish my covenant between me and thee and thy seed after thee in their generations for an everlasting covenant, to be a God unto thee, and to thy seed after thee. And I will give unto thee, and to thy seed after thee, the land wherein thou art a stranger, all the land of Canaan, for an everlasting possession, and I will be their God. (Gen 17:5–8)

The context of circumcision is fruitfulness and procreation, not sacrifice. After Abraham was circumcised, God promised him Isaac, the one through whom his promises would flow. There is no mention of blood in the account of Abraham's circumcision, but some people have clearly imagined the flow of blood as the symbolic "ink" in which the covenant was signed, no doubt because the blood of sacrifice has, traditionally, been considered the means of communication between God and men. Levenson, for example, suggests that it is specifically blood that is important in the ritual; he relates it to the blood of the paschal lamb, which redeemed the firstborn sons of the Israelites as God smote the firstborn sons of the Egyptians. "The blood of circumcision functions within the larger redacted story of Moses and Pharaoh as a prototype of the blood of the lamb" (Levenson, 1993:50–1). God instructed the Israelites to sacrifice a lamb and to daub the lintels and doorposts of their houses with its blood, "and when I see the blood, I will pass over you" (Exod. 12:13). In other words, it is the blood, in this case of the lamb, that is salvific. As we shall see, this line becomes important in midrashim about the "sacrifice" of Isaac. But is it the blood of the lamb or that of the Egyptian firstborn that substitutes for the firstborn of the Israelites? Abraham's relation to circumcision has disappeared in Levenson's interpretation.

Levenson then suggests that circumcision might be considered along with the paschal lamb, the later dedication of the firstborn to Levitical service, and the much later practice of *pidyon haben*, the redemption of the first born with monetary payment as "a sublimation for child sacrifice in ancient Israelite religious practice" (Levenson, 1993:51).[11] But, if so, all of these substitutions or sublimations imply that "the impulse to sacrifice the first-born son remained potent" (ibid.:52); they also imply that the impulse to sacrifice the firstborn son is a natural desire. Levenson is in good company, for this has been a common interpretation among those with a psychological, even Freudian, orientation, as we shall see in chapter 9. Such a position was also discernible in the statement made by a New York rabbi, in a widely read column in the Sunday *New York Times Magazine*, 13 March 1994. Rabbi Joshua Hammerman claimed that the rite of circumcision ritualizes the jealousy and murderous wishes of a father toward the son. He implied that those feelings are natural. Neither he nor Levenson nor Freud considered the way the meaning of paternity and the rite of circumcision may foster those feelings.

More is going on with regard to circumcision than merely the spilling of blood. When circumcision is first mentioned, in Genesis 17, the context is not sacrifice but fatherhood and generativity. The sign of the covenant is inscribed only on males, and on the very member that is imagined as the "fountain of life," or at least the means through which life is transmitted (Speiser, 1964; Delaney, 1977). It is "a cut on the male sex organ: a partial castration analogous to an offering, which in return will bring God's blessing upon *the organ that ensures the transmission of life and thereby the survival of the Hebrew people*" (Soler, 1977:25, emphasis mine). This may be a good representation of ancient Hebrew beliefs, but Soler does not use contemporary knowledge (that both male and female are necessary for the transmission of life) to challenge the system. Unfortunately, and like so many others, he seems unaware that the perpetuation of such notions perpetuates a particular view of gender and procreation that devalues the female role.

Eilberg-Schwartz, an eminent scholar of ancient Judaism, begins with the question that few have asked: why is the covenant signed on the penis? If blood is really the crucial issue, surely the cutting of another part of the body would provide the necessary flow of blood.[12] In a rich and ethnographically inspired chapter, "The Fruitful Cut: Circumcision and Israel's Symbolic Language of Fertility, Descent and Gender," Eilberg-Schwartz (1990) shows a variety of ways in which circumcision is associated with fruitfulness and notions of descent, namely the patrilineage, and the ways in which the symbolic language of the Bible draws numerous analogies between fruit/agriculture and human generativity. Especially significant are the biblical references to uncircumcised trees and how pruning makes them more fruitful: "Cutting away the foreskin is like pruning a fruit tree. Both acts of cutting remove unwanted excess and both increase the desired yield. One might say that when Israelites circumcise their male children, they are pruning the fruit trees of God" (ibid.:152).

There are other references to uncircumcised organs—hearts, ears, and lips—which are closed up and unable to perform their God-ordained task. Similarly, says Eilberg-Schwartz, circumcision "enables the penis to more effectively discharge its divinely allotted task . . . to impregnate women and produce offspring" (ibid.:149). It is questionable whether circumcision really enables the penis to perform better, but the Israelites may have thought so. In any case, such performance is associated more with manhood and virility than with infancy. In cultures where circumcision is practiced—not just in pagan cultures, but also, as we shall see in chapter 7, in Islamic cultures—it is not usually performed on infants but as a puberty or initiation ritual. The question that remains, then, is why Jews perform it on the eighth day.

The Eighth Day

After Abraham was circumcised, God said to him: "he that is eight days old shall be circumcised" (Gen. 17:12; see also Lev. 12:3). The eighth day is also the day on which the firstborn shall be given to God—"both of man and of beast, it is mine" (Exod. 13:2). Scholarly exegesis often makes a connection between circumcision and sacrifice, since both involve the eighth day. Eilberg-Schwartz departs from this tradition and associates the significance of the eighth day to issues of birth and menstrual blood rather than sacrifice: "after the birth of a male child a woman is in a state of impurity as severe as when she has her menstrual period" (Eilberg-Schwartz, 1990:174), that is, for seven days and these days, in turn, are associated in Leviticus, with circumcision: "If a woman has conceived *seed*, and born a man child . . . in the eighth day the flesh of his foreskin shall be circumcised" (Leviticus 12:2–3, emphasis added). Eilberg-Schwartz notes that a woman's impurity during this time means that she contaminates anything she touches, thus one "can infer from these rules that during the seven days following a birth, a male infant is also unclean and would contaminate any man who performed the circumcision" (Eilberg-Schwartz, 1990). This is clearly a place where Mary Douglas's critique (1966) of "medical materialism" (the idea that proscriptions like those in Leviticus were built on a firm knowledge of health) is appropriate. From the standpoint of health, it is far more likely that a man touching an infant would be the contaminating party, not the infant, but as Douglas cogently argues, notions of pollution are related to a symbolic system, and not to hygiene.

Women's blood is considered "filthy, socially disruptive, and contaminating . . . women's blood is symbolically associated with death," whereas male blood "is clean, unifying, and symbolic of God's covenant" (Eilberg-Schwartz, 1990:174). He goes on to say that the rite of circumcision "marks the passage from the impurity of being born of woman to the purity of life in a community of men" (ibid.:175). Israelite circumcision was, in his view, a rite symbolizing not manhood and virility but fertility. Fertility, however, was not merely the result of the natural process of maturation; instead, "a boy's procreative powers were granted by God as a privilege for having been born into Abraham's line" (ibid.:176; cf. Jay, 1992).

But perhaps there is a price to pay for this privilege, and perhaps the line between circumcision as symbolic of sacrifice and circumcision as symbolic of fertility is not as distinct as Eilberg-Schwartz draws it. If the child is considered the fruit of the organ that is imagined as the pure channel through which God's chosen people come, then anxiety over paternity and legitimacy remain. Recall Speiser's comment that "the integrity of the mission was to be safeguarded in transmission, the purity of the content protected by the quality of the container" (Speiser, 1964:93–4). Circumcision could, then, be seen as *pars pro toto*, a part of the child for the whole of the child; it could symbolize the sacrifice of the child, or the idea of the sacrifice of the child created by the anxiety generated by the notions of paternity and the problem of illegitimacy. At the same time, circumcision would also symbolize that, despite these anxieties, the child is accepted.

Although this interpretation is attractive, it is problematic because the institution of circumcision occurs *before* the demand that Abraham sacrifice his son, *before* Isaac is even born. In the chronology of the narrative, circumcision could hardly be seen as a substitute for sacrifice. Indeed, the issue of the sacrifice of the firstborn does not occur until Exodus (and later Leviticus). In this context it is well to recall that Isaac was not the firstborn. Rather than a substitute for sacrifice, circumcision, like sacrifice, can be imagined as an integral part of the ideology of paternal power—marking the organ of (pro)creation and all those who belong to the patrilineage.

After Abraham is circumcised, God tells him he will be exceedingly fruitful, yet he must remember that creative, even procreative, power ultimately rests with God. Through submission to God, the father becomes the channel through which God's creative power flows to earth. Although circumcision may draw attention to procreative power, it simultaneously represents the "cutting" of it, in recognition of the fact that the power of the father derives from God.

The emphasis on the eighth day may relate to a similar emphasis in ancient Greek society. The eighth day was the day on which a father could exercise his *patria potestas* (paternal power)—his right to accept or reject a child. In Israelite society, the rite of circumcision appears to recognize the power of the father as it is transmitted from God by means of the male organ. In the Greek example, the father alone has that power, whereas in Israelite society, the father has that power through the grace of God. Abraham is the means for the transmission of that idea and that power. Those who refuse to recognize God's power, and submit to it, will be punished, for they have abrogated to the self that which is rightfully God's. The power of the father is, of course, reinforced, with the full weight of God behind it.

Eilberg-Schwartz demonstrates the close associations between notions of male procreativity and notions of circumcision, and he details the gendered nature of the associations, but he does not further develop his analysis to ask what makes the associations possible. Neither he nor Speiser, and certainly not Levenson, have examined the *theory* of procreation—the cultural construction of the roles of male and female in the process of "coming-into-being." It is clear from Genesis and other books in the Hebrew Bible (and the New Testament, for that matter) that the male is imagined as the "pro-creator," that is, the one who engenders. The female, in contrast, is imagined as the nurturer. Her role is important, to be sure, but it is of a very different nature and value.

Genesis, then, can be seen as the legitimating document for this theory of procreation, for Genesis, in particular, is concerned with genealogy, paternity, patriline, and the right "seed," through which God's line will continue (see fig. 3). But if the concepts of *seed* and *genealogy* are intimately related to theological conceptions, then a gender analysis does not merely point this out, it strikes a serious blow to these conceptions.

Is Genesis 22 an Injunction Against the Practice of Child Sacrifice?

The idea of the sacrifice of children plays a number of roles in the Hebrew Bible. One problem I have with the use of these other examples to explain Genesis 22 is that they are narratively later than the story of Abraham, and thus the context is quite different. Abraham's story is the initial story and, therefore, unlikely to be the representation of an injunction against the practice. In the Bible, the Abraham story is the first instance of such an idea or practice—and it was an idea powerful enough to found a new notion of god and faith. Perhaps it was heuristic, a device to communicate a particular kind of faith and fear of god; then, perhaps at a later time, it was taken literally. Or perhaps it symbolized the construction of paternity with monogenesis and monotheism as two aspects of one theosocial system.

Let us imagine, for a moment, that the story was, as some have imagined, a late invention inserted to combat contemporary practices among the Canaanites and perhaps also among the Israelites themselves—constructed, that is, in competition with those who practiced such a rite. By showing that the Israelites would be willing to go to such lengths to prove their love of their God, they could also show that their God was better because he did not demand follow-through. This is an ingenious explanation, but it does not alleviate the implications inherent in Abraham's willingness to kill his son. Because, if he was willing, how does that make him different from, or better than, his neighbors who, supposedly, were also willing, and did go through with the sacrifice? How, in other words, does this make Abraham unique? For it is his *willingness* to do it that makes him Father of Faith, not the fact that God put an end to the practice. And God blessed him *because* he did not withhold his son (Gen 22:16–8). If the story was meant as a prohibition or modification of the practice of human sacrifice, God could have said as much, or the biblical authors could have represented him making such an injunction.

Although the story is often interpreted in the context of a discourse on sacrificial rituals, especially blood sacrifice, this is not, I believe, the most appropriate context. Ritual is something that involves a community, something that is done regularly—this is what makes it a *ritual*. But the Akedah is considered a unique event in the Hebrew Bible, just as the

CHILDREN OF ABRAHAM

Fig. 3. (Above) Genealogical chart: The Children of Abraham. English version of Fils d'Abraham. Belgium: Brepols Publishers. (Below) Details showing the index of sects and the schematic of the tree.

LIST OF COMMUNITIES

Adventists	Dawudis	Lollards	Presbyterians
Aglipayans	Disciples of Montfavet	Lutherans	Priscillianists
Ahmadiya	Dönmehs	Mandaeans	Quakers
Alawites	Dolcinists	Manichaeans	Raskolniks
Anabaptists	Doukhobors	Mariavites	Reorganized Church of J.C. of latter Day Saints
Anglicans	Druses	Maronites	Sabbateans
Antoinists	Essenes	Mar Thoma Syrian Church	Sadducees
Arians	Ethiopians	Mennonites	Salvation Army
Armenians	Exclusive Brethren	Methodists	Samaritans
Arminians	Falashas	Moravians	Seveners
Azalis	Frankists	Mormons	Seventh-day Adventists
Azraqis	Friends of Man	Mustalis	Shi'is
Babis	Gnostics	Nestorians	Sikhs
Baha'is	Hafizis	Nestorian Church of Trichur	Sulaymanis
Baptists	Hasidaeans	New Apostolics	Sunnis
Bogomils	Hasidim	Nizaris	Syrian Anglicans
Calixtines	Hinschites	Nusayris	Syrian Catholics
Calvinists	Hutterian Brethren	Old Apostolics	Syro-Malabarese
Caodaists	Ibadis	Old Believers	Syro-Malankarese
Cathari	Imamis	Old Catholics	Taborites
Catholics	Irvingites	Old Episcopalian Church	Tayyibis
Catholic Armenians	Islam	Open Brethren	The Living Church
Catholic Copts	Ismailis	Orthodox	Twelvers
Catholic Ethiopians	Jacobites	Palaioimerologites	Uniates (Byzantine and Melkite)
Chaldeans	Jehovah's Witnesses	Palmarists	Unification Church
Children of God	Judaism	Paulicians	Unitarians
Christian Scientists	Karaites	Pentecostals	Utraquists
Christianity	Karmatians	Pharisees	Waldensians
Church of Anjur-Thozhiyur	Kharijites	Pietists	Yezidis
Congregationalists	Khazars	Plymouth Brethren	Zaydis
Copts	Kimbanguists	Pneumatomachians	Zealots
Darbyites	Little Church	Polish National Catholic Church	

Crucifixion is in the New Testament. Rather than interpreting the story within the context and discourse of sacrifice, as have most commentators, we need to begin with the story. The story of Abraham is not about the end of a practice but about the beginning of a new faith, symbolized by Abraham's submission to a higher authority, even if it means the sacrifice of his son. The faith traditions, to which we now turn, have recognized the religious and theological significance of the story. In the following three chapters, I discuss a range of interpretations of the Abraham story in each tradition, some of the debates that have arisen about it, and the variety of ways in which it pervades people's lives.

PART THREE

Religious Defenses and

Their Silences

Religious Defenses: Prolegomenon

REGARDLESS of whether the story of Abraham represents the end of the practice of child sacrifice, religious interpreters have had to valorize Abraham's willingness to offer up his child. For this is the theological point of the story, the foundation stone of the new kind of faith. The next three chapters are discussions of Jewish, Christian, and Muslim interpretations of the story. Interpretations migrate from religious tradition to religious tradition, and from religious to secular culture, yet despite the fact that these religions share so much, they are mutually exclusive. Adherents of each tradition consider their own tradition distinct and complete in itself, and assume a direct connection and inspiration from Abraham, without any intermediary.

Aside from those who believe that the Bible (or the Qur'an) is the direct word of God, interpreters generally assume that, no matter how divinely inspired the stories may be, they are ultimately human constructions elaborated in relation, as well as in opposition, to what was culturally accepted, including notions of human coming-into-being. The stories may incorporate aspects of the society from which they originated, but they also project a *vision* of society as the authors wished it to be. The stories are, in short, ideological, for they incorporate and project the ideas, values, and aspirations of a particular group.

Interpretations are dually situated. They come after the fact and are affected by the background assumptions, preoccupations, and knowledge available, and by the commitments, aims, and position of the interpreter. Most commentary has been situated within a specific religious tradition, each with its own emphases and concerns. These will be taken up in each chapter. Yet some of the concepts—obvious ones, such as God, father, and sacrifice, but also those of Creation and time—are shared. Interpretations proceed from these background assumptions, which have been molded by the tradition they comment on. Because they are taken for granted, however, and imagined as part of reality, these concepts have been held as separate and separable from the stories that constitute them.

Until quite recently, most commentary has been written by men, for only men have been empowered to study and interpret sacred texts. They have not questioned the ways in which power is vested in their gender and how this may have influenced the questions and concerns that have shaped their commentary. Since the nineteenth century when Elizabeth Cady Stanton and a circle of women compiled *The Woman's Bible*, feminists have been raising new questions about biblical stories. For the past twenty-five years or so, with the increase in the admission of women to seminaries and divinity schools, and the appointments of women to teaching positions in them, feminist analyses have achieved a hearing and been accorded the respect they deserve; in some places they have become a permanent part of the curriculum. Similar attention has increasingly been directed to Qur'anic texts.

Feminist interpretations vary as much as the people who make them. Some feminists wish to point out gaps or oversights in previous interpretations, others attempt to fill in the gaps and rewrite the story, still others assume there is another, perhaps truer, story outside the narrative. Some are committed to the traditions that they simultaneously criticize, whereas others have become disillusioned. Regardless, all of us take the religious traditions and their histories seriously, for we are all aware of the impact these have had on the lives of ordinary men and women and the societies in which we live. In turn, our efforts are making an impact on theology, religious texts, rituals, personnel, and society at large. Without the examples of the many women who have been engaged in the work of feminist interpretation, I might not have had the courage to write this book.

Unlike many other interpreters, I do not argue from the perspective of a single tradition, even though I was born and raised in a culture heavily affected by Christianity. In addition, I have analyzed the story for what it reveals about gender; I do not assume that I know what men and women are, or were, in the time of Abraham (whenever that may have been).

Traditional, as well as feminist, exegetes of Genesis 22 do not question God's command. They take that for granted. All simply proceed from the text, assuming that, because God asks Abraham, that is all there is to it. None of them has asked: Why did God ask only Abraham and not both parents? Or, cast in human terms, what gave Abraham the right to take the child without asking his mother? Would God ask only Abraham if He knew that the child belonged to the mother as much as to the father?

If God is omniscient as well as just, then, clearly, he could not be confined to the ancient and now outmoded theory of procreation in which the child belonged to the man because he was the father's seed. If seed comes from two sources (a combination of both ovum and sperm, each gender contributing half the seed as we now believe, then God could not have asked Abraham, alone, for the child, for the child was not his alone. (If God had asked him alone, then interpretations would have to provide a rationale, but they have not.) Nor, of course, would Abraham have had the right, unilaterally, to take the child. Rather than an act of great faith, it would have been a heinous crime—kidnapping with the intention to kill.

What I am striving to point out is that the concept of God and the story of Abraham are mutually constitutive; together they constitute a notion of creativity expressed at both the divine and human levels, which by its very nature is authoritative and gendered. He who is *author* has authority and the power to command obedience. The story expresses the nature of fatherhood and the hierarchical order of patriarchal authority.

In addition to these common features, others become important in each tradition. For example, in Judaism, Abraham's faith is felt to ransom all future generations from God's wrath, and the story is invoked when the community is threatened. The sacrifice story is felt to be related to, and interpreted in the context of, circumcision and the redemption of the firstborn. In Christianity, the story prefigures the Crucifixion. It also represents the idea of faith above works, and it became connected with the Protestant ideal. In Islam, the story of Abraham is so powerful that Muhammad not only recalls people to that original faith but often seems to walk in Abraham's footsteps. The "sacrifice" establishes a "blood" brotherhood. All three traditions struggle over the patrimony; who is the rightful heir of the promises, who *is* the seed of Abraham? As their battle over religious patrimony has become more deadly in recent years, it is even more important to return to this foundational story.

My purpose in these chapters is threefold: (1) to discuss the meaning and place of the story in each tradition, (2) to examine a range of interpretations in each, and (3) to point out the common assumptions about gender and their theological implications. Simultaneously, the gender analysis undermines all of them.

FIG. 4. Marc Chagall, *The Sacrifice of Isaac* (1960–66).
Musée National Message Biblique Marc Chagall, Nice, France.
© 1998 Artists Rights Society (ARS), New York / ADAGP, Paris.

CHAPTER FIVE

Jewish Traditions

I N JEWISH TRADITION, the story in Genesis 22 is referred to as the *Akedah*, a word that refers to the binding of Isaac.[1] This form of the word appears nowhere else in the Bible. The use of the word *to bind*, which is from the same root as that used to tie up animals for sacrifice, implies that the intention was sacrifice. And the type of sacrifice was ʿ*olah*, a whole burnt offering.[2] Throughout the ages, the story has traditionally been understood as a command from God to Abraham to sacrifice his son. It celebrates obedience to authority in return for the protection and favor of a mightier power.

The Akedah story, placed in the middle of Genesis, in the midst of other stories, is not mentioned again in the Hebrew Bible/Old Testament. The dearth of references to it should not lead one to assume that it is therefore of little consequence, but, rather, should be taken as a sign of its uniqueness.[3]

The Akedah stands as a banner or beacon to all future generations (Genesis Rabbah, 55:1), for it holds up a model of faith that has affected not only Jews but Christians and Muslims as well. Abraham did not hesitate, did not argue, did not waver in his intention to follow God's will. The story is austere in the extreme; there are no irrelevant details and no descriptions of Abraham's or Isaac's emotional state.[4] Yet it is these very gaps and silences that resound with the questions that have called forth the voluminous commentary, including this one. Before turning to Jewish interpretations, I will explain briefly the sources of Jewish tradition about the story.

SOURCES OF JEWISH TRADITION ABOUT
THE STORY OF ABRAHAM

Genesis is, of course, the primary source of Jewish tradition about the story, but it is only the beginning. Commentary on the story is vast and derives from a number of sources; all have been influential for Jewish thought. *Tradition*, here, ought not be taken in the sense of a coherent, fixed, canonical set of interpretations, meanings, and practices, but instead as a reference to the variety of Jewish commentary—all of which is, or was at some time, part of Jewish tradition. The multiplicity of interpretations derives from the multiplicity of sources held as legitimate and valid; these, in turn, derive from works of individuals or of groups (like academies), namely, the *tannaim* and *amoraim* who were devoted to the translation, interpretation and codification of biblical texts, legal material, and legends. In addition there are a few noncanonical but biblical-type books, namely 2 and 4 Maccabees and Jubilees.

Dating of these sources is difficult because the actual, extant written texts are, in most cases, not the original; the "original," whatever that may have been, is also assumed to incorporate layer upon layer of (mostly oral) accretions from earlier times. For rabbinic literature, it is not really appropriate to speak of an original text, because oral traditions had a long history before being committed to writing. In any case, whatever may have been original would take on new meanings when inserted into a new context.

The earliest commentary on the story might be found *within* the biblical text itself, in lines 15 through 18, according to R. W. L. Moberly (1988). These lines have long been recognized as late additions to what is basically a complete story by line 14.[5] As a late interpolation, these lines are commonly treated as secondary or inferior (ibid.:313). They are attributed to the J source, although the rest of the story is assumed to be from the E tradition;[6] yet even this classification is not definitive, as references to Yahweh occur in lines 11 and 14. Although a number of scholars have noticed the anomaly, Moberly claims that few have pondered them at length. That is a moot point, however. R. J. Daly has argued that even though the divine blessings promised to Abraham are mentioned in several places, "this is the *only* one in which these blessings are explicitly presented as a reward of a *particular* virtuous act on the part of Abraham" (Daly, 1977:47). (In my opinion Abraham's acts in Genesis 15 and 17 could also be interpreted in this way.) Nevertheless, Daly links this notion of reward to what he considers a principal theological tenet of Judaism, namely "the idea of justification by works of obedience to the Law" (ibid.). In these lines, God says, "because thou hast done this thing, and hast not witheld thy son, thine only son," he swears upon himself that he will keep his promise of the blessings of seed and nation. And this is, ultimately, Moberly's conclusion. Moberly emphasizes that elsewhere in Genesis the blessings have been a unilateral and unconditional offer from God to man (Moberly, 1988:318), whereas in these verses "human obedience . . . can be taken up by God and become a motivating factor in his purposes towards man" (ibid.:321). This is a profound theological shift, for the promises depend no longer only on God but on Abraham's obedience. And that is, surely, what is emphasized in later Jewish interpretations and uses of the story.

Another, perhaps not insignificant, point is that, although other promises to Abraham from God have mentioned seed and land, in these verses only seed (and the nations that will spring from that seed) is mentioned. The emphasis is further enhanced by the fact that, although the images of both stars and sand have occurred previously to describe the number of descendants, they have been used separately; in Genesis 22 they are used in conjunction. Finally, it is in this passage that God speaks, for the last time, to Abraham.[7]

Given the multiplicity of sources and the system of citations, the reader will benefit, as I have, from a key. The few explanatory paragraphs that follow are meant to be such a key and should make the discussion and further exploration more accessible.

Among the the earliest sources about the story are (1) *De Abrahamo*, written by Philo of Alexandria, who lived from 20 B.C. to A.D. 5,[8] and (2) Josephus, a first-century Jewish historian and general living in Rome, who retells the biblical story in narrative form in his *Jewish Antiquities*. His telling includes a number of details not in the biblical version but which may not have been his own invention. (3) Pseudo Philo's *Liber Antiquitatum Biblicarum*, apparently contemporary with the Gospels, is the source of a number of unusual views about the story. Both Jubilees (4) and 4 Maccabees (5) develop the theme of Isaac as a protomartyr. Jubilees is felt by most scholars to be a fairly early work (between 500 and 100 B.C., with most favoring a date circa 200 B.C.[9]), as it appears to have been an influence on the community at Qumran. A number of documents found there seem to depend on it. *Four Maccabees* is thought to have been written between A.D. 30 and 40, possibly in Antioch. (6) The Targums are another important source of information. The verbal form, *tirgem* means to explain or teach, but when it is used as a noun it means translation. Today it is generally used to refer to the translations (and there are several) of the Bible into Aramaic. The extant versions are Targum Onkelos, thought to date from second century A.D.; the Palestinian Targums, including Neofiti and Genizah fragments which are thought to date from the third or fourth century A.D.; and finally Pseudo Jonathan, which is felt to be quite late, perhaps the seventh or eighth century A.D. All of the dates are provisional and all of the Targums, regardless of date, are presumed to incorporate earlier material.

In addition to these individuals, books, and translations, there were also sages referred to as *tannaim* and *amoraim*, who were active after the destruction of the temple in Jerusalem A.D. 70. They gathered, codified, and commented on much of traditional law (*midrash halakhah*) and lore (*midrash aggadah*). The difference between these types of exegesis concerns different orientations: the *halakhah* concerns laws derived from the biblical text and custom,[10] whereas *aggadah* is concerned more with the specific content—the words, phrases, figures of speech, and message of the biblical stories. *Midrash*, originally a general term that meant to search or seek in the Bible for God's truths, came to refer to works other than the legal material, especially homilies, stories, and *aggadah* commentaries on the Bible.

There were five generations of *tannaim*, and their work, known collectively as the Mishnah, came to an end around A.D. 200. At the completion of the Mishnah, another group known as *amoraim* continued, for several generations, the work of collecting, compiling, and commenting, now also on the comments of the *tannaim*. Some of them worked in Palestine, others were in Babylonia, and their work resulted in the Jerusalem or Palestinian Talmud and the Babylonian Talmud, dated to the fourth and fifth centuries, respectively.[11]

Each generation of sages passed down its wisdom and traditions to the next. These transmissions were imagined genealogically, even though they were not necessarily between a father and son—that is, the idea of male generativity and patriarchal succession had both physical and mental expressions. "He who teaches Torah to his companion's son is considered by scripture as if he had sired him" Sanhedrin 19B (Babylonian Talmud, cited in Goldberg, 1987:107). Goldberg argues that the "Perpetuity of *seed*, and the perpetuity of the Torah are closely associated" (ibid.:112, emphasis added).[12]

In addition to the legal material, there is a vast amount of exegetical commentary on the Pentateuch (the five books attributed to Moses). This midrashic work covers a range of types from exegeses, homilies, and sermons, to *aggadot*. The latter take off from the biblical text with great poetic license; they leap in fanciful twists and turns with the purpose of exciting interest and dive straight for the heart. Although these stories may diverge from the more conventional interpretations, they are often the ones most remembered.

One of the earliest midrashic works is Genesis Rabbah or Bereshit Rabbah, dated to the period of the classical Palestinian *amoraim* (A.D. 400–500), although some scholars believe there was a proto-Genesis Rabbah in existence early in the third century. Genesis Rabbah (often cited as Gen. Rab.) is a verse-by-verse interpretation of, and commentary on, the book of Genesis.

Midrashic activity continued into the Middle Ages with commentaries on other books of the Bible and, later, anthologies of these. This activity was supplemented by poetic and liturgical works, and no doubt the style of, and talent for, midrash continues in the work of contemporary Jewish storytellers. It would be impossible to mention, let alone discuss, all of the sources informing modern Jewish consciousness, and that is not my purpose here; most modern Jews are, perhaps, even more familiar with the medieval commentaries by Rashi, the great rabbi in twelfth-century France, and Ramban, also known as Nachmanides, in Christian Spain. These include and comment on some of the earlier traditions, at the same time adding opinions of their own. I will note them when appropriate. Today, there are several excellent and readable works that are compilations of these ancient traditions, and they are presented in continuous narrative form. One is Louis Ginzberg's *Legends of the Jews* in nine volumes; and one that specifically focuses on the *Akedah* is Shalom Spiegel's *The Last Trial: On the Legends and Lore of the Command to Abraham to Offer Isaac as a Sacrifice: The Akedah*.[13]

"And God Tried Abraham"

Why did God try Abraham in the first place? Some translations use the word *tested*, but that conjurs an image of an examination; others use *tempted*, but that is even more problematic for modern readers, as it is usually associated with Satan rather than God. In a couple of Jewish as well as Muslim commentaries on the story, Satan does try to tempt Abraham away from his duty (see below). *Tried* relates to Abraham' s ordeal, which is most often referred to as his *trial*; it also continues the theme of this book. Because God knew that Abraham's faith (*emunah*) was steadfast, why did he taunt and torture him in this way? One early tradition, which continues to the present, has it that God tests only the righteous (Gen. Rab. 55:2).[14] This tradition has puzzled Jews for a long time, and some of the earliest commentaries insert reasons for the test that purport to take the onus off of God.

The angels, or Satan, or the evil Prince Mastema in Jubilees 17, ask God to punish Abraham because he gave a huge banquet to celebrate Isaac's weaning and forgot to make a sacrifice (Gen. Rab. 55:4). Targum Pseudo Jonathan, Genesis Rabbah, and Rashi include a story wherein the test comes as a result of competitive boasting between Ishmael (son of Abraham with Hagar) and Isaac. Ishmael tells Isaac that he, Ishmael, is the one who ought to inherit because he is the firstborn.[15] Isaac retorts that Ishmael is only the son of a handmaid, whereas he, Isaac is the legitimate son. Ishmael then goes on to prove his worthiness by saying that he was circumcised when he was thirteen and thus at an age when he could have resisted but, instead, consciously chose to submit to his father's will.[16] Isaac was only eight days old and could neither resist nor consciously submit. Isaac responds by saying that even if God should ask for all of his members, he would give them all willingly, whereupon God takes him at his word.[17] In these interpretations, however, the motive of trying Abraham is lost.

More conventionally, this trial of Abraham is thought to be the ultimate trial, the last of ten, a tradition that is referred to in the title of Spiegel's book, *The Last Trial*.[18] None of the previous trials or tests of faith were quite enough to prove Abraham's obedience or to satisfy God. "Since the time of God's first call to him in Haran, no experience of his proved that his devotion to God was unconditional and boundless, not influenced by the many glorious promises he received or the wealth he achieved" (Sarna, 1989:393).

Another opinion is that God did not really put him to a test at all; it puts the onus on Abraham's misunderstanding. "What, do you think I meant for you to slay him? No! I said only to take him up. . . . and now I say take him down" (Gen. Rab. 56:8). Following this line of thought, a modern Jewish thinker suggests that God must sometimes mislead man because, if everything were clear, people would be like automatons and the most timid would be the most pious. God wants only the free to be his (Rosenzweig, 1971); Abraham's freedom, however, is conditional upon the total submission of his will to God.

The very fact of the test, a test God knew Abraham would pass, disturbed medieval thinkers as well. Rashi repeats the midrash above and Maimonides interprets this part of the story as "a test case of the extreme limits of the love and fear of God" (from Maimonides, *Guide to the Perplexed*, cited in *Encyclopedia Judaica*), which Shlomo Riskin, formerly a New York rabbi and now chief rabbi of Efrat and dean of the Ohr Tora institutions, has interpreted to mean that "Abraham was asked to do what all subsequent generations of Jews . . . would be asked to do" (Riskin, 1983:31). "The paradox in Jewish history," he notes elsewhere, "is that, had we not been willing to sacrifice our children for God, we would never have survived as a God-inspired and God-committed nation" (ibid., 1994). My question which, as we shall see, echoes that of a number of modern Israelis is: Is nationhood worth more than one's children?

If the point of the story was to prove Abraham's faith and obedience, why not have him sacrifice himself? Apparently, that would not be enough, for, as Sarna asserts (1989:393), Abraham would be willing to sacrifice himself in order to save his son and therefore the motive would be mixed. (Surely, it is easy to imagine that the motive is mixed in the sacrifice of his son; see, for example, Abramovitch, 1994:122.) In any case, if he had been willing to sacrifice himself to save his son, why does he do nothing at all to try to save him? Why doesn't he argue with God, as he did when trying to save Ishmael from banishment and Sodom from destruction? A moment of hesitation on Abraham's part is registered only in Genesis Rabbah (55:7), when he stalls and asks two questions of God. He feigns confusion and asks, "Which son?" When God says, "Whom thou lovest," Abraham queries: "Is there a limit to the affections?" Second, he asks God how he can perform the sacrifice, since he is not a priest. In this instant, God makes him a priest and says, "Thou art a priest forever."

Abraham is, nevertheless, revered not because of any heroic arguing with God on behalf of his son but precisely because he "concedes nothing to the tie of relationship, but his whole weight is thrown into the scale on the side of acceptability with God . . . he did not incline partly to the boy and partly to piety, but devoted his whole soul through and through to holiness and disregarded the claims of their common blood" (Philo, 1959:97). This theme, articulated several centuries earlier than the rabbinic commentary cited above, constitutes another powerful and continuing strand in both Jewish and Christian thought. Curiously these were the same terms, though with emphasis reversed, that the district attorney used at the trial of Cristos Valenti—"If he had stopped at the first cut, had thrown his weight on the side of the child, the child would be alive today." The sentiments expressed by Cristos, in contrast, followed more closely the ancient, religious model. That model—to be able to detach oneself from affective ties, not to let emotions get in the way of duty—is not just a model about the love of God; it has also been a model used to define masculinity.

Abraham is a heroic figure *because* he was able to cut that affective tie. As Abraham "suppressed his compassion in order to perform Thy will with a perfect heart," so God is asked to let his compassion suppress his anger when it is set against the children of Israel. These lines from Genesis Rabbah (56:10) and Leviticus Rabbah (29:9) are inserted into a prayer of supplication during the services of Rosh Hashanah; they petition God to remember the Akedah and to turn away his wrath. So, too, does the line from Targum Neofiti (1992:119), "Remember today the Binding of Isaac with mercy unto his seed."

The analogy between God and Abraham doesn't quite work because of the reversal of what is being stressed. Abraham must overcome his compassion whereas God must overcome his anger. Today, it strikes a discordant note, for it is a reversal in the emotional qualities more commonly associated with humans (anger) and God (compassion). Yet it directs attention to the idea that God is a jealous God. Far more troubling is the implication that it is good as well as necessary for Abraham to be able to overcome his compassion in order to do God's will. Why isn't compassion, especially love of one's child and fellow humans, stressed rather than suppressed? Why can't Abraham's love of God be shown by his unconditional love for his child? Why should there be a conflict between them? Why must loyalty to God be proven at the expense of one's child rather than expressed *through* one's love and care for one's family and fellows?

The prayer also implies that humans can chide God to act compassionately. When God is about to wreak his vengeance upon them, they can call out and tell him to remember the Akedah in a way that makes them equivalent to counselors of God. By this prayer they can bind God to his promise to Abraham.

Despite the general belief that the sacrifice was not completed, it counts *as if* it had been. Because of Abraham's willingness and, as we shall see, Isaac's submission, it counts as a perfect sacrifice. Abraham's perfect obedience, the "willingness of the founding father to sacrifice his son as proof of his devotion to God created an inexhaustible store of spiritual credit upon which future generations may draw" (Sarna, 1989:394; see also Milgrom, 1988:151).

The whole theme of obedience and disobedience characterizes the relation between God and humans in Genesis, beginning with Adam. Abraham's perfect obedience can be interpreted as making up for, redeeming, Adam's disobedience (see Chaim Lewis, 1973). The result is that obedience comes to be seen as an expression of love—at least in hierarchical relations. As Abraham shows his love of God by his obedience, so too does Isaac show his love of his father by his obedience. But what kind of love is that? Why *is* obedience valued so highly? Might not *disobedience* to such a command be a more appropriate response? These issues will be taken up later. Here, it is important to stress that, in Jewish tradition, Abraham's obedience is precisely why the Akedah comes to have a redemptive quality that allows it to function, for Jews, in a way somewhat analogous to Jesus' Crucifixion.

Whether the Akedah story had that meaning and served that function before the advent of Christianity, and thus served as a model for the theology of the Crucifixion, or whether it took on these meanings and functions in response to Christian theology is a vexing question of deep theological and historical significance; it will be addressed in the next chapter.[19] Here, I wish to bring out more of the Jewish associations and understandings of the Akedah, so that I can refer to them when I turn to the Christian material.

If Isaac is considered an expiatory offering, one might expect the Akedah to be associated more with the holy day of Yom Kippur, the Day of Atonement, but it is not.[20] Today, and for centuries, the Akedah is commemorated on Rosh Hashanah, the New Year. Rosh Hashanah falls in the autumn month of Tishri when, according to one tradition, all great events allegedly occurred—the creation of the world, and the birth and death of the patriarchs—and it is, therefore, suitably the time of Abraham's heroic deed. Rosh Hashanah is a "Day of Remembrance, a day for the blowing of the *shofar* (ram's horn); a holy convocation, as a memorial for the departure from Egypt" (from Rosh Hashanah Service). Although there is mention of the Exodus, Rosh Hashanah focuses more on the Akedah. Genesis 22 is recited in its entirety during the service, and other reminders are cited throughout. The shofar, a vital element of Rosh Hashanah, symbolizes, among other things, the horn of the ram sacrificed in Isaac's stead, a ram that, in midrash, was created on the evening of the sixth day of Creation and was waiting in the wings, so to speak, until its grand performance at the Akedah. The sounding of the shofar also represents a clarion call, reminding people of God's rule over his creation, and it is a reminder that the shofar will sound again in the last days, when the dead are resurrected. The sound of the shofar is also said to have accompanied God's revelation to Moses on Sinai; thus it links the beginning and the end of time, Abraham and Moses, and, implicitly, Rosh Hashanah and Passover.

Rosh Hashanah may not always have been the holiday to which the Akedah was attached, and some (e.g., Davies, 1979, Levenson, 1991; Sandmel, 1956; Segal, 1984) believe it was, at one time, associated with Passover. Passover falls in the spring, the time of new beginnings and new life and thus also, a suitable time for the New Year. The Mishnah records the rivalry between sages over whether Tishri or Nisan should be the new year, and thus to which of these months the same great events should be attributed (Spiegel, 1969:54–5). For some Jewish groups, according to Rosenberg, "the connection of the offering of Isaac with the Passover was more important than the observance of the holiday as a memorial of the exodus from Egypt"(Rosenberg, 1965:386). Segal acknowledges that the book of Jubilees "does contain an explicit connection between the sacrifice of Isaac (or Akedah, loosely speaking) and the Passover" (Segal, [1984]1987:114). This is important for (some) Christians who argue for the coincidence of Passover and Easter, the Akedah and the Crucifixion.

Jubilees, a book concerned with the Jewish calendar, attempts to prove the patriarchal origin of certain feasts (here *patriarchal* refers to the patriarchs). Jubilees retells the biblical story from the beginning of the world; it is told by an angel of God to Moses on Sinai, expressing thereby the long-held belief that God revealed the Torah to Moses. Each chapter of

Jubilees begins with a statement of the month and day, situating the events of which it tells at a particular time. The Akedah is placed so as to fall at "the precise time of the precise day when the paschal lambs for Passover are slaughtered in the Temple" (Daly, 1977:55). As we shall see in the next chapter, some Christians have used the calendrical system of the book of Jubilees to confirm that Jesus was the Messiah. Perhaps the Akedah and Passover became linked in Jewish imagination because the theme of the redemption of the first born is common to both (Swetnam, 1981:39).

The sacrificial feast of the paschal lamb that commemorates the passing over of Israel's firstborn became associated not just with the ram offered in Isaac's place, but with Isaac himself.[21] When God is set to destroy the firstborn of the Egyptians, Jews are instructed to spread blood on the lintels of their doors as a sign to God of their identity so that, "When I see the blood, I will pass over you" (Exod. 12:13), and when he saw that blood, he is thought to have seen the blood of the binding of Isaac, the blood that protects the Jews. This tradition is said to derive from the Mekilta d Rabbi Ishmael (7:78–82), thought to be a fourth-century text (Swetnam, 1981:67).

"The saving virtue of the Passover lamb proceeded from the merits of that first lamb, the son of Abraham, who offered himself on the altar" (Vermes, [1961]1973:215). It seems as unreasonable to claim that there is no relation between the Akedah and Passover as it would to assert that there is no relation between the two great holy days of Rosh Hashanah and Passover.[22] In addition, there are other associations to the Akedah that may or may not be related to either of the holidays; these include associations regarding Moriah, the "blood of Isaac," and the "ashes of Isaac."

MORIAH, THE BLOOD OF ISAAC,
AND THE ASHES OF ISAAC

Although the location of Moriah is unknown, symbolically it has been identified with the Temple Mount in Jerusalem since at least the beginning of the first century and probably earlier. Today, the Temple Mount is covered by a Muslim mosque, the Dome of the Rock (see chapter 7), the rock from which Muhammad ascended to Heaven for a vision of God. Early Muslim tradition implies that it is the site where the sacrifice of Abraham's son allegedly took place, before that tradition moved to Mecca. In any case, it is no wonder (some) Jews want it back, and no wonder (some) Muslims refuse.

Moriah is also, in other traditions, associated with Sinai. In one midrash, Sinai is said to have broken away from Moriah as a piece of dough broken off from the rest (Schoeps, 1946:388, n. 12). Sinai, however important, never became a major shrine, but Moriah, equated with the Temple Mount, did. A modern interpretation reasons that it is because, at Sinai, God comes to man, whereas, at Moriah, a man and his son express willingness to commit themselves, body and soul, to God (Riskin, 1983). Others assert that Sinai could not have happened without Moriah, that theologically the events at Moriah preceded and prepared the way for those at Sinai (Milgrom, 1987; 1988:159).

Isaac's status as sacrificial victim, in combination with the idea that there can be no expiation without the shedding of blood (Talmud, Yoma 5a), may have led to the idea that Isaac was an expiatory offering and to the *aggadic* tradition that his blood *was* shed. Abraham was so zealous in proving his devotion that when the angel called out forbidding him to lay a hand upon the lad, Abraham is thought to have begged to let him bring forth at least a drop of blood (Gen. Rab. 56:7). But the angel said, "Don't do anything to him." A more elaborate *aggadah* says Isaac gave one-fourth of his blood (see Spiegel, 1969:47–9). Because that was the amount thought to keep a person alive, it would have been sufficient to stand in for Isaac—it would be as if he were sacrificed. This midrash implies, of course, that Abraham not only laid his hand on Isaac but that he slashed him with the knife (see Davies, 1989:59).

Isaac was afraid he might flinch at the sight of the knife and asked his father to bind him tightly so that he would not resist and thereby render the offering unfit (Targum Neofiti and Pseudo Jonathan). As noted earlier, the word for *binding* is exactly the word used to refer to the binding of the lambs for the Tamid sacrificial offering at the Temple—offerings that were, unlike the paschal lambs, whole burnt offerings. These offerings were made morning and night, and, in midrash, are thought to be in memory of the Akedah. Here, it is clear that ritual sacrifice is not the context for interpreting the Abraham story but that the Abraham story is the context for interpreting sacrifice. Some rabbis have wondered why daily sacrifices in the Temple were necessary if Isaac's sacrifice atoned for all time, but one scholar suggests that they are "perpetual reminders of Isaac's self-oblation" (Vermes, 1961:209).

It will be immediately apparent to the perceptive reader that, in some of the midrashic traditions, the focus on Abraham and his piety dramatically shifted to Isaac as the perfect sacrifice. Suddenly it is Isaac who is thought to have offered himself on the altar. Some scholars, notably Davies and Chilton (1978), believe this shift in focus could only have occurred after the destruction of the Temple and in response to Christian theology.

The connection with the Tamid offering may also have led to the tradition of the "ashes of Isaac," a tradition that implies Isaac was consumed as a burnt offering. The petition "O, do thou regard the ashes of Father Isaac heaped upon the top of the altar, and deal with thy children according to the Mercy attribute" (Spiegel, 1969:38–42) is part of a prayer at Rosh Hashanah. Yet perhaps it is only *as though* the ashes of Isaac were spread on top of the altar, or perhaps it was the ashes of a ram named Isaac who was substituted in Isaac's place (ibid.:40–1). In the Middle Ages a custom arose of putting ashes on one's head on fast days that were called for in times of distress. This custom did not spring up in the Middle Ages, but was known at least in the first generation of the *amoraim* (ibid.:42).[23]

An unusual midrash (ibid.:35) portrays the rabbis discussing the proper order of events in preparation of the altar for sacrifice: first the fire is laid, then wood, and finally the victim. As there is no mention of laying the fire in Genesis 22, but only that of laying of the wood (Gen. 22:9), they assume the fire had already been laid. Therefore, they reason that Abraham would not have to lay a hand on Isaac to slay him, in that he is already the perfect sacrifice, already consumed by fire. If that were the case, the ashes of Isaac would have "stored up *merit* for atonement generation after generation" (ibid.:27).[24]

Mostly, when it is believed that Isaac was slain, it is also believed that he was revived immediately, restored to life by the "dew of resurrection." In this way the Akedah comes to be associated with the idea of resurrection (ibid.:29), which may be why the ashes of Isaac are referred to in the *aggadah* about the prayers of Benediction for the dead (ibid.:32–7).[25]

Beyond the fact of whether or not Isaac was sacrificed, commentators also discuss whether he would have been a perfect sacrifice if he had not himself been a willing victim. The free consent of the victim, as emphasized in Pseudo Philo, is what makes Isaac's sacrifice "the sacrifice *par excellence*, whose lasting benefits would be felt for all time" (Vermes, [1961]1973:206).

Early on, some thinkers were clearly disturbed by the idea that Isaac should be sacrificed without his prior knowledge or consent. A few even wondered aloud how Abraham could bind a man of thirty-seven without his consent (Gen. Rab. 56:8).[26] When Isaac asked the most poignant question: "My father . . . Behold the fire and the wood, but where is the lamb for a burnt offering?" (Gen. 22:7), midrash amplifies Abraham's answer and lets Isaac know what is going to happen. "God will provide himself the lamb, O my son; and if not, thou art for a burnt offering" (Gen. Rab. 56:4). Josephus says that "Isaac received these words with joy" (Josephus, *Jewish Antiquities*, 1961:115), and he goes on to say that even "were this the resolution of his father alone, it would have been impious to disobey" (ibid.,). Isaac has become the willing victim in accordance with his father's wishes; the motives of the two coincide. Some of this Jewish concern may have found its way into the community of those who would become Muslim, for in the Qur'an Abraham says: "My son, I see in a dream that I shall sacrifice thee; consider, what thinkest thou?" (Sura 37:102) And his son replies: "My father, do as thou art bidden; thou shall find me, God willing, one of the steadfast" (ibid.).

In an attempt to get Abraham to desist from fulfilling his duty, Genesis Rabbah (56:4) has Satan speaking the words of commonsense morality. He tries to talk Abraham out of doing this terrible thing. He says something like, "What has happened to you, old man? Have you gone crazy? How can you even think of doing such a thing? How do you know it is God? Maybe tomorrow he will change his mind and call you a murderer." But Abraham resists. The temptation that Satan offers him, namely, to turn away from following God's order, becomes a prominent part of a Muslim ritual—the stoning of Satan—during the Hajj.

Satan is asking a very important question: How *did* Abraham know it was God who was asking? How did Cristos Valenti know it was God? Why do we believe it in one case and not the other? Why should we just take it on faith that God spoke to Abraham? Curiously, these questions have not been very central in the commentary. One of the few to raise them was Kant in a late and quite obscure little book, *The Conflict of the Faculties*.

> If God should really speak to man, man could still never *know* that it was God speaking. It is quite impossible for man to apprehend the infinite by his senses, distinguish it from sensible beings, and *recognize* it as such. But in some cases man can be sure the voice he hears is *not* God's; for if the voice commands him to do something contrary to the moral law, then no matter how majestic the apparition may be, and no matter how it may seem to surpass the whole of nature, he must consider it an illusion (Kant, [1798]1979:115).

Kant's voice in this case is not unlike that of Satan; he is taking the voice of reason and of human morality. Kant felt that in these circumstances, Abraham should have said a resounding "No." Kant does not let him off the hook as does Kierkegaard in *Fear and Trembling*. Kierkegaard allows Abraham to suspend the ethical—that standard of morality that applies to us all; for Kierkegaard, Abraham is above the law because of his faith. His faith "is a paradox which is capable of transforming a murder into a holy act well-pleasing to God" (Kierkegaard, [1843]1941:64).[27] Today, as we have seen, such faith is considered a sign of madness.

When it became clear that Satan was getting nowhere with Abraham, he approached Isaac and told him what was about to happen. But like

father, like son: Isaac said, "I accept my fate." Satan then went to tell
Sarah what her husband was about to do, whereupon Sarah cried out in
anguish and died of a broken heart. This may have been one way to explain Sarah's death in Genesis 23.

Numerous commentaries interpret Genesis 22:8, "and they went both
of them together," as an indication that they, both Abraham and Isaac,
were of one mind and went with quiet hearts, resolved to do God's will.
"The one who slaughters does not hesitate, and he who is being slaughtered stretches out his neck" (Neofiti, 118; cf. Gen. Rab. 56:4).

Although the dominant tradition is that Isaac was not sacrificed, the
fact that Abraham returned alone gave rise to speculation. "So *Abraham*
returned unto his young men, and they rose up and went together to
Beersheba and Abraham dwelt at Beersheba" (Gen. 22:19, my emphasis).
Where is Isaac? This question may have motivated traditions that Isaac
was sacrificed or merely reinforced those already in existence. Genesis 22
ends with a recitation of the lineage established not through Isaac but
through Abraham's brother Nahor; it is as if Isaac had ceased to exist.

Spiegel (1969:4–5) discusses several midrashim that attempt to account for Isaac's absence. One relates that Isaac was whisked away to
Paradise for three years to recover from his wounds and await his marriage to Rebecca. Although there was no Torah at the time of Abraham,
it figures anachronistically in several midrashim. One is that he was taken
to the house of Shem to study Torah. According to a related midrash, this
was the pretext Abraham used with Sarah in order to take Isaac away
with him.[28] Abraham is said to have told Sarah that Isaac was too old to
be spending so much time with her, that it was time he went to school to
study Torah. Had Abraham used this excuse, he would have been a liar.
Another midrash has Isaac confronting his father on Moriah: "So this is
the Torah I was to learn at school?" (cf. ibid.:49; Graves and Patai, 1966:
174–5; Ginzberg, 1909). This is one of the few suggestions that Isaac
rebelled—that for a moment, at least, he was not the willing victim.

Regardless of whether Isaac was sacrificed, tradition designates him
the perfect, expiatory sacrifice that accrued merit for all generations.
"The Akedah became in Jewish thought the supreme example of self-
sacrifice in obedience to God's will and the symbol of Jewish martyrdom
throughout the ages" (*Encyclopedia Judaica*, 1979, vol. 2:480). Whose
self-sacrifice? Over time it seems that Abraham's submission to God and
Isaac's submission to his father, Abraham's willingness to sacrifice his son
and his son's willingness to be sacrificed, have been conflated, have come
to represent the same thing. It is, however, a dangerous conflation, because it conceals both the hierarchical structure of the relationship and
the dimension of (paternal) power. As we shall see, a number of contem-

porary Israeli Jews are rebelling against the model; they condemn the father and refuse to identify with the submissive, self-sacrificing son. But they have not yet analyzed the relevance of gender.

The Akedah as Model

The story of Abraham has served as a model of the man of faith for millennia, and it has been used to fortify and inspire others.[29] It is, according to Wineman, an archetype, not in the sense of a universal pattern but in the sense of "the presence of an older literary source which resounds in a later work" (Wineman, 1977:6). The most famous and probably the earliest example of this is in 4 Maccabees, which takes up and repeats a story from 2 Maccabees of Eleazar and the woman and her seven sons. In 4 Maccabees, their trials are associated with the Akedah. The stories relate to a time of persecutions under the Seleucid Antiochus IV (167–4 B.C.), during which the Jews were asked to eat the meat from Roman sacrifices. Eleazar refused to do so; bound and scourged, he wanted to set a good example for other Jews. "O children of Abraham you must die nobly for piety's sake" (4 Macc. 6:23). He also asked God to consider him a sacrificial victim: "Make my blood their purification and take my life as a ransom for theirs" (4 Macc. 6:29–30). This is an early, pre-Christian notion of vicarious expiatory sacrifice.

An important concern of the Hellenistic author(s) of 4 Maccabees, noted by a number of commentators, appears to have been the mastery of reason over the passions, so that Abraham's readiness to sacrifice Isaac becomes the model of the victory of reason over parental love. Usually reason is identified with masculinity and passion with femininity; that is why it is even more striking that the same sentiment is put in the mouth of the woman who saw her seven sons tortured to death and then followed them. "Not even her affections for her young caused the mother, whose soul was like Abraham's, to waver" (4 Macc. 14:20).

A midrash has the mother of seven making the following retort: "Go tell Father Abraham not to puff up his heart, if he made an Akedah of one son, I made an Akedah of seven" (Lam. Rab. cited in Spiegel, 1969:16). Once the Akedah became the supreme model of faith, subsequent faithful would be expected to model themselves upon it. Thus, rather than trying to develop a different model of faith, some women adopted the model and strove to fulfill it. Abraham's stoic heroism is more valued than the compassion of weeping women. In order to be considered faithful, a woman must become like a man: "she took her womanly thoughts and fired them with manly spirit" (2 Macc. 7:21).

The model was again consciously invoked in the Middle Ages, during
the persecution of European Jews by the Crusaders—in 1096 at Mainz,
Speyer, Worms, Cologne, Trier, and elsewhere (see Marcus, 1982), and
again in 1146.[30] Jews were again asked to relinquish their religion and
convert, and when they refused they were tortured. Rather than convert
or be tortured, a great number of them are said to have killed their children and themselves—"everyone of them like the Akedah of Isaac, son of
Abraham" (Spiegel, 1969:25). This response to the Crusaders' persecutions was primarily the response of the Ashkenazi Jews of central Europe.[31] Spiegel's well-known book on the legends and lore surrounding
the Akedah are meant primarily to prepare the reader to understand the
allusions to these terrible days in a poem by a twelfth-century rabbi,
Ephraim of Bonn. In the poem, the Akedah was the model for their acts:
"Both the sacrificer and the victims saw as the crowning act of their role
the performance of the Fathers Abraham and Isaac" (Spiegel, 1969:25).
Yet the poem, as well as the acts it commemorates, implies that Isaac was,
in fact, sacrificed.

The theme of substitution, however, was also current in the Middle
Ages. The ram substituted in Isaac's place was considered the preeminent
substitution. The traditional explanation that the lamb substitution was
meant to symbolize both the end of human sacrifice and the institution of
animal sacrifice was dealt with in chapter 2. In a rite called *kapporah*,
practiced in Geonic times (seventh to eleventh centuries) among Jews of
Eastern Europe, a cock was swung three times around the head while the
donor recited: "This be my vicarious offering, my atonement. This cock
shall meet death, but I shall find a long and pleasant life of peace" (*Encyclopedia Judaica*, 10:756).[32] In the fourteenth century, children took
palm-leaf baskets planted with seeds of various kinds and swung them
around their heads, saying: "This be in lieu of me; this is my substitute
and my exchange," and then threw them into the river (ibid.). Yet no
matter how many substitutions are made, no matter how the child, especially the firstborn, is redeemed, the message is that the child is the
appropriate sacrifice, a message that is epitomized in the central event of
Christianity.

Spiegel's book is primarily a compendium of the traditions related to
the Akedah as they inform the interpretation of the medieval persecutions; he is not so concerned with the legacy of those interpretations—
how they shaped the psychological and moral outlook of the community
for subsequent generations. This *is* the concern of Allan Mintz (1984); he
argues that the Askhenazi Jews identified with and used the story of the
Akedah to symbolize and explain their suffering but that they used it in a
very new way. Nowhere in the Talmud or Jewish tradition is human sacrifice encouraged or enjoined as a religious obligation. Martyrdom at the

hands of others, the willingness to be killed for the "Sanctification of the Name," that is, for the sake of God, had been a perennial theme since the times of the Maccabees. But that is quite a different matter from the consensual decision undertaken by the medieval community to commit homicide and suicide for the glory of God.

During the medieval persecutions, a different theological idea emerged in relation to suffering, an idea that has persisted in certain forms to this day. Previously suffering, especially of such catastrophic proportions, was interpreted as punishment, primarily for disobedience. But because of the nature of the destruction at Mainz, Speyer, and Worms and the confidence of that generation in their piety and observances, they had to find an alternative explanation. "The solution was to adopt the concept of 'afflictions from love'" (Mintz, 1984:6), a concept that saw the "suffering of exemplary righteous individuals as a sign of divine favor. This is an idea that goes back to Abraham's trial in the Akedah and to the doctrine among the Rabbis of 'chastisement out of love.' The idea holds that, paradoxically, God tests the faith of those he knows to be already faithful. The trial is an indication of worthiness, not punishment, and its purpose is to strengthen further those who are already strong" (ibid.:91–2). This was not a new theme in Jewish tradition, but Mintz claims this was the first time it was "mobilized as the dominant explanation for a historical catastrophe" (ibid.:92) and applied not to an individual but to collective misfortune. Destruction could be unhinged from sin, and martyrdom could be transfigured into a triumphant religious act. The present sacrifice could be understood as fulfilling what had preceded or prefigured it.[33]

Mintz's interest focuses on the way the actual events came to be symbolized in the discrepancy between the historical record and collective memory or, as he puts it, in the "transactions of the literary imagination with history" (Mintz, 1984:102). His goal is not like that of historians and archaeologists, who try to uncover from the layers of literary and mythologized material some kind of "historical actuality" (ibid.:90). Instead, he is concerned with the poetic transformations of the events that have left their mark on the emotions and morals of people, in this case the survivors and their descendants ever after, for about eight hundred years. Of all the possibilities available from the biblical text to represent the catastrophe at the hands of the Crusaders, it was the Akedah that captured the attention of the medieval poets. Indeed, a new genre of *piyyut* (a kind of hymn that was recited in the synagogue) became known as *Akedah*. By drawing an analogy between contemporary events and the trial of Abraham, the poets helped to collapse the distance between the suffering of the medieval faithful and that of Abraham as well as to give meaning and a sense of grandeur to it. The "events on Mount Moriah continued to structure perceptions and influence behavior. The choice of analogy imparted both a biblical sanction and a sense of election to the martyrs of Mainz" (Roskies, 1984:43).

At the same time, Mintz thinks the comparison was perverse. Their faithful performance of the deed could be seen as a claim to moral superiority over Abraham and thus an expression of pride that was inappropriate. He notes that the point of the Akedah was "to signal the supersession of human sacrifice . . . that what counts in God's eyes is the *readiness* to sacrifice one's firstborn, not the deed itself" (Mintz, 1984:91). He might have gone further and asked why even the readiness to so do should be considered virtuous.

Yet perhaps perversity can also be seen in the interpretation of their trial as an "opportunity given by God . . . a kind of spiritual compliment to the generation" (ibid.:92), which precluded any complaint, reproach, or rebellion on the part of the people against God. As Isaac had to be made into a willing victim, so too did these medieval Jews: "there was not a whisper of complaint" (ibid.:92). Mintz also points out that the Akedah could not fully encompass the triumphant emotional quality expressed in the poems about the medieval catastrophe. In the poems, the contemporary events and the murders and suicides were symbolically assimilated into the Tamid sacrifices. These were the daily animal sacrifices offered at the Temple before its destruction, and, as we have seen, the Akedah has sometimes been associated with them. Nevertheless, the exuberance of the detailed depictions of blood, bones, and dismembered bodies in the medieval poems went far beyond the actual events and called for some explanation. Mintz claims these elaborations were not a perverse expression of an obsession with blood, but a desire to understand their sacrifices as (perhaps more than) comparable. There *is* something perverse, however, in describing in minute detail the way children were slaughtered at the hands of their own fathers and mothers and then describing the outcome of the slaughter as a marriage in which the mingling of blood was the final consummation or union with God. Because that *was* the understanding, Mintz entitled the chapter about these persecutions "Medieval Consummations." Yet this conflation is not as bizarre as one may think. When we come to the Muslim material, we shall see how the story of the Akedah, as well as the actual bloody slaughter of a ram, is inserted into the marriage ritual in Morocco.

HOLOCAUST

The Akedah has also figured in some Jewish interpretations of the Holocaust. What follows should be understood as no more than an outsider's gleanings from scholars with far greater competency to discuss these matters; yet to ignore this world-shattering event would be irresponsible.

First, it is important to point out that the term *holocaust* is the Greek translation, rendered into English, of the Hebrew ʿolah. The word alludes to "going up" in flames, and it has traditionally been taken to refer to a type of sacrifice that is a whole burnt offering, the type Abraham was asked to make of Isaac. At a later time, it was also a type of sacrifice performed at the Temple. The word *holocaust* in reference to the Nazi extermination of the Jews was apparently used for the first time in 1942 in a British newspaper, but it did not become a common term until the late 1950s. The Hebrew terms referring to the same events are *shoah* or *hurban*, both of which mean catastrophe.[34]

The Holocaust has been, and continues to be, a turning point in the interpretation of the Akedah and one that seems to have polarized the Jewish community. A number of Jewish writers "agree in viewing the Nazi Holocaust as a reenactment of the *akedah* and the *akedah* as a prefiguration of the Holocaust" (Brown, 1982:103), but there is little agreement in the interpretation of the analogy. Some continue to admire the patriarchs, Abraham in particular, and see in his model of faith a means of preserving dignity in the face of adversity.[35] They would try to emulate his heroic courage. According to Cohen, Steinsaltz—a renowned Talmudic scholar—"tells us that if we accept the fatherhood of God, we must obey His every command. This vision is compelling enough to elicit the consent of hundreds of millions of men and women of all nations and religions who are able, on faith alone, to accept as the voice of God a command to sacrifice their sons" (Cohen, 1990:54). Significantly, Steinsaltz does not consider the relationship between the notion of fatherhood and obedience, but neither does Cohen who has an opposite response.

Cohen and a number of others are "appalled by this response to the Akedah, to the theology that underlies it and to its ethical implications" (ibid.:55). Cohen suggests that we need to change the model and theology of the Akedah and "to learn how to project our imaginations toward an all-embracing vision of cosmic peace and seek out a path to it" (ibid.:60). His conviction is based on his belief, surely not held by all, that our image of God is a human convention (ibid.:59). Because it is a human convention, or human conception, it can be changed. The Holocaust has forced many Jews to reexamine traditional theology and the models of God and faith through which it is conveyed. "Can a set of values which demands the sacrifice of life be worthy of our absolute committment?" (ibid.:51) The answer for some is "no."

According to Michael Brown, a literary critic, authors Gilboa and Alterman "view the *akedah* and the Nazi Holocaust as enormities to be avoided by rebellion against God. Their Abrahams do not slaughter and their Isaacs are not sacrificed, not because God intervenes, but because they refuse to hear the command that Biblical Abraham heard" (Brown, 1982:105). Similarly, he claims that Agnon and Wiseman "perceive

Europe's Jews as having been bound on the altar of Jewishness by their faithful ancestors" (ibid.). Their faith, not their faithlessness, has resulted in their destruction, an interpretation that clearly draws on the medieval transformation of the meaning of punishment not as divine disfavor but as the trials of the righteous. At the same time, they make it clear that they no longer accept that view. Brown points out that in a number of contemporary Jewish sources, "Abraham and Isaac no longer serve as role models to be emulated . . . but as object lessons to be avoided" (ibid.: 111). This also seems to be the conclusion reached by Neil Gordon in his recent (1995) novel, *The Sacrifice of Isaac*. Nevertheless, there are surely also numerous Jews who find meaning and comfort in thinking of the deaths of their loved ones as sacrifices for their faith, perhaps even so that their descendants might finally have a homeland.

THE AKEDAH IN ISRAEL

The Akedah must also have been invoked to inspire people to fight for and, if necessary, sacrifice themselves for the land of Israel. Immediately after the War of Independence, "the image settled on Isaac as the young *sabra* sacrificing himself on the national altar, with the connivance of his father, Abraham" (Abramson, 1990:107). Yet, while the "post-Holocaust Israeli generation views the *Akedah* story exclusively from the point of view of the sacrificed Isaac" (ibid.), it is a model and role they reject. This rejection became even more noticeable after the Six Day War, when "soldiers explicitly refused to accept the notion of self-sacrifice represented by the *Akedah* . . . and directed their anger at the fathers who had sent them into battle" (ibid.:108). Said one: "I am not willing to be an eternal Isaac climbing onto the altar without asking why, or understanding" (T. Gidᶜon, quoted in ibid.:109).[36] The Akedah has functioned to justify sending sons off to war, and not just among Israelis. It was used during World Wars I and II and Vietnam, and its use helped to construe these wars as holy. (Construing the victims, symbolically, as sons also obliterates the numerous daughters who lost their lives fighting these wars.) According to Cohen, the Akedah has allowed "Man . . . to weasel his way out of the responsibility for eliminating war, hatred and violence of all kinds," but as far as Cohen is concerned, man "is no longer justified, in any way, to putting God's stamp of approval on his resort to arms" (Cohen, 1990:59).

There can be no question that the Akedah, as model, regardless of the interpretation, "has begun to appear again with force and frequency in Israeli writing" (Abramson, 1990:103). Indeed, as long ago as 1971, a symposium was held in Israel to ascertain "the relevance of the Akedah-tradition to Israel's struggle for survival" (Wineman, 1977:8). Even if there is no consensus about the relevance of the story or about which interpretation is most appropriate, the contemporary writers and artists demonstrate that the Akedah story/model is clearly not one that is confined only to the ancient world or to religious contexts but is a powerful myth that people and nations have lived by.

Often the model is secularized to portray problems between fathers and sons, and the lack of understanding between the beliefs and values of the older generation and the younger. Some stories attempt to take Abraham's point of view; they sympathize with a father "bewildered by his son's defection for all he, the father had done was to obey God's command, which in historical terms meant fidelity to God's law" (Abramson, 1990:112). In stories by Amos Oz and A. B. Yehoshua such a father is treated quite differently: there he is portrayed as one who "has never understood or accepted the son's own cultural development, and has tried to impose his own standards on him" (ibid.:113). That fate, of course, is hardly confined to Jews, but the cultural availability of the Akedah has given these experiences mythical as well as deep historical significance.

In Oz's poignant story entitled "The Way of the Wind," the father is "unable to tolerate a son who turns out to be something other than an extension of the father himself" (Wineman, 1977:116). Not too surprisingly, the emphasis focuses on reproduction and the lineage the father wishes to establish. He thinks of the grandsons "who will bear his image and his name." It is quite clear he is thinking of a patrilineage, as he does not countenance the possibility of a daughter and, indeed, seems to exclude women from the process altogether—he disposes of his wife as soon as she has borne him a son. His grandsons will have two fathers: "my son will be the biological father, I'll implant the spirit in them" (ibid.:117–8).[37] This is an interesting example of the psychological effects of patriarchal ideology and the notion that the father is the one who transmits both life and spirit; but in this instance, the grandfather arrogates to himself the godlike role as he relegates to his son the merely biological one normally associated with women in the reproductive process. Here the distinction between spirit and matter is divided between men. In the story, the father purposely deceives the boy's mother by signing the paper that permits the son to join the air force. The son wants to escape from the father, but he cannot escape from his father's desire that he prove himself a man and a worthy son. This internalized desire leads to his death. The sins of the fathers shall be visited upon the sons from generation unto generation. Perhaps it is true that the "Akedah has become a national symbol representing the tragedy of Israel in general and of sons in particular" (Abramson, 1990:114).

The following two poems by contemporary American Jewish women incorporate some of my thoughts about the Akedah; Ostriker's presents it as a "Gentlemen's Agreement" and alludes to the power inherent in it, whereas Wilner's suggests an alternative—a new map that entails new implications and scenarios. Even though a different choice is voiced by the mother, this need not lead to any conclusion about the essential attributes of women; rather, women in patriarchal society have come to symbolize the virtues of compassion and nurturance and have been socialized to promote them. The choice can be made by all of us, men and women alike, but it demands a rejection of the Akedah model and all that it implies. It demands a complete transformation of the model, its values, and our social arrangements. It would mean a moral revolution.

In numerous modern Jewish stories, and in the painting by Chagall, the distinction between the Akedah and the Crucifixion has become blurred. Despite the fact that in Genesis 22 Isaac is not sacrificed, psychologically it is as if the sacrifice has occurred. Abraham's willingness is the core that is left when all the other layers of interpretation are peeled away. In the next chapter I address the ways the story has shaped the Christian tradition.

The Story of Abraham
ALICIA OSTRIKER

I started by reading the banner headline
The way you read the big print at the eye doctor's.
It said I AM THE LORD GOD
ALMIGHTY AND I LOVE YOU ESPECIALLY. No problem. Very good.
One line down it said PACK UP, I'm SENDING YOU OVERSEAS. It said
YOU WILL HAVE AS MANY CHILDREN AS THERE ARE SANDS IN THE
SEA AND STARS IN THE SKY.
THEY WILL POSSESS THE LAND AND
I AM PERSONALLY GOING TO BLESS THEM.
The smaller print said: I am going
To bless them as long as they obey me.
Otherwise there may be
Certain repercussions. The even smaller
Print explained how we needed
A memorable logo for our organization
And he had just the ticket, a mark of absolute
Distinction, it would only hurt for a minute.
The print kept getting smaller and blurrier,
The instructions more bizarre.
Hold on, I interrupted. I'd like to check

Some of this out with my wife.
NO WAY. THIS IS BETWEEN US MEN.
AND IF YOU HAPPEN TO BE THINKING
ABOUT LOOPHOLES
FORGET IT, MAN. It said they preferred
Not to use strong arm techniques. It said
I'd already signed on.

Sarah's Choice
ELEANOR WILNER

A little late rain   *The testing*
the desert in the beauty of its winter   *of Sarah*
bloom, the cactus ablaze
with yellow flowers that glow
even at night in the reflected light
of moon and the shattered crystal of sand
when time was so new
that God still walked
among the tents, leaving no prints
in the sand, but a brand burned into
the heart—on such a night
it must have been, although
it is not written in the Book
how God spoke to Sarah
what he demanded of her
how many questions came of it
how a certain faith was
fractured, as a stone is split
by its own fault, a climate of extremes
and one last drastic change
in the temperature.

"Go!" said the Voice. "Take your son,
your only son, whom you love,
take him to the mountain, bind him
and make of him a burnt offering."
Now Isaac was the son of Sarah's age,
a gift, so she thought, from God. And how
could he ask her even to imagine such a thing—
to take the knife
of the butcher and thrust it
into such a trusting heart, then

light the pyre on which tomorrow burns.
What fear could be more holy than the fear of *that?*

"Go!" said the Voice. Authority's own.
And Sarah rose to her feet, stepped out
of the tent of Abraham to stand between
the desert and the distant sky, holding its stars
like tears it was too cold to shed.
Perhaps she was afraid the firmament
would shudder and give way, crushing her
like a line of ants who, watching
the ants ahead marching safe under the arch,
are suddenly smashed by the heel
they never suspected. For Sarah,
with her desert-dwelling mind, could
see the grander scale in which the heel
might simply be the underside of some Divine
intention. On such a scale, what is
a human son? So there she stood, absurd
in the cosmic scene, an old woman bent
as a question mark, a mote in the eye
of God. And then it was that Sarah spoke
in a soft voice, a speech
the canon does not record.

"No." said Sarah to the Voice.   *The*
"I will not be chosen. Nor shall my son—   *teachings*
if I can help it. You have promised Abraham,   *of Sarah*
through this boy, a great nation. So either
this sacrifice is sham, or else it is a sin.
Shame," she said, for such is the presumption
of mothers, "for thinking me a fool,
for asking such a thing. You must have known
I would choose Isaac. What use have I
for History—an arrow already bent
when it is fired from the bow?"

Saying that, Sarah went into the tent
and found her restless son awake, as if
he'd grown aware of the narrow bed in which he lay.
And Sarah spoke out of the silence
she had herself created, or that had been there
all along. "Tomorrow you will be
a man. Tonight, then, I must tell you

the little that I know. You can be chosen
or you can choose. Not both.

The voice of the prophet grows shrill.
He will read even defeat as a sign
of distinction, until pain itself
becomes holy. In that day, how shall we tell
the victims from the saints,
the torturers from the agents of God?"
"But mother," said Isaac, "if we were not God's
chosen people, what then should we be? I am afraid
of being nothing." And Sarah laughed.

Then she reached out her hand. "Isaac,
I am going now, before Abraham awakes, before
the sun, to find Hagar the Egyptian and her son
whom I cast out, drunk on pride,
God's promises, the seed of Abraham
in my own late-blooming loins."

The
unbinding
of Isaac

"But Ishmael," said Isaac, "how should I greet him?"
"As you greet yourself," she said, "when you bend
over the well to draw water and see your image,
not knowing it reversed. You must know your brother
now, or you will see your own face looking back
the day you're at each other's throats."

She wrapped herself in a thick dark cloak
against the desert's enmity, and tying up
her stylus, bowl, some dates, a gourd
for water—she swung her bundle on her back,
reached out once more toward Isaac.
"It's time," she said. "Choose now."

"But what will happen if we go?" the boy
Isaac asked. "I don't know," Sarah said
"But it is written   what will happen   if you stay."

FIG. 5. Andrea Mantegna, *The Sacrifice of Abraham*. Monochrome painting: imitation of relief. (c. 1490). Kunsthistorisches Museum, Vienna, Austria. Erich Lessing/Art Resource, N.Y.

Christian Commentary

FOR CHRISTIANS, generally, the "sacrifice" of Isaac is thought to prefigure the Crucifixion, which they believe is the most important event in world history. In Genesis, God asks Abraham to sacrifice his son, his only son, the one whom he loves, but at the critical moment God interrupts the sacrifice. It is as if that deed, left unfinished, is finally completed when God the Father sacrifices his only begotten son for the redemption of the world.

The notion of prefigurement establishes a theological as well as psychological connection between the two events. But it also entails a conception of the world in which the Bible is presumed to record a continuous and unitary history of salvation punctuated by specific salvific events such as the Akedah (Frei, 1974:3). It is a view in which everything "that happens in the world can only be conceived as an element in this sequence; into it everything that is known about the world . . . must be fitted in as an ingredient of the divine plan" (Auerbach quoted in ibid.).[1] The notion of prefigurement is an important strategy for the Christian encompassment of Hebrew Scripture; the Hebrew Bible is no longer something separate and autonomous but is transformed into the Old Testament, into that which prefigured the New Testament.

Although the Crucifixion is thought to have superseded the Akedah, it does not erase it from Christian awareness. Christians are reminded of it in numerous ways: (1) by direct reference and allusion in the New Testament, (2) in sermons and liturgy, especially at Easter time when Genesis 22 is traditionally recited, either on Good Friday or during the Easter Vigil,[2] (3) in Sunday school and Bible study classes, (4) in noncanonical early Christian works such as "The Testament of Abraham," (5) in the writings of the Church Fathers such as Origen, Tertullian, and, of course, Augustine, (6) in medieval works—it was apparently a major theme in all the important medieval morality plays, (7) in works by the Protestant reformers, (8) in modern scholarly literature, both religiously motivated and secular, (9) in spontaneous reflections of contemporary ministers and lay people, and finally (10) in religious and secular works of art. It is one of the most common themes in Christian religious art; the Princeton Index of Medieval Art, for example, lists more than 1450 entries up to the Middle Ages alone. The story of the near sacrifice of Isaac continues to be depicted in literature, sculpture, painting, music, and film. In these many ways, it has been a constant image in Christian consciousness since the beginning, and through artistic media, especially, it has permeated the consciousness of people living in Christian cultures, whether or not they are believers.

In the way that many of us are affected by a wide range of commentaries and images—often without being aware of their provenance—I will draw on the range of sources above without overly cataloging them or trying to tie them to their original context. This book is not meant to be a compendium of references to Abraham and Isaac. Indeed, it would be impossible to encompass them all in one book and presumptuous for one person to try.

It is also difficult, though important, to keep in mind the distinction between Christian commentary on Genesis 22, as it is in the Hebrew Bible (Old Testament), and Christian commentary on the way Genesis 22 figures in the New Testament. The distinction is more conceptual than practical, as these lines are often blurred in practice.

When I spoke to people about the story, the most spontaneous response was that the Akedah prefigured the Crucifixion. A Baptist pastor was more explicit: "It is an example of the 'law of first mention'—that is, when a person or concept is first introduced in the Bible. The story of Abraham and Isaac is clearly a type of Christ and Crucifixion. . . . there is also present the theme of deliverance from death because God could have raised Isaac from the dead if Abraham had sacrificed him."[3] He did not know that such an idea was elaborated in some rabbinic commentary; instead he quoted from the New Testament book of Hebrews: "By faith, Abraham when he was tried, offered up Isaac, and he that had received the promises offered up his only begotten son. . . . Accounting that God was able to raise him up, even from the dead, from whence he also received him in a figure" (Heb. 11:17,19). This is the most explicit reference to the Akedah story in the New Testament, and it incorporates a number of themes to be discussed: faith, promises, and resurrection.

The Baptist pastor is not alone in thinking that the Akedah prefigures the Resurrection as well as the Crucifixion, as we shall see, but more common ways to illustrate prefigurement are the attempts to make superficial analogies between the two events. For example, "Isaac," said Tertullian, "when delivered up by his father for a sacrifice, himself carried the wood . . . and did at that early date set forth the death of Christ, who when surrendered as a victim by his Father carried the wood of his own passion" (Tertullian, *Against Marcion* 3:18:225; also Tertullian, *Answer to the Jews*, 13:250–1). Similar notions can be found in most of the early Church Fathers and was reproduced spontaneously by Cristos Valenti's minister in 1991 in California: "Abraham laid the wood upon Isaac just as the cross was laid upon Jesus."

Others have noted the parallels between the liminal three-day journey of Abraham and Isaac from their home to Mt. Moriah and the liminal three-day period between the Crucifixion and the Resurrection. And a few have commented that there were two other lads along with Isaac, as there were two other men crucified along with Jesus.

The ram suspended in the thicket has often been seen as an analogy for Christ hung on the Cross, and Tertullian implies that the thorny crown encircling Jesus' head recalled the brambles of that bush (Tertullian, *Answer to the Jews*, 13:251). Many, too, have noted the analogy between the male lamb sacrificed in Isaac's stead and the appellation of Jesus as "The Lamb of God" (John 1:29[4] and 1 Peter 1:19–20). That lamb "who was foreordained before the foundation of the world" recalls the ram that was created on the sixth day of Creation and had been waiting in the wings until its appointed time—to be sacrificed in Isaac's stead. To my knowledge no one has noted the similarity between the ass that accompanied Abraham and Isaac and the one that Jesus rode into Jerusalem on Palm Sunday.

Another parallel, of course, concerns the language of the "beloved son" (cf. Levenson, 1993). Still others have noted the similarity in the miracle of the conceptions of both Isaac and Jesus—in each case the conception was announced by an angel or messenger of God. Although that situation has provoked centuries of commentary about the suspicions of both Abraham and Joseph regarding paternity, no one has remarked that the *monogenes* (only begotten son), as Jesus is known, implies a "monogenetic" theory of procreation. The seed-child comes from only one source, in this case, only from God. Mary is merely the carrier and nurturer, not co-creator. A graphic example of this is illustrated in a late fifteenth century painting, The Annunciation (see fig. 6). The child (Jesus) is imagined as coming down *whole* from God; that is, Mary is impregnated with the whole child—she does not contribute to its form or identity, but contributes only the physical earthly, nurturant material. The *theory* of procreation is the same whether divine or human; the difference is whether God the Father or a human male is progenitor. The role of the mother is the same whether it is Mary or an ordinary woman (Delaney, 1986).

Prefigurement as a mode of interpretation—for example, the way the Akedah prefigures the Crucifixion—seems much closer to the spirit of the

FIG. 6. *The Annunciation* (c. 1480). Master of the Retable of the
Reyes Catolicos. Spanish. Oil on pine panel. Fine Arts Museums of San Francisco.
Gift of the Samuel H. Kress Foundation.

early Christians and to "fundamentalists" than it is to contemporary Biblical scholarship, which is concerned primarily with understanding the story in its ancient historical context. The latter is a worthwhile pursuit, but it ignores the fact that although the story is situated in the past, it continues to have emotional resonance in the present. The emphasis on historical reconstruction has helped to blur Jewish and Christian differences (of the scholars), but it also defuses the theological, cultural, and psychological significance of the story. The outcome of such a strategy is what scholar of Christian origins, Larry Wills, has called "exegesis across a chasm" (personal communication), meaning that much contemporary exegesis is directed to resurrecting the historical context with little regard to its continuing power to affect millions of people every year. Such an approach contributes to the perception that the story belongs in remote antiquity and is not a myth we live through, and by, today.

This perception may also recapitulate the experience of individual Christians, who generally first hear the story of Abraham when they are very young—that is, in their own prehistory. A number of informants told me that they first heard the Abraham story in Sunday school and that it was among the earliest Bible stories they had heard or remember hearing. Genesis is indeed the book best known to Christians. The stories of the Garden, Adam and Eve, Cain and Abel, and Abraham are as well known to Christian children as is the nativity of Jesus, probably better known than the Passion narrative and Crucifixion. Some people recalled an overwhelming feeling of fear and dread when they first heard the Abraham story—a feeling set down at a time when children have no defense or little means for discussing it with their adult teachers, who try to explain it as a story of love. There it remains, unquestioned, as part of the taken-for-granted cultural background.[5] It is, I think, a strange way to learn about love. Love, in that context, has to do with obedience in a hierarchical relationship. "By consenting to offer to God his only son, Abraham proved his perfect love, and his example became the cornerstone of the whole Jewish theology of love" (Vermes, 1973:193). This notion of fatherly love is, of course, reinforced by the idea that "God so loved the world he gave his only begotten son" (John 3:16). It is difficult to imagine that Christians would not make the connection between the two cases. It is also important to consider what the story has bequeathed about the meaning of love.

For most Christians, it is clear that the story of the sacrifice of Isaac is the prefiguration of the Crucifixion—yet what seems obvious to lay people is not so obvious to scholars. "Despite its significance, the Akedah has, until recently, not attracted much scholarly attention" (Daly, 1977: 74). And the recent debate turns on whether the story of the sacrifice of Isaac influenced the development of Christian theology or, conversely, whether the theology of the Crucifixion provoked Jewish reinterpretation of the story. Although the debate appears to focus on issues of dating of sources and the meaning of certain references, it is also fueled by religious commitments. It is extremely difficult to assign dates to much of the material from what Christians call the "intertestamental period." Christian theologians perhaps want to minimize the influence of Jewish ideas and models of what they hold as the unique event in world history. Jews, on the other hand, could easily view these maneuvers by Christians as yet another means of denying the dependence of Christianity on Judaism and of co-opting a centrally meaningful story from Jewish tradition.

All interpretations, whether divinely inspired or not, are human constructions. They do not occur in a vacuum, nor are they created ex nihilo, and they always depend on the prior context of interpretations common to the culture—even as they may be transformed. "How was it that this infamous death could so quickly become interpreted as a representative, atoning, sacrificial death and in what interpretive framework was such an understanding possible at all?" (Hengel, 1981:1). The Akedah surely seems a likely model for the interpretation of the crucifixion. Yet, because there are few explicit references in the New Testament (e.g., Hebrews, Romans, and James) and a relatively small number of possible allusions, some scholars assume it could not have served as the model. On the other hand, it could also be argued that it was so well known to the Jews who followed Jesus that even the slightest allusion would evoke the story. After all, the story was not mentioned again in the Hebrew Bible, yet its significance can hardly be debated. A number of scholars, both Jewish and Christian, feel that "by NT times the Akedah had become practically a summary of Jewish sacrificial soteriology" (Daly, 1977:74), and furthermore, "that the sacrificial soteriology of the NT can no longer be discussed without consideration of the Akedah" (ibid., 75).

Others, notably Davies and Chilton, disagree. They think that the elaboration of the Akedah was part of a rabbinic polemic against Christianity. They base their argument on the fact that the term *Akedah*, to refer to the story in Genesis 22, did not come into discourse until the late second century. When they say "the NT does not even attest the existence of the Aqedah, much less show its influence" (Davies and Chilton, 1978:515) they mean very narrowly the *aggadic* interpretation of Isaac as vicarious atonement in which he either was reduced to ashes or shed his blood.[6] Using the term *Akedah* to refer to Jewish understandings of the story before the Christian era, or to early Christian uses of the story, may be anachronistic; nevertheless, it seems extreme to assume that the story, was not influential (Segal, [1984]1987:113).

Schoeps, standing almost alone at midcentury, believed that the story served as a model for Paul's theology yet it has scarcely been noticed in the vast bibliography of Paul (Schoeps, 1946:385). "The significance of the Cross for Paul cannot be fully understood without his tacit reference to the sacrifice of Isaac: Paul's exegesis is here rabbinical" (ibid.:392). Indeed, much of the evidence Schoeps brings to bear on his point derives from (later) rabbinic commentary, which, therefore, may be somewhat anachronistic. It is also possible, of course, that such commentary reflects earlier, oral traditions. Nevertheless, as we shall see, Abraham was extremely important for Paul, and it is unlikely that he was unfamiliar with the story. Vermes asserts that the story was well known in the first century and used by Paul to interpret the death of Jesus as atonement (Vermes 1973:218).

Vermes believes that at some point before and during the period around the time of Jesus, the focus of emphasis in the story shifted from Abraham to Isaac. Rather than passive victim, Isaac became an active participant and the exemplar of the Jewish martyr. "Isaac offered *himself* to be a sacrifice for the sake of righteousness" (4 Macc. 13:12, emphasis added). This self-offering, according to Vermes, served as the "key to the doctrine of atonement or Redemption" (Vermes, 1973:193).

Although the interconnected themes of martyrdom and resurrection had been developed in pre-Christian works, "the motif of Isaac's sacrifice as the example *par excellence* of martyrdom does not appear until the first century, pre-eminently in the book of 4 Maccabees dated to the early 30s but devoid of Christian influence" (Segal, [1984]1987:117). It seems but a short step to associate Isaac as martyr with the notion of the "suffering servant" and, though Segal doesn't see that relation, Vermes and Rosenberg do. The latter, in fact, suggests that "in Jewish tradition Isaac is the prototype of the 'suffering servant' bound upon the altar" (Rosenberg, 1965:385). Because Jesus is so often associated with the Suffering Servant in Christian exegesis, this would make clear the link between Isaac and Jesus.

Rosenberg bases his conclusion, in part, on the passage in Maccabees quoted above, for the "righteous one" is how the "suffering servant" is known in Jewish tradition. If this were proved, it would be good evidence that the theology of Jesus was modeled not only on the suffering servant, as a number of Christian theologians emphasize, but also on the exegetical tradition of the time, regarding Isaac. Given the strong association between the Akedah theme and the servant motif in Judaism and, according to Vermes, in "the oldest pre-Marcan stratum of the Christian *kerygma*," he asks "whether Jesus himself was conscious of his destiny as being the fulfillment of Isaac's sacrifice" and, thus, whether "the introduction of the Akedah motif into Christianity was due, not to St. Paul, but to Jesus of Nazareth" (Vermes, 1973:223).

Rosenberg has elaborated the relation between "Jesus, Isaac and the Suffering Servant" (Rosenberg, 1965), and he also introduces another interesting idea. Numerous scholars have noted that the story of the sacrifice of Isaac appears in the book of Jubilees, where it is associated with Passover. Rosenberg pushes it much further and connects Jubilees with the Gospel of Matthew.

Jubilees, a pre-Christian Jewish book, incorporates the dating of events and a calendar that divides history into sequences of Jubilee periods—seven years times seven years and a major Jubilee every fifty years. A generation is equivalent to a Jubilee. The calendar was used by the Essenes, and Rosenberg notes that there is considerable evidence that Jesus and his disciples followed that calendar (Rosenberg, 1965:386). More important, evidence that the Akedah served as a model for the interpretation of Jesus' death is found in the connections Rosenberg sees between Jubilees and Matthew. Matthew 1:17 records fourteen generations from Abraham to David, fourteen from David to the Babylonian exile, and fourteen from the Babylonian exile to Jesus—comparable to the forty-two Jubilees from Creation to Abraham. "The sacrifice of Jesus becomes exactly parallel to the offering of Isaac, for the book of Jubilees (13:16; 17:15; 19:1) indicates that the offering of Isaac had taken place just prior to the beginning of the forty-second jubilee after the Creation of the world" (Rosenberg, 1965:387). Jesus and his disciples believed the Messiah would come during the Jubilee year in which they were living—the eighty-fifth Jubilee after Creation—adding weight to the idea that Jesus may have imagined himself not only as the Messiah but also as the sacrificial victim. (The tradition that the Messiah would come in the eighty-fifth Jubilee after Creation is also preserved in Sanhedrin 97b.)

Jubilees, as one of the books that associates the Akedah with Passover, implies, according to Segal, that the story is related not only to the liberation from Egypt but to all future liberations. Nevertheless, liberation or redemption appears to be associated, at least in several important places—in the Akedah, in the Passover, and in the Crucifixion—with human sacrifice:

> In either case, however, the festival is involved with the theme of human sacrifice; either Isaac, who was saved from death upon the altar by the offering of a ram in his place, or the first born of Israel in Egypt, who were redeemed from death at the hand of the הַמַּשְׁחִית ("the Destroyer") by the blood of the paschal lambs slain in their stead. It was therefore fitting that Jesus, the Lamb of God, should meditate before going to his death at Gethsemane on the Mount of Olives, the site to the east of Jerusalem that in Jewish folklore was sacred to the "Destroyer." (Rosenberg, 1965:386)

If the Akedah was associated with Passover at some time or by some groups of Jews then the strong connection between Passover and the Last Supper/Crucifixion-Eucharist would provide a strong psychological and theological link between the two events.[7] To deny these links seems at times to be no more than scholarly petulance.

The themes of expiation, atonement, martyrdom, and suffering, as well as the concept of the Messiah, were all present by the time of Christianity (cf. Segal, [1984]1987:122–3; Hengel, 1981:1), but whether all were tied together into a specific theology and then focused on and exemplified by the Akedah is a question. Was it an active model around the time of Christ or was it merely an ancient story recalled in certain disparate instances? During the confusion of the intertestamental period, the Temple was destroyed and the Jews were persecuted and dispersed. There was also a proliferation of millennial separatist sects (Essenes, Qumrani, Gnostics, and who knows how many others), some expressing extremes of behavior and seeking new ways, new beliefs, and rituals. Out of the turmoil emerged new religious sensibilities—both the conceptual system of Christianity, in a variety of forms, and renewed forms of Judaism. Both emerged in relation to each other; it was not the end of one and the beginning of another, as Christian theology assumes and as Christians tend to think.

Regardless of the issues of provenance—which will continue to fuel heated debates among historians, theologians, and believers—and far more important for this book is the fact that the Akedah and its associations have been part of the *common* heritage of Jews and Christians for nearly two millennia.[8] Not all of the associations and versions of the story are known to all Jews and Christians, but they are available as a common store of images, ideas, names, and objects. Yet just "because many of the motifs which dominate Christian exegesis are present in Jewish exegesis," one need not assume that "Christianity merely took them all over, effecting no transformation in the traditions as it employed them" (ibid.:122). No doubt the early Jewish-Christians, following Jesus himself, felt that they were cleansing and simplifying Judaism, but with time and the mutual resistance between this new community and other Jews, it became not another form of Judaism but a new vision, a new formulation of the world—the New Covenant. This New Covenant, however, was joined to, and dependent for its meaning on, the Old.

PROMISES OF ABRAHAM

Because Christ claimed to fulfill the "promises" adumbrated in the Old Testament, nascent Christianity had to clarify the nature of the promises and to make the case that Christians were the rightful heirs. The story of Abraham became pivotal—not only to convince other Jews to embrace the new covenant, but also, oddly enough, to convince Gentiles.

"In thy seed shall all the nations of the earth be blessed because thou has obeyed my voice" (Gen. 22:18). The question turns on: who is the seed of Abraham; who are the children of Abraham; who are the rightful heirs of the promises given to him? Would *seed* refer only to the descendants of Isaac and Jacob, that is, to the Jews (the circumcised), or would it also refer to the "many nations" including even the uncircumcised Gentiles?

The very first sentence of the New Testament appears to answer that question: "The book of the generations of Jesus Christ, the son of David, the son of Abraham" (Matt. 1:1). The lineage is not traced to Noah or to Adam, who might figure more easily as general, universal ancestors, but specifically to Abraham, the first patriarch, the one credited with being aware of the one God, the one with whom God made a covenant symbolized by circumcision, and the one willing to sacrifice even his son if that were demanded by his God. The genealogical link collapses all intervening generations but David, and he was apparently included in order to establish Jesus' claim to be the Messiah.

Paul makes the link more explicit in his letter to the Galatians, as he also radicalizes it: "Now to Abraham and his seed were the promises made. He saith not, And to seeds, as of many; but as of one, And to thy seed, which is Christ" (Gal. 3:16).[9] Jesus Christ is heir to the promises because he is figured as the true seed/son of Abraham. Paul's interpretive strategy was momentous. With one word (*seed*) he established a direct link between Abraham and Jesus and securely anchored Christianity in the Jewish heritage, while simultaneously rendering the intervening period between Abraham and Jesus irrelevant. The collapsing of generations is a masterful interpretive strategy and exactly the opposite of that of modern biblical historians. Rather than collapsing the chasm, modern interpreters widen it by placing Abraham in his ancient context and trying to keep him there. The early Christians wanted to bring him closer, and they foreshortened history by collapsing the distance between Abraham and Jesus. At the same time, without any mention of the Akedah, the formulation of Jesus as the true seed/son of Abraham identifies Jesus with Isaac, automatically evoking the Akedah story and hinting at the possibility of Jesus' own sacrifice.

The other Gospels open differently, but in all of them the figure of Abraham is of critical importance in trying to define the new community and legitimize its claims. Although the New Testament opens with the Gospels, they were apparently of later composition than Paul's letters. Incorporated into the canon, Paul's letters may provide the earliest Christian commentary about Abraham. Paul refers to Abraham nineteen times in only three letters—more than to anyone else except Jesus. He uses Abraham to discuss the nature of faith and the relation between Christian and Jew. For Paul, Abraham is father of faith not only for Jews but for all believers (Rom. 4:11–8). Neither physical descent nor keeping Jewish law would be the decisive factor, however; instead, those who exhibited the kind of *faith* that Abraham did would be included in the new community, the new covenant.

Jews who merely followed the law and practices were enslaved, according to Paul; only belief in Jesus Christ would set them free. In a statement that was later incorporated into an early sermon by Augustine (Sermon 2, [c. 391 A.D] 1990:180), Paul said: "Abraham had two sons, one by a slave and one by a free woman. But the son of the slave was born according to the flesh, the son of the free woman through promise. Now this is an allegory: these women are the two Testaments" (Gal. 4:22–4). This allegory compares Jews to Ishmael, son of Abraham via Hagar, thereby illustrating the Jews' enslavement to the law. (This identification would surprise many Muslims who claim their descent from Ishmael, son of Abraham by Hagar.)

In early Christian discourse the word *law* was often used as a kind of shorthand for circumcision, which was interpreted as the sign that Jews are bound to, or enslaved by, the law. Christians were free, liberated from the yoke of slavery. Moreover, Paul's assertion that the children of Abraham through Hagar were "children of the flesh," whereas those through Sarah were "children of the promise" (Gal. 4:23), elaborates the distinction between physical and spiritual kinship and also sets the stage for much of early Christian theologizing. It could also be understood and interpreted by Jews as a ploy by Christians to steal the birthright away from the Jews.

Although Paul still included Jews as chosen by God and, therefore, in a privileged position for recognizing the divinity of Jesus, they could no longer automatically consider themselves the heirs to the promises. He demanded that they reform and believe in Jesus. Such a demand could be considered the beginning of attempts at "disinheriting the Jews,"[10] but it was even more pronounced in John. The eighth chapter of the Gospel of John, which focuses on Abraham, picks up the theme of bondage. He has the Jews answer: "We are Abraham's seed and were never in bondage; how sayest thou Ye shall be made free?" (John 8:33). Jesus appears to agree that they are children of Abraham but says that if they were, they would do the works of Abraham (John 8:39), namely exhibit his kind of faith. Because they do not, he says, "Ye are of your father the devil" (John, 8:44), in what is perhaps the first instance of the demonizing of the Jews. Almost two thousand years later Wharton asks: "Is it a necessary article of faith to *deny* that Jews are legitimate, continuing children of Abraham? For nearly 2,000 years the answer is yes" (Wharton, 1988: 385). The disinheriting of the Jews did not happen all at once but was the logical consequence of some of the early claims of the Christians. Abraham was a pivotal figure in the gradual transformation from Jewish Christian to Gentile Christian.

One early attempt can be clearly glimpsed in the work of Melito, Bishop of Sardis (c. A.D. 150–180), who was writing before there was a Christian canon, authorized tenets of faith, or regularized practices, and in a place and time when there was a well-established Jewish community. The content as well as the direction of his thought was shaped by interaction with that community. But rather than taking a defensive stance, he went on the offensive. In his Paschal Homily, for example, he viciously attacked the Jews for killing Jesus, and, even more, for not knowing whom they had murdered. In Melito's work, at least what survives from it, the Akedah becomes central in showing that the new dispensation overrides the old. Melito's three surviving fragments relating to the Akedah are "the first genuine evidence we have of the direction Christian thinking on the Akedah would take. At a later date the conflict [between Jews and Christians] would become more apparent, but the outlines of the debate are already present in Melito" (Wilken, 1976:68). Melito "attempts to rescue Isaac for the Christians" (ibid. 62), by drawing an analogy between Isaac and Christ and emphasizing that Jesus' sacrifice is the more perfect and complete because he died, whereas Isaac did not. In another fragment, the ram is the analogue of Christ; as the lamb redeemed Isaac, so too does the Lord redeem the world. In the Christological interpretation of the Akedah, the meaning of the story can be found only in Jesus. In this interpretation, Abraham becomes, in a sense, the first witness for Christ.

CHURCH FATHERS

The story of the "sacrifice" of Isaac achieves even greater prominence in the patristic writings than in the New Testament, and it becomes central in the developing Christian piety. Almost all of the early Church Fathers commented on it:

> Origen, writing in the early third century, devoted a large section of his homilies on Genesis to the figure of Abraham; Ambrose in the fourth century wrote two books on him; Gregory of Nyssa, Chrysostom, and others preached about him regularly; Cyril of Alexandria in the early fifth century discusses him extensively in a book on Genesis and in an Easter sermon; Augustine devotes a dozen chapters to him in *The City of God*, and numerous other writers hold him up as a model and example for Christians. (Wilken, 1972:724)

A complete study of the commentaries of these early Christian writers would make fascinating reading, but it would be an enormous undertaking, and it far exceeds the scope and purpose of this study.[11] Here I can give only a sampling. In one of his homilies Origen addressed the fathers in the congregation, especially those who had lost sons during the ordinary course of life. He tells them to learn from Abraham: "show that your faith in God is stronger than your human feelings. For Abraham, though he loves his son, preferred the love of God to human love" (Origen [c. A.D. 185–254] 1982, 8:7). The intent may be noble, but the implication of that way of thinking is, to my mind, perverse. Essentially it admonishes those who grieve overmuch.[12] The child is in heaven and all is well. The child is not *represented*; he or she has no voice, is silenced and obliterated. We are encouraged to focus our attention on God, or on the father, not on the child.

Irenaeus talked of Abraham as a model in Christian life, not just for Christ, but also for God!

> Righteously also do we, possessing the same faith as Abraham and taking up the cross as Isaac did the wood, follow Him. . . . For in Abraham man had learned beforehand and had been accustomed to follow the word of God. For Abraham, according to his faith, followed the command of the Word of God, and with a ready mind delivered up, as a sacrifice to God, his only begotten and beloved son, *in order that God also might be pleased to offer up for all his seed His own beloved and only-begotten Son, as a sacrifice for our redemption.* (Irenaeus [c. A.D. 120–202] 1903:467, emphasis added)

In other words, it appears that God's eventual sacrifice of His Son depended on Abraham's prior willingness. This theme was also taken up in some medieval plays; as Kolve points out, "the fulfillment *depends* upon the figure" (Kolve, 1966:74), namely, that which prefigured or foreshadowed the later event. One of the messages, surely, was that Abraham prefigured God the Father giving His own Son, but also emphasized was Isaac's obedience, his submission to his father's will, as a type of Christ figure. But regardless of exactly *how* Abraham and Isaac are portrayed, they were a prominent part of English medieval play cycles. Indeed, the story of the sacrifice occurred in all of those that included a section on the Old Testament. In four extant plays the section on Genesis ends with Genesis 22. In some cases, such as the Brome cycle, the Abraham story may have stood alone as a separate independent play.[13]

The centrality of the Abraham story for medieval English piety cannot be overlooked. Perhaps for that very reason it has continued to strike a particular resonance in the English-speaking world. But it was clearly present even earlier. Apparently three versions of the story survive in Old

FIG. 7. Filippo Brunelleschi, *Abraham in the Act of Sacrificing Isaac* Museo Nazionale Bargello, Florence, Italy. Alinari/Art Resource, N.Y.

FIG. 8. Lorenzo, Ghiberti, Gilded bronze relief of the sacrifice of Isaac by Abraham. Museo Nazionale del Bargello, Florence, Italy. Alinari/Art Resource, N.Y.

English and must have been written prior to Aelfric, who wrote a commentary on it.[14] Its place in the medieval play cycles may have been achieved in part because it was prominently depicted in paintings, stained glass windows, psalters, and literature. When Old Testament history was depicted at all, Genesis was often the only text included, and it usually ended with Genesis 22. It is also "at this point that the Old English poem, *Genesis*, comes to an end, and Bede's commentary on Genesis does not extend beyond this point. The propriety of this stopping place is self-evident: the effects of the Fall have by then been fully displayed and the Redemption has been fully foreshadowed" (Woolf, 1972:63–4).

The figural tendency that is so strong in these medieval works is attributed by Kolve (1966) to the emphasis on history and on the God who shows himself in time. It is very different from an allegorical tendency. The figural tendency is not a new invention but was already evident in Tertullian: "he insisted on the historical validity of Old Testament events: for him the *spiritual* sense lay in perceiving the relationship between two apparently disconnected historical happenings. In his terminology the fulfillment (or second event) is spoken of as *veritas* and the figure that announces it as *umbra* or *imago*" (Kolve, 1966:65). Regardless of when it originated, this mode of interpreting the text has been, and continues to be, a very important strand in Christian thought (cf. Daniélou, 1960; Frei, 1974; Handelman, 1982).

Because the story of the "sacrifice" of Isaac "had always been taken by Christian theologians to foreshadow the sacrifice of Christ" (Hartt, 1975: 127), it became the subject of a sculptural competition in Florence in 1401. Seven sculptors were chosen to submit plans for the panels on the doors of the Florentine Baptistery; among them were Brunelleschi and the young Ghiberti, whose plan won (see fig. 7 and 8).[15]

WHO SHALL INHERIT?

Because Christians claimed that Jesus was the fulfillment of the law and the prophets—that the new dispensation abrogated the old—the identity of the proper descendants/heirs of God's promises to Abraham became an uppermost concern. A tension between physical and spiritual descent clearly existed. Some claimed that physical descent (being Jewish) gave them a privileged position, and others claimed that only faith in Jesus Christ mattered. The latter position was surely designed to include the Gentiles in the community. But if they were to be reckoned children of Abraham, a means other than circumcision had to be found. For the mark of being Jewish was not only following certain laws and practices, but, quintessentially, circumcision. It is not clear whether the Gentiles refused to be circumcised, whether they vehemently opposed the practice, or whether their unwillingness was simply assumed. Although the wording of the following passage from Romans is obtuse, the message Paul wants to convey seems to mean that Abraham "is the common father of Jew and Gentile alike according to faith alone" (Siker, 1991:59).

> He received the sign of circumcision, a seal of the righteousness of the faith while *he had yet* being uncircumcised: that he might be the father of all them who believe, though they be not circumcised; that righteousness might be imputed unto them also: And the father of circumcision to them who are not of the circumcision only, but who also walk in the steps of that faith of our father Abraham, which *he had* being *yet* uncircumcised. (Romans 4:11–2)

Circumcision alone, therefore, was not to allow Jews to claim Abraham as father; they also needed faith.

Oddly, Abraham, the first to be circumcised, became the vehicle for the inclusion of the uncircumcised, that is, the Gentiles. According to Paul and presumably to many early Christians, Abraham's faith was independent of the law; he was reckoned righteous before the law (Gen. 15:6), before the institution of either circumcision or later Mosaic law. The covenant established by means of circumcision was interpreted as a physical sign of his faith, which had preceded it. Therefore, neither circumcision nor all the rest of Jewish law was necessary in order to be included among God's people.

Christian critique of circumcision did not, however, extend to an investigation of the meaning and implications of its gendered specificity. Early Christian thinkers and leaders did not explain (perhaps did not need to explain) why the sign of the covenant was inscribed only on male flesh, for they, too, believed that the penis was *the* organ of generativity, fatherhood, and transmission of the line. Although they might dispense with circumcision, associations between spirituality and male generativity were metaphorically transferred and reinforced; the focus was no longer the physical line but the spiritual line, and the means of transmission not semen but the seminal word—the *logos spermatikos*.

A passage in James seems, on the surface, to contradict Paul's view when he says that "faith without works is dead" (James 2:20) and uses the Akedah as the example. But it could also be interpreted to mean that the fruit of faith is works, that they give outward expression of an inner condition; not that one is justified by following certain practices but that one's practices are the expression of faith (cf. Siker, 1991:98–9). And clearly, for James, the Akedah is the example par excellence: "Was not Abraham our father justified by works when he had offered Isaac his son upon the altar?" (James 2:21). James seems to have concluded that faith is completed by works.

Faith is the important term for Paul and for other early Christian writers. In Hebrews it occurs more than in any other book in the New Testament; in chapter 11 alone it occurs twenty-four times and begins eighteen sentences. "By faith Abraham, when he was tried, offered up Isaac: and he that had received the promises offered up his only begotten son, Of whom it was said, That in Isaac shall thy seed be called" (Heb. 11:17–8). Although others are mentioned who also have faith, it is generally felt that Abraham is the focal point. He is held up as the model for all those who believe. "The seed which was promised to Abraham seems to have been further realized in the eyes of the author of Hebrews not merely in the numerous offspring which come to Abraham through Isaac and his physical descendants as a result of the promise, but in the spiritual seed composed of all those who, like Abraham, have faith when they are tested" (Swetnam 1981:128). These individuals are chosen one-by-one by God—they are the ones who constitute the "seed" of Abraham (ibid.: 104). They are the children of the promise; they inherit the promises. "Chosenness" was no longer relegated to a specific *ethné* (group of people) but was acquired, through divine election, by specific individuals.

In addition, the promises are transformed from physical blessings to purely spiritual ones. God's promises to Abraham were seed (many descendants) and land; in Christianity these are transformed into spiritual seed (of saved souls) and the Heavenly Home. Tertullian draws attention to the difference, which he claims was prophesied in the promise to Abraham. The promise of descendants as multiple as "the sand on the seashore and the stars in heaven" was for him "an intimation of an earthly as well as a heavenly dispensation" (Tertullian, *Against Marcion*, 249). So, too, is the land spiritualized; it becomes eschatological. The citizenship of the true children of Abraham is in heaven; they will inherit that home and sit at the banquet table with their father Abraham (Matt. 8:11–2). If not at his table, then in his bosom. "Abraham's Bosom," according to Tertullian, was a kind of waiting place—neither heaven nor hell—but a place for the reception of the souls of his *sons* even from among the Gentiles (Tertullian, *Against Marcion*, 455).

Faith is intimately related to belief in the resurrection, which, according to some rabbinic midrashim, as well as Christian interpretation, was first hinted at in Genesis 22 (see chapter 5). Abraham, they say, was willing to go through with the sacrifice of Isaac because he was convinced that God would bring him back or could raise him from the dead if necessary. That interpretation could make it seem like Abraham was only going through the motions. It also gives too much specificity to

Abraham's faith and seems to vitiate other views of his faith—that it was precisely a "leap" of faith, a leap into the unknown, a leap with the confidence, no doubt, that his God knew what was best for him. One might also interpret his faith as an active stance, not merely as belief *in* something. Additionally, if his faith consisted in the belief that God would resurrect his son, his faith would have been focused more on resurrection than on God, related ideas surely but different nevertheless.

If Abraham's faith was, and continues to be, the model of faith, one could ask what theological need there is for Jesus? Yet the answer seems implicit in the question, for from a developed Christian point of view, at least, Abraham has the kind of faith in God that Christians ought to have in Jesus. Jesus is the one to whom this faith ought to be directed. From the Christian point of view, he completes what was begun with Abraham. In the Gospel of John, Abraham *is* a witness for Christ. "Jesus said unto them, Verily, verily, I say unto you, Before Abraham, I was" (John 8:58). This is a claim not only for the preexistence of Christ but primarily for his divinity.[16]

In any case, "Abraham is thus seen as the focal point for all of the OT heroes, even for those who preceded him. And the aspect of Abraham which is central is the sacrifice of Isaac. To this pole of history is opposed the death and resurrection of Christ which acts as an opposing pole" (Swetnam, 1981:129). *Opposing* here does not mean in opposition but more that Abraham and Jesus are the alpha and omega that encompass biblical faith.

That was also the position of Martin Luther, whose church at Wittenberg contains a huge triptych above the altar, one panel of which depicts the "sacrifice" of Isaac. Luther began his commentary on Genesis 22 on 27 October 1539, during a period of the plague.[17] In his struggle against Catholic orthodoxy and its increasing involvement with "works," such as acts of penance and indulgences, Luther claimed that one is saved by faith alone. And Abraham became important for his exposition. God's blessing comes only through the seed of Abraham which is Christ, he said, citing Paul's statement (see above). For Luther, Abraham was justified by faith; he must have understood the resurrection of the dead because he believed in the promise but was commanded to kill his son. "Life and death are alike for the godly," one must keep faith no matter what God does or asks (Luther, [1539–41]1964:120). Once you get a command from God you cannot do anything but obey, and you must undertake the task without hesitation or trepidation. This sounds very close to what Cristos Valenti said at his trial. Luther does not elaborate on how this command would come, and he also denounces those Catholics who boast that they have heard the voice of God: because Jesus has come there is no more need of voices, miracles, apparitions; one is saved by faith alone.

Inextricably linked with faith is obedience. Obedience was exhibited not just by Abraham but also by Isaac. Luther appears to equate Isaac with Christ in his obedience to his father's will. Referring to Isaac, Luther says: "With the exception of Christ we have no such similar example of obedience" (ibid.:114). At the same time, Luther warns that Abraham's extraordinary example should not be dragged along as a precedent to be followed. Instead we should imitate his obedience and his faith. "Because of God, Abraham is willing to give up not only his son, Sarah, his inheritance, his house and his church but even his own life" (ibid.:98). Although Abraham had twice given Sarah up (Gen. 12, 20; see Speiser, 1963), there is little evidence that he was willing to give up his inheritance, house, church, or his own life; furthermore there is a difference between giving up things and taking another person's life, a difference Luther does not address. Nor does he ask what right Abraham had to involve other people in such a unilateral decision.

He does, however, express some concern about the deception of both Sarah and Isaac. When he speculates about Sarah, he reveals what we would call "sexist presumptions": Abraham must have concealed from her what he was about to do because she was too weak to withstand the great shock it would cause (ibid.).[18] He is more concerned about the deception of the son, and he thinks Abraham must have told him he was to be the lamb but that this conversation was omitted by Moses. (This passage shows that Luther believed that the Pentateuch or Torah was written by Moses; it also shows his flexible way of reading between the lines.)

There is much more one could say about Luther's commentary and the way Abraham figures in it. But I want to draw attention to his theological use of the word *seed*. Although Abraham is important in Luther's theology, this is primarily because of Abraham's relation to Jesus, his seed. "The blessed Seed alone delivers from death" (ibid.:165). Throughout the English translation of Luther's commentary, *seed* is always capitalized; it is reified in the true sense of the word, for *the Seed is Jesus who is God*. In the King James version of the Bible, references to seed in the Old Testament are starred, as prophetic announcements of Christ. Seed is divine; it is identified with God. No wonder Luther can say: "Nowhere is there light, life or salvation except through this Seed" (ibid.:177). There is an unbroken stream, a "gushing fountain" (ibid.:151) of the divine lineage through Abraham to Christ who is also God. It is clearly a relation between father and son, whether Abraham and Isaac on the human plane, or God the Father and Christ the Son on the divine. The use of the language of procreation for theological conception has a long history, and Luther's use of it seems quite deliberate.[19] Although he uses procreative language theologically, he is unaware that he is using a *theory* of procreation.

THE "SEED" OF ABRAHAM: (KINSHIP)

Questions of what constitutes a Christian cannot be separated from who is a Christian. These questions have to do with inheritance and kinship but are framed in terms of seed (*sperma* in the Septuagint, a Greek translation of the Old Testament made sometime in the third century B.C. and usually referred to as *LXX*). Other scholars have focused on the referents of seed in Genesis 22:18 (and elsewhere, in relation to Abraham). Swetnam, in particular, has a number of sections on the meaning of *seed* in various books of the New Testament, but meaning for him is clearly referential—that is, who is being referred to. He does not ask *what* is the meaning of *seed*. My concern has been with the constitutive meaning of *seed* and with the theological and social implications.

Seed encapsulates the biblical notions of procreation as biblical scholar, Robert Alter has noted. In speaking of the importance of the divinely chosen lineage in Genesis, he says: "nothing is allowed to detract our focused attention from the primary, problematic subject of the proper channel for seed (since this is thought of both figuratively and in the most concretely physical way, I have translated it literally throughout)" (Alter, 1981:6). I wish others had done the same, for the translation of *seed* as posterity, descendants, or progeny conceals that these are a matter of seed. Although Alter recognized the symbolic importance and specificity of seed, he seemed oblivious to the gendered implications. Writing in the late twentieth century, he cannot be excused for neglecting that women, too, have "seed"; but because he did, he also lost the opportunity to challenge the theology that is so interdependent with it. That is, although most of the commentators accept the idea that *seed* means progeny and that only men produce seed, they are not self-reflexive: *they do not examine the way gender is inextricably bound up with theological conceptions.* The gendered meanings are so obvious and yet have been overlooked by all of the commentators.

The entire theology is wrapped up with the construction of masculinity as it is related to fatherhood; both circumcision (for Jews) and seed focus on, and highlight, male pro-*creative* abilities. Denaturalized, male generativity is used symbolically to describe God's creativity; conversely, God's creative power is naturalized in the notions of male generativity. The notion of masculinity (what a man is) has, in the West, been intimately involved with notions of paternity—a point Mary Daly seems to have missed in her otherwise groundbreaking critique of the gender of God, *Beyond God the Father* (1973). Despite the title, she does not really explore the meanings of fatherhood and the way paternity is a *concept* embedded in a theory of procreation. Instead she assigns fatherhood to the category of the natural, and this leads her to attribute the negative aspects of patriarchy to male nature rather than to a particular construction of it.

Just because the notion of masculinity has involved a notion of male generativity, this does not mean that any particular man has to become a father in order to exercise his power. Rather, every man is imagined as endowed with the ability to produce seed, and it is this ability that bestows maleness with life-giving, authoritative, god-like power. It has to do with notions of paternity and thus with an entire *theory* of procreation. Abraham, who receives the promises, is able to pass them down, able to transmit them to his seed and, through his seed, to him who Christians claim is Heir, to Christ himself. As the idea of procreation becomes spiritualized or, as I would prefer, metaphorized (as is done in the theological conceptions), maleness and paternity are essential features. Exceptions are often useful to point out the more general assumptions.

One passage that has perplexed commentators for some time is Hebrews 11:11: "Through faith Sarah herself received strength to conceive seed." The English translation *conceive seed* obscures the Greek connotations whereby the words "must be understood in an active sense, and in all normal Greek usage can only refer to the active operation of the male in generation" (Black quoted in Swetnam, 1981:99, n. 59). Such an understanding has raised questions about the intentions of the author of Hebrews. Did he (or she) think (a) that Sarah had become like a man, as Hannah was said to have done when she let her sons be sacrificed, (b) that the passage was evidence of a two-seed theory of procreation, or finally (c) that it implied primarily that her *faith* was so strong. "What has failed to be suggested so far is rather simple: the word . . . is being used in a spiritual sense" (Swetnam, 1981:100). Van der Horst (1990, 1992), on the other hand, thinks it reveals a glimmer of a two-seed theory of procreation. He briefly reviews material on procreation from 500 B.C. to A.D. 500, but he also notes that a two-seed theory does not necessarily imply that the female seed is generative or equal.[20] In other words, textual evidence alone is not sufficient. Perhaps it could also be interpreted to mean that in her old age Sarah was given the strength of a man to be able to conceive seed, in the sense of being able to hold onto it.[21] Men do not conceive seed, they produce it.

Despite the fact that Swetnam and Van der Horst (and no doubt others) noticed the peculiarity in that one passage, they failed to use it to question the usual interpretations—that the male is the one who produces seed and thus pro-creates. They failed also to see the implications for and about women and the way it has been integral to theological conceptions. In the painting of the Annunciation we have already seen how it has been expressed visually.

Whether fatherhood is physical or spiritual, whether Abraham or God is father, it is still fatherhood, not motherhood, that bestows identity and symbolizes divinity. "To speak of one's paternity reveals one's basic identity" (Siker, 1991:135), as Jesus himself appears to indicate, when he says repeatedly in the Gospel of John that he knows *where he comes from and where he is going*: from and to the "Father." Notions of identity cannot be separated from notions of origin: who you are is related to where you come from, whether conceived physically, socially, or cosmologically; each level is gendered. Jesus can speak with the voice of the Father because, basically, Father and Son *are* one. As Isaac is the son of Abraham in a way he is not the son of Sarah, so too is Christ the son of God the Father in a way that he is not considered the son of Mary. Mothers are not equal parents; there is really only one parent. Father and Son are one, they are of the same essence (see especially John 5:18ff.); mother and son are not. Nor are mother and daughter of the same essence because a daughter also proceeds from the father; women, in this view, lack the ability to pass on themselves. It is paternity, not maternity, that confers identity; knowing who your father is legitimates you as a full person. Although for John, and Christianity generally, physical, genetic descent is not the determining element in whether one is a child of Abraham, paternity in the conceptual/spiritual sense is. It is important to understand why this is so and what this implies, not just for and about women, but also regarding the essentially gendered nature of theology.

INTERPRETIVE STRATEGIES

It is not enough merely to take a woman's or a mother's point of view, as a number of feminist scholars working with the biblical text have done (cf. Schüssler-Fiorenza, 1992; Trible, 1984; Bach, 1993). That assumes the meaning of *woman* or *mother* is self-evident; such a stance may redress the imbalance of attention, but it does not question the essential premises. To resurrect women's voices, especially the cry of the mothers—Hagar, Sarah, Mary, and the Mary at the contemporary trial—is important. But these women can only react; their reactions are predetermined by the structure of power between the genders. This hierarchical order is premised on the meaning of gender in the context of procreation which, in turn, is connected to a wider system of meanings of coming-into-being.

If, indeed, a monogenetic theory of procreation—in which the life-giving element, the identity, even the soul, comes from (or is transmitted by) only one (masculine) source—is correlative with the theological doctrine of monotheism, then gender and theology are inextricably entangled. For example, if the child came equally from both God and Mary, Mary would be co-Creator along with God, but she is not. Had she been so, the concept and meaning of God and of the female procreative role would be vastly different from what they are.

A feminist strategy for interpretation, in my view, must focus not on what a religious tradition has to say *about* women and men, but on the way female and male are constructed *by* the theology, and vice versa. Rather than analyzing the story from a perspective that takes the genders for granted, we need to ask, instead, how the story itself constructs and reinforces the meanings of gender so as to appear natural, inscribed in the very nature of the universe.

Such a strategy, however, is difficult for those for whom God is a constant—somehow separate from, impervious to, and unentangled in human meanings—and who also have a vested interest in preserving the religious tradition. They have a number of other options: (a) to retreat and reinforce the system as a scheme given by God and therefore not open to change, (b) to try to change some of the institutional arrangements, for instance by admitting women to the priesthood or the rabbinate, or (c) to try to change the language so as to be more inclusive. As noted earlier, however, a particular theory of language is being implemented, a theory that assumes that meaning exists separate from language and is not constituted by and through language (see note 23, chapter 1). We have already seen what gets swept under the rug when such a seemingly simple word as *seed* is changed to *children*.

Some feminists have also suggested a notion of Mother/Father God as a way to resolve the problem of male bias, but, given the argument of this book, it is clear that that would only perpetuate and reinforce the stereotypes of maternity and paternity we have been discussing. Rather than salvaging theology, we need to rethink the entire system and the structures and values that are embedded in it. But if we are to begin to construct more humane theories of human existence, it is of crucial importance to rethink these powerful religious traditions, their foundational stories, and the underlying assumptions.

Focusing on God rather than Abraham, a few feminist scholars (e.g., Brown and Parker, 1990; Brock, 1990; Kraemer, 1992) have begun to question why the sacrifice of the son should be a model of faith and the supreme example of love and absolution. Kraemer, for example, suggests that "those preoccupied with Christianity might do well to reflect on the differences between a religion whose central myth is that of the separation and ultimate reunion of mother and daughter beloved of one another, and that of a religion whose central myth is of a father who requires the painful sacrificial death of his only son" (Kraemer, 1992:208).[22] This is an attack on the central idea, the central performative act of Christianity: "God so loved the world, he gave his only begotten son." Along with Kraemer, Brown and Parker ask whether we should continue to accept such a model. "Throughout the Scriptures is the idea that Jesus died for our sins. Did he? Is there not another way for sins to be forgiven: Why an idea of original sin? Christianity has functioned to perpetuate the Fall, for without it there is no need for a savior" (Brown and Parker, 1990:2). Their concern is for the way this ideology has affected women. They argue that throughout Christian history women have more often than men been identified with Christ, have been called upon to be self-sacrificing and to suffer in silence as Jesus suffered in obedience to his father's will.

The model of the Crucifixion conveys the message that suffering is redemptive; Brown and Parker have also begun to see in it a model of abuse: "Divine child abuse is paraded as salvific and the child who suffers 'without even raising a voice' is lauded as the hope of the world" (ibid.). This is serious stuff; they are courageous for even voicing it. The model they criticize has implications not just for women but for men, and especially for children. Their critique demands a total revaluation and reordering of human society and social ethics. But it extends beyond the strictly Christian context they are working in. Except for a brief mention of Abraham in relation to the power of blood to atone for sin, they do not consider the structuring power of this story for the Christian one. Had they related their observations to the story of Abraham, they would have realized that the same theme is common to all three monotheistic religions, and they might, then, have been able to broaden their critique of Christianity to include a critique of monotheism and the notion of a Creator God.

FIG. 9. A Turkish postcard of the "Kurban."

CHAPTER SEVEN

Muslim Interpretations

$\mathbf{M}$UHAMMAD'S mission was to recall the people to the monotheistic faith of Abraham, a fact about Islam of which many Westerners are unaware. Yet it is essential. Because Islam shares many figures, concepts, and practices with both Judaism and Christianity, some people assume it is a synthesized and therefore distorted version of them. The historical framework of biblical religious tradition fosters such a view—that Islam, being a relatively recent arrival on the religious scene, seeks to upstage Judaism and Christianity. Yet, because it goes back to Abraham, Islam is, in its own view, the original of which both Judaism and Christianity are distortions. For example, Muhammad attempts to persuade the People of the Book, "Why will you argue about Abraham, when the Torah and the Gospel were not revealed until *after* him?" (Qur'an 3:65 emphasis mine). For "Abraham was not a Jew, neither a Christian, but he was a pure monotheist (*hanif*) and one who submitted (*muslim*) to God; certainly he was never of the idolators" (Qur'an 3:67).

In pre-Islamic times Abraham was known as *hanif*, a true monotheist, and he is referred to in that way even today. The term *muslim* means submission to God, and simply describes one who recognizes that everyone and everything is dependent on Him.[1] Because Muslims assume that dependence is self-evident, it is incomprehensible to them why Jews, Christians, and others reject Muhammad's teaching. Their rejection is interpreted not merely as nonbelief but as active rejection of obvious truth.

Islam, then, can best be described as a new/old religion (Firestone, 1990:157); Muhammad was the newest (and the last) in a long line of prophets, but because he was trying to restore the old, original religion of Abraham, Islam is both new and old, the alpha and omega of true religion, not *a* religion. Jews and Christians will not be convinced, but the idea is important for any understanding of Islam. A grave misunderstanding was perpetrated, for example, when Islam was referred to as Muhammadanism, for Muhammad does not have the role and function Jesus does in Christianity. And Abraham is at least as important as Muhammad for Islam.

Abraham, the "Friend of God" (*al-Khalil*)—an epithet that may derive from the Bible (2 Chron. 20:7; Isaiah 41:8; see Firestone, 1990:141, n.46; see also James 2:23, and the Epistle of Clement, 11:1)—is not a shadowy figure relegated to the mists of time, but absolutely central to Islam. Hardly just an ancient hook on which to hang a new prophetic mantle, his life and deeds are inextricably woven into the very fabric of Islam.

> The spiritual presence of Abraham is always felt in Arabia, as in the whole Muslim world, not only in the frequency with which his name (in its Arabic form *Ibrahim*) is given to children, but also in the ever-recurring remembrance, both in the Koran and in the Muslims' daily prayers, of the patriarch's role as the first conscious preacher of God's Oneness: which also explains the great importance given by Islam to the annual pilgrimage to Mecca, which since earliest times has been intimately connected with the story of Abraham (Asad, 1954:377).[2]

As we shall see, the meaning and rituals of the pilgrimage (*hajj*) refer to events in the life of Abraham. The Hajj culminates in the Feast of the Sacrifice (Arabic: *Id al-Adha*; Turkish: *Kurban Bayramı*), the holiest day in the Muslim calendar. That day commemorates Abraham's willingness to sacrifice his son at God's command, and, in commemoration of Abraham's deed, each male head of household slaughters a ram (or other appropriate animal substitute). In Mecca tens of thousands of animals are sacrificed on that day; it is not just in Mecca, however, that the sacrifice occurs, but throughout the Muslim world.[3]

Etched viscerally into the sentiments of all Muslims is the sight, sound, and smell of that sacrifice. Children in the village in Turkey where I lived for nearly two years used to tell me that "if God had not provided Ibrahim with a ram, fathers would still be slaughtering their children."[4] They were steeped in the notion that it is because of God's mercy that fathers no longer sacrifice their sons—a lesson that encourages both their thanks and their indebtedness to God and that reinforces the notion of patriarchal power. When children misbehaved, for example, the most common threat was "You'd better be good or I'll make a *kurban* out of you." *Kurban* (Arabic *qurban*) means sacrifice, but refers to and evokes Abraham's near-sacrifice of his son and his actual sacrifice of the ram.[5]

My understanding of the importance of Abraham for Islam has been conditioned by my fieldwork in Turkey. My interpretation of his significance is therefore more immediate and more ethnographically grounded than my accounts of his place in Judaism and Christianity. That may be fortunate, as his role in Islam is less familiar to most Americans and Europeans, who, I suspect, will be the readers of this book. It is first necessary to give a brief description of the sources of Muslim interpretation.

SOURCES OF MUSLIM INTERPRETATION

In addition to Muhammad himself the sources of interpretation are primarily the Qur'an, the holy book communicated to Muhammad from God through Gabriel (*Jibril*); the *hadith* or traditions of the Prophet as remembered and passed along by friends; and a vast array of medieval (eighth to fourteenth century) exegetical commentaries or "tales of the prophets."[6]

Muhammad

Muhammad was born c. A.D. 570 in Mecca to Amina; Abdullah, his father, had died while she was still pregnant. Muhammad's mother died when he was six, and he went to live with his paternal grandfather 'Abd al-Muttalib, who belonged to the tribe of the Qureysh. (An early biography of Muhammad relates that al-Muttalib made a vow to sacrifice him [Firestone, 1990:110], but this assertion does not seem to be much elaborated). Upon the death of his grandfather two years later, Muhammad was taken care of by his paternal uncle, Abu Talib. Muhammad got to see some of the world when he worked for the widow Khadija, a wealthy merchant, and she was so impressed by his trustworthiness that she proposed to him. Although she was fifteen years older (he was twenty-five and she was forty), their marriage of twenty-six years was, apparently, a happy one.[7] They had a number of children but only the girls survived infancy. After Khadija's death, Muhammad took other wives, but with them he had no children (except for a son Ibrahim by a concubine Mary; this son also died in infancy).

Muhammad used to take Khadija and the children to a cave in the mountains (Mt. Hira) for a month of meditation—the month was *Ramadan* (the "Scorcher"), which at that time meant the month of heat. In Islam it would become the month of fasting and would no longer be associated only with the summer. The Muslim calendar is a lunar one, and thus holy days and holy periods, such as Ramadan, move relative to the solar year and, vis-à-vis the solar calendar, are celebrated ten days earlier each year. Also, holidays are not fixed to a particular season, as are Christmas, Easter, Yom Kippur, or Passover, but move around the year and make a complete revolution every thirty-three years. I have suggested elsewhere (Delaney, 1991:291) that this contrapuntal rhythm helps to emphasize the separation between the things of this world and those of the spirit.

In Islam, Ramadan commemorates the month in which the Qur'an began to be revealed. Muhammad was forty at the time.[8] One night when he was asleep or "dead to the world" in meditative trance, he heard a voice call out: "Read."[9] Muhammed is said to have responded, "But I can't read." He was illiterate. The voice called out again, and Muhammad responded the same way. The third time he asked: "What can I read?" And the voice responded:

> Read: In the name of thy Lord Who createth.
> Createth man from a clot.
> Read: And it is thy Lord the Most Bountiful
> Who teacheth by the pen,
> Teacheth man that which he knew not.   (Qur'an 96:1–5)[10]

This was the first revelation, but it is not the first *sura* (chapter) in the Qur'an. Instead it is number ninety-six—a first indication of a major difference between the Qur'an and the Bible. When Muhammad shook himself awake, the words were as if inscribed upon his heart. Soon afterward he heard the voice again: "O Muhammad! Thou art Allah's messenger, and I am Gabriel." Much shaken by this experience, he was later to be assured that he had received a divine call to be the Messenger of God.

Muhammad reported what he heard to his friends; they, in turn, wrote down what he said. These written suras were dispersed among some of his followers, and a number of people committed them to memory. When some of them were killed in a battle, those remaining collected the suras and arranged them in the form the Qur'an has to this day. The accepted tradition is that all of the suras were written down while Muhammad was alive; this is a fact of which Muslims are proud. They contrast it with the Gospels, which, as Turkish villagers explained to me, are obviously distortions of the Word because there are four somewhat different versions of the same story and all were written after the Crucifixion.

Qur'an

Despite scholarly debates about the composition of the "canon," the popular as well as the theological position is clear: the Word is One, undiluted.[11] The Qur'an is not merely inspired by God, it *is* the word of God. The Qur'an is not a record of the events of His people or His interventions among them; it is an exhortation to remember that God is God.

Because the Qur'an is the word of God, the sacred words must be learned in the language in which they were communicated, namely Arabic. The Qur'an cannot really be translated; all "translations" are called *interpretations*, for clearly they are human attempts to render the word of God. In countries where Arabic is not the native language, such as Turkey, people nevertheless learn the Arabic text. Because the emphasis is on knowing the exact words, there has always been a great stress on memorization. Throughout the Muslim world there are people, including illiterate villagers, who have committed the entire Qur'an to memory. This appears to be a very different sense of learning and education than that of Western Enlightenment, which imagines education as a drawing out of truth through the process of reasoning (see Eickelman, 1978).

Although the Qur'an is a historical book in the sense that much more is known about the date and mode of its composition than about the Hebrew Bible or the New Testament, it is not a historically constructed book. By that I mean that it is not constructed chronologically, as is the Bible, which begins with Creation and proceeds to recount the history of God's people. To people accustomed to the narrative style of the Bible, the Qur'an is very disorienting. There is "very little narrated history (in fact, very little narration at all) and, in the standard order of the suras, it is a disjunctive and discontinuous book of lessons, warnings, instructions, and exhortations" (Waldman, 1986:51). The style is more poetic than narrative, a style that is more conducive to recitation and memorization.[12] The "Qur'an, despite its having a written form, presents itself as essentially an oral composition" whereas "whatever the oral qualities and the dimensions of the Hebrew Bible, it has come down to us as a written composition" (ibid.).[13]

Although many biblical figures, such as Abraham, Joseph, and Mary, are found in the Qur'an, they do not appear in the same order as in the Bible and their characters are not as fully developed, leading many Westerners to conclude that Muslims got it all wrong. But that would be to misunderstand the differences between the Bible and the Qur'an. Muhammad's task was not to tell the story of his people but to call them (back) to God, to turn them from their supposedly pagan, idolatrous ways. The familiar biblical characters are intended, it seems, to be representatives of a type, to be used for didactic purposes. The Qur'an warns Muslims about their fate if they do not heed the message, and it gives instruction about the conduct of daily life.

Hadith *and Other Traditions*

The *hadith* are collections of traditions about Muhammad—things he said and things he did—as recounted by relatives and friends and passed down over generations. There are a number of collections of *hadith*; some are more respected than others because of the *isnad* or line of transmission. That is, the authenticity of a tradition is only as good as the authenticity of the transmission. It is a lineage, even a patrilineage, and even though it is not biologically based, the stress on authenticity in this realm is comparable to the stress on authentic paternity in the biological one. Some traditions have no authentic or trustworthy line of transmission, and these have an aura of illegitimacy about them.

In addition, numerous tales and traditions are recounted in medieval commentaries such as Ibn Ishaq's *Sirah*, which is a "Life" of Muhammad set in a world-historical schema, and Al-Tabari's *History*. Newby (1989) suggests that the *hadith* and the tales are really two different kinds of biographies of Muhammad; the *hadith* are fragmented, whereas the tales try to situate the life of Muhammad in the context of the lives of other prophets. Some of these tales incorporate a great deal of pre-Islamic (Jewish, Christian, Persian, and Arab) material (cf. Firestone, 1990). Those that refer to biblical figures were not just "borrowed" from Jewish and Christian scriptures, however, nor even from direct oral transmission by Jews and Christians; instead a great many of these tales had been circulating for centuries in that area of the world, and therefore each tradition could incorporate them as it wished. The fragmentary nature of the references to biblical figures in the Qur'an and *hadith*, however, must have been a motivation for Muslim scholars to search out the biblical referents, especially Abraham, given his importance for Muhammad (cf. Newby 1989:13–4). These traditions should not be considered pale reflections of their biblical referents. Once elaborated and inserted into a new theological/historical scheme, they are really new versions.

With regard to the story of Abraham and its interpretations, I do not argue for one correct version over others; indeed, as most collections include a variety of versions, even contradictory ones, the idea of a canonical version is alien to Islam. Nor do I try to place any particular version in its specific historical or social context, except for anecdotal material from my own fieldwork. Instead, my concern is with some of the features of the myth—what has appeared to be significant about Abraham in Islam—rather than with any particular instantiation of it. No doubt some features have been more important to some groups at some times and other features to other groups at other times. I do not suggest that all features have been known by all Muslims at all times any more than I suggested that all Jews know all the various Jewish interpretations of the story. Even fewer Jews and Muslims are aware that their versions of the Abraham legend overlap a great deal, especially stories involving Abraham's astronomical knowledge (Qur'an, 6:76ff.), his iconoclasm (Qur'an 21:58ff.), and the story of Nimrod and the fiery furnace (see below). On these points the influence is not one way, that is from Jewish to Muslim, for it is also possible that Muslim elaborations of the stories influenced later rabbinic, midrashic material.

Certain individuals or groups have no doubt possessed and promoted their own interpretations, but certain features are indispensible and do not change very much. Central texts exist, central practices continue to be practiced, and both are continually taught and promulgated. This is true of the story of Abraham and the sacrifice.

The references to Abraham in the Qur'an—all two hundred forty-five of them—are scattered throughout; they do not form one coherent story situated at a chronologically appropriate place. The fullest account concerns the sacrifice story, found in Sura 37:100–13.

> 100. My Lord! Vouchsafe me of the righteous.
> 101. So We gave him tidings of a gentle son.
> 102. And when (his son) was old enough to walk with him, (Abraham) said: O my dear son, I have seen in a dream that I must sacrifice thee. So look, what thinkest thou? He said: O my father! Do that which thou art commanded. Allah willing, thou shalt find me of the steadfast.
> 103. Then, when they had both surrendered (to Allah), and he had flung him down upon his face,
> 104. We called unto him: O Abraham!
> 105. Thou hast already fulfilled the vision. Lo! thus do We reward the good.
> 106. Lo! that verily was a clear test.
> 107. Then We ransomed him with a tremendous victim.
> 108. And We left for him among the later folk (the salutation):
> 109. Peace be unto Abraham!
> 110. Thus do We reward the good.
> 111. Lo! he is one of Our believing slaves.
> 112. And We gave him tidings of the birth of Isaac, a Prophet of the righteous.
> 113. And We blessed him and Isaac. And of their seed are some who do good, and some who plainly wrong themselves.

Much in this telling of the story is familiar to readers of the Bible: the test;[14] the calling out at the last minute saying that he had fulfilled the test; the ransom by substitution of another victim, although it does not specify that it was a ram;[15] and the blessing to him and to Isaac and the mention of their seed. But much is different. Most notably, unlike the biblical version, Abraham tells his son what is to take place, and the son responds in the way that he does in some of the Jewish commentary, for example in Josephus (see chapter 5). There is no mention of the place, nor of the accoutrements of sacrifice—the fire, the wood, and the knife; these are, however, elaborated in the stories. The Qur'an specifies the position of the son and the fact that Abraham flings him down on his face (or in some versions his forehead). This is a position that deviates from the way an animal would be sacrificed (Firestone, 1990:119). The Qur'an mentions the seed of Abraham, but the blessing is not that the seed will become a great nation; rather, it is a statement that some seed will be good and some will not, perhaps an allusion to the Parable of the Sower in the Gospel of Matthew. It is clear that Abraham is a model of the righteous man, one who surrenders totally to God. And so, too, is his son.

CONFLICTING LEGENDS

The meaning of the story is not contested: Abraham's great faith was proved by his obedience/submission to God—that is, by his willingness to sacrifice his son at God's command. But there are conflicting stories about when the sacrifice story and practice entered the Hajj tradition and about the details: (1) Which son is the intended victim—Ishmael or Isaac? (2) Where did the sacrifice take place—in Syria, Jerusalem, or Mecca? And much less clearly, (3) when did it take place: (a) before or after the building of the Kaʿba (the huge stone shrine in Mecca toward which Muslims pray, and which is the goal of pilgrims, see below), (b) before or after Ishmael's marriages, which would have made him more than a boy "who was old enough to walk with him," or (c) before or after the institution of the pilgrimage?

That there has been any question about such issues may come as a surprise to many Muslims who assume Ishmael was the son to be sacrificed and for whom the traditions associating Abraham with Mecca and the rituals of the Hajj appear to be rooted in immemorial custom. Indeed, the conflicting details of the stories may be of interest only to scholars; ordinary Muslims no doubt learn whatever version is told in their community. And though the contradictory, even mutually exclusive accounts, may interest Muslim scholars, the contradictions may not overly trouble them. If the goal is primarily heuristic, and Muslim interest and concern are directed to the archetypal, exemplary model in the story, rather than to an ascertaining of the accuracy of the historical details, as Crow (1986:27) and others assert, then the details may be threads to elaborate rather than to unravel. Such a method may be an indication of a very different scholarly style and motivation.

Despite the fact that he is mentioned only twelve times in the Qur'an, Ishmael, son of Abraham by Hagar, is, in Muslim tradition, considered the ancestor of the Arabs. Apparently there is no mention of either of them in pre-Islamic Arab traditions. Although there is precedent for it in Jewish (and Christian) tradition, the creation of this genealogy for Arabs was apparently the work of Muhammad.[16] By this means, Muhammad created an identity for Arabs that was at once ethnic and religious. The earliest biography of Muhammad (Ibn Ishaq) traces his lineage back to Abraham via Ishmael and then back to Adam. By placing Muhammad in the sacred lineage, he was able to give a new direction to sacred history— for the "underlying claim of the text is that there is a new dispensation and a new line of inheritance" (Newby, 1989:66). Ibn Ishaq gives him a biological genealogy as well as the more prophetic one in which the divine light is bestowed by God to the chosen ones; it is in a sense a divine genealogy.[17] Once again we see the symbolic conflation of divinity, light, and seed—a connection also pointed out by Eliade (1971), who did not, however, draw out the assumptions about, and implications for, gender.

Kisa'i, a twelfth-century scholar who wrote an engaging "Tales of the Prophets," conflates the biological and prophetic genealogy. Abraham's father heard a voice say to him: "Your wife's youth has been restored to her that she may produce the brilliant light that is in your seed" (al-Kisa'i, 1978:136). As soon as they had completed the sexual act in which Abraham was conceived, a voice proclaimed: "There is no god but God alone who hath no partner" (ibid.). This is also what Abraham is said to have proclaimed at the moment of his birth (al-Kisa'i, 1978:137).

The divine light that is transmitted in the sacred lineage, as well as the precociousness of Abraham, reappears in the stories about Muhammad's birth, especially in a long poem, the *Mevlidi Serifi* by Suleyman Celebi (d. 1421). In Turkey it is traditionally recited forty days after a death and thereafter on the anniversary of a person's death (Delaney, 1991; Tapper and Tapper, 1987). In addition, by continually drawing attention to the fact that God has no partner, especially in reference to human procreative activity, I feel that Muslim interpreters do protest too much; I take it as a sign of interest in both the differences and similarities between procreation and creation.

Although Ishmael is rarely mentioned in the Qur'an, he is, today, the one most Muslims assume was the intended sacrifice. Yet a renowned Muslim scholar of the tenth century, Al-Tabari, notes: "The earliest sages of our Prophet's nation disagree about which of Abraham's two sons it was that he was commanded to sacrifice. Some say it was Isaac, while others say it was Ishmael" (Al-Tabari, [c. 915]1987:82). And he goes on to list those who have sided with one or the other. Firestone has searched a number of traditions in addition to Al-Tabari and says that when "all the traditions are collated we find a surprisingly close count. One hundred thirty authoritative statements consider Isaac to be the intended victim; one hundred thirty-three consider it to have been Ishmael" (Firestone, 1990:135).

The difference of opinion has to do primarily with the source of a particular tradition. Although all of these stories were collected by medieval Muslim scholars, many of them obviously pre-dated the Muslim era. Crow (1986) and others suggest that the ones that focus on Sarah and Isaac are pre-Islamic and that those focused on Hagar and Ishmael are Muslim. That does not mean, however, that everywhere in the Muslim world Ishmael has supplanted Isaac in the popular imagination. Westermarck noted in 1933 that some Moroccans still believed it was Isaac (cited in Firestone, 1990:151, n. 123). Ironically, the process of homogenization and unification progresses as the diverse traditions become better known through the spread of literacy and education.

One unusual story relates that the caliph 'Umar, in the area of Syria quite close to Haran, the traditional home of Abraham, thought his Muslim companions were mistaken to think Ishmael was the intended sacrifice. So he called in a Jewish scholar, who allegedly had converted to Islam. He also seemed to have converted his former traditions. When asked which son Abraham was commanded to sacrifice, he answered: "Ishmael . . . the Jews know that, but they are envious of you, O Arabs, because it was your father who was named in God's command and to whom God ascribed such merit for his steadfastness in obeying God's command" (Al-Tabari, [c. 915]1987:88; cf. Newby, 1989:77).

Ishmael is presumed to be the intended sacrifice in part because of his association with Abraham in the building of the Ka'ba. Although there is just the merest mention of it in the Qur'an—"And when Abraham and Ishmael were raising the foundations of the House . . ." (Qur'an, 2: 127)—that part of the Abraham legend is elaborated in the stories. But we must back up a bit and say a little more about some of the main features of Abraham's life as recounted in Muslim tradition, in order to see where some of the various pieces fit.

ABRAHAM'S CHARACTER

Abraham was born in Mesopotamia, specified in some versions as Kufah in what is now southern Iraq, during the reign of Nimrod of Babylon. Nimrod was given an oracle that a boy born in his time would grow up and break the idols of his religion and thus his rule. So he had all the newborn boys slaughtered—all except Abraham whose mother hid him in a cave. Similar oracle motifs, and attempts to thwart them by Pharaoh and Herod, are found in the birth narratives of Moses and Jesus.[18] Whether these motifs were transferred to Abraham or whether he was the source of them, I do not know; in any case, they can be used by Muslims to show that his birth and his trials prefigure those of Moses, Jesus, and Muhammad.

Abraham's iconoclasm is well known in both Jewish midrash and Muslim legend. His father was supposedly a maker of idols. Abraham was even thought to have peddled them, but he knew they were worthless. One day he went to the factory and smashed all but the largest, and into its hand Abraham put the ax so it would appear that the great idol had smashed the others. When questioned about the destruction he said: "Ask them," referring to the idols. The interrogators said: "But they cannot speak." Abraham made his point: "Then why do you worship them?"

Muhammad is also said to have smashed the idols—in Mecca. In pre-Islamic Arabia, this city had been a traditional pilgrimage site for the various tribes who came to worship there. Mecca was the home of numerous idols, some say as many as three hundred sixty, but the most famous were the three female deities, al-Lat, al-Uzza, and Manat, who are named in the Qur'an (53:19–20).[19] In this and in a number of other ways Muhammad is clearly being assimilated into the model and figure of Abraham. Whether Muhammad consciously modeled himself after him is impossible to know, but after his night journey (mir'aj) to heaven, where he met the other prophets, including Abraham, he is thought to have said: "I have never seen a man more like myself than Abraham" (Newby, 1989:19).[20] The elaborations of their lives in stories and legends show so many parallels and overlaps that it is often difficult to keep them apart.

Abraham's monotheism was apparently the product of deduction, crystallized when he realized that the luminaries he had worshipped—the stars, the moon, and even the sun—set. "Lo! I have turned my face toward him Who created the heavens and the earth, as one by nature upright, and I am not of the idolaters" (Qur'an 6:80). Abraham's astronomical knowledge may have been attributed to him because of the existence of an observatory at Haran (see fig. 10). As in biblical tradition, Haran is alleged to be Abraham's home or at least a major stopping place on his hijra that ultimately took him to Mecca. Hijra means emigration and is most often used in reference to Muhammad's departure from Mecca to Medina in A.D. 622. It is the date that begins the Muslim calendar. Year one A.H. (after Hijra) is not the date of either the birth or death of Muhammad but of the departure of the faithful from the city in which it had become impossible to practice their faith; thus it also represents the consolidation of the first faithful Muslim community in Medina. Hijra can be used today to legitimate a person's or people's emigration from a land of disbelief.[21]

FIG. 10. Remains of the observatory at Haran, Turkey. Photo by author.

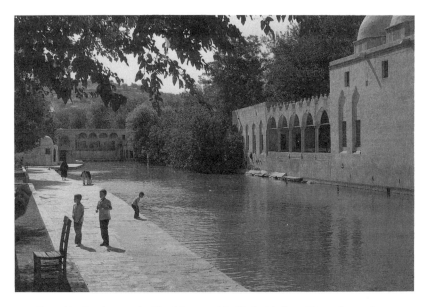

Fig. 11. Pool near the Ibrahim *cami* in Urfa, Turkey. Photo by author.

Abraham's proclamation of the one God brought him into open conflict with Nimrod. When he was about forty, Gabriel descended to him and told him he must fight Nimrod. Abraham was the same age as Muhammad when the same angel, Gabriel, appeared to him. Abraham shouted out: "O people! Say that there is no god but God and that I, Abraham, am God's apostle" (al-Kisa'i, 1978:142). This is similar to what is claimed for Muhammad in the confession of faith: "There is no god but God and Muhammad is his Messenger." Nimrod attempted to cast Abraham into the fiery furnace and so do away with him. Because of his steadfast belief, however, God protected him. Numerous legends place this event near Haran. These legends are still very much alive in Urfa, a town near Haran, where people told me that the pit of fire turned into a pool of cool water and the embers into goldfish. Today these sacred fish are still being fed in the beautiful pool near the Ibrahim *cami* (mosque). (See figs. 11 and 12.)

Abraham married Sarah, the daughter of his paternal uncle, not his half-sister as in the biblical account (see Firestone, 1990:29). The biblical stories of her barrenness and of her giving Hagar, her handmaid, to Abraham are also common in Islam. So too is the story in which Abraham casts out Hagar and Ishmael. In the biblical account the destination is unknown, whereas in some of the best-known Muslim accounts, Abraham accompanies them to Mecca and helps to settle them there. Not only does this feature perform a valuable exegetical function, joining the bibli-

FIG. 12. Painting depicting legends relating to Abraham. Urfa, Turkey.
Photo by author.

cal-Syrian aspect of the story with the Muslim-Mecca aspects, it also adds
a more compassionate element to Abraham's character than the one portrayed in the Genesis account. Nevertheless, Hagar and Ishmael are still
left to fend for themselves in desert country. The story of Hagar's frantic
search for water has been memorialized in a ritual of the Hajj whereby
pilgrims run between al-Safa and al-Marwah, desirous of drinking from
the well of Zamzam and taking some of it home for their relatives and
friends.

   Although Abraham must return to Sarah in Syria he often visits Hagar
and Ishmael in Mecca. In some traditions, al-Kisa'i for instance, Ishmael
grows up and marries, and Hagar dies, all before the building of the
Ka'ba. One popular theme in a number of traditions is Abraham's view
of Ishmael's wife. When Abraham arrives at Ishmael's home, he is out
hunting. His wife is inhospitable to Abraham and offers him neither food
nor water. He leaves a message for his son: "Change the threshold of your
house," meaning "get rid of this woman"; the message also confirms my
belief that *threshold* or *gate* can refer to female genitals. The next time
Abraham visits, he finds a different woman. She invites him in, offers

food and water, and washes his head or, in some versions, anoints it with oil. Some suggest that while this was done he stood on a stone that was called the *Maqam Ibrahim* because his footprint became imprinted in it (cf. Firestone, 1990:77)—a tradition that, as we shall see, conflicts with the one that places the Maqam Ibrahim next to the Ka'ba. Abraham is pleased with the new wife and tells her to inform Ishmael that "his threshold is sound." On the third and last visit of Abraham to Ishmael, the al-Kisa'i tale recounts the story of the building of the Ka'ba, after which Ishmael is said to live and prosper for one hundred thirty-seven years. Only in a later chapter is the sacrifice story told; it occurs in Syria and the son to be sacrificed is Isaac.

In the reconstructed account of Ibn Ishaq, felt to be one of the earliest collections of tales within a biography of Muhammad, the sacrifice occurs in Mecca, the intended victim is Ishmael, and the event occurs after the building of the Ka'ba and the institution of the pilgrimage. After Ishmael is redeemed by the animal sacrifice, he goes on to marry. The details may not matter much; indeed al-Tabari includes them all! What is important are the various elements—the building of the Ka'ba, the pilgrimage, and the sacrifice. No doubt the desire to transpose them to Mecca is motivated by a desire to distinguish and reinforce the specifically Muslim character of the traditions.

When Abraham visits his Meccan family, he allegedly is transported by the miraculous horse, Buraq. Much later, the same miraculous horse is said to have transported Muhammad from Mecca to Jerusalem for the night journey (*mir'aj*). The ascension is said to have taken place on the former site of the Jewish temple, the site that, in other legends, is said to be the one where Abraham attempted to sacrifice his son.[22] This extraordinarily sacred spot for both Muslims and Jews (as well as for Christians) is now covered by the Muslim shrine, al Haram al Sharif, also known as the Dome of the Rock (see fig. 13). At the beginning of his mission, Muhammad had Muslims orient their prayers toward Jerusalem rather than Mecca. Only after rebuilding and purifying the Ka'ba was the direction changed.

ABRAHAM, MUHAMMAD, AND THE KA'BA

When Muhammad rebuilt the Ka'ba he reenacted Abraham's deed. Abraham was ordered to build God's "house" (temple) and was shown the way by the Sakina (related to Hebrew Shekhina), a two-headed wind that could speak or, in other versions, coiled up around the spot where the first temple had been. When Abraham brushed off the sand that had covered it up, he revealed the stone of the original temple—that which Adam

FIG. 13. The Dome of the Rock (al Haram al Sharif). Jerusalem, Israel.
Photo by Sandra Razieli.

had built. Some versions claim it was where God left his print. During the flood the Ka'ba was taken up to heaven where the angels flitted about it, as the circumambulation by pilgrims is meant to replicate.

Upon that spot Abraham and Ishmael raised the foundations of the Ka'ba. When Abraham got tired or had to reach too high, Ishmael brought a stone for him to stand on; it is now known as the *Maqam Ibrahim* for the footprint Abraham left on it. In a number of the building stories Ishmael comes off as somewhat incompetent and Abraham somewhat impatient. When Ishmael was sent to find the cornerstone, he could not find one, or the one he found was not good enough, or he was too late, and Abraham berated him and said, "God would not entrust such a thing to you, my boy!"

The Black Stone, nestled in the Ka'ba, is not the *Maqam Ibrahim*; it is said by some to be the eye of God; alternatively it is his hand, which blesses all who touch it—reason enough that all pilgrims to Mecca endeavor to touch or kiss it. It is also alleged that it is the only relic to have come down from the time of Adam, and that it was originally white and contained the voices (souls) of all the living.[23]

One version claims that Gabriel brought a white sapphire from India, which Adam had brought down from Heaven, but the sapphire turned black, either because women menstruated over it or because of the sins of mankind (Firestone, 1990:87; for other excellent accounts of legends about the Black Stone, see Esin, 1963, and Lazarus-Yafeh, 1981). The Black Stone is today encased in a frame of silver which, to me, has the appearance of a vagina complete with labial folds. I was unaware that anyone else made this association until I spoke with several people who had recently made the Hajj and who independently told me of their associations. Whether the majority are of the same opinion I do not know. Nevertheless, the belief that it turned black because of menstrual blood supports such a view. The female symbolism of the Kaʿba has also been noted by Lazarus-Yafeh (1981:30), who cites several texts in which the Kaʿba is imaged as a bride who, on Judgment Day, will be led to her wedding; those who are able to catch hold of her covers will enter Paradise with her. The *kiswa* or covering of the Kaʿba is referred to as its veil. Extending out from the Black Stone and the Kaʿba, Mecca is felt to be the "mother of towns," the first dry ground floating upon the waters from which the rest of the earth spread out.[24]

After the Kaʿba was restored, a number of stories allege that Abraham had a vision telling him to sacrifice his son. The fact that Ishmael had helped him build it is taken by some as evidence that he was the son to be sacrificed. It is also evidence that he had reached the "time of running"— that is, of being able to help Abraham with his work. In other versions, however, and not necessarily the earliest, the vision occurs in Syria and the son is Isaac (see for example, al-Kisaʾi, 1978:160–62); in still others the intended sacrifice is said to occur either in Jerusalem, perhaps at the site that, in Jewish tradition, is associated with the site of the ancient temple or, if near Jerusalem, perhaps in the vicinity of the Valley of Hinnom.[25]

As in Jewish midrash, there is also, in Muslim legend, the story of Satan trying to dissuade Abraham from his horrible deed and, as in the Jewish case, he gets nowhere. Ishmael is represented as obedient and willing—the perfect model of the perfect sacrifice. But, just as in Jewish midrash, there are hints that he was anxious:

> make my bonds fast, for if death is hard, I do not believe I will be able to endure it when I feel death's touch. Hone your knife so that you can finish me off and release me. When you lay me down to sacrifice me, lay me on my face; do not lay me on my side, for I fear that if you look at my face, you will turn soft and abandon the command of God. If you wish, *return my shirt to my mother*, for it might be a consolation to her. (Newby, 1989:78, emphasis added)

Reading that part of the story, I was reminded of the shirt Cristos Valenti gave his mother (via his lawyer) every day and of the fresh one she handed back to him.

God is said to have turned the knife to its blunt side, to have pushed it away and indicated what was to be sacrificed instead. Muslim art shows a ram being led or held by an angel, usually said to be Gabriel (Jibril).[26] The Muslim story al-Kisa'i tells replicates the Jewish midrash whereby the ram is "the ram of Abel son of Adam, which he sacrificed to his Lord and which He accepted. I have grazed in the meadows of Paradise for forty autumns" (al-Kisa'i, 1978:162).

HAJJ[27]

When Abraham had completed building the Ka'ba, he was commanded to go to the top of a nearby hill and call all humankind to the pilgrimage. His voice was said to have been amplified so that it was heard all over the earth. This may be the origin of the Muslim idea that originally all peoples had true religion but some forgot. But "Everyone who makes the Pilgrimage is today of those who answered Abraham" (Newby, 1989: 75).

Muhammad's role in establishing the pilgrimage is pretty well effaced; in this perception he has become merely the conduit for reinstating the original pilgrimage instituted by Abraham. That pilgrimage, according to Muhammad, had fallen into disuse and, over time, had been distorted by the Arab tribes who made a pilgrimage to Mecca for the purpose of worshipping their idols. Whether by divine inspiration or clever strategy, Muhammad's reinterpretation of this pilgrimage as a distortion of the ancient pilgrimage instituted by Abraham, rhetorically, at least, subsumed the Arab tribes in his plan. It did not allow for a separate and different religion; they were cast as infidels rejecting the true faith. Only after consolidating the Muslim community at Medina did Muhammad revisit Mecca. It was then that he was said to have cleansed the temple area of idols, rebuilt the Ka'ba, and declared thereafter the Hajj. Muhammad made a pilgrimage back to his home, but he never again returned there to live.

In making the Hajj, then, pilgrims not only fulfill one of the obligations of faith incumbent upon all who are financially and physically able, they also simultaneously make a journey to the center of faith (cf. Turner, 1972–73). Mecca represents an image of their ultimate home, for Mecca is the *axis mundi*, felt to be the city nearest to heaven. It is an earthly mirror reflecting their heavenly home.[28] Making the Hajj is meant to be the ultimate expression of a life of faith, regardless of the other reasons a particular person has for undertaking it and regardless of its other benefits. By following in the footsteps not just of Muhammad but also of Abraham, they signify, at least in theory, a devotion reminiscent of Abraham's.

Muhammad inscribed a number of these legendary events into the rituals of the Hajj and thereby inscribed them into the lives of Muslims. Those who actually go on the Hajj have already learned by heart the myth and the ritual: they circumambulate the Ka'ba seven times counterclockwise, as the angels are said to circulate around the Throne of God; they pray on the Maqam Ibrahim; they touch or kiss the Black Stone nestled in its corner. They run between al-Safa and al-Marwah remembering the distraught Hagar seeking water for her son. They stone three pillars in Mina to remind them of Satan's attempt to divert Abraham from his duty (others say the three pillars represent the three pre-Islamic goddesses, see above); they stand on the plain of 'Arafat from noon to sunset and praise God. Finally, at the end of the Hajj, the rituals culminate in the Feast of the Sacrifice, when each male head of household sacrifices a ram (or substitute) as Abraham did. In Mecca hundreds of thousands of animals are slaughtered; but because the sacrifice is replicated throughout the Muslim world, it becomes the mimetic means by which Muslims everywhere are joined in a community of faith as well as blood.

ABRAHAM AS MODEL

Abraham is the exemplary model, the quintessential model of a man of faith. Muhammad clearly drew upon (or constructed) this model to pattern his own behavior and beliefs. In stepping into the footsteps of an archetypal figure, however, Muhammad tends to merge his personality with that of Abraham, or perhaps Abraham's tends to merge with Muhammad's. What each may lose in distinctness they gain in the combined power of their mission. Although Muhammad clearly had a major part in shaping Islam, he is cast merely as the Messenger, the instrument for transmitting or revealing the original message given to Abraham. As Muhammad attempted to insert himself into the mythic pattern, the sacred precedent, so too do others attempt to model their behavior and beliefs upon the *sunna* (behavior) of the Prophet. His character and behavior, as recorded in the *hadith* and tales, are the basis for daily life as well as the law, *shari'a*. All Muslims should be following the model laid down not just by Muhammad but by Abraham.

Yet the model is clearly a male model. Only males can legitimately step into it, and only males are participants in the sacrifice. It may be true that the ritual establishes a community of faith and blood, but that identity is performed and transmitted by men. This, I believe, is not an incidental detail but at the heart of the sacrifice. It is both similar and dissimilar to the Christian Eucharist for which, traditionally, only a male priest (or minister) could perform the ritual and transmit the sacred power. That power, it is believed, has been transmitted only in a consecrated line of males that began with the Apostles. In Christianity, sacred power is held by the few. In Islam, each and every male head of household can himself have intercourse with the sacred when he performs the sacrifice that substitutes for and symbolizes Abraham's son, an act that ritually enacts and reinforces patriarchal power.

The implications of the story and model are worked out in somewhat different ways in various Muslim communities (cf. Bowen, 1992). Perhaps nowhere is the story so elaborated as in Morocco. "For Muslims, the myth of Ibrahim is humanity's archetypal interaction with God, an awesome act involving awesome players" (Combs-Schilling, 1989:248). There an innovation has been introduced into the ritual. About three hundred years ago the monarchs of the "ʿAlawi dynasty began the practice of having the blood-descendant king sacrifice a ram on behalf of the community of believers as a whole" (ibid.:222). By means of this dramatic innovation (which for some approaches blasphemy) the "monarchs became the sacrificial link between God and nation, the means by which God could see the collectivity's faith and grant his favor. Through the performance, the Moroccan monarchs inserted themselves into the single most powerful canonical ritual in Islam and into the mythic foundations upon which it rests" (ibid.). When the king slits the throat of the ram on behalf of the people, he becomes an intervening link or mediator between the people and, through Muhammad and Abraham, ultimately, God. Conversely, he becomes the vehicle that channels creative power to earth. He places himself in the line that begins with Abraham, goes through Muhammad, and then passes down to each head of household—a patriline that transmits sacred power. The king becomes both the symbolic representative of the community and its link to transcendence. In this way the performance of the Great Sacrifice becomes "the most powerful ritual support of the Moroccan monarchy" (ibid.:223). But it does much more than that.

It also reaffirms patriarchal power by means of the metaphorical equivalence—between the highest and lowest males—established in the ritual. In the ritual, "the identity of the king is intermingled with that of the household heads. . . . For individual heads of households to undercut the authority of the overarching ruler would be to undercut their own power base" (ibid.:252).

The patriarchal power inherent in the Great Sacrifice is also reenacted and reinforced during the wedding ceremonies of a first marriage, which,

Combs-Schilling claims, is metaphorically equivalent and helps to bring out the sexual and gender-based elements in the ritual.[29] The symbolic parallels she draws accord, to a great extent, with what I observed in Turkey, and are no doubt common in much of the Muslim world.[30] In Morocco, however, the bridegroom becomes not just a generic "king for a day," he becomes symbolically the embodiment of "the Moroccan king, the blood descendant of Muhammad who reigns from Morocco's throne" (ibid.:190). The bridegroom does not embody the living ruler so much as what the ruler symbolizes: (pro-)creativity.

A similar meaning is conveyed in Turkish wedding festivities (Delaney, 1991:86, 140) and these, in turn, are connected to the symbols, ceremonies, and practices related to circumcision. Circumcision is the event that initiates the boy into manhood and symbolizes his potential to reproduce; it also simultaneously initiates him into the Muslim brotherhood. The same word, *düğün*, is used for both the circumcision and the wedding festivities. In addition, a phrase, *mürüvvet görmek* (to see the good day of your child), is said to the parents of the boy on the occasion of his circumcision as well as to the parents of the wedding couple. *Mürüvvet* means abundance, munificence, possibly also manliness, but it implies reproductive wealth, symbolized by the coins thrown at the wedding.

The innovation in the Moroccan marriage ritual may have come about during the reign of Mawlay Isma'il, for apparently his "reproductive prowess was unparalleled" (Combs-Schilling, 1989:191); he is said to have produced seven hundred sons.[31] The monarch's creative role is linked to procreative power, which, she suggests, is symbolized by the sword. When they "wish their leader good luck and hope that he is girded with a sufficiently powerful sword so that creation can begin" (ibid.:194), they are referring simultaneously to the sword that protects the people and the other "sword," or phallus, that creates them. The image of the sword figures in the sayings and songs recited during the wedding rituals. I found similar imagery, although not so pronounced, in Turkey (Delaney, 1991:138ff.).

As the previously subservient young male is transformed into the phallic king, the young woman is transformed into a passive bride. With her white gown and eyes rimmed in black, just like the sacrificial ram, she is laid on the bed where the bridegroom "enters, and in an act of some violence, he forces his way into her, causing the lifeblood to flow" (Combs-Schilling, 1989:188). The bloody sheet is often displayed after this act of intercourse. If no blood flows, it is assumed she is not a virgin, and she can be slain, in which case she would become the literal sacrifice. Although this does not happen often, it does happen.[32]

In the Moroccan wedding ceremony, the bride has come to symbolize the ram sacrificed in lieu of the son—that is, an equivalence has been established between the son, the ram, and the bride. Although the gender difference is notable, the hierarchical structure is maintained—as a man (even a king) must submit to God, and a son to his father, so should a woman to her husband. We might also recall that in the Bible, Israel is referred to both as God's firstborn son and as his bride.

In any case, the idea that the girl could be punished unto death for her transgression serves as a powerful sword held over her head. Through the spilling of the woman's blood at first intercourse, the man controls the powers of life and death; through intercourse he will produce children that will continue the "earthly community of Muslims through the regeneration of men's patrilines on earth" (ibid.:205). Procreation, Combs-Schilling claims, is for the glory of God. Before sacrificing, and at the moment of ejaculation during sexual intercourse, a man should call out the name of God, the "Bi'smi'llah." She argues that sacrifice by the knife is mimetic to sexual intercourse, with the male taking the role of the actor in each case. In turn, by modeling itself on the actions that bring about life in this world, sacrifice becomes a symbolic pathway to eternal life.

Combs-Schilling has given a rich and convincing account of the meaning of blood sacrifice in Moroccan Islam and its relation to the story of Abraham. Nevertheless, she, like Jay, assumes, rather than challenges, the meaning of paternity. Despite the plethora of evidence regarding its meaning as creativity, she does not use that to examine its constructedness within a theory of procreation and, thus, loses an opportunity to reevaluate the meanings of paternity, maternity, and (the imagined lack of) female generativity. In her book she, like Jay, assumes procreation has to do primarily with biology, with the natural, and insists on maintaining a strict distinction between the world of nature (biology) and the divine realm. But this distinction is, itself, part of the gendered conception of the world that is, I suggest, intimately related to the theory of procreation I have been discussing. In this theory, let us recall, it is the male who imparts the divine spark of life while the female represents and contributes the material nature—and this is *not* just a theory of biology.

From Sacred to Secular

Although we tend to think about procreation primarily, if not exclusively, as a biological, natural event that has little to do with culture and even less with the divine, that context is not adequate, for it cannot explain the valuations of the roles of each gender nor their symbolic elaboration in other contexts. While certain physiological processes are universal, the way they are conceptualized varies considerably. Western cultures have elaborated an integrated system wherein creativity, imagined as masculine in character, is the connecting link between the divine and human worlds. Procreation is not just about biology and the natural, since the male's contribution (seed) has been imagined as the conduit for the divine; his is the creative role that bestows life and identity. Only women's role as providing the nurturant material has been imagined as within the realm of the natural. Creation and procreation are not separate, but are deeply interconnected.

A different way of conceptualizing procreation, therefore, demands a different way of conceptualizing both the spiritual world and the natural world—in short, a different cosmology or world view. In the monotheistic cosmology, there is only one principle of creation, symbolically masculine, and it is manifest on both human and divine planes. Monotheism and monogenesis constitute one integrated and mutually reinforcing system. And in this system, the story of Abraham is central.

Because Islam is conceptualized as a return or recall to the one, true, original religion given in the beginning to Abraham, his story may be more actively present in Islam than in either Judaism or Christianity. That is especially true when, annually, a man sacrifices an animal in commemoration of the ram sacrificed in place of his son; but it is also true as pilgrims retrace his footsteps and reenact some of the dramas of his life that have become part of the rituals of the Hajj.

In all three monotheisms, however, the story has been a primary structuring force and a powerful influence on human psychology and the dynamics of history. On the psychological level, it has figured in notions of faith and steadfastness, sacrifice and love, authority and obedience, gender and family relations. On the stage of history, it figures in conflicts over territory, cities, and shrines that continue to this day. These conflicts are as volatile and violent as they are (and can easily become more so) because they ultimately return to the question of who *is* the true seed of Abraham, who *is* the true heir and, therefore, who has the right to the patrimony. It would be a great step toward peace if these "sons" could acknowledge their joint claims and agree to work out ways to share it. But it would be a much greater step if they could recognize the assumptions about gender and procreation without which the story and all its consequences could not make sense. Then the choice becomes clearer: can we allow new stories, new social arrangements, new values to emerge, or will some continue to demand, despite the bloodshed and the inequalities, a return to these older values and structures?

In the next section I focus on one of the ways some of these values and structures have become secularized and seen as part of the human condition rather than the outcome of particular historical, theosocial systems. Freudian psychoanalysis has been another powerful mode of interpretation of human behavior and the dynamics of history, and, again, the dynamics turn on the relations of sons and fathers. Oddly, Freud did not explore or include as integral to this theory either the relation of fathers to their sons or, more important, how the meaning of *father* is partly responsible for the dynamics. In chapter 8 I will show how Freud assumed, but did not examine, a particular notion of paternity and how this systemic neglect bequeathed a distorted and incomplete vision of gender, the family, and the motive of history. In chapter 9 I critically analyze the work of some of his followers who have tried to correct his blind spot and thereby salvage his theory.

PART FOUR

The Testimony of

Psychoanalysis

CHAPTER EIGHT

Freud's Blind Spot

T HE STORIES in the Bible and the Qur'an have had, and continue to have, an enormous impact on human psychology and society. They affect the way we live and what we value. In a very broad sense they are the myths we live by, whether in specifically religious contexts or as they have been transformed into secular narratives. It is all the more curious, then, that Freud—the great mythmaker of modern times—passed over a biblical story in favor of a Greek myth as the paradigm of human psychology and society, especially when he admitted that biblical stories had had a profound effect on him.[1]

Drawing on the ancient Greek myth of Oedipus, he created a modern analogue that he felt explained both individual and social dynamics. For him, it represented the foundation of society and something ever-present in the human condition. Today, it is a myth by means of which many people interpret their lives—not only through the process of psychoanalysis but also because of its diffusion into popular culture. And yet there is a glaring *scotoma* or blind spot.[2] Freud focused primarily on the son, and the son's feelings and relation to the father, and gave little attention to the father, and the father's feelings toward the son. This exclusive focus seems to have blinded him to the importance of including the father in his theoretical frame. Moreover, it prevented him from seeing that the meaning of *son* is constituted in relation to that of *father* and vice versa. Freud's neglect is systemic, not a minor oversight but a major distortion that has far-reaching implications for his theory, and ours—about the person, about religion, and about the nature of culture. In Freud's theory and practice, the father is unassailable; his absence is omnipresent but invisible, analogous to that of the father God. His absence serves to reify and reinforce patriarchy.

Although the dominant myth in Freud's work is Oedipus, toward the end of life he turned to the biblical story of Moses. In this chapter, I continue the exploration of monotheism, Abraham, and fatherhood, oddly enough, through an analysis of Freud's *Moses and Monotheism*. The question that began my investigation is really quite simple—even absurdly so. Why did Freud focus on *Moses* and monotheism rather than on Abraham? Abraham, not Moses, is traditionally the man associated with monotheism in all three monotheistic religions—Judaism, Christianity, and Islam.[3] The more I investigate *Moses and Monotheism*, the more that question cries out. Why did Freud fabricate a story out of whole cloth, as it were, about the symbolic sons killing their father instead of using and analyzing the story that is actually *in* the biblical text—that of a father willing to kill his son if God demanded? Why did he ignore the biblical text and substitute his own version? What did his substitution reveal? Although Freud may have thought the tradition was a distorting screen through which one could see only dimly the "real, true" events, his normal method would have been to analyze the manifest content as a means to arrive at the underlying, latent meaning. In this case, he changed the manifest content, the tradition.

The book is flawed historically and theoretically; it is not written in his pellucid style, and it is extremely repetitive. That, in itself, is significant, at least according to Freud, for he felt that repetitions often pointed to an unresolved issue of obsessive concern. This was Freud's last major study, as he himself seemed to be aware; it presented him with an opportunity to reflect on his life's work as well as to revise some of the more discredited ideas and concepts developed in *Totem and Taboo* on which *Moses and Monotheism* depended. Instead, he repeated and reinforced them, vigorously.

Rather than viewing *Moses and Monotheism* as an embarrassment, as evidence of Freud's advancing age, as many did when it first appeared, or as a personal, though veiled statement about his Jewishness or about his relationship with his father, as more recent scholarship proposes,[4] I suggest it is a key to his entire corpus. It is the culmination and integration of some of his major ideas—the Oedipus complex, the transmission of cultural memory, the correlation between individual and cultural development—directed in this instance to an investigation of the psychological underpinnings of the society in which he lived. It should be taken seriously if for no other reason than that Freud took it seriously.

It may never be possible to know exactly why Freud neglected the Abraham story, and this glaring oversight may ultimately relate to Freud's Jewishness or to his father complex. I am not suggesting it was purposeful; on the contrary, a blind spot is something one is not generally aware of. Nor is it my purpose to psychoanalyze Freud, even though I do occasionally speculate about his personal motivations. If, as I believe, *Moses and Monotheism* is a key to his entire corpus, it also, inadvertently, provides the key for questioning these ideas.

My investigation does not depend on searching for new, or as yet un-discovered, external evidence for some clues that will help to answer my initial question. For me, the clues are internal; they lie scattered throughout his work. Following Freud's example, I pay close attention not just to what he says but also to what he leaves unsaid, and I ask questions that he himself might easily have asked. If, as he notes in *Moses and Monotheism*, distortions in a text are like a murder, what did he (try to) cover up and why? He has not covered his tracks very well, as he himself admitted (Freud, 1939:52, SE 23:43). What do the "striking omissions, disturbing repetitions, palpable contradictions" (ibid.) reveal?[5] Where do they lead us?

The striking omission of Abraham, like Ariadne's thread, leads into the labyrinth of Freud's thought and to a major theme at the very heart of his work. Hidden away, ignored, neglected (dare I say repressed?), this theme could be considered the dark, unanalyzed side of the Oedipus complex. The Abraham story is more about the father than the son, about the father's willingness to kill the son, whereas in Freud's interpretation of the Oedipus drama, the focus is on the son and his killing of the father. Freud then uses that story as a means to talk about unconscious desires that he claims are universal. Oedipus's "destiny moves us only because it might have been ours—because the oracle laid the same curse upon us before our birth as upon him. It is the fate of all of us, perhaps, to direct our first sexual impulse towards our mother and our first hatred and our first murderous wish against our father" (Freud, SE 4:262). Does this really refer to all of us or only to males? If the latter, the complex cannot be considered universal. In addition, Oedipus did not know, at first, that it was his father he had killed (or, for that matter, that it was his mother he had married); the son's murderous wish as well as his incestuous sexual desire is Freud's idea, Freud's addition to the myth.

The first murderous wish *in* the myth belonged to the father. Anyone familiar with the Oedipus myth, and Freud surely was, for he wrote a paper on it while at the Gymnasion, knows that Laius, the father of Oedipus, first tried to get rid of his son; indeed that was the act that set the drama in motion. Laius pierced Oedipus's foot with a nail—the name *Oedipus* means swollen foot—and abandoned him or, in some versions, gave him to a servant to dispose of. Yet Freud puts the action in the passive voice (Oedipus was abandoned), concealing the father's active role.[6] Perhaps it is the father's murderous wishes that activate them in the son; at the very least, they ought to be considered relationally. But in his psychological interpretation and use of the myth, Freud did not develop a theory in which the actions and wishes of father and son are inter-related. It is not that the father is absent, he is simply not implicated or interrogated.[7] As Freud ignored the role of the father in the Greek drama so, too, did he ignore it in the Bible.

Instead of using the story of Abraham to question and perhaps revise his earlier ideas, he used his earlier ideas as the framework to construct his own version of the biblical myth. *Moses and Monotheism* was the culmination of Freud's more general theory of religion and society, the final chapter, so to speak, of the book he had written twenty-five years earlier, *Totem and Taboo*. In order to fully understand *Moses and Monotheism*, it is necessary to recapitulate the thesis of *Totem and Taboo*.[8]

Totem and Taboo (1913) was Freud's first foray into anthropology; he drew upon (certain) anthropological sources[9] and wished to make a contribution to theory about the origin of religion, morals, and social organization.[10] Freud was deeply concerned about origins and in this he was much closer to his nineteenth-century forebears than to his contemporary theorists (see chapter 1). Like them, Freud thought that a specific type of religion, in this case monotheism, would have its roots in the origin of religion itself, and that is what he set out to discover in *Totem and Taboo*. Like his nineteenth-century predecessors, he thought the origin of religion could be found in what was considered the most primitive religion known, that of the Australian aborigines, for there we might discern "a well-preserved picture of an early stage of our own development" (Freud, SE 13:1).[11]

Using texts of Darwin, Atkinson, and Robertson Smith, Freud constructed his own origin myth. Freud's equivalent of Genesis, his origin story, begins not with the Word but with the Deed and, unlike Genesis, this assertion, taken from Goethe's *Faust*, is the last line rather than the first in the book: "In the beginning was the Deed" (Freud, SE 13:161).

Freud's Origin Myth

The story in essence is as follows: Once upon a time there was "a violent and jealous father who keeps all the females for himself and drives away his sons as they grow up. . . . One day the brothers who had been driven out came together, killed and devoured their father, and so made an end of the patriarchal horde" (Freud, SE 13:141, and repeated in Freud, 1939:102–3 [SE 23:81]).

In order that the sons not have this overthrow repeated against themselves, they formed what Freud considered *the* social contract, in which they: (1) renounced their rights to all of the women hoarded by their father, (2) began the first communal society based on laws, (3) set up a taboo on murder, and (4) began to worship the totem surrogate for the father.[12] In this way, "The dead father became stronger than the living one had been. . . . They could attempt, in their relation to this surrogate father, to allay their burning sense of guilt, to bring about a kind of reconciliation with their father" (Freud, SE 13:143–4).

It is a good story and it makes sense, especially because acceptance has been prepared by the web of associations that Freud has built up in the preceding chapters on incest, totemism, ambivalence, and taboo. The associations and evidence begin to unravel, however, as soon as the story is subjected to an anthropological critique. Yet even then, I believe the most obvious and most important problems remain unseen, perhaps precisely because they are so transparent, so much a part of his and our common-sense assumptions—the myth we live by. An excellent summary of the anthropological response already exists, so I shall not attempt to recapitulate it here except where it becomes relevant to my critique.[13] In what follows I take up each point of his story in turn.

"*A violent and jealous father.*" Here, Freud assumes that violence, at least among males, is a primary instinct and that it is tied to male sexual jealousy. It should more appropriately be called "innate male sexual greed," for the desire to possess and hoard all the women is taken for granted as self-evident. Aggression and sexuality do combine in his notion of *libido* or active sexuality, which Freud characterized as masculine regardless of whether it was displayed by men or women. In addition, and rather surprisingly given Freud's own ideas about the polymorphous nature of human sexuality, there is an assumption of innate heterosexuality—for each of the sons "would have wished, like his father, to have all the women to himself" (ibid.:144). Perhaps Freud took heterosexuality for granted in this case because he thought it was the most "natural" society, that is, the closest to nature; still, this assumption contradicts his belief that such a society would not yet have instituted repressions necessary for the dominance of heterosexuality. Curiously, he does not consider the supposedly frustrating situation of the sons as a possible reason for the development of homosexuality.

Others such as Marx and Engels have argued that sexual jealousy is related to a desire to ensure children of undisputed paternity. Although Freud does not speak of sexual jealousy in these terms, I believe it is an unexamined assumption in his theory.

"*Who keeps all the women to himself.*" Few question Freud's silly idea that the primal male could have kept all the females to himself even if he wanted to.[14] Freud assumed that the primal father was so powerful that he could subdue the women and keep the sons at bay until he drove them away. This goes against all common sense: (a) What could have prevented the women from fleeing? Does the assumption of male power mask another, unstated assumption of primal, essential female passivity and immobility? (b) On the other hand, if the primal father had helpers in keeping a rein on his harem, who and where were they? (c) In all probability, the sons were stronger than the father; surely, together, they could have overpowered him—as indeed, they eventually did. (d) The sons might also have joined forces with the women and together plotted to do away with the tyrant. This solution would have involved women in the deed. Greek mythology includes several well-known examples of this scenario—Cronos plots with his mother to castrate the father and, later, Zeus plots with his mother to overcome the father. Freud knew of these examples, for he refers to them in other contexts (e.g., Freud, SE 4:256, SE 5:619).

The sons could also have taken foreign women, as they did after the murder. What prevented them from doing that earlier, especially given their supposedly insatiable desire? What was so special about those particular women? If Freud presupposed the erotic attachments of the sons to their mothers, he needed to say more about the basis of that assumption—are the attachments in this case "natural," or are they possibly provoked by the behavior of the father? Would the jealous father have permitted such erotic attachments to develop?

If the father was so threatened by the sons, and if he was so powerful, why did he wait until the sons had grown up to drive them away? He could simply have killed them off when they were born. This theme, too, figures in Greek mythology. In this case, perhaps Freud thought Greek mythology was not applicable, because the primal family was not quite human; indeed, it was the murder of the father and its consequences that he felt ushered in full humanity.[15] On the other hand, if fathers' murderous wishes are included in Greek mythology, why are they not also useful for considering the mental endowments of humanity? Why is the myth of Oedipus, alone, so considered and, even then, only the story of the son's (not the father's) murderous wishes? If primitives were cannibals as Freud believed, why didn't the father simply gobble up his sons as they were born?

"*One day the brothers who had been driven out [of the horde] came together, killed and devoured their father. . . . United they had the courage to do and succeeded in doing what would have been impossible for them individually*" (Freud, SE 13:141). But what had prevented them from uniting *in* the horde? Of course, getting together for a common purpose presupposes language and society, and Freud even presupposes some cultural or technical advance that would have given them the sense of power necessary to do the deed. Yet the deed, itself, is supposed to be the origin of society and culture.

"*Cannibal savages as they were, it goes without saying that they devoured their victim as well as killing him*" (Freud, SE 13:142). Freud simply assumes that they devoured the father because he assumes that the most primitive peoples were cannibals, and he repeats this belief in *Moses and Monotheism* (Freud, 1939:103 [SE 23:81]). There is no evidence at all for this supposition, but the idea was, and still is, a popular belief about primitives, especially archaic ones; the idea is perpetuated in much psychoanalytic writing, for example, by psychoanalyst Martin Bergmann (1992). In any case, eating the father was, according to Freud, the origin of the totem feast; by incorporating the flesh of the father the sons became identified with him. For Freud, then, the original sacrifice was human; the animal (totem) was already a substitute.

For Freud, the sons' deed marked the end of the patriarchal horde. But the very notion of the primal horde, taken from Darwin and Atkinson, "is merely hypothetical. It is a mere guess that the earliest organization of man resembles that of the gorilla rather than that of trooping monkeys" (Kroeber, [1920]1952:302).[16] Beyond that, however, is the question of whether one can legitimately read from animal behavior to human. For is it not the case that what we read of animal behavior has already been endowed with analogies from human behavior and social organization? Once human forms have been inscribed onto animal life, we then read back what these animals tell us about ourselves (Marx in Sahlins, 1976: 53; Haraway, 1989).

Second, and for my purposes more important, how can there be a patriarchal horde without a notion of patriarch? It was essential for Freud that the primal male was the father; otherwise neither the story nor the consequences that he believed flowed from the deed would make sense.[17]

Freud presupposed a notion of father; yet therein lies a "palpable contradiction" in his theory. For it was precisely the "discovery" of paternity that, for Freud and others, marked a major advance in civilization. How then, could such an idea have been present, *ab origine*, in that most archaic society?

> A great advance was made in civilization when men decided to put their inferences upon a level with the testimony of their senses and to make the step from matriarchy to patriarchy. The pre-historic figures which show a smaller person sitting upon the head of a larger one are representations of patrilineal descent; Athena had no mother, but sprang from the head of Zeus. A witness who testifies to something before a court of law is still called "Zeuge" (literally "begetter") in German, *after the part played by the male in procreation*. (Freud, SE 10: 233, n. 1, emphasis mine)[18]

The problems with his view about paternity and the momentous shift from matriarchy to patriarchy that he and many others assume occurred have already been dealt with (chapter 1). Here, it is important to point out that the errors of these assumptions had momentous implications for his theory, and through him, for contemporary theory about gender, social organization, and the symbolization of power.

Parenthetically, it is important to note that Freud not only ignores the story, recounted in Hesiod, that Athena did have a mother by the name of Metis; he also ignores how it came about that Athena was born from the head of Zeus. Zeus was afraid of Metis because she was said to be greater than all the other gods, and so he gobbled her up when she was pregnant with Athena and then passed her daughter off as his own creation (see chapter 7, n. 18).

More relevant to our discussion, however, is that if the "discovery" of paternity represents a step forward in civilization, as Freud asserts, how can he presuppose its existence at the dawn of society? Put more forcefully: *if there was no idea of paternity, how could there have been a primal father?* There could only have been a primal male.

Without the notion of father as "begetter," as the one who engenders the sons, the killing of the male head of the horde could not possibly have had the power and meaning Freud attributed to it. It would have been simply homicide—horrible, but unfortunately, a fairly frequent event. The deed that supposedly generated religion, society, and morals would instead only tell us something about the supposed propensity of males to kill (innate male aggression); it could not have been a patricide—a crime that Freud feels is far more weighty.[19]

Without a notion of paternity or father in the primal horde, could the meaning of *son* possibly carry the same valence? And why would these "sons" feel such a "burning sense of guilt" about a man whom they hardly knew, who had treated them cruelly and banished them? Yet the remorse these "sons" allegedly felt was so profound it (a) was repressed and unconsciously projected onto an animal totem—the substitute for the father which ultimately, through a series of transformations, becomes the great Father God—and (b) left a generalized feeling of guilt that was bequeathed to all subsequent generations. These we shall take up shortly.

The killing of the father and the religion that developed from this deed could not possibly have the same meaning and relevance for women as they have for men. Freud does not consider this difference, but implies that culture is entirely male-generated. In Freud's script of the deed that sets humanity on its course, women are hardly mentioned except as passive pawns in the action that takes place between father and son.[20]

For that is finally what the origin story comes down to: "the beginnings of religion, ethics, society and art converge in the Oedipus complex. . . . [These and] the problems of social psychology are soluble on the basis of one single concrete point—a man's relation to his father" (Freud, SE 13:156–7). At the very least, why not also a father's relation to his son? I shall leave to one side Freud's idea that the origins of religion and society stem only from the relationship between fathers and sons, rather than from that between mothers and daughters, or fathers and daughters, or mothers and sons. Here I want to focus on the father-son relation.

Had Freud raised the question about a man's relation to his son in addition to that of a man's relation to his father, he might have developed a theory that implicated fathers in the problems of their sons (and daughters). Such a question might have led him to develop a theory about fatherhood and, in turn, might have prompted him to ask another, vitally important question: What is the meaning of father and upon what does that meaning depend? It is a question he could very easily have asked; he had all the answers, but he never put them together. Had he done so, I believe it would have been necessary for him to revise his conclusions about the Oedipus complex, about the nature and origin of culture, and about religion and monotheism in a way that would have resulted in a book very differerent from *Moses and Monotheism*. I will postpone the implications of this failure until after we have a better sense of what he did do, namely to repeat the thesis formulated in *Totem and Taboo* as the basis for the story he constructs in *Moses and Monotheism*.

From Totem and Taboo to
Moses and Monotheism

For Freud the origin of society rests on a murderous deed committed in primeval times. It was a deed so horrible that it made a powerful impression on the perpetrators—so powerful, in fact, that it left a permanent mark.[21] It became an acquired characteristic of the human race as the human race passed from barbarity to society. At the very end of *Totem and Taboo* Freud had the courage to ask himself whether "the mere hostile *impulse* against the father, the mere existence of a wishful *phantasy* of killing and devouring him, would have been enough to produce the moral reaction that created totemism and taboo. In this way we should avoid the necessity for deriving the origin of our cultural legacy, of which we justly feel so proud, from a hideous crime, revolting to all our feelings." (Freud, SE 13:160). Yet because of his distinction between primitives and modern neurotics, namely that the latter are inhibited, that with them thought substitutes for action whereas primitives are uninhibited, that with them "thought passes directly into action," he finally says "it may safely be assumed that 'in the beginning was the Deed'" (ibid.:161).[22] Although several years previously he had abandoned the notion of a causative *deed* in relation to the development of neuroses in individuals, he held fast to the idea of such a deed when it came to his cultural studies.

In *Moses and Monotheism*, he confesses that perhaps the story he told in *Totem and Taboo* had been too condensed, "as if what in reality took centuries to achieve, and during that long time was repeated innumerably, had happened only once"(Freud, 1939:102 [SE 23:81]). Whether there was one deed or a number of them, it (they) occurred in primeval times and the knowledge of the deed(s) was repressed. In the long period of time between the primal horde and the early history of the Jews, there was a gradual return of the repressed (ibid.:169–170 [ibid.:132ff.]).[23] In historical times, "the mental residue of those primeval times has become a heritage which, with each new generation, needs only to be awakened, not to be reacquired" (ibid.:170 [ibid.:132]). The repetition of the primal crime on the person of Moses enabled the emotional fervor attaching to the original murder and its consequences to be reawakened, reacquired, and reinforced. That is the power of the story he tells in *Moses and Monotheism*.

MOSES AND MONOTHEISM

Freud creates his own version of the story of Moses in three separate but repetitive essays—the first two published in 1937 and then together in book form with the third in 1939. In these essays Freud brings all of his work on individual psychology (the Oedipus complex) and its relation to the origin and structure of society to bear on the origins of his own society and, specifically, on the conflict between Judaism and Christianity that was threatening to shatter his world.

Freud was deeply concerned about the rise of anti-Semitism under Hitler. *Moses and Monotheism* can, at least in part, be read as Freud's attempt to answer the questions: What is it about Judaism and Jews that provokes such hatred? How to explain it, and more important, how to defuse it? (Cf. Gilman, 1993). These queries provided strong, but clearly not the only, motivations for Freud to take up the question of the origin of Judaism. Also motivating his quest was the possibility of demonstrating his conviction that "religious phenomena are to be understood only on the model of the neurotic symptoms of the individual" (ibid.:71 [ibid.:58]). Thereby, Freud could use what he learned of the latter to theorize about the former. In the development of a neurosis, he says, there is an "early trauma—defence—latency—outbreak of neurosis—partial return of the repressed material" (ibid.:101 [ibid.:80]), and this is the periodization he uses to develop his theory about the rise and power of Mosaic monotheism.

With the contributions of Meyer, Sellin, and Rank, Freud spins a web of associations and conjectures that can be quite mesmerizing. The first clues are linguistic: he argues, quite persuasively, and using evidence from Meyer and others, that the very name of Moses is Egyptian. That, however, does not mean that the man Moses *was* Egyptian, but this is the conclusion Freud draws. He notes a discrepancy between the two Biblical accounts of Moses—Moses in Egypt and Moses among the Midianites— and suggests that there has been a conflation of two quite separate traditions, each of which involved a man named Moses (ibid.:41 [ibid.:36]). But he does not see how that undermines his thesis about the name: if this second Moses acquired *his* name by borrowing it from the first, as Freud implies, why couldn't the Egyptian Moses have borrowed his name?

The second clue is the way the Moses story contravenes the standard version of the myth of "the birth of the hero," as described by Otto Rank. In the typical form of the myth a child is born of noble parents; his "conception is impeded with difficulty" and, most important, the father receives a warning—an oracle or dream—that his son will be a danger to him. In response to the oracle, the father typically exposes the infant to the elements or in some way tries to get rid of the child, who is taken in by a humble couple and then, after many adventures and trials, emerges victorious to avenge his father and claim fame and fortune for himself (ibid.:7–8 [ibid.:10–11]). This *is* the Oedipus story.

The Moses story as portrayed in the Bible, Freud says, is the reverse: Moses is born into a humble family and brought up among nobility. But rather than a reversal, it may simply represent a difference between Greek and biblical myth. In the stories of both Isaac and Jesus, for example, the children are born of humble parents and their conceptions are unusual. Nevertheless, with regard to Moses, the "reversal" is not as simple as Freud would like. Moses "is the child of Jewish Levites" (ibid.:11 [ibid.: 13]), and although Pharoah's daughter does draw him out of the water, she turns him over to a wet nurse who, it turns out, is actually his own mother (Exod. 2:9). Jewish tradition holds that the Levites were the group (class or caste) of priests: they would hardly have been of the more humble or poorer classes, although Freud might have meant that they were humbled because of their captivity. More important, how could they be Jewish Levites without Judaism? If Moses is the father of the Jewish people, as Freud says, the one who brings or gives the religion of Judaism, then how could he be from a family of Jewish Levites? Indeed, before Judaism, what could that mean? Faced with such a "palpable contradiction," Freud simply changes the tradition and claims that *that* "seems a transparent distortion of the actual state of affairs: the Levites were instead, Moses' people." He was not born *of* Levites—instead, they were the retinue he brought with him during the Exodus, "his nearest adherents, his scribes, his servants" (Freud, 1939:45 [SE 23:38]). That still does not explain their Jewishness.

Nevertheless, the reversal is significant for Freud in the same way he thinks reversals in dreams are significant; they lead to a (distorted) truth. By analogy with individual psychology, he surmised that the same phenomenon was operative in myth, the collective dreams of a people. The truth that the reversal hides, Freud conjectures, is that Moses is an Egyptian of high rank, probably associated with the court, who lived in or near the time of Ikhnaton.

Ikhnaton was originally called Amenhotep IV after his father, Amenhotep III. The *Amen* part of the name refers to the god Amon, and the *aton* in Ikhnaton refers to the god he elevated to the prime position, Aton, the Sun-God, whom he worshipped "not as a material object, but as a symbol of a divine being whose energy was manifested in his rays" (ibid.:23 [ibid.:22]). According to Freud, Ikhnaton "ascended the throne about 1375 B.C. . . . (and) undertook to force upon his subjects a new religion, one contrary to their ancient traditions and to all their familiar habits. It was a strict monotheism" (ibid.:21 [ibid.:20]), imposed with harshness and intolerance. Such "religious intolerance, which was foreign to antiquity before this and for long after, was inevitably born with the belief in one God" (ibid.).

Freud's picture of Ikhnaton is in stark contrast to the one that his friend and colleague Karl Abraham painted earlier (1912), and which Freud knew about, as we shall see. From Karl Abraham we learn that Ikhnaton was only nine when his father died and that the kingdom was ruled for a time by his mother and by regents. Ikhnaton was a frail and poetic type, interested more in the arts of leisure than in conquests and battles, and he was devoted to his beautiful wife, Nefertiti, until his death at the age of twenty-five.

Freud imagined that *his* Moses was a follower of the Aton monotheistic religion and that he had hopes of rising in the Egyptian hierarchy. With the early death of Ikhnaton and the destruction of the Aton cult, these dreams or hopes of Moses were also dashed.[24] Freud imagined that Moses had been put in charge of the Jewish people, and that, with the return to power of the enemies of Ikhnaton, there were persecutions, which provided a reason for the Exodus. Freud suggests that Moses chose these Jews as his people, successfully led them out of Egypt, and then tried to reinstitute the Aton religion. While wandering hungry in the desert, they began to "murmur" and rebel and one day rose up against him and killed him.[25]

As with the murder of the primal father recounted in *Totem and Taboo*, the guilt or remorse after this terrible deed led them to reify, if not deify, Moses and made them adhere even more strictly to his rules. The repetition of the primal crime is what gives such power to Jewish monotheism and its "child," Christianity. Freud believed the murder was repressed. But if the murder of Moses was repressed (Freud, 1939:86 [SE 23:68]), why didn't Freud consider the possibility that the literal "sacrifice" of Isaac had been repressed?

The murder, according to Freud, was repressed; only traces—distorted, displaced, and transformed—remained, and those are what he claims to have unraveled. At the same time, he leaves as many traces or clues for us to unravel.

First, Moses is not the father of those who murdered him except perhaps in a symbolic sense. This might have alerted Freud to the fact that the primary issue is authority, not biology, and that revelation might have led him to rethink his thesis in *Totem and Taboo*. Moses is not referred to as father (*avinu*) in Jewish tradition. Indeed, according to Rice, "no patriarchal qualities were ever attached to Moses" (Rice, 1990:161); Moses is referred to as teacher (*rabeynu*). The title of father is reserved for Abraham, and it is from him, not Moses, that Jews (as well as Christians and Muslims) claim their descent. In addition, Freud makes no case for the incestuous desires of these "sons" for the wife of Moses or for the women he did not, in any case, hoard. Yet these were the prime motives for the primal crime, the residual traces of which Freud believes have been deposited in every male's Oedipus complex. But if the "father" and "sons" in this case are symbolic rather than biological and the motive primarily authority and obedience, what kept Freud from using this insight to critique his earlier theories about the Oedipus complex and its social ramifications in *Totem and Taboo*?

Second, Freud attributes the rise of Egyptian monotheism, before Ikhnaton, to political, especially imperial motives: already during the time of Thothmes III "Egypt had become a world power. . . . This imperialism was reflected in religion as universality and monotheism" (Freud, 1939: 22 [SE 23:21]). In the third essay, Freud states this even more clearly: "In Egypt monotheism had grown—as far as we understand its growth—as an ancillary effect of imperialism; God was the reflection of a Pharaoh autocratically governing a great world Empire" (ibid.:80 [ibid.:65]). But if Freud assumed that, for the Egyptians, the idea of uniting under one god was a very useful means to consolidate a multicultural empire, why should the foundation of *Jewish* monotheism depend on a repetition of the primal crime, the murder of the father (see Coward, 1983:214–5)? Conversely, does he see no contradiction in his explanation of the original Egyptian monotheism? By stretching the theory a bit, Freud attributes to Ikhnaton the Oedipal tendencies that rightly needed to be applied to the earlier florescence.

Perhaps it is true that Ikhnaton substituted a God (Aton) for his father and "directed his efforts to effacing all traces of the god for whom his father and he *himself* were named" (Abraham, [1912]1935:551, my emphasis), namely Amon. If one is to interpret his deed as a wish to murder the father, then one would at the same time have to interpret it as a suicide. Instead, Ikhnaton's erasure of the names with Amon affixed seems to have been motivated more by his hatred for the god Amon than by hatred for the father he hardly knew. The "return of the repressed" god, Aton, did not involve a murder, remorse, or the deification of the murdered father but had, at least according to Karl Abraham (1912), much to do with Ikhnaton's mother and her women friends, who had been devotees of Aton.

One cannot rule out the possibility that Egyptian monotheism might have emerged in relation to a repetition of the murder of the primal father, but since Freud considered other factors such as imperialism and authority, these should have been taken into account in considering the rise of Jewish monotheism.

Third, as there are many violent and horrible deeds recorded in the Bible, particularly in Genesis and Exodus, why was the murder of Moses, alone, repressed? Why should the murder of Moses be more horrific than his order for the murder of three thousand of his compatriots because of their disobedience (Exod. 32:28)? Why should the murder of the father be more significant than the murder of the son? Finally, why didn't Freud consider the possibility that the repressed murder in the Bible was not of the "father" but of the son, Isaac?

CHRISTIANITY

If the repressed murder had been that of the son, Isaac (as even a few biblical scholars assert), Freud might have made more sense of Christianity than he did. Not only did he dismiss and distort Jewish tradition, he also did violence to Christian tradition. The murder of Jesus became for Freud not the completion of the suspended sacrifice of Isaac or its possible repetition, but the expiation of the original crime, namely the murder of the Father. He attributed it to "a growing feeling of guiltiness . . . as a precursor or the return of the repressed material" (Freud, 1939:109 [SE 23:86]). He claimed that Paul rightly traced it to its primeval source and "this he called original sin; it was a crime against God that could be expiated only through death" (ibid.). Original sin was transformed by Freud into murder (of God the Father); he ignored both Jewish and Christian religious tradition, which interpreted it as disobedience. He also failed to take into account a traditional Jewish interpretation of Abraham's deed—that his obedience to God made up for, atoned for, Adam's disobedience. Abraham's deed (willingness), we may recall, bestowed merit upon Jews that redeemed them from God's wrath. Freud might have asked why God should be so angry, why the sacrifice of a child would be the appropriate propitiatory response, or why obedience was so important, but he did not. Such an exploration might even have provided a suitable rationale for the murder of the father.

He ignored the tradition altogether and substituted his own psychoanalytic explanation of events. At least in his individual case studies, he describes the patient's story; here he dispenses with it. In his terms, Jesus' death is an expiation for the original murder; therefore, Christians are liberated from *guilt* because his death amounts to their admission that they have killed God (the Father). Christian doctrine, on the contrary, teaches that through Christ's death Christians are liberated from *sin*—his death atones for their sin. Freud does not ask why "an all-powerful God can find no other way to absolve us from sin but to sacrifice his own beloved son" (Bergmann, 1988:251).

Freud's explanation changes the terms, for example from sin to guilt, and reduces the significance and meaning that Christ's death has for Christians. In fact, Freud blames Jesus for what happened. "That the Redeemer sacrifice himself as an innocent man was an obvious tendentious distortion. . . . [He] could be no one else but he who was most guilty, the leader of the brother horde who had overpowered the Father" (Freud, 1939:110 [SE 23:87]). Freud goes on to say that Christ was either "the heir of an unfulfilled wish-phantasy [or] his successor and his reincarnation" (ibid.:110–11 [ibid.:87]); in other words, he was the son who had usurped the father's place "just as in those dark times every son had longed to do" (ibid.:112 [ibid.:88]). Christianity is the triumph of the sons, the brother-band; it is, according to Freud, a son-religion, whereas Judaism remained a father religion.

Jews could not or would not join the brother-band; they obdurately refused to acknowledge the murder of the father (ibid.:114 [ibid.:90]) and, instead, compensated ever more persistently by their adherence to the strict regime required by the father.[26] This is Freud's tortuous way of explaining the terrible accusations Christians throughout the centuries have hurled at the Jews, namely that they are "Christ-killers"; no doubt such accusations were being heard again in Freud's Germany. When Christians say to Jews: "You have killed our God," Freud interprets it to mean, not Christ the son, but "the archetype of God, the primeval Father and his reincarnations" (ibid.:115 [ibid.:90]), an interpretation that would probably serve only to arouse their ire as Freud, himself, seemed to be aware.

Freud's contorted explanation ignored other possibilities that resonate much better with both historical and theological traditions. First, it was Jesus' own disciple, Judas Iscariot, who betrayed him; true, he was a Jew, but so too was Jesus; the traitor was one of his own. It is not as if a Jew killed a Christian, for there were no Christians at the time, there were only followers of the Jew, Jesus. A disciple betrayed him and "he was crucified under Pontius Pilate," as the Christian "Confession of Faith" repeatedly reminds believers. Although the Gospels portray Pilate as washing his hands of the whole affair (Matt. 27:24; Mark 15:15; Luke 23:24), he, nevertheless, did ultimately allow it to happen. Others have noted that the Jews could not have killed Jesus because "crucifixion was a Roman punishment for rebels, Jews would have stoned him" (Bergmann, 1988:252), or similarly, that only the Sanhedrin (the highest judicial and ecclesiastical council of the ancient Jews) could have sentenced him but that they would not have met during Passover.

Far more important, Freud ignored the theological interpretation of the death of Jesus: that God the Father sacrificed his only begotten son. One could easily imagine either that the Crucifixion repeated the Akedah, and thus acknowledge what had been covered up, or that it completed a deed that had been left unfinished; in either case, one is much closer to tradition and perhaps to the psychological complexes it bequeathed. Psychoanalytically, Freud might then have interpreted the Crucifixion as the repetition and coming to consciousness of the original repressed murder—that of Abraham's son. If that were too strong, he might have interpreted it as the fulfillment of an original repressed wish. In a general sense Christians interpret their religion as the culmination of the law and the prophets, the fulfillment of Judaism; more specifically it is the fulfillment of the promises given to Abraham.

In a book on a biblical figure and on a story of "sons" killing the "father," it is hard to imagine that Freud could *not* have thought of the story of Father Abraham and his willingness to kill his son. An initial question must be whether Freud knew of the story of Abraham. The Abraham story is one that I wager all children with even the most minimal of religious educations—in Judaism, Christianity, or Islam—eventually hear. And, "every male child who has been exposed to the story has been affected by it because of the universality and timelessness of its theme. Sigmund Freud was no exception" (Rice, 1990:161). I am not convinced of the universality of its theme, but it has persisted in certain cultures for several thousand years and its effects are felt not just by male children. It is not clear on what Rice bases his assumptions about Freud, but it is true that Freud had at least minimal acquaintance with Judaism and the Bible.[27] Most scholars think Freud had more than that, that he was intimately acquainted with biblical stories. Rice, for example, thinks young Sigmund was sent to Jewish primary school (ibid., 1990:181f.) and Yerushalmi imagines that his father may even have taught him Hebrew and

German as he told his son stories from their family bible (Yerushalmi, 1991:64).[28]

Listening to the biblical stories and peering at the family Bible—the Philippson's illustrated Bible with its full-page engraving of Moses holding the stone tablets as frontispiece (see fig. 14) and numerous illustrations of Egyptian scenes, objects, and motifs—it is not difficult to surmise that Freud's attachment to Moses and to all things Egyptian was forged in his childhood or youth.[29] Krull (1986:163) even makes the interesting suggestion that the adult Freud may have tried to replicate the Egyptian drawings with the collection of statues and figurines that filled his study in Vienna.

The Bible and its stories were, it seems, part of his childhood. His acquaintance with Greek myth and language came later, when he was a student at the Gymnasion. It was there that Freud first translated *Oedipus Rex* as part of his classical education. Freud confessed in his *Autobiography*: "My deep engrossment in the Bible story (almost as soon as I had learnt the art of reading) had, as I recognized much later, an enduring effect upon the direction of my interests" (Freud, SE 20:8).[30] Again, why did he choose a Greek myth rather than a biblical one as the human archetype?[31]

We can safely assume that Freud knew the story of Abraham. In fact, we do not really need to seek outside confirmation, as Freud himself lets us know that he was aware of it. He mentions it in his work, though only three times in his entire corpus, and then in a very offhand, casual way. On the surface it seems it did not affect him the way Rice thought it should. But the casualness and brevity of his citation could have been an indication of what he might, in others, have called an "avoidance reaction."

The first time Freud mentions Abraham is in the case study known as "Wolfman" (Freud, 1914, published in 1918). It was the child who actually mentioned it; Freud simply quoted him. "God had treated his son harshly and cruelly, but he was not better towards men; he had sacrificed his own son and had ordered Abraham to do the same" (Freud, SE 17: 65–6). The boy became terrified of God. Freud goes on to say, "The boy had some kind of inkling of the ambivalent feelings towards the father which are *an underlying factor in all religions*. . . . [H]is opposition soon turned instead directly against the figure of God" (ibid.:65, my emphasis, because this is hardly established fact). The ambivalent feelings may have arisen during the boy's initial obsession with questions about procreation and where babies come from and therefore may have been directly related to the Oedipal complex. The boy's statement may also have been a way to talk to Freud about his fear of his father and/or of cruelty experienced

FIG. 14. *Moses* etching from the Philippson Bible. *Mikra Torah Neviim
U-Khetuvim- Die Israelitische Bibel. Enthaltend den heiligen Urtext,
die deutsche Uebertragung, die allgemeine ausfurliche Erlauterung mit mehr
als 500 englischen Holzschnitten.* Leipzig: Baumgartner, 1858.
From Andover-Harvard Theological Library of Harvard
Divinity School, S.C.R. 391 Philippson.

or expected. That is, the son's ambivalent feelings may have arisen not only from his Oedipal wishes; they may have been due, in part, to behavior of the father. Freud should have been more attentive to the connections the child was drawing between notions of fatherhood, Abraham, and God.[32]

Freud mentions Abraham only two other times, both in *Moses and Monotheism*, and in neither case does he mention the sacrifice story. That seems extremely odd in a book that creates a story about "sons" killing the "father." In the first instance Freud thinks Abraham can be dispensed with because he is a legendary figure, an invention and projection of later prophets. But what an odd reason for Freud to reject him; after all, Freud uses another legend, that of Oedipus, as a way of analyzing universal complexes, so why not the story of Abraham? It has the additional merit of being a story that is repeated year after year—at Rosh Hashanah, at Easter, and during the Muslim Hajj—and generation after generation; it could, therefore, much more easily be understood as having shaped Western attitudes about the relation between fathers and sons. No society repeats the Oedipus story in a ritual context. But, for Freud, psychological complexes had to be anchored in something more solid than a notion of cultural transmission; he felt it necessary to elaborate his idea of some kind of genetic inheritance, albeit an initially acquired characteristic. Finally, if the first page of *Moses and Monotheism* is any indication, Freud seems to have regarded Moses as only relatively less legendary. For Freud, however, it was not only that Abraham was legendary: he believed he had been invented with a specific purpose, namely to displace the acts of Moses onto Abraham in order to cover up the *fact* that Moses was Egyptian.

One of the most important acts that Freud attributes to Moses, rather than Abraham, is the introduction of the custom of circumcision to the Hebrews. The Bible, he believes, covers this up: "the Biblical account, it is true, often contradicts it [and] dates the custom back to the time of the patriarchs as a sign of the covenant concluded between God and Abraham" (Freud, 1939:29 [SE 23:26]). The Bible specifically states that circumcision was first introduced by Abraham and is a sign of the covenant: "This is my covenant, which ye shall keep, between me and you and thy seed after thee; Every man child among you shall be circumcised" (Gen. 17:10). Can such an important Biblical story on which Hebrew identity and other events hinge be dismissed so easily? The practice was common among the Egyptians, and Freud takes this as further proof that Moses, too, was an Egyptian who later introduced the practice to his "chosen" people, the Hebrews. He seems never to have imagined that Abraham, during his sojourn in Egypt (Gen. 12), may have introduced circumcision to the Egyptians, and monotheism, too. In other words, we might more easily trace the genealogy of monotheism from Abraham to Ikhnaton rather than from the latter to Moses. Freud ignored this possibility, which adheres more closely to the biblical text, and instead proposed that it was Ikhnaton's monotheism that Moses attempted to revive. Freud's avoidance of Abraham appears to be overdetermined.

PERSONAL OMISSION

There is another, more personal, explanation for Freud's avoidance of Abraham that is closer to home and should not be overlooked. Although my purpose here is primarily to point out the relation betweeen the personal and the theoretical, some of my observations may contribute to the efforts of those who try to psychoanalyze Freud.

"Freud had forgotten that—as with Moses—an 'Abraham' had preceded him in Egypt" (Shengold, 1972:134). Shengold attributes Freud's omission of the biblical Abraham to a paraphraxis (a psychologically motivated slip) in relation to his associate Karl Abraham. Freud had conveniently forgotten that Karl Abraham had written an article on the Egyptian King Ikhnaton and monotheism long before Freud's *Moses and Monotheism* was even begun. Shengold thinks Freud's lapse stems from the psychologically motivated "death wishes" he harbored toward some of his own symbolic "sons," that is, his followers. Jung had been the favorite "son," chosen to succeed Freud, but after his defection, the honor was bestowed on Abraham. As we shall see, however, events precluded his succession.

Abraham's paper psychoanalyzes Amenhotep IV and, in a number of ways, anticipates Freud's theses in *Moses and Monotheism*: "Ikhnaton's doctrine not only contains the essential components of Old Testament Jewish monotheism but in many respects is in advance of it" (Abraham, [1912]1935:553).[33] For example, because Ikhnaton did not visualize his god, he "forbids any pictorial representation of the god—which command becomes a forerunner of Mosaic law" (ibid.). Further on, he notes that the intangible, invisible god would be a weakness of the religion because such a god would never appeal to the masses. This theme becomes a major point in *Moses and Monotheism* and is proffered as a reason why Christianity, with its profusion of images, became so popular. Abraham also discussed the similarity between the names Aton and Adonis, which may have prompted Freud's discussion of Aton and Adonai (ibid.:540).

Freud, who was usually so scrupulous in citing the work of others, clearly should have credited Abraham, as he did Sellin, Meyer, and Rank, for some of the ideas in his book. The fact that Freud cited Rank, another of his associates, does not excuse him for failing to cite Abraham's work, as Kanzer (1972:160) proposed.[34] Abraham's paper was well known to Freud and had been a subject not only of their correspondence but also of a small conference of his associates. Abraham first wrote to Freud on 11 January 1912, to tell him of his new paper on a "theme that will interest you: about Amenhotep IV and the Aton cult." He goes on to acknowledge his "first introduction to Egyptology that I enjoyed in Vienna in December 1907" (Abraham and Freud, 1965:111–2).

Freud's answer, written three days later, begins with the exclamation: "Just think of it, Amenhotep IV in the light of psychoanalysis. That is surely a great advance in orientation" (ibid.:112). By 3 June 1912, Freud writes, "I have read your Egyptian study with the pleasure that I always derive both from your way of writing and way of thinking, and should like to make only two criticisms or suggestions" (ibid.:118).[35] Abraham took them into consideration, and Freud wrote again 21 October 1912, saying: "I like your Amenhotep in its revised form much better" (ibid.: 124).

Abraham's paper was discussed at a meeting of the main members of the psychoanalytic circle in Munich a month later, in November 1912. Presciently, the issue of citation and attribution came up during the meeting. Jung felt that too much was being made of the erasure of Ikhnaton's father's name.[36] Freud's testy response was that Jung had not cited *him* in some recent work, implying that he, too, was trying to efface his "father." When Jung began to defend himself, Freud fainted. It was the third time he had fainted in *that* room in the Park Hotel (the other two times were in 1906 and 1908). Jung was also present on those two occasions and both times they had been discussing the death wishes of son to father. Although Freud accused Jung of having death wishes toward him, he did not appear to acknowledge his own.[37] It does seem as if Freud found it difficult to tolerate disciples who had independent opinions and who did not adhere strictly to his theory. He seemed to want to put his stamp on them as had the "Great Man" (see *Moses and Monotheism*, 1939:136–42 [SE 23:107–11]). Any straying was felt as betrayal.[38]

Ten years later, Freud was again reminded of Abraham's paper, for he made allusions to it in a letter he wrote to Abraham, 4 March 1923, thanking him for some clippings about the discovery of Tutankhamen's tomb (Abraham and Freud, 1965:334). Not long after that (on Christmas Day 1925) Abraham, although twenty-one years younger than Freud, was dead, and Freud was deprived of his chosen successor. Yet it seems that Freud had already become ambivalent about his decision, for sadly, during Abraham's illness, their exchange of letters had become fairly frosty and Abraham even complained that he was beginning to feel the brunt of Freud's hostility. Freud's reaction may partly be explained by the fact that Abraham's doctor during his illness was Fliess, the very man with whom Freud had had an intimate relation, then quarreled and broke with. Although Freud had once recommended Fliess to Abraham, he may have felt some jealousy as well as betrayal when Abraham communicated to Freud how highly he regarded Fliess. Freud had not taken Abraham's illness very seriously and had jokingly written: "I feel your illness to be a kind of unfair competition." When Abraham died so precipitously, Freud may have felt guilty; perhaps he realized, unconsciously, or could not acknowledge, that his "death-wishes" had been fulfilled. Did Freud find it significant that his chosen son had died on the day Christ was born?

Freud should have acknowledged Karl Abraham in *Moses and Monotheism*. And his name ought to have jogged a memory of the biblical Abraham (Yerushalmi, 1991:5). Indeed, when Freud first met Karl Abraham, he asked whether he was a descendent of his namesake Abraham—a way of asking whether he was Jewish yet contradicting his belief that Jewishness comes from Moses not Abraham.[39] Furthermore, the fact that Christians and Muslims also claim Abraham as their father might have led Freud to consider the foundational story that unites all three monotheisms—the story of a father willing to sacrifice his son.

Freud's avoidance of Abraham points to a much larger issue—his reluctance to hold fathers partly responsible for the problems of their children, or to consider their role and their (possibly ambivalent) feelings toward their children. Had he done so, he would have been forced to consider whether "father" and "son" refer to relationships given in nature or whether they are interrelated terms that derive their meaning from a particular theory of procreation. He might then have been led to the realization that the terms, their meanings, and the myths about them are *not universal* but relate to a particular social, historical, and cultural context. That, as we saw in chapter 1, is what the "virgin birth controversy" is all about, namely, whether the Trobriand Islanders (among others) had a *concept* of paternity and, if not, how the absence of it affected their social life and religious conceptions. Ernest Jones, a colleague of Freud and promulgator of psychoanalysis in England, became one of the interlocutors in that debate with his paper, "Mother-right and the Sexual Ignorance of Savages" (Jones, 1924). Other of his successors turned to the figure of the father in attempts to correct Freud's blind spot. However, they carefully adjusted the lens but left the frame intact. They turned their attention to the figure of the father but did not scrutinize the meaning of "father."

CHAPTER NINE

Sa(l)vaging Freud

T HE ABSENCE of the father in
Freud's work has not gone unnoticed by his successors, but their correctives stay within the psychoanalytic paradigm. Some even stay within the
Greek mythological context and suggest, for example, a "Laius complex"
to complement the "Oedipus complex" (Devereux, 1953). Others suggest
a biblical context but emphasize a story other than Abraham—for example, the story of Cain and Abel (cf.Yerushalmi, 1991:92; Rieff, [1959]
1979:195) or the Garden of Eden (Mazlish, 1969)—without taking into
account the foundational place of the story of Abraham in the monotheistic religious traditions. Nevertheless, a handful of psychoanalytically
trained doctors and scholars have focused on the Abraham story as a
corrective to Freud's emphasis both on Greek myth and on the son over
the father.[1]

Their perspectives highlight a dimension that was not brought out in
Freud's work, but they see it as merely additive. They are salvage attempts—the story of Abraham is interpreted as balancing or completing
Freudian theory. Like their counterparts in biblical scholarship, these analysts have a vested interest in recovering the story for the tradition, in
this case psychoanalytic tradition, rather than exploring the ways the
story of Abraham challenges it. Fundamental to the psychoanalytic, as to
the religious, interpretations is the unquestioned assumption that "father" or "paternity" means merely the social acknowledgment of a biological tie to a child rather than a social construction relative to a particular *theory* of procreation—a theory that imputes creativity and agency to
the male at the expense and devaluation of the female role.

Because my interpretation of Freud's blind spot diverges widely from
these psychoanalytic revisions, this chapter is not intended as an extended
review and critique of their work—a tack that would take us way off
course. By picking my way around them and pointing out the hidden

dangers in their commonplace assumptions, I use them to chart my own course. The route may be somewhat tedious and of interest mostly to specialists, but it illuminates the depths to which Freudians have gone to salvage his theory, and it highlights the significance of my critical departure. Readers who wish to investigate these byways further should consult the references.

DEVEREUX

I begin briefly with Devereux because he was one of the first "to note that psychoanalytic theory pays exceedingly little attention to certain complexes which . . . complement the Oedipus complex" (Devereux, 1953: 132), especially what he calls the Laius complex. He attributes Freud's scotoma vis-à-vis the father both to the authoritarian structure and atmosphere of nineteenth-century families and to "the adults' deep-seated need to place all responsibility for the Oedipus complex upon the child; and to ignore, whenever possible, certain parental attitudes which actually *stimulate* the infant's Oedipal tendencies" (ibid., emphasis added). I do not know on what grounds Devereux postulates "adults' deep-seated need," but the failure to implicate fathers in their children's neuroses rests with Freud.

Freud had actually started out on that path because of the stories his female patients told about being "seduced" by the father or by a father substitute, such as another male relative. Even here, however, one can glimpse Freud's effort to excuse the father, for what was at stake was hardly seduction but incest or rape; indeed, the girl/daughter was the one labeled "seductive." When he abandoned the "seduction theory," he developed the thesis that neurotic symptoms were the fulfillments of wishes or fantasies on the part of the child (in this case the female child) rather than the inscriptions of faults of the fathers or their surrogates. Perhaps he was unwilling to believe that so many fathers, or their substitutes, could be abusing their daughters, even though in several of the cases there was corroborating evidence. It is even stranger to consider that although the patients he was dealing with were female, the theory he eventually elaborated—the Oedipus complex—focused on males, a double abandonment. In any case, his theory changed from being interpsychic to intrapsychic, from seeing psychological problems as social to locating them within the individual.[2]

This change occurred during a period of time immediately following the death of Freud's own father. Perhaps, as a number of scholars have suggested (Krull, 1986; Robert, 1976; Balmary, [1979]1982; Rice,

1990), Freud was unwilling or unable to confront his father and thus recognized that if he had left stones unturned, he would now have to deal
with the consequences by himself. Perhaps he also realized that he had
stepped into his father's place and was now invested with the authority to
which he had aspired, and he did not want to relinquish it.[3] For me, these
personal factors, however interesting, matter less than the implications
they had for his theory and practice, and for what they tell us about the
implicit cultural theory he produced.

By detailing the unsavory character of Laius, Devereux attempted to
historicize and particularize the Oedipus complex. He suggested that
Laius had brought on himself the fate he confronted at the crossroads
because of his own belligerent behavior (a) by exposing the infant Oedipus, and (b) even earlier by the homosexual rape of Chrysippus, the son
of King Pelops. For Devereux, at least, the Oedipus complex is activated
by the desires and actions of the father at least as much as it is by those of
the son.

WELLISCH

Although in agreement with the last comment, Wellisch breaks out of the
Greek script for psychoanalysis with his book *Isaac and Oedipus* (1954),
in which he suggests that "the Akedah motif . . . is the Biblical extension
of the Oedipus complex" (Wellisch, 1954:113) and is more appropriate
for the psychology of modern man. Modern psychology, he observes, is
based on nonbiblical ideas, yet the Akedah is "the fundamental event on
which the whole Bible stands" (ibid.:57) and is basic to the religious development of Judaism, Christianity, and Islam. It has, he asserts, been far
more influential in molding family values and psyches than have the
Greek tragedies. A very good point indeed.

Isaac and Oedipus is hardly a direct critique of *Moses and Monotheism*; the latter book is not mentioned at all and the few references to
Moses are biblical ones. Nevertheless, because it presents the Akedah, the
story of Abraham's near sacrifice of Isaac, as the complement to Freud's
interpretation of Oedipus, it is relevant here.

For Wellisch, "the Akedah story describes *the resolution of the Oedipus conflict*" (ibid.:78, emphasis in the original). Unlike what might be
called a Laius complex, the Akedah resolves the Oedipus complex with
love, establishing thereby a new relation between parent and child (ibid.:
23). This relation transcends the solution that might be effected by the
addition of a Laius complex to the Oedipus complex. For Wellisch, the
addition would not be a solution but more like a balancing act "between

the opposing tendencies of the wish to possess the child completely or even to kill him and the desire not to do so" (ibid.:4). The reconciliation between parent and child, by which Wellisch actually means father and son, is brought about by the father's "abandonment of his possessive, aggressive tendencies and especially infanticidal tendencies and their replacement by a covenant of love" (ibid.). We shall see in a moment what he means by *love*.

Wellisch's argument, however, rests on a few untenable, or at least highly questionable, assumptions embedded in a theory of sociocultural evolution popular in the nineteenth century but discredited by most twentieth-century anthropologists. One must be suspicious of a theory that depends, as his does, on an evolutionary schema that posits a unitary, universal cultural evolution consisting of stages: (1) primitive, (2) oedipal, and (3) Akedah.[4] On the very first page he states: "The first and most primitive stage is characterized by intense aggression and possessiveness of the parents. This aggression is particularly severe in the father and is directed mainly to his sons . . . [I]t not infrequently culminated in infanticide" (ibid.:3–4). Not only does he assume an infanticidal impulse; he projects it back to the dawn of history, which both he and Freud assumed was mean, brutish, and cannibalistic. He gives no evidence for these assertions but seems to have carried them over directly from Freud, who, without mentioning the word infanticide, and without any explanation, indicates that those most vulnerable to male aggression are newborn babies, menstruating and birthing women, and the dead (Freud, SE 13:33).

Correlative with the assumption of a barbaric past is Wellisch's assumption of some kind of primordial (male) aggression that automatically would be directed to a man's children, especially his sons. He claims that infanticide has been practiced "all over the world by all races and nations" (Wellisch, 1954:11) in *historic* times, and cites a number of myths to support his claim. His belief in evolutionary progress leads him to conclude that if infanticide was practiced in historic times, then it must have been practiced even more assiduously in primeval times. Yet he might just as easily have asserted a more Edenic past and considered that infanticide or child sacrifice (which he does not really distinguish) may have arisen *with* civilization. As discussed in chapter 3, all evidence for child sacrifice is in complex, civilized societies, not simple ones, and from times much later than the story of Abraham. Wellisch's statement is a prime example of evolutionary reasoning: he simply assumes that earlier means barbaric and historic means civilized—in the sense of an advance in moral development. The historic instances of infanticide are, in this kind of reasoning, seen as "survivals" of a more brutish past.[5] In the same way, he simply assumes that human sacrifice preceded that of animals (ibid.:30). These assumptions are so common that they are rarely questioned; it is difficult to persuade people that they are interpretations, not fact—interpretations that derive from a *conception* of the past, as well as of the present.[6]

Wellisch does, however, point out that "if one considers the possibility of the sons having killed the primordial father," as Freud did in both *Totem and Taboo* and *Moses and Monotheism*, then "one can infer that this was due to the father's behavior. One can assume that in the beginning was infanticide" (ibid.:10). Wellisch's statement, like Devereux's, has the merit of raising the question of why Freud did not really consider how the father's behavior provoked the sons' action and how the father, therefore, is inextricably implicated. Wellisch leads us to expect some discussion on the development of the father complex, but that does not occur. Instead he moves to religion and the idea of a higher power.

Wellisch's theory is rendered even more suspect by his examples of the new covenant between parent and child, which he calls *love*. "The readiness of the child to be sacrificed at his parent's command plays a great role in the development of filio-parental relationships. It . . . reached its noblest fulfillment in the attitude of Isaac towards Abraham" (ibid.:12). Note the singular *parent*; he really means the son's submission to the father: "By the surrender to the father's command, the son is greater than the father" (ibid.:94).

For Wellisch, the *child's* self love is therapeutic and brings about a more harmonious family relationship. He cites a chilling example from his clinical practice. A man who had returned from World War II began to exact military discipline from his wife and two sons. "He had very strict ideas about what is right and wrong and his ethics centred around discipline and doing what one is told. These ideas he linked with his belief in God, the Church, law and order" (ibid.:106). He was obsessed with duty and obedience and expected the same from his family. When the sons rebelled, they were punished. Wellisch does not question the destructive behavior of the father in this instance, nor the basis of the father's authority; instead he advises the family to submit to his authority and discipline because these are derived from principles rooted in religion. (The work of Philip Greven on Christian childrearing practices, cited in chapter 10, is again relevant.)

Although this solution may have calmed the tensions in that household, we must wonder what psychic violence was further perpetrated on the sons. The wife's collusion was solicited; she was encouraged to accept her husband's values and to use her influence to get the sons to accept them as well. Wellisch's theory and therapy ends, like Freud's, by supporting the father at the expense of the son. It reinforces rather than challenges the themes of authority and obedience that are so central to the Akedah.

BAKAN

David Bakan, a Canadian psychologist and professor, and a longtime student of Freud, has also discussed the relevance of the Abraham story for modern psychology. Like Wellisch, he assumes an "infanticidal impulse" and attributes its mitigation to the Abraham-Isaac story. "*Infanticide is, in the wider sense of the term, primitive. It would be obscuring reality to call this trait 'instinctive.' It is not common to all mankind. Yet it comes so near being inherent in the primeval parent-child relationship that one is tempted to say of it: 'here, if anywhere, is a bit of behavior natural to primitive man.'*" (Bakan, 1971:56, emphasis in the original). Although Bakan admits that infanticide is not universal, it is close enough for him. The attribution of such an impulse to archaic societies is purely speculative—there can be no empirical evidence. Nor does he investigate contemporary "primitive" societies,[7] but he theorizes that infanticide and child abuse are related to the so-called discovery of paternity, which eventually all peoples must acquire as they ascend the evolutionary ladder. The "discovery" of paternity is thought to evoke an impulse to infanticide because of concern over legitimacy, that is, whether a specific child is really a man's own, and the entailed responsibility for that child. The Bible, he claims, is the document that depicts the crisis precipitated by this discovery, and the Abraham story mitigates it.

Because the themes and issues Bakan and I discuss appear similar, it is of critical importance to distinguish our very deep differences. For this reason, I devote slightly more space to him. We agree that "Paternity is one of the most frequent themes in both the Old and the New Testaments. . . . [T]he authors of the Bible were extremely preoccupied with fatherhood" (Bakan, 1974:205). Where we differ is on whether the Bible reflects the *crisis* of paternity or symbolizes, instead, the establishment and elaboration of the *notion* of paternity, the patriarchal family, and the values that support it, making them appear as if they are rooted in the structures of the universe rather than in a particular culture. The Akedah, for me, could hardly represent the mitigation of an "infanticidal impulse," but it might possibly represent the beginning of an infanticidal impulse.

Paternity, according to Bakan, has both positive and negative sides: on the one hand the "biblical mind discovered children could be created at will . . . [that] *men* truly became as gods in this respect" (ibid.:206, emphasis added). Although human men were not immortal as were the gods, they saw the "possibility of achieving biological immortality by means of the willful *creation* of offspring" (ibid.:207, emphasis added). In the preface to *Slaughter of the Innocents*, his book about child abuse, Bakan claims that the "dawn of civilization must have been when man learned that through planting seed, in the ground or sexually, he could create life at will" (Bakan, 1971:ix), and armed with that knowledge, men could also assume the right to take life or take control over it. But is this *knowledge* or a particular construction of procreative events? Bakan has perpetuated without question the idea that it is *men*, not women, who create children. Because he fails to use contemporary knowledge of procreation to reveal the assumptions embedded in these ancient beliefs, he has no basis from which to criticize them, and thus he reinforces them. He does not consider the possible effects on women or whether there might have been some struggle over this interpretation of creativity. Did women object to being likened to soil? Did they also desire immortality? Nor does he consider that not all cultures have been seed-planting ones, nor have all made an analogy between agriculture and procreation, between semen and seed. This view of procreation and the emphasis on the male role is a theory, a *construction*, not a "discovery." But it is here that his conflation of biological relationship and male creativity is most baldly stated.

The idea of paternity as male (pro-)creativity makes sense of the patrifiliation or identification of children with the father, but it entails other problems. Bakan believes that the "difficulties arising from men's assuming responsibility for *their* children also gave rise to a temptation to kill their children" (Bakan, 1979:15) because:

> First, the offspring might not be loyal, might not continue to provide, might not continue to obey, and might even kill their parents. Thus arises the obedience morality of the Bible. . . . Second, the simple burdensomeness of raising children under conditions of shortages of resources was itself a threat. . . . Third, the biblical mind was compromised by the possibility of lack of authentic paternity . . . (and) was especially uneasy about the first born, because the first born is ever of dubious paternity if the gestation period is not known. (ibid.:)

Although Bakan does not specify sons, that is who he is thinking about. The ambivalence toward the firstborn, he believes, is illustrated by the commandment "sanctify unto me all the firstborn," in which the firstborn sons are dedicated to God.[8] The focus on sons becomes immediately understandable if one believes that the son is, via seed, the incarnation of the father and the one who carries on his line; a father had to be sure a son was his own.

Bakan argues, quite rightly, that the emphasis on obedience is intimately related to paternity. Even if the son should not rise up and usurp the father's place violently, he keeps in front of the father the idea that he will ultimately succeed him. By demanding obedience from the son, the father can determine when that will be. It should be pointed out that obedience is required of the wife as well as the son, for upon her fidelity lies the guarantee of authentic paternity. (The obedience of wives is still part of traditional marriage vows.) Bakan asserts that the "covenant of God and Israel is of the same order as the covenant *extended* to a woman in marriage" (ibid.:163, my emphasis). Israel sometimes figures as the wife or bride of God; in this patronizing statement it is clear that there is an ascending hierarchy of obedience and the feminine is subordinate. Bakan even talks of the "effeminization" of the son in relation to the father, and of the father in relation to God (cf. Eilberg-Schwartz, 1994).

The consequence, however, of the son's submission to the father and the father's to God is that God's power and authority is channeled through males. Circumcision, the sign of the covenant given to Abraham "may be understood," according to Bakan, "as representing God's having delegated his procreative prerogative to man" (Bakan, 1979:141). Yet it is not to *man* but to men; the covenant was signed on the penis, on what was considered *the* generative organ. There was no comparable covenant with women. Bakan reinforces the patrilineal ideology when he notes that the sexual-generative ability, bestowed by God, is transferred from father to son throughout the generations.

All of these themes are exemplified in the story of Abraham, which Bakan sees as the mitigation of the infanticidal impulse. In fact, he asserts that "the essence of Judaism and Christianity is the management of the infanticidal impulse . . . and a binding of the father against acting out the impulse" (Bakan, 1974:208). The use of the term *binding* is a clear reference to the Akedah but for Bakan it is the father, not the son, who is bound.

The "infanticidal impulse" emerges with the "discovery" of paternity; its transcendence, which the Akedah supposedly symbolizes, has the result of men taking responsibility for their children. A number of additional assumptions are entailed in this interpretation, but they are merely stated, not examined. First, Bakan assumes that it is only with the "discovery" of paternity that men would be involved in child care at all. Before the discovery, he had assumed that it was women's function to "provid[e] maintenance, protection and education of the young" (Bakan, 1979:28). In this way, he gives agency to biology; biology determines social arrangements, especially the strict division of labor based on biological function. He assumes that previous to the "discovery" only women were biologically involved, thus only women would have had the responsibility of caring for children. There are grave problems with this argument; had he not dismissed anthropological evidence and theory so summarily, he might have avoided some of them. In all cultures, regardless of whether there is an ideology of biological relation at all or of paternity in particular, men participate in the rearing of children (see Introduction). All kinship systems, even matrilineal ones, have a role and function for the male vis-à-vis the children of the woman he marries or lives with. Bakan's assumption that men will assume care only for children who are biologically their own merely replicates and reinforces our own cultural ideology—it is not universal.

The logic of his argument forces him to come out in support of patriarchal religion and, by implication, patriarchal society. The Akedah represents for Bakan "the establishment of a patrilineal and patriarchal ideology" (ibid.:134) consequent on the "discovery" of paternity; at the same time, the Akedah also represents a mitigation of an infanticidal impulse brought about by this "discovery." He concludes that patriarchy is an advance because it "is associated with what is perhaps the most important step toward the *reduction* of male-female sex role difference in the history of civilization" (ibid.:166, emphasis added), namely that men take responsibility for children. His conclusion is contrary not only to anthropological evidence, but also to the evidence he brings from contemporary Western societies (Bakan, 1971) where many men have abandoned, hurt, or destroyed their children (see chapter 10). Nevertheless, the logic of his argument leads to the conclusion that we have forgotten the message of the Akedah, which, for him, mitigates the "infanticidal impulse." But it also demands the obedience and submission of the child (and the wife); the implications of his theory imply a return to patriarchal family values rather than a radical questioning of them. My argument that the story represents the construction, establishment, and naturalization of sex role *differences* makes much more sense of the evidence.

BALMARY

Marie Balmary, a French psychoanalyst, also recognized that Freud had a problem with incorporating the psychology of the father into his theory of psychoneuroses. She thought that by *Psychoanalyzing Psychoanalysis* (1979) she might be able to locate his "hidden fault." She, too, begins her investigation with the observation that Freud ignored the figure and character of Laius in his construction of the Oedipus complex. She believes that whatever patricidal and incestuous wishes Oedipus had were intimately related to the character and actions of his father. Although she focuses on the loathsome character of Laius, particularly in his betrayal of Pelops's hospitality (by the homosexual rape of his son Chrysippus), she puts very little emphasis on the fact that Laius first tried to get rid of Oedipus. Freud may not have known about the Chrysippus episode but he did know of Laius's attempt to dispose of his son.

In any case, Balmary says that the Oedipus myth is about the intimate links between father and son and asks why, then, does Freud focus on Oedipus alone. Why not a theory of the father's hidden fault (Balmary, [1979]1982:27)? She, like a number of others, notes that Freud had originally started in that direction, but then stopped rather abruptly. Again, like a number of others, she realizes that the abandonment of the "seduction theory" was intimately related to the death of Freud's father. Balmary thinks that the abrupt shift in the direction of his thought had to do with Freud's inability to confront his father about his past, particularly his relationship with the hidden woman, Rebecca.[9] Jakob Freud's secret was a sexual one—a liaison or brief marriage with a woman who then disappeared without a trace. Balmary claims that behind the sexual fault is murder or, at least, actions that led to another's death, and that this is the fault of Freud's father that neither he nor Freud could acknowledge. How "could Freud reveal the fault of his father just when his father was appearing before his judge?" (ibid.:41) that is, just at the time his father was dying. His secret went with him to his grave but its effects are transmitted from generation to generation, for "the patient does not suffer from his own faults but from those of the dominating if he cannot denounce them" (ibid.:87).[10]

Like a detective, Balmary presents detailed evidence of the three weeks in Freud's life during which he made that "great transition." In the process, the father's fault was carried to the son, and its effects are known by its absence in his theory. And, as has become clear since Freud's death, the effects have been transmitted to several generations of analysts who have continued to deny the "fault" of the fathers, a denial that has had particularly damaging effects on women patients (e.g., Herman, 1981; Lerman, 1986; Masson, 1984). Even though Balmary may have pinpointed the fault of Freud's father and Freud's reluctance to confront him with it, and outlined the way the fault was transmitted to his theory and practice, this does not explain the "faults" of numerous other fathers.

Balmary is aware of this problem and attempts to resolve it with the idea that "the origin of neurosis is not sexual desire alone nor even sexual trauma alone, but all the faults committed by the very people who present the law to the child" (Balmary, 1979:164). For her, symptoms are demands for recognition, and the cure consists in connecting the deed, or betrayal, to the one who committed it (ibid.:128), to discover the witness to what we had known alone (ibid.:162). This, surely, is an important therapeutic idea. In this work she locates the cause of neurosis externally either in the father or, in a Lacanian mode, in the law he represents. What she does not do is ask why the father represents the law or, conversely, why the law represents the father. These are questions that neither Lacan nor his numerous, even feminist, followers have satisfactorily answered. They assert that the phallus symbolizes the law of the father, but they deny that the meanings of *the phallus* are derived from the physical penis. On the contrary, I suggest, that precisely because the penis has been imagined as the primary instrument of human generativity or creativity, it can become "larger than life" as *the phallus*.

Balmary's more recent book, *Le sacrifice interdit* (The Forbidden/ Interrupted Sacrifice, 1986), is a psychoanalytically influenced reading of the story of Abraham's sacrifice. Although she retains the interpersonal aspect of her theory and focuses more on Abraham, the father, than on Isaac, the son, she does not use it as a foil for Freud's Moses nor as a complement to the Oedipus complex. She does not find fault with Abraham but instead elevates him into a modern existential hero struggling with the issue of separation and individuation, coming to autonomous selfhood free of encumbering relations.[11] This is signaled, she thinks, by God's command to Abraham, "Go forth," which she interprets to mean something like: "Go find yourself." She believes that one cannot become a full autonomous being if one is ensnared in relationships that one is not willingly committed to. Her interpretation is conditioned by modern psychoanalytic theory and especially by the valuation of autonomy and individuation, which may not have been cultural ideals when Genesis was written and which have recently come under a great deal of feminist criticism. The ideals of autonomy and independence, in contrast to interdependence and caring, are heavily involved with social contract theory, which, as recent criticism (Pateman, 1988; Glendon, 1991; Fraser, 1989) has shown, is built on a masculine model.

Abraham *is* identified with his son, but I do not think the story mitigates that identification; instead I think it inscribes it. Balmary thinks Abraham must cut the ties that bind so that they can come together again, allied in a relationship freely chosen. These echoes of social contract theory versus patriarchalism seem particularly inappropriate and anachronistic in the case of Abraham, who is symbolically, culturally, and religiously the first patriarch.[12] According to Balmary, when Abraham responds to three calls from God, he cuts the ties that bind him—to his parents, to his wife, and to his son (Balmary, 1986:205). What he cuts in the "sacrifice" is not Isaac himself, but the *relation* that ties them, thus freeing Isaac to become his own person, not just a reproduction of his parents. But the story does not free Isaac. She seems to have forgotten that after their trial on the mountain, Abraham descends alone. Moreover, Isaac does not become much of a person in his own right after the Akedah; it is as if all life had been taken out of him. These facts have been noted by a number of biblical commentators, and a few have taken them as evidence that perhaps Isaac was really killed (see chapter 5). Balmary retreats from considering such a possibility and instead goes off in an equally speculative direction even more at variance with centuries of tradition.[13]

She also overlooks what Steinmetz (1991) and others have recognized: that the son in this story is imagined as of the same essence as the father. He is Abraham's seed—seed that will become a great nation and inherit the land. The ability to pass on this essence is given only to males—the fault line is the patriline.

She arrives at her conclusion by denying that the command was to sacrifice. She rightly says that the word for *sacrifice* is not in the text, that God asked only that Abraham *offer up* Isaac. Yet the word ʿ*olah* (burnt offering), which is in the text, signifies a sacrificial offering, and this "mistake," she says, has been inscribed in the tradition. Therefore, she thinks that Abraham was in great danger of misunderstanding God's command.[14] He had to wake up to what was meant—namely that he separate himself from his son psychologically. "You did not withold your son" means, for her, "you did not hold onto him." That might be fine for Abraham and perhaps it might free him from his attachment, but it seems to me that there might be other ways to illustrate this point without such trauma to the son.

In *Le sacrifice interdit* Balmary repeats the same fault she accuses Freud of when she claims that "the *Interpretation of Dreams* is the result of Freud's refusal to reprove the father" (Balmary, 1979:79). She does not reprove the father; her interpretation of the Abraham story is an apologetic interpretation. Like Freud, she ends by upholding and justifying the system that upholds and justifies the father.

MILLER

The only voice crying from the psychoanalytic wilderness is that of the Swiss psychoanalyst Alice Miller, in a chapter entitled "When Isaac Arises from the Sacrificial Altar" in *The Untouched Key: Tracing Childhood Trauma in Creativity and Destructiveness* (1988; English trans. 1990). When she examined a number of paintings depicting the scene of the sacrifice, she noticed that Abraham never looked directly at Isaac and "there is no pain to be seen in Abraham's face, no hesitation, no searching, no questioning, no sign that he is conscious of the tragic nature of his situation. All the artists, even Rembrandt, portray him as God's obedient instrument, whose sole concern is to function properly." She goes on to ask: "Why did they all take it for granted that the Bible passage could not be questioned?" (Miller, 1990:141).

Although astonished by their failure to doubt the received text, she attributes their lack of nerve to a "fundamental fact of our existence": that all of us have had firsthand experience of being at the mercy of our fathers, so much so that the "moral expressed in the story has almost been accorded the legitimacy of a natural law" (ibid.). Regardless of whether we have all experienced paternal abuse, paternal authority has had the status of something akin to natural law in that it has been culturally legitimated through religious texts, secular institutions, and modes of behavior. Such a moral structure demands the obedience and submission of women and children but is often symbolically rendered through sons.

Miller deplores this state of filial passivity and calls for "sons" to wake up, not to take the law into their own hands and kill the father, which would only perpetuate the problem, but to begin to question the law and its legitimacy. She constructs a dialogue between Isaac and Abraham that echoes my own childhood questions about the story as well as some of the dialogue between Cristos and his small daughter.

> Isaac will ask, "Father, why do you want to kill me?" and will be given the answer "It is God's will." "Who is God?" the son will ask. "The great and benevolent Father of us all, Whom we must obey," Abraham will answer. "Doesn't it grieve you," the son will want to know, "to have to carry out this command?" "It is not for me to take my feelings into account when God orders me to do something." "Then who are you," Isaac will ask, "if you carry out His orders without any feeling, and Who is this God, Who can demand such a thing of you?" (Miller, 1990:144)

Like the child who pointed out the obvious in the tale about the emperor's new clothes, it is about time we asked such obvious questions, especially of our sacred tales, the myths we live by. Miller's confrontation with the Abraham-Isaac story resulted in a radical questioning of psychoanalytic theory and practice, with which she had been involved for a quarter century. In her own theory and practice she has taken the side of the child and worked to expose abuse personally, theoretically, institutionally, and culturally.

BERGMANN

The latest book by a psychoanalyst on the Abraham story, that by Martin Bergmann, *In the Shadow of Moloch: The Sacrifice of Children and its Impact on Western Religions* (1992), takes no note whatsoever of his analytic colleagues Miller, Bakan, or Balmary.[15] Such an oversight makes one wonder about his research methods. It is also the latest example of what results when psychoanalysts enter into the realm of anthropology without any acquaintance with anthropological theory since Frazer and W. Robertson Smith. Bergmann does make passing reference to Levi-Strauss but turns him into a cultural particularist instead of the comparativist he is.

Bergmann first wrote about the Abraham story in 1988 and discussed it again when he played the part of the psychiatrist in Woody Allen's film *Crimes and Misdemeanors*. In the film he asks how it was that the early

Israelites conceived of a God who cares and demands that we act morally but, at the first opportunity, asks Abraham to sacrifice his son. That question is not answered in the film, but an attempt is made in Bergmann's book. He begins with the unsubstantiated assumption that ritual infanticide was a "ubiquitous custom" practiced long ago by those cannibal savages. Furthermore, he contends that "the struggle against this custom has been a driving force in the development of Western religions" (Bergmann, 1992:1). This could be a statement taken directly from Bakan, whom Bergmann does not cite. He travels down the predictable path, stating that *survivals* of this custom continue to exist in the unconscious and in certain religious rituals such as the Eucharist. He does not imagine, let alone ask, whether they might emerge relative to a specific concept of paternity and to a Father God.

With the exception of Miller, it seems that all of these theorists reached a limit—the *terminus ad quem*—beyond which they could not go. The limiting concept is the father who, for them, seems like the sun in a heliocentric universe; they revolve around it, blinded by its power.[16] In order to move beyond, they need to get a new perspective, they need a new theory, and especially they need a better anthropology.

The limit seems insurmountable, but it is not. What is needed is more attention to the meaning and definition of father. This, of course, would not prevent particular fathers from abusing their power and their children, but it would enable us to see this abuse as an extreme case of "acting out" or acting upon what is implicit in an entire system that institutionalizes, naturalizes, and legitimates paternal power.[17]

FATHERHOOD, MONOTHEISM, AND ABRAHAM

Although Freud thought that the concept of *God* was a projection of the feared and admired qualities of the human father, he also seemed to attribute godlike qualities to human fathers. He appears to have put fathers, or at least the idea of the father, on a pedestal, and he approached but seemed afraid to touch it. In fact, he noted that "the sacred is obviously something that must not be touched" (Freud, 1939:154 [SE 23: 120]), which may explain why he could not approach/reproach his father. Finally, he concluded "that what is sacred was originally nothing but the perpetuated will of the primeval father" (ibid.:156 [ibid.:121]) who was larger than life—as is every father to his small child.

The image of the father that Freud presumed we all carry around with us is an image that creates both fear of the father's authority and longing for it. This idealized image is sometimes enlarged into the "Great Man," like Moses, and ultimately into God, but it originally develops from one's own father.

> The decisiveness of thought, the strength of will, the forcefulness of his deeds, belong to the picture of the father; above all other things, however, the self-reliance and independence of the great man, his divine conviction of doing the right thing, which may pass into ruthlessness. He must be admired, he may be trusted, but one cannot help also being afraid of him. We should have taken a cue from the word itself; who else but the father should in childhood have been the great man? (ibid.:140 [ibid.:109–10])

Surely not all fathers possess or are seen to possess such qualities. Or is it that, despite their individual differences, each partakes of the *imago* of the great man? Freud seems to conflate or confuse the *imago* with its real-life embodiments, which may help to explain why he appears to exonerate fathers, to let them off the hook, so to speak, for each in his own way represents the "Great Man" and each deserves a portion of the respect, both love and fear, owed to such a one. Freud's image of the father is not unlike that of a Christian theologian who stated: "there is something divine in the father, seeing that there is something fatherly in God" (Quell, 1967, vol. 5:965). Both are drawing on deep-seated cultural beliefs.

For Freud, the elevated place of the father is tied to his interrelated ideas about renunciation, paternity, and cultural advance. The very idea of father, for Freud, is bound up with the renunciation of instinctual gratification. Yet this is contradicted by his description of the primal father who indulged his instincts, both aggressive and sexual. The father may have forced renunciation on the sons, but Freud stressed that it was the brothers who imposed it on themselves after the murder. Not only did they renounce all the women of the horde, they also renounced, if not the desire, at least acting upon the desire to hoard women. Each man would have a woman for himself.

RENUNCIATION

Despite the contradiction at the heart of Freud's theory of renunciation, renunciation is, nevertheless, portrayed as a male achievement; those who renounce are men; those who are renounced are women and what they symbolize, namely, sensuality and instinctual gratification. Men's renunciation becomes identified with rationality and progress, and it is exemplified by the idea of the Great Man.[18] Moses' capacity for renunciation and the strict rules he imposed on his followers provided them with a motive to kill him; their guilt, arising from the murder, caused them to reinstate his precepts. For Freud, the stringent precepts of Judaism represent the renunciation of instinctual gratification and this is, for him, what gives Judaism its masculine character. No doubt some of his effort to construct Judaism as masculine lay in his reaction to some of his contemporaries who portrayed it as feminine (e.g., Weininger, 1903; cf. Eilberg-Schwartz, 1994; Gilman, 1993). Perhaps Freud's construction represents his own "flight from the feminine."[19]

The gendered associations are not just about men and women but are intimately connected with the notions of maternity and paternity we have been discussing. Because men were thought capable of lifting themselves out of their dependence on sense perception, "to put their inferences upon a level with the testimony of their senses," the great leap forward was made possible. Freud is referring to the so-called discovery of paternity as well as to the commonplace idea that "maternity is proved by the senses whereas paternity is a surmise and a premise." This "turning from the mother to the father . . . signifies above all a victory of spirituality over the senses—that is to say, a step forward in culture" (Freud, 1939:145–6 [SE 23:114]). Freud reiterated, without quite the same flair, what Bachofen had said eighty-five years earlier. Today, echoes of these ideas are heard behind numerous statements about gender, appropriate sex roles, and intellectual ability.

For both Bachofen and Freud, the "discovery" of paternity marked not just an intellectual advance but also a spiritual one—it had to do with men and women and notions of divinity, deity, and morality—illustrating that for them, at least, gender has ethical and cosmological implications. Marx and Engels eschewed the religious dimension, but they, too, subscribed to the belief that the "discovery" of paternity and the conjectured "overthrow of mother right" ushered in the new age of patriarchal institutions based on property, among which a man could henceforth count his children.

Freud clearly reiterated what many others assumed and continue to assume without question, namely that maternity is self-evident, a matter evident to the senses, an obvious fact of nature, rather than a term that gives a particular meaning to the fact that babies come out of the bodies of women. Paternity, he assumed, was an inference that demanded abstract thought and sophisticated rational processes. Because rational processes have been ranked higher than those of the senses, the notion of paternity marked an intellectual advance by those who made the "discovery."

MATERNITY-PATERNITY

Freud, like so many others, conflates the fact that babies come out of the bodies of women with the *concept* of maternity. What is lost in the conflation is the specific meaning of maternity: it has meant giving nurture and giving birth; it has not meant creation or co-creation. Freud assumes even more about paternity, which he describes but does not examine. In order to make the assumptions more obvious, I return to the work of Bakan because he examines paternity in somewhat more detail and unwittingly allows us to see where the problematic assumptions are. Like Freud, he believes that monotheism is intimately related to paternity and that both represent a cultural advance. The problems stem from the lack of specificity about the meaning of paternity. Bakan gives several commonplace definitions but does not pursue them. In a number of places he states something similar to: "Paternity is the biological fact that men are necessary for the birth of children" (Bakan, 1979:12). Elsewhere he recognized that "in the blush of the biological discovery, men tended to believe that the total genetic endowment was theirs. They were, of course, unaware of what we know today" (ibid.:166).

That, however, is the crux of the problem in several ways, and Bakan failed to understand any of them. He did not explain why men should assume that they provided the entire "genetic" endowment, or why women would accept that explanation. Second, the problem is not just with the ancients and their lack of knowledge. It is also that *we* fail to realize that the absence of genetic theory did not prevent the ancients from constructing a concept of paternity. They weren't just hanging around until genetic theory was invented. Nor did its absence prevent *any* human group from constructing a social role for men.

In other words, Bakan does not realize that paternity was culturally constructed, not discovered. The difference between discovery and construction is vast—it entails different conceptual frameworks for the interpretation of the past as well as the present. To discover something means "to obtain knowledge through observation" (American Heritage Dictionary); it is applicable to science and the investigation of the natural world. To construct something means to build, create, or put an interpretation upon it. Today a growing group of scholars recognizes that scientific observation is, itself, culturally mediated—that scientific knowledge proceeds from, and is relative to, the construction of meanings. The danger in not comprehending this is that cultural notions of gender (and race) often become inscribed in what is usually imagined to be the neutral area of scientific theory.[20]

Paternity is obviously a concept that includes but is not limited to a biological connection. The biological definition has blinded us to the fact that paternity has also meant the primary creative role. The meaning of *father* emerged in relation to a *theory* of procreation; the male was imagined as progenitor, the creator (with God's help) and transmitter of life, and this was encapsulated in the notion of *seed*. For Bakan, male identity was tied to the notion of *seed*, and this was a positive image for him because it conveyed "man's effort to extend the boundary of his ego to include his seed" (Bakan, 1966:202).

Although it may be beneficial for a man to extend his ego boundary, Bakan does not take into account the effect on the female ego beyond acknowledging that the notion of seed "tends to make the male even more important than the female, as seed is the determining factor of the nature of the plant, with the soil, water, and sun playing only an enabling role" (ibid.:202–3). He goes on to say that the "very concept of semen as 'seed' which is deposited in the ground is suggestive that the ego has moved to include the semen" (ibid.:202–3). He means, but does not say, that the ego is male, and ignores "what we know today," that seed is composed of both male and female elements, namely, genes.

No doubt the image of seed helped a man identify with his semen and his child, but that identification was done at the expense of women (could women have an ego?). Women became symbolically equated with the soil, with the material and therefore renewable and exchangeable aspects of existence. Bakan assumes that previously only women were identified with children and therefore only women cared for them; he assumes that only when men imagine themselves *biologically* identified with their children will they begin to care for them. The identification of a man with his seed implied, for Bakan, a "motherization" of the male (ibid.:203) and a reduction in male-female sex role polarity, and it is this image of male-female relations that, he believes, is deposited in the Bible. Rather than causing a reduction in sex-role polarity, I believe this theory of procreation exaggerates it; to me, Bakan has completely misunderstood the implications of what he has said.

I am not arguing that there is no physiological connection between a man and child, but the problem has been that we tend to conflate that understanding with the one that implies that a man, by means of his seed is *the* begetter, the creative agent, the one who has the potential to create and transmit life. The simple, natural image of seed conveys enormous power. Embedded in stories that have been told for generation upon generation, the meaning of *paternity* has been operative not just in the first blush, as Bakan imagines, but for several thousand years.

MONOTHEISM

For Freud, the genesis of monotheism depends on the murder, not the definition, of the father; indeed, he states that without the two murders, the genesis of monotheism would have been impossible (Freud, 1939: 129–30 [SE 23:101]). In his last work, Freud atavistically clung to the idea of an original deed, whereas in regard to his studies of individual psychology he had abandoned that idea long ago. The murder of Moses was the historical repetition of the primal crime, a deed that, for Freud, laid the foundation for human society and morals. What was true of religion in general must be true of what he considered the most advanced type of religion, namely, monotheism. The repetition of the original crime reinforced the pattern of guilt, reification, awe, and worship that characterized the formation of what he claimed was the original god image. At the same time it was an abstraction and condensation of the image of all fathers. So, too, is Abraham.

FREUD'S BLINDNESS—ABRAHAM

Abraham is considered the father of the three monotheistic religions and the Akedah the foundational story. It was, therefore, the obvious place to begin an investigation of monotheism. Freud's own theories as well as his identification with Moses got in his way. Instead of hypothesizing an original murder of the father by the sons, Freud might have considered the attempted sacrifice of the son by the father and speculated about what that might represent. Had he considered Abraham, he might have thought about infanticidal impulses or of a primal murder of the son by the father. And that might have led him to take into consideration the role of Laius in the fate of Oedipus, and he might, then, have given us a theory of the interrelations of father and son. But he might not have stopped there; he might have pushed further and asked about the nature or, better yet, the meaning of fatherhood. Had he done so he would have realized that the relation between father and son has to do with meaning, not just about biology and sexuality, but also about authority and obedience. Indeed, he *did* recognize that in *Moses and Monotheism* but he did not use that insight to rethink his theory of individual psychology.

When Isaac was about to be sacrificed to Abraham's God, he did not cry out; at least no cry has survived. All that remains in the text is silence—silence enough to construct theological and psychological explanations. Usually Isaac's silence is interpreted as his acquiescence—that he performed his filial duty, obeyed his father as his father obeyed God. But maybe he did cry out and maybe his cry was muffled and then obliterated in the text. After all, there was no one there but Abraham to report it.

Freud did not consider Isaac and the Akedah nor its relation to the sacrifice at the heart of Christianity. Had he done so, he might have been led to wonder why Oedipus, unlike another whose feet were pierced with a nail, failed to cry out: "Father, father, why have you forsaken me?" Through the ages, theologians and, more recently, psychoanalysts have tried to drown out that cry as over and over children are sacrificed to the will of the father(s).

PART FIVE

The Social Legacy

CHAPTER TEN

Sacrificing Our Children

TODAY we do not ritually sacrifice children to a deity (if, indeed, such a practice was ever widespread). Yet every day we open the newspaper to learn of another way in which the hopes, trust, opportunities, and lives of children have been sacrificed by the people they depend on and the social, cultural, and religious systems they are taught to have faith in. In this chapter I sketch some of the connections between patriarchal power, as epitomized in the Abraham story, and ways in which children are sacrificed today, for example, through physical and sexual abuse, poverty and the welfare system, and war. To hold the story of Abraham responsible for these contemporary sacrifices would be both ridiculous and an abdication of our own responsibility. But it has had an influence, which, though subtle, is relevant.

This story, at the foundation of the three monotheistic religions, has shaped the social, cultural, and moral climates of the societies animated by them. It provides the supreme model of faith, and it incorporates notions of procreation, paternity, the family, gender definitions and roles, authority, and obedience. It is a symbolic representation of patriarchal power, and the structure, roles, and values that support it. Once these ideas, structures, and values have been internalized psychologically, rationalized philosophically, codified legally, and embedded in institutions such as marriage and the family, the military, and the church, they become part of the reality we live. Examining the assumptions in this foundational story illuminates some of the connections between these seemingly disparate areas and enables us to glimpse the outline of the myth that has shaped our lives and the social legacy we have inherited. Only then do we have the possibility of changing it. Placing contemporary social issues in a wider theosocial context opens up new avenues for research and new ways for revisioning our world.

My purpose is not to imply that religion is essentially or primarily *about* abuse. But it is about power and authority, the abuse of which is all too common. The belief that one has the single, true, right way is easy justification for forcing others to conform or punishing those who remain outside and opposed. More than that, however, power, authority, and sacrifice of the child are embedded in some of the major symbols and stories of Judaism, Christianity, and Islam. Specifically, it returns us to the Akedah, the Crucifixion, and the Kurban—the willingness of the father to sacrifice his child, and the child's obedience and submission to the father.

The story of Abraham is about both faith and male (pro-)creativity—two aspects (sacred and profane) of patriarchal power. These two aspects are related to two different modes of the sacrifice of children: on one side, the sacrifice is morally justified; on the other an extension of paternal right. Abraham showed his love for God by his willingness to kill his son. But what about his love for his *son*? The message to humans, affirmed in all three religious traditions, is that love of God must come first. Without denying that message, something else is added in Christianity—God the Father so loved the world he gave his only begotten son. But what about his love for his *son*? Jesus' will, like that of Isaac, is portrayed as at one with the Father, a complete submission of the will of the son to that of the Father. Theological interpretations of this "at-one-ment" abound; here, I focus on the implications of this sacred model of paternal power for human behavior and morality.

This model implies that to be faithful, fathers ought to be willing to sacrifice their sons if God, or some other transcendent authority, such as the State, demands. The story has been used to justify fathers sending their sons off to war—especially when the war can be imagined as "holy." The faithful *man* is a man whose faith in an abstract, transcendent concept (God) takes precedence over his earthly, emotional tie to his child; his faith renders him invulnerable to human claims.[1] This kind of psychological detachment can be very dangerous, for it can lead to a devaluation of human life. The story also communicates something to sons: it is their duty to obey. Those who do not obey should be punished, for they threaten not just the authority of fathers but also the system that supports them. The model is thoroughly authoritarian.

The authority of the father is, however, rooted in notions of paternity. The father, imagined as the author (with God's help) of human life, as God is of life in general, is symbolically allied with divine power. The child is his, is his seed; the child belongs to him. The logical consequence is that he who creates life has, implicitly at least, the power (and the right) to take it. That *is* God's prerogative as we are constantly reminded in both the Bible and the Qur'an. It has also been men's prerogative: throughout history human males have been the ones to take life—both of animals and other humans, and, more generally, have had the power (and assumed the right) to determine and control the lives of children.[2]

Patriarchal power is what connects the sacred story of the sacrifice with the more mundane but real sacrifices of real children. Obviously, not all fathers abuse their power; this is not a critique of men as people. I do not think that male violence is necessarily inherent in masculine nature; this is not an essentialist argument. Instead, I think the problem lies with the *meanings* of "father" and the ways these meanings have been institutionalized. A man need not be a father to partake of patriarchal power. His procreative ability is part of the definition of masculinity. Nevertheless, children *are* sacrificed in the name of the father, whether that father is the child's own or a surrogate, a priest, or the "fathers of state." This is not to exempt or excuse mothers, but, overwhelmingly, abuse is at the hands of fathers or other men. When it does occur at the hands of mothers it is interpreted differently. It is also predominantly "fathers of state" who make the decisions to send their sons (and now daughters) to war. In the United States, these same fathers recently decided to sacrifice an entire generation of children by cutting off their welfare benefits, thereby depriving them a modicum of access to life, liberty, and the pursuit of happiness.

In the following sections I briefly reflect on the relation between paternal power and these contemporary sacrifices of children. I start with personal and intimate occasions in which paternal power is exerted on children, and move to wider social and global issues. Abraham is not the cause of these sacrifices, but what ties them together are the interrelated meanings of God, paternity, and authority that are given their first symbolic expression in that story. Because the three monotheistic religions that have sprung from the story have exerted enormous power over numerous societies for a very long time, the meanings have been generalized, even secularized.

PHYSICAL ABUSE

Out of every ten children murdered in the world, nine lived in the United States (United Nations Children's Fund Report, see *San Francisco Chronicle*, 23 September 1993);[3] every fourteen hours it is a child under five, every five hours a youth between the ages of fifteen and nineteen (Sidel, 1992, citing Children's Defense Fund report, 1991). Every day we hear that a child has been killed or maimed. It happens all across the country and among all classes of people. It happens on a scale and with means unimaginable in what we so condescendingly call "primitive" societies. Instead, in the most modern, most advanced, most affluent country in the world:

> Children have been whipped, beaten, starved, drowned, smashed against walls and floors, held in ice water baths, exposed to extremes of outdoor

temperatures, burned with hot irons and steam pipes. Children have been tied and kept in upright positions for long periods. They have been systematically exposed to electric shock; forced to swallow pepper, soil, feces, urine, vinegar, alcohol, and other odious materials; buried alive; had scalding water poured over their genitals; had their limbs held in open fire; placed in roadways where automobiles would run over them; placed on roofs and fire escapes in such a manner as to fall off; bitten, knifed, and shot; had their eyes gouged out (Bakan, 1971:4).

Such appalling events would never have been predicted for late twentieth-century America, certainly not by Freud or those influenced by his thought. Freud, as we have seen, believed in evolutionary advance and in the notion of civilization as something won at great cost, mainly by men, through their ability for renunciation. Primitives were assumed to act out their aggressive impulses; in modern society these impulses are supposedly bound. Modern men can only fantasize and become neurotic. And yet an argument diametrically opposed to Freud's could be made—that civilization is the progressive unleashing of aggressive tendencies inflicted anonymously on a large scale as well as on those nearest and dearest (see also Diamond, 1974).

A common assumption is that aggression is *natural*, and thus an inherent part of human nature. This obscures both the *cultural* differences in the expression of aggression and the different *kinds* of aggression, for example, those that are activated (a) in response to direct threats to one's own life or that of one's family, (b) in relation to abstract concepts such as the enemy, the nation, or God, and (c) as a result of anger or frustration. Direct aggression against children probably falls most often under (c), but it need not be carried out in the heat of anger; some punishment is done cooly and rationally. In order not to lay the blame for child abuse at the feet of particular fathers, Bakan situates it in an "infanticidal impulse" that was activated by the "discovery" of paternity. But it was not a discovery about the male's biological contribution to the formation of a child, it was a specific cultural *belief*—that by planting his "seed" he created life, like God. Nevertheless, Bakan's entire discussion is situated in the context of human evolution and human nature, rather than culture.

Bakan does not consider that not all cultures have been seed-planting ones, and that those that are do not necessarily equate semen with seed, or make the seed-soil analogy for human procreation. In Western culture, however, it has served to naturalize male power, prestige, and privilege, and it is woven into the most sacred of origin myths. Human problems are not simply reflexes of human nature, or of economic or political conditions alone, but are related to specific cultures and religious traditions, especially to the stories we tell ourselves, and come to believe, about human nature and the human condition. There is no way of knowing human nature outside of culture, outside of particular cultures.

The sacrifice and betrayal of children is, I suggest, bound up with patriarchal authority, which, in turn, is bound up with the foundation story of our culture. If Abraham was willing to sacrifice his beloved son, how much easier it is to assent to the sacrifice of children who are not loved, not claimed, not "owned." Children hurt today are often not beloved, though that is not always the case; some children are singled out precisely because they are loved, and the abuse, especially sexual abuse, is done in the name of love. Others are hurt or killed because they misbehave or are perceived to misbehave. For example, James Austin, a Pennsylvania man allowed to procure a baby by "surrogacy" despite his evident lack of preparation for parenting, killed his five-week-old son because he was not behaving properly, i.e., he was crying (*New York Times*, 9 August 1995). Other children are punished because they are disobedient, and here, too, punishment can be done in the name of love or in "the best interests of the child." A jury in Texas voted to acquit Forrest Grigg in the murder of his son; the father said, "I did it for him." The son had been smoking marijuana and drinking wine, and for the father "any drugs are dangerous." His son, allegedly, was his pride and joy, but confronted with his disobedience, the father admitted that "There wasn't any question about me killing him" (see *Chicago Tribune*, 17 January 1977).

Still other children are hurt or killed because they are no longer under the father's authority. This was true in several particularly horrible cases in 1995. In Alabama, Stanley Kidd killed his fourteen-month-old twins by strapping them into their car seats and pumping the car full of carbon monoxide. He did this to avoid child support payments and to collect their life insurance (*New York Times*, 2 August 1995). Alan Gubernat killed his three-year-old son when the mother, to whom he was not married, refused to give *his* name to the child (*New York Times*, 16 May 1995). These stories appeared in small columns and could be easily overlooked. The case that received the most media coverage and riveted national attention was of a mother who also put her two children in a car and sent it rolling into a river where they drowned. Only Susan Smith became the target for the accumulated moral outrage of the nation. Her actions were seen as unnatural. But what does the lack of attention and outrage about the crimes of the fathers imply?

Although hardly generalizable, my experience in the 1980s in Chicago, as a volunteer counselor with people accused of child abuse, made me aware of how readily the abuse was justified in terms of the patriarchal authority embodied in religion. The most noticeable characteristic of my clients' stories was the stress they placed on the *obedience* of children and the religious justifications for it, including the story of Abraham.[4] The abuse, among my clients, was most often at the hands of fathers or their surrogates—uncles, brothers, friends. Mothers were not, and are not, exempt, of course, but they are structurally in a very different position. Even though we think of mother and father as equivalent, both equally parents, the argument of this book has been that the meanings and values of the terms and the roles are not only different but hierarchically ordered, and thus, the damage they inflict, even when similar, is interpreted differently.

To my clients, punishment was justified because the parents felt that obedience was their due. Citing sermons from their preachers or the Bible, these people expected that children should be brought up to obey their parents and that they, as parents, could demand obedience. They were acting in place of God and they construed their actions as in the best interests of the child. Although not always explicitly stated, they seemed to have an idea that a child is born bad;[5] therefore it is the parent's role, in fact the parent's *duty*, to train them to be good. Training and discipline were most often accomplished with corporal punishment. And the "most enduring and influential source for the widespread practice of physical punishment, both in this country and abroad, has been the Bible" (Greven, [1990]1992:6).

While these Chicago parents may have overstepped the fine line between punishment and abuse, their views can hardly be considered aberrant since they form a continuous strand in American Christianity since the founding of the nation. Philip Greven, a historian at Rutgers University, has documented the pervasiveness of beliefs about obedience, discipline, and punishment in Christian childrearing manuals and diaries from the seventeenth century to the present in the United States. For example, Jonathan Edwards, a well-known protestant minister-theologian in seventeenth century New England, and his pious wife Sarah believed "that until a child will obey his parents, he can never be brought to obey God" (ibid.:21). And they advised parents to begin to discipline a child early, at least by the time it was six months old, or at the first sign of self-will.

The goal of such punishment is to "break the will" of a child. A child should not have a will of its own but its will should coincide with that of the parent, just as we have been taught Isaac's will coincided with that of Abraham, and Jesus' will with that of God the Father. This obsession with obedience and breaking the will of infants and children continues in a number of contemporary Christian childrearing manuals: "The only issue in rebellion is will; in other words, who is going to rule—the parent or the child. The major objective of chastisement is *forcing the child's obedience to the will of his parents*" (Fugate, 1980 cited in ibid.:67, emphasis added). Another contemporary Christian pedagogue states that the chastisement "should be painful and it should last until the child's will is broken" (Hyles, 1977, cited in ibid.). Hyles tells parents to: "Require strict obedience. This obedience should always be immediate, without question or argument. . . . Obedience is the foundation for all character. It is the foundation for the home. It is the foundation for a school. It is the foundation for a country. It is the foundation for a society. It is absolutely necessary for law and order to prevail" (Hyles, 1977, in ibid.:71).[6] This vision of a totally authoritarian system, in which the will of the father is paramount, seems hardly the foundation for an emergent democracy. Any challenge to the will of the father is felt as a threat to the entire system that supports his power and, therefore, must be dealt with swiftly and forcefully.

SEXUAL ABUSE

Sexual abuse is a more intimate example of physical abuse, in which patriarchal power is specifically but inappropriately aimed at the reproductive part of the body. It has taken us a long time to believe that such abuse was happening, in part because of the belief in the supposedly universal "incest taboo," and in part because of the legacy of Freud. This is not the place to go into lengthy discussions of either the incest taboo or of the Freudian literature about incest, except to say that although all cultures have prohibited marriage and/or sexual relations between certain people construed as relatives, the specific people vary cross-culturally, and, in any case, the prohibition has not prevented the widespread incidence of incest perpetrated primarily by the father.[7] Because of the heterosexual bias and the belief that sex is for the purpose of procreation, theorists did not immediately contemplate incest between father and son. But the "growing awareness that many more boys [than previously thought] are also sexually abused by their fathers makes it impossible to maintain the comparison between human sexual activities and the breeding behavior of animals, to regard the incest taboo as a mechanism which prevents genetic defects in offspring or ensures their evolutionary fitness" (LaFontaine, 1987: 286). In other words, homosexual incest undermines the biogenetic explanations for the incest taboo.

Furthermore, many theorists assumed that "sexual relations between parents and children would subvert parental (paternal) authority" (ibid.: 269). Not until the early 1980s and the emergence of feminist critiques of previous theories, did people begin to understand paternal incest as an *expression* of paternal power and authority (Jenkins, 1992:107ff.; McKinnon, 1995; LaFontaine, 1987). Furthermore, it "was only a mild exaggeration of normal male behavior" (Glaser and Frosh, 1988; cited in Jenkins, 1992:110). Anthropologist Susan McKinnon has observed that the most remarkable aspect in discussions of incest was "the repeated refrain of normalcy. . . . The incestuous father is virtually indistinguishable from any other man in American culture. . . . The high moral and religious profile of incestuous fathers is repeatedly mentioned" (McKinnon, 1995:28). Conventional theorists did not see pathology or perversion on the part of the fathers, but blamed, instead, the "seductive" daughters and the "collusive" mothers (ibid.:31–6).

Freud's theory that the child (usually the daughter, but see the case of Schreber in Freud, [1911]SE 12) harbored sexual fantasies directed to the father exonerated fathers. He did not explore the sexual fantasies of fathers toward their daughters (or sons), or how these may have activitated them in their children. More important, his theory "ignores the issue of power," as Judith Herman, a Boston-based psychiatrist, was one of the first to point out (Herman, 1981:27). A child is "powerless in relation to an adult, she is not free to refuse a sexual advance," and, in any case, "the parent's authority over the child is usually sufficient to compel *obedience*" (ibid., emphasis added).

Incest, of course, is only one form of sexual abuse. Most nonrelative sexual abuse is, nevertheless, committed overwhelmingly by males who are often relatives or "surrogates" for the father—uncles and friends.[8] The issue of power and authority is as pertinent in these types of sexual abuse as in incest, and it is as relevant for boys as it is for girls.This has become especially clear after the revelations of numerous cases of sexual abuse of boys (and some girls) by priests.

Roman Catholic priests, referred to as "Fathers," are the very men who represent God the Father, or at least his will, on earth. They are channels for God's power; they act in his name; they are revered, respected, trusted, and looked up to for moral guidance; the abuse of that trust is, therefore, all the more reprehensible.[9] Because of priests' position, it is perhaps not so surprising that it took so long for anyone to believe that the abuse was really happening.[10] The glacially slow reaction of the church has shown that the church's primary objective was to protect the priests (fathers) identified with the institution, not the children who were hurt and abused. "The *primary* consideration in dealing with cases like these has always been keeping the affair as quiet as possible. The parents and the victims in these cases were more or less ignored," said Rev. Doyle, speaking with amazing candor to *The Boston Globe* (24 October 1992, emphasis added) about the case of James Porter, a priest accused of numerous acts of sexual abuse in several states.

These fathers, hidden behind the legitimating systems of patriarchal authority,[11] are above suspicion, beyond question; they are protected and let off the hook. For the children, however, it is a double betrayal—first by the particular "father" who perpetrated the abuse and second by the church, which, by not believing the child and hiding the abuse, has taken the side of the priest against the child.[12]

POVERTY AND WELFARE

Although physical and sexual abuse captures the imagination and indignation of society, most maltreatment of children is not as depicted in these lurid cases. Summarizing a 1983 report by the American Humane Society, anthropologists Scheper-Hughes and Stein note: "The greatest threat to child well-being and survival in our society today is from neglect, which is broadly defined in child welfare discourse as the 'deprivation of necessities,' or, in other words, poverty" (Scheper-Hughes and Stein, 1987:352). This is reiterated by Penelope Leach, a well-known British child psychologist: "Poverty," she says, "is the single most predictive indicator of risk for children" (Leach, 1994:188) or, more dramatically, "more American children in any five-year period die from causes directly related to poverty than American soldiers during the Vietnam War" (ibid.:185; see also Edelman, 1987, and Funiciello, 1993:17, who claims that poverty is "the number one killer of children in the United States"). All point out how much easier it is to focus on and pathologize a few spectacular cases of abuse than to deal with the more pervasive social and economic problems of poverty. Although poverty does not *cause* violent, physical child abuse, its stress can exacerbate situations in which it is far more likely to occur (cf. Garfinkel, 1992).

Poverty sacrifices the potential of children by depriving them of adequate care and the necessities needed to flourish (food, shelter, clothing, health care, and education). Ironically, during the 1970s and 1980s, when the country became obsessed with child abuse, Republican presidents severely slashed welfare, food stamps, and health and education benefits (Scheper-Hughes and Stein, 1987). One analyst referred to this as a "Time of Sacrifice" (DeMause, 1984), meaning that children were being sacrificed to "Reagonomics." He could not have foreseen that this trend would reach its denouement on 22 August 1996, when President Clinton signed the *Personal Responsibility and Work Opportunity Act*. With one flick of the pen, President Clinton ended "welfare as we know it," established in 1935 as part of a widespread program of social security. His action did not put an end to the problems welfare was designed to alleviate; indeed, the "welfare wars," as Nancy Fraser named them (Fraser, 1989), are just beginning. In signing the act, President Clinton merely fired the first shot.

In order to gain some perspective on the issue of welfare, we need to ask why, in the richest country in the world, millions of children live in poverty without adequate housing, food, child care, health care, and education.[13] Many scholars agree that providing adequate support for all children in the United States is economically possible; indeed, the United States could significantly alter the welfare of all children in the world. What is lacking is the social will to do so (Katz, 1986:272; Leach, 1994: 174). A number of studies have found that the United States does less than almost any other Westernized, industrialized nation in helping to defray the costs that parents shoulder in rearing children.[14] This is a shocking indictment of the social will.

Children's poverty in the United States is increasingly associated with single motherhood and with welfare (AFDC—Aid to Families with Dependent Children). The onus for poverty is placed on the character of the mothers rather than on the abdication of the fathers. Instead of analyzing the social and economic shifts that have made it difficult even for two parents to raise a child and to what Diana Pearce (1978) called the "feminization of poverty," we scapegoat the most vulnerable. The very late and desultory attention to "deadbeat dads" has never reached the level of excoriation poured on welfare mothers. Yet nonsupport of children by fathers is the major cause of women seeking AFDC. Welfare, more accurately, should have been imagined as a *government subsidy of fathers*, instead of a handout to mothers, for it is fathers' income, not mothers' care that it is meant to compensate. That interpretation might have produced more sympathy and support for mothers and children.

We are all aware that it "takes two to tango," a sperm and an ovum to begin the process that results in a child; children of welfare mothers are not the products of "virgin births." Nor are their mothers usually among those seeking the services of new reproductive technologies, sperm banks, artificial insemination, or adoption; they are girls and women who got pregnant by the traditional method, and who, for whatever reason, have been abandoned by the fathers of the children. "A woman who leaves her newborn in the hospital and never returns for it still makes headlines. You'd need a list as thick as the New York City phone book to name the men who have no idea *where* or *how* or *who* their children are" (Pollitt, 1995:20). Most women do not abandon their children; they *are* being responsible, doing what mothers have always done (caring for children or trying to), but in the face of poverty, stigma, and public scorn. Although it may be true that children in single-parent families are at greater risk, are they at risk because there are not two parents (specifically a father) or because there is no money? A number of studies have shown that children in single-parent families do as well and, in many cases, better than those brought up in two-parent families provided there is adequate financial, social, and emotional support (Stacey, 1994; Leach, 1994; Inglis, 1978; Young, 1995). If we were really concerned with the welfare of children, the marital status of the mothers would not be at issue, and we would think of creative ways to nurture and support them.

Economics is not the issue, for many of those who oppose welfare seem willing to spend their tax dollars (1) to put children in orphanages at a cost per child of $40,000 to $60,000 a year—many times an average welfare stipend (*Newsweek*, 12 December 1994); (2) to keep a young prisoner in jail at a cost of $200 a day ($73,000 a year) (*New York Times*, 16 May 1994), but balk at giving his mother $200 a week, a grant that might be enough to help her keep him out of trouble, and, perhaps more telling, (3) to pay foster mothers three to six times what welfare mothers receive to care for their own children. Nationally, AFDC has accounted for only 1 percent of the federal budget, or about $22 billion a year (compared to $300 billion for the military, some of it for things neither necessary nor wanted), yet it receives a disproportionate amount of public attention. Clearly, something besides economics is at stake in the welfare debates.

The almost exclusive focus on welfare mothers has obscured both the physical absence of fathers and, more important, their powerful, symbolic (omni-)presence. Throughout the welfare debate we have been barraged with stereotypic images of the welfare mother—a young, black woman with several children born out of wedlock. Welfare mothers are characterized as irresponsible, lazy, dependent, and the cause of contemporary social ills such as teenage pregnancy, out-of-wedlock births, crime, drugs, and violence. In this view, welfare mothers clearly represent a serious threat to the social fabric. Despite numerous facts that contradict the stereotype, it is, nevertheless, the stereotype that informs popular opinion as well as government policy.[15] It also reduces to one type the diversity of women on welfare and the different paths that led them there—for example, death of a spouse, divorce, disabilities of partner or child, unwed motherhood, inadequate health and child care, and lack of jobs that pay a "family wage."[16]

Single mothers (whether ever married or not) are being punished in proportion to belief in another stereotype—the "traditional" family, felt to be both natural and ordained. Although the word *family* originally meant all those dependent on a male head, and although it still carries some of that meaning, today it usually refers to a nuclear family composed of a married, heterosexual father and mother biologically related to their children. Regardless of whether such a family was really traditional (and a number of studies suggest it was not), it has been resurrected by a group of mutually citing social scientists connected with the Institute for American Values who, despite their conservative rhetoric, convened to inspire the "family values" agenda of the Democratic Party (see Young, 1995; Stacey, 1996). For them, fatherless families are the problem, and their solution is to put a man back into the picture. But they have few suggestions for how to do this or how to make fathers more responsible (Blankenhorn, 1995). Instead, their portrait of the ideal family holds millions of women and children hostage to a standard against which they are measured and found wanting.

The "traditional" family, according to Barbara Dafoe Whitehead, a prominent member of the aforementioned institute, is "responsible for teaching lessons of independence, self-restraint, responsibility, and right conduct, which are essential to a free, democratic society. If the family fails in these tasks, then the entire experiment in democratic, self-rule is jeopardized" (Whitehead, 1993:84). It follows that those outside the "traditional" family cannot teach these values and, therefore, are to blame for the deterioration of society. But it is the welfare mothers, not the absent, and irresponsible fathers, who threaten democratic society; they must be eliminated, at least from public consciousness. No wonder there is a "War on Welfare Mothers."[17]

The double standard runs very deep. Because women have traditionally been held responsible for emotional relationships, they are blamed for not being able to "hold onto a man." Women have also been held responsible for birth control—either they should not have sex or they should be prepared to take the consequences.[18] Studies have shown that more than two-thirds of teenage girls are impregnated by men who are between the ages of twenty and fifty, that is, by men who are far more likely to know about the biology of reproduction and can more easily obtain contraceptive devices such as condoms. A girl might harbor romantic notions of marriage and family, but the men seducing these young women have sex, not marriage, in mind—indeed, many of them may already be married. Nevertheless, there is strong resistance to penalizing the unwed dad. "The attempt to make casual sexual partners behave like fathers sends the wrong message. . . . [I]t is bad policy for the state to enforce a contract that does not exist" (Schiffren, *New York Times*, 10 August 1995). Restated: *fathers are not responsible for their children unless they are married, but mothers are.*

Out-of-wedlock births have been blamed on women, and the term *illegitimate* has been reinvigorated to refer to their children. That term is both ideological and patriarchal, for it means that a child has no man to name and claim it. But why should a child be stigmatized for the "sins" of its parents which are, however, blamed only on the mothers? Why shouldn't every child be legitimate by virtue of being born?

Men have been able to exercise their paternal power (*patria potestas*) choosing which children to acknowledge and care for. There are plenty of men who father numerous children with different women and who take care of *none* of them, yet there is far greater reluctance to infringe on men's reproductive rights, including those of sex predators, than on women's (Bordo, 1993).[19] Men seem to have an inalienable right to reproduce, women only when they are dependent on a man. I have heard of no proposals to limit the reproductive freedom of unwed fathers, but people discuss, quite complacently, the sterilization of welfare mothers, a requirement to have Norplant inserted, and the cutting off of their benefits if they have another child while on welfare.

Even women who have been married can end up on welfare, and the marriage contract does not count for much once they divorce, as the dismal record of child support attests.[20] Child support orders are generally very low to begin with—often less than a man's car payment (Yee, cited in Pearce, 1990:268; Glendon, 1987:92)—but failure to pay is as common among professional, affluent men as among poor, working class men, among white men as among black men. For women, the "average drop in income after divorce or separation is 50 percent" (Garfinkel, 1992:1), and it can drop much lower depending on a variety of circumstances. Nationally the amount of unpaid child support approaches fifty billion dollars, more than enough to offset the AFDC budget. There are, and always will be, some men who are unable to pay because of disadvantages of race, education, disability, and especially lack of jobs, but the same excuses are not extended to the mothers. They are expected to shoulder the traditional male breadwinner role in addition to the traditional mothering, housekeeping role, while men have been relieved of both.

This is the crux of the problem. Women's gender roles and expectations have changed in the past twenty-five years, but men's have not. Rather than face the problems of the family "as we know it," it has been easier to blame and punish the women who, for whatever reasons, are outside of it.

Welfare is, I believe, the fissure that exposes the deep subterranean fault of patriarchy; it is the visible sign of the decline and fall of the "traditional" (patriarchal) family and the values that sustain it. The problem facing our nation has to do with values—there *is* a crisis of values. It is not, however, the loss of "family values" that is the problem, but those values themselves, especially their gender definitions, and the way in which they structure power and authority. "Historically, stable marriage systems have rested upon coercion, overt or veiled, and on inequality" (Stacey, 1996:68). William Julius Wilson, a Harvard social theorist, agrees that "without coercion . . . divorce and single motherhood rates will remain high" (ibid.). The choice facing the nation (and numerous other societies) is whether to coerce women into the "traditional" family and prevent their full personhood, or to develop creative, supportive alternatives for nurturing children. The choice is whether to perpetuate, by force if necessary, the notions of procreation, gender, and family that have been around since the Abraham story.[21] Rather than trying to rein*force* that model, the welfare issue provides an opportunity to examine its underpinnings.

Our culture, especially the religious culture, has long extolled the virtues of motherhood; it is simultaneously a sacred calling and a natural role. It is what women were created for. Freud reinforced this idea when he said: "anatomy is destiny," meaning that women are made to be mothers and that it is in their nature to nurture. The socially important job of childrearing has been perceived as simply one of the "functions" women perform (cf. Okin, 1979:241ff.). The work they do as mothers is a labor of love; it cannot and should not be compensated, which helps explain the difference in attitudes about paying foster mothers but not biological mothers for the same work. Women's "dependency work" (Young, 1995), that is, all the caretaking work expended on children, the sick and disabled, and the elderly, has been done mostly by women, mostly in the home, and it is, therefore, mostly unpaid. *To the extent that men have been exempt from "dependency work," they are dependent on the women who do it*. Men's dependence on women's work is never seen this way, however, because that work has been imagined as an inseparable part of women's nature and role, and thus has not been theorized in either capitalist or socialist economics. Society in general and governments in particular have been getting (quite a lot of) something for nothing.

Carl Degler, a social historian at Stanford, writes: "The historic family has depended for its existence and character on women's subordination . . . [meaning] that a woman will subordinate her individual interest to those of others—the members of her family." He goes on to say that "the equality of women and the institution of the family have long been at odds with each other" (Degler, 1980: vi–vii). The family, quite simply, has depended on "traditional" gender roles, regardless of whether the wife-mother also worked outside the home. Not only was that work imagined as secondary and supplementary, the woman still generally had a "second shift" of housework to do when she got home (Hochschild and Machtung, 1989). Today, whether women work because they have to or because they wish to pursue a career, they cannot do so without a great deal of rearrangment in the family. The problem has to do with the nature of work and careers that have all along been patterned on a male model (Hochschild, 1975)—a model in which the man is relieved of all the "dependency work," free to devote himself singlemindedly to his job. Women are expected to be "like men" in the labor force, but they are not relieved of the dependency work—that is simply subsumed by their gender definition.

Women are handicapped in the labor force because: (a) they have not been raised to think they will be the sole supporters of a family and have often not acquired the skills to obtain a high-paying job, (b) there are not enough jobs, and the kinds of jobs available to women tend to have long hours, and be routine, inflexible, lower-paying, temporary, and often without benefits, and (c) there are unfair wage differentials. Women's wages continue to be lower than men's whether they are doing the same or comparable work. In addition, women must pay for child care which, not infrequently, consumes more than half of their income, despite the fact that child-care workers are often paid less than parking attendants.

Outside the "protection" of the family, a woman with a child or children is expected to fulfill *both* gender roles. Mary Jo Bane and David Ellwood, President Clinton's advisors on welfare, considered this an unreasonable demand: "One parent shouldn't be expected to do the job of two" (Bane and Ellwood, 1994:150), and they resigned when the euphemistically phrased *Personal Responsibility and Work Opportunity Act* was passed. Nevertheless, their assessment of the issues, their goals and solutions were hardly different from those who ratified it. Even though a woman's dependence on a man is considered natural in a marriage, it becomes pathological once outside of it (on the issue of dependence see Fraser, 1989; Fraser and Gordon, 1994; Kittay, 1996). Welfare mothers must be made self-sufficient and independent, and the cure, according to almost all welfare "reformers," is full-time work, thereby depriving the child of the time and attention of the one remaining parent.

Our extreme valorization of self-sufficiency and independence obscures the fact that we are all (inter)dependent—on parents, on each other, on employers, and on government subsidies and contracts. Ultimately, we are all dependent on the children, for they are the ones who will care for us, for the nation, and for the world. We sacrifice them at our peril.

WAR

Since the seventeenth century more than one hundred million people have been killed in war, over 90 percent in the twentieth century (Goldson, 1993:18), and in modern wars, the majority of deaths are of civilians, many of whom are children. "Over the past 10 years, two million children have been killed in wars," others were maimed, were starving, or ill, and still others have witnessed the murder, torture, or rape of their parents, siblings, and friends.[22] War, and preparing for war, consumes people, energy, and money. Worldwide spending on armaments in 1985 was more than $980 billion. Edward Goldson, of the Children's Hospital in Denver, cited a report by Robert Sidel calculating the effects of military spending on children's welfare. He noted that

> it would cost only 1 hour's worth of the world arms spending to eradicate smallpox, that the annual budget of the World Health Organization costs about 3 hours of arms spending, and that the cost to immunize the world's children against common infectious diseases would cost less than 1 day's expenditures on arms. He went on to report that 1 year's spending on Star Wars research could provide an elementary school education for 1.4 million Latin American children, and that the cost of one Trident submarine could fund a 5-year program for universal immunization against six major deadly diseases. (Goldson, 1993:4)

In the United States, a fraction of the $300 billion annual military budget could truly eradicate the poverty of America's children. Instead of funding life, the "military-industrial complex" is taking all of us into its vortex of death. The man alleged to have coined the phrase knew very well the relation between war, welfare, and the sacrifice of children: "Every gun that is made, every warship launched, every rocket fired signifies . . . a theft from those who hunger and are not fed, those who are cold and are not clothed. This world in arms is not spending money alone. It is spending the sweat of its laborers, the genius of its scientists, the hope of its children" (Dwight David Eisenhower 16 April 1953, cited in Edelman, 1987:95). There has been a great deal of feminist theorizing about the nature and causes of war;[23] I wish only to draw attention to the relation betweeen war and the values and structure of the Abraham story. In war, sons (and now daughters) are sacrificed for the "fatherland,"[24] even though it involves killing the sons and daughters of others. Fathers seem to have a right to determine the lives of their sons and to expect obedience or submission to their will. Women are unloyal and unpatriotic if they refuse to go along with this plan. Women's duties are to give birth to future soldiers and to encourage and support war efforts. The sacrifices incurred by war are legitimated with honorable motives and sanctified with the claim that God is on our side (the most recent example is the Gulf War when both the United States and Iraq made similar claims). The job of the sons is to carry out the will of the fathers. Those who balk at the idea or refuse to serve are disobedient and unmanly. To be a real man means to be a fighting man—witness the public debate over President Clinton's avoidance of military service during the Vietnam War.

The story of Abraham was clearly behind *Who Asked Isaac?*, Robert Herhold's 1995 dramatization of the conflict between a father and son over Vietnam. The father wanted the son to join the army and fight in

Vietnam; *his* honor seemed dependent on it. The son did not want to go, but risked losing his father's love and respect if he did not. The son said poignantly, "I thought the first job of parents is to protect their children." The father responded: "I'll love my son when he proves he's a man. How can I love a wimp?" and acknowledged that he would be proud if his son died in the army.

The duty of soldiers is to protect the nation and its patrimony, primarily its land, and this duty is presented as a great honor. War is glorified and the soldiers imagine themselves as heroes (Miedzian, 1991; see also Oliver and Steinberg, 1995, regarding similar sentiments among young Muslim martyrs).[25]

But what is it, asks Benedict Anderson, about that invention of imagination—a nation—that so many millions have been willing to die for? (Anderson, 1983:129) Although the nation-state is a modern invention, the roots of the idea return us to religion and specifically to Abraham.

> Nationalism, as a collective emotional force in our culture, makes its first appearance, with explosive impact, in the Hebrew Bible. And nationalism at this stage is altogether indistinguishable from religion; the two are one and the same thing. God chose a particular people and promised them a particular land. . . . "God said to Abraham: 'Lift up now thine eyes, and look from the place where thou art northward, and southward, and eastward, and westward: For all the land which thou seest, to thee will I give it, and to thy seed for ever.'" (O'Brien, 1988:2–3, citing Gen. 13:14–5; see also Kohn, 1960; and Schwartz, 1997).

This promise of land to Abraham's seed is repeated several times in Genesis; it is the *same* land that is being fought over today. The idea of the unity between a particular people and a particular piece of land is also part of the notion of the modern nation-state.[26] What is often not recognized are the gendered aspects of this configuration.

The land flowing with milk and honey has functioned symbolically as female; those who possess it are symbolically, and often literally, male. If the land is imagined as female, then it is not surprising that male honor can be aroused to protect her virtue and her boundaries from the defilements and penetrations of others. Because sexual metaphors are bound up with nationalism (Delaney, 1995; Mosse, 1985), they are prominent in war (Cohn, 1987; Lakoff, 1990–1; Miedzian, 1991). Sexuality used metaphorically derives from the theory of procreation in which women are likened to soil, land, fields, whereas men are those who possess it, work it, and claim the result. It is in the self interest of men to protect the land and to ensure that the sons do the same.

Sons are not allowed to question: "Theirs not to make reply, / Theirs not to reason why, / Theirs but to do or die."[27] Their duty is to follow orders of their superiors, generally older men. Obedience is perhaps the primary virtue and value in the military. This was brilliantly exposed in the film "A Few Good Men," in which, under orders from their commanding officer, but against their own desire and better judgment, two young men harassed another to death. They were acquitted of murder because the defense argued that they were being good, obedient soldiers following orders; the verdict thus upheld the authoritarian, hierarchical structure of the military.

At the very top of that structure is the president. In the midst of a democracy where the consent of the people is required by the Constitution before going to war, the Father of State, nevertheless, holds godlike power in his hands. He has the right of first strike with nuclear weapons—whose destructive power has been assimilated metaphorically, in a classic instance of "doublespeak," to birth and Creation (Cohn, 1987; Easlea, 1983). He alone can set in motion forces that could annihilate millions of people, if not the entire world.[28] Who will stay his hand? It should come as no surprise that the last chapter in the novel *Fail-Safe* (Burdick and Wheeler, 1962) is entitled "The Sacrifice of Abraham." In it, the president of the United States makes a decision to drop four nuclear bombs on New York City, thereby sacrificing millions of his own countrymen, including his wife and children, in order to honor a deal he struck with another Father of State. An honorable man, he kept his "gentlemen's agreement," legitimating his action by reference to Abraham. Like Abraham's knife held perpetually over our heads, war, and the threat of war, keeps us in submission to patriarchal power.

The Abraham story is, clearly, not just an ancient story but a vividly contemporaneous one. It has, I believe, formed a continuous substrate of moral consciousness for millennia. In times of crisis it is said to resurface to remind people of their faith and to give them courage in their trials. We must ask whether this is the model of faith and the kind of courage we want now.

Conclusion

IN order to stem the tide of sacrifice—of the hopes, trust, health, and lives of children—we need more than economic solutions, we need a revolution in values. We need a new moral vision, a new myth to live by—one that will change the course of history as profoundly as did the Abraham story. I cannot provide such a myth—no one person can do that. Myths are collective enterprises; they emerge from people's experiences of the discrepancies between their personal lives and the myths with which they try to make sense of those lives. Yet, myths, like scientific theory, do not emerge *de novo*, they are always constructed out of old ones. My task has been a critical one, but criticism is not my only goal. By illuminating the assumptions built into the Abraham myth, we can better go about the task of reconstruction.

Abraham is both the father of faith and, symbolically, the first father. His story begins the patriarchal narratives but also dramatically presents the establishment of patriarchy. It is not accidental that the story revolves around a male-imaged god, a father, and a son, rather than female characters, for it involves a new understanding of masculinity, which emerges from a theory of procreation. The story symbolizes the incorporation of the assumption that the male is the generative agent in the procreative process—that by means of his seed he transmits the divine spark of life. The concept of God as creator and male as pro-creator are two aspects of the same system; indeed, I have suggested that the concept of God is a denaturalized or reified paternity, and that of the father, a naturalized divinity. These represent the two poles of an intricately intertwined system that is at once natural and divinely ordained.

In this system, definitions of male and female partake of the order of the universe, yet we know they are mutable and can be changed. Gender roles, if not definitions, are changing, but the process has not been easy. Our theory of procreation has also changed, but the changes have not yet been incorporated religiously, culturally, or emotionally. We assume that procreation is about biology and relevant primarily in medical or scientific contexts. We have failed to see that notions of procreation (coming-into-being) are bound up with a cosmological-religious system. You cannot change one without changing the other, yet the two domains are rarely brought together.

Changes are occurring also in theology and religion. In the past twenty-five years or so, more and more women have been admitted to divinity schools and seminaries. Feminist theologians, ministers, and rabbis are challenging the texts, the concepts, the rituals, the liturgies, and the institutional structures. Others, both men and women, are exploring new forms of spirituality and are forming new religious and spiritual groups. We do not know where all this ferment is leading, but it is through just this sort of process that new myths and metaphors will be forged. There is a sense of excitement but also of crisis—the old verities have become unhinged and there is yet no sight of a new anchor.

The turn of a century, and even more so the turn of a millennium, is a time of anxiety and hope. It forces people to consider both the past and the future—where we have come from and where are we going. Not surprisingly the past few years have shown a heightened interest in the stories of Genesis—there have been several new translations, and the stories have been topics of talk shows, news articles, and television dramas. Most of this recent interpretative effort has been expended to make them relevant to contemporary life, even as they seem like episodes in a soap opera (Rothstein, 1996). Historians of religion, in contrast, attempt to place the stories in their historical context, but in so doing often ignore their ability to escape historical limits and to move from religious contexts to secular ones. Anthropologists have something to contribute here.

Anthropologists have long been aware that "Myth lies at the basis of human society," as historian William McNeill (1986:23) acknowledged. Unlike historians, however, anthropologists analyze people's myths not so much for their historical truth but for the assumptions, categories, and symbols with which people imagine themselves and their world. In addition, anthropologists' lived experiences in other cultures create an awareness that there are viable alternatives to the myths we live by. Such an awareness is related to the often critical perspective anthropologists have on their own society, but it is also liberating—the way things are is not the only possible way.

As we stand at the brink of a new era, more aware than ever that we will all flourish or perish together, we are faced with a choice—to continue along the course charted thousands of years ago, or to try to chart a new one. In contemplating this choice, I ask that people consider deeply the question that motivated this book: Why is the willingness to sacrifice the child, rather than the passionate protection of the child, at the foundation of faith? I ask that people imagine how our society would have evolved if protection of the child had been the model of faith. If I have not completely convinced you with my analysis of the Abraham story, I hope I have at least, raised a reasonable doubt.

Notes

INTRODUCTION

1. Cristos Valenti is a fictitious name, but the man is real and his story is true. It will be told in chapter 2. Anthropologists are required to disguise the identities of the people they study. I chose the name Cristos because of its similarity to Christ, which was, in fact, the real nickname of the defendant.

2. The concept of the "Abrahamic" religions was put to use at the 1992 Summer Olympics in Barcelona. An Abrahamic Religious Center was built, and Jews, Christians, and Muslims worshipped under one roof, albeit at different times. *The Wall Street Journal*, 2 August 1992.

3. In speculating about the impact of the story of Abraham, E. A. Speiser, the well-known commentator on Genesis, contemplated "whether the course of recent history would have changed much if . . . Letizia Bonaparte had given birth to a girl instead of a boy . . . the chances are that the deviation from the original course which the advent of Napoleon brought about would have righted itself in due time. But in the case of Abraham, the detour became itself the main road" (Speiser, 1964:lii).

4. Kierkegaard's *Fear and Trembling* (1843) is the prime example of this type of interpretation.

5. In Islamic tradition it is generally, but not always, believed that the child to be sacrificed is Ishmael, son of Hagar, not Isaac, Sarah's son. This will be discussed in more detail in chapter 7.

6. Another foundational text is Aristotle's *Generation of Animals*. Although it appears to be primarily a zoological text (and thus by today's standards, outdated), the zoology is encompassed by wider cosmological assumptions about "coming-into-being." I am not alone in recognizing the importance of this theory and its consequences for gender definitions. See for example: Maryanne Cline Horowitz (1976) "Aristotle and Women," in *Journal of the History of Biology* 9(2):183–213; Shadia Drury (1987) "Aristotle on the Inferiority of Women," *Women and Politics* 7(4):51–65; Lynda Lange (1983) "Woman is Not a Rational Animal: On Aristotle's Biology of Reproduction," in Sandra Harding and Merrill B. Hintikka, eds., *Discovering Reality* (Dordrecht, Holland: D. Reidel Publishing Co.); The Biology and Gender Study Group (1989) "The Importance of Feminist

Critique for Contemporary Cell Biology," in N. Tuana ed., *Feminism and Science* (Bloomington: Indiana University Press); Nancy Tuana (1989) "The Weaker Seed: The Sexist Bias of Reproductive Theory," in N. Tuana, ed., above; Anne Fausto-Sterling, *Myths of Gender: Biological Theories about Men and Women* (New York: Basic Books, 1985). These feminist scientists and philosophers have rarely addressed the wider, cosmological implications. Feminist theologians, on the other hand, have addressed the gendered images of deity, but few try to bring together these two realms (religion and reproduction) so often imagined as antithetical. For exceptions see Børrensen (1991); Buell (1995); and Hultgård (1991).

7. The man who raises the issue in the film is, in "real life," a psychiatrist who has written about the story; see chapter 9. In addition to the film, Woody Allen wrote a short story about Abraham, as did Philip Roth and numerous other modern writers of fiction. Scott Turow's comments on the story at the end of his book *The Laws of Our Fathers* (1996), closely parallel mine. I only became aware of this after my manuscript was finished, and wish to thank Thomas Slaughter for showing it to me.

8. The term *gate* is often used to refer to female genitals; if other lands or cities are intended by the phrase "thy seed shall possess the gate of his enemies," perhaps they are being figured as female—an allusion that is still very common.

CHAPTER ONE
ABRAHAM ON TRIAL: CASE FOR THE PROSECUTION

1. A variety of feminist approaches to the Bible have been proposed, e.g., Bach (1990, 1993); Bal (1986, 1987, 1988); Bird (1981); Buchmann and Spiegel (1994); Newsom and Ringe (1992); Niditch (1992); Pardes (1992); Schüssler Fiorenza (1985, 1992); Schwartz (1990, 1997); and Trible (1984). But feminist interpretations have, by and large, passed over the Abraham story (e.g., Niditch [1992]; Pardes [1992]; Buchmann and Spiegel [1994]). The latter is a case in point. In their recent edited volume of essays by twenty-eight feminist interpreters of the Bible, not one of them discusses Abraham. *The Woman's Bible*, a nineteenth-century feminist critique of the Bible, especially of Genesis, also does not discuss this story.

2. David Bakan, a psychologist whose work will be discussed more thoroughly in chapters 9 and 10, has recognized the importance of paternity for the story of Abraham, but he thinks the story represents the "discovery" of paternity rather than a particular construction put on the male role in the process of procreation. The difference between *discovery* and *construction* is vast, as will become clearer as we proceed.

3. Cf. Feldman who claims that because the "Hebrew Bible channels all its

'paternal energy'. . . into the image of the heavenly father, it leaves little room for paternal authority within its human drama" (Feldman, 1994:16). However, she does not consider the way Abraham is a channel for God's power—he is assimilated to it so that his acts (and those of other fathers) are imbued with supernatural power.

4. There is, in Jewish tradition, a strand that acknowledges a feminine *aspect* of God, referred to as *Shechinah*.

5. Leach (1961, 1969) and Dundes (1988) are among the very few who have dared to deal with Genesis; a few others have looked at Biblical themes (Douglas, 1966; Feeley-Harnik,1981; Paul, 1996). Even fewer have considered the way in which Genesis may have provided the paradigm for anthropology, albeit in secularized form. George Stocking's unpublished lecture in the Anthropology Department at the University of Chicago in the early 1980s, "Genesis: Anthropology's First Paradigm," suggested that Genesis could be imagined as the paradigm for some of anthropology's concerns, especially the early focus and concern with origins. Genesis incorporates important notions about genealogy and kinship that, I feel, have served as models for constructing genealogies of languages and of human origins, not to mention the anthropological study of kinship as practiced, for example, by Morgan, Rivers, etc. Yanagisako and I (1995) argue that these secular and scientific concepts are transformations from the biblical model.

6. It is not so surprising that it is also precisely the one that has moved in to fill the gap created by the collapse of some of the others, especially the Marxist-communist vision.

7. This idea is commonplace but the use, specifically, of *splendor* is attributed to the Babylonian Talmud, where it is found in a number of places. See Wilken (1976:69) and Spiegel (1969:117, note 148).

8. A particularly engaging and easy-to-read discussion of the parallels is Sarna's *Understanding Genesis* (1966). See also Pritchard (1950); Speiser, (1964).

9. The trials of Abraham have been elaborated primarily in Jewish midrash and will be discussed in chapter 5. There are a number of different lists, and some include material that is not in the Bible, but all of them include circumcision and the sacrifice story.

10. Scholars have argued that the patriarchs could not have been monotheists because the idea did not develop until later. That does nothing to undermine my argument because my point is that monotheism frames the entire biblical story, "In the beginning God created . . . " It was within this guiding framework that the story of Abraham was redacted and given its theological significance.

11. Nor is the story of the sacrifice of Jephthah's daughter (Judges 11:29–40) foundational (cf. Trible, 1978). A story closer in sentiment to that of the two women judged by Solomon is the story of Moses (Exodus 2) where the mother relinquishes her son, the daughter watches what becomes of him, and Pharaoh's daughter rescues him and arranges that he be nursed by his biological mother.

12. This is an example of what Spivak is trying to get at in "Can the Subaltern Speak?" (Spivak, 1988). That is, how does one go about reading texts in which certain voices do not appear? A number of feminist theologians attempt to fill in the absent voices, to reconstruct possible dialogues, or, at least, to register the way women might have reacted.

13. See Yanagisako and Delaney (1995) for an elaboration of this idea. My thinking on this matter was sparked by a lecture given by George Stocking; see note 5.

14. Following are just a few of the relevant books published in the last half of the nineteenth and early twentieth centuries, but they give an indication of the concern with origins: Darwin, *Origin of Species* (1859); Lubbock, *Origins of Civilization* (1871); Morgan, *Ancient Society* (1877); Tylor, *Researches into the Early History of Mankind* (1878); Engels, *Origin of the Family, Private Property and the State* (1884); Kohler, *Prehistory of the Family* (1897); Durkheim, *Elementary Forms of the Religious Life* (1915); and Westermarck, *Origin and Development of Moral Ideas* (1917).

15. Cultural evolution is not to be confused with biological evolution, but means instead an idea that there is some ideal trajectory for human culture to which all cultures will and must conform. It is the kind of theory that permits people to say *preliterate* rather than *nonliterate*, as if literacy were dictated as part of evolution. There are other arguments with the theories of biological evolution.

16. Non-anthropologists often conflate matrilineal with matriarchal, but the two are not equivalent. There are a number of matrilineal societies, but the notion of matriarchy is problematic, most notably because it assumes a reversal of patriarchal society in which women, not men, hold positions of power. This view does not take into account the very notions of hierarchy and power that are supposedly endemic to patriarchy. More important, however, it presumes a notion of "mother" as prior to "father" (I argue that they are simultaneously constructed within a specific theory of procreation) and falls prey to the idea that matrilineal and patrilineal are the only possibilities for thinking of descent.

17. Kinship is an enormously complicated study, and debates continue among anthropologists. For very different views the reader might consult Fox (1967), Schneider (1960, 1972, 1984), and Scheffler (1972).

18. McLennan (1896:273) was a lone voice suggesting that kin terms are merely terms of address; nevertheless, he still believed that kinship *itself* was a matter of sex and blood.

19. For background to this debate, see the bibliography in Leach's paper. Cf. Malinowski (1927); Ashley-Montagu (1937); Jones (1924); Spiro (1968); and my critique of the debate, Delaney (1986).

20. A woman in Madagascar told anthropologist Gillian Feeley-Harnik that the "penis water" is like food that feeds and strengthens a child, like vitamins (personal communication).

21. Marilyn Strathern has said something quite similar with regard to the taken-for-granted division between "nature" and "culture" (1980). Nature has meant something quite specific in the West; I would say it has meant the created universe, created by God. It has a special relationship and specific meaning in monotheistic cultures that also allowed it eventually to be treated as merely the material, physical world by scientists. In other cultures where what we call the *natural world* has different ontological status and place in an overall system, there could not possibly be the dichotomy "nature-culture" as we have come to think about it.

22. If there were alternative theories, they are all but suppressed in the text. Jay (1992) believed she discerned evidence for a matrilineal descent system, but does not speak of what the procreation theory may have been. Her analysis is flawed, however, because she too often conflates kinship with biology. Beginning with the premise that the "mother is always known," she does not ask the further question: what is meant by "mother" and do all peoples have the same concept?

23. Theorists who have been major influences for this position are Saussure (1966), Whorf (1956), Sapir (1951), Benveniste (1971), and Langer (1942). For example, Saussure used a notion of a piece of paper in which one side represented the verbal image and the other the concept, and he noted that you cannot cut one without cutting the other. Moreover, he suggested that the meaning of words emerges in relation to other words; it is not a matter of reference. More recently interest has focused on context, but that hardly excludes the linguistic environment. The work of Fernandez (1986, 1991), Friedrich (1979, 1986, 1991), and Lakoff (1980) on ways that metaphor figures in the imagination is pertinent. David Schneider's work on kinship also loosened the notion that the world we live in is the same world cross-culturally; translation is not merely a matter of changing the labels—different cultures construct different conceptual worlds. See also Handelman (1989) who contrasts rabbinic-Jewish and Hellenic-Christian modes of interpretation.

24. Shelley made that statement to her husband, Holling, on the popular television program *Northern Exposure*. The imagery of seed was further reinforced by his taking up gardening at that time and getting obsessed with the seeds he was planting.

25. Denise Buell's (1995) doctoral dissertation at Harvard is a detailed study of the theological uses of procreative imagery in Clement of Alexandria. She also refers to similar practices among a number of ancient theologians, both Jewish and Christian. Others, notably DuBois (1988), have worked on procreative imagery among Greek philosophers.

26. Another recent example of this thinking can be found in Frymer-Kensky's book *In the Wake of the Goddesses* (1992). For her, paternity means only the awareness that males had a role in procreation, and she dates this discovery to about 9,000 B.C.! She has misunderstood the meaning of *paternity* and thus its relevance to biblical structures and values.

27. Many cultures appear to be male dominant; whether they are really *patri-archal*, having to do with the power of the idea of father, needs to be examined in each case. An article by Seth Mydans in the *The New York Times* (6 May 1997) showed that although men dominated in certain areas of Papua New Guinea, there was no idea that the male was the agent in procreation or that he had any biological tie to the child. Regarding patriarchal societies, we might also consider whether the notion of the male as the primary agent in procreation swept across many cultures at roughly the same time but was incorporated somewhat differently, depending on what had been the prevailing theory among each group.

CHAPTER TWO
ABRAHAM AS ALIBI? A TRIAL IN CALIFORNIA

1. As noted in the introduction, anthropologists are required to disguise the identities of the people they study. *Cristos Valenti* is a pseudonym; it has an unspecifiable, non-Anglo-Saxon ethnic character. A discussion of ethnicity would no doubt have made this a more richly nuanced study and would have explained some of the stereotypes and feelings of the jurors, but it is not the focus of this essay, nor did it ultimately affect the verdict. Neither the deed, nor the reactions to it, are the preserve of any particular group. The specific time and place of the deed and trial have been similarly disguised.

2. An exploration of the historical, archaeological, mythological, and religious interpretations of the story formed a major part of my study at Harvard Divinity School (1973–76) and resulted in an article, "The Legacy of Abraham," in 1977. I intended to write a book on the topic at some time in the future. With this case, that time seemed to have arrived. As I was finishing this book, two similar cases came to my attention. Robert Blair, of Concord, New Hampshire, killed his son (and wife) on 25 March 1996 because "God wants me to sacrifice him to Him—like Abraham and Isaac" (*Concord Monitor* [New Hampshire] 22 October 1996). He, like Valenti, said he "walked in God's grace" because he had done the right thing. Avi Kostner, of New Jersey, killed his two children (25 June 1996) by slowly (over fourteen hours) gassing them in his car. He did it after his divorce because he feared his ex-wife would convert them to Christianity. "I killed them because I loved them and didn't want them to grow up to hate me and Judaism," he said (quoted in Israeli paper, *Yediote Ahronote*, 7 March 1997, p. 21; translation by Sandra Razieli). It was the judge, Jonathan Harris, who made the reference to the Akedah and likened Kostner's son Ryan to the angel who stayed Abraham's hand. The child had called out repeatedly pleading with his father to stop. The Judge said he "violated every commandment in Judaism, in whose name he supposedly acted, in order to justify the murder to himself." (*Yediote Ahronote* 23 May 1997, p. 41).

3. Descriptions of trials are very rare in the anthropological literature. James

Clifford's "Identity in Mashpee," in his *The Predicament of Culture* (Cambridge: Harvard University Press [1988]), is a partial exception. The anthropology of law has been more concerned with customary law in nonstate societies (Max Gluckman, *Custom and Conflict in Africa*, Glencoe, Il.: Free Press, 1959; Sally Falk Moore, *Social Facts and Fabrications: "Customary" Law on Kilimanjaro, 1880–1980* Cambridge: Cambridge University Press [1986]); different legal systems (Lawrence Rosen, *The Anthropology of Justice: Law as culture in Islamic Society*, Cambridge: Cambridge University Press, 1989; June Starr, *Law as Metaphor: From Islamic Courts to the Palace of Justice*, Albany: State University of New York, 1992); the effects of law on differentially located groups (Laura Nader, *No Access to Law*, New York, 1980; Sally E. Merry, *Getting Justice and Getting Even: Legal Consciousness among Working-Class Americans*, Chicago: University of Chicago Press, 1990; Jane Collier, *Law and Social Change in Zinacantan*, Stanford: Stanford University Press, 1973; John Comaroff and S. A. Roberts, *Rules and Processes: The Cultural Logic of Dispute in an African Context*; Chicago: University of Chicago Press, 1981; the construction of legal facts (Clifford Geertz, "Local Knowledge: Fact and Law in Comparative Perspective," in *Local Knowledge: Further Essays in Interpretative Anthropology*, New York: Basic Books, 1983); legal language (Donald Brenneis, "Language and Disputing," *Annual Review of Anthropology* (1988) 17:221–37.); and more recently on court personnel and procedure (Barbara Yngvesson and Carol J. Greenhouse, *Law and Community in Three American Towns*, Ithaca: Cornell University Press, 1994). Truman Capote's *In Cold Blood* (New York: Random House, 1965), may be somewhat closer to what I am attempting.

4. Because ancient Israelites performed blood sacrifice, Jews are, or have been, considered—in the minds of some Christians—more primitive. This prejudice has had disastrous social effects; it has also influenced theoretical work in the history of religions. See Howard Eilberg-Schwartz (1990), for an excellent discussion of this phenomenon.

5. Regarding the sacrifice of animals, see Reynolds v. United States 98 U.S. 145 (1878) and the Massachusetts case *Commonwealth v. Rogers*, 48 Mass. (7 Metc.) 500 (1844), both of which are cited in the *Case of Guiteau*, 10 F. 161 (D. D.C. 1882). See also *State of Missouri v. Roland* 808 S.W.2d 855 (Mo. App. W.D. 1991); *State of Missouri v. Clements*, 789 S.W.2d 101 (Mo. App. S.D. 1990); *State of Oregon v. Rose*, 801 P.2d 839 (Or. 1990); and the case of the *Church of the Lukumi Babalu Aye, Inc. v. City of Hialeah*, 508 U.S. 520 (1993). For a fictionalized account to test the religion clauses, see Stephen L. Pepper, *The Case of Human Sacrifice* (23 *Arizona Legal Review* 897, 1981).

6. Her observation may have reflected some of her class and ethnic stereotypes; the jurors knew that Cristos worked a lot with his hands and did manual labor. They may have expected a dark, swarthy man with large rough hands.

7. The role of the judge is to be an arbiter of the law, that of the jury to be arbiters of the facts. The judge aids the jury on points of law to enable them to

come to a reasonable view on the basis of the evidence. The prosecuting attorney represents the State's interests, not the victim's, and the role of the defense attorney is to puncture the prosecution narrative. I am indebted to Paul Rock for clarifying these points for me (see also Rock, 1993).

8. Trends in anthropology to let the voices speak for themselves (e.g., Kevin Dwyer, *Moroccan Dialogues: Anthropology in Question*, Baltimore: Johns Hopkins Press, 1982; James Clifford, *The Predicament of Cultures: Twentieth Century Ethnography, Literature, and Art*, Cambridge, Mass.: Harvard University Press, 1988) are admirable but problematic because they must always be contextualized. The quest for accurate representation is endless, but it is also selective.

9. Such an argument has been put forth for mediums, particularly female mediums of the nineteenth century. See Alex Owen, *The Darkened Room: Women, Power and Spiritualism in Late Nineteenth-Century England* (London: Virago, 1989).

10. Although several different ethnicities were represented on the jury, there were no obvious racial differences. The three jurors who were of the same ethnicity as the accused were his harshest critics; they thought he had brought shame on the group.

11. A very nice statement of what anthropologists and theologians have noted as the double nature of the holy, and Freud would call the ambivalence of the sacred—something set apart and taboo, something sacred and blessed as well as accursed and worthy of disgust, something respected and feared. Freud (SE 23: 121–2 [1939]). See also Durkheim (1915); and Otto (1923); as well as Freud (SE 13:18–74 [1913].

12. LPS is the Lanterman Petrus Short Act, a mental health law that entitles people who exhibit signs of mental illness to a court hearing; relatives cannot just put them away.

13. The history and thought about trials by jury makes for fascinating reading. Especially colorful is Lloyd Moore ([1973]1988) *The Jury: Tool of Kings, Palladium of Liberty*, Cincinnati: Anderson Publishing Company. But see also *Trial by Jury* (1877), John Proffatt reissued by Fred B. Rothman & Co. (Littleton, Colo., 1986); and more recently, *Twelve Good Men and True: The Criminal Trial Jury in England 1200–1800*, J. S. Cockburn and Thomas A. Green eds. (Princeton: Princeton University Press, 1988); *Juries on Trial*, Paula Di Perna (New York: Dembner Books, 1984); *The Jury Under Attack*, Mark Findlay and Peter Duff eds. (London: Butterworths, or Massachusetts: Butterworth Legal Publishers, 1988); John Singleton (1989), "Trial by Jury: History and Preservation" (*Trial*, 25[7]:90[6]); John M. Mitnick, "From Neighbor-Witness to Judge of Proofs: The Transformation of the English Civil Juror" (*American Journal of Legal History*, 1988, 32[3]:201–35); Lord Griffiths, "The History and Future of the Jury" (*Cambrian Law Review*, 1987, 18: 5–13); James Russell Gordley, "Law and Religion: An Imaginary Conversation with a Medieval Jurist" (*The Journal of Law and Religion*, 1986, 4[1]:193–209); George B. Johnson, "The Development of Civil

Trial by Jury in England and the United States" (*Simon Greenleaf Law Review*. 1984, 4:69–92); James E. Rooks Jr., "In Defense of the Freedom That is Our Birthright: Sources of Trial by Jury in America" (*Trial*, 1983, 19[9]46[6]); Roger D. Groot, "The Jury in Private Criminal Prosecutions before 1215" (*American Journal of Legal History*, 1984, 28[2]:147–63); D. O'Connor, "The Transition from Inquisition to Accusation" (*Criminal Law Journal*, 1984, 8[6]: 351–72. More recently, Jeffrey Abramson, *We, the Jury: the Jury System and the Ideal of Democracy* (New York: Basic Books, 1995) and Stephen J. Adler, *The Jury: Trial and Error in the American Courtroom* (New York: Times Books, 1994). A must for the history of Western law in general is Harold Berman's masterful *Law and Revolution: The Formation of the Western Legal Tradition* (Cambridge, Mass.: Harvard University Press, 1983).

14. That was the assumption of the anonymous author of *A Guide to English Juries by a Person of Quality*, attributed to Lord Somers (London 1682). He alludes to the Bible regarding twelve jurors: the Prophets were twelve, the Apostles were twelve, the Judges were twelve (pp. 9–11). He also noted that "the process by which the 'modern' jury evolved, where jurors ceased to be witnesses [for character] and became judges of fact, began in the thirteenth century" (p. 56) and was largely completed by the end of the fourteenth. Moore (1973, see note 13) cites an account in Greek mythology in which Ares was acquitted by a tie verdict of twelve gods.

15. These dichotomies (rationality versus emotion, objectivity versus subjectivity) and notions of their validity are deeply rooted in Western culture. The classic texts are Plato's *Republic* and Aristotle's *Politics*, but similar views were expressed by Freud in his 1932 letter "Why War?" See also Lakoff (1980).

16. There is extensive theory about jury selection that lawyers learn in law school and through practice, for example, Thomas A. Mauet (1988) *Fundamentals of Trial Techniques* (Boston: Little Brown and Co.); S. S. Diamond (1990) "Scientific Jury Seleciton: What Social Scientists Know and Do Not Know" (*Judicature* 73:178–3); J. M. Van Dyke (1977) *Jury Selection Procedures: Our Uncertain Commitment to Representation Panels* (Cambridge: Ballinger). Since the defense generally has the more difficult task in a murder trial, I asked the public defender what his criteria were for choosing or disqualifying jurors. He said he looked for people who were compassionate and sympathetic and a little unorthodox and independent in their thinking, and he tried to avoid the more rigid law-and-order types.

17. Cf. S. S. Diamond, "What Jurors Think: Expectations and Reactions of Citizens Who Serve as Jurors." In R. E. Litan, ed., *Verdict: Assessing the Civil Jury System* (Washington, D.C.: Brookings Institution, 1993).

18. Cf. Douglas's definitions of *holy* and *impurity*. Dirt or impurity is matter out of place (Douglas, 1978:35) and "Holiness means keeping distinct the categories of creation" (ibid.:53). Keeping the boundaries separate and distinct is part of what the sacred is all about, not just the content.

19. The effect of the structure of space and time on court procedure has been dealt with in great detail by Paul Rock (1993).

20. Ritual has been a central concern of anthropologists. Processual theories of ritual begin with Van Gennep, *Rites of Passage* (1909), and were most elaborated by Victor Turner, *The Ritual Process: Structure and Anti-Structure* (1969), *Dramas, Fields and Metaphors: Symbolic Action in Human Society* (1974), and *From Ritual to Theatre* (1982). See also Sally Falk Moore, *Law as Process* (1978); and Rosaldo *Culture and Truth* (1989).

21. Jurors were also given a set of written instructions to help in their deliberations. Court instructions, and particularly the convoluted and confusing language of such instructions, have become the focus for recent research. See Diamond (1993), "Instructing on Death: Psychologists, Juries and Judges" (*American Psychologist*, 48[4]:423–34); I. J. Severance and E. G. Loftus (1988), "Jury Instructions: A Persistent Failure to Communicate" (*North Carolina Law Review*, 67:77–109). The goal of clarification, however, appears to be to make the outcomes of jury trials more predictable. But if the outcomes of jury trials were more predictable, what would be the purpose of a jury trial?

22. Involuntary manslaughter is also an unlawful killing of a human being. It occurs "during the commission of a misdemeanor which is inherently dangerous to human life . . . or in the commission of an act, ordinarily lawful, which involves a high degree of risk of death or great bodily harm, without due caution or circumspection" (CALJIC 8.45). This definition did not apply to the case at hand.

23. "Our collective conscience does not allow punishment where it cannot impose blame." This is a statement by Judge Bazelon in *Durham v. United States*, 214 F.2d 862 (D.C. Cir. 1954) cited in Morris, 1992:126. Was Cristos to blame for the killing? For sacrifice? For believing in God? For taking biblical stories too literally, for being insane?

24. What's in a name? Names do have psychological resonance. Did the close association of his name with Christ as well as his job as a carpenter predispose him to dwell more on religious topics than he might have otherwise?

25. Jephthah promised that if he won the war he would sacrifice "whatsoever cometh forth of the doors of my house to meet me" (Judges 11:31). It was his daughter. He might have known it would be she or his wife or thought about that when he rashly made the vow. But a sacrifice in fulfillment of a vow is, according to most interpreters of the biblical stories, different from sacrifice that proceeds from God. Jephthah had asked God's help in winning the war; it was an exchange. Such is not the case with Abraham. Although one could argue that he stood to gain everything, this is not the case made by commentators. Instead, they stress that rather than a man keeping his promise by fulfilling the vow, it is God who promises Abraham everything if he proves his faith by being willing to kill his son. The Abraham story is about faith and obedience, and about recognition

of and following a higher authority, a higher law. Cristos was not fulfilling a vow, he was obeying a higher authority.

26. From Christian Scientists who refuse to take their children to the doctor and Amish who refuse to send their children to secular, public schools to the more fanatical cults of the Jim Jones, David Koresh variety, where does one draw the line? Can it be drawn, should it? The definition of religion as belief, rather than practice, is a particularly Protestant notion of religion and conflicts not only with Jewish and Muslim practices but also with those of Native Americans (for example, the peyote trials), Rastafarians, and, more recently, the case of the *Church of the Lukumi Babulu Aye, Inc. v. City of Hialeah*, 508 U.S. 520 (1993) about a Florida group who practice ritual animal sacrifice. Clearly the "free exercise" clause of the religion statutes needs clarification.

27. A curious twist on this idea was related to me by a friend living in Thailand. She told me that the state is encouraging people, especially women, not to make sacrifices *for* their families but to sacrifice their families for the good of the country; to put the nation before their loved ones.

28. Recent cases concerning abortion rights, rights of "surrogate" mothers versus the contracts of the sperm fathers, as well as the rights of the latter in several custody cases against adoptive parents, do give one pause, for they tend to support paternal over maternal rights.

29. Cross-examination is another framing device that can be artfully exploited in trials. The focus of the questions and the way they are framed determines the kind of response one is likely to get. I am grateful to Elizabeth Traugott of the Linguistics Department at Stanford for references on cross examination: for example, James Gibbons, *Language and the Law* (1994); Roger Shuy, *Language Crimes* (1993).

30. In recent years, the public (and the legal profession) has become more interested in the rights of victims to speak at murder trials and at sentencing hearings.

31. Many men, of course, choose not to fulfill that responsibility, as the dreadful state of child support and welfare testifies. Only very recently has there been any attention focused on these "deadbeat dads." Women may not want the responsibility, either, but they do not opt out in such numbers, and they often end up caring for *and* supporting their children.

32. In cases like this the ancient system of *wergeld* makes considerable sense. Then the family of the accused, in this case his parents and siblings, would make reparations to the victim or the victim's family.

33. *M'Naughten's case*, 8 Eng. Rep. 718 (1843) , sometimes cited as M'Naghten. See also *Jones v. United States*, 463 U.S. 354 (1983); *People of California v. Drew*, 583 P.2d 1318 (1978), and *People of California v. Skinner*, 704 P.2d 752 (1985). In the past few years, the insanity defense has undergone renewed scrutiny. Several states (Montana, Utah, and Idaho) have abolished the insanity

defense and others, such as Pennsylvania, allow a verdict "guilty but mentally ill." In that case, the convicted person will receive psychiatric treatment and then serve out his sentence. (*New York Times*, 4 March 1996 in relation to the trial of John Salvi who killed two receptionists at abortion clinics.)

34. Norval Morris, a professor of law at the University of Chicago has written an extraordinary book on "parables of the law" (Morris, 1992). He uses the "persona" of Eric Blair (George Orwell) and descriptions of life and legal cases during his years in Burma to construct stories that will illuminate contemporary legal issues. One chapter, entitled "Ake Dah," is clearly a reference to the *Akedah*. There is also much in it that parallels the California trial, including the issue of voices and the M'Naughten rule. Morris, himself, feels "there should be no special defence of insanity to a criminal charge. The sole issue as to the accused's mind should be: did he, with a mind that was or was not 'sick,' intend or willfully risk this killing? If yes, he is responsible for it; if no, he is not" (Morris, 1992: 124).

35. Barbara Johnson cited in Bal (1988). We should keep in mind who controls the use of language and speaking and remember that in biblical tradition, God created with the Word.

36. While the prohibitions are, apparently, listed in the Talmud, I have also been told that any activities that can be interpreted as transformative through human labor are forbidden, for on the Sabbath the Lord rested. Yet the prohibition about using pens (creation by the Word) or turning on light switches ("let there be light") seem, at least to this observer, to have more to do with imitating acts of creation than they have to do with work. In any case my notes were, of necessity, jotted down from memory when the meeting was over.

CHAPTER THREE
CHILD SACRIFICE: PRACTICE OR SYMBOL?

1. For those wishing to explore theories of sacrifice, the following provide a good beginning: Beers (1992); Frazer (1890, 1913, 1919); Girard (1977); Hubert and Mauss (1898); Jay (1992); Smith (1889); Valerio (1985); and Strensky (1996), and for totemism, the book by that title by Claude Levi-Strauss who provides all the earlier references relative to the debate.

2. The strange division of animals in Gen. 15:9–17 may be a sacrifice, but the reasons for it are very obscure, and it differs from the others in that it is not an offering nor are the animals burnt.

3. The problems with this assumption were pointed out by W. Robertson Smith in his *Lectures on the Religion of the Semites* (1889). Because his conclusion rests on the now discredited theory of totemism, it cannot be taken as fact. Yet it is important for its recognition that the common assumption is dubious at best. "When the full kinship of animals with men was no longer recognized in

ordinary life, all this became unintelligible, and was explained by the doctrine that at the altar the victim took the place of a man" (Smith, 1889:346). The assumption that the ancients were barbaric and would "naturally" practice human sacrifice is particularly noticeable among psychoanalysts, as we shall see in chapters 8 and 9. Freud, for example, thought that the beginnings of society, morals, art, and religion came about through the sacrifice of the primal father.

4. But see Wineman (1980) for a different opinion.

5. A continuous narrative has been constructed from what are considered the "J" documents, *The Book of J* (translated by David Rosenberg, interpreted by Harold Bloom, 1990). It received undue notoriety because Bloom claimed "J" was written by a woman. I heartily disagree. If it had been written by a woman, I think she would not have been so complacent about the notions of procreation, the patriline, and the emphasis on male genitals and fathers and sons.

6. Although many people have begun to use B.C.E. (before the common era) instead of B.C. (before Christ), I have chosen to retain B.C. primarily because I feel that B.C.E. is a euphemism—the commonality still turns on the birth of Christ. Furthermore, Muslims would not consider this a "common" era even though they have much in common with both Judaism and Christianity. B.C. and A.D. can also serve to point out the imperialism of the Christian West. In order to rectify the bias, we need far more drastic means of reconceptualizing time.

7. See *Gods, Graves, and Scholars: The Story of Archaeology* by C.W. Ceram ([1949]1972, N.Y.: Bantam Books) for a very readable account of the work of Schliemann and others whose archaeological discoveries and deciphering skills transformed our knowledge of ancient Greece and the Near East. For a different, and more recent, assessment of Schliemann, see David A. Traill's *Schliemann of Troy: Treasure and Deceit* (1995).

8. Silberman (1982, 1989) has explored the ideological contexts in which biblical archaeology developed.

9. That, too, was the conclusion I had reached quite independently, from speculations concerning a different kind of material, namely a theory and symbols of procreation (Delaney, 1977).

10. Although Genesis 11:31 states that they went forth from Ur of the Chaldees, scholars have debated whether this refers to the famous Ur, in modern Iraq, uncovered by Leonard Woolley between 1922 and 1934, or some other place.

11. See archaeological reports, for example, Lloyd and Brice (1951); Prag (1970).

12. In an earlier article (1977), I made the suggestion that a conflict between different notions of kinship, affiliation, and procreation occurred in Haran in the late third, early second millenium and that the Abraham story reflected the outcome. This is a fascinating topic for scholars of the ancient Near East, but my own interests have shifted from trying to unearth ancient procreation theories to demonstrating the theological significance and social implications of ideas about gender, kinship, and procreation that are expressed in the Bible.

13. Some of this may be related to the suggestion by Parrot (1968:36) that the name Sarah, or more accurately Sarai, is the equivalent of an Akkadian word for *Queen*. The notion of Sarah's possible high status has been used by feminist scholars for a number of purposes. For example, Teubal (1984) imagined her a priestess but situates her in Hebron (in Palestine) rather than in Haran, and Jay (1992) called her a matriarch. Jay may have been influenced by W. Robertson Smith (1889:52, 1903) who argued that the ancient Semites were matrilineal.

14. One might also wonder whether there was a parallel regarding Inanna, the Queen of Heaven, so important in Ur and Akkad as enshrined by Enheduanna, priestess, daughter of Sargon (King of Akkad c. 2250 B.C.) and her lament about the destruction of her temple at the hands of invaders (Hallo and van Dijk, 1968). Kramer discerned a progressive demotion of female goddesses in Sumer over the same period, see "The Goddesses and the Theologians: Reflections on Women's Rights in Ancient Sumer" (Paper presented at the 23rd International Meeting of Assyriologists, September 1974, and at the University of Chicago later that year [personal copy in author's files]).

15. Instead, the remains conveyed an image of an orderly gathering, even a party, for some of the people seemed to have been playing music, others drinking wine. It is possible that they were poisoned; perhaps they were duped but perhaps they submitted willingly. Neither case really qualifies as sacrifice. A more recent example is the mass suicide of Heaven's Gate followers, which were not sacrifices and with which there was no evidence of violence.

16. The phrase is from Harding (1991) in reference to the way mainstream Christians and Americans view "fundamentalists." It is curious, surely, that the latter hurl accusations of ritual sacrifice (including of children), excessive sexual abuse, and Satanic worship at others yet in so doing enliven the idea of these in the minds of their own children.

17. I wish here to acknowledge once again the information, erudition, and material that Professor Jo Ann Hackett of Harvard University generously shared with me.

18. In cases of triple interments, they note that two of the three children were twins (always the stillborn or newborn) without any awareness or discussion of the long-standing, widespread ambivalence, even taboo, regarding twins in a number of African societies.

19. For opposing opinions see Cartun (1975), Weinfeld (1972), Moscati (1983). Several Europeans (especially Italians and French) argue against the practice, whereas Americans argue for it. Both interpretations are ideological and incorporate implicit assumptions; much of this debate reminds me of the debate among anthropologists, discussed in chapter 1, about whether certain "primitive" peoples knew about paternity.

20. Levenson (1993) says the statement should be read ironically. Yet the distinction between murder and sacrifice is often what the exegesis regarding the Abraham story turns on; see, especially, Kierkegaard.

21. Gordon Newby informed me that the two different spellings derive from two different dialects of Phoenician, both of which were transmitted to the classical authors.

22. I do not know where the first child was buried. But if there is a special burial ground in Urfa, there would, in this case, already be infant bones with the bones of the sacrificed sheep, and if the new child also died, his or her bones would also be added.

23. JoAnn Hackett informs me, however, that many of the inscriptions appear to preclude that possibility, because they are predominately in the past tense, a kind of "do et des" or thank you for service rendered. Still, presenting it as if already rendered may have been the proper way to make such an offering. Her work-in-progress on some of these inscriptions will help clarify such matters.

24. Weinfeld claims that there is "no evidence of its existence in Phoenicia" (1972:140). But more recently Sader (1991) reports that a few stelae have been found in Tyre that she thinks resemble those at Carthage. The dates cannot be confidently assigned because the finds were the result of illicit digging. Nevertheless, she speculates that they are seventh to sixth century B.C. with one possibly from the ninth century, and she further assumes that the finds belong to a child cemetery, which she calls a *tophet*. Whether it was a sacrificial site is, of course, another question.

CHAPTER FOUR
CHILD SACRIFICE IN THE BIBLE

1. I am pleased to be able to thank a friend from my Harvard Divinity School days, Jeremy Cott, who made a list of possible examples: a man in the time of Ahab (1 Kings 16:34); by Ahaz (2 Kings 16:3); by Manasseh (2 Kings 21:6); by Jephthah (Judg. 11:31); as an example of breaking covenant (Ezek. 20:26; Jer. 7:31; 19:5; 32:35); by Mesha, king of Moab, who sacrificed his son, also in relation to war, like Jephthah (2 Kings 3.27); and to the god Molech (Jer. 18.10; 32.35).

2. I would like to thank Joan Frigole (Barcelona) for calling my attention to several contemporary practices of "passing through the fire." In parts of Greece, Spain, and Portugal, rituals to purify or cure sick children consist of passing the children through the fire, having them jump over the fire, or, in one case, putting the child in an oven (cf. Handman, 1983; Tolosana, 1979).

3. Day (1989:94) cites Cazelles (1957) and Vaux (1964), and notes that with regard to Vaux this was a development of his position since 1961, when he understood *molek* to mean merely a divine name without connection to the Punic *molk*.

4. As God generally addresses men not women, this kind of admonition could mean several things: (a) indirectly it is a warning to women; or (b) a warning to men to keep watch over "their" women; or (c) that men are symbolically put in

the position of women vis-à-vis God (see Eilberg-Schwartz, 1994, for the consequences of this position for the male psyche).

5. Traditionally, in Turkey, if you asked: "How many children do you have?" the answer would give only the number of boys. Girls were not counted in everyday conversation nor in the census.

6. That is precisely how Levenson responded, when I asked him, after his public lecture in April 1993 at Harvard Divinity School. Not only did he take for granted what needs to be proved or at least explored, but he assumed that social organization can be imagined as separate and prior to its ideological and cultural expression. Such a view presupposes something natural about gender, about family, about social organization that exists prior to or outside of culture. Ultimately, it is a psychological point of view.

7. Some also see parallels in the Sumerian story of the courtship of Inanna and Dumezi, in which Inanna favored the farmer but was encouraged to marry the shepherd. Regina Schwartz sees the story as paradigmatic of the violence of monotheism where identity is constructed in opposition to an Other who is excluded. Her book, *The Curse of Cain: The Violent Legacy of Monotheism* (1997) came out just as this was going to press; our critiques of monotheism are complementary.

8. Jay (1992) is one of the first to address the issue of blood sacrifice and gender. She argues that it is primarily men who are engaged in blood sacrifice—a ritual, she claims, that is as powerful and evident to the senses as giving birth. Indeed, she theorizes that it is a ritual instituted in compensation for being born of women. Through blood sacrifice men establish a transcendent paternity and patrilineage that cannot be impugned by the vagaries of procreation. Nevertheless, a *notion* of paternity is presupposed; she did not explore what it means but only talked about the difference between biological and social paternity, the latter being a symbolic form of the former. Furthermore, she assumed the biological basis of kinship and, thus, the self-evidence of maternity (see chapter 1 for discussion of these points). Because her work is on gender and sacrifice it appears to be very close to mine, yet the differences are significant. Her primary interest is in sacrifice; she begins with the notion/category of sacrifice, which is, she admits, difficult to define cross-culturally. I begin with the foundation story of the three religions which, as I stated in chapter 3, does not have much to do with ritual sacrifice.

9. Weinfeld (1972) argues that "sacrifice" is not intended, at least not for the human being. Instead, he believes that the animals were sacrificed, but that the sons were merely dedicated to priestly service. Others, such as Smith (1975:478) strongly disagree.

10. Ezekiel 20:25–26 claims that God did the same thing with the Israelites, but there is debate about whether this should be taken literally (cf. Vaux, 1961: 444).

11. With regard to Levitical service, Cartun (1975) suggests that after the "passover" all Israelites were devoted to the service of Yahweh because Israel itself is spoken of as the firstborn son of God. When the Levites took over the function of priestly service, other firstborn sons could be redeemed. In his view redemption of the firstborn is not redemption from sacrifice but from priestly service.

12. Even if there is blood from cutting the penis, it can mean very different things depending on culture. The penis, itself, does not have same symbolic meaning cross-culturally. For example, as Bettelheim (1962) and others have remarked regarding the customs of some Australian aboriginal tribes, the penis is purportedly subincised as symbolic of *female* organs. The blood that flowed was apparently meant to be analogous to menstruation. See also Turner (1967) and Renaat Devisch (1993); however, a discussion here of these various practices would deflect the focus of our discussion.

Chapter Five
Jewish Traditions

1. Akedah comes from the root 'aqd meaning "to bind." When the term *Akedah* came into use as the title of this story is a matter of some dispute. Davies and Chilton (1978), for example, argue that it developed in response to Christian theology. For that reason they propose the more neutral "Offering of Isaac." Jews, however, refer to it as the *Akedah*.

2. The term 'olah in Genesis 22:13 is from the root 'alh and means "that which goes up," but it is generally taken to refer to a whole burnt offering (see *Encyclopedia Judaica*, 1979, vol. 14, p. 600).

3. Another possibility, of course, is that the story did not assume real importance until post-biblical times and in relation to developing Christian theology. For reasons discussed in the previous chapter, here, and in subsequent chapters, I am not convinced that this is an adequate answer.

4. The classic statement about this is in Auerbach's *Mimesis* (1957), but this quality is often true of biblical narrative. See also Alter (1981).

5. For a contrary opinion see, C. W. Coats (1973). Van Seters notes that it is usually accepted that verses 15 through 18 are a later addition, but he goes on to say: "The fact that such a notion of an addition is very plausible is not enough to conclude that this is actually the case" (Van Seters, 1975:228–31).

6. If the J source is somewhat earlier than E, then Moberly's idea that these lines are a late insertion is called into question. The apparent contradiction could be resolved if one presumed that they were inserted by an editor drawing on the earlier tradition of J, and maybe that is what he intended. Curiously, the only lines from Genesis 22 mentioned in Bloom's *The Book of J* are 22–4.

7. A few midrashic commentaries suggest that the reason is that Abraham got it all wrong; he misunderstood God's command. Shari Seider, a doctoral candidate at Stanford, informed me that the orthodox Jews in Argentina with whom she worked also took this view.

8. See chapter 3, note 6, regarding use of B.C., A.D. versus B.C.E. and C.E..

9. But for a dissenting opinion see Davies and Chilton (1978). The *Genesis Apocryphon*, the earliest version of Genesis extant, was found at Qumran; unfortunately it breaks off at the announcement of the birth of Isaac.

10. There is a tradition of a parallel oral law handed down to Moses at Sinai along with the written one, as perhaps the basis for customary practice and its codification in the *halakhah*.

11. This group was known as *saboraim* and their work was continued in Babylonia until the eleventh century by those called *geonim*.

12. The same idea exists in Plato's *Symposium*, where older men are imagined to inseminate the minds of their young pupils; both mirror an ideology of procreation wherein the male is imagined as the creative, life-giving agent. See also Eilberg-Schwartz (1994); compare with discussion of ritual fellatio among the Sambia of New Guinea by Herdt (1981, 1982).

13. Jo Milgrom's *The Binding of Isaac: The Akedah* (1988) is another compilation of the earliest sources. For more scholarly work, see Swetnam (1981) and Siker (1991).

14. See, also, commentaries by Nachmanides and Rashi as well as some of the literature regarding the medieval pogroms (e.g., Mintz). The idea of testing the righteous has been used in some interpretations of the Holocaust, see below.

15. The *Encyclopedia Judaica* says that in Jewish law the firstborn is the rightful heir, and this stricture is supposed to apply in polygamous households regardless of the status of the mother. The encyclopedia notes that primogeniture was disregarded in Abraham's case. I suggest, however, that perhaps it did not exist at that time, as all the firstborn sons in Genesis were passed over. See discussion in chapter 4.

16. In Islam, boys are usually circumcised some time between the ages of eight and thirteen. The ritual not only admits them into the brotherhood of Islam but also serves as an early test of masculinity.

17. This story occurs in both Genesis Rabbah and Pseudo Jonathan. Pseudo Jonathan is considered to be later, because it includes the names of Isaac's wives, which turn out to be the same names as those of Muhammad's wives, and thus the work could not have been completed until after the Muslim conquest. Of course, these names could also have been a late insertion.

18. The ten trials are variously listed in the different sources (see Milgrom, 1988:34–45, for an excellent list of the parallels). All include the following trials: leaving the land and home of his father, circumcision, twice passing off his wife as his sister, the banishment of Hagar and Ishmael, and, of course, the Akedah. I

heard about two others while I was in Urfa (Turkey), a town near Haran that was Abraham's home before the migration to Palestine. These are extrabiblical legends involving King Nimrod (Ginzberg, 1909; Firestone, 1990). Because I heard them in a Muslim context, I recount the story in chapter 7.

19. A number of scholars (e.g., Vermes, Hengel, Daly) think that the theological ideas embedded in the Akedah had a powerful shaping influence on Christianity. Davies and Chilton (1978), in contrast, think that Christian theology predates the full development of the Akedah themes and, thus, that the term *Akedah* should not be used prior to rabbinic interpretations.

20. Spiegel notes (1969:55, n. 14) that the Akedah may have been associated among the Kabbalists with Yom Kippur.

21. Melito, a Christian writing in the second Christian century in Sardis, a town in Asia Minor (now Turkey) with a sizeable and ancient Jewish community, made the connection between the Akedah and Passover (Wilken, 1976:58, n. 25), but whether that association came from the Jewish community or whether it was his own way of theologizing the Crucifixion is not clear.

22. Vermes (1961) and others argue for close relationship; Davies and Chilton (1978) think those who assert one are "skating on thin ice"; Swetnam (1981) thinks both go to extremes and argues for a more moderate approach. In addition, "a classical midrash relates that God split the Red Sea for the Israelites departing from Egypt as a reward to Abraham, who had split the logs for his own son's sacrifice" (Brown, 1982:99; cf. Miller, 1983:38), indicating that a strong connection has been imagined for quite some time. See also Genesis Rabbah and Spiegel (1969:114) for other sources.

23. It would be of interest to know the relationship between this custom and the Christian Ash Wednesday, when, at the beginning of Lent, ashes are placed on the forehead. They symbolize the recognition that we are but ashes and to ash we shall return, and they refer to the death of carnality (on Mardi Gras) and the beginning of the life of the spirit.

24. The merit is not just for redemption of sins; it is also attributed to the safe rescue of Israel's firstborn sons through the Red Sea (see note 22, above). This is a good illustration of the idea that Abraham's deed in one place led to an effect in another (Miller, 1983:37). The merit is also thought to have saved Jerusalem, in David's time, from the Destroying Angel, to have garnered forgiveness for the apostasy represented by the Golden Calf, and, finally, to have enabled the resurrection of the dead (Vermes, 1973:206–7). Nevertheless, the notion of merit is felt by some to be in contradiction with the whole tone of the Hebrew Bible; Jews are thought to be saved because of divine patrimony, not by the deeds of a man. Yet, see statement about Abraham's obedience, above.

25. See also Levenson (1993) who includes this idea in the title of his book, *The Death and Resurrection of the Beloved Son.*

26. Some traditions assert that Isaac was seven, whereas others conclude that he had to have been about thirty-seven.

27. It should be clear that I disagree with Kierkegaard's interpretation. To analyze it fully would take up too much space. Briefly, I agree with his desire to find the meaning *in* the existential situation, not in the conclusion. But I do not agree with his eulogy to the individual person, nor with the analogy he makes between what Abraham was going to do and what a mother does in weaning her infant. In one case, the child is to be sacrificed, in the other the mother is helping the child make a transition to the food he will need to grow. Kierkegaard also makes an analogy between what Abraham was going to do and what he, Kierkegaard, did in breaking his engagement with his fiancée. He could not stand her dependence on him and decided to set her free. He needed to see what he did as sacrificing his "own dear girl," and the method he chose to "wean" her from him was to act like a scoundrel. He imagined himself as the heroic martyr. See Walter Lowie's *Kierkegaard* (London: Oxford University Press, 1938).

28. Cristos Valenti used a somewhat similar excuse when he said he wanted to take his daughter with him to AA.

29. Abraham serves as a model in another way; I have been told that when one makes an orthodox conversion, one's parents become Abraham and Sarah.

30. The most popular discussion of the persecutions is S. Spiegel's *The Last Trial* ([1950]1969). But see also S. Eidelberg, ed., *The Jews and the Crusades: The Hebrew Chronicles of the First and Second Crusades* (1977); A. Mintz, *Hurban* (1984); D. Roskies, *Against the Apocalypse* (1984); and I. Marcus, "From Politics to Martyrdom: Shifting Paradigms in the Hebrew Narratives of the 1096 Crusade Riots," in *Prooftexts* (1982, 2[1]: 40–52).

31. Mintz (1984:84–5) claims that their response was different from that of the Sephardim who, faced with similar persecutions, apparently accepted a superficial conversion. This, rather than geographical dispersion, he believes, is the cause of the cultural and moral rift between the two communities.

32. The rite was apparently practiced on the Day of Atonement or on the day before Rosh Hashanah. Dr. Jorunn Buckley has informed me that this rite was being practiced in the United States until soon after World War II. In Yiddish, the expression is something like "kippeh shlagen," which means "throwing the chicken." The rabbi whirled the hen over his head and threw it into the river—it was a "scape-bird."

33. This is not unlike a similar notion in Christian interpretation—the idea that certain events prefigure or foreshadow what is to come, what will be fulfilled. As we shall see, the Akedah is thought to prefigure the Crucifixion. Mintz does not take a stand on whether this mode of interpretation was influenced by Christianity or existed separately.

34. An interesting study might focus on the way the different terms shaped the interpretation of the event and whether, for example, the use of *Holocaust* predisposed English-speaking peoples to think of the events of World War II in relation to the Akedah. Although Israelis also make the analogy, it does not spring directly to mind from either *shoah* or *hurban*. In Turkish, *kurban*, which may be related

to *hurban*, refers specifically to Abraham's (Ibrahim's) sacrifice, and when used more generally, it always evokes that allusion.

35. Among them Wiesel, Zeitlin, Roskies (see Brown, 1982) as well as Steinsaltz (see Cohen, 1990).

36. Compare with sentiments of the young Muslim martyrs, see chapter 7, note 5.

37. A different translation reads "my son can take care of them, and I'll take care of their ideas." See Oz's *Where the Jackals Howl* (translated by Nicholas deLange and Philip Simpson, 1981:49).

CHAPTER SIX
CHRISTIAN COMMENTARY

1. This may be a sacralized theory of progress; conversely, the notion of progress could be considered a secularized version of salvation history. There are, I believe, connnections between this logic and certain forms of the theory of evolution, especially sociobiology.

2. On Easter Sunday and Monday 1994, a film entitled *Abraham* was shown on television.

3. The earliest references to Isaac as a type of Christ are found in The Epistle of Barnabas (7:3) and in the work of Melito of Sardis (cf. Wilken, 1976). It also became a theme in the works of some of the major church fathers, such as Clement of Alexandria, Irenaeus, Tertullian, and Origen. See Schoeps (1946:386).

4. Origen apparently was the first to connect "The Lamb of God" (John 1:29) with the ram of Genesis 22.

5. My own experience is probably neither unique nor particularly common. I vividly remember being punished for asking impertinent questions, such as what kind of God would demand such a thing, what kind of father would obey. And when the answers were unsatisfactory I also recall saying that I could not love that God. So I was punished.

6. See Hayward (1990) for the view that the blood of Isaac has meaning in Jewish religious life independent of any Christian influence.

7. Anthropologist Gillian Feeley-Harnik has elaborated the parallels in *The Lord's Table: Eucharist and Passover in Early Christianity* (Washington, D.C.: Smithsonian Institution Press [1981]1994). The book discussses the significance of commensality and food symbolism in both Judaism and Christianity.

8. A suggestion by Spiegel (1969) regarding provenance seems to make the most sense. He says it is not necessary to assume sequential borrowing; these ideas may have been circulating during the time of the Roman persecutions and they may have developed differently in the different communities of interpretation. Many of the ideas were also common among the Greeks; the hero tradition, whereby the sacrificial death of the hero sometimes expiated the sins of the city,

began in the classical period and continued down to the time of Aesop, who was a contemporary of Jesus. See Larry Wills (in press); Gregory Nagy (1979); Hengel (1981).

9. When I speak of Paul in this way I am referring to St. Paul, the Apostle Paul, the Jew known as Saul who converted to Christianity on the way to Damascus and who wrote a number of letters that are included in the New Testament following the Gospels. He is also credited as being *the* theologian of early Christianity.

10. For an especially thorough documentation of this process, see a book with the same title, *Disinheriting the Jews: Abraham in Early Christian Controversy*, Jeffrey Siker (1991).

11. Interested readers might begin with Daniélou (1960); Lerch (1950); and a special issue of *Cahiers Sioniens* (1952), or they might begin a search in the *Ante-Nicene Christian Library* of works by commentators such as Tertullian, Origen, and Irenaeus.

12. There was, apparently, a strong moral emphasis among the Hellenistic philosophers, particularly those partial to the Stoics; perhaps it is not too surprising to find that tendency in Origen. I am grateful to Robert Gregg, Dean of Memorial Church, Stanford University, for pointing this out to me. The bias against grieving overmuch continues today in certain kinds of "fundamentalist" thinking (see Harding, 1987). It was also implicit in the court trial, where our attention was focused on the killer and not on the mother or child. The mother's grief over the child could not become palpable or legitimately recognized.

13. Curiously, in that play, perhaps alone of all the plays, Isaac wondered whether God had really ordered the sacrifice or whether it was his father's idea. If the latter, then perhaps Abraham would go through with it at another time. (Kolve, 1966:260). Isaac was portrayed as a boy and was not privy to the voice of God.

14. See Creed (1967: 69), and S. J. Crawford, ed., *The Old English Version of the Heptateuch, Aelfric's Treatise on the Old and New Testament and His Preface to Genesis* (1922).

15. I wish to thank Judith Brown (Rice University, formerly of Stanford) for bringing this material to my attention.

16. Jesus could be imagined as waiting for the critical moment to save the world, analogous to the rabbinic idea that the lamb sacrificed in Isaac's stead had been waiting for that moment since the Creation.

17. See volume 4, pp. 81–186 in his *Lectures on Genesis* ed., Jaroslav Pelikan (St. Louis: Concordia Publishing House, 1964).

18. Philo characterizes Sarah's acquiescence to the sacrifice as an act of courage and describes her attitude as manly. See my comments chapter 5. I am indebted to Robert Gregg for pointing out to me that the Greek word *andreia* means courage and derives from *andro* meaning man.

19. See Denise Buell's 1995 Harvard doctoral dissertation on the "seminal"

use of procreative imagery in theological conceptions both Jewish and Christian. The dissertation focuses primarily on the work of Clement of Alexandria, a Christian, but comparisons are made with Philo of Alexandria, a Jew. Another doctoral student, Rachel Rasmussen, shows how these images persist into twentieth-century theology, especially in the work of Paul Tillich. She is working on a theology of birth.

20. This is the position of Galen, as opposed to Aristotle, who thought women had no seed. It is also exactly what I found to be the case during my fieldwork among contemporary village Turks (Delaney, 1986, 1991). Most talked only of the male seed, but in the few cases where someone said that women, too, have seed, they were quick to point out that it was not generative, but merely lubricative. A very strange "two-seed theory" that has been circulating since the 1920s has recently surfaced among the extreme right-wing group called the Freemen. For them the "two-seed theory" does not mean that a man and a woman each contribute a seed to the formation of a child; instead it indicates Jewish versus Christian descent. "God created white gentiles as a superior race, descended directly from Adam and Eve, but . . . Jews descended from a sexual union between Eve and Satan"; that is, the line is still established via the male, either Adam or Satan. This is what the "two-seeds" refer to (*New York Times*, 12 April 1996).

21. If men are thought to produce seed, a woman's capacity has to do with whether she can hold onto it. That is how Turkish villagers explained the roles to me; they did not know of the genetic theory of procreation.

22. Kraemer acknowledges Ann Loades for suggesting this to her. Her own study of ancient Greek religion and society prevents any illusion that there is a direct correlation between religious myth and the actual treatment of women, but the question is nevertheless important.

CHAPTER SEVEN
MUSLIM INTERPRETATIONS

1. "This day I have perfected your religion for you and completed My favor unto you, and have chosen for you as religion Al-Islam," (Qur'an 5:3). *Islam* means surrender to God.

2. I prefer to use the spelling Qur'an rather than *Koran*, but when *Koran* appears in a quoted text I shall defer to that. Similarly, except in quotations, I will use God instead of Allah, Muhammad rather than Mohammed, Muslim instead of Moslem, and for consistency, Abraham instead of Ibrahim even though he is known as the latter in Muslim tradition.

3. The meat is supposed to be eaten immediately and the rest given away or disposed of. In order to deal with both the excess of meat and the health hazards, the Saudi government has recently enabled the meat to be frozen and shipped to poorer Muslim nations, and it has also expended great effort in dealing

hygienically with the carcasses. I wonder why one central sacrifice could not symbolically stand for all, and I also wonder what some future archaeologist will make of the burial sites of millions upon millions of (mostly) sheep bones.

4. I lived and worked in a central Anatolian village, from August 1980 through July 1982, conducting anthropological fieldwork. Prior to the fieldwork, from September 1979 through August 1980, I spent time in Ankara. See Delaney (1991). And I have revisited (July 1986, June 1993, and December 1997). While there, I saw a film called *Adak* (vow) based on the true story of a man who sacrificed his child because of a vow he had made to God. This event occurred in the late 1970s; I had hoped to obtain newspaper accounts to compare with the story of Cristos Valenti but I was unable to.

5. The concept of *kurban* has also been used in time of war. For example, Atatürk, the founder and first president of Turkey, encouraged his soldiers to be willing to become a *kurban* for the country he was trying to create. Anderson (1983) believes that such sacrifice is necessary for the establishment of a nation. The idea is also related to the notion of martyrdom embraced by numbers of "fundamentalist" Muslims; see Oliver and Steinberg (1995), who also point out that the *self*-sacrifice of young boys is, nevertheless, done at the *command* of an older leader. The rhetoric is not dissimilar to that used during the Israeli War of Independence, and the story of Abraham is never far removed.

6. A well-known one is Al-Tabari's (d. 923) *History*, which has recently been published in English. See also the Appendix in Firestone (1990), which lists some of the most popular.

7. Information about Muhammad's life comes from numerous biographies and tales. An early Life of Muhammad was written by Ibn Ishaq (d. 768); for an account of it, see chapter 4 in F. E. Peters (1990). See also Michael Cook, *Muhammad* (Oxford: Oxford University Press, 1983); Sir John Bagot Glubb, *The Life and Times of Muhammad* (New York: Stein and Day, 1970); Alfred Guillaume, *New Light on the Life of Muhammad* (Manchester: Manchester University Press, 1960); Mohammed Rauf, *The Life and Teachings of the Prophet Muhammad* (Kuala Lumpur: Longmans, 1964); Maxime Rodinson, *Mohammed* (New York: Pantheon Books, 1971); Montgomery Watt, *Muhammad: Prophet and Statesman* (London: Oxford University Press, 1964).

8. Forty is a very significant number in Islam as well as in Judaism and Christianity: forty days and nights the ark weathered the flood, Jesus was forty days in the desert, Muhammad was forty when the Qur'an began to be revealed, and apparently Abraham was forty when he began to do battle with Nimrod. On the significance of forty, see Stanley Brandes (1987, *Forty: The Age and the Symbol*, Knoxville: University of Tennessee Press). In the Turkish village where I worked, the forty days after a marriage, birth, or death were considered auspicious as well as dangerous; traditionally the soul "opened" or was thought to be deposited by God forty days after conception.

9. Some versions say that the opening word was *Recite*, but he was supposed

to recite what was presented as written. Since he could not read, it comes down to the same thing.

10. Qur'anic quotations are taken from the popular English version, *The Meaning of the Glorious Koran* (translated by Mohammed Marmaduke Pickthall, published as a Mentor Book from the New American Library, undated). Compare with *The Holy Qur'an* (translated by A. Yusuf Ali, published by the Islamic Propagation Centre International, Durban, 1946).

11. Newby (1989:25 n. 7), for example, cites a number of traditions about its composition.

12. See K. Nelson's *The Art of Reciting the Qur'an* (1986) and compare with R. Alter, *The Art of Biblical Narrative* (1981).

13. See Walter Ong, S. J., *Orality and Literacy*, for an excellent account of the differences between oral and written literature.

14. But note the difference in the kinds of tests from those in the Bible. See Al-Tabari ([c.915]1987:99) for accounts of the tests. According to one, "Abraham was tested with ten Islamic practices: rinsing the mouth, cleansing the nostrils with water, trimming the mustache,* using the toothstick, plucking the armpit,* paring the nails,* washing the finger-joints, circumcision,* shaving the pubic hair,* and washing the rear and the vulva." He goes on to say that "Others have said the same, except that they said that six of the ten commands were to do with the body and four of them were to do with the cultic stations." The six concerning the body include the five starred items plus bathing on Friday, and the four cultic stations are "walking around the Ka'bah, running between al-Safa and al-Marwah, stoning the pillars, and hurrying" (ibid.:100).

15. Although the Qur'anic text does not specify a ram, this is elaborated in both story and art. Unlike the biblical account, however, the ram is portrayed being brought by an angel, specifically Gabriel (Jibril). See Schapiro ([1943]1979) for a fascinating account of the differences between Muslim and Jewish-Christian depictions.

16. Dagorn (1981); but for a contrary view see Crone and Cook (Patricia Crone and Michael Cook. (1977) *Hagarism: The Making of the Islamic World*. Cambridge: Cambridge University Press). F. E. Peters (1990:25), also notes that "the genealogy of the Arabs as descendants of Ishmael was well established, and widely disseminated, long before the coming of Islam." But he does not say whether it was accepted by Jews and Christians or among pre-Islamic Arabs themselves.

17. When the Saracens crossed the Alps in A.D. 970 and captured the Abbott of Cluny, they apparently told the medieval French that Christ had descended from Abraham through Ishmael. See Schapiro ([1943]1979:305) quoting eleventh-century Rodulfus Glaber.

18. In Greek tradition the same kind of oracle was given to Kronos, to Zeus, and to Laius. One of the myths about the baby Zeus is that he was hidden in a cave on the island of Crete. When he grew up he, too, was told that a child would be

born who would surpass him. That child was Athene and her mother was Metis, the goddess "who knew more than all the gods or mortal people. But when she was about to be delivered of the goddess, grey-eyed Athene, then Zeus . . . put her away inside his own belly . . . in order that no other everlasting God, beside Zeus should ever be given the kingly position. For it had been arranged that, from her, children surpassing in wisdom should be born" (Hesiodus, 1959:176–77). The story we remember is that Zeus gave birth to Athene by himself, from his head.

19. See Lazarus-Yafeh (1981) for a good analysis of the pre-Islamic pilgrimage and attempts to Islamize it. Sabbah (Fatna Sabbah. (1984) *Woman in the Muslim Unconscious.* Mary Jo Lakeland, trans. New York: Pergamon Press) describes these goddesses, thought to be the daughters of God, who were worshipped in Mecca before Islam. Some Muslim and Western scholars think verses indicating that Muhammad recognized them have been omitted from the Qur'an; these verses have been known as "the satanic verses"—a term revived in the title of Salman Rushdie's novel. For a more scholarly treatment of the origins of Mecca as Muslim sanctuary, see Hawting (1982).

20. Newby is quoting from Guillaume's translation of Ibn Hisham's "Life of Muhammad," which, in turn, is a recension of the earliest biography of Muhammad, that by Ibn Ishaq. Ibn Ishaq was born in Muhammad's city of Medina about seventy-five years after Muhammad's death and thus must have been privy to numerous stories about him. It is thought that his biography was written during his time at the court of al-Mansur in Baghdad.

21. It has also been used, for example, "by Egyptian fundamentalists in the 1970s for their strategy of withdrawing from corrupt secular society until such time as the state could be overthrown" (Fischer and Abedi, 1990:159). In mystical Islam *hijra* can be the inner migration of the soul away from worldly things that are thought to foster unbelief.

22. According to Newby the rock is, in Hebrew, "the foundation stone." "God is supposed to have stood on this rock and left his footprint there when he formed the earth. In Christian legend Jesus is supposed to have ascended to heaven from this rock, and the footprint is his. In Islamic lore Muhammad stood on this rock on his way to heaven, leaving his footprint. Many Jews believe that the rock supported the Holy of Holies when the Temple stood. The Islamic shrine of the Dome of the Rock now covers this rock. It can be noted that Abraham left his footprint near the Kaʿbah in Mecca when he made his pilgrimage there, thus equating the two sites" (Newby, 1989:30, n. 89). Other stories say that Abraham left his footprint on the stone when he was building the Kaʿba.

23. I am reminded of the humming black monolith that opens and closes the film *2001.*

24. I have argued elsewhere (Delaney, 1991) that the physical, earthly elements that house the divine are symbolically female, whereas the divine that is eternal and transcendent is symbolically male, and furthermore, that these symbolic associations reinforce meanings of human gender.

25. The disparity between the different names, times, and places reminds me

of an incident that occurred in the village in Turkey just before my arrival there
and resulted in a court procedure that continued the entire two years I was there
(see Delaney, 1991:226, and n. 21). There were conflicting statements about
when the incident occurred (the Turkish children's holiday or May Day?), about
what song was played (the "Internationale" or the Turkish national anthem?),
and about who instigated it (the teachers or certain villagers?). This was a recent
incident that all the villagers knew about, yet the recollections did not coincide.
Why then do we assume that there should be consistency with regard to ancient
stories?

26. Schapiro (1979[1943]) notes that this motif is usual in Islamic portrayals
but rare in Jewish or Christian ones; nevertheless it occurs. His research on that
motif in Jewish and Christian art is a fascinating piece of reconstructive history.
Questions—such as, how did the ram get caught in the thicket? was he newly
created in a twinkling?—pose grave theological problems for those who think
God's creative activity was confined to the first six days. The ram in the thicket
symbolized for Christians Christ hanging on the Cross, and the thorns symbolized
the Crown of Thorns.

27. I have written about the Hajj in more detail (Delaney 1990, 1991).

28. Not unlike Augustine's notion of the *City of God*, of which the earthly city
is a mere reflection.

29. I cannot here reproduce all of the details of the marriage rituals any more
than I can those involved in the performance of the Great Sacrifice; for those who
seek to explore this further, consult Combs-Schilling (1989).

30. John Bowen (1992) criticizes Combs-Schilling for the emphasis she gives
to the patriarchal character of the ritual, and cites evidence from Indonesia and
other parts of Morocco to point out alternative interpretations and the ways in
which women participate. But he does not really ask why sacrifice, why this story?
That is the question that concerns me and Combs-Schilling, even though our answers differ slightly.

31. Similar claims about procreative prowess and spiritual power were also
made by David Koresh, Elijah Muhammad, and no doubt others.

32. In order to insure that there will be a bloody sheet, some people give a
couple a chicken or a pigeon to kill so that its blood can substitute for that of the
girl. They seem unaware that girls/women do not always have "intact" hymens
even if they are virgins.

CHAPTER EIGHT
FREUD'S BLIND SPOT

1. In this and the next chapter I am approaching Freud as mythmaker. I recognize that there is a division in the scholarly work on Freud, and rarely is the work
in one cross-referenced by the other. The first group I classify roughly as those
who are concerned more with the scientific or unscientific aspects of his work,

for example, Sulloway (1979); Masson (1984); Neu (1991); Grünbaum (1993); Robinson (1993); and those interested in the relation of his work to his personal and religious beliefs, for example, Bakan (1979); Bergmann (1992); Eilberg-Schwartz (1994); Gilman (1993); Paul (1996); Rice (1990); Robert (1976); Yerushalmi (1991). I am interested in the work of the former, but the latter have been more relevant to my own work. Although gender has been an issue for a number of them, few from either group have considered the importance of a notion of paternity, and those who have, such as Bakan, have conflated it with biology and have not examined its constructedness in relation to a particular theory of procreation. Much of what follows is adapted from my unpublished master's thesis at the University of Chicago (1978), a draft of which had been completed as a term paper at Harvard Divinity School (1975).

2. *Scotoma* means an area of pathologically diminished vision within the visual field, that is, a blind spot (*American Heritage Dictionary*, 1991). The word was used by Devereux (1953) to point out Freud's omission of Laius in his theory.

3. This is not to suggest that the claim is historically accurate, for theologians and historians debate whether or not monotheism, in the sense we think of it today, could have existed for either Moses or Abraham. But it was surely the guiding theme of the redactors who put the stories together in the form we have received. Abraham *is* the first monotheist in the three monotheistic traditions.

4. Notably, Yerushalmi (1991) and Rice (1990), who even link the names of Freud and Moses in the title, but see also Gresser (1994), Geller (1993), and Paul (1996), and articles by Bergmann (1988) and Kaplan (1990).

5. Quotations from *Moses and Monotheism* are from the popular Vintage Books edition translated by Katherine Jones. The wording is somewhat more vivid than in the Standard Edition (SE), but the meaning has not been changed. I have included references to the SE in each case, and use it for all other works by Freud.

6. The passive voice is in the original: *Ich meine die Sage vom Konig Odipus und das gleichnamige Drama des Sophokles. Odipus, der Sohn des Laïos, Königs von Theben, und der Jokaste, wird als Säugling ausgesetzt, weil ein Orakel . . .* (Freud. 1972[1900] "Die Traumdeutung." *Studienausgabe*, vol. 2:265, Frankfurt am Main: S. Fischer Verlag). *Säugling* means a nursing infant and *ausgesetzt* can mean abandoned. I am grateful to Judith van Herik, who graciously checked these points for me and provided the nuanced meanings to some of the words.

7. It may be that with the abandonment of the "seduction theory" (described below), which had focused on actions of fathers against daughters, he did not pursue the role of the father vis-à-vis the son in the construction of the Oedipus complex. Perhaps it also marked his growing focus on intrapsychic as opposed to interpsychic phenomena, a shift more coordinate with his hydraulic model of psychic functioning.

8. *Totem and Taboo*, in turn, followed directly on an analysis of a case of religious delusion (the case of Schreber) in which Freud began to see a relationship

between the Oedipus complex and religion. Curiously, Schreber imagined that he had to become a woman in order to bring forth the new race of humans.

9. For a detailed analysis of the sources used by Freud, see *Freud and Anthropology* by Edwin R. Wallace, 1983.

10. Such claims would be certain to attract the attention of anthropologists. Yet no German, French, or English anthropological review of *Totem and Taboo* appeared until 1920, almost seven years after its publication. Some of this lapse may be due to fact that there were no English translations until 1918, or French until 1923, but that does not excuse the absence of a German review. Some of that lapse may also be attributed to World War I. The response of anthropologists over this century has been ambivalent, to say the least, but many of us, like Kroeber ([1939]1952:309), "though remaining unconverted, have met Freud (and) recognize the encounter as memorable." In all honesty I cannot add the final phrase, "and herewith resalute him."

11. The Australian aborigines became the ultimate "Other" for the West, and every major theorist discussed them—Durkheim, Freud, Malinowski, Lévi-Strauss, etc. See Burridge (1973) for a discussion of this phenomenon. This is not the place to enter into discussion of what defines *primitive* or whether primitive material culture can be equated with primitive social organization or conceptual schemes. In fact, especially in the case of the Australian peoples, the opposite case can be made (cf. Diamond, 1974; Spencer and Gillen, 1899; Ashley-Montagu, 1937; Bell, 1983; etc). Nevertheless, the idea that Australian aborigine religion was *the* most primitive was very popular, and it was assumed by numerous social theorists, for example Durkheim (1915).

12. See Pateman (1988) for a critique of the notion of the social contract. She argues that it is really only between males, that prior to it and behind it is what she calls *The Sexual Contract*.

13. The most important critique was that by Kroeber (1920, 1939). But see also Malinowski (1927). An important summary of the debate is Wallace (1983). My own critique leaves to one side the whole problem of totemism, which has been superbly dealt with by Lévi-Strauss (1962).

14. Freud conflates *wives* with *females* (compare Freud, [1913]1950, pp. 125 and 141). Darwin said *wives*; if that is really what he meant, however, it would presuppose culture, because marriage is a sociocultural ritual. And that would obviate Freud's point that the horde was in a state of nature.

15. Malinowski made a number of excellent points in this connection. Because the primal family was, in Freud's view, not quite human, their behavior would have more closely resembled animal behavior. If that is the case, Malinowski asks: "Why should the father have to expel the sons if they naturally and instinctively are inclined to leave the family as soon as they have no more need of parental protection?" Why would they bother to return to the paternal horde and "attempt to accomplish the cumbersome and unpleasant act of killing the old male?" (Malinowski, 1927:164). Malinowski notes that Freud burdens this

prehuman family with habits and attitudes that would have been lethal for any animal species.

16. The more recent work of Dian Fossey (1983. *Gorillas in the Mist*, Boston, Mass.: Houghton Mifflin) might also challenge some of their assumptions about gorilla behavior.

17. This oversight (or lack of understanding) helps to underscore a point, so often overlooked even by feminists, that male dominance and patriarchy are not synonymous even though they may be related phenomena (see chapter 1, n. 27). Patriarchy demands a notion of *patriarch*—that is, *father*—and *father* is a meaningful term within a specific *theory* of procreation. Paul's (1996) conflation of meaning and biology leads him to conflate *father* with *senior male* and then to naturalize his behavioral traits.

18. In English, the words *testimony* and *testament*, also meaning to bear witness, are derived from *testes*. These associations may ultimately go back to Abraham, for in Genesis a servant swears an oath by placing his hand on Abraham's testicles (Gen. 24:9). The testicles were assumed to be *the* source of human generativity, an inference that was, originally, a matter of faith and belief. Although scientific theory has confirmed the testes to be the source of sperm, it has also shown the ovum to be the other indispensible source of generativity. Even modern interpreters such as Bakan or Paul tend to ignore the role of the ovum. In law, to witness something was originally also a matter of faith, not observation.

19. Indeed, the killing of the father ought to be called *patricide* not *parricide* as so many commentators have done, as it is most definitely not just the killing of a parent, but the killing of the father. Of course, perhaps they, along with Aeschylus, Clement, Augustine, Aquinas, etc., are thinking that the father is the *true* parent. Freud also makes brief reference to the *Oresteia* in connection with the supposed shift from matriarchy to patriarchy, a reference that has become popular in such discussions: "the mother is no parent of that which is called her child, but only the nurse of the new-planted seed. . . . [T]he parent is he who mounts" (Aeschylus, [c.458 B.C.], 1953, Richmond Lattimore, trans. Chicago: University of Chicago Press, 158).

20. See Rubin (1975) and Coward (1983) for excellent critiques of this position.

21. Could Freud have been thinking about the mark of Cain? This insight was provided by Bill Maurer. Perhaps it is also relevant that Freud was, and remained, a Lamarckian to the end of his life (cf. Rieff, 1979:199ff).

22. One could read chapter 1 of *Totem and Taboo* as providing contradictory evidence. In it Freud discusses the extent of *restrictions* on sexual, especially incestuous, behavior among so-called primitives. They were inhibited, he suggests, by their great fear. Anthropologists, generally, eschew psychological motivation and view such rules as relative to the cultural categories that make up a particular sociocultural world.

23. A new twist on this theme has been given by Robert Paul (1996), a psycho-

analytically trained anthropologist. He suggests that the entire Old Testament is an allegory of the primal horde. Furthermore, he thinks Genesis is really only an overture to the main events that happened in Egypt. This is surely an imaginative reading, but it ignores the centrality of the Abraham story and the model of faith and, perhaps more surprising in the contemporary intellectual climate, does not grapple with the gendered aspects of the biblical story nor with their theological or social implications.

24. Perhaps Freud was thinking, unconsciously, of the early death of Karl Abraham—his selected successor—and the continual threats of dissolution of the analytic circle. This conjecture will become clearer as we proceed.

25. Freud does not explicitly state that they also ate him; yet if this was meant to be a repetition of the primal crime, one might conclude that they did. A suggestion has also been made that the manna in the desert symbolizes the body of Moses . . . and later is transformed into the Christian Eucharist.

26. This is related to the theme of renunciation that is so important for Freud's notion of the virile strength of Judaism. See Van Herik (1982) for a superb analysis of the meaning and role of renunciation in Freud's work.

27. His father Jakob, son of Reb Schlomo, had been brought up in a *shtetl*, a Jewish community in Tysmenitz, a town in the East European area of Galicia in which there were Orthodox and Hasidic Jews as well as a group of *maskilim*, members of the Jewish Enlightenment or Haskalah (see Krull, 1986:74–91). Freud himself says that his father "did indeed come from a Chassidic background" (ibid.: 90; *Letters of Sigmund Freud.* Tania and James Stern, trans., New York: Basic Books, 1960:394). Although Jakob Freud tried to leave some of that background behind when he moved from Tysmenitz to Freiburg, he nevertheless continued the study and practice of Jewish traditions. Only when they moved to Vienna, when Sigmund was about three, did Jakob Freud begin to drop dietary observances.

28. Robert (1976:37) argues that it was the stories, not the various social, political, and intellectual movements, that interested Freud.

29. Jakob may first have had the 1848 edition, but the 1858 edition was found in Freud's library. I have seen a copy of the 1858 edition with the engraving; I do not know whether it was included in the 1848 edition.

30. By *Bible story* Freud meant the entire story of the Jewish people as told in the Hebrew Bible. The *Autobiography* was written in 1925 and did not include the line quoted; it was inserted in 1936, no doubt because of his work on *Moses and Monotheism*.

31. The reasons Kaplan adduces for why the psychoanalytic establishment did not take more seriously Wellisch's (1954) argument for a biblical psychology may also apply to Freud: (1) the traditional split between psychology and religion, (2) Freud's own adult opinions about religion, (3) attempts by psychoanalysts to appear scientific, and (4) the general academic idealization of ancient Greek life (Kaplan, 1990:74).

32. Especially as Freud had come across something quite similar not long before, in the case of Schreber (SE 12). Schreber was fixated on the torture inflicted on him by God, even though he could not call it torture. In his illness, Schreber's descriptions of the "rays" of God's love replicated the real tortures inflicted on the child by the father in the form of mechanical devices to improve his posture, keep him from touching his penis, etc. Rather than interpreting that aspect of Schreber's illness as a body hallucination, Freud interpreted it as a defense against homoerotic impulses toward his father. Schreber's father was a famous pedagogue who had written numerous works describing punitive methods of child training, including the torturous items just noted. Freud did not make a connection between the father's intrusive methods and the son's illness; instead, he just assumed the famous father was a good man and an appropriate object of desire. For a more complete analysis see Niederland (1951, 1959a, 1959b, 1960); Schatzman (1972, 1973); and Delaney, Master's thesis, University of Chicago, 1978.

33. That paper, "Amenhotep IV (Ihknaton): A Psychoanalytic Contribution to the Understanding of His Personality and the Monotheistic Cult of Aton," was first published in *Imago* in 1912 and reprinted in the *Psychoanalytic Quarterly* (1935) and in Karl Abraham's collected papers (1955).

34. Kanzer goes on to talk about the theme of the patriarchs bestowing their blessings on one of the sons, and he relates this to Freud's ongoing concern regarding the establishment of his own successor.

35. (1) Freud did not think that Abraham was justified in calling Ihknaton neurotic, for "we all have these complexes and we must guard against calling everyone neurotic" (Abraham and Freud, 1965:118). (2) Freud felt that there was no evidence for Abraham's assertion that if the mother was an important figure, the conflict with the father would be milder. But he did not object to Abraham's assertion that she was an important figure in Ihknaton's life—he was only ten when he ascended the throne and only twenty-eight when he died (Abraham, 1935:543; others say he was twenty-five years old when he died)—nor did he object to Abraham's suggestion of her role in the invention or development of monotheism. This is particularly odd, because Freud felt that monotheism was connected to masculinity.

36. A more virulent fate awaited the images of Ihknaton upon his death.

37. Shengold suggests that he did have such feelings toward Fliess, his former colleague and intimate friend, and that he associated Munich with Fliess, concluding that all these connections brought about Freud's faint.

38. Several of his letters reveal that he also wanted to put the stamp of his ideas on his wife. Regarding betrayal, he once told Rank, in relation to his theory about birth trauma: "with an idea like that any one else would set up on his own" (Abraham and Freud, 1965:352). Rank did eventually set up on his own, as did Fliess, Jung, Stekel, Ferenczi, and others, and it was interpreted as betrayal. "All my life I have been looking for friends who would not exploit and then *betray* me" (Shengold, 1972:143, emphasis in original.) Abraham, the one he seemed to

trust most, the one with whom he felt free to discuss these betrayals, finally received some of the same accusations himself.

39. Ironically, Abraham wrote a paper on the importance of names.

Chapter Nine
Sa(l)vaging Freud

1. Notably Wellisch (1954); Bakan (1971, 1974, 1979); Arietti (1981); Balmary (1979, 1986); Rice (1990); and Bergmann (1992).

2. The change may also relate to Freud's "hydraulic" view of internal psychosexual functioning. Regardless, there is still a social dimension if only because of the need to recognize an "other" and become aware of "difference."

3. In a slightly different vein, Schorske suggested some time ago (1973) that Freud overcame his father by making politics an epiphenomenon of psychic forces because his father had wanted him to have a political career.

4. A much more egregious example of evolutionary-stage thinking is found in Schlossman, (1972:47–9). Sulloway (1979) argues that Freud's thinking was suffused with evolutionary theory; it is, therefore, not so surprising that his followers perpetuated it.

5. The notion of *survivals* figured quite prominently in nineteenth-century anthropology, for example, Spencer, Tylor, Morgan, and McLennan, but it has been discredited by contemporary anthropologists.

6. Such assumptions are encountered in most of the psychoanalysts who attempt to enter the area of anthropology, perhaps none more outrageously than Schlossman, who asserts, as if it is a well-known *fact*, that "matriarchal societies and religions tended to be orgiastic, castrating and cannibalistic." Matriarchal societies, which he uses interchangeably with matrilineal socioreligious cultures, "may have have existed as a transitional stage after the Old Stone Age" (Schlossman, 1972:46). He seems to be unaware that there are a number of matrilineal societies still in existence that answer to none of these outrageous descriptions. Such is the persistence of myth.

7. Had he done so, he would have found considerable evidence that child abuse is absent in a number of "primitive" societies, even if infanticide, especially of babies with gross deformities, is a feature. This is not the kind of infanticide of girls that exists in several highly civilized societies such as China and India.

8. Schlossman makes the interesting point that a firstborn is the first besides the father to pass through the woman's genitals (1972:38–9) and could, therefore, arouse a father's jealousy. Yet he needs to explain why this is important only in the case of firstborn sons, not daughters.

9. She was the third woman in Jakob Freud's life, squeezed between the two that Sigmund knew of. Jakob had been married once, before he married Sigmund's mother, and that marriage gave Freud a number of older half-siblings. Before Jakob married Freud's mother, it appears he had an affair with, or perhaps

even a secret marriage to, Rebecca. This liaison appears to have interfered with Jakob's marriage to Amalia Nathanson, as Freud's birth certificate was altered, indicating that Amalia had been pregnant at the time of her marriage. See Krull (1986); Robert (1976); and Rice (1990).

10. Elsewhere Balmary says that "what the dominating does not want to recognize the dominated cannot know"; the result is that when the dominated tries to question the dominating, to learn the truth, he or she might be told: "That's crazy," or "You're crazy." This is just what happened in the case of Dora and Schreber. For fuller analysis of these case histories, see Schatzman (1972, 1973); Niederland (1959a, b); and my Master's thesis (University of Chicago, 1978).

11. I thank Gaylord Brunolfson for help with translation and discussion of *Le sacrifice interdit*. See Arietti (1981) who calls Abraham the first modern man, proposing that he is the first to have separated spirit from matter and to have raised the issue of human choice for good or evil. Abramovitch (1994) uses a theory of developmental psychology to interpret Abraham as a "spiritual revolutionary."

12. The debate between social contract theorists and patriarchalists can best be studied in a comparison between Locke's *Second Treatise on Government* and Filmer's *Patriarcha* (1680). Yet from a feminist point of view, the debate is spurious, because both focus on, and take for granted, male dominance. Women are excluded from their theorizing. Pateman's critique (1988) is essential reading.

13. Balmary proceeds with a Lacanian discussion of "othering" and "lack" that itself lacks a theory of culture in the construction of difference. This omission becomes most noticeable in her discussion of gender, which is both essentialist and heterosexist because it is based on the essential features of sexual difference—namely, that each has what the other lacks. This is a noticeable problem with a number of the so-called French feminists, and it may be attributed only in part to the lack of distinction in French between sex and gender.

14. So, too, did Woody Allen in his brief reading of the story: When Abraham is ready to sacrifice Isaac, God calls out in a deep, resonant, well-modulated voice . . . "Do you listen to every crazy idea that comes thy way?" Abraham pleads, "But doesn't that prove my love for you?" And God responds, "It proves that some men will follow any order no matter how asinine, as long as it comes from a resonant, well-modulated voice." ("Scrolls" in Woody Allen. [1975] *Without Feathers*, New York: Random House, 26–27).

15. I will not address the work of Abramovitch (1994) in this context, as he is a social anthropologist using the psychological, not psychoanalytic, theory of adult life stages described by Levinson (see Delaney, 1996). He does not question the notion of father/paternity nor discuss *Moses and Monotheism*.

16. Freud discussed the sun in relation to God and paternity in a number of places, for instance, in the case of Schreber (SE 10:81) and in *Moses and Monotheism* (1939:147).

17. Susan McKinnon (1995), for example, argues that father-daughter incest in America is not something totally alien and pathological, but only one extreme along a continuum. See chapter 10.

18. For a much more nuanced discussion of renunciation and its relation to femininity and faith, see Van Herik (1982).

19. In the nineteenth century, genius was thought to be masculine in character; women could play supporting roles such as the muse. Otto Weininger, a psychologist contemporary with Freud, wrote an influential book called *Sex and Character*, which was translated into English in 1906. Aware of Aristotle's tripartite division of soul (and one might wonder about Freud's tripartite division of the psyche), Weininger reinterpreted it in slightly more modern terms: "A woman has an unconscious life, a man has a conscious life, but the genius has the most conscious life. . . . A female genius is a contradiction in terms, for genius is simply intensified, perfectly developed, universally conscious maleness" (Weininger, 1906:189). One can see the echoes of Aristotle's vegetative, sentient, and rational souls. Some of these ideas appear to emerge in Freud's notions of hysteria (the wandering womb) and appropriate occupations for women . . . especially that too much education was psychologically dangerous. See case of Dora, for example, and her final rebellion. (I discussed this in my Master's thesis.)

20. See Ruth Hubbard, *The Politics of Women's Biology* (New Brunswick, N.J.: Rutgers University Press,1990); Sandra Harding, *The Science Question in Feminism* (Ithaca: Cornell University Press,1986); Anne Fausto-Sterling, *Myths of Gender: Biological Theories about Men and Women* (New York: Basic Books, 1985); Emily Martin, *The Woman in the Body: A Cultural Analysis of Reproduction* (Boston: Beacon Press,1987), and "The Egg and the Sperm: How Science Has Constructed a Romance Based on Sterotypical Male-Female Roles," (*Signs* 16: 485–501, 1991); Verena Stolcke, "New Reproductive Technologies: The Old Quest for Fatherhood" (*Reproductive and Genetic Engineering* 1(1):5–19); Sarah Franklin, "Romancing the Helix: Nature and Scientific Discovery" (in *Romance Revisited*. [1995] Lynne Pearce and Jackie Stacey eds., London: Falmer Press). This dynamic becomes especially disturbing when biology is reduced to genetics (cf. Marilyn Strathern, *Reproducing the Future: Essays on Anthropology, Kinship, and the New Reproductive Technologies,* Manchester: Manchester University Press,1992; Adrienne Zihlman, "Misreading Darwin on Reproduction: Reductionism in Evolutionary Theory" in Faye D. Ginsburg and Rayna Rapp, eds., *Conceiving the New World Order*, Berkeley: University of California Press, 1995) and ultimately to "information" (Stefan Helmreich, "Anthropology Inside and Outside the Looking Glass Worlds of Artificial Life," Ph.D. dissertation, Department of Anthropology, Stanford University, 1995).

CHAPTER TEN
SACRIFICING OUR CHILDREN

1. This was expressed in the emotionless response of an Israeli father whose wife and son were killed 13 December 1996 in Hebron by a Palestinian. Just as Abraham was asked to give his son, so, too, this man imagined that he was asked

to give his son for the cause. Emotional detachment has been a mark of the spiritual man for a long time, and it is also an integral part of the model of masculinity. This is the quality Freud stresses in "Why War?" (Freud, SE 22). "More care should be taken to educate an upper stratum of men with independent minds . . . whose business it would be to give direction to the dependent masses . . . a community of men who had subordinated their instinctual life to the dictatorship of reason. . . . Nothing else could unite men so completely and tenaciously even if there were no emotional ties between them" (ibid.:212–3). Freud also applies emotional detachment to love, clearly from the male point of view: "the instinct to love, when it is directed towards an object, stands in need of some contribution from the instinct for *mastery* if it is in any way to obtain *possession* of that object" (ibid.:208, emphasis added).

2. This theme is quite pervasive in literature and film; a recent example is the 1996 film *Shine*.

3. This figure excludes death due to war, which will be discussed below. It is unclear whether the figure includes female infanticide but I presume it does not. Sidel (1996) notes that in 1992, in the United States, 5,279 children were killed by guns.

4. At that time, there were reports in the press about Christian summer camps where a number of children were punished, some unto death, for disobedience.

5. There is no concept of "original sin" in Islam; children do not begin to accumulate sin until puberty. I do not know the status of this belief or its relevance for child rearing among Black Muslims.

6. Alice Miller ([1988]1990) noticed similar patterns in her study of such beliefs in Europe. Both she and Greven discuss the influential theory and practices of the child pedagogue, Daniel Schreber; Freud's misanalysis of Schreber's son's illness; and the commentary about it. See also Delaney (1978) and Inglis (1978).

7. Those interested in the topic might begin with Herman (1981), LaFontaine (1987), and Masson (1984), and consult their references.

8. Freud's (mis)analysis (and betrayal) of Dora is an extreme but obvious example. I have reanalyzed it at length in my Master's thesis (1978). See also Lerman (1986:43–9).

9. A similar abuse of trust was also purportedly committed by nearly two thousand leaders in the Boy Scouts, an organization whose purpose is the development of both the physical and moral attributes of boys. Most of them have since have been removed on charges of molestation.

10. The Church's reaction is not unlike that of the psychiatric, especially psychoanalytic, profession in its refusal to acknowledge that the sexual abuse of children by fathers and father-surrogates was, and is, widespread.

11. The Roman Catholic Church is, of course, another primary example of an authoritarian, hierarchical, and patriarchal system. The pope can command obedience from priests and lay people alike.

12. This was also true in the abuse of children by priests and nuns at the Mont

Providence Orphanage in Quebec, among others. "By declaring the orphans mentally deficient, Quebec and the church had found a way to line their coffers," since the government "paid the church more than twice as much for caring for psychiatric patients as it did for orphans" (*New York Times* 21 May 1993). The greed of the priests who ran the institutions led them to redefine their wards as mentally retarded, a definition and stigma that would follow the children all their lives. One of those children, Hervé Bertrand, now fifty years old, recalls that schooling just stopped. No longer students, they became inmates in a mental institution. Some of them *became* retarded because of the kind of treatment and (lack of) education they received. He and numerous others have described in intimate detail the physical as well as sexual abuse that went on there (see Gill, 1991, and a 1995 television documentary).

13. According to a report prepared for the Carnegie Foundation, at least one quarter of the children in the United States live in poverty (*New York Times* 12 April 1994.) Millions more live near or just above the poverty line. The gap in income between the richest and poorest is widest in the United States and has been growing wider every year (*New York Times* 15 July 1996). In any case, AFDC grants are so low that they have often been half, or less, of what the government has considered the poverty level; in no state have benefits ever reached the official poverty level.

14. See the *New York Times* 14 August 1995 citing the Luxembourg Income Study; see also the Carnegie Report (1994); Handler (1995); Kamerman (1984); Kamerman and Kahn (1989, 1994); Katz (1986); Leach (1994); Sidel (1986, 1996). The two countries that do less than the United States are Ireland and Israel, and, in both, family policies are dominated by religious groups and ideologies.

15. Here are a few well-known facts that have done little to change the myth of the welfare mother: (1) More than half of welfare mothers have been married. (2) Most of the women are working, or have worked, but cannot support their families on their wages. (3) Of women on AFDC the percentage of white women is slightly higher than black, 38 percent versus 37 percent, respectively (Bane and Ellwood, 1994); admittedly, this represents a higher proportion, in relation to their own group, of black women on AFDC than white. (4) Of children born out of wedlock, the percentage to white women is almost 60 percent and to black women about 40 percent (Young, 1995:539, taken from *Statistical Abstracts, 1993–4*, U.S. Bureau of Census). (5) Less than 3 percent of poor families are headed by women younger than nineteen. (Women's Committee of One Hundred, *New York Times* 8 August 1995. MacCurdy and O'Brien-Stain's recent California study revealed that almost no AFDC families have ever had a teenage mother, *San Francisco Chronicle*, 11 February 1997, and *Stanford Report*, 19 February 1997.) Teenage pregnancy has actually been decreasing since the 1950s. What is different is that teens are having the babies and keeping them. (6) Most welfare recipients have one or two children, about the same as, or slightly lower than, the national average. And (7) the average time on welfare has been about

two years (see Bane and Ellwood [1994], and the Women's Committee of One Hundred, cited above).

16. Men have been the beneficiaries of the "family wage," established in the late nineteenth century to enable men to support a family (cf. Sapiro, 1990; Folbre, 1991). Because of views of women's roles, primarily as mothers, women's wages remained low relative to men's and, like their role in procreation, were imagined as secondary and supportive. In addition, women were, until quite recently, barred from many of the more lucrative professions. Since so many women are now the sole supporters of their families, a kinder, gentler solution would be to pay women the "family wage."

17. It might we worthwhile to ask what has happened between President Johnson's "War on Poverty" and the current "War on Welfare Mothers" (cover of *Time* magazine 20 June 1994). Why war? Why mothers?

18. *Metro* (a weekly paper in California's Santa Clara Valley) featured a cover story (14–16 November 1996, 12[3]), "Do Men Have A Choice?" in which men claimed "entrapment" and no legal escape from the obligations of "accidental" fatherhood. However, since none of the men cited were taking responsibility for birth control, fatherhood was hardly accidental.

19. See the *New York Times* (27 August 1996) discussing a proposal to use drugs to decrease the sexual desire of felons convicted of child molestation. The use of the term *castration* is inflammatory for it is not castration that is being proposed. The drugs are related to hormones used for female birth control and menopause. Those opposed to this procedure claim it interferes with men's *right* to procreate. Such opposition was not raised when proposals for chemical or surgical sterilization of welfare mothers was discussed.

20. Noncompliance with court-ordered child support can mean anything from zero compliance to partial and sporadic compliance. The *New York Times* reported 17 July 1997 that failure to pay court-ordered child support occurs in four out of five cases. Until quite recently the money was generally paid directly to the woman; thus, it became her responsibility to hire a lawyer and sue if she did not receive the support. Without any money, that is extremely difficult. A few states now require payments to go through the court, which enables the states to pursue fathers (and some mothers) who do not comply with the court order. But the above mentioned article noted that "Federal efforts to help states increase compliance rates have failed," and several Congress members have proposed turning collection over to the IRS. In California, a few state congress members have proposed making nonpayment a felony.

21. Margaret Atwood's *The Handmaid's Tale* is a powerful and terrifying vision of just what this might entail. Although the book is a work of fiction, Atwood has stated that she took many of the separate parts from stories in the contemporary press; that is, many of the parts already exist. Moreover, the story is grounded in biblical forms and values.

22. Anthony Lewis, *New York Times* (29 December 1996), citing a report

entitled "The Impact of Armed Conflict on Children." He also reported that in Angola alone, eight thousand children have had "limbs amputated after land-mine explosions" and notes that there "are still 10 million mines under Angolan soil." Many other children are being used as soldiers. (See also "Valentina's Nightmare," *Frontline's* report on Rwanda).

23. Generally, the theorists relate war to dominant notions of *masculinity* that encourage certain attitudes and behaviors. For a start see Cohn (1987); Enloe (1990); Elshtain and Tobias (1990); Jeffords (1989); and Miedzian (1991).

24. *Fatherland* refers more to the conceptual reality of the nation; the soil, itself, is still very much figured as symbolically female. So even when the term *motherland* is used, as in Turkey, it generally refers to the physical aspects of the nation while *father* symbolizes the state (cf. Delaney, 1995).

25. The "fathers of state" who commit their "sons" (and daughters) to war have, more often than not, never experienced the horrible day-to-day combat and trench warfare (Miedzian, 1991).

26. In Christianity, the idea was allegorized, and the Promised Land came to mean Heaven, although it also figured prominently in the imaginations of the first explorers and settlers of America.

27. Lines 13 through 15 from Alfred Lord Tennyson's 1854 poem, "The Charge of the Light Brigade," depicting a sacrificial battle ([1951] *Selected Poetry of Tennyson*, Douglas Bush, ed., New York: The Modern Library, Random House, pp. 253–4).

28. "During his own impeachment proceedings, Richard Nixon said to a group of Congressmen, 'I can go into my office and pick up the telephone and in 25 minutes 70 million people would be dead'" (Scarry, 1992:25).

Select Bibliography

Abraham, Hilda C. and Ernst L. Freud, eds. (1965) *A Psycho-Analytic Dialogue: The Letters of Sigmund Freud and Karl Abraham 1907–1926*. New York: Basic Books.

Abraham, Karl. ([1912] 1935) "Amenhotep IV (Ikhnaton). A Psychoanalytic Contribution to the Understanding of His Personality and the Monotheistic Cult of Aton." *Psychoanalytic Quarterly* 4:537–69. First published in German (1912) in *Imago* 1:334–60 and reprinted in Abraham, K. (1955), 262–90.

———. (1955) *Clinical Papers and Essays on Psycho-Analysis*. New York: Brunner/Mazel.

Abramovitch, Henry Hanoch. (1994) *The First Father. Abraham: The Psychology and Culture of a Spiritual Revolutionary*. Lanham, Md: University Press of America.

Abramson, Glenda. (1990) "The Reinterpretation of the Akedah in Modern Hebrew Poetry." *Journal of Jewish Studies* 41(1):101–14.

Albright, William. (1950) *The Biblical Period*. Pittsburgh: Biblical Colloquium.

Allegro, John M. (1970) *The Sacred Mushroom and the Cross*. New York: Doubleday.

Alter, Robert. (1981) *The Art of Biblical Narrative*. New York: Basic Books.

Anderson, Benedict. (1983) *Imagined Communities*. London: Verso.

Anderson, Bernhard. (1988) "Abraham, the Friend of God." *Interpretation*. 42(4):353–66.

Arieti, Silvano. (1981) *Abraham and the Contemporary Mind*. New York: Basic Books.

Asad, Muhammad. (1954) *The Road to Mecca*. New York: Simon and Schuster.

Ashley-Montagu, M. F. (1937) *Coming into Being among the Australian Aborigines*. London: George Routledge and Sons.

Auerbach, Erich. 1953 *Mimesis*. Willard R. Trask, trans. Princeton: Princeton University Press.

Augustine. ([c. A.D. 354–430] 1990) *The Works of St. Augustine: The Sermons on the Old Testament*, part 3, vol. 1. E. Hill, trans. New York: New City Press.

Bach, Alice, ed. (1990) *The Pleasure of Her Text: Feminist Readings of Biblical and Historical Texts*. Philadelphia: Trinity Press.

Bach, Alice. (1993) "Signs of the Flesh: Observations on Characterization in the Bible." *Semeia* 63:61–79.

Bachofen, J. J. (1973) *Myth, Religion, and Mother Right*. Ralph Manheim, trans. Princeton: Princeton University Press. (From *Das Mutterrecht*, published 1861.)

Baird, William. (1988) "Abraham in the New Testament." *Interpretation* 42(4): 367–79.

Bakan, David. (1966) *The Duality of Human Experience: Isolation and Communion in Western Man*. Boston: Beacon Press.

———. (1971) *Slaughter of the Innocents: A Study of the Battered Child Phenomenon*. Boston: Beacon Press.

———. (1974) "Paternity in the Judeo-Christian Tradition." In *Changing Perspectives in the Scientific Study of Religion*. A. Eister, ed. New York: John Wiley, 203–16.

———. (1979) *And They Took Themselves Wives: The Emergence of Patriarchy in Western Civilization*. San Francisco, Calif.: Harper & Row.

Bal, Mieke. (1988) *Death and Dissymmetry: The Politics of Coherence in the Book of Judges*. Chicago: University of Chicago Press.

Balmary, Marie. (1982) *Psychoanalyzing Psychoanalysis: Freud and the Hidden Fault of the Father*. Ned Lukacher, trans. Baltimore: Johns Hopkins University Press. (Originally published in French, 1979.)

———. (1986) *Le Sacrifice Interdit: Freud et la Bible*. Paris: B. Grasset.

Bane, Mary Jo, and David Ellwood. (1994) *Welfare Realities: From Rhetoric to Reform*. Cambridge, Mass.: Harvard University Press.

Baron, Salo. (1939) Book Review of *Moses and Monotheism*. *American Journal of Sociology* xlv(3) 471–77.

———. (1969) "A Review of Freud." in R. J. Christen and H. E. Hazelton, eds. *Monotheism and Moses*. Lexington, Mass.: D. C. Heath.

Beers, William. (1992) *Women and Sacrifice: Male Narcissim and the Psychology of Religion*. Detroit: Wayne State University Press.

Bell, Diane ([1983]1993) *Daughters of the Dreaming*. Minneapolis: University of Minnesota Press.

Benveniste, Emile. (1971) *Problems in General Linguistics*. Coral Gables, Fla.: University of Miami Press.

Bergmann, Martin. (1988) "The Transformation of Ritual Infanticide in the Jewish and Christian Religions with Reference to Anti-Semitism." In *Fantasy, Myth and Reality—Essays in Honor of Jacob A. Arlow, M.D.* H. P. Blum, Y. Kramer, A. K. Richards, A. D. Richards, eds. Madison, Conn.: International Universities Press.

———. (1992) *In the Shadow of Moloch: The Sacrifice of Children and Its Impact on Western Religions*. New York: Columbia University Press.

Berman, Harold. (1983) *Law and Revolution: The Formation of the Western Legal Tradition*. Cambridge, Mass.: Harvard University Press.

Bettelheim, Bruno. ([1954]1962) *Symbolic Wounds*. New York: Collier Books.

Bimson, J. J. (1980) *Essays on the Patriarchal Narratives*. A. R. Millard and D. J. Wiseman, eds. Leicester, England: Inter-Varsity Press.

Blankenhorn, David. (1995) *Fatherless America: Confronting Our Most Urgent Social Problem*. New York: Basic Books.

Bloom, Harold. (1990) *The Book of J*. David Rosenberg, trans. New York: Grove Weidenfeld.

Bordo, Susan. (1993) *Unbearable Weight: Feminism, Western Culture and the Body*. Berkeley: University of California Press.

Børrensen, Kari Elisabeth, ed. (1991) *Image of God and Gender Models in Judaeo-Christian Tradition*. Oslo: Solum Forlag.

Bouhdiba, Abdelwahab. (1985) *Sexuality in Islam*. Alan Sheridan, trans. London: Routledge and Kegan Paul. Originally published in French (1975).

Bowen, John. (1992) "On Scriptural Essentialism and Ritual Variation: Muslim Sacrifice in Sumatra and Morocco." *American Ethnologist* 19(4)656–71.

Bright, John. ([1959]1972) *A History of Israel*. Philadelphia: Westminster Press.

Brinner, William and Stephen D. Ricks. (1986) *Studies in Islamic and Judaic Traditions*. Atlanta: Scholars Press.

Brock, Rita Nakashima. (1990) "And a Little Child Will Lead Us: Christology and Child Abuse." In *Christianity, Patriarchy, and Abuse*. Joanne Carlson Brown and Carole R. Bohn, eds., 42–61.

Brown, Joanne Carlson and Carole R. Bohn eds. ([1989]1990). *Christianity, Patriarchy and Abuse: A Feminist Critique*. New York: The Pilgrim Press.

Brown, Joanne Carlson and Rebecca Parker. (1990) "For God So Loved the World?" In *Christianity, Patriarchy, and Abuse*. Joanne Carlson Brown and Carole R. Bohn, eds., 1–30.

Brown, Michael. (1982) "Biblical Myth and Contemporary Experience: The Akedah in Modern Jewish Literature." *Judaism* 31(1): 99–111.

Buchmann, Christina and Celina Spiegel, eds. (1994) *Out of the Garden: Women Writers on the Bible*. New York: Fawcett Columbine.

Buell, Denise Kimber. (1995) "Procreative Language in Clement of Alexandria." Ph.D. diss., Harvard University.

Burdick, Eugene and Harvey Wheeler. (1962) *Fail-Safe*. New York: McGraw Hill.

Burridge, Kenelm. (1973) *Encountering Aborigines: Anthropology and the Australian Aboriginal*. New York: Pergamon Press.

CALJIC (5th edition, 1988) [California Jury Instructions, Criminal]. St. Paul, Minn.: West Publishing Co.

Carroll, Michael. (1987) "'Moses and Monotheism' Revisited—Freud's 'Personal Myth?'" *American Imago* 44(1):15–35.

Carter, Jimmy. (1985) *The Blood of Abraham*. Boston: Houghton Mifflin.

Cartun, Mark Gregory. (1975) *Humans as Sacrificial Victims in Ancient Semitic Cultures*. Thesis. Hebrew Union College—Jewish Institute of Religion.

Caspi, Mishael. (1995) *The Binding: Akedah and its Transformation in Judaism and Islam*. Lewiston, N.Y.: Mellen Biblical Press.

Chilton, B. D. (1980) "Isaac and the Second Night: A Consideration." *Biblica* 61(1):78–88.

Coats, C. W. (1973) "Abraham's Sacrifice of Faith: A Formcritical Study of Genesis 22." *Interpretation* 27:389–400.

Cohen, Jack. (1990) "Is this the Meaning of My Life? Israelis Rethink the *Akedah*." *Conservative Judaism* vol. xliii(1), 50–60.

Cohn, Carol. (1987) "Sex and Death in the Rational World of Defense Intellectuals." *Signs* vol. 12 (4):687–719.

Combs-Schilling, M. E. (1989) *Sacred Performances: Islam, Sexuality, and Sacrifice*. New York: Columbia University Press.

Coward, Rosalind. (1983) *Patriarchal Precedents*. London: Routledge and Kegan Paul.

Creed, Robert. (1967) "The Art of the Singer: Three Old English Tellings of the Offering of Isaac." In *Old English Poetry*, Robert Creed, ed. Providence, R.I.: Brown University Press.

Cross, Frank Moore. (1973) *Canaanite Myth and Hebrew Epic*. Cambridge, Mass.: Harvard University Press.

Crow, Douglas K. (1986) "The Amplification of Abraham in Islam," In *Face to Face: an Interreligious Bulletin*. vol. xii, 21–28. (Special volume on Abraham in Judaism, Christianity and Islam).

Dagorn, R. (1981) *La Geste D'Ismael d'apres l'Onomastique et la Tradition Arabes*. Geneva: Librairie Droz.

Daly, Mary. (1973) *Beyond God the Father: Toward a Philosophy of Women's Liberation*. Boston: Beacon Press.

Daly, Robert J. (1977) "The Soteriological Significance of the Sacrifice of Isaac." *The Catholic Biblical Quarterly* 39:45–75.

Daniélou, Jean. (1960) *From Shadows to Reality: Studies in the Biblical Typology of the Fathers*. London: Burns and Oates.

Davies, P. (1979) "Passover and the Dating of the Aqedah." *Journal of Jewish Studies* 30:59–67.

Davies, P. and B. Chilton. (1978) "The Aqedah: A Revised Tradition-History." *The Catholic Biblical Quarterly* vol. 40: 514–46.

Day, John. (1989) *Molech: A God of Human Sacrifice in the Old Testament*. Cambridge: Cambridge University Press.

Degler, Carl. (1980) *At Odds: Women and the Family in America from the Revolution to the Present*. Oxford: Oxford University Press.

Delaney, Carol. (1977) "The Legacy of Abraham." In *Beyond Androcentrism*. Rita Gross, ed. Missoula, Mont.: Scholars Press.

———. (1978) "Freud and the Father: Systematic Distortion in Psychoanalytic Theory and Practice." Master's thesis, University of Chicago.

———. (1986) "The Meaning of Paternity and the Virgin Birth Debate." *Man* 21(3) 494–513.

———. (1990) "The Hajj: Sacred and Secular." *American Ethnologist* 17(3) 513–30.

———. (1991) *The Seed and the Soil: Gender and Cosmology in Turkish Village Society.* Berkeley: University of California Press.

———. (1995) "Father State, Motherland, and the Birth of Modern Turkey." In *Naturalizing Power: Essays in Feminist Cultural Analysis.* S. Yanagisako and C. Delaney, eds. New York: Routledge, 177–199.

———. (1996) Book Review of *The First Father. Abraham: The Psychology and Culture of a Spiritual Revolutionary.* Henry Hanoch Abramovitch. *American Ethnologist* 23 (1).

DeMause, Lloyd. (1984) *Reagan's America.* New York: Creative Roots.

Devereux, Georges. (1953) "Why Oedipus Killed Laius." *International Journal of Psychoanalysis* 34:134–141.

Devisch, Renaat. (1993) *Weaving the Threads of Life: the Khita Gyn-eco-logical Healing Cult among the Yaka.* Chicago: University of Chicago Press.

Diamond, Stanley. (1974) *In Search of the Primitive: A Critique of Civilization.* New Brunswick, N.J.: Transaction Books.

Diodorus of Sicily. (1954) Russel M. Geer, trans. Loeb Classical Library. Vol. x, Cambridge, Mass.: Harvard University Press.

Douglas, Mary. (1966) *Purity and Danger.* London: Routledge and Kegan Paul.

Driver, S. R. (1904) *The Book of Genesis.* London: Metheun and Co.

DuBois, Page. (1988) *Sowing the Body: Psychoanalysis and Ancient Representations of Women.* Chicago: University of Chicago Press.

Dundes, Alan. (1984) *Sacred Narratives: Readings in the Theory of Myth.* Berkeley: University of California Press.

———. (1988) *The Flood Myth.* Berkeley: University of California Press.

Durkheim, Emile. (1915) *The Elementary Forms of the Religious Life.* New York: The Free Press, Macmillan Publishing Co.

Easlea, Brian. (1983) *Fathering the Unthinkable: Masculinity, Scientists, and the Nuclear Arms Race.* London: Pluto Press.

Edelman, Marion Wright. (1987) *Families in Peril.* Cambridge: Harvard University Press.

Education for Ministry. (1979) Book 1: The Beginning; Part 2: The Patriarchs (The Abraham Saga). The School of Theology, University of the South. (Course book for teaching in Episcopalian Church Schools.)

Eickelman, Dale. (1978) "The Art of Memory, Islamic Education and its Social Reproduction." *Comparative Studies in Society and History*, 20(4) 485–516.

Eilberg-Schwartz, Howard. (1990) *The Savage in Judaism.* Bloomington: Indiana University Press.

Eilberg-Schwartz, Howard. (1994) *God's Phallus and Other Problems for Men and Monotheism*. Boston: Beacon Press.

———. (1996) "The Father, the Phallus, and the Seminal Word: Dilemmas of Patrilineality in Ancient Judaism." In *Gender, Kinship, Power*. Mary Jo Maynes, Ann Waltner, Birgitte Soland, and Ulrike Strasser, eds. New York and London: Routledge.

Eissfeldt, O. *Molk als Opferbegriffim Punischen und Hebraischen und das Ende des Gottes Moloch*. Halle.

Elshtain, Jean Bethke, and Sheila Tobias. (1990) *Women, Militarism, and War: Essays in History, Politics, and Social Theory*. Savage, Md.: Rowman and Littlefield Publishers.

Elwell, Walter A., ed. (1984) *Evangelical Dictionary of Theology*. Grand Rapids, Mich.: Baker Book House.

Encyclopaedia of Islam (1960–93), Leiden: E. J. Brill.

Encyclopedia Judaica. (1971) Jerusalem: Keter Publishing House.

Engels, Frederick. ([1884]1972) *The Origin of the Family, Private Property and the State*. New York: International Publishers.

Enloe, Cynthia. (1990) *Bananas, Beaches, and Bases*. Berkeley: University of California Press.

Esin, Emel. (1963) *Mecca, the Blessed, Madinah, the Radiant*. London: Elek Books.

Eusebius. ([c. 260–340] 1903) *Preparation for the Gospel*. Edwin H. Gifford, trans., Oxford: Oxford University Press.

Feeley-Harnik, Gillian. (1981) *The Lord's Table: Eucharist and Passover in Early Christianity*. Philadelphia: University of Pennsylvania Press.

Feldman, Yael. (1994) "And Rebecca Loved Jacob, But Freud Did Not." In *Freud and Forbidden Knowledge*. Peter L. Rudnytsky and Ellen Handler Spitz, eds. N.Y.: New York University Press, 7–25.

Fernandez, James. (1991) *Beyond Metaphor: The Theory of Tropes in Anthropology*. Stanford: Stanford University Press.

Filmer, Sir Robert. (1680) *Patriarcha or the Natural Power of Kings*. London: printed for Ric. Chiswell, Matthew Gillyflower, and William Henchman.

Firestone, Reuven. (1989) "Abraham's Son as the Intended Sacrifice (al-Dhabih, Qur'an 37:99–113): Issues in Qur'anic Exegesis," *Journal of Semitic Studies* 34:95–131.

———. (1990) *Journeys in Holy Lands: The Evolution of the Abraham-Ishmael Legends in Islamic Exegesis*. Albany: State University of New York Press.

Fischer, Michael M. J. and Mehdi Abedi. (1990) *Debating Muslims: Cultural Dialogues in Postmodernity and Tradition*. Madison: University of Wisconsin Press.

Folbre, Nancy. (1991) "The Unproductive Housewife: Her Evolution in Nineteenth Century Economic Thought." *Signs* 16(3):463–84.

Foster, Benjamin (1989) "Western Asia in the Second Millenium." In *Women's*

Earliest Records From Ancient Egypt and Western Asia. Barbara Lesko, ed., Atlanta: Scholars Press, 141–43.

Fox, Robin. (1967) "*Totem and Taboo* Reconsidered." *The Structural Study of Myth and Totemism.* Edmund Leach, ed. London: Tavistock Publications. 161–178.

Fraser, Nancy. (1989) "Women, Welfare, and the Politics of Need Interpretation." In *Unruly Practices.* Minneapolis: University of Minnesota Press.

Fraser, Nancy and Linda Gordon. (1994) "Dependency Demystified: Inscriptions of the Poor in a Keyword of the Welfare State." *Social Politics: International Studies in Gender, State, and Society* 1(1):4–31.

Frazer, Sir James George. (1890) *The Golden Bough.* London: Macmillan.

———. (1913) *The Scapegoat.* London: Macmillan.

———. (1919) *Folk-Lore in the Old Testament.* New York: Macmillan.

Frei, Hans W. (1974) *The Eclipse of Biblical Narrative.* New Haven: Yale University Press.

Friedman, Richard (1987) *Who Wrote the Bible?* New York: Harper and Row.

Friedrich, Gerhard, ed. (1967) *Theological Dictionary of the New Testament.* vol 5:965. Grand Rapids, Mich.: Wm. B. Eerdmans Publishing Company.

Friedrich, Paul. (1979) *Language, Context and the Imagination.* Stanford: Stanford University Press.

———. (1986) *The Language Parallax.* Austin: University of Texas Press.

Freud, Sigmund. (1900) *Interpretation of Dreams.* vol. 4. In *The Standard Edition of the Complete Psychological Works of Sigmund Freud.* James Strachey, ed. 24 vols. London: Hogarth Press, 1953–74 (hereafter SE).

———. (1909) "Notes Upon a Case of Obsessive Neurosis." SE 10.

———. (1911) "Psycho-analytic Notes on an Autobiographical Account of a Case of Paranoia (Dementia Paranoides)." SE 12.

———. (1913) *Totem and Taboo.* SE 13.

———. ([1914]1918) "From the History of an Infantile Neurosis." SE 17.

———. (1924) "An Autobiographical Study." SE 20.

———. (1933) "Why War?" SE 22 (Einstein's letter included).

———. (1939) *Moses and Monotheism.* Katherine Jones, trans. New York: Vintage Books, and SE 23.

Frymer-Kensky, Tikva. (1992) *In the Wake of the Goddesses.* N.Y.: Free Press.

Funiciello, Theresa. (1993) *Tyranny of Kindness: Dismantling the Welfare System to End Poverty in America.* New York: The Atlantic Monthly Press.

Garfinkel, Irwin. (1992) *Assuring Child Support: An Extension of Social Security.* New York: Russell Sage Foundation.

Geertz, Clifford. (1973) *Interpretation of Cultures.* New York: Basic Books.

Geller, Jay. (1993) " "Paleontological View of Freud's Study of Religion: Unearthing the *Leitfossil* Circumcision." *Modern Judaism* 13 (1): 49–70.

Genesis Apocryphon of Qumram Cave I. (1971) Joseph Fitzmyer, SJ., trans. Rome: Biblical Institute Press.

Genesis Rabbah: The Judaic Commentary to the Book of Genesis: A New American Translation. Jacob Neusner, trans. 1985, Atlanta: Scholars Press.

Gibson, Joan. (1992) "Could Christ Have Been Born a Woman?" *Journal of Feminists Studies in Religion* 8(1) 65–82.

Gill, Pauline. (1991) *Les Enfants de Duplessis*. Montreal: Libre Expression.

Gilman, Sander L. (1993) *Freud, Race, and Gender*. Princeton, N.J.: Princeton University Press.

Ginzberg, Louis. (1909) *Legends of the Jews*. (7 vols.) Philadelphia: Jewish Publication Society of America.

Girard, Rene. (1972) *Violence and the Sacred*. Baltimore: Johns Hopkins University Press.

Glaser, Danya and Stephen Frosh. (1998) *Child Sexual Abuse*. London: Macmillan Education/British Association of Social Workers.

Glendon, Mary Ann. (1987) *Abortion and Divorce in Western Law: American Failures, European Challenges*. Cambridge, Mass.: Harvard University Press.

———. (1991) *Rights Talk*. New York: Free Press.

Glueck, Nelson. (1955) "The Age of Abraham in the Negeb." *The Biblical Archaeologist* 18:2–9.

Goldberg, Harvey (1987) "Torah and Children: Symbolic Aspects of the Reproduction of Jews and Judaism." In Harvey Goldberg, ed. *Judaism Viewed from Within and Without*. Albany: State University of New York, 107–138.

Goldson, Edward. (1993) "War Is Not Good For Children." In *The Psychological Effects of War and Violence on Children*. Lewis A. Leavitt and Nathan A. Fox, eds. Hillsdale, N.J.: Lawrence Erlbaum Associates, 3–22.

Gordon, Neil. (1995) *The Sacrifice of Isaac*. New York: Random House.

Graves, Robert and Raphael Patai. ([1963]1966) *Hebrew Myths: The Book of Genesis*. New York: McGraw Hill.

Green, Alberto R. (1975) *The Role of Human Sacrifice in the Ancient Near East*. Missoula, Mont.: Scholars Press.

Gresser, Moshe. (1994) *Dual Allegiance: Freud as a Modern Jew*. Albany: State University of New York.

Greven, Philip ([1990]1992) *Spare the Child: The Religious Roots of Punishment and the Psychological Impact of Physical Abuse*. New York: Vintage Books.

Grünbaum, Adolf. (1993) *Validation in the Clinical Theory of Psychoanalysis*. Madison, Conn.: International Universities Press.

Hackett, Jo Ann. (1987) "Women's Studies and the Hebrew Bible." In *The Future of Biblical Studies: The Hebrew Scriptures*. R. Friedman and H. Williamson, eds. Atlanta, Ga.: Scholars Press, 141–164.

Hallo, William W. and J. J. A. van Dijk. (1968) *The Exaltation of Inanna*. New Haven: Yale University Press.

Handelman, S. (1982) *The Slayers of Moses: The Emergence of Rabbinic Interpretation in Modern Literary Theory*. Albany: State University of New York Press.

Handler, Joel F. (1995) *The Poverty of Welfare Reform*. New Haven: Yale University Press.

Handman, Marie-Elisabeth. (1983) *La Violence et la Ruse. Hommes et Femmes dans un Village Grec*. La Calade, Aix-en-Provence: Edisud.

Haraway, Donna. (1989) *Primate Visions: Gender, Race, and Nature in the World of Modern Science*. New York: Routledge.

Harding, Sandra. (1990) "Starting Thought from Women's Lives: Eight Resources for Maximizing Objectivity." *Journal of Social Philosophy* 21 (2/3): 140–49.

Harding, Susan. (1987) "Convicted by the Holy Spirit: the Rhetoric of Fundamental Baptist Conversion." *American Ethnologist* 14:167–181.

———. (1991) "Representing Fundamentalism: the Problem of the Repugnant Cultural Other." *Social Research* vol. 58(2):373–393.

———. (1992) "The Afterlife of Stories: Genesis of a Man of God." In *Storied Lives*. G. C. Rosenwald and R. Ochberg, eds. New Haven: Yale University Press, 60–75.

Hartt, Frederick. (1975) *History of Italian Renaissance Art*. N.J.: Prentice Hall.

Hawkesworth, M. (1989) "Knowers, Knowing, Known: Feminist Theory and Claims of Truth," *Signs* 14(31):533–557.

Hawting, G. R. (1982) "The Origins of the Muslim Sanctuary at Mecca." In *Studies on the First Century of Islamic Society*. G. H. A. Juynbull, ed. Carbondale: Southern Illinois University Press.

Hayward, C. T. R. (1990) "The Sacrifice of Isaac and Jewish Polemic Against Christianity." *The Catholic Biblical Quarterly* 52:291–306.

Haywood, Robert. (1980) "Appendix: The Aqedah." In *Sacrifice*. W. F. C. Bourdillon and Meyer Fortes, eds. London: Academic Press.

———. (1981) "The Present State of Research into the Targumic Account of the Sacrifice of Isaac." *Journal of Jewish Studies* xxxii(2):127–150.

Hengel, Martin. (1981) *The Atonement*. Philadelphia: Fortress Press.

Herdt, Gilbert. (1981) *Guardians of the Flutes: Idioms of Masculinity*. New York: McGraw-Hill.

——— ed. (1982) *Rituals of Manhood: Male Initiation in Papua New Guinea*. Berkeley: University of California Press.

Herhold, Rev. Robert M. (1995) "Who Asked Isaac?" Unpublished play performed 27 October 1995. University Lutheran Church, Palo Alto, Calif.

Herman, Judith with Lisa Hirschman. (1981) *Father-Daughter Incest*. Cambridge, Mass.: Harvard University Press.

Hesiodus. ([8th cent. B.C.] 1959) *Works and Days, Theogony, the Shield of Herakles*. Richard Lattimore, trans. Ann Arbor: University of Michigan Press.

Hill, Dorothy. (1957) *Abraham: His Heritage and Ours*. Boston: Beacon Press.

Hocart, A. M. (1973) "Kinship Systems." In *The Life-Giving Myth*. London: Tavistock Publications.

Hochschild, Arlie. (1975) "Inside the Clockwork of Male Careers." In *Women and the Power to Change*. Florence Howe, ed. New York: McGraw Hill.

Hochschild, Arlie and Anne Machtung. (1989) *The Second Shift: Working Parents and the Revolution at Home*. New York: Viking Penguin.

Hultgård, Anders. (1991) "God and the Image of Woman in Early Jewish Religion." In *Image of God and Gender Models in Judaeo-Christian Tradition*. Kari Elisabeth Børrensen, ed. Oslo: Solum Forlag.

Inglis, Ruth. (1978) *The Sins of the Fathers: A Study of the Physical and Emotional Abuse of Children*. New York: St. Martin's Press.

The Interpreter's Bible. (1952) George Arthur Buttrick et al, eds., New York: Abingdon-Cokesbury Press.

Irenaeus. ([c. A.D. 120–202] 1903) "Against Heresies." In *The Ante-Nicene Fathers*, vol. 1, N.Y.: Charles Scribner's Sons.

Jay, Nancy. (1992) *Throughout your Generations Forever: Sacrifice, Religion and Paternity*. Chicago: University of Chicago Press.

Jeffords, Susan. (1989) *The Remasculinization of America: Gender and the Vietnam War*. Bloomington: Indiana University Press.

Jenkins, Philip. (1992) *Intimate Enemies: Moral Panics in Contemporary Great Britain*. New York: Aldine de Gruyter.

Jones, Ernest. (1924) *Essays in Applied Psychoanalysis*. London: Hogarth Press.

Josephus Flavius. ([c. A.D. 30–100] 1961) *Jewish Antiquities*, Vol. 4, Book 1:222–36. Cambridge, Mass.: Loeb Classical Library, Harvard University Press.

Kamerman, Sheila B. (1984) "Women, Children, and Poverty: Public Policy and Female-headed Families in Industrialized Countries." *Signs* 10(2):249–271.

Kamerman, Sheila B. And Alfred J. Kahn. (1989) "Single-parent, Female-headed Families in Western Europe: Social Change and Response." *International Social Security Review* 1:3–34.

———. (1994) "Family Policy and the Under-3s: Money, Services, and Time in a Policy Package." *International Social Security Review* 47(3–4):31–44.

Kanzer, Mark. (1972) "Discussion of Leonard Shengold's Paper." *American Imago* 29(1)160–64.

Kant, Immanuel. ([1798]1979) *The Conflict of the Faculties*. Mary Gregor, trans. Lincoln: University of Nebraska Press.

Kaplan, Kalman. (1990) "Isaac and Oedipus: A Re-Examination of the Father-Son Relationship." *Judaism* 39(1)73–81.

Katz, Michael. (1986) *In the Shadow of the Poorhouse: A Social History of Welfare in America*. New York: Basic Books.

Kertzer, David. (1993) *Sacrificed for Honor: Italian Infant Abandonment and the Politics of Reproductive Control*. Boston: Beacon Press.

Kierkegaard, Søren. ([1843] 1941) *Fear and Trembling*. Walter Lowrie, trans. Princeton: Princeton University Press.

al-Kisa'i, Muhammed ibn Abd Allah. ([11th cent.] 1978) *Tales of the Prophets of al-Kisa'i*. Translated from the Arabic, with notes, by W. M. Thackston, Jr. Boston: Twayne Publishers.

Kister, M. J. (1971) "Maqam Ibrahim: A Stone with an Inscription." *Le Museon* (84):477–487.

Kittay, Eva. (1996) "Human Dependency and Rawlsian Equality." In *Feminists Rethink the Self*. Diana Tietjens Meyers, ed. Colo.: Westview Press.

Kohn, H. (1960) "Hebrew and Greek Roots of Modern Nationalism." In *Conflict and Cooperation Among Nations*. Ivo Duchacek, ed. New York: Holt, Rinehart and Winston, 39–41.

Kolve, V. A. (1966) *The Play Called Corpus Christi*. Stanford: Stanford University Press.

Koran, The Meaning of the Glorious. Mohammed Marmaduke Pickthall, trans. New York: A Mentor Book, n.d.

Kraemer, Ross J. (1988) *Maenads, Martyrs, Matrons, Monastics: A Source Book on Women's Religions in the Greco-Roman World*. Philadelphia: Fortress Press.

Kritzeck, James. (1965) *Sons of Abraham: Jews, Christians and Moslems*. Baltimore: Helicon Press.

Kroeber, Alfred L. ([1920]1952) "Totem and Taboo: An Ethnologic Psychoanalysis." *The Nature of Culture*. Berkeley: University of California Press, 301–5.

———. ([1939] 1952) "Totem and Taboo in Retrospect." *The Nature of Culture*. Berkeley: University of California Press, 306–9.

Krull, Marianne. (1986) *Freud and His Father*. New York and London: W. W. Norton.

LaBarre, Weston. (1958) "The Influence of Freud on Anthropology." *American Imago* 15(3) 275–328.

LaFontaine, J. S. (1987) "Preliminary Remarks on a Study of Incest in England." In *Child Survival*, Scheper-Hughes, ed. 267–290.

LaHurd, Carol Schersten. (1990) "One God, One Father: Abraham in Judaism, Christianity and Islam." *Dialog* 29(1)17–28.

Lakoff, George. (1980) *Metaphors We Live By*. Chicago: University of Chicago Press.

———. (1990–91) "Metaphor and War." Paper circulated on computer networks, December 1990; presented at Stanford University, January 1991, during the Gulf War.

Langer, Suzanne. (1942) *Philosophy in a New Key*. Cambridge, Mass.: Harvard University Press.

Lazarus-Yafeh, Hava. (1981) *Some Religious Aspects of Islam*. Leiden: E. J. Brill.

Leach, E. (1961) "Levi-Strauss in the Garden of Eden: An Examination of Some Recent Developments in the Analysis of Myth." *Transactions of the New York Academy of Sciences* 23:386–395.

———. (1967) "Virgin Birth." In *Proceedings of the Royal Anthropological Institute, 1966–67*, 39–48.

Leach, E. (1969) *Genesis as Myth.* London: Jonathan Cape.

Leach, Penelope. (1994) *Children First: What Our Society Must Do—And Is Not Doing—For Our Children Today.* New York: Alfred A. Knopf.

Lerch, David. (1950) *Isaac's Opferung Christlich Gedeudet.* Tubingen: Verlag J. C. B. Mohr.

Lerman, Hannah. (1986) *The Mote in Freud's Eye.* New York: Springer Publishing Co.

Levenson, J. (1991) "The Good Friday-Passover Connection." *New York Times* March 3.

———. (1993) *The Death and Resurrection of the Beloved Son.* New Haven: Yale University Press.

Lévi-Strauss, Claude. ([1962]1963) *Totemism.* Rodney Needham, trans. Boston: Beacon Press.

Lewis, Chaim. (1973) "From Adam's Serpent to Abraham's Ram." *Judaism* 22(4) 392–99.

Lloyd, Seton and William Brice. (1951) "Harran." *Anatolian Studies.* 1:77–111.

Longton, Joseph. (1987) *Fils d'Abraham: Panorama des Communautes Juives, Chretiennes et Musulmanes.* Belgium: Editions Brepols.

Luther, Martin. (1539–41) *Luther's Works: Lectures on Genesis* (Chapters 21–5). Jaroslav Pelikan, ed. Saint Louis: Concordia Publishing House, 1964.

Malinowski, Bronislaw. ([1927]1985) *Sex and Repression in Savage Society.* Chicago: University of Chicago Press.

———. ([1929]1982) *Sexual Life of Savages in Northwestern Melanesia.* London: Routledge and Kegan Paul.

———. ([1948]1954) *Magic, Science and Religion.* New York: Doubleday Anchor Books.

Marcus, Ivan. (1982) "From Politics to Martyrdom: Shifting Paradigms in the Hebrew Narratives of the 1096 Crusade Riots." *Prooftexts* 2:40–52.

Masson, Jeffrey M. (1984) *The Assault on Truth: Freud's Suppression of the Seduction Theory.* New York: Farrar, Straus and Giroux.

Mazlish, Bruce. (1969) "Freud as Philosopher of History." In *Monotheism and Moses.* R. J. Christen and H. E. Hazelton, eds. Lexington, Mass.: D. C. Heath and Company.

McGrath, William. (1974) "Freud as Hannibal: Politics of the Brother Band." *Central European History* 7(1).

McKinnon, Susan. (1995) "American Kinship/American Incest: Asymmetries in a Scientific Discourse." In *Naturalizing Power: Essays in Feminist Cultural Analysis.* Sylvia Yanagisako and Carol Delaney, eds. New York: Routledge, 25–46.

McLennan, J. F. (1896) *Studies in Ancient History.* London: Macmillan and Company.

McNeill, William. (1986) *Mythistory and Other Essays.* Chicago: University of Chicago Press.

Miedzian, Myriam. (1991) *Boys Will Be Boys: Breaking the Link Between Masculinity and Violence*. New York: Doubleday.

Milgrom, Jo. (1987) "From Moriah to Sinai, From Abraham to Moses, From a Man to a People." *Moment* 12(6):37–41, 59.

———. (1988) *The Akedah: A Primary Symbol in Jewish Thought and Art*. Berkeley: The Bibal Press.

Millard, A. R. and D. J. Wiseman. (1980) *Essays on the Patriarchal Narratives*. Harmondsworth, England.: Inter-Varsity Press.

Miller, Rabbi Alan. (1983) "The Binding of Isaac." *The Jewish Spectator* Fall: 37–9.

Miller, Alice. ([1988]1990) *The Untouched Key: Tracing Childhood Trauma in Creativity and Destructiveness*. New York: Anchor Books—Doubleday.

Mintz, Allan. (1984) *Hurban*. New York: Columbia University Press.

Moberly, R. W. L. (1988) "The Earliest Commentary on the Akedah." *Vestum Testamentum*. 3(3), 302–323.

Montagu, Susan. (1983) "Trobriand Gender Identity." *Mankind* 14(1):33–45.

Morgan, Lewis Henry. (1870) *Systems of Consanguinity and Affinity of the Human Family*. Washington, D.C.: Smithsonian Contributions to Knowledge.

———. ([1877]1974) *Ancient Society: or Researches in the Lines of Human Progress from Savagery through Barbarism to Civilization*. Gloucester, Mass.: Meridian Book, The World Publishing Co.

Morris, Norval. (1992) *The Brothel Boy and Other Parables of the Law*. New York: Oxford University Press.

Mosca, Paul. (1975) *Child Sacrifice in Canaanite and Israelite Religion*. Ph.D. diss., Harvard University.

Moscati, Sabatini. (1983) *Carthage*. Milan: Jaca Book.

Mosse, George. (1985) *Nationalism and Sexuality*. New York: Howard Fertig.

Musallam, Basim. (1983) *Sex and Society in Islam: Birth Control Before the Nineteenth Century*. New York: Cambridge University Press.

Nachmanides (Moses ben Nahman; Ramban). ([c.1195–1270] 1971) *Commentary on the Torah*. Rabbi Dr. Charles B. Chavel, trans. New York: Shilo Publishing House.

Nagy, Gregory. (1979) *The Best of the Achaeans*. Baltimore: Johns Hopkins University Press.

Neu, Jerome. (1991) *The Cambridge Companion to Freud*. Cambridge: Cambridge University Press.

Newby, Gordon Darnell. (1989) *The Making of the Last Prophet: A Reconstruction of the Earliest Biography of Muhammad*. Columbia, S.C.: University of South Carolina Press.

Newsom, Carole A., and Sharon H. Ringe. (1992) *The Women's Bible Commentary*. London: Westminster; Louisville, Ky: John Knox Press.

Nicholls, David. (1993) "Addressing God as Ruler: Prayer and Petition." *British Journal of Sociology*. 44(1):125–41.

Niditch, Susan. (1992) "Genesis." In *The Women's Bible Commentary*. Carole A. Newsom and Sharon H. Ringe, eds. Louisville, Ky.: Westminster/John Knox Press.

Niederland, William G. (1951) "Three Notes on the Schreber Case." *Psychoanalytic Quarterly* 20.

———. (1959a) "The 'Miracled-up' World of Schreber's Childhood." *Psychoanalytic Study of the Child* 14. New York: International Universities Press.

———. (1959b) "Schreber: Father and Son." *Psychoanalytic Quarterly* 28.

———. (1960) "Schreber's Father." *Journal of the American Psychoanalytic Association* 8.

Noonan, John Thomas. (1965) *Contraception: A History of its Treatment by the Catholic Theologians and Canonists*. Cambridge, Mass.: Belknap Press of Harvard University Press.

Novak, Michael. (1993) "Women, Ordination, and Angels." *First Things* April.

O'Brien, Connor C. (1988) *God Land: Reflections on Religion and Nationalism*. Cambridge, Mass.: Harvard University Press.

Okin, Susan. (1979) *Women in Western Political Thought*. Princeton: Princeton University Press.

Oliver, Anne Marie and Paul Steinberg. (1995) "Embodied Imperative: the Command of Death in the Underground Media of the Intifada." Unpublished paper at Center for Middle Eastern Studies, Harvard University.

Orlinsky, Harry. (1969) "Abraham and Moses." In *Monotheism and Moses*. R. J. Christen and H. E. Hazelton, eds. Lexington, Mass.: D. C. Heath and Co.

Otto, Rudolph. (1923) *The Idea of the Holy*. Oxford: Oxford University Press.

Oz, Amos. ([1965]1973) "The Way of the Wind." *Where the Jackals Howl and Other Stories*. New York: Harcourt Brace Jovanovitch, 39–60.

Pardes, Ilana. (1992) *Countertraditions in the Bible: A Feminist Approach*. Cambridge, Mass.: Harvard Univerity Press.

Paret, Rudi. (1978) "Ibrahim" and "Ishma'il." *The Encyclopaedia of Islam*. Leiden: E. J. Brill.

Parrot, Andre. (1968) *Abraham and His Times*. James H. Farley, trans. Philadelphia: Fortress Press. (First published in French, 1962).

Patai, Raphael. (1986) *The Seed of Abraham: Jews and Arabs in Contact and Conflict*. Salt Lake City: University of Utah Press.

Pateman, Carole. (1988) *The Sexual Contract*. Stanford: Stanford University Press.

Paul, Robert. (1996) *Moses and Civilization: The Meaning Behind Freud's Myth*. New Haven: Yale University Press.

Pearce, Diana. (1978) "The Feminization of Poverty: Women, Work, and Welfare." *Urban and Social Change Review* (Winter/Spring):28–36.

———. (1990) "Welfare is NOT for Women: Why the War on Poverty Cannot Conquer the Feminization of Poverty." In *Women, the State, and Welfare* Linda Gordon, ed. Madison: University of Wisconsin Press, 265–279.

Pesikta Rabbati. (1968) William Braude, trans. New Haven: Yale University Press.

Peters, F. E. (1982) *Children of Abraham.* Princeton: Princeton University Press.

———. (1986) "The Children of Abraham and Sacred History." *Face to Face: an Interreligious Bulletin* xii:4–8. (Special volume on Abraham in Judaism, Christianity and Islam).

———. (1990) *Judaism, Christianity, and Islam.* Vol. 1. Princeton: Princeton University Press.

Philo of Alexandria. ([c. 20 B.C.–A.D. 50] 1959) *De Abrahamo.* F. H. Colson, trans. Cambridge, Mass.: Loeb Classical Library, Harvard University Press.

Phipps, William E. (1989) *Genesis and Gender: Biblical Myths of Sexuality and their Cultural Impact.* New York: Praeger Publishers.

Piske de Rabbi Eliezer. (1965) G. Friedlander, trans. New York: Hermon Press.

Plaut, W. Gunther. (1974) *The Torah: A Modern Commentary.* New York: The Union of American Hebrew Congregations.

Pollitt, Katha. (1995) "Subject to Debate." *The Nation.* January 30, 20.

Prag, Kay. (1970) "The 1959 Deep Sounding at Harran in Turkey." *Levant: Journal of the British School of Archaeology in Jerusalem.* 2:63–94.

Pritchard, J. B., ed. (1950) *Ancient Near Eastern Texts Relating to the Old Testament.* Princeton: Princeton University Press.

Quell, G. (1967) Entry on "pater" in the Old Testament. In *Theological Dictionary of the New Testament.* Geoffrey W. Bromiley, ed. Grand Rapids, Mich.: William B. Eerdmans Publishers, 807–08.

Rashi. (1929) *Pentateuch with Rashi's Commentary.* Rev. M. Rosenbaum and A. M. Silbermann, trans. London: Shapiro, Vallentine.

Reid, Stephen. (1972) "*Moses and Monotheism:* Guilt and the Murder of the Primal Father." *American Imago.* 19(1):11–34.

Rice, Emanuel. (1990) *Freud and Moses: The Long Journey Home.* Albany: State University of New York Press.

Riddle, John. (1992) *Contraception and Abortion from the Ancient World to the Renaissance.* Cambridge, Mass.: Harvard University Press.

Rieff, Philip ([1959]1979) *Freud: The Mind of the Moralist.* Chicago: University of Chicago Press.

Riskin, Shlomo. (1994) "The Akeda: A Lesson in Martyrdom." *The Jerusalem Post* October 21.

Riskin, Shlomo, Sheldon Zimmerman and Alan W. Miller. (1983) "The Binding of Isaac: Three Rabbis Study and Teach a Text." *The Jewish Spectator* Fall.

Robert, Marthe. (1976) *From Oedipus to Moses.* Garden City, N.Y.: Anchor Books.

Robinson, Paul. (1993) *Freud and His Critics.* Berkeley: University of California Press.

Rock, Paul (1993) *The Social World of an English Crown Court.* Oxford: Oxford University Press.

Rosaldo, Renato (1989) *Culture and Truth*. Boston: Beacon Press.

Rosenberg, R. (1965) "Jesus, Isaac, and the 'Suffering Servant.'" *Journal of Biblical Literature* 84:381–88.

Rosenzweig, Franz. (1971) *The Star of Redemption*. New York: Holt, Rinehart and Winston.

Roskies, David G. (1984) *Against the Apocalypse: Responses to Catastrophe in Modern Jewish Culture*. Cambridge, Mass.: Harvard University Press.

Rothstein, Edward. (1996). "A Beginning Stripped of Awe." *New York Times* December 1.

Rubin, Gayle. (1975) "The Traffic in Women: Notes on the 'Political Economy' of Sex." In *Toward an Anthropology of Women*. Rayna Reiter, ed. New York: Monthly Review Press, 157–210.

Sader, Helen. (1991) "Phoenician Stelae From Tyre." *Berytus Archaeological Studies*. Vol. xxxix:101–26.

Sahlins, Marshall. (1976) *Culture and Practical Reason*. Chicago: University of Chicago Press.

———. (1981) *Historical Metaphors and Mythical Realities*. Ann Arbor: The University of Michigan Press.

Samuel, Raphael and Paul Thompson, eds. (1990) *Myths We Live By*. London: Routledge

Sandmel, Samuel. (1956) *Philo's Place in Judaism: A Study of the Conceptions of Abraham in Jewish Literature*. Cincinnati: Hebrew Union College Press.

Sapir, Edward. (1951) *Culture, Language, and Personality*. David Mandelbaum, ed. Berkeley: University of California Press.

Sapiro, Virginia. (1990) "The Gender Bias of American Social Policy." In *Women, the State, and Welfare*. Linda Gordon, ed. Madison: University of Wisconsin Press, 36–54.

Sarna, Nahum. (1966) *Understanding Genesis*. New York: McGraw Hill.

———. ed. (1989) *The JPS Torah Commentary: Genesis*. Philadelphia: The Jewish Publication Society.

Saussure, Ferdinand de. (1966) *Course in General Linguistics* New York: McGraw Hill.

Scarry, Elanie. (1992) "The Declaration of War: Constitutional and Unconstitutional Violence." In *Law's Violence*. Austin Sarat and Tom Kearns, eds. Amherst Series in Law, Jurisprudence, and Social Thought, 23–76.

Schapiro, Meyer. ([1943]1979) "The Angel with the Ram in Abraham's Sacrifice: A Parallel in Western and Islamic Art." *Late Antique, Early Christian and Medieval Art*. New York: George Braziller, 289–318.

Schatzman, Morton. (1972) "Paranoia or Persecution: The Case of Schreber." *International Journal of Psychiatry* 10(3).

———. (1973) *Soul Murder: Persecution in the Family*. New York: Random House.

Scheffler, H. W. (1972) "Systems of Kin Classification: A Structural Typology." In *Kinship Studies in the Morgan Centennial Year*. P. Reining, ed. Washington, D.C.: American Anthropological Society.

Scheper-Hughes, Nancy, ed. (1987) *Child Survival: Anthropological Perspectives on the Treatment and Maltreatment of Children*. Dordrecht: D. Reidel Publishing Company.

Scheper-Hughes, Nancy and Howard Stein. (1987) "Child Abuse and the Unconscious in American Popular Culture." In *Child Survival*. Scheper-Hughes, ed. Dordrecht: D. Reidel Publishing Company, 339–58.

Schiffren, Lisa. (1995) "Penalize the Unwed Dad? Fat Chance." *New York Times* August 10.

Schlossman, Howard. (1972) "God the Father and His Sons." *American Imago* 29(1):35–52.

Schneider, David. (1968) *American Kinship: A Cultural Account*. Englewood Cliffs, N.J.: Prentice-Hall.

———. (1972) "What is Kinship All About?" In *Kinship Studies in the Morgan Centennial Year*. P. Reining, ed. Washington, D.C.: The Anthropological Society, 32–63.

———. (1976) "Notes Toward a Theory of Culture." In *Meaning in Anthropology*. Keith H. Basso and Henry A. Selby, eds. Albuquerque, N.M.: University of New Mexico Press, 197–220.

———. (1984) *A Critique of the Study of Kinship*. Ann Arbor: University of Michigan Press.

Schoeps, H. (1946) "The Sacrifice of Isaac in Paul's Theology." *Journal of Biblical Literature* (65) 385–92.

Schorske, Carl E. (1973) "Politics and Patricide in Freud's *Interpretation of Dreams*." *The American Historical Review* 78(2).

Schüssler-Fiorenza, Elisabeth. (1985) *In Memory of Her: A Feminist Theological Reconstruction of Christian Origins*. New York: Crossroad Publishing Co.

———. (1992) *But She Said: Feminist Practices of Biblical Interpretation*. Boston: Beacon Press.

Schwartz, Regina. (1990) "Introduction: On Biblical Criticism." In *The Book and the Text: The Bible and Literary Theory*. R. Schwartz, ed. Cambridge, England: Basil Blackwell, 1–15.

———. (1997) *The Curse of Cain: The Violent Legacy of Monotheism*. Chicago: University of Chicago Press.

Scott, James C. (1990) *Domination and the Arts of Resistance: Hidden Transcripts*. New Haven: Yale University Press.

Scudder, Lewis R. (1990) "Ishmael and Isaac and Muslim-Christian Dialogue" *Dialog*. 29(1) 29–32.

Segal, Alan F. ([1984]1987) "The Sacrifice of Isaac in Early Judaism and Christianity." *The Other Judaisms of Late Antiquity*. Atlanta, Ga.: Scholars Press.

Shariati, Ali. (1980) *Hajj*. Houston, Tex.: Free Islamic Literature Inc.

Shengold, Leonard. (1972) "A Paraphraxis of Freud's in Relation to Karl Abraham." *American Imago* 29(2):123–59.

Sheppard, Gerald. (1986) "The Presentation of Abraham in the Christian Tradition." *Face to Face: An Interreligious Bulletin*. Vol. xiii:14–20.

Shulman, David. (1993) *The Hungry God: Hindu Tales of Filicide and Devotion*. Chicago: University of Chicago Press.

Sidel, Ruth. ([1986]1992) *Women and Children Last: The Plight of Poor Women in Affluent America*. New York: Penguin Books.

———. (1996) *Keeping Women and Children Last: America's War on the Poor*. New York: Penguin Books.

Siker, Jeffrey S. (1991) *Disinheriting the Jews: Abraham in Early Christian Controversy*. Louisville, Ky.: Westminster/John Knox Press.

Silberman, Neil Asher. (1982) *Digging for God and Country: Exploration in the Holy Land, 1799–1917*. New York: Doubleday, Anchor Books.

———. (1989) *Between Past and Present: Archaeology, Ideology, and Nationalism in the Modern Middle East*. New York: Doubleday, Anchor Books.

Smith, Morton. (1975) "A Note on Burning Babies." *JAOS* 95:477–79.

Smith, W. Robertson. (1889) *Lectures on the Religion of the Semites*. New York: D. Appleton & Co.

———. (1903) *Kinship and Marriage in Early Arabia*. Boston: Beacon Press.

Soler, J. (1977) "Dietary Prohibitions of the Hebrews." Elborg Forster, trans. *New York Review of Books* 26:10 (June 14), 24–30.

Speiser, E.A. (1963) "The Wife-Sister Motif in the Patriarchal Narratives." In *Biblical and Other Studies*. A. Altmann, ed. Cambridge: Harvard University Press.

———. (1964) *Genesis*. Translation and commentary for the Anchor Bible, New York: Doubleday & Co.

Spencer, W. B. and F. J. Gillen. (1899) *The Native Tribes of Central Australia*. London: Macmillan.

Spiegel, S. ([1950]1969) *The Last Trial*. Judah Goldin, trans. New York: Schocken Books.

Spiro, Melford. (1968) "Virgin Birth, Parthenogenesis, and Physiological Paternity: An Essay in Cultural Interpretation." *Man* New Series (3):242–61.

Spivak, Gayatri. (1988) "Can the Subaltern Speak?" In *Marxism and the Interpretation of Culture*. Cary Nelson and Lawrence Grossberg, eds. Urbana: University of Illinois Press, 271–313.

Stacey, Judith. (1994) "Dan Quayle's Revenge: The New Family Values Crusaders." *The Nation*, July 25/August 1, 119–22.

——— (1996) *In the Name of the Family: Rethinking Family Values in the Postmodern Age*. Boston: Beacon Press.

Stager, Lawrence. (1982) "Carthage: A View from the Tophet." *Phönizier Im Westen*. H. G. Niemeyer, ed. Mainz am Rhein: Verlag Philipp Von Zabern.

Stager, Lawrence and Samuel R. Wolff. (1984) "Child Sacrifice at Carthage: Religious Rite or Population Control?" *Biblical Archaeology Review* 30–51.

Stanton, Elizabeth Cady, ed. ([1895]1974) *The Woman's Bible*. Seattle: Coalition Task Force on Women and Religion.

Starting Points: Meeting the Needs of Our Youngest Children. April 1994. Carnegie Corporation of New York.

Steinmetz, Devora. (1991) *From Father to Son: Kinship, Conflict, and Continuity in Genesis*. Louisville, Ky.: Westminster/John Knox Press.

Strathern, Marilyn. (1980). "No Nature, No Culture: The Hagen Case." In *Nature, Culture, and Gender*. Carol MacCormack and Marilyn Strathern, eds. Cambridge: Cambridge University Press, 174–222.

Strenski, Ivan. (1996) "Between Theory and Speciality: Sacrifice in the 90s." *Religious Studies Review* 22(1):10–20.

Sulloway, Frank J. (1979) *Freud, The Biologist of the Mind*. New York: Basic Books.

Swetnam, James. (1981) *Isaac and Jesus*. Rome: Biblical Institute Press.

Syren, Roger. (1993) *The Forsaken First-Born: A Study of a Recurrent Motif in the Patriarchal Narratives*. Sheffield, England.: Sheffield Academic Press.

al-Tabari. ([c. 915] 1987) *The History of al-Tabari: Prophets and Patriarchs*. W. Brinner trans. Albany: State University of New York Press.

Talmud, Hebrew-English Edition of the Babylonian, Yoma. (1974) Rabbi Dr. Leo Jung, trans., Rabbi Dr. I. Epstein, ed., New York, London, Jerusalem: The Soncino Press.

Tapper, Nancy and Richard Tapper. (1987) "The Birth of the Prophet: Ritual and Gender in Turkish Islam." *Man* 22(1):69–92.

Targum Neofiti. (1992) Martin McNamara, MSC, trans. Minneapolis., Minn.: Michael Glazier Book Liturgical Press.

Targum Pseudo Jonathan: Genesis. (1992) Michael Maker, MSC, trans. Minneapolis, Minn.: Michael Glazier Book Liturgical Press.

Targum Onqelos. (1988) Bernard Grossfeld, Wilmington, Del.: Michael Glazier.

Tertullian. ([c. A.D. 160–230] 1970) "An Answer to the Jews." *Ante-Nicene Christian Library*. Vol. xviii. Edinburgh: T. & T. Clark. 201–53.

———. (1972) *Adversus Marcionem*. (Books 1–5) Ernest Evans, ed. and trans. Oxford: Clarendon Press.

———. (1970) "Adversus Praxean." *Ante-Nicene Christian Library*. Vol. xv. Edinburgh: T. & T. Clark.

Teubal, Savina. (1984) *Sarah the Priestess: The First Matriarch of Genesis*. Athens, Ohio: Swallow Press.

———. (1990) *Hagar The Egyptian: The Lost Tradition of the Matriarchs*. San Francisco: Harper and Row Publishers.

Thompson, Thomas L. (1974) *The Historicity of the Patriarchal Narratives: The Quest for the Historical Abraham*. Berlin: Walter de Gruyter.

Tietjen, John. (1988) "Hebrews 11:8–12." *Interpretation* 42:4, 403–07.

Tolosana, C. Lisón. (1979) *Brujería, Estructura Social y Simbolismo en Galicia.* Madrid: Akal.

Tonkinson, Robert. (1978) "Semen vs. Spirit Child in a Western Desert Culture." In *Australian Aboriginal Concepts.* L. R. Hiatt, ed. Atlantic Highlands, N.J.: Humanities Press.

Trible, Phyllis. (1978) *God and the Rhetoric of Sexuality.* Philadelphia: Fortress Press.

———. (1984) *Texts of Terror: Literary-Feminist Readings of Biblical Narratives.* Philadelphia: Fortress Press.

Turner, Victor. (1967) *The Forest of Symbols.* Ithaca: Cornell University Press.

——— (1972–3) "The Center Out There: Pilgrim's Goal." *History of Religions* 12:191–230.

Van der Horst, P. (1990) "Sarah's Seminal Emission: Hebrews 11:11 in the Light of Ancient Embryology." In *Greeks, Romans and Christians: Essays in Honor of Abraham J. Malherbe.* Minneapolis, Minn.: Fortress Press, 287–302.

———. (1992) "Did Sarah Have A Seminal Emission?" *Bible Review* 8(1) 35–9.

Van Herik, Judith. (1982) *Freud on Femininity and Faith.* Berkeley: University of California Press.

Van Seters, John. (1975) *Abraham in History and Tradition.* New Haven: Yale University Press.

Vaux, Roland de. (1961) *Ancient Israel: Its Life and Institutions.* John McHugh, trans., New York: McGraw Hill.

Vermes, Geza. ([1961]1973) *Scripture and Tradition in Judaism.* Leiden: E. J. Brill.

Waldman, Marilyn. (1986) "New Approaches to 'Biblical' Material in the Qur'an." *Studies in Islamic and Judaic Traditions.* William Brinner and S. Ricks, eds. Atlanta, Ga.: Scholars Press, 47–64.

Wallace, E. R. (1983) *Freud and Anthropology: A History and Reappraisal.* New York: International Universities Press.

Weiner, Annette. (1976) *Women of Value, Men of Renown.* Austin, Tex.: University of Texas Press.

———. (1978). "The Reproductive Model in Trobrand Society." *Mankind* 11:175–86.

Weinfeld, M. (1972) "The Worship of Molech and of the Queen of Heaven." *Ugarit Forschungen* 4:133–54.

———. (1978) "Burning Babies in Ancient Israel: A Rejoinder to Morton Smith's Article in JAOS 95 (1975)." *Ugarit Forschungen* 411–13.

Weininger, Otto. ([1903]1906) *Sex and Character.* London: W. Heineman; New York: Putnam.

Wellisch, Erich. (1954) *Isaac and Oedipus.* London: Routledge & Kegan Paul.

Wenham, G. J. (1980) "The Religion of the Patriarchs." In *Essays on the Patriarchal Narratives.* A. R. Millard and D. J. Wiseman, eds. Leicester, England: Inter-Varsity Press, 157–88.

Westermann, Claus. (1981) "Genesis 22:1–19, Abraham's Sacrifice." S. J. Scullion, trans. In *Genesis 12–36, A Commentary*. Minneapolis, Minn.: Augsburg Publishing House, 351–65.

Wharton, James A. (1988) "On the Road Again: Abraham and Contemporary Preaching." *Interpretation*. Vol. xlii (4):381–92.

Whitehead, Barbara Dafoe. (1993) "Dan Quayle Was Right." *Atlantic Monthly* 27(4):47–84.

Whorf, Benjamin. (1956) "The Relation of Habitual Thought and Behavior to Language." In *Language, Thought and Reality*. Cambridge, Mass.: M.I.T. Press.

Wilken, R. (1972) "The Christianizing of Abraham: The Interpretation of Abraham in Early Christianity." *Concordia Theological Monthly* 43:723–31.

———. (1976) "Melito, The Jewish Community at Sardis, and the Sacrifice of Isaac." *Theological Studies* 37(1) 53–69.

Wills, Lawrence M. (in press) *The Quest of the Historical Gospel: Mark, John, and the Origin of the Gospel Genre*. New York: Routledge Press.

Wineman, Lawrence. (1977) *The Akedah-Motif in the Modern Hebrew Story*. Ph.D. diss., UCLA.

Wiseman, D. J. (1980) "Abraham Reassessed." In *Essays on the Patriarchal Narratives*. A. R. Millard and D. J. Wiseman, eds. Leicester, England: Inter-Varsity Press, 139–56.

Wolkstein, Diane, and Samuel Noah Kramer. (1983) *Inanna: Queen of Heaven and Earth*. New York: Harper and Row.

Woolf, Rosemary. (1972) *English Mystery Plays*. Berkeley: University of California Press.

Wright, G. Ernest. (1960) *Biblical Archaeology*. Philadelphia: Westminster Press.

Yanagisako, Sylvia and Carol Delaney. (1995) *Naturalizing Power: Essays on Feminist Cultural Analysis*. New York: Routledge.

Yerushalmi, Yosef. (1986) "Freud on the 'Historical Novel': From the Manuscript Draft (1934) of *Moses and Monotheism*." *International Journal of Psycho-Analysis* 70:375–95.

———. (1991) *Freud's Moses: Judaism Terminable and Interminable*. New Haven: Yale University Press.

Young, Iris. (1995) "Mothers, Citizenship, and Independence: A Critique of Pure Family Values." *Ethics* 105:535–56.

Zeligs, Dorothy. (1954) "Abraham and Monotheism." *American Imago* 11(3) 293–316.

Index

Abel, 21, 72, 94, 141, 179, 211

Abraham: as before and above the law, 68, 123; Freud's references to, 205, 207; as friend of God, 163; God's promise to seed of, 14, 20, 23, 96, 109, 113, 117–18, 132, 134, 145–48, 151, 153, 168–69, 249; as having misunderstood God, 116, 222; as heroic figure, 117, 221; lineage of, 92, 124, 146, 170; as model of faith, 7, 14, 19, 101, 104, 123, 233–34, 251, 264n.25; as model of faith, in Christian community, 5, 6, 21–22, 59, 111, 147, 153–56, 250; as model of faith, in Islamic community, 5, 6, 59, 111, 180–83; as model of faith, in Jewish community, 5, 6, 21–22, 59, 125–28; Muhammad's parallels with, 172, 174, 179; paternity concerns of, 139; as patriarch, 17, 23, 119–20, 221; as Protestant figure, 58, 154–56; as sole possessor of child to be sacrificed, 7, 18, 22–23, 32, 59–60, 108–9, 234; submissiveness of, to God, 22, 44, 111, 116, 117, 162, 169, 222, 264n.25; ten trials of, 116, 272n.18; tomb of, 20; willingness of, to sacrifice his child, 6–7, 101, 107, 118, 124, 146, 149, 163, 169, 191, 234, 237; as witness for Christ, 148, 154. *See also* Abraham story; circumcision; Hagar; Isaac; Ishmael; Sarah

Abraham (television miniseries), 9, 275n.2

Abraham, Karl, 200, 202, 208–10, 285n.24

Abraham story (Akedah): absence of women from, 17–18, 60–63, 251; in art, 10, 110, 136, 138, 140, 150, 161, 175,

222; Christian references to, 137–60; contemporary uses of, 9, 130–35; as a cultural text, 9–10, 34, 74, 141; destructive legacy of, 13–14, 20–21, 109, 184, 233–53; in fiction, 9, 130–31, 256n.7; as foundational story for Judaism, Christianity, and Islam, 5, 6, 17, 20, 21–23, 73, 90–91, 101, 107, 162–63, 190, 210, 229, 233, 237, 255n.2; Freud's ignoring of, 189–210, 229; impact of, on children, 9, 50–51, 141, 163, 204, 233–50, 275n.5; as injunction against child sacrifice, 13, 33, 71, 101, 104, 218, 219; Jewish and Muslim overlaps concerning, 167–68; in Middle Ages, 126–28, 149–51, 170–71; as most patriarchal of stories, 12; obedience as theme in, 14, 32, 85, 104, 111, 116–18, 127, 129, 132, 154–55, 215, 222, 233; paternity concept established in, 94; in *piyyut*, 127; in popular culture, 9, 10, 132–36, 138; power of, 6; as precursor of Crucifixion story, 8, 46–47, 75, 109, 118, 119, 132, 137, 138–39, 141–44, 151, 153–54; psychoanalytic views of, 211–29; rationality vs. emotionality in, 49, 117, 125, 223, 234, 289n.1; redemptive quality of, 118, 120; and resurrection, 122, 138–39, 143, 153–54, 183, 273n.24; self-sacrifice vs. child sacrifice in, 22, 116–17; separation and individuation themes in, 221–22; succession as theme in, 85, 100–101; as test of faith, 21–22, 73, 115–20, 127, 168, 279n.14; as universal, 77–78, 90; in Valenti episode, 5, 53, 56, 59; Vedic

About the Author

Carol Delaney is Associate Professor of Anthropology at Stanford University and has a master's degree in theological studies from Harvard Divinity School. She is the author of *The Seed and the Soil: Gender and Cosmology in Turkish Village Society*.

the last time i saw you

the last time
i saw you

 A NOVEL

ELIZABETH
BERG

RANDOM HOUSE / NEW YORK

The Last Time I Saw You is a work of fiction. Names, characters, places, and incidents are the products of the author's imagination or are used fictitiously. Any resemblance to actual events, locales, or persons, living or dead, is entirely coincidental.

Published in the United States by Random House, an imprint of The Random House Publishing Group, a division of Random House, Inc., New York.

RANDOM HOUSE and colophon are registered trademarks of Random House, Inc.

LIBRARY OF CONGRESS CATALOGING-IN-PUBLICATION DATA
Berg, Elizabeth.
The last time I saw you: a novel / Elizabeth Berg.
p.   cm.
ISBN 978-1-4000-6864-7
eBook ISBN 978-1-58836-892-8
1. Class reunions—Fiction.   2. Reminiscing—Fiction.
I. Title.
PS3552.E6996L37 2010
813'.54—dc22   2009040008

Printed in the United States of America on acid-free paper

www.atrandom.com

2 4 6 8 9 7 5 3 1

First Edition

Book design by Susan Turner

For Phyllis Florin
and
Marianne Quasha

High school, those are your prime suffering years.
You don't get better suffering than that.

—UNCLE FRANK (Steve Carell), *Little Miss Sunshine*

Every parting gives a foretaste of death
as every reunion a hint of the resurrection.

—ARTHUR SCHOPENHAUER

Maybe one day I can have a reunion with myself.

—SEBASTIAN BACH

the last time i saw you

ONE

DOROTHY SHAUMAN LEDBETTER SHAUMAN IS STANDING IN front of the bathroom mirror in her black half-slip and black push-up bra, auditioning a look. Her fortieth high school reunion, the last one, is one week away, and she's trying to decide whether or not to draw a beauty mark above her lip for the occasion. It wouldn't be entirely false; she does have a mole there, but it's faint, hard to see. She just wants to enhance what already exists, nothing wrong with that; it's de rigueur if you're a woman, and it's becoming more common in men, too. Wrong as that is. Dorothy would never have anything to do with a man who wore makeup or dyed his hair or carried a purse or wore support hose or cried or did any of those womanly things men are appropriating as though it's their god-given right. No. She prefers an all-American, red-blooded male who is not a jerk. They're hard to find, but she holds out hope that she will have some sort of meaningful relationship with one before she's six feet under.

She regards herself in the mirror, tilts her head this way and

that. Yes, a beauty mark would be fun, kind of playful. She pencils in the mark gingerly, then steps back to regard herself. Not bad. Not bad at all. *Sexy.* Just like she wanted. *Helloooo,* Marilyn. She pictures Pete Decker looking up from his table full of jocks when she walks into the hotel ballroom and saying, *Va va va voom!* And then, *Dorothy?* Dorothy *Shauman?*

"Uh-huh," she will say, lightly, musically, and walk right past him. Though she will walk close enough to him for him to smell her perfume. Also new. One hundred and ten smackeroos. She got perfume, not cologne, even though her personal belief is that there is no difference. She'd asked the counter woman about that. She'd leaned in confidentially and said, "Now, come on. Tell me, *really.* If you were my best friend, would you tell me to get the perfume over the cologne?" And the woman had looked her right in the eye and said, "*Yes.*" Dorothy was a little miffed, because the woman had acted as though Dorothy had affronted her dignity or questioned her ethics or something. Like the time Dr. Strickland was telling Dorothy to get a certain ($418!!!) blood test and she'd said, "Would you tell your *wife* to get it?" And Dr. Strickland had drawn himself up and quietly said, "I would." Dorothy had been all set to give him an affectionate little punch and say, "Oh, come on, now; don't be so *prissy,*" but then Dr. Strickland had added, "If she were still alive," and that had just ruined everything. It wasn't *her* fault the woman had died! Dorothy had been going to refuse the test no matter what, but when he said his wife was dead, well, then she had to get it. Those dead people had more power than they thought.

Dorothy has never gone to a high school reunion. She'd been married when they had them before, and who wanted to bring *that* to a reunion. Now she is divorced, plus she saw that movie about saying yes to life. She steps closer to the mirror and raises her chin so her turkey neck disappears. She'll hold her head like this when she walks by Pete Decker. Later, when they're making

out in his car, it will be dark, and she won't have to be so vigilant. Oh, she hopes he drives to the reunion; she happens to know he lives a mere three and a half hours away. She knows his exact address, in fact; and she Google-Earthed him, which was very exciting.

In high school, Pete had a four-on-the-floor metallic green GTO, and Dorothy always wanted to make out with him in that car. But she never even got to sit in it. She bets he has something like a red Lexus coupe now. And she bets that at the reunion he'll watch her for a while, then come up to her and say, "Hey, Dots. Want to take a walk?" And she'll say, all innocent, "Where?" And he'll get a little flustered and say something like "You know, just a *walk,* get some *air.*" She'll hesitate just for a second, just long enough to make him think she might refuse, and then she'll shrug prettily before she agrees to accompany him outside. They'll go right to his car and he'll open the passenger-side door and raise an eyebrow and she'll say, "*Pete!*" like she's offended at the very notion. But then she'll get in, will she ever. She likes this part of the fantasy best: She'll get in, he'll come around and get in on his side, and then, just before he lunges at her, he'll look at her with smoke practically coming out of his eyes. And in her eyes, a soft *Yes, I know. I, too, have wanted this for years.*

Dorothy does plan on being a little mean to Pete at first; she has finally learned it can be a good thing to be mean to men. Apparently they like it; it's supposed to appeal to their hunting instinct. That's why she's going to walk right by him when he first sees her and notices how attractive she is. Considering.

Her daughter, Hilly, is the one who told her about being mean to men. She said you do it just at the beginning and then every so often, just to keep up a level of intrigue, like immunization shots. And it works, too, because when Hilly started doing it, wasn't she *engaged* in what seemed like ten minutes! She's getting married in Costa Rica next month, and Dorothy thinks it's a

wonderful idea, the destination wedding. Thank God Dorothy's ex will pay for everything. Poor he was not. She supposes he'll bring his new wife to the wedding, and pander to her every single second. Holding her hand, as though they were teenagers. Bringing her drinks, as though the woman is incapable of doing anything for herself. Staring into her eyes like the secret of the universe is written there. It's nauseating, the way they behave, anyone would say so. Hilly calls them the Magnets, though she might only do that to offer some kind of support to her mother, who lives alone now and must take out the garbage and figure out whom to call for repairs and check the locks at night and kill centipedes in the basement and everything else. Dorothy suspects the truth is, Hilly actually likes her stepmother. She hasn't said so directly, but she did say that she's happy for her dad, and wasn't that just like nails on a chalkboard. But Dorothy did the noble thing and said yes, she was, too. Uh-huh, yes, he did seem happy now, Dorothy said, and she just wanted to throw up.

Hilly's fiancé is a doctor. A proctologist, specializing in the wonderful world of buttholes and rectums, but still. Dorothy is working up to asking the question that—come on!—must occur to everyone to ask him: What exactly made you choose this line of work? When Dorothy tried to ask her daughter about it, all Hilly did was get mad. It is true Dorothy could have used a more sensitive approach—what she'd asked Hilly was "Why in the wide, wide world would you ever want to look up people's *heinies* all day?" Still, Dorothy doesn't see why Hilly had to take such offense. Her daughter had said something like perhaps Dorothy should consider the fact that preventing and treating cancer is a pretty noble goal. But that still didn't answer the *question,* did it?

Dorothy thinks it was a book her daughter read that taught her about being mean to men. Who knows, if Dorothy had been mean to Pete Decker in high school, they might have gotten mar-

ried. They went out once—well, not a date technically, but they did spend some time together on the class trip to Washington, D.C., and Dorothy was *awfully* nice to Pete and then of course that was that, he never called her. But if they had gotten married, they probably would have gotten divorced, and then she wouldn't be looking forward so much to going to her high school reunion. Apart from her friends Linda Studemann and Judy Holt, she's really only going to see him. And, to be honest, to show off her recent weight loss. That was the one nice thing about her divorce: During the grief part, before she realized how much better off she was without her husband, she lost twenty-three pounds. She bets she'll look better than the cheerleaders, and even better than Candy Sullivan, who had been queen of everything. Not that Candy Sullivan is coming. According to Pam Pottsman, who is the contact person for this year's reunion, Candy came to the five-year reunion and hasn't come to any since. "Is she dead?" Dorothy asked, ready to offer an impromptu eulogy praising Candy's good points, even though Candy never gave Dorothy the time of day. But Pam said no, Candy wasn't dead, apparently she just thought she was too good to come, and then they both started talking about what a snob Candy always was, and she wasn't even really all that hot. "Did you know she stuffed her bra?" Pam said, and Dorothy said, "*Really?*" and felt that delicious rush, and Pam said, "Yup, I sat across from her in Mr. Simon's psychology class and I saw Kleenex coming out of the top of her blouse one day and I whispered to her that it was showing and she got all embarrassed and stuffed it back in and wouldn't look at me."

"But wait a minute," Dorothy said. "I saw her naked in gym class, and she didn't need any Kleenex."

"What year?"

"Senior. And she did not need Kleenex."

"Well, that psychology class was sophomore year," Pam said, and she sounded a little disappointed that Candy Sullivan had

outgrown her need for bra stuffing. But then she told Dorothy how a lot more people were coming this year than ever before, probably because it was the last reunion their class was going to have; and she named several of their classmates who had signed up. Dorothy thinks it will be fun to see poor Mary Alice Mayhew, who is coming for her very first reunion, just as Dorothy is. Though there the similarity ends, thank you very much. Such a little mouse Mary Alice was, walking down the hall and looking at the floor, all hunched over her schoolbooks. She wore awful plaid dresses, and she never wore nylons, just thin white ankle socks, not even kneesocks. And loafers that were *not* Weejuns, you could tell. From a mile away, you could tell. Poor thing. And wait, didn't she put *pennies* in them? There's always one of them, and in their school, it was Mary Alice Mayhew.

Oh, and Lester Hessenpfeffer, who was screwed the moment he was christened. Lester's uncle, who was present at his birth, had just changed his own last name to Hess, and he suggested that Lester's father do the same for the sake of his newborn son. Lester's father reportedly screamed, "Change our name! Change our *name*? Why should we change our name? Let the rest of the world change *their* names!" Lester had told that story once when someone teased him about his name. You had to give Lester this: he was always an affable guy who didn't ever seem to take things personally.

Poor Lester. Never dated. He had such a cute face, but he was too much of a brain, and too sensitive. He probably ended up in computers. Maybe he got rich, like that homely Microsoft guy. And if so, you can bet your boots that Dorothy will be saying hello to him, too.

If Mary Alice Mayhew really comes to the reunion, Dorothy will make a point of being nice to her. Yes she will. She'll buy her a drink; oh, what a hoot to think of buying Mary Alice Mayhew a drink. So odd to think that they're *old* enough to drink now.

Mary Alice had silver cat-eye glasses with rhinestones on them and her hair always looked like she'd taken the rollers out and not brushed it. Dorothy has heard plenty of stories about how ugly ducklings come to their high school reunions as swans, but she'd bet money that Mary Alice looks much the same, only with wrinkles. She wouldn't be the Botox type. Dorothy's position on Botox is *Thank God*. Who cares if you can't move your eyebrows around like caterpillars on a plate?

"Is Pete Decker coming?" Dorothy asked Pam.

"He is."

"And his wife, too?"

"He only registered himself. You know Pete. Oh, I can hardly wait to see him again. What a dreamboat he was."

"Oh, did you think so?" Dorothy studied her nails casually, as though she and Pam were talking in person. If you wanted to sound a certain way, even on the telephone, it was good to act a certain way—the feeling crept into your voice. You were supposed to smile when you were talking on the phone if you wanted to sound friendly. A lot of the people who made recordings for telephone prompts seemed to do that, though such recordings always make Dorothy want to bang the phone against the wall until the wires fall out.

"I thought Pete Decker was the most handsome boy in the school!" Pam said. "Didn't you?"

"I don't know. I guess a lot of people found him attractive." Dorothy sniffed then, and changed the subject. No need for Pam to know of Dorothy's designs on Pete; Pam was quicker than Twitter at spreading things around.

Dorothy turns and views herself from the side: not bad. The bra, bought yesterday on her final stop for putting together a killer outfit, is doing what it promised; her breasts are hiked up and perky, rather than hanging down so low they appear to be engaging in conversation with her belly button. Eighty-five dol-

lars for a bra! At least it's French. Dorothy always likes it when things are French. In the dressing room, she'd sniffed the bra to see if it smelled like Chanel or something, but no, it smelled like rubber. Not for long. Dorothy will have *everything* perfumed when she goes to that reunion, even her you-know-what. But she'll have to remember to *pat* it on down there; last time she sprayed, she gave herself a urinary tract infection and, oh, does she hate cranberry juice.

She steps back from the mirror, then leans in to darken the beauty mark. Perfect. She should take a picture of herself to remember to do it just like this on Saturday night. They're having a Saturday night dinner followed by a dance, complete with a DJ who's supposed to be really good and not tacky, and then there's a Sunday brunch. Two times for a final try at glory.

Dorothy's stomach growls, and she puts her hand over it and says aloud, "*No.*"

TWO

L ESTER HESSENPFEFFER AWAKENS ON A BATH RUG STUFFED into the corner of a gigantic cage and stares into the open eyes of the bull mastiff. The dog wags his tail once, twice, and Lester feels his chest tighten with joy. Just before he fell asleep, he'd been preparing a speech for the dog's owners about how he'd done his best, how he'd tried everything, but . . . Samson had ingested a few Legos the day before, which the owners' great-grandchildren had left lying about. One had perforated his intestine. By the time he was brought to Lester's clinic, the dog was in shock and the prospects for saving him were almost nil. Lester had slept in the cage with him to provide comfort not so much to the dog as to himself. He'd known Samson since he was a puppy, and he was very fond of the owners, an elderly couple who thought Samson hung the moon. They'd wanted to spend the night at the clinic, but after Lester told them he'd be literally right beside the dog, they reluctantly went home. Lester had hoped they'd get some sleep, so that they could more easily bear the news he was pretty certain he'd have to deliver in the morning.

This is always the worst part of his job, telling people their pet has died. Sometimes they know it, at least empirically; on more than one occasion someone has brought a dead animal into the office hoping against hope that Lester can revive it. And when he can't, he must say those awful words: *I'm so sorry.* He's noticed a certain posture many people assume on hearing those words. They step back and cross their arms, as though guarding themselves against any more pain, or as though holding one more time the animal they loved as truly as any other family member, if not more. Oftentimes, they nod, too, their heads saying yes to what their hearts cannot yet accept.

But here Samson is, alive and well enough to give Lester's face a good washing with a tongue the size of a giant oven mitt. "Hey, pal," Lester says. "You made it! Let's have a look at that dressing." He rises to his knees and very gently turns the dog slightly onto his side. Samson whimpers and holds overly still, in the way that dogs often do when they're frightened. There's a lot of drainage, but nothing leaking through. He'll give Samson something for pain and then call Stan and Betty. By the time he's done talking to them—he can anticipate at least a few of the questions they'll have—he'll be able to change the dressing without causing the dog undue distress. He thinks Samson will be able to stand and move about a little this afternoon, and imagines him lifting his leg with great dignity against the portable fireplug his staff uses for cage-bound male dogs (the girls get Astroturf). The portable bathrooms had been Jeanine's idea; she was always coming up with good ideas. She had the idea for Pet Airways before they came up with Pet Airways, although her suggestion was that pets and owners fly together—cages would be installed next to seats so that an owner could reach down and scratch behind an ear, or speak reassuringly, or offer a snack. This was a much better idea for alleviating the stress caused to animals when they fly, and Lester advised Jeanine to write to Pet Airways suggesting

it. She said she'd rather keep the idea for herself because she wanted to start Dog Airways, as it is her belief that only dogs *really* care when their owners are gone. She is by her own admission a dog chauvinist, but she's good to all the animals who come to the clinic, even the hamster whose hysterical owner brought her in because she was gobbling up her babies as soon as she gave birth to them.

Jeanine also had the idea that Lester should attend his high school reunion. When the invitation had come to the clinic, Jeanine had opened it, and then immediately begun a campaign to get her boss to go. Lester knew what she had in mind—she wanted him to find a woman.

When he was twenty-nine years old and had been married for only a year, Lester's four-months-pregnant wife, Kathleen, had been killed in a car accident. Since that time, not only has he not remarried but he has not dated. Oh, he has some women friends, and he's pretty sure some of them have had little crushes on him. But despite the charms of this woman or that, there's never been anyone who moved him the way his wife did. He had just opened the clinic when she was killed; Kathleen had worked as the receptionist for the grand total of four days before he lost her. It doesn't hurt the way it did at first—how could anyone survive such a thing?—but there is a place for Kathleen in his heart that leaves no room for anyone else. He is at peace with the idea of living the rest of his life alone, even if Jeanine isn't.

But he did finally agree to go to the reunion. It might be interesting to see all those people again, even though he'd never really been close to any of them. He'd pretty much kept to himself, for many reasons. He wonders if any of his classmates look anything like they used to, or if at the reunion they'll all walk around squinting at name tags, then looking up with ill-disguised disbelief into a person's face. He feels *he* still somewhat resembles the boy he used to be, but then he guesses that everyone does

that, sees in the mirror a mercifully edited version of themselves different from what everyone else sees.

Lester was very pleased to see that, on check-in at the reunion, he would be given a box lunch. He feels about the words "box lunch" the way Henry James felt about the words "summer afternoon"—that they are the most beautiful words in the English language.

But mostly Lester agreed to go to the reunion so that he could get Jeanine off his back. He'd even asked her if she'd like to accompany him. Jeanine is married, seemingly happily so, but Lester thought she might get a kick out of going. He'd told her her husband could come, too; they'd find a way to sneak him in. Or maybe they wouldn't have to sneak him at all—anyone who looked to be in their late fifties would probably be able to walk right in, once people deserted their posts at the registration table. "That's true," Jeanine had said. "I used to think sometimes about crashing high school reunions, walking around asking people, 'Do you remember me? You remember *me,* don't you?' just to see what they'd say. But no, you need to go alone or you'll never meet someone. Not a wife, just someone to go to the movies with. It's your *last reunion*!" What she had not said, but what Lester heard, is, "You're getting old, now. It's not funny. You're going to *need* someone."

"All *right,*" he'd finally said. "I'll *go.*" And Jeanine had clapped her hands together and asked if she could pick out what he should wear and he'd said no, thank you. She'd asked if she could refer him to a good hairstylist, and he'd said all right because he actually did need to find someone new to cut his hair—his barber's cataracts had gotten so bad, Lester always came out of the shop looking a little electrocuted.

As soon as Lester agreed to go to the reunion, he'd actually started looking forward to it. Not because he was thinking of meeting someone he could go to the movies with, no. He doesn't

need anyone to go to the movies with, he likes going alone, in fact. He likes sitting there with his popcorn and small Coke ("small" being roughly the size of a silo) and watching movies and thinking about them on his walk home. He likes putting in a garden every spring, nourishing it every summer, and putting it to bed every fall. He likes traveling to Europe every October. He loves reading, mostly history or biography, but classics, too; he never tires of rereading Proust or Dickens or Tolstoy or Flaubert. He also likes sitting in the living room of his small, well-tended two-bedroom house, listening to jazz while he enjoys a little scotch. He likes the way Rosaria changes his sheets every Thursday, the way the bed always smells so good then. He'd asked her once what she did to make the sheets smell so good and she'd put her hand up over her mouth, over her gold-filled teeth, and giggled. "Nothing especial; is detergent only, Doctor," she'd said. And he'd said no, it was something more, it must be that she had magical powers, yes, that must be it, and she had giggled again.

Rosaria had worked for him for many years, and occasionally he accepted one of her frequent invitations to have dinner at her house—both she and her husband, Ernesto, were inspired cooks, and Lester also enjoyed the company of their ever-expanding family, especially the black-eyed grandchildren who crawled all over him and brought him their stuffed animals to examine and treat. Rosaria had tried for a while to fix him up with various single women she knew—she would invite women to dinner on the nights he came, all kinds of women—but he never felt drawn to pursuing a relationship.

Over and over, it seems, he has to explain that his life is fine. He has his work and his friends and the beauty of the rotating earth. He does not feel he lacks anything, and he certainly does not think going to a high school reunion will put him on the path for finding a replacement for Kathleen. No, he's going to the reunion because there is something about it being the last one; and

he also wants to go because, after he spoke to Pam Pottsman, he learned that Don Summers had become a vet, too. He wants to talk shop in a way he feels he couldn't do otherwise—surely a high school reunion permits a kind of honesty one does not often encounter in one's adult life. A high school classmate might be the equivalent of family in terms of offering an intimate access, as well as a lowering of the usual defenses. Lester imagines leaning against a makeshift bar and talking to Don about a lot of things: The ethics of chemo for extending the lives of suffering animals. The increase in aggressive behavior in dogs—is it from them being put in cages and left alone for so long? How many immunizations are now proven to be carcinogenic? Lester also wants to ask Don if he doesn't feel a little like a bullshit artist when he advocates brushing pets' teeth. Especially under anesthesia. Lester himself can't recommend it. Give a dog a marrow bone, give a cat a break.

If he were going to be completely truthful, Lester would have to admit that there is one other person he is interested in seeing at the reunion, one he's not thought about since he left high school, but now that he has been reminded of her, he wants very much to see what kind of woman she became. He hopes she shows up, but he'll keep it to himself, that kind of hope.

In his office, Lester dials the number for Stan and Betty Kruger. It rings several times and then Betty answers in an uncharacteristically soft voice.

"Betty?"

"Oh, God," she says.

"No, it's *good* news," Lester says, and Betty begins to cry.

"STAN!" she yells. "He MADE it! Samson's OKAY!" To Lester, she says, "We're coming right now. I'm in my robe and pajamas. Don't look."

After Lester hangs up, he sits back in his chair, his hands clasped behind his head. He thinks about a man he met on a train

in France last year. The man, Hugo, asked him what the saddest experience he ever had as a vet was, and Lester said it was the day he had to tell someone whose son had died of cancer that the son's dog, whom the father had adopted, had developed the exact same disease. It happened more often than people knew, that dogs developed the same illnesses as their owners: diabetes, adrenal diseases, cancers. It was one of those mysterious things.

"And the happiest experience?" Hugo asked, and Lester said the happiest came after one of the saddest: he'd made a house call to put down a fourteen-year-old tricolor collie named Mike whom Lester had often seen standing with the family's kids at the end of the driveway while they waited for the school bus. Their mother had told Lester that Mike would go to the same spot and wait for the kids to come home in the afternoon, always at precisely the right time. "We never tell him the kids are coming," she'd said. "He just knows. He'll go to the door and bark to be let out, and the kids will arrive right afterward, without fail." One Easter, the family had gotten a duckling, and he and the dog had become best friends—they'd slept together every night until the duck died, and Mike often visited the duck's grave, his tail wagging on the way there, hanging low on the way back. On the day Lester came to put the dog down, the family had Mike lying on a quilt and had just offered him beef tips, which the dog had refused. Four months later, the owners had returned to Lester's clinic with a new puppy, a beautiful female tricolor.

"So. This is life, eh?" Hugo said. "We lose something here, we get something there. The trick is to stop looking in the old place to find the new thing."

Lester nodded, and then he stared out the window of the train at the countryside as they traveled through it. Sometimes it was hilly; sometimes it was flat; always, in one way or another, it was beautiful.

THREE

MARY ALICE MAYHEW PUTS THE SOFT-BOILED EGG INTO the bright blue porcelain holder she bought at the thrift shop yesterday. Presentation is all. If Einer Olson finds his breakfast good-looking, maybe he'll eat it. She adds a bud vase with a half-opened yellow rose, though this is more for her benefit than for his. Einer is indifferent to flowers. He says all they do is die.

She carries the breakfast tray into his fusty-smelling bedroom. He insists on eating in his bedroom, sitting in an armchair next to the window where he can look out onto the street below. She places his meal on the TV tray before him, and cracks open the window. "It's beautiful out there today," she says.

"Is it?"

"Seventy-six degrees, no humidity. None. Perfect September day."

"Huh." He picks up his spoon, taps it against the egg. "I don't think I can eat this. Why don't you have it?"

"I already had an egg for breakfast. It was delicious. That one's for you." She moves over to his bed to make it. It appears

he had a restless night: the sheets are twisted, the pillows flung onto the floor.

"I can't get it out of the shell."

She smiles over at him. "Sure you can."

He sits staring at the egg. Then, after a few tries, he slices off the top, dips the spoon in, and takes a bite. "That's enough." He pushes the tray away.

Mary Alice comes over to stand before him. "One more bite, and a half slice of the toast. It's Swedish rye, from Uppman's Bakery. You love their bread."

He looks up at her, his eyes magnified hugely by his glasses. It seems hard for him to breathe today: through the thin fabric of his shirt, she can see the muscles in his shoulders moving to help him. And has he gotten paler overnight? She feels a rush of anxiety, and it comes to her that Einer is her best friend. She doesn't want to think about what life will be like without him. She pushes his tray closer to him and speaks gently. "Eat just a little more. Then we can go out on the porch and read the newspaper and you can gripe."

He looks out the window, considering. "No more egg. A bite of toast. One bite."

"Two bites of toast, and a big drink of orange juice."

"You drive a hard bargain," he says. But then he mutters, "Deal."

Einer is ninety-two years old and Mary Alice's next-door neighbor. Two years ago, when Mary Alice moved back to town and into her parents' vacant house, he'd hired her for caregiving services, though he claimed he didn't really need help with anything except weeding the garden. She'd worked for him for a few weeks, then moved on to another job. Einer has a full-time caregiver named Rita Essinger now, but Mary Alice still comes over at least once a week to help out. While she takes care of Einer, Rita runs errands or just takes some time for herself. She always

thanks Mary Alice profusely, but the truth is, Mary Alice offers relief for a selfish reason. She doesn't want Rita to burn out and quit. It's important that Einer have the right kind of person caring for him, and Mary Alice doesn't want to have to go through another round of seemingly endless interviews on his behalf anytime soon.

Mary Alice had been working as a research assistant in a laboratory in Cincinnati when the economy went bonkers in 2008. After a few months of trying unsuccessfully to find another job in that city, she had moved back to Clear Springs. It only made sense—she could live in her parents' house rent free, and besides, someone needed to take care of the place. Mary Alice's mother had died only a few weeks after Einer's wife had—Einer said it was because the two of them just *had* to have their coffee klatch every day, and if it meant Mary Alice's mother dying in order to continue that, well, so be it. "They're up there in heaven, sitting with their mugs and stollen and not letting God get a word in edgewise," he'd told her.

After Mary Alice's mother's death, the house had sat empty for months. It was only partly because of the real estate crisis that had accompanied the country's economic collapse. The house had problems. Not structural ones—it was a beautiful American foursquare, built at a time when there was a lot of integrity in both materials and contractors, and it had been well maintained. But it was reportedly haunted, and in a small town like this, word had spread; even the realtor had said she had a legal obligation to disclose this odd fact to potential buyers who hadn't already heard the rumor. In addition to that, the interior had not been remodeled since it was built in the thirties; the one bathroom had a chain used for flushing the toilet, its tank up high against the wall. The kitchen had no dishwasher, no fancy stove and refrigerator, no granite counters. Mary Alice liked it that way. She especially liked the large walk-in pantry with the

cabbage-rose-flowered drape that she and her sister used to make into a theater curtain when they put on shows. And she liked the ghost. All it did was occasionally make walking sounds on the creaky floors—it was like a roommate who kept you company but didn't run up the grocery bill. So she came back to live in this house she'd grown up in, a place full of memories.

Sometimes when Mary Alice lies in bed in what used to be her parents' bedroom, she thinks about the day her father died. It happened on a cold winter day, when she was a junior in high school. She'd gone to the auditorium for band practice after school. The sky had been dark and menacing all day, and she'd been watching through the high, dirty windows for the predicted snow to start falling. She'd been worrying about her mother having to come to school to pick her up—her mother was a terrible driver under the best of circumstances. But then the office secretary had come and spoken quietly to the music teacher, who told Mary Alice she needed to go to the principal's office for a message. She remembers the other kids in the band falling silent to watch her walk off the stage and then across the polished floor, her footsteps echoing, her clarinet case bumping into her knee. Someone had whispered, "*What's* her name?" and she had felt a shameful blip of hope that now she might finally be known for something.

She had suspected that the principal was going to deliver bad news, but she'd never anticipated how bad. Mr. Spurry told her there'd been an emergency involving her father and he'd been asked to give her a ride home. "Okay," she'd said immediately, and then immediately regretted it, as though her easy acceptance of the fact made it more true than she wanted it to be.

Mr. Spurry had accompanied Mary Alice to her locker to get her coat and her books. Then he'd walked with her out to the teachers' parking lot. He'd opened his car's passenger door for her, which had embarrassed her. She'd sat stiffly upright in the

front seat, her hands folded on her knees, her knees pressed tightly together, afraid that anything more casual might be seen as rude, or inappropriate; or that it might bring bad luck. She'd kept silent, and so had he. She'd listened to the music that played low on the radio, thinking that she didn't want to know this much about Mr. Spurry: what he drove, what station he listened to, how his car smelled slightly of something like hamburger grease.

When she'd come into the house, her older sister, Sarah Jane, and her mother had been sitting at the kitchen table. Her sister wouldn't stop crying and her mother was starkly dry-eyed, and each had seemed to Mary Alice to be equally bad. After Mary Alice found out what had happened to her father—an aortic aneurysm had burst; he'd never had a chance—she'd gone into her parents' bedroom and sat for a while on her father's side of the bed. She'd held his pillow and sat looking out the window as the sky abruptly lightened—the storm had never come. Later, she'd made fried egg sandwiches for the three of them for dinner. It was when her mother was washing the dishes from that dinner that she'd finally started to cry. She'd stood in her apron, her head bowed over the sink, her hands dripping at her sides, and she'd said, "Oh, *Gerald*," as though her husband had grievously disappointed her, and then she'd cried and cried. Mary Alice had put her arms around her mother and rocked her in place. Her sister had sat bent over in her kitchen chair watching them, her hands shoved between her knees, and she was rocking, too, moving in that same universal rhythm. Mary Alice had looked at the bent heads of her mother and her sister and a thought had come to her: *You'll have to be the father, now.* So she had not cried. Not then, not that night, and not for many days afterward. The day after the funeral, her mother had gotten a job at the dime store, and the girls had helped out with babysitting and paper route money, so they were able to keep the house.

And here Mary Alice was again. The first day she worked for Einer, she'd told him she was glad to be back, she'd always liked Clear Springs.

Einer hadn't quite believed her. He said it had seemed to him that she'd led an awfully lonely life, sitting out there on the porch steps with her book and her glass of red Kool-Aid almost every summer afternoon when all the other kids, including her sister, were at the pool, or the movies, or hanging around downtown. And later, when she grew older, spending most Saturday nights at home with her mom instead of going out with some fellow.

"You know what, Einer?" she told him. "I had a very happy childhood." And when he frowned, deepening his already deep wrinkles, she said, "I did!"

Oh, it's true that Mary Alice had had her moments, growing up; sometimes she sat outside Sarah Jane's bedroom door listening to her gab on the phone and wondering if anyone would ever call her and inspire her to talk in that excited, girlfriendy way, full of gasps and exclamations; or in that low, seductive voice Sarah Jane used when she talked to boys.

As it happened, no one did call her. "Well, why don't *you* call someone?" her mother used to ask, and Mary Alice couldn't explain why not. It was . . . It was that something had to happen *before* you called, and that something had simply never happened to Mary Alice. So she learned—and came to like, really—a certain self-reliance. The world engaged and excited her; she looked forward to each day despite the injustices she endured in high school. She had been lucky to have a friend in her ninth-grade English teacher, a gay man, she realizes now, who'd told her that high school was good for getting a ticket into college, and that was all. Unless you counted the macaroni and cheese this school's cafeteria served twice a month. That was good, too. Otherwise, put everything in perspective, he'd told her. Life is long; you'll be fine, he'd said, and she was.

Mary Alice now works at a day-care center, in the toddler room. Her specialty is kids who bite—she somehow gets them not to. If a child bites someone, she takes them into the corner and talks to them in a very quiet voice and they almost never bite again. The other workers call her the Toddler Whisperer.

She has a way with children in general, she's discovered; she, more than anyone else at the center, can make them laugh, and there is no tonic like the sound of children laughing. No pleasure quite so pure. She doesn't make much money, but she's happy surrounded by children and glue and blunt-nosed scissors and fat crayons and Play-Doh. She likes the stuffed animals, the colorful balls, the blocks. In the reading corner are an oversize rocking chair and kids' books galore—the illustrations are marvelous, and the stories more intriguing than one might suspect. She likes watching children press their small hands against the sides of the day care's gigantic aquarium and talk earnestly to the fish; and she likes watching them play in the housekeeping corner, roughly dressing and undressing dolls and adorning themselves with costume jewelry and making dinners of plastic peas and pork chops. And if you smack your lips and tell them you like their cooking, oh, how *pleased* they are!

She is heartened by the way the children care for one another: the bending down of one toddler to stare solicitously into the face of another, the outright expessions of concern: *Do you feel sad? Are you going to cry? Do you want a hug?* She likes the art projects, the finger paintings and Popsicle stick sculptures, the Mother's and Father's Day cards so loaded with glue and glitter they flop over in the hand. She likes when the children use cotton balls to make Santa's beard and it looks instead like an odd kind of acne—invariably, the children are as sparing with cotton balls as they are generous with glitter.

She likes taking children for a walk on any kind of day: even a dreary, rainy day offers distinct pleasures, if only in displaying

rainbows in oily puddles. She never would have considered working in day care if she hadn't been let go from her job in Cincinnati; now she's glad she did get fired. She has learned from the inside out the meaning of small pleasures, and she keeps her needs small, too.

Mary Alice used to long for a husband; she used to date a little bit and dream, dream a little bit and date; she had a list of names she would have bestowed upon her children, had she been lucky enough to have them, and had her husband agreed with her choices. Moselle had been her favorite for a girl, after the river. For a boy, she had liked Amos best; she thought it was an awfully friendly name. But the longing for a family of her own has stopped. In the gentlest and most good-natured of ways, she has given up on the prospect of being married or even living with a man. She did get one proposal, on her thirty-ninth birthday, but it was from a widower with four children under six. She felt bad for him, but they didn't love each other, not by a long shot. In fact, the night he proposed, they were at the Wagon Wheel Steakhouse, and he couldn't keep his eyes off their waitress, a buxom blonde with a sexy cigarette voice who had no interest in him other than knowing what kind of salad dressing he preferred.

Mary Alice has a body pillow named David. Her sister, Sarah Jane, gave it to her for Christmas many years ago as a kind of jokey imperative, but now she says she's jealous of Mary Alice for getting to sleep with a body pillow rather than a real live man like her husband, who is guilty of every bed-partner crime known to man. Forever encroaching on her side. Farting. Drooling on the lacy pillowcases. Snoring so loudly Sarah Jane can sometimes hear him from the guest room, where she retreats at least two nights a week so that she can get some rest. She says her husband has violent dreams that sometimes have him kicking her. And eating crackers in bed, he actually does that. He eats crackers with cheese and red onion and horseradish mustard.

Last Sunday afternoon, Sarah Jane had driven the thirty miles from her house in Dayton to visit Mary Alice. While Mary Alice claimed her old place on the top porch step, Sarah Jane sat gently rocking herself on the porch swing, embroidering a face on David, giving him eyelashes to die for. She also brought over some lovely plaid pajamas she'd made for him. She included long sleeves that had been filled with cotton batting, in case Mary Alice wanted the feel of "arms" around her. Mary Alice mostly uses David to back up against and has no use for arms at all, but she didn't tell her sister that. She told her it was a very good idea.

Mary Alice wonders sometimes if Sarah Jane doesn't waste far too much time worrying about her; it makes Mary Alice worry about Sarah Jane. "You don't need to keep coming *up* with things for me," she wants to tell her sister. "You don't have to bore your husband at the dinner table with your concerns about your old maid sister." But in the way of most families, Mary Alice only accepts with gratitude the inappropriate gifts Sarah Jane gives her, aware of the fact that she undoubtedly gives Sarah Jane things her sister would happily do without.

While Sarah Jane sat working on David's face, Mary Alice told her about receiving the invitation to the high school reunion. Her sister stopped rocking, stopped sewing. "God help us," she said.

Mary Alice knew her sister had not enjoyed her own experience at their high school. Sarah Jane was five years older than Mary Alice, so they'd not been at that school at the same time, but they'd had many of the same teachers and knew many of the same people. Sarah Jane had been more popular than Mary Alice—she'd been blessed with better looks, and she knew better than Mary Alice how to behave in various situations. But to say she had been more popular than her sister was not to say she'd been popular per se. She'd been accepted, but she'd not been *in*.

Sarah Jane was the kind of girl who was allowed to sit at the popular kids' table because she would go and get more catsup for them or take individual blame for what was a group infraction. She would spend hours decorating the gym for dances where the elite were honored and from which she was often excluded, for lack of a date.

When she was in high school, Mary Alice had occasionally confided in Sarah Jane about the kind of treatment she endured—the way she was mostly ignored except when she was teased. Once, on Valentine's Day, she'd found fake dog shit put into a candy box and left in her locker. Mary Alice had thought that was kind of funny. It was actually almost flattering, because it was the kind of weird thing some of the popular kids did to each other. She didn't tell Sarah Jane that, though. It used to make Sarah Jane crazy that Mary Alice was so unperturbed about the way kids treated her. Sarah Jane tried to help Mary Alice by offering makeovers or trips to the mall to enliven her wardrobe, but it was no use. Mary Alice made a fair amount of money delivering newspapers, but she would never use any of it on clothes or makeup. At first, she spent it on supplies for her microscope: slide covers and probes and fixatives—Mary Alice had from the age of nine been a card-carrying member of the Junior Scientists of America Club. By the time she was in high school, she spent all her money on record albums and on paperback books—she couldn't get enough of either. Why moon about not being invited to a party when you could listen to Bob Dylan? What date could compete with *Nine Stories*? She held out hope that, when she got to college, she'd be appreciated, and in some respects, she was right: she was appreciated when she was in college. She wasn't popular, but she was appreciated.

"So are you going?" Sarah Jane asked. She kept her voice light, but Mary Alice figured her sister's blood was boiling.

"I thought I might."

There was a thick silence until Mary Alice finally sighed and said, "What."

Sarah Jane looked up. "What? I didn't say anything!"

"Exactly."

"Well, Mary Alice, I mean . . . What can you possibly *gain*?"

"I don't know. These are people I used to know, so long ago! I'm curious to see how they turned out."

"I can tell you how they turned out. They were assholes then, and they'll be assholes now."

"Oh come on. People grow up."

Sarah Jane sniffed. "Some people do." She stabbed at the fabric with her needle. Then she gasped and looked wide-eyed at Mary Alice. "You aren't going there to see some secret *crush*, are you?"

"No," Mary Alice said. "Not at all. No."

"Oh, my God. You are, too! You're going to see *Pete Decker,* aren't you? That guy whose pictures from the newspaper you had up on your bedroom wall. Pete Decker, right? The football player, the prom king, president of the student council."

"Vice president," Mary Alice said. "Tom Gunderson was president."

"Mary Alice, listen to me, for once in your life. Believe me when I tell you: It is not a good idea to go to this thing. Everybody thinks things will be different at a reunion, but they're not: everybody just gets right back into their old roles from high school. It's awful. Those people won't want to see you now any more than they did then. They won't give you a second chance, believe me."

"You went to your fifth- and tenth-year reunions," Mary Alice said, and Sarah Jane said, a little too loudly, "Right! So I know what it's like! I was an idiot to go twice. A *masochist*! I

should have brought Richard, because all I did both times—*both times!*—was sit at a table and eat maraschino cherries from watered-down drinks. I'll probably get cancer from all the red dye I consumed at those reunions."

Mary Alice spoke gently. "It's the *fortieth* reunion, Sarah Jane. And it's the last. It will be my only chance to ever go to a high school reunion. However imperfect it might have been, that time in high school is part of my life. I want to go and somehow revisit it. And I think it *will* be different."

Sarah Jane waved her arm. "Fine. Go, then. I'm just thinking of you. I don't want you to get hurt again."

"Oh, they never hurt me."

Sarah Jane stared at her until finally Mary Alice said, "Look. I appreciate your concern. I really do. But I'll be fine."

"Do you want me to go with you?"

Mary Alice laughed. "No, that's okay."

"Well, are you bringing Marion at least? You'll need an ally, Mary Alice. You'll need someone from your life now who really cares about you. You'll need someone who can defend you if . . . something happens."

Marion, a tall, pleasant-looking Polish man, is the owner of a construction company the next town over. He likes Mary Alice a lot, and occasionally they go out to eat or to a movie. But Marion doesn't speak much English. They mostly communicate with smiles and gestures, which actually suits Mary Alice fine. It seems graceful and kind, the way they talk. It seems *of the essence,* somehow. But she told her sister, "No. I'm going alone." Even as she said this, though, a little doubt crept in and she began to wonder. *Was* it so bad to go alone? *Should* someone go with her, just in case? But just in case *what*? What could possibly happen that would be so harmful?

Her sister is set on not believing it, but Mary Alice feels both

secure and happy. She thinks she was born content, and she's grateful for that. She's not an insensitive person, but she has learned not to let hurt take up residence inside her. Everyone is entitled to their own opinion, but she learned long ago that she doesn't have to buy into what someone else says or thinks about her.

So yes, she is going to the reunion. She has narrowed her choices for what to wear down to two outfits: either a charcoal gray suit with a silvery blue blouse, a pearl necklace, and matching stud earrings, or a long black skirt with silver stars on it—she bought that skirt at a recycled clothing shop on a day she was feeling a little wild. It would be worn with a three-quarter-sleeved black V-necked top, the top quite low. Mary Alice hunched over to hide her breasts in high school, but now she does not hide them because they are beautiful—she blushes every time she thinks of Marion telling her that one night when they were making out in his construction truck. Just a little, they were making out. Each seemed afraid of going very far physically, though not *afraid* afraid. It was more like a don't-let's-break-this-thing-that's-not-broken fear. But that night Marion had kissed her breasts so sweetly and then looked up at her and sighed. He'd sat up and made a cupped-hand, up-and-down motion and said, "Beautiful. Still on high." When she got home, she'd stood naked before her bathroom mirror and thought, *He's right.* And she'd experienced a small rush of surprise, of delight, as if she'd walked into her bedroom and found a gift on her pillow.

"Well . . . *thank* you," she'd told Marion. What *does* one say in a situation like that? Mary Alice had never understood combining talking with sex. Do whatever you're doing and *then* talk, is what she thinks. Otherwise, it's like trying to listen to two conversations at once. In college, she once watched a porn movie with a couple of her dorm mates. One scene showed a woman lying beneath a man saying, "Oh, do it to me, do it to me, fuck

me *hard,*" and Mary Alice had no idea why the man didn't rear up and say, "I *am!*"

Mary Alice stares out Einer's bedroom window and decides that she'll wear the low-cut top and the starry skirt, and she thinks with it she'll wear big silver hoop earrings and many silver bangle bracelets. But then she worries how her glasses will look with that. Oh, enough! She'll decide what to wear on the night she's getting ready for the reunion: an answer will come to her.

Einer has taken one more bite than she asked him to, and she rewards him with a kiss on the top of his head. Then she helps him out onto the porch and begins to read the newspaper's front-page stories to him—he can no longer see to read. She's barely gotten through a paragraph when he starts in: "Oh, what the hell is Congress *doing?* In my day, a man had a thing between his ears called a brain, and guess what? He used it!" He'll settle down by the time she gets to the advice columns. They like to talk about what advice they'd give before Mary Alice reads the answers the columnist actually wrote.

Today, when she gets to the advice columns, she makes up a question. She keeps her eyes on the newspaper, as though she is reading, and says, "I am a middle-aged woman who has been in-vited to a high school reunion. I was not very popular in school and was often picked on. Should I expect that I might have a good time anyway?" She lets the question hang in the air, then says, "Hmmm. What do you think?"

Einer scrunches forward. "Don't you even think about going. Don't give those bastards the pleasure of your company."

"That's what you'd tell her?"

"That's what I'm telling *you.*"

She looks away, and he says, "Everything's shot but my mind. You of all people ought to know that. Don't forget my wife taught music at that high school. She knew what went on. She used to tell me about how those kids treated you and your sister.

So, they're having a reunion, are they? Coming back to the old hometown they couldn't wait to get away from. You're not going, are you?"

"Well, yes. I am."

He grunts, adjusts himself in his chair. Then he leans forward and says, "I'm going with you, then," and she laughs, though a part of her thinks, *Well, why not?* This could be exactly what she needs: an ally who won't get in the way of anything.

"When we're there, if anyone says one snide thing to you, you help me out of my chair and I'll give them what for."

"Okay, Einer."

"I'm serious about this. You think I'm kidding? I'm serious! Where is it, anyway? At the school?"

"No, it's at the Westmore Hotel, out on Thirty-three."

"That's not but ten, fifteen minutes away. Short drive."

"Right."

"When is it?"

"Next weekend."

"Well, if I'm still here, I'm going."

"You'll be here," she says, though she's aware that he might not be, actually.

He sits back in his chair. "Punks," he mutters.

"Some of them were nice," Mary Alice says. "A lot of them were."

"Yeah. We'll sit at *their* table. All two of them."

Rita, Einer's caregiver, pulls up to the curb, and Mary Alice goes to help her carry in groceries.

"You will not believe what happened at the grocery store," Rita says. "I met the nicest man, over by the lettuce; he was all confused about what kind to buy. I helped him out and then we just got to talking, you know? When I said I had to go, he asked for my number, and I gave it to him. Oh, I hope he calls. I hope

he does! Do you know how long it's been since I went out with a man?"

Mary Alice doesn't answer, thinking the question is rhetorical, but then when Rita says, "*Do* you?" Mary Alice dutifully responds, "No. How long has it been?"

"Well, it's been seven *months,*" Rita says. "Isn't that ridiculous?"

Mary Alice does not find this ridiculous. But, "*Wow!*" she says. And then, "I'm sure he'll call you."

"Oh, I hope so. And if he does, promise me you'll stay with Einer? I don't want to turn him down on the first date; I want to say yes to any night he proposes. Will you promise?"

"I promise," Mary Alice says. It's a pretty safe bet she won't have any other plans.

FOUR

PETE DECKER HAS JUST CHEATED ON HIS MISTRESS WITH HIS wife, Nora. Now he sits at her kitchen table, watching her scramble eggs for him. Her ass shakes in that unattractive way that used to practically nauseate him, but now he sees it as comforting. And this woman knows *how* to scramble eggs, as opposed to Sandy, the woman he's been living with for the last three and a half months. That one makes scrambled eggs that come out like hard little yellow balls. He dropped Sandy off at the day spa this morning so that she could have her *stress* relieved. Though what she has to be stressed about, he has no idea. All she does is read magazines and natter on to her girlfriends and watch *The Housewives* this and *The Housewives* that and shop. On his dime. What a terrible mistake he has made. His kids will hardly speak to him, his office mates talk behind his back, and he's having an increasingly hard time getting it up. Never thought it would happen to him. Never! Not so young, anyway—he's only fifty-nine! (Though he's told Sandy he's fifty.) His dad was sticking it to them when he was *eighty*—he got laid the day before he *died*!

Well, Pete's not taking those damn boner pills. One reason is, he heard those things don't always work; two, they can cause vision and hearing loss. Wouldn't that just be perfect: he'd take a pill to amp up his sex life and end up with the trifecta of turnoffs. He'd be a limp-dicked guy, squinting into somebody's face and yelling, "*WHAT'S that?*"

Another reason he's not taking those pills is that it turns out Sandy's not worth it. If only he'd known that she drew on her eyebrows and wore false eyelashes, that she went to bed with purple crap on her face every night, that the vacuousness he had initially found so charming—such a *relief*!—would so soon wear thin. He'd only been living with her for two weeks when she got lazy about her appearance. The truth is, Sandy is a slob and a slacker. If you suffer under the illusion that all women are natural-born housekeepers, well, just come over and have a look at their place. They'd probably get evicted if anyone ever saw the kitchen or the bathroom. Sandy is great-looking, no one can deny that. Built, too, oh, sweet Jesus, built! But a slob and a slacker and a bore. What a terrible mistake he has made.

Nora puts the eggs down in front of him, perfect, fluffy eggs accompanied by the kind of bread that's good for you but tastes good anyway, and a little bowl of fresh fruit all cut up nice. "Thanks," he says. "Sandy mostly gives me Pop-Tarts."

"Well," Nora says. "Her cooking is not why you moved in with her. And you know, you could try cooking yourself sometimes."

It frustrates Pete, the way Nora defends Sandy, frustrates and mystifies him. He supposes it's really a way of getting back at him, a way of saying *You made your bed.* But still, shouldn't a wife be bitter and outraged about a mistress? Nothing's working out the way he thought it would!

"How are the kids?" he asks. He can't look at her when he asks this. It hurts too much.

"Didn't Katie call you?"

"She might have; I haven't looked yet today to see if I have any cellphone messages." This is a lie; he has looked, he's always looking, but his kids never call. If he wants to talk to them, he has to be the one to place the call. And then, when they show him the great honor of picking up, which is about one third of the time he calls, they make it plain they can't wait to get off the phone. They treat him a little like he's nuts. Which he guesses he was. But he's not, anymore. He's back.

"Huh!" Nora says. "She said she was going to call you yesterday."

"Well, what *is* it? Is she okay? Is it something bad?"

"No, nothing bad," Nora says, and then she smiles. "It's really nice news, actually."

"Nora. What is it?"

"I think I should let her tell you."

"Is she . . ." Pete sits back in his chair. "She's pregnant, isn't she? Oh, man, is she *pregnant*?!" Their twenty-seven-year-old daughter has been trying to conceive for two years. Last Pete knew, she was going to wait a couple more months and then start in with a fertility doctor.

Again, Nora smiles, but says nothing.

"No kidding, she's going to have a baby! That's great news!" But then the fact of his daughter's pregnancy suddenly slams into his brain and he realizes that if she's a mother, he'll be a grandfather. Him, a grandfather! Is he ready for that? An uncle, okay, but a *grandfather*? Is Nora okay with it? Is she ready to be a grandmother? Judging by her soft, pleased expression, he guesses she is. He forces himself to smile and says, "I'm going send her the biggest bouquet of flowers they can make. All . . . pink and blue!"

"Wait for her to tell you," Nora says. "I don't want her to

think I betrayed her; she asked me not to say anything. She said she would tell you, and I'm sure she will, when she's ready."

Betray. He looks down at his eggs and takes another bite. "Thanks for making me breakfast, Nora. It's really good. You know?" His throat is tight. What, now he's going to *cry*? He bites down hard on his back molars, swallows away the feeling. "Thanks for everything." Now he looks into her face and smiles. The woman may be thirty-five years older than Sandy, but she has her own eyebrows, for Christ's sake. And her smile is still dynamite. And the sex he just had with her was almost like it was when they first started. What a mistake he has made.

"How are the boys?" he asks. Their older son, Pete Jr., is having problems with his wife, though he's assured his mother he wants to work it out. He and his wife, Karen, are in therapy together. Pete himself has often said he'd never go to marriage counseling. But guess what? He'll do it now. He'll sit there and listen to all the bullshit and promise the moon. And deliver it.

Their younger son, Cal, is trying yet again to start up a business: selling boats, this time, God help him. Cal doesn't know a thing about boats. But he says he'll learn. Cal's a happy, wildly optimistic soul; it takes a lot to make him feel bad or discouraged about anything. His wife, Sunny, is aptly named: she'll go along with anything Cal wants to do. And her family mints money: if worse comes to worst, they can always get a loan from them.

"The boys are okay," Nora says. "Pete and Karen are going to Paris."

"Wow. So their problems are over." Pete imagines his son and daughter-in-law cuddled together on a nighttime flight to Paris. *Business* class. Pete Jr. would no doubt fall for that upgrade bullshit when the truth is that an airplane seat is hell no matter where on the plane it is. Save your money for when you get where you're going, is what Pete would like to tell him. But Paris, that's

nice, he guesses. Very romantic place, he's heard. He should have taken Nora there, she always used to talk about wanting to go to Paris. But then she just gave up.

"No, their problems aren't over," Nora says. "They're just trying really hard. They say they want to work it out, they want to try to stay together. It's hard. But Cal! Cal is *great*! You won't believe it, but in the last week, he got three orders for yachts. Big ones!"

"How in the hell did he do that?"

"Well, he's got his father's charm and he's also connected to a lot of people that Sunny's family knows. And you know how it is; even in a bad economy, the rich still spend money."

Pete wipes up the last of his scrambled eggs with the last bite of toast. Perfect breakfast. "How are you fixed for funds?"

"I'm fine."

"Why don't I leave you a couple hundred?"

"I'm *fine,* Pete." She leans in closer to him. "Pete? Listen, I . . . What we just did? I feel bad about it. And I think you need to tell Sandy that it happened."

"Ah, jeez."

"If you admit it—and I think it's only fair that you do—you'll get to some problems in your relationship that you obviously need to face up to. And I'm going to tell Fred, too."

"You're . . . Fred who?"

"Fred Preston."

Pete can hardly contain his outrage. "You're involved with *Fred Preston*?" The wimpy guy down the block. Widower. Always wearing a hat so he won't get *skin cancer.* Runs every day in *a jogging outfit.*

"Yes, I am. I've been wanting to tell you."

"Fred *Preston?* You are fucking shitting me!"

"Do you mind watching your language?"

"You're kidding me."

"He's actually a very interesting man."

Pete snorts. "Yeah, well, he'd better be. Not much else to recommend him."

Nora stands and starts clearing the dishes. "Not true. I think he's quite good-looking."

"Oh, *please*."

She turns from the sink to look over at him. "Well, you may not think so."

"Oh, come on, Nora. You're *attracted* to him?"

She raises an eyebrow, lifts one shoulder.

"And you're going to tell him we had sex."

"Yes, I am. I am interested in having a completely honest relationship, for a change. I'm going to say I had a little slip, but it won't happen again."

Pete lowers his voice to what he hopes is a sexy register. "Are you sure?" He wishes Nora would look at him. He has gorgeous turquoise eyes, god damn it.

She comes back to the table and sits down with him. "Pete. Listen to me. We're done. I want to finalize the divorce."

Her words actually take his breath away. They make for a deep pain right in the center of his chest.

He speaks rapidly. "But I'm getting out, Nora. I'm leaving her. I was just going to tell you that. You think I haven't been regretting what I've done since the day I left? What we did here today . . . I understand something now.

"I want to come back. I'll tell Sandy this afternoon and then, right afterward, I'll pack my bags and come home. Let me come home, Nora. Everything will be so different, you'll see. I didn't mean all those things I said the day I left. How could I have meant those things? I was just frustrated about . . . I don't know. About everything, I guess. But I didn't mean those things, Nora! Please! Do you believe me?"

"Yes. I believe you."

He closes his eyes, exhales. "Oh, God, thank you, honey. Thank you." He can't wait. He'll pack just a few . . . No. Fuck it. He'll leave everything in that crap condo Sandy couldn't live without. He never wants to go back there again. Let her have everything. All he wants is to have his family back, that's all he wants. Once again, he feels the burn of tears. "I want you to know, babe, that I—"

"Pete," she says. "*Don't.* I know you really meant what you just said. But I mean what I said, too. I'll be your friend, we'll co-parent the kids, but . . ." She shrugs. "It's over. Such a silly word for such a serious thing, it seems like such a cliché to say it, so Roy Orbison. But it's true. We've come to the end, there's no going forward for you and me. And I'm not even . . . I'm not hurt anymore. I'm not bitter or angry. The kids are, but they're working that out. And I'm trying to help them with it. This has been coming for a long time, Pete. I knew it was coming; you must have, too. I guess I had more time to get ready than I'd thought. In the back of my mind, I think I'd resigned myself long ago to our not staying together.

"Look, down the road, I can see us all having dinner together, you and Sandy, and me and Fred, and the kids . . . and the grand-kids! Things will all work out. But, Pete, you have to listen to me, now. You have to hear me. I don't want to live with you again. It wasn't good for me, as it turns out. I'm happier now." She sighs. "I'm sorry, pal."

"Aw, Christ. Don't call me '*pal.*'"

"I always call you that."

"Yeah, but now it means something different." He stares miserably at the table, where the sun has come through the window to illuminate his hands. They are clenched so tightly together his knuckles are white. He separates them and clears his throat. "Hey, Nora? Did you get the invitation to our fortieth high school reunion?"

"Yes. I threw it away."

"You're not going?"

"When have I ever gone to one of our reunions? I didn't RSVP, but Pam will figure it out. Not that she was the brightest girl. *Nice,* though. And always so cheerful! She always said hi to you every time she passed you in the hall, remember? 'Oh, *hi!*' in that real excited way, even if she'd *just seen* you. She'd say hi and wave. Once she started to wave to me and she dropped all her books. I helped her pick them up and we bumped heads and it really *hurt.* And then we couldn't stop laughing, we were just sitting on the floor and laughing and then we were late for class." Nora shakes her head, smiling. "God. Pam Pottsman. I haven't thought about her in years. Maybe I will call and tell her I'm not coming. I'll catch up with her a little bit."

"Don't call!" Pete says, so loudly that Nora jumps.

"Sorry," he says, and smashes down the hair at the back of his head, a nervous habit he hates. "Don't call her," he says again. "Or do call, but say you're coming. Say you're coming with me."

"But I'm not coming with you!"

"Will you? Please? It's the last one!"

"Pete. No."

He gets up and stands before her. He holds her familiar face in his hands—oh, God, look at her. "Nora. I fucked up big-time. I know it. I fucked up for years. I'm *sorry.* I *heard* you, when you said we were done, I heard you, okay?"

She starts to respond and he talks over her. "No. No. Listen to me. We were married for a long time, Nora. A long time, you know? Why don't you just think about going with me? That's all I'm asking. Just think about it. I know it wouldn't necessarily mean anything. But if you'd go with me, I'd be so—"

"Pete, I can't. Fred and I are going on a trip that weekend."

He can't speak. He stares at her and feels again that terrible ripping sensation in his chest.

"We're going to the Grand Canyon," she says.

Oh, for fuck's sake. The *Grand Canyon*. Which she's already seen, she went with a couple of girlfriends not two years ago!

"You know what, Nora? I'll take you to Paris. I will. No strings attached or anything. First class! You can have your own hotel room, if you want. If you need to. We can go—"

"Okay, Pete, enough. Listen, I made a mistake with you this morning, and I am fully prepared to take responsibility for it. I think you should do the same, though I recognize that it's not really my business anymore what you do. But now let's just move on. Let's not see each other for a while. If anything with the kids comes up, I'll tell you. Or, you know, anything else you really need to know about. But let's not see each other for a while. Let's look upon what happened today as a final goodbye, and get on with our lives. Okay?"

"Nora," he says. "I'll do whatever you want. I will. But let me just ask you something. And don't answer yet! Don't answer yet. I want to ask something very important." He sees her mouth tighten and he says, "I'm *going*, Nora, but I just need to ask you this one thing."

She crosses her arms, steps back. "What."

"I want you to consider moving your trip with Fred to another weekend and going to the reunion with me." If she does this, he'll still have a chance to get her back. If not, his goose is cooked.

She starts to speak, and he holds up his hand. "No! Please, don't answer yet! Come on, Nora, can't I even . . .

"It's just that it would mean so much to me. It really would. And also, I think if you do this for me . . . If you do this, then I can start letting you go. I know you want me to let you go. I just want us to end on a pleasant note. You know?" He shudders, then, an autonomic response that humiliates him. He looks away

from Nora, and when he turns back to her, he sees tears in her eyes.

"Okay, so I'll take off," he says. From the corner of his eye, he sees a fork still on the table. He retrieves it and hands it to her. "Here you go."

"Thank you," she says softly.

"Finally helping with the dishes, huh?"

She smiles.

"Do you . . . The lawn's gotten long. Do you want me to mow it? I won't come in after or anything. Nothing like that."

"Pete," she says. "Go home."

I am home, he wants to say. But he's not, anymore.

He walks out to the car on feet that seem to have become numb. Now what? Get some Viagra, he supposes. Then go home and screw the living daylights out of Spa Girl. That's right. That will make him feel better. He climbs into his car, thinks about what he can try with Sandy that he hasn't done yet. Then he rests his head against the steering wheel and stares down at the stupid tasseled loafers she talked him into buying. Nora looked at them when he flung them off before they went to bed, but she didn't say anything. That's what she does when she doesn't like something. That's what she used to do, anyway. Now she speaks up, at least about the important things. Well, so will he. He'll call Pam Pottsman and he knows exactly what he'll say, he can all but see the lines like they're a script. He'll say, "Hey, Pammy, how you *doing,* sweets?" Then she'll *blah blah blah.* Then he'll say, "Listen, I'm going to need another ticket for the reunion. Put me down for two instead of one. A little surprise for Nora, so don't say a word." He bets Pam will think that's romantic. He bets she'll flirt with him on the phone, too, just like she did last time. Any girl in their class would flirt with him, if she had the opportunity. Somebody like Pam Pottsman, that could be a trial. You

didn't want to be rude, but Jesus. Another kind of woman, though, that's another story. Couple of months ago he ran into Beth Hillman at the airport in *Detroit,* for Christ's sake, and she remembered him right away. He remembered her after a minute, too. Head cheerleader. They'd had a few sessions. Oh, yeah, they had. Bethie was a *real* blonde. At the airport, they'd gone to a bar and had a drink, had a real nice talk, too, no time for anything else, but if there had been time, he could have checked them into the adjoining hotel, no problem, he could tell; she was ready steady. "You know, you really haven't changed a bit, Pete," she'd said, and don't think he didn't know what that meant.

He heads out onto the freeway, and when the traffic slows, he regards himself in the rearview mirror. Game so not over, not for this boy. Not by a long fucking shot. He starts to smile, to check out his killer dimples, but his smile becomes a grimace. He grabs at his chest, his hand over his heart and grunts, *Unh! Unh! Unh!* He manages to pull into the breakdown lane, to put the car into park, call 911 and give an approximate location. Jesus, it's hard to talk, it's hard to talk! He snaps the phone shut, then slumps down, closes his eyes, and waits to die.

FIVE

OROTHY CAN HARDLY DIAL THE PHONE FAST ENOUGH.
When her friend Linda answers, Dorothy says, "You
won't believe this! Candy Sullivan is coming to the reunion!"

"Get out," Linda says. "How do you know?"

"Pam Pottsman called me. Just this very minute."

"Does Judy know?"

"No, I called you first."

"Oh, my God. Let's have a conference call tonight. I'll send
Judy an email and tell her. How's seven o'clock?"

Dorothy's favorite television show comes on at seven, but this
is more important. She can always watch it with the sound down.
She wishes she knew how to use the recording device on her television, but it's all she can do to turn it on and off. When her husband was moving out and asked if he could take the TV, she had
hollered, "*No! No! No!* You don't take *one* thing from this house
unless it belongs to *only you.*" And he hadn't. He'd left quietly,
with a great deal of dignity, Dorothy had to admit. She'd been a

screaming banshee, but she is so much better now. Completely recovered. A new person, really.

Hilly said she'd teach her mother how to record shows; it's easy, she's said; but she hasn't shown Dorothy how yet. She hasn't done much of anything lately but talk about her wedding: Should she wear a necklace with her gown? Drop earrings or stud? Are take-home monogrammed cookies for the guests a charming or a tacky idea? Must the hand towels in the ladies' room be linen or is high-quality paper all right? Dorothy wants to help, but she's never been good at this kind of thing. And although she's never told Hilly this, she doesn't really like all the fuss made over weddings. She herself had the thinnest of affairs, and it was all she could do to get through *that*. So far as she is concerned, the whole industry is nothing but a rip-off. Nonetheless, when Hilly told her she was engaged and wanted a big, big wedding, Dorothy ran right over to the bookstore and purchased an armload of bride magazines. But looking at them only depressed her. So many decisions! You see a classic multilayered ivory fondant cake decorated with fresh flowers and wide bands of periwinkle blue ribbon and think, *Oh, that's the one!* Then you turn the page and see a tiered silver server loaded up with purposefully imperfect cupcakes and think, *Oh, but what fun* this *one is!*

It went on and on. Where to have the wedding? At what time of day? How many guests should be invited? What should the meal be? The music? Open or cash bar? And the choice in bridal gowns! Thank God Hilly pretty much knew what she wanted going in. In less than three hours, she chose a floor-length, strapless confection of a gown with a subtle pattern of seed pearls and other shimmering embellishments strewn across the bottom half of the skirt. She's wearing a full-length veil, too, a lacy one with the same kinds of embellishments as the dress. When Dorothy saw the price tag, she had to bite her tongue to keep from

squawking in outrage. But she didn't say anything. She wasn't the one paying the bills, after all. And anyway, Hilly looked beautiful in that dress. She looked absolutely transformed. That was a moment, when Hilly tried the dress on, and their eyes met in the mirror. Dorothy stood behind her daughter, her purse clenched tight up against her middle, and blinked back tears, then let them freely flow. *Oh, my love,* she was thinking. *My little girl.* And so much more, she was overwhelmed with feelings, a curious mix of joy and sorrow. And even though Hilly laughed and made fun of her mother, Dorothy saw tears in Hilly's eyes, too.

Dorothy tells Linda, "A conference call! Great idea. Okay, call me at seven. I'll be right by the phone."

"Here's your assignment," Linda says. "Start remembering stories about Candy so we can have a really good session. Oh! I just remembered one now! I'm going to go write it down."

After Dorothy hangs up, she inspects herself in the mirror again. She's going to have lunch with her daughter, and Hilly can be very critical. Honest, she calls it, and it is honest, Dorothy supposes, but it's also barbed-wire critical.

It bothers Dorothy how much she wants Hilly to like her. She knows it's wrong, she knows you're not supposed to worry about your children liking you, you're just supposed to raise them right, but from the day Hilly was born, she has always wanted her daughter to like her. Not love her, although that, too, but actively *like* her. In the early years, it wasn't much of a problem. Hilly absolutely adored her. Oh, she went through her I-only-want-Daddy! phase when she was a toddler, but Dorothy knew she didn't really mean it. She came soon enough to the knowledge that Dorothy was the one to whom she should really be grateful.

All through Hilly's elementary and junior high school years, she and Dorothy had been like best friends. Hilly told her mother everything: what boy she was crazy over, how her breasts were infuriatingly small, how embarrassing it was when she burped

during math class. And Dorothy told Hilly things she supposed she shouldn't: that she sometimes cried in the middle of the day and didn't know why. That she suspected their neighbor of having an affair with the FedEx deliveryman. That she feared she would be abandoned in her old age. She hadn't said all the mean things she wanted to say about Hilly's father; she knew how damaging it was for a child to hear one parent bad-mouthing the other, and besides that, it could backfire and make Hilly move closer to Team Daddy.

But then, right around age fifteen, Hilly had begun preferring her father to her mother. In every way. Since the divorce, which her father had instigated just after Hilly graduated from college because he found someone who *appreciated* him (God almighty, the woman looks like a *frog*, plus she's older than he is!), Hilly has been a bit nicer to her mother. But heaven forbid Dorothy even think a negative thought about her ex-husband. Pops, Hilly began calling him in her senior year of high school, and every time Dorothy hears it, she wants to roll her eyes.

Dorothy told Hilly about what she's wearing to the reunion: one of those extravagantly ruffled black blouses with sheer sleeves, a black pencil skirt, black nylons, and some heels that will probably necessitate her having back surgery after she wears them. But it's important that she look fabulous and not a victim of collapsing vertebral disks. After she described her outfit to Hilly, her daughter had said, "Hmm," and that's when Dorothy knew she'd done it all wrong. Well, there's plenty of time to get a replacement outfit. She'll see what Hilly suggests, if, as she suspects, she nixes her mother's first choice.

Dorothy hears the front door opening and then the sound of her daughter calling her. "In the kitchen!" she says, and she grabs her purse, a clutch her daughter gave her last Christmas, so she knows it's right.

She meets Hilly in the hallway, and they give each other a

quick embrace. Dorothy doesn't really like embracing people in this way, but you have to, these days. Everybody does that European kiss-kiss thing now, too, and Dorothy thinks it's so fake. Why must people *touch* one another so often? Look at all the germs you're spreading around for no reason. Oh, touching is fine when it's for a reason, but when you're just saying hello? Well, she'd better get used to it. She bets at the reunion they'll be double-kissing like crazy. She'll have to remember to get some of that nonsmear lipstick.

"So!" she says. "Where would you like to go for lunch? We can go anywhere you like!"

"I don't know, Ma," Hilly says. "You pick. I thought you had a place in mind."

"I thought it would be fun for you to choose."

"Fine, Bistro 102."

"Oh, great idea! They have such good food!"

"Not really, but it's close. I need to get over to the wedding coordinator's office by three; she's screwed everything up again."

"What's wrong?"

Hilly waves her hand. "Oh, a million things. For one thing, the videographer I wanted is moving overseas before the wedding, so now I have to choose another one. And there's a bunch of miscellaneous problems you don't want to hear about, believe me. *I* don't want to hear about them!"

"Do you need me to help?"

"No, Ma. Thanks."

"Okay," Dorothy says, "so we'll go eat, and then if we—"

"Didn't you want me to look at your outfit for the reunion?" Hilly says. "I thought you wanted me to come over here so I could look at your outfit!"

"Oh!" Dorothy says. "Right!" She puts her purse down on the hall bench and says, "Come upstairs with me, I'll try it on for you." She's excited; she wonders what Hilly will say.

"Can't you just show it to me?" Hilly looks at her watch.

For a moment, Dorothy thinks of saying, "You know what? Forget the whole thing. Just forget the whole damn thing! You ungrateful child! I used cloth diapers so you'd never get a rash! Everything I fed you I made from scratch! I stayed home to raise you and I played Candy Land with you over and over when other women were forging interesting careers. Who changed your sheets when you vomited all over them? *Pops?*" But she doesn't say that. She says, as evenly as she can, "You have time for me to try it on. You can't really tell me how it looks unless I have it on."

She walks ahead of her daughter up the stairs and hears Hilly say something. "What?"

"You have a *run* in your stocking," Hilly says. "You know, nobody even *wears* those things anymore, and that's *why.*"

And now Dorothy turns around to speak angrily to her daughter but collapses on the steps, just falls on her butt with her legs spread out like a man's so anyone who wants to can see up her skirt, as if. Then, to make matters worse, she starts to cry. Hilly's not the only one whose nerves are on edge. Dorothy has a lot to think about, too!

"Ma," Hilly says. "Jesus Christ."

"Just go!" Dorothy says. "I don't want to have lunch with you! And I don't care what you think of what I'm wearing!" She kicks her leg out angrily, like a toddler, and her shoe falls off.

Hilly retrieves it and sits beside her mother on the steps. She slides the shoe onto her mother's foot and then puts her arm around her shoulders. "Ma," she says, and her voice is softer now. She smells good. She's wearing a black-and-white blouse and black pants and many silver bracelets. Her hair is done in one of those half-up, half-down styles, and it looks very pretty. She has Chanel sunglasses perched atop her head. "Look," Hilly says. "I'm sorry. I am just a mess these days. I'm such a bitch I can hardly stand to be with myself, let alone other people. It's this

wedding crap. All these details to decide, it just never stops, it's like Mickey Mouse in that movie with all the brooms and buckets. I swear, I don't even *want* to get married anymore."

"Don't say that!" Dorothy says, and hastily dries her eyes. He's a doctor, for God's sake, and Hilly is almost forty. This is no time to throw a good fish back into the ocean!

"I mean it, Ma. I don't want to. I don't see why I should. The only reason to get married these days is to have kids, and I don't think I want kids."

Dorothy looks at her. Blinks. "You don't?"

"No. I mean . . . I don't know."

"I think you should have children," Dorothy says. "Oh, Hilly, you can't know how wonderful it is. You never can know, until you're in it up to your eyeballs."

"At which point it's too late," Hilly says, ruefully. "What if you don't *like* it?"

"You'll like it," Dorothy said. Though even as she says it, she recognizes, as if for the first time, the possibility of it not being true. It reminds her of the glib reassurance she was given by a nail tech who talked her into getting those false fingernails. "You'll love them," the woman had said. But they were awful! It hurt when you got them put on, and you had to get them filled all the time and they made your real nails a fragile, peeling mess, and you could never keep them clean under there. Oh, how she cringes when she's handed food by people with nails so long they couldn't clench their fists if their lives depended on it. Those long nails with *things* all over them, like hieroglyphics. She herself finally had the false nails removed, and after a few months her own nails were back to normal. She'd only gotten those nails because she had been relentlessly schooled by her mother in what a girl was required to do: Maintain ten long painted nails at all times. Put your fork down after each bite, and make sure each bite is minuscule. Practice walking with a book on your head to

ensure good posture. (Dorothy actually did that, up and down the hallway, over and over.) Sit with your knees pressed together and your legs slanted to the side. Cream your face, powder your feet, know when to use "who" and when to use "whom." Never let anyone see you in rollers; those women who went out with scarves on their heads weren't fooling anyone.

There were a million rules that Dorothy endeavored to follow and still her mother never seemed satisfied. Or her father. Dorothy's mother had been a bona fide beauty queen, Miss Ohio, and Dorothy had never lived up to her parents' expectations of her, she knew it. She would lie in bed at night vowing that the next day would be better, and it never was. She was the worst in dancing class. The ringlets her mother put in Dorothy's hair were ruined by cowlicks. She fell off her horse the first day she rode and many times thereafter. The one and only time she tried to kiss her parents goodnight, it went so badly, she never tried again. They were not big on touching in Dorothy's little family, which is to say they did not touch at all. They did not praise or say "I love you"; that was too effusive, utterly unnecessary. But one night when Dorothy was four, a summer night, the sky still blue at bedtime, she was overwhelmed with a desire to kiss her parents goodnight. Dorothy remembers every detail: her hair was put up in bobby pins, and she was wearing a new white nightgown, white ribbons and white lace, a ruffled bottom. She remembers how her mother sat stiffly, her hands clenched, when Dorothy embraced her, and how her father smiled indulgently and then pushed her away, saying, "Now, now." And Dorothy had felt full of shame. Full of it. She had understood that you do not do that, no matter how your heart may be calling for it. It was yet another mistake she had made. The only thing she is good at is inspiring a certain kind of friendship and loyalty in some people, and she still doesn't know how she makes that happen.

But children. She recalls a night when Hilly was maybe six years old and Dorothy was tucking her into bed. She pulled up Hilly's covers and kissed her forehead and said, "Now I'm going to make a magic sign so you will have wonderful dreams." She made a kind of swirling motion with her hand and Hilly watched solemn faced, believing absolutely in her mother's powers in the way that children do. Up to a certain age, anyway, after which they believe nothing you say, but never mind. That night, Dorothy had tucked a little blanket she'd made for Hilly's favorite stuffed animal—a bedraggled Snoopy dog, who at that point seemed held together purely by Hilly's love for him— around him. Then she'd kissed his nose and said, "Goodnight, Blackie," and Hilly had said, "Make a sign for Blackie's dreams, too," and Dorothy had; and at that point she'd kind of believed in her powers herself. Hilly had sighed and said, "You're a good mommy." And something had swelled inside Dorothy's chest, and she'd thought, *If I never have anything else, at least I had this.*

But now Dorothy tells Hilly, "You don't *have* to have kids, of course. You can enjoy other people's children. Or live a life that doesn't have much to do with children at all—what's important is that you're honest with yourself."

Well! She said that and immediately she wanted to lock herself in the bathroom and sit on the floor and think what it meant. What did that *mean,* to make your own decisions, independent of all the grabby influences in the world? How did it feel to say, "No, I don't think that's for me," and then simply *not do* what it seemed like everyone else was doing? She couldn't imagine. Yet here is her daughter clearly attempting to be in charge of her own life, to be aware that it is created by the choices she makes, and Dorothy wants to weep in gratitude. It is too late for Dorothy to live a conscious life. She never escaped her mother's iron hand, she had not even *tried* being a hippie except for one time when

she didn't wear makeup or shave her legs. And even then, she returned quickly enough to her learned standards of hygiene. You did your hair and you shaved your legs and you put your face on, no matter what. But Hilly was out from under something huge. Hilly was able to look up and see the sky. And Dorothy had somehow been a part of making that happen.

"I don't know about kids," Hilly says. "But I will get married, I guess. I mean, I kind of have to."

"You mean because of the money?" Dorothy says. "Because we'll lose the deposits? Don't get married for *that* reason! Who *cares* about the money?" *Especially when it's your father's,* she thinks. But she feels certain Hilly's father would offer the same advice.

"No," Hilly says. "It's not because of the money we'd lose." She turns to face her mother. "It's just that . . . I don't think I'll find anyone better than Mark. If I'm going to get married, I guess he's the one. But all of a sudden, it feels so . . . I don't know. *Arbitrary. Dangerous.* I don't see how anyone can ever feel completely convinced that marrying someone is the right thing to do, I don't see how anyone can not be consumed by doubt. Did you feel absolutely sure about marrying Pops?"

Dorothy had felt absolutely sure about being pregnant, that's what she had felt. But Hilly doesn't know that. So she says, "Course I wasn't sure! I was full of doubt, too. I think almost everyone is. You have to be! Who can possibly subscribe to the notion that there's only one person in the world for you? No. But you find someone you care for, that you think you might be able to build a life with, and then you just go for it!"

"And then you get divorced," Hilly says bitterly.

Dorothy speaks carefully now. "No, now, Hilly, you know that's not true. Some people have very happy marriages. I think the biggest problem is people's expectations are so high. And so wrong! People think marriage is going to be so romantic and ful-

filling. They think the other person is going to *complete* them. But that's not what happens. In a good marriage, you complete yourself while sharing a bathroom. You go through life with company, rather than alone, and humans seem to need company. And . . . You remember in *Carousel,* when the doctor tells the high school graduating class not to worry about others liking them, that they should just try to like others?"

"I love *Carousel,*" Hilly says, sighing. "I still love it. Everybody makes fun of me, but I still love it. We used to watch it and eat caramel corn and dill pickles."

"I know," Dorothy says. "But do you remember that part?"

"Of course."

"Well, that's it. That's what you need to do in your marriage. You need to *give* what you *want.* And don't expect so much. That only sets you up for disappointment. If you expect anything, expect that marriage will be hard, that it will be work. And expect that the pleasures will be erratic and often small, but they'll turn out to mean more than you know."

Dorothy's voice has thickened; there is a sizable lump in her throat. *Now* look what she has just said! What is she, Dr. Phil? Or whoever? She wishes someone had told *her* the things about marriage she just told her daughter. Her husband might still be with her instead of with Amphibian Face. It comes to her all at once the lack of generosity she showed her husband all the years they were together. The lack of simple kindness. The way she blamed him for everything.

"Where did you read that?" Hilly says. "I might buy the book."

"Oh, here and there," Dorothy says. "And of course I've had a little experience in learning what *not* to do. Not only in marriage, either." She inspects the tops of her knees. She stares intently at them as though trying to locate a tiny thing she just felt crawling on them.

Hilly speaks in a small voice, stripped of arrogance or defense. "So . . . do you think I'll be okay, then?"

Now Dorothy's heart warms and opens, and she turns to face her daughter. "Oh, sweetie, I think you'll be just fine. I think you'll be great. I think the two of you will have a wonderful marriage. All brides are nervous wrecks in the weeks before their marriage. It's good luck!" She doubts that this is true, really, but what the heck.

Hilly reaches over to hug her mother, and Dorothy hugs her back, and there, *that's* how a hug should be given.

"Let's see that outfit," Hilly says, standing and reaching out a hand to help pull her mother up.

"I don't know," Dorothy says. "Now we've had this emotional exchange, and maybe you won't quite tell me the truth. You'll think you have to spare my feelings."

"You know me; I'll tell you the truth," Hilly says, and so Dorothy gets up and goes into the bathroom and changes into her outfit, complete with beauty mark that she draws in above her lip. She talks to Hilly about Pete Decker through the closed door, how handsome he was, how popular, what a great car he had, how he'd seemed pretty interested in her at one point.

"So I want to just knock him out," Dorothy says. "I just want one more chance with him. And the first time he sees me needs to be really memorable." She opens the door. *"Ta dah!"*

Hilly widens her eyes and bites at her bottom lip. Nods.

"See?" Dorothy says. "You hate it but you won't say so."

"I don't *hate* it," Hilly says. "I think you should wear the blouse with jeans for the breakfast. But for Saturday night, may I make a suggestion? I saw a Stella McCartney the other day that would look terrific on you. Cobalt blue. You look really good in blue. And you've lost more weight, you'd look fabulous in it, you'd look absolutely cachectic."

"Oh, honey," Dorothy says. *"Thank* you."

"You're welcome." Hilly points to her own upper lip. "You've got something on your lip, right here."

"That's my beauty mark. I drew it in. I'm going to wear it to the reunion. Kind of fun."

"Oh."

"No?"

"It's your party, Ma."

"Okay, no." Dorothy rubs it off. But she will wear it at the reunion. Her daughter doesn't know everything. Beauty marks aren't from her time.

Hours later, Dorothy is in her bathrobe and seated on her sofa in front of the television, waiting for her friends to call. She's put egg white on her face—she's going to use a different kind of facial every night before the reunion, and her hairdresser told her raw egg whites work wonders. "It feels like a big glob of snot when you first put it on," she told Dorothy, "but then it tightens your skin like you wouldn't believe, and it gives it a wonderful glow." The egg has indeed begun to tighten her skin—she just saw herself in the mirror and she looks like she used to when she would pull a nylon down over her face for Halloween.

The phone rings, and Dorothy answers by saying, "Hi, it's Candy Sullivan, I can't come to the phone right now because I'm too busy admiring myself in one of my many gilt-framed mirrors." It just pops out. She guesses she's through being all wise and kind and generous in spirit. But she can't help it; gossip is so delicious and, anyway, Candy will never know.

She hears Judy and Linda laugh, and then Linda says, "Okay, I want to go first. Did you guys ever hear about Candy and George Keethler?"

"Nooooo," they say together.

"Well, I heard they were in his car and she was giving him oral sex—"

"No way!" Dorothy says, and sees that her fingers have in-

advertently flown to her breastbone. She reminds herself to make an appointment for a manicure the day before the reunion, the last appointment of the day. "Candy Sullivan? She would never have done that!"

"Oh, yes, she did!" Linda says. "She gave BJs! The whole football team knew it! And she was giving one to George Keethler and the car's engine was on 'cause they needed the heater, and her head bumped into the gearshift and they started rolling and he sat up real fast and she *bit* it!"

Judy is laughing, but she says, "How do *you* know this?"

"The guys on the football team! George showed the bite mark to them! And Ross Duggan was a friend of my brother's and he told my brother, and my brother told me. It was when my brother was pissed off at Candy because she wouldn't go out with him because she had moved on to the college boys. He made me promise not to tell you guys, but I think we're past the statute of limitations."

Out of the corner of her eye, Dorothy is watching a scene on her television show. She reaches for the remote and turns the volume up, just a little. Oh, her life seems suddenly to be an embarrassment of riches. Her daughter and she seem to be getting closer, she's lost weight, she's got a beautiful dress in which to seduce Pete Decker, and she's about to hear more delicious stories about Candy Sullivan. The one she'll share isn't nearly as good. She had science class with Candy, and one day the teacher had asked the question "What is matter?" He had called on Candy even though her hand was not up. Dorothy knew the answer and her hand was up, but Mr. Templeton did not call on her. He asked Candy the question, and she answered, "Nothing." Mr. Templeton's forehead wrinkled and he said, *"Nothing?"*

"Right," Candy said. "Nothing." She was wearing a heather pink A-line skirt that day, Dorothy remembers because she loved that skirt, it had a matching cardigan sweater and Candy wore it

that day with a floral-print, round-collared Villager blouse and the little cheerleading megaphone necklace that she always wore, all the cheerleaders did, God forbid anyone ever forgot for one moment that they were *cheerleaders,* and her hair had been all the way down that day, she had the most unbelievably thick blond hair that hung down past the middle of her back. Really beautiful hair.

Mr. Templeton frowned at Candy and looked over at Dorothy, still waving her hand in the air like she was trying to flag down roadside assistance. "All right, Dorothy," he said. "What is matter?" And she answered breathlessly, "Matter is anything that takes up space and has weight."

"Right," Mr. Templeton said, and then stared pointedly at Candy. She smiled that unbelievably beautiful smile and said, "Oh! I thought you said, 'What's *the* matter?' "

"I've got a story," Judy says, and Dorothy turns the sound back down on the television. They're showing a commercial for food, and Dorothy doesn't want to hear a word of it. She's starving to death but a girl can do anything for four more days.

SIX

"Cooper?" Candy Sullivan Armstrong says, softly. No answer.

"Coop?" She can tell from the sound of her husband's breathing that he's deep in sleep. She won't wake him. He won't be able to give her what she wants, anyway. What she wants is to say that she's scared, and for him to take her into his arms and simply hold her. But if she does say that, Coop will sigh and say, "Why are you *scared*? You don't even *know* anything yet. Go back to sleep." And then he will do precisely that.

The truth is, she does worry too much. On four separate occasions when awaiting medical test results, she diagnosed herself with terrible diseases; and then it turned out she was just fine. But this time is different, it really is. This time it feels as though something has come into her house and sat in her darkened living room, waiting for her to come upon it. And now that she has, it has said, *Ah. There you are. Don't be turning on the light, now.*

She pushes the bedclothes off and sits up, slides her feet into the slippers she keeps at her side of the bed. She reaches for her

robe, pulls it over her nightgown, and stands for a moment looking at the dim outlines of the furniture in her bedroom: the bed,
the night tables and lamps, the antique writing desk, the armoire,
the little French sofa and the table that sits before it. Her eyes follow the sweep of the draperies, the line of the velvet cushion on
the window seat. She can't make out the images in the various
paintings, but she knows full well what they are, and she loves
them, every one. Everything has become precious: the slippers on
her feet—her *feet*! She looks back at Coop, still sleeping soundly,
and tiptoes out of the bedroom.

When she was a girl, she thought of old age as a kind of insulting, almost humorous infirmity. You got gray and wrinkled,
you couldn't run or even walk fast, you couldn't see or hear very
well, you spoke in a voice that trembled and cracked, you rubbed
your aching knees with hands whose knuckles had gone knobby
and high. That was all. It astonishes her now to think how she
was so unaware of the smorgasbord of frightening diagnoses, or
the need for constant doctors' visits, or the mountains of pills required just to keep up the ever-deteriorating status quo. Her own
parents died young, in their late fifties, in a boating accident
when they were on vacation in the Bahamas, so she never saw
them deal with the trials of living a long life. Cooper's parents
also died relatively young. But she has seen her neighbors Harriet
and Arthur Gilbert begin to decline in terrible ways. They were in
their early sixties when she moved here, robustly healthy, very active and happy people who went out often: to friends' houses for
dinner, to the symphony, to art exhibitions and county fairs.
They loved taking long walks around the neighborhood. Now
most of their outings are to doctors' offices. Last week Candy ran
into them as they returned home from the neurologist Harriet
has been seeing, and Candy asked how things were going. "We
didn't get the news we were hoping for," Harriet said. "Nothing
awful, but not the news we were hoping for."

"We decided we are entering the time of life where true courage is called for. True courage and a sense of humor!" Arthur said.

"And *faith*," Harriet said.

"Well," Arthur said. "One always needs that."

In the kitchen, Candy starts a pot of coffee. Then she'll go out to the front porch to see if the newspapers have been delivered yet. She and Cooper get three papers: *The New York Times, The Boston Globe,* and *The Wall Street Journal.* Coop looks at all three, but normally it's all Candy can do to get through the *Globe.* It's because she doesn't like to skim, as her husband does. If she's going to read a newspaper, she's going to *read* it.

She steps out onto the porch and shivers, pulls the edges of her robe closer together. It is still night-cool, a few stars remain in the sky, and the moon looks half erased. The papers are there, lying in a jumbled pile, and she gathers them up with a kind of relief. Today she will read all of them in order to have something to do before she goes to the doctor's office. Her appointment is for nine-thirty. She and Coop are going together to hear the Report. Coop thinks it's unnecessary for him to come along. He said if it were bad news, the doctor would have *told* her to bring her husband along, wouldn't he? But Dr. Johnston hadn't said a word about Coop. He'd just said that there were some things he needed to talk to her about. "He probably just wants to put you on some new medication," Coop said. But in the end, he reluctantly agreed to come along. And Candy thanked him.

Candy can hardly believe the way husbands go with their pregnant wives to routine OB visits these days. Coop and Candy didn't have children, but she bets if they had, Coop wouldn't have gone with her to the doctor for such visits. Of course, back in the day when she would have been pregnant, not many men did. Back then, they were just starting to let husbands witness the birth. She had really wanted children, but Coop hadn't. He'd

made it plain on their first date that he didn't want them, and her initial thought was, *That's the end of* this *relationship!* But she was so attracted to Coop, and she kept going out with him, and finally she thought, *Well, it's all right if we don't have children. We'll have each other.* She has so often recalled the day that she told Coop those very words. It was fall of their junior year, and they'd been sitting on a blanket beside the Charles. Coop was a rower for Harvard, and when he wasn't on the river, he liked to be by it. He was dancing around the idea of marriage and when she told him she didn't need children, he squeezed her hand and said, "Well, finally. A girl almost as smart as she is pretty. We'll be married next June." And she thought, *What do you mean, "finally"? How many women have you proposed to?*

The last time Candy went for her routine physical, she sat on a narrow table in her doctor's office in a blue paper gown that had ripped when she put it on. Over her left breast was a wide opening that looked oddly suggestive, and she kept lightly touching the edges as though this would magically repair the tear.

She hates paper gowns, and she always wears a nice pair of earrings and a bracelet whenever she has a doctor's appointment, so she won't look so horrible in them. She also ties the thin plastic belt tightly around her still enviable waist, and has on occasion even rolled up the sleeves a turn or two—she doesn't like the way the sleeves fall to a neither-here-nor-there place on her arm.

Candy doesn't understand why people being examined by their doctors don't just get naked and lie under a sheet. What, doctors have never seen a naked body before? And wouldn't it be easier than the false modesty offered by gowns that only get pulled far down, or pushed to the side, or lifted way up anyway? Or, if you're going to make patients wear gowns, why not have them be made of bamboo fabric in pale pastels, so they'd be pretty to look at, soft against the skin, and ecofriendly to boot? Candy has a lot of ideas about how medicine should be prac-

ticed. She'd gone to Boston University to become a nurse but had never worked as one. Coop didn't want his wife working. He made enough as a trial lawyer to support five wives. Candy had volunteered at Mass General until the advent of AIDS, and then Coop ordered her to stop, lest she bring home the deadly disease those godforsaken pervs, as he called them, were responsible for creating. She tried arguing with him, but it got her nowhere; not for nothing was he a lawyer who almost never lost a case.

While Candy sat in the examining room listening to the sonorous tones of her doctor talking to a patient in the room next door (a patient who kept *laughing*—oh, how wonderful to hear *that* sound in a doctor's office!), she leafed through a gossip magazine someone had left behind. She felt sorry for the movie stars who were featured. She stared into the eyes of this beautiful person and that, thinking their rise to stardom may have been awfully exhilarating at first—all that excitement, all that money, all that attention; but now look. Now they couldn't even go out to an ice cream stand on a hot summer night, and what was a hot summer night without an ice cream stand? They couldn't even take a walk! No one would ever just nod hello to them and say, "Nice out, huh?" and be done with it. People always *wanted* something from movie stars. They acted foolish around them, too, and Candy thought it must be a lonely feeling to have people act foolish around you all the time.

When her doctor came into the exam room, Candy said, "Boy, *someone's* in a good mood!" And when he looked confused, she said, "I heard you through the walls. I heard your patient laughing. I wondered why in the world he was so happy! Want to know my fantasy?"

Candy finds Dr. Richard Johnston, whom she calls Dick, an inordinately kind man. He has been Candy's internist for over thirty-five years. He's an elegant dresser, and he wears a bow tie with no sense of irony. She used to have a little crush on him, he's

very handsome; and she thought he maybe had a crush on her, too, until the day he told her he was gay. That had been both a comfort and a disappointment to her. Naturally she didn't tell Coop when she found out Dick was gay; she enjoyed the irony.

Dick had his back to her, washing his hands; and she went ahead and told him what she'd imagined about the patient she'd heard laughing. "I decided it was someone going on a fabulous trip to some exotic place; and he came here today to get his shots. And he's so excited, he just keeps laughing."

Dick turned around and gave her one of those raised chin, closed mouth smiles and she realized that it was none of her business. She looked into her lap, embarrassed.

"Not quite that," he said, and asked her to lie down. Then, as though to mitigate her embarrassment, he shared a little information. "That patient's been living with a terminal disease for a while, and has learned some terrific coping mechanisms. He's a pleasure to be around, he's always cheering everyone else up."

"Oh," Candy said, "that's wonderful." But now she felt even worse. She felt as though she'd come onstage to audition after someone really, really good had just performed. Not that this was an *audition,* but didn't one always want to be one's doctor's favorite patient?

Dick asked her to lie down and proceeded to examine her. When he pressed on her abdomen, she felt a sudden, deep pain. "*Ouch!*" she said, then, "Sorry, that just kind of hurt a little."

Dick looked over the top of his bifocals at her. "It *hurt?*"

"No, I guess . . . not really." She waved her hand. "I'm sorry. I think you just surprised me." He pressed again, a little more deeply this time, and she gasped and reflexively pushed his hand away. "What's *under* there?" she said.

"Your ovary, among other things." He spoke in the same soothing voice he always used, but wrinkles appeared between his eyebrows and he began pushing again, here, there; and Candy

clenched her fists and didn't make another sound. At one point he looked at her and said, "Is this still hurting?" and she nodded and looked at the wall. He ordered some blood tests and an ultrasound and an MRI. And she had them all done, praying to the blessed Virgin before and after each one.

About a week later, just after Candy had finished eating lunch, her doctor's office called to say she should come in on Friday morning to get the results. Candy leaned against the kitchen counter and said, "Is it bad?" She looked at the sandwich crust she'd left on the plate, and thought, *I should have eaten it.*

"We'd just like you to come in," the receptionist said. "It's pretty standard procedure."

Pretty standard. "But is it bad?"

"You know, you'll have to talk to Dr. Johnston about the results. I don't even have all the information here. I'm just calling to make an appointment."

"So it's bad," Candy said, and her kitchen suddenly seemed vastly bigger. She made the appointment and then washed her lunch plate and started thinking about what problem she might have that wasn't *so* bad. In the back of her brain, someone stood clanging a big bell, and the bell did not peal but rather spoke, and what it said was *It's very hard to survive ovarian cancer.* It said, *Gilda's fame and fortune couldn't help her one bit.* At that moment, Candy wanted a sibling more than ever before, and she had spent plenty of her growing up years wanting a sister or a brother. She wanted a sibling or her parents. Or a child. But her only family is Cooper. Who has grown tired of her. To put it mildly. Oh, not that he has cheated on her, not to her knowledge. But they've not had sex in years. And for many more years, he has not complimented her, or rushed to tell her anything, or listened with any interest to anything she has to say.

They get along, she supposes she would have to say. They have their routines: Breakfast out every Saturday morning. The

Sunday morning news shows. Plays, the symphony. Trips to Europe twice a year. Candy focuses on the house and garden, her visits to various art museums in the city, her donations to this charity and that, and their bulldog, Esther. Cooper works long hours, and then comes home to their huge Wellesley colonial, eats dinner, and watches television until he falls asleep in front of it. When there are terrible headlines, or terrible storms, or something awful happens to someone they know, they talk then. They come together almost like in the old days, then. What a strange way to find intimacy in a marriage, she always thinks.

Candy doesn't have girlfriends to talk to. Most women don't like her. Men always did. Boys always did. At first it was because she was so pretty—she was awfully pretty for a very long time. But when they got used to the prettiness, as always happened, then they would like her because she was actually a very nice person. But she is no longer beautiful and Cooper is not particularly gratified by his wife's being nice. "What's *that,* being *nice?*" he'd once said, when they were having one of those arguments where she felt compelled to defend her attributes. "How about *interesting,* how about that?" he'd said. "How about *intelligent?*" Well. Maybe he won't have to endure her vacuity for much longer.

She pours herself a cup of coffee and snaps open the *Times* and starts reading the front-page stories. When, after about half an hour, she hears Cooper coming down the stairs, she can't help it, she feels glad. She folds the *Times* back up and puts it on his .side of the table.

He comes into the kitchen, pours himself a cup of coffee, and sits heavily at the table with her. "Damn, that coffeemaker's loud," he says.

Her mouth tightens. *Not today, Coop,* she thinks. *Today* you're *taking care of* me. And yet she hears herself saying, "I'm sorry. Did I wake you up?"

"Well, Candy, what do you think?" He opens the newspaper.

"Do you want some breakfast?"

"Yeah, in a minute, let me wake up." He wipes at something under his nose. "Get me a tissue, would you?" he asks, and she does.

She moves to the center island to begin chopping onions and peppers for an omelet.

"What time did you get up, anyway?" he asks.

"I didn't even look. The sun was just starting to come up. It was two pink clouds after a star." She figures he'll turn around and say, "*What?*" and she'll say, "You know, like two minutes after five, *two clouds after a star.*" But he doesn't turn around. He doesn't do anything.

When she puts his omelet in front of him, he says, "Smells good." So, you know. She sits down. She salts her omelet. She eats it. When she has finished, she will put on one of the beautiful St. John suits he insists she wear. After the appointment, no matter what the news is, she'll tell Cooper that she's going to her high school reunion this weekend. When she got the invitation and asked if he'd like to go, he'd said, "Good God, no. *Clear Springs?* No. Thank you." She waited a day or two, then called the airlines to make a reservation for herself and her dog, and then called Pam Pottsman to say she'd be coming, alone except for her bulldog; and Pam was so excited. "Are you still unbelievably gorgeous?" Pam said, and Candy said, "No, Pam, I am not." Pam said, "Oh, yes you are!" and they both laughed. And it was fun, that moment on the phone. It lifted her heart to hear Pam's voice and to be suddenly enriched by a rush of memories. She saw the wide steps of the high school, smelled that janitorial waxy smell you always noticed when you first came into the building, saw the lit trophy case out in the hall with the photos of outstanding athletes. She saw the crowds of students walking down the hall, the teachers standing at the fronts of their classrooms. She saw the gymnasium at night, decorated for a dance,

felt the pressure of a crown being put on her head as she sat on a plywood throne that had been painted gold. After Candy hung up, she went to look at herself in the mirror, and for the first time in a long time she saw how her blond hair was still thick and lovely (if chemically enhanced), how her wide eyes were still a clear green, how her expensive night creams had kept wrinkles at bay. She thought, I am *still kind of gorgeous.*

She's going to that reunion tomorrow, no matter what. Before, she just kind of wanted to. Now, she needs to. Now, she would go in jeans and a sweatshirt and a shower cap and no makeup, just to sit at a table and be surrounded by people she used to know, just to be near someone familiar in the old way. Someone from before.

SEVEN

LESTER, ON LUNCH BREAK FROM HIS VETERINARY CLINIC, takes the mini Lop from his nine-year-old neighbor, Miranda. He holds the rabbit tight up against his stomach, facing out. "When you examine a bunny," he says, "the thing to do is to hold it like this." The bunny begins to kick wildly. "And when they kick, which they usually do, you rub your hand slowly over their tummies, which sort of hypnotizes them." He demonstrates, and the rabbit does indeed calm down. Lester uses one hand to support the rabbit's bottom and turns him to face his owner.

"Yup. He looks pretty happy, now," Miranda says.

"What did you decide to name him?"

"Custard."

"Ah."

"Because he's gooshy like custard. You're the one who told me to name an animal because of how it *is*." Miranda pulls her T-shirt away from her neck and blows down on herself. It's a warm afternoon. She and Lester have just had lunch, as is their

custom on Friday afternoons. Lester does scheduled surgeries on Friday mornings, and most times there's a couple hours' window before he needs to be back at the clinic for routine appointments. Miranda, who comes home from school for lunch, began eating with Lester on Friday when she was seven, and they alternate preparing the food. Today was Miranda's turn, and she brought a sophisticated roll-up: lemon hummus, lettuce, tomato, onion, and kalamata olives, which were inconsistently pitted.

The little girl is set on becoming a veterinarian herself, and thus far Lester has given her a stethoscope, an otoscope, a white lab coat, a thermometer, empty vaccine bottles, and syringe barrels minus the needles. She brings a notebook on the days they have lunch, and she writes down the things she learns. She has a cat, a dog, and a parakeet, and she taught the bird to retrieve quarters she rolls across a table, something Lester frankly doubted a parakeet could do until he saw it with his own eyes. Just yesterday, she and her parents rescued the rabbit from the humane society. The people who surrendered him had him for only four days before giving him up, saying he had destroyed all the downstairs electrical cords. "Do you think it's really true he did that?" Miranda asked Lester when she first showed him her new pet. And Lester told her that the only thing rabbits like better than electrical cords is birdseed. "Really?" Miranda said, and Lester said yup, that for rabbits, birdseed is like candy. You shouldn't give them too much, though, just like people. A little went a long way. The girl considered this, then asked, "Do *you* like birdseed?" Lester allowed that he had never tasted it. "Should we?" Miranda asked, and Lester said he thought he'd rather have the sandwiches Miranda had brought. "That's not all," she said and showed him the red apples, the entire roll of Oreos, and the napkins she had decorated with rainbow stickers.

Now she lays Custard in her lap and pets him. "Aren't they so luxurious, rabbits?" she says. "They're like you have a mink

coat but you don't have to kill anything." She looked up at him. "I have something to ask you."

"What's that?"

"Tomorrow night? There's a play at seven o'clock in Mr. and Mrs. Pichiotti's basement. This kid Eddie Sandman wrote it. He's twelve. It's about a vampire, and guess who the vampire is?"

Lester strokes his chin. "Hmmmmm. Would it be Custard?"

Miranda giggles. "No!"

"Would it be Eddie Sandman?"

"No, he's the *director*!"

"Hmmmm," Lester says. "Give me a minute. . . ."

"It's *me*!" Miranda says.

"You're *kidding*."

"No!"

"You can *act,* too?"

"Yes! Can you come? I get to suck blood two times. And we have strawberry jelly hidden in a Baggie in my cape and I secretly smear it on and it looks exactly like real."

Lester sits back in his chair and reaches over to pinch off a dying leaf from one of the plants on the windowsill next to the table. He's got a series of glass shelves in lieu of curtains, and they're full of flowering plants. It had been his wife's idea; the window got lots of sun. "I can't come tomorrow night. I'll be out of town."

"Where are you going?"

"I'm going to a high school reunion. You know what a re-union is, right?"

Miranda scratches a mosquito bite at the side of her neck with apparent satisfaction; it makes her mouth draw over to one side. "Yeah, it's really good friends who all come from all over to see each other again."

"Right," Lester says. Though to himself, he thinks, *Well, really good* friends . . .

"What all are you going to do?" Miranda asks.

"We're having a dinner and dance and then brunch the next morning."

"You can *dance*?"

"Why, yes, Miranda, I can."

"I never saw you dance!"

"I never saw you dance, either."

"Well, I can."

"And so can I. For your information, I took ballroom dancing as a young man." Not that it did much good, actually. Lester was an awful dancer. But at least he knew how the steps were *supposed* to go. The fox-trot. The waltz. The cha-cha; oh, how he had hated doing the cha-cha. He had wanted to murder his mother every time he did the cha-cha. There was simply no good way for a guy to hold his hands when he did the cha-cha.

"What *is* ballroom dancing?" Miranda asks.

"Well, literally, it's dancing in a really big room made for dancing. But if it's a class called ballroom dancing, it kind of teaches you everything you need to know. I mean, the basics, anyway."

"Who are you going with?"

"Nobody. I asked Jeanine and her husband to come, but they can't."

Miranda studies his face as though it's a palm she's reading. She worries about him, has told him on numerous occasions that he needs a girlfriend, and has made recommendations ranging from Miley Cyrus to the cashier at BuyLow who told Miranda she loves animals, too. "I can go with you. If you want."

"That's very nice of you. But what about the play?"

She slaps the top of her head. "Oh, yeah!"

Lester looks up at the wall clock and tells Miranda he's got to get back to the clinic, and she back to school.

"Do we have time for Three Things?" she says.

Every week, Miranda is told three things about various animals. Parakeets have about a teaspoon of circulating blood volume; elephants grieve; horses can get sunburned on their noses; dogs sweat through the pads of their feet—that sort of thing. "Well, you have one thing already," Lester tells her. "Rabbits like birdseed." Miranda dutifully writes it down. He notices that she has moved into an elaborate cursive and he's happy to see it. He's heard that many schools aren't teaching cursive anymore, and it makes him unaccountably sad. He still remembers Mrs. Lord in her blue crepe dress and enormous pearl clip-ons, standing over him in elementary school, trying to impress on him that good penmanship was a sign of good character and civility. She used to wear entirely too much perfume, Mrs. Lord, a heavy, spicy scent that reminded Lester of carnations. She wore rhinestone pins on her shoulder every day, and her ankles seemed to spill over her low pumps in what Lester knows now was a sign of congestive heart failure but at the time believed was a kind of *decision* she had made—flesh as accessory—and he wasn't quite sure how he felt about it. He used to look at his mother's slender ankles and wonder if she wasn't lacking somehow.

"What's another thing?" Miranda asks.

"Well, let's see . . . ," Lester says. "How about a cow one? We haven't done a cow one for a long time."

"I've decided I'm not going to be in large animal practice," Miranda says. "I don't want to be driving around all over to farms and to hell and back."

"I see," Lester says.

"Can I *ask* two things?" Miranda says.

"Of course."

"Is it true that dogs can't see colors?"

"No," Lester says. "They can see colors. Just not like you. They see gray, and they see the colors of the world as basically yellow and blue. You know, a lot of people don't know that dogs

don't actually see all that well, period. They rely more on scent and hearing. For some sounds, they hear hundreds of times better than people."

"They are always better than people."

"Well," Lester says.

"It's true! There are hardly any people as good as dogs, you have to admit. Name me one person you ever met who was as good as a dog."

"Oh, I've met a few."

"Who?"

"My wife, for one. And you, Miranda Bryson, if you must know. You are as good as a dog."

"I am?"

"You are."

"If I *think* about it, I guess you are, too."

"Thank you. But listen, we have to go. Hurry and ask me your second question."

"Okay. Okay, it is . . . Oh! Custard keeps rubbing his face on me. Why?"

Lester puts their plates in the dishwasher. "Well, that's for a good reason. He's marking you. Rabbits have scent glands under their chins, and they secrete something from there that only other rabbits can smell. It's totally odorless and only a little bit damp, so you might not have noticed. But he's saying you belong to him. That behavior is called 'chinning.'"

Miranda smiles. "That's a good one."

"I thought you'd like that."

They go out the front door onto the porch, where Lester's dog, Mason, is sleeping in the shade. "Let's go, buddy," Lester says, and the dog leaps up and heads for Lester's truck.

Lester is backing out of the driveway when he hears Miranda calling his name. He leans his head out the window. "*What?*"

"You should wear something *blue* to the renewion!"

He nods, waves, and as he drives toward the clinic, he thinks, *Maybe I will.* His wife used to like him in blue, and since she died, he's purposefully not worn it much. But maybe it's time. *Renewion.* He looks into the rearview mirror, at Miranda fading away in the distance. There was a period in his late thirties when he seriously considered adopting a child, but he worried about whether he'd be able to adequately care for a son or daughter as a single parent. Now it's too late, and in quiet moments, he sometimes feels a profound regret about not having gone through with it. It could have worked. He could have hired someone to help him. It might not have been ideal, but he would have had the experience of raising a child, something he thinks he would have enjoyed for all kinds of reasons. The day after his wife told him about her pregnancy, she'd given him a miniature fishing rod and tackle box. It's still in the back of his closet, and sometimes he takes the little metal box out and looks at all the lures Kathleen had chosen. Their child would have loved it, he's certain.

He supposes, too, that it would have been nice, at this point in his life, when retirement is not so very far away, to think that he belonged to someone, and they to him—to chin and be chinned.

He shifts the truck into third and catches a glimpse of himself in the rearview mirror. There are a few years on him, yes, but he's in pretty good shape. He wonders if Candy Sullivan's coming to the reunion. He used to think about her in a certain way, though he knew it was useless. He used to sit at his desk doing homework and then stop and look out the window and think of her. Maybe he'll have a drink and tell her that.

He walks into his clinic, thinking about how fast time goes by, one's whole life. When Jeanine sees him, she slams down the phone and stands up behind the reception desk. "I was just trying to call you. Samson's back. He's in trouble; his temp and heart rate are sky-high. He's in room one."

EIGHT

"DAMN IT!" COOP SAYS. "I JUST CAN'T BELIEVE THIS!" IT'S eleven o'clock, and Candy and he have just come back to the car after having met with Dr. Johnston. Coop sits slumped behind the steering wheel, his car door open to let out some of the heat that has accumulated—he'd parked the car in the sun, thinking they wouldn't be longer than fifteen or twenty minutes. Candy's door is not open. She doesn't feel the heat. She doesn't feel much of anything but a need to get home and get out of this suit, out of these heels.

Coop looks over at her. "Fuck. I don't know if I can *drive*."

"I'll drive," Candy says and starts to get out of the car.

Coop grabs her arm. "I'll do it." He holds on to her for a moment longer, then closes his eyes tightly and Candy can see he's trying not to cry. "Just give me a minute." She waits, staring out the windshield at the line of cars parked before her, wondering how many other people will walk to their cars feeling weirdly shaken. She wonders if she wins for worst diagnosis for the day.

"Candy, I . . . I'm so sorry for all—"

"Don't," she says. "You don't need to do that. Let's not do that. Let's just go home."

He sighs, puts the key into the ignition, and turns on the engine, the air conditioner. He shakes his head. "I really can't believe it. Can you?"

She shrugs.

Coop puts the car into reverse and begins backing out. "Well, we're not going to listen to that and just assume it's right. We're going to get a second opinion, maybe a third. Let's just see what happens after that. Let's see what *they* say."

"Yes, all right."

"I mean, I literally cannot believe this! You haven't even felt sick!"

She laughs, a small sound.

"What," he says. "What's funny."

"I don't know. Nothing."

They drive in silence for a while, and then Coop says, "He's not that good a doctor, anyway. I don't know why you insist on going to him. Is he even board certified?"

"Coop."

"What?"

"I knew something was wrong."

Now he laughs. "You always think something is wrong! And it never is!" He pulls out onto the freeway and sits back farther in his seat, more relaxed, now. "It's not going to be anything this time, either. It's a mistake, it's got to be. You'll see. They make *mistakes*."

"Okay, Coop."

He looks over at her. "Okay?"

"Yes."

He looks at his watch. "We'll go somewhere nice for lunch."

"I want to go home."

"I'll take you anywhere you want to go."

"I want to go *home*, Coop." In his face, she sees a quick flicker of . . . what? *Annoyance?* Coop doesn't like it when she doesn't take him up on his offers for things he thinks she should like. Once, he told her such refusals reflected her self-loathing.

Remembering this confirms her decision to tell Coop about the reunion tomorrow. She will say that she is going, and that he is not going with her. He might say he'll come now, but she'll say no. She'll say she'll be fine, it's just a weekend. Nothing has changed, except that they've heard some words, a first opinion.

When they pull into the driveway, their neighbor Arthur is outside moving slowly toward his house, carrying what looks to be a heavy bag of groceries. Candy tells Coop to go and help him. When he starts to argue, she says, "I'm fine. Go and help him, please."

Coop gets out of the car and calls to Arthur, saying, "Hey there, need a little help?" For a moment, Candy worries that Arthur might be offended by the offer, but no, his face lights up and he hands his bag to Coop. She hears him say, "Tell you what, there are three more bags in the car. Thanks a million, awfully neighborly of you. It's those big tin cans that'll kill you! Those crushed tomatoes!"

Candy goes into the house and does not acknowledge Esther, though the bulldog greets her at the door and begins snorting and spinning in happy circles. She picks up the mail from the vestibule floor, sorts it by size, and lays it on the table. When she walks into the kitchen, she realizes she has no memory of who sent the mail she just picked up. But what does it matter.

She goes upstairs and into the bathroom and starts water running in the tub. Then she goes to the bedroom and takes off her clothes and puts on her softest bathrobe, the blue one she's had for so many years now. She goes back down to the kitchen and pours herself a glass of Pinot Grigio and gets out a tray on which she arranges fancy cheeses, crackers, a bunch of grapes,

and a bar of Vosges chocolate that features a combination of sweet, salty, and hot, her favorite. She adds a rose from the arrangement at the center of the dining room table and carries the tray up to the bathroom, where she balances it on the wide edge of the tub and turns off the taps. The tub is deliciously full, overfull, and wisps of steam rise and twist enticingly.

Esther has not left her mistress's side, and now Candy pats the top of the dog's head. "Did I ignore you?" she says. "Did I? I'm sorry." She gives Esther a bite of cheese and watches as she swallows it without chewing, then lies down, her chin on her crossed paws.

From downstairs, Candy hears Coop call her name.

"In the bathroom," she calls. *Back to the womb,* she thinks. She has always taken baths when she feels bad, seeking out—and finding—an elemental comfort.

There is an unopened bottle of scented oil on the wide ledge of the tub that Candy's been saving for a special occasion. She opens it now and adds it to the water, then steps in. She looks down at her dear, familiar body, her pale skin and the cheerful scattering of freckles across her chest, down her arms. She lowers herself slowly—the water is wonderfully hot—and feels a dull pain in her knees. She leans against the back of the tub, takes a sip of wine, and sighs. When did she start feeling it in her knees when she bends down this way? Will she never again in her life do a cartwheel? When *was* the last one?

She hears Coop coming up the stairs and then he knocks at the door and speaks through it. "You're taking a *bath*?"

"Yes." Another sip of wine. Very good.

"Didn't you take a shower this morning?"

"Yes, Coop."

"Can I come in?"

She looks again at her body, seeing it in a different way, now.

Having no affection for it at all, and feeling embarrassed by her sagging breasts, her soft belly, the blueness of the veins that run close to the surface.

"Candy?"

"Come in."

He opens the door, and she sees him take in the tray, her blue robe, Esther, then: her, though he looks quickly away from her body and fixes his gaze on her face.

He sits awkwardly at the side of the tub. "So . . . Are you comfortable in there?"

"Yup."

"Need anything?"

"Nope." She looks into his eyes and it is as though she hasn't seen him for a long time. He's a very handsome man, beautiful gray eyes, high cheekbones, and a strong chin. Silvery temples on an otherwise black head of hair. She says, "You know what I was just thinking? I was in a department store the other day and I used the restroom, and there was a receptacle for tampons in the stall. And I thought, *What do they need that for?* You know? I thought that because *I* no longer use tampons, there was no need for a receptacle."

Coop stares at her. He doesn't understand.

Candy sits up and the water makes a sloshing sound. "I mean that I've become so incredibly self-centered that I—"

"You're not self-centered," Coop says. "Arthur was just telling me how you're always running next door to ask them if they need anything, that you bring them turnovers from the bakery and pick up their library books and shovel their snow and everything else."

Candy nods. She wants her husband to listen to what she is saying. She wants him to understand what she *means* by what she says. She may have an opportunity to try to explain herself

now in a way she would not have been able to before. "But I am, Coop. And I've cut myself off from others, from important things, really important things!"

He makes the smallest gesture of impatience, but he does not speak.

She moves closer to him, tries to hold his eyes with her own. "You know, you get a diagnosis like this, and it's like there's a seismic shift or something. A very personal seismic shift. All I could think, after Dick gave me the odds, was, *Oh my God, what I haven't done!* It's as though . . . It's like all around a person, the world goes on, all the time, all the goodness and all the evil. All the living and the dying and we always seem to forget that our time for dying will come, too. We walk in cemeteries and feel sorry for the people who are buried there. Like it will never happen to us! And yet now that I've been told I'll die—"

"That's not what he said!"

She looks at him.

"It's *not*! He gave you some statistics. That's all. And we don't even know if he's right. He could be wrong!"

"Well," she says. "Anyway." She smiles at him. "I'm fine, Coop. Really I am."

"So . . . you want to just stay here for a while?"

She nods.

"Do you want me to read to you or something?"

He used to do that. In the early years, knowing that she loved to be read to, he would ask her now and then if she would like him to read to her. Always, she said yes. But it's been years. It's been a lifetime, truly. She could accept this gift he's offering. But what she really wants right now is solitude. And for once, her needs are going to be honored over his. She says, "Oh, that's sweet of you. But no. Not now. I'd like to just be in here and . . . I want to think. The warm water feels good. And doesn't it smell nice?"

"Yeah."

She doubts he's noticed the smell at all, even now, when she's pointed it out to him. But that's all right. It's for her, and she smells it just fine.

"Want me to bring you anything else?"

"No, I've got everything I need."

"Well . . . Don't you want me to just sit here with you? So you're not alone?"

"I'm okay. You go and do whatever you want. I'd actually like to be alone."

He stands and she can see him trying hard not to look relieved. "All right, so I'll just go and work on the computer. Call me if you need anything."

"Okay. Coop?"

He turns around. "Yeah?"

"I'm going to my high school reunion tomorrow. I really want to. But you don't have to come."

"Well, I will, now."

"I don't want you to."

He stands there, and she says, "What I mean is, I don't *need* you to go. You said you didn't want to when I asked you before, and that's fine. But I want to go. I've got the tickets. I just need you to give me a ride to the airport, and pick me up when I come back. Or I can take a cab."

He puts his hands in his pockets and nods. It's all she can do not to get out of the tub and embrace him. She thinks of how her wet body would imprint on his dry clothes.

Two hours later, he knocks on the door again. "You okay?"

"I'm fine."

"You don't need anything?"

"No."

"Can I . . . do you still want to be alone?"

"Yes. But take Esther out, will you? She needs a good walk."

Many hours after that, Coop comes to the door and says, "I'm starving. You?"

"I'm not getting out quite yet, Coop. You'll have to make your own dinner."

"Well . . . What have we got?"

She almost laughs. "Why don't you *look*?"

Twenty minutes later, he comes into the bathroom with toasted cheese and tomato sandwiches. "Coop!" she says.

"Dinner. I *made* these."

"I know."

"Wasn't that hard, really."

"I know that, too."

"It wasn't *easy*, either."

She looks at him.

"The damn tomatoes were slippery."

"Well. It looks very good."

"But *taste* it."

She takes a bite. "Yes. Very good."

"I used two kinds of cheese."

"Uh-huh."

"Kind of fancy."

"Yes, it is. It's very good, Coop."

They eat their sandwiches and talk a bit, and Coop does not ask again if she wouldn't like to come out of the tub. It's as though she lives there now, like a fish. He brings her a book she asks for, a gardening magazine, sets a radio on the floor and tunes it to the classical station she requests.

Candy lets her mind roam. She thinks about how she wanted to be a horse when she was a little girl. She thinks of a tangerine-colored scarf she wore under a brown leather jacket when she was in college. She thinks of a time when she and Cooper were on vacation. They were staying at an inn on the water in Connecticut, and she had awakened early and taken a walk alone

across a causeway. On the way, she saw two swans sleeping, rocked by the water, their long necks wrapped around their bodies so that their heads could be supported on top of their folded wings. She spoke softly to them, asking them, absurdly, if they were asleep, though she could plainly see that their eyes were closed. It is Candy's habit to speak to almost every animal she comes in contact with; she has a deeply grounded affection for animals similar to that which she has for young children, and she thinks it's for the same reason: they are unapologetically themselves, and their default setting seems to be for happiness. On that same walk, she remembers, she saw a seagull flapping its wings against a strong wind, struggling hard just to stay in one place, and the image now has particular poignancy.

She thinks about how she went into a coffee shop yesterday and sat at a table next to one where an old woman and her daughter were sitting. The old woman was a mess: her hair long and stringy, her face thin and ravaged-looking. She looked homeless, but Candy didn't think she was, not with her daughter sitting there with her official-looking papers. The daughter was dressed in a stained black top and loose-fitting black pants, Clark Kent–style glasses. She was overweight, her hair greasy, and there was a distinct smell of body odor coming from her. The daughter was giving her mother some sort of test, checking for Alzheimer's or something, Candy thought, for she said, "Okay. Concrete is *hard,* or concrete is *soft*?" She repeated the question, and repeated it yet again, with no pause in between. Then, *"Mother!"* she said.

"Concrete is hard or concrete is soft," the mother said quickly. Obediently.

"No, but which *is* it?" the daughter said. "Concrete is *hard* or concrete is *soft*?" And again she repeated the question two more times.

"Concrete is soft," the mother said.

Her daughter sighed. Then she said, "Okay, that's kind of a trick question. Because concrete is soft when they first pour it, isn't it? But *then* it gets hard."

Yes, Candy thought. *One for the mother. Why don't you ask her if a* sidewalk *is hard or soft?*

"Next question," the daughter said. "Mother? Mother, pay attention, listen *carefully.*"

Listen carefully? Candy thought. *The espresso maker is making such loud noises, people keep coming in the door and going out of it, there are conversations going on at every table—how can she concentrate? Take her home, to her own kitchen table. Give her a chance.*

"Okay, next question," the daughter said. "You keep money in a wall or you keep money in a wallet, you keep money in a wall or you keep money in a wallet, you keep money in a wall or you keep money in a wallet?"

I'm going to scream, Candy thought.

"I'm so hungry," the mother said.

"Well, Mother, so am I," the daughter said. "Okay? Now pay attention. Listen carefully. You keep money in a wall or you keep money in a wallet?"

If you say something over and over again, it begins to lose its meaning, Candy thought. *Say anything enough times and it becomes gibberish.* Then she thought, *You could keep money in either a wall or a wallet. You could have a safe.*

The mother said, "You keep money in a . . . ," and Candy didn't move a muscle, waiting to hear the woman's answer, praying that she would get it right, that she would have this small triumph.

"In a wall!" she said, and then, "Oh. No. Did you say . . . ? It's *wallet*!"

"Right!" the daughter said. "Very good! Now listen to the

next question: A *banana* is round, or a *coconut* is round?" She repeated it, repeated it again.

"A banana is round," the mother said, and the daughter said, "*No*, Ma. *Concentrate.*"

But a banana is round! Candy thought. *Depending on where you look at it! A banana slice! What about a banana slice?*

"I'm so hungry," the mother said.

Candy went up to the counter to order a piece of coffee cake for the mother. She would give it to her with a flourish and say, "You can share it with your daughter, if you want." But she ended up ordering two pieces of coffee cake, and two twenty-dollar gift cards, and asked the counter person to wait for her to leave the store before she delivered it all to the women. She thought, *Everyone's in the same boat. Pass the coffee cake.*

At around ten-thirty that night, Candy awakens from having fallen asleep. She shivers; the water has grown cold. She thinks about adding more hot water yet again but decides not to. Instead, she climbs out of the tub, dries off, applies a luxuriously thick orange- and ginger-scented lotion, and pads into the bedroom. She sees that Coop has fallen asleep on top of the bedcovers, legal papers in his hand, the light on. She turns out the light and puts the papers on the floor, then lies down beside him. He turns and pulls her close to him, then closer. It is so unfamiliar now, the feel of him pressed up against her. She has been missing this, yearning for it for so long, yet now she finds it claustrophobic. Still, it's nice. It's a kind of home. Or like revisiting a home she used to love. Neither of them speak. She remembers reading an essay in the newspaper that a woman hospitalized with a terminal illness had written about her ex-husband. Their divorce ten years earlier had been exceptionally acrimonious, and each had felt vastly relieved to be rid of the other. But when the woman was admitted to the hospital for that final time, her ex

sent her a lavish bouquet and a letter, the contents of which she did not disclose. But she did say she'd pressed the letter to her heart for some time before saving it in a zippered compartment of her purse, because she didn't trust keeping it in the hospital nightstand. She said she wanted it for as long as she could have it; and then she wanted her children to have it. She also wrote, "It came to me that the experience of dying didn't necessarily have to be all bad. That parts of it could be glorious."

Candy feels tears slide down her face, and she makes no move to wipe them away. They are a miracle of composition, tears, and they provide a vital and intimate service without ever being asked. She moves her left toes, then her right. They are still working. *Miles to go,* she thinks. *Miles to go before I sleep.* She recalls the earnestness of Mr. Little's face when he tried to show his freshman English class the elegance of the construction of those last two lines of the poem "Stopping by Woods on a Snowy Evening."

"Why does Frost say the line twice?" he asked the class, and they all sat still before him. "Well, why do you *think?*" he said, his pale blue eyes pleading. Finally a boy raised his hand to answer. It had been Lester Hessenpfeffer, who always knew the answer to everything but liked to give others a chance, so he would wait before he raised his hand. Lester answered the question, saying, "Well, one is specific, and one is general. He's talking about getting home and going to bed that night, but he's also talking about dying."

"Very good," Mr. Little said, with obvious relief. And Candy remembers thinking, *That's what I thought! I should have answered; that's what I thought!* She'd smiled at Lester, and he'd blushed and looked down at his desk. His shoes were weird, she remembers, his shoes and his clothes; but he was cute, that Lester. She wonders if he's coming to the reunion. She wonders if Buddy and Nance Dunsmore are coming; they'd had to get mar-

ried; she wonders if they stayed together. She begins remembering more names: Annie Denato, who had such a terrible reputation for being easy; Karen Erickson, who once fainted in home ec
class at the sight of raw liver and banged her head and the am-
bulance had to come and take her to the hospital; Marjorie
Dunn, who won a big prize for writing an essay none of them understood—something about a white bird with one black feather
and a black bird with one white feather. None of the kids had any
idea what it meant but the English teachers were all very pleased.
Tommy Metito was on the swim team and looked like Arnold
Schwarzenegger and this was before steroids, or at least she
thinks it was. Lou Kressel wore an *ascot*; she wonders if he's out
as gay now. She gets more and more excited and then it's like she
runs right into a wall, because she remembers what the doctor
told her this morning. Extraordinary that she forgot, but then the
world is full of surprises. She would like to see some more of
them.

The last thing she thinks of before she falls asleep is a time she
was a little girl outside playing on a summer night. She was the
first to be called in, and she resented it: the sky was violet and
the clouds were pink; the fireflies were just coming out; the taste
of sweat at the bend in her elbow was delectable; and the earth
had given up its heat to the coolness of evening, making the grass
so pleasant to lie in. She complained bitterly to her group of
friends about having to go in, and Mary Nix said, "We'll all have
to go in in a few minutes, anyway. You're just the first." That
made it better. Then, when she got inside, there were clean sheets,
and the light on at her bedside, and the covers turned down, and
the little statue of the Virgin to whom Candy prayed every night
and who Candy believed knew her best. Knew everything, in
fact, and just kept quiet about it.

Death is a beginning or death is an end? Death is a beginning
or death is an end? Death is a beginning or death is an end?

NINE

O N Friday evening, Mary Alice and Einer are in downtown Clear Springs at Styletique dress shop. Late that afternoon, Mary Alice had shown Einer the choices for what she was going to wear to the reunion dinner and dance tomorrow, and he had shaken his head and said, "Absolutely not." Half an hour later, they were here. On the way over, Einer had told her that he himself intends to wear a medium-weight gray suit and an electric blue tie to the reunion. Might be nice if she would coordinate with him and wear a pretty blue dress. Men like dresses, he said, and men like blue. He said, "You ask any man, what's your favorite color, and he won't hesitate. Blue."

Well, Mary Alice likes red. She likes a red so deep it's almost black, and as soon as they walked in the store, she saw a dress in that very color, a kind of satiny number with a crisscross bodice and a full skirt with rhinestone belt buckle, and she likes it very much. When she modeled it for Einer, he only sat still, staring at her, which she took to be a compliment. But apparently not, for he finally said, "Inappropriate. Now try on the blue." For Einer's

benefit, she tried on the midnight blue dress he liked. It is nothing like what she would normally wear. For one thing, it's awfully close fitting. Also, it has cap sleeves, a risky thing for a woman her age. And it's so plain, not a rhinestone or ruffle to be found! But, "Yup, that's the ticket," Einer said, nodding. "Didn't I tell you? Wear that one."

She wants to follow Einer's advice and wear what he picked out; she could always wear a dressy little cardigan with it. She understands that telling her what to wear makes him feel important and gives him something to do. But she so loves the red! How to disagree with him tactfully? He's already crabby; he usually eats at five o'clock and now it's a little after six. Not that he'll eat much, but the man likes his routine.

Maureen Jernoff, the owner of the store, comes back to the dressing room area. "Have you decided yet?" She has managed to keep the impatience from her voice, but her arms are crossed a little too tightly beneath her bosom. It's past closing time. She's probably hungry, too.

"Well, I'm leaning toward the red," Mary Alice says, hoping Maureen will enthusiastically endorse her choice. But no such luck. "The blue was much better on you, you ought to get that one," she says. "Up to you, of course. But hey, listen; are you going to pay cash or charge?"

"I'll charge it," Mary Alice says and reluctantly starts to put the red dress back on the rack. But then she says, "You know what, Maureen? I'll take them both." To Einer, she says, "The red one I can wear another time."

"I thought I'd get the chicken pot pie," Einer says, and Mary Alice guesses he misheard her. Never mind. She's getting both dresses. And she's getting the chicken pot pie, too.

At the Tick Tock diner, Mary Alice is amazed at the amount of food Einer puts away. He eats almost half of a very generous serving of chicken pot pie, and he says he could eat more, but he's

leaving room for pie, as he has been advised to do both by the bold print at the top of the menu and by—especially by—their waitress, Desiree. "You leave room for pie, now," she told him. And then, leaning over so that her considerable cleavage was exposed and the scent of her heavy perfume more apparent, she said, "That way we'll have more time together. Won't that be nice?"

"Yes, it will," Einer said, and glanced quickly over at Mary Alice, who looked pointedly off into the distance. Desiree is a sexily overweight black-haired woman in her late forties who wears wildly colored tights—hot pink or turquoise or fire engine yellow or multistriped or paisley print—with her uniform. She has very pretty and very clear porcelain skin, and she wears deep red lipstick. She *looks* like a Desiree. Mary Alice has a sneaking suspicion the woman has given herself that name, and why not? If Mary Alice were to pick a name for herself, it sure wouldn't be Mary Alice. It would be . . . what? Maybe initials. Initials beg a question, they're inherently mysterious, and she thinks they suggest a certain authority, too. K.C., she might be. She imagines herself at the reunion, someone saying, "Hey, aren't you Mary Alice Mayhew?" and her responding, "It's K.C. now." She wonders how many people go to reunions just to try on another way of being, confident that they'll be able to sustain the ruse for that short amount of time.

Desiree knows both Mary Alice and Einer well, but she pays attention only to the old man. Mary Alice doesn't mind. It's nice to see him engaged in conversation with a woman who is not checking on his bowel status or asking if he would like his pills mixed with applesauce, and it gives Mary Alice time to think her own thoughts.

She hadn't really believed Einer would go with her to the reunion. She thought he'd forget about it, or lose interest, or that some medical ailment—*minor!* she'd imagined, *minor!*—would

develop and he would be unable to go. But no. Rita's man friend had asked her out for this Saturday and so Mary Alice is going to honor her promise and stay with Einer—it just won't be in his house. And Einer's thrilled. He's begun to act like it's *his* reunion, talking about people he remembers from his own senior class. Peggy McClure, who used to slip him brazen love notes in the hallway. Cecil McIntyre, who bore a strong resemblance to the actor Johnny Weissmuller and whose nickname, in fact, was Tarzan. How he went down in a plane crash in World War II a week before he was supposed to go home. Priscilla Embert, in the class behind him, who went to New York City and became a Rockette. Ned Connady, who started out his bitter enemy and ended up his best friend—they'd had a double wedding. Oh, he'd had some times in high school, he said, and he's begun to tell her more and more stories, and to become more and more animated while doing so. Frankly, Mary Alice is beginning to resent it. She wants to think her own thoughts about her high school experiences, imperfect though they might have been. In fact, once one gets older, there's a kind of pride in having survived a bad high school experience; it certainly makes for more interesting conversation when a group of people are comparing notes. What would be the follow-up question, after all, to "I didn't have *any* problems in high school!"? Though she wonders now if anyone ever would say that, if even the most popular kids weren't full of doubt and self-loathing, if they weren't victimized by the same take-no-hostage hormones that plagued everyone else.

Mary Alice also wants to think about how she'd like to approach the man she's going to the reunion to see. Even if nothing happens, it will be interesting to see him. How he has turned out. If his personality is still kind of the same. If he has a huge beer belly or is still fit and trim.

When Einer pays the check (which he insisted on doing—and after Mary Alice saw the size tip he left Desiree, she understood

why), he says, "You'd better get me home; I've got to get my beauty sleep. Now, tomorrow's just registration and then the dinner at seven, right?"

"That's right," Mary Alice says.

"I don't suppose I'd need to go to the registration."

"No. Considering the fact that you're not registered."

He looks sharply at her. "Well, I know that. I guess I know that. Take me out in the backyard and shoot me if I don't know that! But what I was thinking is, do you *need* me to come?"

Mary Alice is suddenly and unexpectedly touched, both by Einer's interest in protecting her and by his excitement at getting out, to go to the reunion with her. She knows this magnanimous feeling probably has to do with the fact that she's about to drop him off at his house and back into the care of his homemaker. Still. "I'll be fine, Einer," she says. "If anyone messes with me, I'll tell you, and then at the dinner you can clean their clock for me."

"I'll rabbit punch them," Einer says. "That'll take any man down."

"What if a woman offends me?"

"Well, I'll rabbit punch her, too. You all want equality, by golly, I'll give it to you." He straightens himself in the booth. "What are we having for dinner, anyway?"

"Surf and turf."

Einer is quiet.

"Do you like that?" Mary Alice says. "I thought it might be good to get two things. You know, more choice, since we have to share."

"Well, to be honest, I'd have preferred the chicken, there must have been a chicken dish. Seems like people always have chicken."

"I'll see if I can change it," Mary Alice says. She likes chicken, too. She just hopes there's no garlic in it.

After Mary Alice gets home, she plays back the two messages

on her answering machine. The first one is from Pam Pottsman, saying that there's a problem with dinner on Saturday night. There aren't going to be enough surf and turfs, the hotel just called; somebody screwed up on the ordering. Would Mary Alice mind very much having the chicken instead? Pam herself was going to have to change her order; there just wasn't enough surf and turf, but oh well. She would assume it was okay with Mary Alice unless she heard otherwise, and she can't *wait* to see her tomorrow night, she is so *excited,* isn't Mary Alice?

Perfect, Mary Alice thinks. And perhaps a sign, too, of how well things are going to go generally? Maybe all she'll have to do is sit back and good things will happen of their own accord.

The second message is from Marion, asking her if she'd like to go with him to the Olde Warsaw Buffet next Saturday night. Of course she would. Unless there's someone new in her life by then. Who knows, there could be. There really *could* be! She had done a little research. She knows what he does, where he lives. No reason they couldn't have a relationship with some miles between them. Why not take a little road trip to visit a special friend? Who might become more than that? Though even just a friendship would be fine; Mary Alice needs more friends, as Einer is always quick to point out.

She goes upstairs and into her closet and finds her senior yearbook. She turns to the page he's on and looks into his eyes, assesses for the billionth time his open smile. A man at peace with the world, and in love with it, and she'll bet anything he's still like that. As is she. "Hey," she says softly to the picture. "It's Mary Alice Mayhew. Remember me?"

That's what she'll really say, and now she runs through possible responses. A blank—though kind—look, mixed with a mild curiosity. Or a blank look followed by sudden recognition and a friendly hug. *Immediate* recognition followed by a warm hug, and him saying, "Well, of course I remember you!" Finally, her

favorite: grateful recognition, followed by a lingering hug and him saying low in her ear, "Gosh, I'm so glad you came! I was hoping you'd come!" Then he'd step back a bit from her and look into her eyes and say, "The last time I saw you, you were walking out of the gymnasium on graduation day. Where'd you go, anyway? Why didn't you come to the party?" This last, she knows, is a bit unlikely, but she plays it out in her mind anyway. She feels pretty certain that, when they talk, he will ask her what she's up to now, and she will answer by saying she has just moved back to Clear Springs. She won't reveal that she knows where he lives. She'll just say, "How about you?" And he'll tell her where he lives and she'll say, "Really. Well, that's not so far. We ought to get together sometime." She knows about his wife, and that he's single, now.

Before she goes to bed, Mary Alice tries on both dresses again. Here at home, in different light, she decides that Einer is right—the blue brings out her eyes and doesn't fight so much with her glasses. It isn't so much plain as elegant. She turns to the side, then grabs a hand mirror to inspect the rear view. Yes. The blue. She leaves the dress hanging in the bathroom, as though to discourage herself from changing her mind, and then lays out on a chair in her bedroom the outfit she'll wear to register in: black pants, a white blouse, a string of pearls her mother wore on her wedding day. Simple, but pretty. And surprise: red shoes, with four-inch heels. She might not see him there, but she'll see somebody. And they'll see her. "Mary *Alice*?" they'll say.

When she gets into bed, she closes her eyes and for a moment she wonders about the meaning of this sudden . . . silliness. She is being so silly! But silliness is in everyone; so far as Mary Alice is concerned, it's a pleasant common denominator. She remembers once meeting a distinguished professor of Asian studies on an airplane; a woman whose eyes held such fierce intelligence. And what did they talk about? Gregory Peck's unending appeal, and

laundry detergent. For some reason, Mary Alice jokingly (if truthfully) told the woman that she herself used a brand of detergent Tim Gunn from *Project Runway* recommended, and the woman asked why, and then asked many more questions and finally pulled out a Mont Blanc to write down "Tide Totalcare. Renewing Rain scent."

Mostly, Mary Alice thinks, her silliness is Einer's fault. The way he's after her all the time to enrich her life. "Get out there!" he says. "Do things while you still can! Blink a couple of times and you'll be an old fart like me, with memories your only entertainment. You think I'm kidding? I'm not kidding! You'd better *make* some memories before it's too late!"

As angry as he has made her, picking away at her like this, now she is grateful to him. It isn't too late for some things. It isn't! She may have gray hair and a few brown spots and her memory may not be quite as excellent as it once was, but the taste of a good vanilla ice cream cone or the sound of church bells on a Sunday morning or the sight of a red sky still thrills her. And in those moments of appreciation she, like all people, becomes ageless.

TEN

"I THINK I CAN MAKE YOU FEEL A WEENSY BIT BETTER, BABY." It's ten-thirty on Saturday morning, the day of the reunion, and Sandy is talking in the pooched-lip baby voice that Pete used to like so much. Now she reaches under the sheet for his penis.

He pushes her hand away. "Cut it out," he says. "This is a *hospital.*"

But it's not because he's in a hospital that he doesn't want her to touch him. It's because his heart is breaking—again, and in the more painful way, having nothing to do with a myocardial infarction, which is why he's here. He'd had a heart attack. A *heart attack,* a man like him! After he was stabilized in the emergency room and the doctor told him the news, Pete had yelled "*What the fuck!*" before he could stop himself, and his doctor—a female, not bad looking, Indian chick—had pressed his chart to her bosom and stepped back.

"Sorry," he'd said, and she'd given him one of those tight-ass smiles and nodded. He saw right away he wouldn't have any fun with this one; with this one, he'd have to play by the rules.

"Sorry," he'd said again, and then listened dutifully as she explained what the EKG had shown, the cardiac enzymes. She'd given him some stupid pamphlet called "You and Your Heart." He'd listened, he'd promised to read the pamphlet, but mostly he was thinking, *This is bullshit. I'm fine. I don't need anything except to get the hell out of here. This was a fluke, that's all.* The doctor had told him about how he'd need more tests, how he'd be on this medication and that medication. Jesus Christ. She'd told him he'd have to be in the hospital for at least a week, and when he got out, he'd need to wear one of those weird MedicAlert bracelets, what a babe magnet that was. Not that he gives a shit about babes anymore, but still.

Earlier this morning, his wife came to visit him. His kids, too. Nothing like a near-death experience to make everybody suddenly get along. Katie left after only a few minutes—she'd had to go to a birthday party—and the boys left soon afterward. Still, when the kids were there, they were loving and kind. Forgiving. Cal put his hand on Pete's shoulder and invited him to dinner next Sunday. Pete Jr. told him about some tickets he scored for a baseball game and invited him to go along. It made Pete think having a heart attack wasn't all bad. The MedicAlert bracelet will be a continual reminder to everyone that he is vulnerable, even if he doesn't seem like it.

After the kids left and Pete was alone with Nora, he said, "Listen, I can't go to the reunion today. They won't let me out until Monday. But I'd like to ask you to go for me. Would you, Nora? Please. I signed us both up, it's all paid for, all set."

She looked into his face with a kind of gentle weariness. "Oh, Pete. Why would you want me to go without you?"

Because he wanted her to think about him in the old way, that's why. He wanted her to be among their classmates, who knew them both back in the day. He thought this might provide the tiniest chink in the wall, a way for him to begin the arduous

process of trying to make his way back into her life. He's determined to get back what he has lost, a woman whose honesty and character he admires, someone who from day one saw through his bullshit to the good that lives inside him, and helped make him a better person than he is able be on his own. Nora was so pretty when he first started dating her, a raven-haired girl with big brown eyes, a heart-shaped face with deep dimples, a cute little figure. It is true that she is no longer a head turner. But her spirit. Her soul. He wants what he has come to see matters most. Which is not Sandy, though, God bless her, she's knocked herself out trying to look hot today. And has succeeded. Sprayed-on jeans would look like elephant skin compared to what that girl has slithered into today. The orderly nearly had a heart attack himself when he came in and saw her, he couldn't keep his eyes off her ass. And Sandy, in her inimitable way, made it possible for him to get a good look the whole time he was in there, leaning over Pete to adjust his sheet when it needed no adjustment, standing with her back to the guy to read the couple of cards taped to the wall, even though she had sent both of them.

"I just really wanted to go to that reunion," Pete told Nora. "I wanted to see what happened to all our classmates. Wouldn't you like to see that?"

She shrugged. "I don't know. Not really. The only people I'm interested in are the ones I've kept up with anyway."

"But . . . Lester Hessenpfeffer!" Pete said, and then he started madly thinking of whatever names he could remember. "Trudy Lebbing! Tommy Metito! Aren't you even a little curious?"

She didn't have to answer. He saw it in her eyes. She picked up her purse, stopped short of sliding the strap over her arm. "*Any*way . . ."

He tried one more time. He shifted himself as though he were really uncomfortable but bravely trying to hide it from her. He

made his voice just the tiniest bit pinched. "Nora," he said. "It's one night in your life. A few hours! And it's the last reunion!"

"Well, you *know*, Pete, you never wanted me to go before."

"Everything's different now, Nora." He considered getting a little short of breath here, then dismissed it for being too over the top. But he did try another idea, a brilliant one, he thought, that had suddenly come to him. "Ah, never mind," he said. "I'm being a selfish prick again, aren't I? Of course you don't need to go, just to tell me what everybody's up to. I'm sorry for asking. You don't have to put yourself through that."

She stood silent for a moment, thinking, and then, by God, it worked. She said, "Oh, all right, I'll go! Just for tonight's dinner, though, I'm not doing the whole thing. I'll go just to the dinner and that's all; I'm not even going to stay for the dance."

Yes, she will, he thought. Never mind, he still knows her. She'll get to talking, and she'll end up staying, if for no other reason than to talk some more. And all the girls—well, women, now, he supposes—will be asking her if Pete is still so handsome, if he's still so much fun. Which he is.

He mocked grateful surprise. "Aw, honey—*sorry!*—I mean, *Nora*. Thank you. Oh, man, that's so nice of you. Thank you. Fly United, and use my miles for the ticket; I've got more miles than I know what to do with. You know my password. And if you have any problem at all, just put it on my card. There's a flight that leaves in two hours, that's the one I was on, you can make it."

"It's less than a four-hour drive. And I really like to take road trips, as you know. And so does Fred."

Pete's smile froze. "What?"

"I'm going to bring Fred. You registered for two, right?"

"Well . . . Yes, but—"

"I don't want to go alone, Pete. I'm bringing Fred. End of dis-

cussion. I'll call you tomorrow and let you know how everybody was." She kissed his forehead. "I'm sorry. Feel better. I've got to go."

"*Petey?*" Sandy says, and Pete snaps back into the ugly present.

"What."

"I *said*, do you want me to bring you something special for dinner?"

He looks up at her, her big hoop earrings, her drawn-on eyebrows. "Listen, I need you to do something for me."

She blinks once, twice. Then she smiles and moves her face closer to his. "*Sure.* What'll it be, baby?"

He looks around her to be certain there's no one in the hall, and lowers his voice. "Get me my clothes. I'll watch to make sure nobody's coming while you get my things out of the closet and put them in the bathroom. I'll go in there and change while you stand guard, and then we'll make a break for it."

Her eyes widen. "You can't do that!"

"Sssh!" he says, then whispers, "Yes, I can. They're just keeping me for observation. I'm not even wired anymore. I can observe myself."

"If you leave a hospital before you're supposed to, you have to sign something. When Uncle Tony left after his hernia repair, he had to do that. It's an ANA form."

"What's that?"

"It's a form you have to sign if you leave before you're supposed to."

"I *know*, but what does ANA stand for?"

She consults the ceiling. "I think it's . . . *against* something?"

"Oh," he says. "Right. I know. AMA. Against medical advice."

"That's it. That's right. So anyway, you can't go without signing that."

He sits up, swings his legs over the side of the bed. "Watch me."

"Pete, I can't—"

"Just get the clothes and put them in the bathroom," he says. "I'll watch to make sure nobody sees. You can leave after that, leave before me, and nobody will know you did a thing."

"No, but I . . . What I'm trying to tell you is that you don't have any clothes here!"

He sits there. Stares at her. Then he says, "Why not? Where are my clothes? What happened to them?"

"I'm washing them."

"You're *wash*ing them?"

She scratches her arm, and her bangle bracelets jingle. "Well, not this very minute. But I'm going to. I'm going to wash them for you so you can have all clean clothes to come home in."

He looks off to the side, nodding. "All right. All right. Just bring me some other clothes. Pack me a bag with a casual outfit and a nice suit, some pajamas, my toiletries."

"Where are we going?"

"Not we. Me. I've got a business meeting. Very important. How soon can you get the stuff over here?"

"Well, I don't know. I have a therapist's appointment this af-ternoon; I could get them for you after that."

"You have a *therapist's* appointment?"

She shrugs.

"What the hell are you seeing a *therapist* for?" She doesn't have enough of a brain to be picked!

She shakes her finger at him. "Now, see? That's where I draw my boundary line. It's not your business. It's my business. It be-longs to me, and I'm not telling you."

"What are you seeing a therapist for?"

"Self-esteem issues."

He shakes his head. Sighs. "Well, cancel it, and go to the

condo and pack my bag and bring it back here. Don't bring the suitcase in the hospital, just bring my clothes to change into. Please."

"I can't cancel my appointment this late; she'll charge me!"

She'll. Couple of women sitting around man-bashing, one of them getting paid big bucks for it.

"I'll pay for it," he says.

And to his amazement, Sandy says, "No."

"Sandy."

"No! I'm doing this for me and I will pay for it myself. And also you can't bully me. Not anymore."

Fuck! He makes his tone soft, placating, sexy. "Come on, baby."

"I have to go now," she says, and damned if she doesn't leave. *Click, click, click* on her white high heels, right out the door.

Pete looks at his watch. If he leaves right now and gets out to the airport, he can make his flight and be at the reunion ahead of Nora and Fred. He can register himself and Nora and then, so sorry, no room for Fred. Oh, he'll be perfectly cordial to Fred— Have a few drinks on me in the hotel bar, pal; Nora will be back later. He'll tell Nora the doctor sprang him after all, and he decided to surprise her. He looks down at himself. He's wearing surgical scrubs, thanks to the kindness of one of the nurses who went for him big-time. None of those ridiculous tie gowns for a guy like him.

He goes over to the door and peers out into the hallway. No one in sight. In the little metal locker at the side of the room, he finds his trench coat—thank God it had been a cool morning when he went to see Nora. He slips on his socks and loafers, puts on his coat, collects his wallet from the little bedside table. He wonders for one second where his car keys are before he remembers that Pete Jr. has his car.

Again he checks the hall. The elevator is some distance away, but the exit to the stairway is two doors down. He walks rapidly to it and starts down the steps. He forces himself to go slowly, which isn't hard, because he's kind of dizzy.

Credit card, driver's license, he's thinking. Twenty minutes to the airport. Boarding pass at the kiosk in the walkway from the garage to the terminal. He'll buy an outfit to wear on the plane at the pro shop—there's a golf store at the airport. He can get a razor and toothbrush and comb at the hotel.

Right outside the hospital is a line of cabs. *Piece of cake,* he thinks, and climbs in the one in front.

"Airport," he says.

The cab pulls away from the curb and the driver looks at him in the rearview mirror. "Where you off to, Doc?"

The scrubs, Pete supposes. "Going to visit my parents," he says. Then, warming to the situation, he says, "They're having their sixtieth wedding anniversary." That's what he and Nora will have.

"That right?" the cabbie says. "Wow, that's something special. What all you going to do for them?"

"Oh, the works," Pete says, and then, "I gotta tell you, I'm beat. Don't mind me if I keep quiet. I've been up all night—just finished with a major operation."

The driver looks again in the rearview. "Oh yeah? What kind, if you don't mind my asking."

"Brain surgery," Pete says. "Tough case, but the guy's out of the woods now."

"Good for you," the cabbie says. "Okay, you take it easy. Sleep, if you want. I'll wake you up when we're at the airport."

"Yeah, good. Thanks." Pete closes his eyes and feels his pulse racing. *Calm down.* He takes in a deep breath, and imagines Nora in his arms, dancing with him, falling in love with him all

over again in spite of herself. She'd say that very thing: "Oh, Pete, I'm falling in love with you all over again in spite of myself."

And if she does say that, he'll pull her closer. He'll say, "Nora, I'm a changed man."

He'll be so tender to her, all night. So kind. So *listen-y*. And when they go back to the hotel room, he'll make love to her like she's never seen. Like *he's* never seen. At some point, she'll remember Fred, and he'll say, "I'll take care of it, sweetheart." And Nora will say, "Don't be *mean*," and he'll say, "I won't," and he won't be, because he will have won.

The cab has been sitting still for too long. Pete opens his eyes and sees a long line of cars stalled behind what appears to be an accident. He starts to get angry, but then doesn't. Nothing really great has ever come to him without *some* effort. Plus, what if him getting all upset blows a gasket or something? He wishes he'd brought that pamphlet about the heart. He'll look up some stuff on the hotel computer, everything's on the computer now. He closes his eyes, unclenches his fists. By God, relaxes. He *is* a changed man. The cab begins to move again. Pete closes his eyes, but he's never been so wide awake.

ELEVEN

Dorothy Shauman sent four bouquets of flowers to herself at the Westmore Hotel, and now she goes around checking them before she unpacks. You have to watch these people, to be sure they don't send out some second-rate bouquet and think you won't do a thing about it, but Dorothy will, you'd better believe it. But the flower company has done right by her: each bouquet is just fine. They're not big bouquets, but they're pretty, and there are no wilted carnations or yellowing baby's breath or those awful supermarket alstroemeria snuck in there. She doesn't want supermarket flowers, no. As she always explains when she orders flowers, if she wanted supermarket flowers, she'd buy them herself from the supermarket, duh. She doesn't say it that meanly. She makes a little joke of it, and usually the people laugh back. Not the gay men, but gay men never like her. And she doesn't know why because she likes *them*.

The hotel has put all four bouquets on the desk in the corner, and now she happily distributes them: the pink one to the bathroom, the white one to the nightstand, the yellow one she puts on

the little table with the lamp stationed near the door, and the blue one she leaves on the desk. Next, she opens the sheer curtains to see what her view is. Well, it's the parking lot, but never mind. Could be interesting to see who all is coming and going.

She's left word for Judy and Linda, who are sharing a room, to call her when they arrive; until then, she'll unpack and eat her box lunch: tuna sandwich and red grapes and peanut butter cookies. She suspects some of the people will get together to eat their lunch, but she wants to save herself. Besides that, she has a lot to do to get ready. She and her girlfriends have booked themselves a hot stone massage at the hotel spa, and then they're getting their hair done at the adjoining salon. Dorothy has availed herself of the salon's makeup service, too, which provides partial false eyelashes, which Hilly has told her are all the rage. She's a little worried she won't like it and then what? But if that happens, she'll just take it all off and do her makeup herself. Judy and Linda said they would never pay to have makeup put on, but they'd stay with her while she did it. Well, here's what Dorothy knows: if she looks good when she's done, Judy and Linda will fall all over themselves getting it done, too; and then she'll have to wait for them. She's glad she made the appointments for early in the afternoon; she wants no rushing as she prepares to see Pete.

A dark cloud comes onto her psychic horizon: what if Pete's wife is there after all? When Dorothy checked in, she'd quietly asked Pam Pottsman if Pete had arrived yet, and Pam had told her in her nine-billion-decibel voice that, yes, he'd arrived—alone, even though he'd registered for both himself and Nora. "I am going right up to him tonight and asking for a dance," Pam had said. "It's my very last chance, and I'm doing it!" That had made Dorothy kind of mad, and nervous, too. Not because Pam was any kind of competition—please—but because she'd take time away from Dorothy and Pete, and Dorothy had a lot of

work to do in a short amount of time, especially if she went according to plan and ignored Pete at first.

If Nora comes, everything will be harder. That damn Nora, she'd been popular and pretty and smart, all three. And she'd never liked Dorothy, Dorothy knew it, even if Nora never said it. Whenever Dorothy tried to talk to her, Nora just acted tired. Surely Pete wouldn't bring her, he's just not the type, he's never been the type, and even if he does, well, he's *Pete Decker*. He would never turn down a ripe peach. So to speak. Especially at a last high school reunion, where *everything* is almost *required*, isn't it?

She didn't see anyone else when she was registering. It was just Pam Pottsman, with her three chins and badly dyed red (??) hair, acting like she was the queen bee just because she organized this whole thing. Which *was* something, Dorothy supposed. Credit where credit's due. Once everyone's registered, though, Pam will be left in the dust, just like in high school, when she used to organize all the dances and then not be invited to go to any of them. But you couldn't ever discourage that girl! She loved life! She loved everything! And she doesn't seem to have changed one whit, sitting there behind the registration table smiling and laughing and acting like everyone she sees is her long-lost friend.

In a way, Dorothy is glad there weren't a lot of people registering when she arrived. She never looks very good after a plane ride; she needs time to rehydrate and rest after a flight. She did pass Ben Small on her way to the elevator. Ben was in the drama club and everyone thought he'd be a great actor but no; when Dorothy asked him about it, he laughed and told her that what he did was sell products for people who were incontinent. Imagine having to say that over and over again tonight! If Dorothy were Ben, she'd say she was in the medical supply business and let it go at that. Ben always did share too much; he was needy that way. You'd say, "How's it going, Ben?" and he'd *tell* you!

As she was heading down the hall to the elevator, she saw Nance and Buddy Dunsmore—they'd hardly changed at all! Thank God they didn't see her. They were the Cute Couple in high school; everyone liked them. Nance was a cheerleader who wasn't all that pretty, and Buddy was the football player that nobody got all that excited about. They were just *cute,* like Karen and Cubby in the Mouseketeers. And they'd been together forever, since fourth grade, everyone knew. Buddy used to walk Nance slowly to every class, which made him late for his own, but the teachers all tolerated it because they were *Nance and Buddy.*

In the winter of her senior year, Dorothy was at a party and went into the bedroom to get her coat to go home, and there Buddy and Nance were, she resting back on her elbows at the end of the bed, her skirt shoved up and her garters revealed, and he kneeling before her with his face shoved between her thighs. . . . Well, you can just imagine how it felt to walk in on *that.* Dorothy had never seen such a thing; it gave her a sick and vaguely discouraged feeling, like when she saw dogs' red penises sticking out, and she did what she had to: she told the boy hosting the party that there was lewd behavior going on between Buddy Dunsmore and Nancy Greene right in his parents' bedroom. Plus, okay, she told a few other people. She thought it was indecent! She thought people needed to know so that they could leave, too! Word spread quickly and someone must have alerted Nance and Buddy because, very soon afterward, they came out of the bedroom, hastily rearranging their clothes, Nance all shamefaced and crying, as well she should have been, Dorothy had thought. But Buddy was mad. He'd come rushing up toward Dorothy and scared her so that she reached out and slapped him preemptively and also inadvertently scratched him. It was a bad scratch, he bled a lot and later there was a scar on his cheek, and she was horrified at what she'd done. She was sorry, too, that she

hadn't just gotten her coat and said nothing to anyone and quietly gone home. But she remembers thinking, *If your neighbor's
house is on fire, you tell him!* There Nance and Buddy were, de-
filing the party, behaving in what she believed at the time was an
immoral way that, really, affected everyone else who was there.
Everyone was guilty by association! Dorothy had wanted no part
of it, and she'd assumed that, if the others knew, they'd want no
part of it, either. She'd imagined, in fact, that everyone would
leave, talking about how they were so grateful that Dorothy had
walked in on Nance and Buddy, because otherwise there they
would have been with *that* going on not twenty feet away. But afterward, all the kids stayed at the party anyway, and they were
mad at Dorothy, as though she'd been the one behaving in such a
disgusting way. Which of course was true.

If only people were given the opportunity to behave differently at certain times in their lives! That party would be a time
that Dorothy would revisit. Never mind the popular sentiment
you heard every five minutes these days: *Everything that's happened in your life has helped to make you who you* are! No,
Dorothy would like to be back at that party, and she would open
the door to the bedroom, and she would see Nance and Buddy,
and she would quietly close the door. She would wait until they
came out of the bedroom to get her coat, and then she would go
home without having said a word to anyone about what she had
seen. Not because she thought what they did was all right, but
because it was none of her business.

Not long after that party, Nance got pregnant (the night of a
church social, of all things, Dorothy had heard). The whole
school knew about how she had lain in bed crying night after
night when her period didn't come, and how she'd then tried to
solicit advice for how to get rid of it. Lynn Donnelly told her to
take hot, hot baths. Debbie Goodman said to drink vinegar three
times a day. Joyce Ulrich told her to stick a chopstick up there,

and Nance had reportedly started to, but then she got scared and ended up telling Buddy she was going to have the baby. And he'd said, well, they'd just get married, then; and he'd get a job after graduation and take care of her, no problem. He said that, even though he had gotten a football scholarship and was all set to go to college. He just kept on loving her, and he treated her even *better* after he knew she was pregnant, like glass! Nance had come to graduation with that bump showing, wearing her wedding ring with the microscopic chip of a diamond, everybody trying to act like it was okay, but it was not, not in those days.

Buddy got a job bagging groceries at SaveMore and had to wear a white shirt and black pants and a red bow tie and a green apron. He'd always looked so sexy in his letter jacket, moving down the hall with the other jocks and carrying his books at his hip. And then there he was, looking like a little Christmas elf or something. Dorothy saw him in the store a few times before she left for college and she was just mortified on his behalf. He didn't seem much different, though, still the same smiling, affable guy, but, oh how sorry Dorothy felt for him. To be married at eighteen! Surely he felt a terrible shame! And how could a marriage like that ever last? How? And yet there they were, still together and holding hands, for goodness' sake! And they were still very nice-looking people, just the tiniest bit overweight.

Dorothy ran into Karen Erickson when Karen was getting off the elevator, and they chatted for a while. Karen reminded her that they were in chorus together, though Dorothy had no memory of that, not at all. She would look Karen up in the yearbook later; she had brought along the yearbook for just such things. Karen Erickson was Karen Slater now. Her husband was not there, but Karen made sure she let Dorothy know that he was an orthodontist, and Dorothy raised her chin and said *"Oooh!"* appreciatively, even though who the hell cared.

Karen asked if Dorothy had seen anybody else yet, and

Dorothy said she'd talked to Ben Small, and she'd caught a glimpse of Buddy and Nance but hadn't spoken to them. "Oh?" Karen said. "Well, I've kept in touch with Nance. She and Buddy own a few Subway franchises and they have five children, can you imagine? They're a very close and happy family. Two of their children, a daughter and a son, work at NASA. One is an English professor and one is an actor on a soap opera, very successful. And the youngest has just become an executive chef at some fancy hotel in Milwaukee, where they live."

Dorothy said, "Huh," and her spirits sagged a bit. Other people's happiness could do that, put a pin to your balloon, you'd think people could keep good news to themselves instead of acting like those god-awful trumpeting Christmas letters: *Look at US!* But never mind. Buddy and Nance had their happiness; Dorothy was about to enjoy her own. Dorothy said she'd see Karen later, and she got into the elevator and quick punched the button so she wouldn't have to talk to anyone else, she had a lot to do.

In her room, Dorothy opens her suitcase and starts unpacking. When she goes into the bathroom, she catches a glimpse of herself in the mirror and is actually shocked to see herself as a fifty-eight-year-old woman. She'd been thinking of herself as that high school girl in her plaid skirt and kneesocks and circle pin, but no, *here* is who she is. Fifty-eight years old. She really can't believe it. Oh, she believes the changes in herself physically, but inside she still feels like a girl. She does! Aaron Spelling's wife, Candy, feels that way, too; Dorothy heard that, in some interview, she described herself as a child who happens to be sixty-something. Dorothy could probably be friends with Candy Spelling, because she feels exactly the same way. She wonders if they were friends, if Candy would pay for everything all the time—she's so rich!—even though Dorothy *would* offer to pay for herself.

Dorothy leans in closer to the mirror and looks deep into her own eyes. She experiences a sudden descent into what feels like the center of herself. She is aware of a lonely regret: she isn't that high school girl any longer; and she can't do a single thing in her life over again—though she wonders if, given the opportunity, she really *would* do anything over. One is given one's own particular box of tools; one does what one must at various points in one's life. She supposes she might have been a little kinder in high school. She wasn't very kind, then. Though who was, in those days? What adolescent could be described as being *kind*? An aberrant one, that's who. Well. Nothing for it but to make the best of what one has, at the moment. Which is exactly why she's here.

On the shower rod, Dorothy hangs all the clothes that she'll wear tonight and to the breakfast tomorrow: the steam from her bath will make the few wrinkles fall right out. On the counter go all the things for personal hygiene, including the new bottle of Chanel No. 5 she bought that had necessitated her checking her bag. Checking her suitcase had made her very nervous—what if it got lost?—but she had sat by the window and watched as the bags got loaded into the plane, and there was her suitcase on the conveyor belt, the handle tied with a hot pink ribbon you couldn't miss. She leaned back against the seat after that, relieved, and refused the offer of peanut M&M's from her seatmate, even though she was dying for some. There would be time enough for peanut M&M's after the reunion, unless she was still seeing Pete, in which case she would still be dieting, but it would so be worth it. She wonders what Hilly would think of Pete, wonders if her Mom Stock wouldn't go up if her daughter saw her with such a handsome man. It could be their time, Dorothy and Pete's. Reunions are breeding grounds for just that sort of thing. Divorces happen all the time in the wake of reunions. She

wonders if you can get divorced online; it seems to her that you can do everything online, these days. Soon no one will venture out of their house for anything, ever.

The phone rings and Dorothy actually jumps, then laughs at herself. She's so nervous! Or *excited,* or something! It's Linda and Judy calling from their room. They want to know if Dorothy has eaten her box lunch yet, it actually looks pretty good. They suggest coming up to Dorothy's room and they'll all have lunch together. And then she has to come with them to look at the ballroom—it's decorated so cute, in their high school colors, all burgundy and white! There are Kleenex carnations at every table, felt pennants. On the wall there are blowups of photos that had been in the senior yearbook. There's a cheerleader outfit and a football uniform hung up there, too; and there are posters made to look like the ones that used to hang in the halls when people ran for things.

"Never mind all that," Dorothy says. Those damn cheerleaders; would their glory *never* fade? They'd be in a *nursing* home and everyone would still be fawning over them because they were *cheerleaders.* "We're due at the spa in less than half an hour."

"It's right here at the hotel," Linda says. "We'll have plenty of time. Relax!"

But Dorothy says, "We can't be late. Why don't you guys eat and then come and get me and we'll all go over together. I'll see the ballroom tonight. I'd rather see it tonight anyway, it will be more romantic."

Judy says, "It's hardly romantic! There are plastic *horses* on every table, for the Mustangs. And the crepe paper is twisted and hung up all swoopy, you've got to see it."

"We don't have time," Dorothy says. And since she remains the boss of their little group, the women agree, and Dorothy finishes making ready her room. She puts her pajamas in the bureau

drawer, sprays her pillowcases lightly with Chanel, removes the dust from the window ledge. Those maids. All they do is watch soap operas and begrudge you extra bottles of lotion.

When her friends come, Dorothy knows they'll comment on all the flowers in her room, and she isn't sure she should tell them she sent them to herself. Then she decides she will admit to it; she might as well get back into the habit of telling them everything, because if she gets her way, she'll have plenty more to tell them. Not for nothing did she opt out of staying with them, and get a single. It had been fun to think about making out in Pete's car, and they still might, some, but for the grand finale, no. A bed, please, they probably both have joint issues.

She pulls the blackout curtain, then lies on the bed to practice her Kegels. No one can tell when you're doing that, they say you can even do it when you're sitting at your desk, but still. She lies in the exact center of the bed, closes her eyes, and squeezes, releases, squeezes, releases. Dorothy could never do this sitting at her desk. For heaven's sake! It gets you hot! If she gets to be intimate with Pete, she's got to remember not to get on top no matter what. All the loose skin on her face will fall forward like ice cream sliding off a plate. And besides, when she lies flat her belly looks . . . containable.

After a few minutes, Dorothy hears a knock at the door. She gets off the bed and opens the curtains, then opens the door, and there they are, Linda and Judy, squealing *Hi!* and *Oh, my God!* and *Can you believe it?* They are wearing bright orange feather boas, and after they come into Dorothy's room they offer one to her. Which she takes and wraps gaily around her neck, then immediately removes and lays on the table. No boas. Next they'll be suggesting red hats. No.

"Who are all the *flowers* from?" Judy asks, and Dorothy admits that she sent them to herself. Judy and Linda have a good laugh about that, though Dorothy doesn't know why—she

doesn't think it's so astounding that a woman would send flowers to herself, she thinks it shows a kind of spunk.

Linda sits on the edge of the bed and says, "Guess who *we* just saw?"

Dorothy presses her lips together and tries to contain her emotions. "Pete Decker?"

"*Yes!*" Judy and Linda squeal, together. "He was going into his room and no one was with him! He's three doors down from us!"

"Oh, my God," Dorothy says. "Is he still handsome?"

"He is *so* handsome!" Linda says, and she shakes her hands like she just burned them. Linda is still cute, Dorothy realizes, blond, petite, her big blue eyes still huge in her face and no lines around them, thank you Mr. Botox. Judy's not bad-looking, either, tall and slender, with front teeth crossed in an endearing way, brunette hair still long and thick, and those great boobs that are now and always were 100 percent natural. Dorothy hopes her friends have no interest in Pete.

"He was wearing doctor pants," Linda says. "Did he become a doctor?"

"No," Dorothy says. "He's a stockbroker." Facebook.

"Well, he's wearing scrubs."

"It's probably some cool fad or something," Judy says. "He was always starting fads; whatever Pete did, a whole bunch of other guys did."

"I'm going to hit on him," Dorothy says.

Linda rolls her eyes. "We *know.*"

"So don't either of you."

"We're *not,*" Linda says, but Judy says, "I might." When Dorothy's mouth drops, she says, "Just kidding. I do think I might hit on Buddy Dunsmore, though."

"He's still married to Nance, and she's here with him!" Dorothy says, and Judy shrugs and says, "It's a reunion. That's

what these things are *for*. Although I also just saw Lester Hessenpfeffer. And he is *really* hot. But he's, you know, Lester *Hessenpfeffer*. Ew."

They all laugh, and then Dorothy looks at her watch and says it's time to go to the spa. When she walks down the hallway toward the elevator, she feels oddly outside herself. Here it comes, the reunion is here, it's all starting to happen! This is the *before* before the *after*.

When they get off the elevator, they start heading toward the spa. But then Judy suddenly stops in her tracks. "Look!" she says, pointing toward the registration table down the hall.

Dorothy gasps. "Is that . . . ?"

"Oh, my God," Judy says.

"Mary Alice Mayhew," Linda says. "I can't believe it. Why would *she* ever want to come back and see any of *us*?"

They watch as Mary Alice chats with Pam, then fills out two name tags.

"She's bringing someone," Judy says.

"Where is he?" Dorothy asks.

"I'll bet it's not a he. I'll bet she's a lesbian," Linda says. "I'll bet her partner is unloading the car and that they brought sex toys. A feather and a dildo!"

"Stop that!" Dorothy says, and then they start laughing.

"Damn, I wish she hadn't come," Linda says. "I was going to put her name on a tag and pretend to be her!"

Dorothy stops walking. "You still can! In fact, why don't you change tags with her?"

"Nah," Linda says. "She wouldn't do it."

"She might," Judy says. "People change."

"Here's one thing I'd stake my life on," Linda says. "Mary Alice Mayhew has not changed. Not one bit. People like that? They don't change. Even if they change. Put Mary Alice Mayhew

in red stilettos and she's still Mary Alice Mayhew. To us, anyway, because we knew her when."

They reach the door to the spa, a frosted door with elegant silver script on it, and all the women quiet down. They want to get in the mood.

Dorothy opens the door and gestures to her friends to go ahead of her. *"Après vous,"* she says, in an accent she's sure their high school French teacher, Mademoiselle Florin, would have appreciated.

"Hello, ladies," the receptionist says, and Dorothy wants to smack her. *Ladies,* that condescending catchall greeting used for women of a certain age. She wants to say to the receptionist, "You think you'll never get old, but you will." Instead, she joins her friends in a weak chorus of *"Hiiiii."* It is almost like a question, the way they say it. It is almost as though they're asking for permission for something. As they kind of are, Dorothy thinks. Really, they kind of are.

TWELVE

LESTER SITS ON THE SIDE OF HIS HOTEL BED, THINKING, HIS unpacked suitcase beside him. He checks for messages again, even though his cellphone has not rung. No messages. Samson had developed a massive infection after his abdominal surgery; but his wound has been debrided, he's been resutured, he's been given an antibiotic bolus intravenously and now is getting oral doses every four hours. He's staying in the clinic a couple of days for close observation. He should be fine.

Dumb dog. Rolling in fertilizer when his belly had just begun to heal. Lester imagines him in the cage in the back room, his chin on his favorite stuffed animal, his brown eyes shifting left and right, watching what little activity occurs there. He should be fine. Still, Lester calls his clinic, and when Jeanine answers, he says, "I'm coming back."

"*No!*" There are three loud banging sounds and then Jeanine says, "Did you hear that? That was the sound of my head hitting my desk."

"That was not your head."

"It might as well have been."

"Listen, Jeanine. It's not important that I be here. It's important that Samson be monitored very carefully, and I'm—"

"How long have I been working for you?" She sounds angry now; she's speaking in the cool, clipped tone she uses on the phone with her husband when they're fighting.

"I'm not saying a thing against you and your complete and utter competence," Lester says. "It's just that I'll be thinking of him the whole time, anyway, so I might as well—"

"Dr. Hessenpfeffer. Lester. You're *an hour* away!"

"Ninety minutes," Lester says. "Without traffic."

"Samson is just fine. He's afebrile. His heart rate and blood pressure are perfect. His dressing is dry. He's alert. I had to give him a squeaky toy because he's *bored*."

Lester sits still on the bed, stops his knee from bouncing.

"*And:* Miranda said she'd sleep with him tonight."

Well, yes. That's what Lester wants, is for someone to sleep with Samson. But he can't have Miranda in the cage with the dog. Insurance and whatnot. But before he can voice his objections, Jeanine says, "I'll make up a cot for her right outside his cage. And I'll make up one for me, too. We'll *both* be there. He'll be fine. And I promise you, if the least little thing happens— a whimper!—I'll call you right away. You need to learn to take some time for yourself."

"I take time! Every year!"

Jeanine sighs. "You know what I mean. Now, will you promise me that you'll stay there?"

"All right. Fine. I *promise*. But put him on the phone."

"Who, Samson?"

"Right."

"Hold on."

She puts Lester on hold and then he hears her voice sounding a bit far off, saying, "Okay, you're on speakerphone, go ahead."

"Hey, Samson!" Lester says.

"He's wagging his tail and cocking his head," Jeanine says. "Aw."

"You hang in there, buddy, and I'll see you tomorrow."

"Now he's trying to get *up*!" Jeanine says. "Lie down, Samson, Doctor's not here. Lie down, buddy. Good boy! Stay, okay? Stay there. *Good* boy." To Lester, she says, "Don't you say anything else, you're getting him all excited and he needs to keep still. He's all right. I just irrigated his incision and it's clean as can be. You go and enjoy yourself."

Lester stands to look out the window. There's a striking blonde crossing the parking lot, pulling her luggage behind her. Candy Sullivan? He squints to see better. Yes, it's Candy all right. And she's still . . . Candy Sullivan.

"Call me if there's *anything*," he tells Jeanine.

"I will."

"Any other news?"

"Nothing. Routine shots today. Oh, and Pia is pregnant again."

Lester sighs. "They need to spay that dog."

"Duh. But you know, she throws the cutest puppies. I might even take one this time."

"Then you're just encouraging them."

"I know, but remember the last litter? The runt that looked like he came off the set of *The Little Rascals*? I want one like that. I want to name it Spanky."

"Go down to the shelter and you'll find a *bunch* of Spankys." He looks outside to see what door Candy is headed toward. "All right, I'll call you later."

"Dr. Hessenpfeffer?"

"Yes?"

"*I'll* call *you* if I *need* you. If you call me, I'll quit. I swear to God, I will flat-out quit."

"You'll never quit."

"I know, but *don't call me.*"

Candy disappears into the hotel door closest to the registration table. She'll be there in just a few seconds. No one is with her. He grabs his box lunch and heads for the elevator. He'll see if she'd like to have lunch and catch up. He supposes he'll have to tell her who he is. Which is fine.

But by the time he gets to the ground floor and then to the registration table, there is no sign of Candy Sullivan. There's only Pam Pottsman, sitting at the table and looking at her watch, and some other woman sitting on a chair in a conversational grouping of furniture a little ways down the hall. She must be a classmate; she's eating her box lunch.

He approaches Pam and asks quietly, "Did Candy Sullivan register?"

Pam laughs, then bellows, "Good grief! She's *still* the most *popular girl*! Yes, she just went up to her room."

"Did she take her lunch?" Lester asks, then immediately regrets asking.

"No, she said she wasn't hungry. Do you want it?"

Actually, he would like it. He's hungry, and the lunch doesn't appear to be all that big. "Sure," he says. "I'll take it. Thanks."

Pam reaches into a large bag and pulls out a lunch. There is only one more box left in the bag. Almost everyone has come, then. She hands him the box, then points to the woman eating alone. "You remember Mary Alice Mayhew?"

He remembers the *name*. And then, looking over at the woman, well, of course he remembers Mary Alice. One of the uncool nerds, like him. Kids used to be pretty mean to her. He remembers a time a group of jocks made catcalls after her as she walked down the hall. He'd wanted to defend her—what was the *point* in that kind of cruelty?—but hesitated out of fear of being attacked himself. But then he saw that she didn't seem in need of

being defended: she'd held her head high and walked steadily on, seemingly impervious to their taunting. And there that knot of thick-necked boys stood: utterly ignored, suddenly looking sort of foolish.

Mary Alice still has the same hairdo: mid-neck length, but salt and pepper now. It's styled more attractively now, not sort of lumpy like it always used to be. She's gotten to be rather nice looking; she seems to have grown into herself. Her glasses are certainly better. As are his.

He walks over and smiles at her, holds out his hand. "Hey, Mary Alice. I'm Lester Hessenpfeffer. Do you remember me?"

Her mouth is full and she smiles apologetically, holds her index finger up, swallows. Then, "Hi, Lester," she says. "Of course I remember you. The last time I saw you, you were giving the valedictorian speech. *To creating our destinies!*"

Lester nods. "My Sally Field Oscar moment," he says. "Ah well. All I meant to say—"

"Oh, no," Mary Alice says. "I loved what you said. The idea that you could create your destiny, that you weren't imprisoned by some preordained set of circumstances. It was a wonderful speech, Lester."

They regard each other, each of them doing their own *then* and *now,* Lester supposes. Then Mary Alice says, "I see you have your lunch. Want to join me?"

"Well. Lunch*es,*" Lester says.

"If one's good, two is better," Mary Alice says. "And it actually is good."

He sits in the chair next to her and opens one of the little boxes. There on top, a folded paper napkin, red-and-white-checked. "I love these things," he says. Then, looking over at Mary Alice. "Box lunches."

"Me, too," Mary Alice says. "I always think I know who made them."

"A grandmotherly type with a drooping apron top who takes her time folding the napkin?" Lester asks and Mary Alice laughs and says, "Exactly!"

Her laugh is clear and genuine, a nice sound.

"The only thing we're missing is a train ride," she says.

"Okay, let's be on a train. Where are we going?"

Mary Alice tilts her head. "Where are we going. . . . Hmmm. I don't know! Where do you want to go?"

"Along the Mississippi, I should think."

"The West Coast being too obvious?"

"Exactly." Lester bites into his sandwich. One slice of bread is white; one is whole wheat. Something for everyone. And there's a crosshatched peanut butter cookie and fruit. If the sandwich were wrapped in wax paper instead of plastic wrap, his happiness would be complete. He looks over at Mary Alice and smiles. She has the kind of brown eyes that seem lit by little golden lamps. She has dimples at the corners of her mouth, he'd never noticed that.

"Are you here with someone?" he asks.

"Not really. I'll be bringing a friend with me tonight. An older gentleman I work with sometimes. He's taking a nap, and then I'm going to go and pick him up for the dinner and as much of the dance as he can stay awake for."

"He lives here in Clear Springs?"

"Yes. I do, too."

Lester talks around a bite of sandwich. "You stayed, then."

"No, I left. But I came back. I like it here. I like small towns." She points to the corner of her own mouth, and Lester wipes off a crumb of bread from his.

"I'm not far away," Lester says. "I live over in Hopkins. I have a veterinary practice there."

"That figures. You were the one who was so utterly respectful whenever we had to do dissections in science class. Remember

how the other guys would fool around with things, how a couple of them took that fetal pig and switched around all the organs? But it always seemed kind of *sacred* to you."

Lester looks at her. "Yes."

"You were right."

Two people walk up to the table and Lester hears Pam say, "Just in time! I was just going to give up on anyone else coming. Now, who are you guys?"

The man points to himself and says, "I'm just a friend." He puts his arm around the woman. "This is Nora Decker."

"Nora Hagman Decker," Nora says.

Pam squeals and leaps up. "Nora! Oh my God, I can't believe I didn't recognize you!" She shakes her finger at Fred. "It was you who threw me off." She comes around the table and hugs Nora, then tells Fred, "Co-captain of the cheerleading squad, did you know that?"

"I did not know that," Fred says, in a terrible, terrible Johnny Carson imitation, and Nora looks down. "Fred," she says.

"Well, welcome!" Pam says and hands them a box lunch. "Gosh, you just missed Pete."

Nora and Fred exchange glances and Pam frowns. "No?" she says. "Uh-oh."

Lester looks over at Mary Alice, who shrugs.

"*Hmmm,*" Lester says quietly. And then, looking out the window at the beautiful warm day, "You feel like a walk, Mary Alice Mayhew? *Is* it still Mary Alice Mayhew?"

Mary Alice smiles. "It is. And I know a great place to walk, red-winged blackbirds so thick you think you might have to beat them off with a stick. But we'd have to go a ways to get there."

Lester finishes his cookie, stands. "I'm all yours."

Mary Alice's face grows serious. Almost shyly, she says, "I'll have to walk barefoot. These are not good walking shoes."

"Barefoot girl and a box lunch. You can't get much better than that."

Mary Alice smiles. "I'll just have to get back in time to get ready for dinner."

"Me, too," Lester says. Candy Sullivan is *in* the building. Doing what, he wonders. Maybe napping. He thinks of her lying on her side, her yellow hair spread out against the pillow. He thinks of how beautiful women look when they lie like that, and some sleeping thing inside him opens one eye.

THIRTEEN

Candy Sullivan lets Esther out of her little carry-on, and the dog runs excitedly around the room, sniffing deeply at this place and that. Candy and Cooper once watched a documentary on hotel cleanliness—or lack thereof—and Coop said, "You see why I don't like to travel?" But it wasn't true that he didn't like to travel—he relished his getaways with his male friends. It was traveling with her that gave him pause. She had figured that out, finally, and only last year went to Paris alone, which at first scared the hell out of her, but then she actually enjoyed it quite a bit. To linger before a painting in the Musée d'Orsay or over a platter of cheese at an outdoor café, to watch the waters of the Fontaine d'Agam or sit in the stained-glass-colored light of a cathedral, without worrying about someone else's level of tolerance for such things! To take in a sunset while sitting beside the Seine and allow it to be the religious experience that it was, to come to tears over the astonishing beauty in a to-tally uninhibited way! She ate three croissants with raspberry jam for breakfast one day, and had no breakfast at all the next.

She deliberated over a little painting for sale at a gallery on Rue des Beaux-Arts, worrying and worrying about the cost of just under two thousand dollars, but then got it anyway, and after she brought it back to her hotel room and propped it up so that she could see it from the bed, she decided it was worth three times what she'd paid for it. It was of a rolling field of lavender in late afternoon, the sun a deep gold wash, and she wanted to be buried with it, she told Coop on the phone the next day, when she called to check in. That was when the idea of being buried was still an abstraction.

He'd said at that time that he missed her, that he was eager for her to come home, but then when she came home, he didn't seem so glad after all. The first thing he said to her after she cleared customs was, "Christ, what *took* you so long?" When they got home and she showed him the painting, he said, "Huh. *How* much was that?" Later, he just seemed sad—sighing over his dinner, seeming to avoid her by planting himself in front of the television and then his computer, and when finally she called him on it, he said, "Oh, for fuck's sake, here we go again. Don't blame your moodiness on me!"

She considered not responding, but then she said, "I'm only asking you to tell me what's going on. You seem upset. Or sad, or something. If I'm wrong, you can tell me. You don't have to get mad."

"*You're* the one who's *mad*!" he said.

She stared at him, her stomach aching, then said, "And yet you're the one who's yelling."

He shook his head wearily, his eyelids at half-mast. Then he lowered his voice to a chilling level and said, "I'm not *yelling*, Candy." He stood back from her, put his hands on his hips, and shouted at the top of his lungs, "*THIS IS YELLING! See the difference?*"

She walked away, and—how to say it?—feared for her back

as she did so. She walked away and straightened some things in her desk drawer. She sat at the edge of the bed and contemplated her knees. She took a bath. She went to bed.

There is a knock at the door. For one second, she thinks it might be Coop, and she looks around the hotel room with his eyes, thinking about how he'll disapprove of the tacky artwork, the floral bedspread. She straightens her suit jacket and skirt and goes to the peephole to look out. It's someone from the hotel, an awkward-looking young man in a uniform that's way too big for him, and he's holding a massive bouquet of flowers. Candy sighs, presses her forehead against the door, and then opens it. "My goodness!" she says. "Aren't they lovely!"

The man—boy, really—holding the flowers seems barely aware of them. After Candy exclaims over them, he gives them a quick look, then smiles at her. "Yeah, these are for you," he says. "You're Candy Armstrong, right?"

"Right." She takes the flowers from him and breathes in the scent of one of the lilies. "Wait right there," she says, and puts the flowers on the dresser, then goes to her purse for a ten-dollar bill.

"*Thanks!*" he says. "You need anything else? Ice? I could go and get you some ice for your ice bucket."

"No thanks."

"You know how to work everything in the room?"

Probably not. The alarm clocks they put in hotel rooms by-passed her level of competence years ago. The television she never bothers with. But she tells him yes, she's all set. She'll figure out what she needs to know, or she'll get help later. She wants to lie down for a while now, and then she wants to take a walk with Esther. Since the time she was a little girl, sleep and nature have been fail-safe tonics. And besides, the dog will be left in the room tonight, and Candy wants to be sure Esther will be too worn-out to make trouble. This hotel is dog friendly and Candy wants to

do her part to keep it that way. There is a room service menu for dogs: chicken and rice, or beef and gravy, or a hamburger. There are dog cookies in the shape of fire hydrants. You can order a tennis ball or a Kong toy, too. Candy brought Esther's usual kibble, but maybe she'll give her a treat tonight and get her a burger.

Her cellphone rings and she looks to see who's calling. Cooper. She contemplates not answering. But he'll know her plane has arrived, he always tracks her flights, and he'll keep calling until she does answer. She opens the phone and says, "Hi."

"You get there all right?" She can hardly hear him. He must be in the car and using his earpiece. It comes to her that she has no desire to know where he is or what he's doing, but she nonetheless asks, "Where are you?"

"Just running some errands," he says. "Are you okay?"

"I'm fine. The flight was perfect; I actually arrived early. A lot of people are here already. I saw—"

"I mean, 'cause I was thinking, you didn't plan on being there with all this *stuff* going on."

"I'm fine, Coop. I was just going to take a nap."

"Did you get something from me?"

"Oh! Yes! So sorry, of course; I got the most beautiful bouquet of flowers—they just arrived. Thank you."

"Yeah, I told 'em, you know, spare no expense. Should be a pretty over-the-top bouquet."

"It is."

"Like a million different types of flowers."

"Uh-huh, yes."

He waits, and so finally she says, "There are roses and lilies, and gerbera daisies and delphinium—"

"Yeah, blue, did they send blue delphinium? I know you like the blue ones. That's what I told them to send."

She sees herself in the mirror across the room, her shoulders drooping, her mouth thin and drawn. In the hotel with her are

the people she went to high school with, the ones who knew her when. She straightens herself so that she is standing tall, untucks the hair that has fallen down her collar, and tosses her head. "You know what, Coop? I'm so sorry, but I am just beat."

"Well, I was just making sure the *flowers* I sent you had arrived. I wanted to make sure they were what I ordered. I paid enough for them."

"I'll bring them home and you can see them."

"I doubt you can get them through security." There is a kind of petulance in his voice.

"I'll get them through," she says. "The vase is the problem. But I'll wrap them in wet newspaper and plastic; I'll get them home. I'm going to lie down now, Coop. I'm *tired*. I'll call you tomorrow."

"We'll talk later tonight," he says.

She turns off her cellphone and puts it in her purse, takes off her suit and lies on the bed. She realizes she has never turned off her cellphone when she's been away from home. It's not *that* radical—he knows what hotel she's in. He can call the general number and ask to be connected to her room if he really needs her.

She picks up the hotel phone and asks for the front desk. "I wonder if you could hold my calls until further notice," she says, and the man says, "My pleasure, Ms. Armstrong," and as soon as he says it, she feels a thrilling zip of energy that all but eliminates her fatigue.

She lies back down anyway, and pats the space beside her for Esther to come up. But the bed is higher than the one at home, and so Candy has to reach down and help lift the dog. As she does, she notices a swelling on either side of Esther's abdomen and now she feels a deep stab of fear. Esther noses around, snorting and turning in tight circles, and finally lies down. Candy presses lightly on the dog's sides. Yes. A definite swelling, on both

sides. Oh, please. It can't be. She presses harder, and Esther raises her head and licks Candy's hand.

She moves her face close to Esther's, looks into the dog's eyes. "Are you okay?" Esther licks Candy's nose and wags her stumpy tail. Candy pulls the dog closer to her and lies back down. Esther has been eating, drinking, sleeping, peeing, pooping. It's nothing. It can't be anything. It *isn't*.

She thinks she can probably take a good half-hour nap, and then she and Esther will take a walk (she'll watch the dog's gait, any change in her level of endurance) and then she'll get ready for the dinner and dance. She has a new dress for the occasion, one that she rather than Cooper selected.

She regards the mammoth bouquet on the dresser, the small white card stuck in it. She hasn't even bothered to look at the card; that's not right. Maybe, despite everything, he's trying. Maybe he wrote something romantic, some overture meant to try to get them onto a different path. She gets off the bed and goes over to the dresser to pull the card out of the little envelope. "Call when you get this. Coop."

She props the card against the vase, then throws it in the trash. She moves to the window and leans her head against it, considers again the information she was given by her doctor. She will seek a second opinion, even a third. But if she is dying, well, then she's going to live first. On her own terms. On the night-stand is her purse and in it is a chocolate bar and she gets it out. She breaks off a large square and carefully positions it in the exact middle of her tongue. Then she moves herself to the exact middle of the bed to let the candy slowly melt. While it does, she runs her hands over her abdomen, then up across her breasts and down her arms. She touches herself in a way that has nothing to do with eroticism and everything to do with simply acknowledging—thanking!—a body that has been ignored for a very long time, by Cooper and by herself, too. *Don't go,* she thinks.

At three-thirty, the bedside clock alarm goes off. Candy starts awake, then reaches over to shut the thing off. Who would set their alarm for three-thirty in the afternoon? Someone taking a nap, she supposes. Or someone like her, who distrusts the off switch and is wary of an alarm going off at five in the morning and so sets it for three-thirty in the afternoon. It makes Candy smile, thinking of someone else doing that, sitting on the side of the bed and fiddling with the alarm clock, arming themselves against what are supposed to be conveniences. She would like to meet someone like that; they could probably be friends, having lunch and complaining about the demise of hands-on reading and the way you can never get a live person on the line when you're trying to take care of some pressing business matter. On one particularly bad day when Candy had to call about a problem with her refrigerator, she got a recording offering endless choices for things she didn't want; and then she was rerouted to the beginning of the recording when she pressed 0. Same deal when she pressed *. And when she pressed #. Finally, Candy yelled into the phone, "I WANT A *PERSON,* I WANT A *PERSON,* THIS IS SO DE*HUMANIZING,* GIVE ME A *PERSON!*"

Later that afternoon, when she went out to deadhead the flowers in her garden, her neighbor Arthur was in his backyard. He saw her and waved, and Candy waved back. Then he came up to the fence and asked quietly, "Everything all right?" Candy flushed—he must have heard her screaming on the phone—and said brightly, "Yup!" It seems to her now that she might have shared with him her exasperation with recordings on the telephone and he would have understood. It seems like he would have nodded grimly and said, "It gets my goat, too, I'll tell you. The world's going to hell in a handbasket." And then she could have shared with him her idea for being a person whose job is to simply be a real person on the line. Not to do anything; just to be a real live voice, for the *relief* of it all. He would have laughed at

that, Arthur, and his bright blue eyes would have disappeared into his face the way they did when he laughed. Such a nice man, Arthur. A kind man.

Esther is sitting before her, staring expectantly in her pop-eyed way. Candy pets her, and checks to see if the lumps are still there or if they have somehow disappeared. Still there. How has she not noticed this before? She tells the dog, "Okay. I know. I'm going to take you out. Just let me take myself out, first."

She uses the toilet, brushes her teeth, then goes to the window to look outside. Still sunny and warm, it appears, no one wearing a sweater or a jacket. She puts on a pair of white linen pants and a black linen blouse, a gold cuff bracelet, low-heeled sandals. She pushes the room key into her back pocket. Then she snaps Esther's leash on and goes out into the hall.

Standing at the elevator is a man whose face she thinks she recognizes. "Pete?" she says. "Pete Decker?"

"Aw, Jesus, *Candy Sullivan*? The last time I saw you, you were drunk at our graduation party."

She laughs. "Right back at you. How are you?" Oh, it's nice to see him. Pete Decker, all grown up. He looks fine—graying hair, a few wrinkles, a little looseness at the jawline, but he really looks fine.

"I'm great!" he says, and she can see that he is taking in her collateral damage in the same way she just quickly assessed his. He bends down to pat Esther. "How you doing there, Sparky?" He looks up at Candy. "What's his name?"

"Esther. She's a girl."

He laughs. "Great name. Great-looking dog. I like bulldogs, they always put you in a good mood." He leans closer to Candy to say, "*You* look fan*tas*tic!"

"Thanks. You do, too."

The elevator comes, and Pete holds the door for her and Esther, then steps in after them.

"You play golf?" Candy asks, as they lean on opposite walls of the elevator.

Pete looks down at his yellow knit shirt, with its little embroidered golfer teeing off at nipple level. "Well, yeah, I do; but I don't usually wear golf *clothes*. This was just . . . I spilled something on my clothes at the airport, whole cup of Coke, some kid knocked into me, so I had to quick buy a change of clothes. I was wearing jeans and a blue Zegna shirt. You know. These pants don't even fit me." He pulls with some pride at the waistband to show her the pants are too big, and Candy nods. They are also a bit short, she sees.

"I'm going to try to quick buy a suit somewhere," he says.

"Your suit got wet, too?"

He looks confused. "Oh. No! That, I . . . Would you believe it, I forgot to pack it!" He smacks his forehead. "Left it hanging in my closet!"

The elevator doors open, and Pete looks to the right and the left before he exits. "You seen anybody yet?" he asks. "'Sides me, I mean. Course, *I'm* all you *need* to see!"

She smiles. Same old Pete. She tells him, "Just Pam, when I registered." But now she sees a couple standing outside, about fifty feet from the entrance. "Is that anybody?"

Pete squints. "I think that's . . . Oh my God, I *think* that's Lester Hessenpfeffer and Mary Alice Mayhew! Isn't it?"

Candy looks again. "I think you're right!"

"*There's* a match made in heaven!" He shakes his head.

Candy starts to say she always liked them both but felt inhibited in the old days from showing it, and why had they all been like that? But Pete's in a hurry and steps briskly down the hall, and Candy decides the people to talk to are Lester and Mary Alice, not Pete. She suspects if she asked Pete about why they marginalized people in that awful way back then, he'd say, "Well

they were *nerds*." And then he'd look over at them and probably say, "Still are, come on."

But Lester and Mary Alice are engrossed in what appears to be a rather personal conversation, standing there with their heads bent close together, and she decides not to bother them. She'll tell them tonight, one way or another, that she regrets not having gotten to know them better in high school. She'll ask Lester for a dance. If she drinks enough, she may ask Mary Alice for one, too. It comes to her that she'd like to tell her the News, that Mary Alice would be the kind of person you'd want for your friend, if things got bad. Or even if they didn't. How can she feel this way, when she has not exchanged a word with Mary Alice in all these years? She never talked to her much when they were in school together, either. Still, she has this feeling about her.

Candy goes out the far door of the hotel and into the sunshine. She'll walk Esther for as long as there's time. Then she'll come back and get ready.

She takes a few steps, then suddenly stops and says, "*Essie!*" The dog looks up at her. She reaches down to pet her, avoiding touching her abdomen. "Good girl," she says. "You're a *good girl*! You ready?"

A snort.

"You *ready*?"

A few steps backward, and she barks.

"*Okay!*" Candy says. "Me, too. Me, too. Let's go."

FOURTEEN

A FEW MINUTES BEFORE THE DINNER IS SCHEDULED TO
start, Pete Decker gets off the elevator and runs smack
into his wife and that nincompoop, Fred Preston. Fred is wearing
a suit you'd wear to a funeral: something muddy-colored and
plain, with no style at all, and his tie is a nightmare. What is that,
cats on there? Not that Pete should talk. Damn it. He was not able
to find a suit, and so he's stuck wearing these stupid golf clothes.
His shirt is untucked to disguise the fact that the pants are so loose
at the waist. He, Pete Decker, Mr. GQ, looks like hell. That's
right. He looks worse than Fred! But to put a new spin on an old
axiom, even in tacky golf clothes, tomorrow morning he'll still be
Pete Decker and Fred Preston will be the dickwad that he is, no
matter what he wears. Nora has stopped in her tracks to stare at
Pete, and he raises his hand in a little wave. "Hey," he says.

"Pete! What are you doing here? Why aren't you in the hospital?"

He shrugs. "Yeah, funniest thing. Right after you left, the doc
came in and sprang me after all."

God, Nora looks good. She's wearing some blue-green dress with a short skirt that shows off her legs, and her shoulders are bare. She looks beautiful. She has on a necklace he didn't give her and hopes Fred didn't, either; he hopes she bought it for herself. It's blue-green, too, something made of glass or crystal or some such thing, and it has a very classy and contemporary look, like the jewelry Hillary Clinton wore when she was running for president. It's a youthful look. He remembers how Nora used to comment on how swell Her Hillaryness looked every time she spoke on the campaign trail, and he would think, *Yeah, well, maybe you should pay attention to the content and not the costume,* but the truth was that Nora did pay attention; she retained more about what the candidates said than he did. Another thing he'll do when he moves back in is give her the respect she deserves.

Fred reaches out his hand, and Pete reluctantly (though *graciously!*) shakes it. "Nice to see you, Pete," Fred says, and Pete says, "You, too," and aren't they both full of shit.

"Play a few rounds today?" Fred asks, smirking, and Pete looks down at himself and says, "Yeah, the airline lost my bag, what can you do." He feels himself blushing and tightens his buttocks as though that might stop it.

"Well, we'd better get going," Nora says, and there is—is there?—just the softest hint of regret in her eyes. Pete guesses that she wishes she were with him, that she has begun to feel exactly what he wanted her to, on account of all the memories being stirred up. He stares back at her, his high school sweetheart, the girl who wore his letter jacket, his wife, the mother of his children, his *friend,* and he feels two parallel lines in his throat begin to ache.

"Hey, Nora," he says. "Can I just . . . Can I talk to you in private for just a second?"

She hesitates, and Fred takes her arm and says, "We were just going in, Pete."

And God bless Nora, she pulls her arm away and says, "It's okay, Fred. You go ahead, and I'll be right there."

"I really don't know anyone, Nora," Fred says. "This is, after all, *your* high school reunion."

Right, Pete thinks. *Hers and mine. Not yours.* He wonders how Fred got a ticket, anyway. That damn Pam Pottsman. She probably just told him he could come for free, giggling the whole time.

Nora's right eye twitches, which it always does when she's getting annoyed. Not that Fred knows this. Or anything else. She says, "Well, could you just wait for me at the entrance to the ballroom? You might try speaking to someone. They're all friendly people." Her tone softens, then, and she says, "Just give me a second, okay? I'll be right there."

Oh, man, this is suddenly the happiest day of Pete's life. He won't take her from Fred right away. Let them have dinner, then he'll request that the DJ play "The Way You Look Tonight," which was the first song he and Nora screwed to, and then he'll walk right over and ask her to dance. She might get weepy, that would be good. But in any case, they'll dance a little and then he'll say, "Why don't you dump the excess baggage and come upstairs with me?" and maybe she will. He bets she will.

Nora comes over to him and he says softly, "How you doing, babe?"

She crosses her arms and sighs, and he sees that the scenario he just imagined is not going to happen. She's with another man. She's wearing a dress he's never seen before. A new scent.

He blows air out of his cheeks. "Okay, well, I don't have anything, you know, special. I just wanted to say that you look so beautiful. You really do."

"Well . . . Thank you. Thanks, Pete." She starts to walk away.

This can't be it! There's got to be something he can say that

will get to her! He gently takes her arm and says, "Nora? I also wanted—" The cellphone in his pocket vibrates, making a buzzing sound, and he tries to ignore it, but she hears it, too.

"Better get that," she says, and there is something in her tone that makes him think she's pretty sure it's Sandy. He wants so much for her not to think that. He points to the phone and says, "Bet that's one of the kids."

Her eyebrows rise to the *Oh?* position.

He takes the phone out and looks to see who's calling. Damn it, it *is* Sandy. "I'll call them back," he says, but Nora knows. She smiles, turns away, and walks down the hall toward Fred, who's probably going to act like he's saving the damsel in distress. Asshole. He can't even play touch football. He doesn't *like* sports. Or cigars. Or *cars!* He "kiddingly" referred to Pete's Porsche as generic Viagra. And what does Fred drive? A *Nissan Cube,* an absolute joke of a car, and in the driver's seat he has some sort of wooden-beaded *orthopedic* device for his *back.*

Well, Nora is still his wife. They're not divorced yet, she is still his wife. He opens his still-buzzing cellphone and says, "What."

"Okay," Sandy says. "I have to do this while I'm feeling strong enough to do it, so please just listen. Okay. I want to say something. Which is: I don't think we should continue our relationship. It is too damaging to my esteem."

He pulls the phone away from his ear, looks at it, tries to think of what to say, and then just snaps it shut. It buzzes again, and when he answers, Sandy says, "Did you hear me?"

"Sandy," he says.

There is a long silence, and he hears her snuffling. "I'm sorry," she says. "I know this comes as a shock. I'm sorry to hurt you. But I just don't know if we can work this out."

Pete rolls his eyes. "I understand. We're done. Be happy. Goodbye."

"You *always* hide your *true* feelings," she says.

"Not this time," he says. "Take it easy."

He stands in the hall and watches his classmates come out of the elevator and head for the ballroom. He calls out to some of his football buddies, wonders who some of the other people are. There goes Pam Pottsman in her triple-X-size emerald green dress and her hair ratted up real high. She's wearing blue shoes. Women used to get their shoes and purses dyed so everything matched; now they seem to pride themselves on these outrageous color combinations. You have to pay attention to women; they're always shifting things around, always *changing* things. A guy can never trust that the chair that he has positioned perfectly for watching television will be left alone.

Dorothy Shauman gets off the elevator with her two girl-friends who always hung with her like she was the Queen of Sheba and they were her slaves. They're all still okay looking; the brunette, especially, what was her name, Jennifer, he thinks, something *J*. Anyway, he made out with her but good one night at a Homecoming bonfire. And the blonde, Linda, he had a session with her in the bathroom at a party he brought Nora to on their first date. He still feels kind of bad about that. The J woman and Linda say hi, but Dorothy hardly looks at him, what's her problem? He made out with her, too, one time, and it actually wasn't bad, she was most accommodating. Maybe she forgot. It's possible. He doubts it, but it's possible.

He recognizes Ben Small, who gets off the elevator alone, talking on his iPhone. That guy had been a really good actor. *Really* good. Pete watches him walk to see if he turned out queer. Hard to tell; Ben's got an easy, long-legged stride that could go either way. Same with the clothes: elegant, casual, expensive look-ing, but not sissy. He'll buy Ben a drink, see what's up. He might have become some Broadway star, who knows? The last time he saw Ben Small, it was the August before most of them left for col-

lege and Ben was mowing the lawn in front of his little white house. Pete had driven by with a handful of buddies and they'd all called out, "Hey, Small!" and Ben had waved and then stood still, watching them go. Everybody wanted to be in Pete's crowd in those days. Everybody did.

He looks at his watch and starts for the ballroom. Coming around a corner near the opposite end of the hall, Pete sees a woman in a blue dress pushing some old geezer in a wheelchair. The guy's all decked out in a suit Pete wishes he had on, nice blue tie, too. As they get closer, he sees it's Mary Alice Mayhew. God damn. She actually looks kind of nice! She recognizes Pete and smiles, waves. He waves back, then goes over to meet her and what he presumes is her father. He'll ask if he can sit with Mary Alice for dinner. She'll be a safe haven from where he can watch the crowd. Well, not the crowd. Nora. Nora Jane Hagman Decker, born September 9, 1952, at 7:07 A.M. via cesarean section. Favorite color: green. Favorite movie: *All About Eve*. Favorite food: sauces, the woman loves sauces, always asks for extra sauce on the side. It will be good for Pete to sit with Mary Alice Mayhew. If Nora sees him, she'll know he's *behaving* himself.

"Hey, what's up, Mary Alice," he says when he's beside her.

"Hi, Pete." She leans over and gives him a little kiss. She smells good, like just-cut grass. "How are you?"

"I'm fired up!" he says.

Mary Alice puts her hand on her father's shoulder. "This is my friend Einer Olson."

"Nice to meet you," Pete says, and thinks, *Hmm, not her father. Is he her* date?

He always did feel sorry for Mary Alice, but this takes the cake.

"Bet *you* were a senior superlative!" Einer says, looking him up and down. The dude's glasses must be three inches thick.

Pete smiles. "Pardon?"

"Senior superlative! Didn't you people have them? When I was in school, we had senior superlatives. They were the young men and women who truly excelled in one way or another. We had one guy, Cecil McIntyre, oh, that guy could throw a football, I'll tell you! Good friend of mine."

"Yeah, I played football," Pete says.

"No, he's been gone for years now," Einer says.

"No, I said, 'I played football,'" Pete says, loudly.

"That so? What position?"

"Quarterback."

Einer tilts his head back to scrutinize Pete more fully. "Well, the girls always like the quarterbacks, don't they?"

"Yes, sir, they do."

"I was a track man, myself."

"Nothing wrong with that."

"I could *play* football, just wasn't my strong suit."

"Einer, I'm starving," Mary Alice says.

"Move along, then! I'm not the one driving!"

Mary Alice pushes him slowly into the ballroom, and it seems to Pete that she's carefully scanning the crowd.

"Looking for someone?" Pete has to raise his voice to be heard over "Crimson and Clover," which the DJ is playing a little too loudly.

"Oh, no," Mary Alice says.

"She is, too," Einer shouts. "She told me on the way over that she really wants to talk to Bert Small."

"*Ben* Small?" Pete says. And then, pointing, "He's right over there. Let's go and sit with him; there's room at his table."

Now Mary Alice speaks quietly. "That's okay, Pete."

"Aw, come on!" Pete smiles the old killer smile. Let this be his good deed of the night: get Mary Alice Mayhew and Ben Small together. He doesn't remember ever seeing her with anybody in

high school. In fact, now that he thinks of it, he recalls that kids were kind of shitty to Mary Alice. Oh, not Pete—he had bigger fish to fry. He picked on other jocks, especially those from other schools. Put a little spray paint a few places it shouldn't go, that kind of thing.

Pete takes over pushing the wheelchair for Mary Alice, and when they get to Ben's table and ask if they can sit there, he says absolutely, and seems happy. Pete sees in one instant that Ben Small is not gay. Sensitive, maybe, but not gay. He's not sure Mary Alice can see it, though. She's looking in another direction altogether. She's looking two tables over, where Candy Sullivan—Jesus, *gorgeous* in that white dress—is sitting with none other than Lester Hessenpfeffer. Mary Alice is probably worried about Candy moving in on Ben. All the girls used to worry about Candy Sullivan.

The dance floor is empty but for a couple Pete doesn't recognize—a couple of white-haired people dancing to "Proud Mary." The music isn't quite so loud now; Pete thinks maybe the couple asked them to turn it down.

"I had a lot of fun in high school," Einer says, and Pete moves closer to him. He'll make do having conversation with the old man during dinner. It's fine. The guy's kind of funny—interesting, too—and Pete has a clear view of Nora, who is engaged in intense conversation with another woman at their table—Gloria Gelman? Is that ancient-looking woman the formerly sexalicious Gloria Gelman?—while Fred sits there like some kind of stick-in-the-mud. That's because he *is* a stick-in-the-mud, a total loser, a namby-pamby, pissant girlyman, which, if Nora hasn't learned by now, she soon will. All Pete needs to do is take his time and play it cool. And oh, baby, he knows what cool is.

"I was a bit of a ladies' man until I met my wife," Einer says. "She was the editor of the school newspaper. Real bright girl."

"That right?" Pete says.

"Yup. So who do you think signed on to be a reporter?"

"Einer Olson?"

"Bingo," Einer says. And then, "Say, Pete, do you think you could get me a gin martini?"

"Einer," Mary Alice says. "I don't think you can drink with your medication."

Einer leans back in his chair and slaps his hands on his knees. "You're right. And guess who hasn't taken his medication the last couple of days?" He turns back to Pete. "How about it, son?"

"My pleasure," Pete says. And then, to Mary Alice, "What can I get you?"

"Well, a gin martini, I suppose."

"Ben?"

"I'm set," Ben says, and holds up what looks like a glass of Coke, complete with compensatory slice of lemon. He's probably an alkie. A lot of sensitive types end up alkies.

"Be right back," Pete says. He takes a path to the bar that will bring him close enough to see Nora better without her seeing him—she's sitting with her back to him. She's having red wine, and so is Fred. He hates that they're having the same thing. Fred looks over and sees him and his stupid smile disappears and his expression becomes tense and unhappy. *That's right, buddy.* Pete smiles, waves, and steps up to the bar to order the drinks, loosens his shoulders. Yup. He's starting to have a good time now. He looks back over at Fred, who has turned away from him and emphatically put his arm around Nora.

Pete leans against the bar and looks around the room. There's Kim Birch, she was a smart one, went to Wellesley. He sees Hodder Carter, weird name, great wrestler. He'll catch up with him later. He's talking to a woman Pete thinks is Angie McNair, who Hodder had a big crush on, and Angie would never go out with him. She told him if he'd just lose weight, he'd be a lot more pop-

ular and then she would go out with him. Well, who needs to lose weight now? Angie looks like *she's* the wrestler now, heavy-weight division. Look at the neck on that woman!

Some guy Pete doesn't recognize is standing at Candy Sullivan's table, talking to her. Wait. Is that . . . ? It's Buddy Dunsmore! Damn! Poor Buddy, he really got shafted, having to marry Nance. Pete would bet money that they are long divorced by now. So Buddy's going to go after what every guy in school wanted: Miss Candy Sullivan, who looked every day like she walked right out of the pages of a magazine. *Beautiful* girl, and really very nice, too. Buddy never got her—hell, even *Pete* never got her, not even one kiss. She dated very few guys from their school, she mostly dated boys from the private school a couple of towns over, and by senior year was dating college guys exclusively. Nobody from their high school ever nailed her. She moved out East right after high school, she was going to become a nurse. She probably married a surgeon or something.

Candy was one of those happy types, always in a good mood. He'd enjoyed running into her earlier today and talking for the little bit that they did. There was something about Candy now, though. He couldn't put his finger on it, but she had a look in her eyes—or maybe behind her eyes—that reminded him of how his then five-year-old daughter looked one time when he'd yelled at her to put something back and he'd yelled way louder than he meant to. Katie had jumped, and she'd put the thing back very carefully, and then she'd looked over at him and her hands were clasped tightly together and she was smiling but she was scared as hell. Overcome with guilt, he'd held out his arms and said, "Aw, I'm sorry; come here, baby," and she had, but she'd kept that look on her face until he'd held her a long time. Candy had a look like that, only sadder.

The salads are being delivered. Pete pays for the drinks and

starts to carry them carefully back to the table. A hugely over-weight man comes up and punches him lightly in the arm. "Hey, Decker, you asshole!"

"Hey!" Pete says. "How you doing?" The guy's not wearing his name tag. Pain in the ass. Pete's not wearing his name tag, ei-ther, he hates those things, but he doesn't *need* one.

"Remember me?" the guy says.

Pete smiles, says nothing.

"Aw, man, you don't remember me?"

"I'm sorry," Pete says.

"Benny Westman!"

"Oh, sure!" Pete says. *Who the hell is Benny Westman?*

"For fuck's sake, man! I can't believe you didn't recognize me. Although I look a little different now, huh?"

"I guess we all do." *Benny Westman. Benny Westman.* Oh yes, he remembers now. Tight end. Kind of a jerk. Always real mean to his girlfriends, or at least about them—revealed plenty of secrets in the locker room. Stuff a girl for sure wouldn't want known about herself. Stuff the other guys didn't want to hear, al-though of course they never admitted that, they just laughed and shook their heads.

"Few of us lettermen are getting together after dinner in the parking lot for a little recreational toot," Benny says. "Want to join us?"

"Yeah, sure, we'll see." Pete gestures with his chin to his table. "I'd better get back and deliver these drinks." *Lettermen.* He's got to remember to request "The Way You Look Tonight."

Benny looks briefly toward Pete's table, then turns back to him, his eyes wide. "Is that fucking Mary Alice *Mayhew*?"

"It is."

"You're sitting with *that* skank?"

"Yeah, I am. You know what? It's been forty years, Benny. You want to give her a break?"

Benny's face changes. "Oh, Jesus, sorry, man. Are you like . . . *with* her?"

"No, she's just a friend."

"You and Nora are still together, right?"

"She's here," he says, and then, "I'll see you later, Benny."

He returns to the table, passes out the drinks, clinks glasses with everyone. He watches Benny lumber back to his table and put his arm around a washed-out looking blonde. She's wearing a tacky black strapless dress, and she still has her purse hooked over her shoulder, a brown leather purse on which she has put her name tag. It's one designed for the spouses, and it says, "Hi! I'm with _____." He feels sorry for the spouses. Nobody wants the spouses there, unless they went to the same school. In fact, all of a sudden he feels sorry for *everybody*. Here they all are, all these people, all these years later just . . . what? Trying, he guesses. Just trying.

"Mary Alice!" he says.

"Yes!"

"Dibs on the first dance!"

She smiles. "How about the second? Einer beat you to the first."

"Well, the best man won," Pete says, and holds his glass up to toast Einer. Einer holds his own glass up, his hand trembling.

When Nora and Pete were still together, Pete had noticed Nora beginning to pay a lot of attention to old people. She would watch some bent-over octogenarian painstakingly making her way across the street. Or she'd stare at an old lady selecting a little can of beans from the supermarket shelf, or standing in line with a walker waiting for a prescription. "That'll be me in five minutes," Nora would say. And he would laugh. He didn't understand why she said that. Now, suddenly, he does. Einer, the high school star, holding a forbidden drink in his trembling hand.

Someone bumps into the back of Pete's chair, and he feels cold liquid spilling onto his shirt.

"Oh, *sorry!*" a woman says.

"It's okay," Pete tells her, dabbing at the mess with his napkin, and now he's got *orange salad dressing* on the shirt as well. What the hell. Nothing can make it look any worse.

"Are you . . ." The woman smiles. "Oh my God. Pete Decker!"

"Hey, Susie." Susie Sussman. *She* wore her name tag, like a sensible person. She was okay in high school, pep squad, cute little figure; he made it to third base with her, something like that. He knows her underpants were on his car floor, anyway. Hers or her sister Patsy's. They were twins. He got them both, but he never made out with them at the same time, which guys were always daring him to do. Patsy died the day after graduation in a motorcycle accident, Pete found that out at the five-year reunion, where Susie showed up looking like a million bucks. They'd had a nice little boozy kiss in the hall that year, couple of kisses, nothing else since. Susie looks a bit worn at the edges now. Well, she looks like hell, really. A good thirty pounds overweight, big circles under her eyes, one of those awful too-short spiky haircuts that women seem to think make them look younger but only make them look like Marines. He saw her at the last reunion, and she still had something, then. All gone now. Nada. Not that she seems to know it. Once in the Club, always in the Club, he supposes.

"How the hell *are* you, Pete?"

"Good," he says, nodding. "Yup."

"You look great!"

"Thanks. You, too." *What the hell.*

"Save me a slow dance, will you?"

"I will!"

She moves away without having acknowledged one other

person at the table. It was high school behavior she'd reverted to; the people at Pete's table had never made the cut then and apparently don't now, either. Pete feels ashamed, as though it's his fault Susie ignored them. He supposes that, in part, it is. He should have made introductions. Well, add it to the mea culpas. Add it to the long and ever-growing list. He drains his drink, looks over at Nora. It appears she hasn't touched her salad. Too busy talking, laughing. Look what a good time she's having, a Kleenex carnation pinned to her hair. See that? He knew she would enjoy herself like this, he *knows* her. What a smile she still has. He smiles back at her, though clearly she is not smiling at him.

FIFTEEN

"Now, there's someone I can get along with," Einer tells Mary Alice, as he watches Pete wend his way through the crowd toward the bar.

"He *is* a nice guy," Mary Alice says.

"Should have hung around with *him* when you were in high school!"

"Well." She smiles at Einer. "Yes, I suppose so."

Einer's having a great time. She hasn't seen him so enlivened since . . . since she doesn't know when. She herself is not exactly thrilled with the way things are going. She'd hoped—expected, really—that she'd be eating dinner with Lester, but there he is sitting next to none other than Candy Sullivan. Well, that's the end of that. Candy is wearing a simple white dress that sets off . . . everything. She remains a dazzlingly beautiful woman. Her hair is in a loose upsweep, and she wears a large pair of diamond studs that twinkle every time she moves. Her shoulders are bare, her arms, but she has a gossamer wrap draped loosely about them. Mary Alice sighs the tiniest of sighs. She can't justify

getting angry: Candy doesn't know she has feelings for Lester; and what man could resist her? Moreover, Candy Sullivan never did a single nasty thing to her in high school and, on one momentous day, actually chose Mary Alice first to be on her field hockey team in gym class. There was a collective gasp when she did that, and at the time Mary Alice wondered if her being picked first wasn't as bad as being picked last—different stares, different whispers, but stares and whispers all the same.

No, and she doesn't blame Lester, who sits with his chair turned at an angle toward Candy, his legs outstretched, his arms crossed. Mary Alice puts a great deal of stock in body language, and would like to think that Lester's crossed arms indicate a certain unwillingness to let Candy in. But look at his face: open, friendly, and awfully attentive to whatever Candy is saying. At the moment, their conversation is exclusionary; everyone else at the table is talking to each other. Nance and Buddy Dunsmore. Sheila Grommer, class secretary. Linny Waterman, who, as captain of the cheerleading squad, wore a star on the sleeve of her sweater and could do multiple backflips and impossibly high jumps. Marshall Kind, whose father more than once got kicked out of his son's wrestling matches for arguing with the refs. Erik Betterman, a huge, burly guy who was rumored to be a fool over his ancient cat. Mary Alice remembers every single one of them. Still the popular table, except that Lester and Pete Decker ought to change places.

Einer rises a little ways out of his wheelchair to reach for the salt, and Mary Alice watches carefully. She won't help him unless she has to; she appreciates the fact that his own memories have erased many of his years, if only in his mind. After she "dances" with him, she suspects he'll have his choice of partners. The truth is, he looks adorable, his tightly knotted tie and gold cuff links, his stick-out ears and duck-fluff hair. She bets someone will end up in his lap.

Mary Alice sighs and contemplates her hands, clasped together in her lap. She and Lester had had such a lovely time together this afternoon. They had talked easily, their conversation running smooth and lively and seemingly unstoppable. They are aligned politically; they both like pancake breakfasts; he likes Beethoven over Mozart, just as she does. They both like line dancing, though Lester says he's better at watching it than doing it. And when it came to high school memories, well! Didn't they understand each other in that regard! The name-calling, the spitballs, the nasty notes shoved into locker doors, the "accidental" knocking of books from their arms, the churlish comments about them in slam books. Yet both of them had let go of all that, had in fact let go of it long before they graduated. "Did you even *care*?" Lester had asked, and Mary Alice had thought for a while before she'd answered. Finally, she'd nodded and said, "Yes. But I cared about other things more. The world was quite a bit bigger than the halls of Whitley High School."

"It sure was," Lester said.

He had told her about his wife, briefly, mostly by way of explaining why he'd devoted himself more to work than to pursuing a relationship. There'd been one time when they were standing in the middle of the field—which, as promised, had been full of red-winged blackbirds—and Lester's hand had rested on Mary Alice's shoulder when he showed her one of the birds sitting motionless on a wire and looking up at the sky. "It's like he's contemplating the cloud formations," Mary Alice said, and Lester laughed and said, "It's true! I have never seen a bird do that. Have you?" Mary Alice turned toward him and allowed as how she had not. Their faces were very close together then, and the moment was charged not so much with any kind of sexual energy as with *ease*. Lester asked if she'd ever been bird-watching in a more formal way, if she'd ever risen before dawn, slung binoculars around her neck, and headed out to join a group that

moved together like one organism, whispering and pointing and then going out for a breakfast that felt more like lunch. No, she said, she had never done that. And he said, well she really ought to. That moment hung in the air, it felt like an invitation from Lester was forthcoming, inevitable; and then she made a mistake. She looked at her watch, which prompted him to look at his own and say that they'd better get going. *No, that's not what I meant!* she wanted to say. *I was looking because I wanted* more *time!*

But she'd figured she'd have an opportunity to bring up the subject again. He'd said, "See you at dinner?" and the late afternoon had been gilding the side of his face and making the tips of his eyelashes seem to glow; and besides looking handsome, he'd looked kind and capable and rich in the soul, and she'd said yes, she would see him at dinner. Yes, she'd said, and she'd wondered how she would look to him in her new dress.

She went home and got ready in a kind of grounded ecstasy, and applied a little makeup to the best of her ability. And she thought she looked quite nice. She looked in the full-length mirror at her front and back and sides; and she approved of herself in a way that was new to her. She sang "It Had to Be You" under her breath, and laughed at herself for her presumptuousness, then decided she wasn't being presumptuous at all, she was just being hopeful—realistic, even!—and responding to the encouragement she'd been given.

She called Einer before she left home, telling him she was on the way to pick him up, and he could release Rita to leave for her dinner date with the man she'd met in the grocery store. Rita had promised to come back in a couple of hours; she and Mary Alice had incorrectly assumed that Einer wouldn't want to stay for long at the reunion.

When Mary Alice arrived to pick up Einer, he was still in his bathrobe. He told her he was sorry, but he had to use the bathroom before he finished getting dressed. *Finished?* Mary Alice

had thought. *You haven't even started!* But she stood in her heels and perfume, clutching the little evening bag she'd borrowed from her sister, and Einer shuffled to the bathroom at his turtle pace, the newspaper under his arm, and what could she do? The choice was to be furious and unhappy or to make herself useful. She'd put her purse on the nightstand and turned down Einer's bedcovers invitingly and plumped his pillows. She'd gone down to the kitchen to get a glass of water to put on his nightstand. Then she'd sat at the foot of his bed with her back straight, her knees together, breathing in and breathing out and feeling grateful that she never had to give her bowels a second thought. Einer farted explosively several times, and then called out "Sorry!"

"It's all right!" she called back.

"I'm having a little trouble getting going!"

"Take your time," she said.

"What?"

"It's *okay;* take your *time,*" she said, and looked out the window at the darkening sky. She would not give him a suppository. Absolutely not.

As it happened, Einer succeeded on his own ("Now you're talking!" she heard him mutter), and soon he came shuffling out of the bathroom. He dressed slowly and with great deliberation, and then he fussed with the knot in his tie, and then he combed and combed his sparse hair while he squinted into the mirror. Next he deliberated over which cologne to wear, citrus or spice? By then it was all she could do not to drag him out of his room by the scruff of his neck. "Women like citrus," she told him, and he looked at her doubtfully, but then shrugged and put on that scent.

At last, he was ready, and she helped him out and into the car, and they headed for the hotel. And then what? A freight train!

Once Mary Alice walked into the hotel, she calmed down and was most accommodating to Pete Decker, who asked if he might

sit with them. She'd always found him lovely to look at, the photo of him had looked nice on her bedroom wall, but a crush? No. Despite what her sister thought, she had never had a crush on Pete Decker. No reason for him not to sit with them, though. He was still lovely to look at.

Mary Alice had told Einer on the way over that she wanted to talk to Ben Small because she did want to talk to Ben Small, but only because she was curious about whether or not he'd ever become an actor. But now look.

She turns and glances again at Lester, who is still engrossed in conversation with Candy. What are they *talking* about? Each so serious. She doubts he's even noticed that she is here.

Pete comes back to the table and delivers the drinks, and Mary Alice takes such a large first gulp of hers, it gives her the hiccups. She's embarrassed by this, but Ben Small puts his hand on her arm, nicely, and she leans back in her chair and smiles. Then she hiccups again and he laughs and so does she. What can you do? Love the one you're with. The main courses are placed before them by grim-faced waitstaff who are banging the platters down in a way that is not exactly gracious: *Here! Here! Here's your food!* They want to get this dinner over with, it's clear; and so does Mary Alice. Because although she has missed her opportunity to have dinner with Lester, there's still the rest of the night to come; the DJ is already setting up for the dance in the corner of the ballroom. In third grade, Mary Alice once asked the most popular boy in the school to dance. And what do you think he said? *Okay,* that's what he said.

There is the sound of a spoon against a water glass, and the loud chatter in the room gradually quiets. Pam Pottsman is over by the DJ, and she takes his microphone. "May I have your attention?" she says. "Now, I know you just got your dinners, and I want you to go ahead and enjoy them. But I have a surprise. I think most of you know that Walter Vogel has passed on; his

class photo is over on the memorial table, you probably saw it. And gosh, we all remember Walter Vogel, don't we?" She leads the audience in a confused kind of applause.

Mary Alice has not yet looked at the memorial table, and she suspects she is not the only one who is putting off doing so. But she has no memory of Walter Vogel. Not one memory. *Walter Vogel,* she thinks. *Walter Vogel.* And then she remembers: a thin boy in ill-fitting clothes who had seemed pathologically shy— he'd never talk to or even look at anyone. He lived alone with his father; his mother was dead, and there were rumors that his father beat him with a board. He did poorly in school; Mary Alice remembers that he had a driver's license long before the rest of them, because he'd been left back a few times. Unike her or Lester, Walter wasn't picked on. He was simply ignored. Unseen, really.

Pam continues talking exuberantly into the microphone, though it's obvious she's not quite sure what she's doing—or should do. "Right! Okay! So, Walter Vogel, he . . . You know, he was quite the . . . And of course I think he also played on the basketball team! Walter unfortunately died of cancer two years ago, and—" She looks off to the side, where a young man stands in the shadows. "Pardon? . . . Oh, I'm so sorry, it was three years ago, but anyway, the good news is that his son, who was the one who got the invitation to the reunion and then called and told me about his dad's passing, *he* has come here tonight, and he would like to say a few words. It's just a wonderful *surprise* for *all* of us, and, well, here he is, Ron Vogel. Walter's son."

The young man steps into the light, and now Mary Alice remembers his father clearly; his son is his spitting image. Ron is wearing jeans and a plaid shirt, a sweatshirt jacket, heavy work boots. "Okay," he says. "Well, first off I just want to say thank you to everyone for letting me talk to you. Which I did not plan

to do, to be honest. But I remembered you all were going to be here tonight, and I thought . . . Well, I just wanted to come over.

"My dad, he was not an easy guy. I guess that's what you'd say. He was a hard dude to live with, he wasn't so nice to us kids. He was real nice to my mom, he always was, he treated her like she was a princess or something.

"What I really wanted from my dad was a way to know him. I never did *know* him, he wouldn't hardly ever talk to me. Or anybody, for that matter. He never did. But I think you all must have known him. He used to talk about this group of guys he hung around with in high school. Glory days, you know, that is the one thing he would talk about is this group of guys he hung around with in high school. Pete Decker is the guy he talked about most, he just loved Pete Decker. Is Pete Decker here tonight?"

"Over here," Pete says. He's smiling, but his eyebrows are furrowed, and Mary Alice suspects he, too, is trying to remember who Walter Vogel was.

Ron says, "Hey, Pete! Good to meet you, man! Wow. Okay, so . . . I just want to . . . I just want to thank *all* of you, really, for being such an important part of my dad's life. It's good to know he *had* a time when he was . . . you know . . .

"Well, I'll let you get back to your party now, and thank you very much."

"Hold on!" Pete says. He gets up and heads over to where Ron is standing. He puts his arm around the younger man's shoulders and takes the microphone from him. "I did know your dad, we all did, and we all really liked him, too. And I'll tell you, back in those days, one of the things he talked about most was how he couldn't wait to get married and have a kid. We got a six-pack one night, and we went down by the river, did he ever tell you about that night?"

Ron shakes his head no.

"Well, *I'll* tell you about it. So . . . we got a six-pack, your dad talked some guy going into the liquor store into buying us a six-pack. I was too chicken to do it, so your dad did it. We drove over to the river and drank it, and your dad opened up about what he hoped would happen in his life. And you know, he didn't say one word about jobs or money or status or any of that stuff. What he really wanted was a son. He said he wanted to make sure his son got taught the things he'd never been given the opportunity to learn. He said he could hardly wait to see his boy grow up in front of him, his own son would be . . . would be just the best thing that ever happened to him. He could not wait for you to arrive. And I was . . . you know, I was still young and a little wild, and the last thing on my mind was marriage and family. But when I heard him talk about it that way, even I wanted it."

A few people laugh, and Pete holds up his hand. "No, really. The way he described it made me want it, too. So your dad knew exactly what he *wanted* to do. He had big plans. But as I'm sure you know, Ron, sometimes things in real life don't work out the way they do in our imaginations. And men aren't always so good at showing emotion, at showing appreciation for the things that mean the most to them. We *feel* those things, but we don't show them. Although I think your generation is a lot better at that. I guess our generation was told that real men don't do this and real men don't do that, but your generation, you know better. And that's good. It's important to tell the people closest to you how much you care, and not to take them for granted. Because otherwise you might lose them."

Mary Alice steals a look over at Nora, who is staring into her lap.

Pete takes his arm from around the younger man's shoulders and faces him. "I guess there's a lot we don't do in our lives, no

matter who we are. I guess there's a lot of important things we mess up. But I want you to know that, even if your dad didn't share much of himself with you, he *wanted* to. I hope that counts for something. And I want to tell you, too, that I was proud to call Walter my friend." Pete offers his hand to the young man, who shakes it, and everyone applauds. Then he starts back to the table, refusing to meet anyone's eyes. Ron calls out a final "Thank you!" and leaves the room.

Immediately afterward, Mary Alice hears the questions start: "*Who* was he?" "*Our* class?" She hears someone else say, "Not on the basketball team. He wasn't on any team." And she hears, "Pete Decker and *Walter Vogel*? No way."

When Pete sits back down, Mary Alice puts her hand over his, and when he looks up, she nods.

By the time they are through with the entrees, both Einer and Pete have finished their second martinis, and Einer is slumped decidedly to the left, though he keeps telling Mary Alice that it's only because he's trying to hear Pete better. Mary Alice has mostly talked to Ben Small, who *did* try to be an actor in New York, but mostly ended up working as a waiter in a deli that got shut down for having rats in the kitchen, and that was the final straw: Ben left behind the city and his dreams of becoming an actor. She's enjoying talking to Ben, but she's having trouble hearing him, because the music is so loud. And then there's the exuberance displayed by Einer talking to Pete. Once she heard Einer say, "Right back *at* it!" and now he lifts himself partway out of his chair to yell, "Well, son, that's exactly what I'm saying! You decide what's worth fighting for, and what isn't! That's the critical decision you got to make! And once you make it, why, then you stand up and be a man!"

"Einer," Mary Alice says.

"*What?*"

Pete looks over at his wife, then at Mary Alice. "You know what? He's right." He says loudly to Einer, "You are absolutely right!" and begins to pound his fist lightly against his thigh.

"Tell you what, I'll help you," Einer says. "All right? I will help you. I'll be right by your side! I'll be the commander and you be the infantry, by God!"

"Einer?" Mary Alice says.

He turns to her, his face flushed. "Look here, Mary Alice. Have you heard this man's story? Do you have any idea what he's going through?"

"Are you *okay*?"

He stares at Mary Alice, and then leans back in his chair. "I have never been finer. I've got a mission. I and my friend Pete. Which we are going to run right after I have one more martini."

Mary Alice puts her hand on Einer's arm and leans in close to him. "Einer, please don't. You've had too much already. I know you're having fun, but I'm afraid of what might happen if you drink another martini. Please don't do that. I feel responsible for you."

"You're not responsible for me! Rita's responsible for me! That's why I pay her, is to be responsible for me!"

"Rita is out on a date tonight! I'm responsible for you until she comes home! And I don't know when that's going to be! She still hasn't called!"

Einer squints at her, and she knows he's thinking about whether or not to fight her on this one. But finally he says, "Oh, all right. All right! Let me get back to my friend now, you don't have to babysit me. I'm through drinking, all right?"

"I'm not!" Pete says. "I'm going for a refill. Mary Alice?"

"I'm fine, thank you."

"Ben?"

"Just another Coke, thanks."

Mary Alice leans back in her chair to let the server remove

her dinner plate. "Still working on this?" he'd asked, and Mary Alice had, as usual, despaired of hearing that particular turn of phrase. Whatever happened to "Still enjoying this?" or "Have you finished?" or "May I remove this?" "Still working on this" always reminds her of pigs at a trough. Oh, but why fuss about such things? She supposes she's getting old and cranky.

She watches Pete as he talks to this person and that on the way to the bar. He glad-hands all the men, charms all the women. The man holds his liquor well, she has to give him that. Except for an overemphasis on certain words, he seems fine. He just showed everyone at their table photos of his children, of his wife and himself. Mary Alice, aware now of what's going on, feels bad for Pete. It can't be easy, sitting there in tacky golf clothes, across the room from a man who is dressed in a well-made suit and overtly courting your wife. She has switched from sneaking looks at Lester and Candy to sneaking looks at this Fred person. He has kept his arm around Nora the whole night, except when he cut his meat. And now she sees Pete go over to the table and say something to Fred and Nora. Whatever he said makes Nora look down and Fred leap up. Nora grabs Fred's arm, and Fred flings her hand off angrily, then steps closer to Pete and punches him in the face. Someone screams and the room goes deathly quiet.

Pete carefully puts the drinks he's still holding down on the table. Before he can straighten up, Fred has punched him again, hard enough that Pete actually falls onto the floor. "Stop it!" Nora yells, she and several others, and now people are all standing, trying to see what's happening. And then Einer takes off in his wheelchair.

"Einer!" Mary Alice calls after him. "Come back here!"

It's useless; the man is hell-bent on rushing to the aid of his new friend. Mary Alice looks around for Lester. He's not a doctor, but he's a vet; if something happens, he'll be better than nothing. But Lester is not at his table any longer, nor is Candy

Sullivan. Mary Alice doesn't see either of them anywhere. *When did they leave?*

She looks back at Einer and sees him trying to stand, then giving up and instead trying to kick Fred. And then he suddenly slides out of his wheelchair.

Mary Alice tries to push her way over to him. "Hey! Hey!" the DJ says. "Let's everybody calm down, now. Just calm down."

People start talking; it gets louder and louder. Someone says, "What's going *on?*" and someone else yells, "Is there a doctor in the house?"

"I'm perfectly all right!" she hears Einer say, and then she finally reaches him. He's resting on his elbows, his hair sticking straight up, and Pete is lying flat beside him. And then Pete slowly gets up and wipes the blood from his upper lip. He bends down to lift Einer back into his chair, and then wheels him toward their table, saying, "It's okay, everybody, it's all over. No problem. No problem."

But when they get back to the table, Mary Alice sees that Einer is not all right. He's pale, and she sees him putting his finger to his wrist, checking his pulse. She grabs her purse. "I'm taking Einer to the hospital," she says, and Pete says, "I'm coming," and Einer says, "I'm not going anywhere until this thing gets settled! Now, let's re-strategize!"

Mary Alice leans into his face and says, "Einer? We're going to the hospital," and he says, "Fine. Suit yourself," and gingerly touches his cheek, where a bruise is already beginning to form.

In the parking lot, Pete says, "I'm awfully sorry, Mary Alice," and she shrugs. Then—who can account for why?—she starts laughing. And then Einer does. And then Pete does. "Well, that was a good time," Einer says.

They drive the short distance to the hospital, and the ER is empty, so Einer is brought into the examining room right away.

Pete and Mary Alice sit quietly in the waiting room. Mary Alice points to a new stain on Pete's shirt and says, "Is that blood?"

Pete puts his hand to his nose and then looks at his shirt. "Guess so."

"I'll bet Einer would lend you a shirt."

"I don't think it would fit," Pete says. And then, looking down at his chest again, he says, "Ah, what the hell. Badge of honor."

They sit quietly for another minute or two, and then Pete says, "Damn. We missed dessert."

Mary Alice smiles. "I know."

"It was red velvet cake with cream cheese icing, too."

"Yes."

Pete crosses his arms and bounces his knee, looks around the waiting room. Scratches the side of his neck. Then, his face brightening, he asks, "Would you like a candy bar? There's a vending machine down the hall. I saw it when we came in."

Mary Alice smiles. "Why, yes, I would. I would like a Snickers with almonds. Or if they don't have that, Oreos. Or if they don't have that, Skittles. And also I would like you to help me get Einer home."

"Done," Pete says, and heads off for the vending machine, and Mary Alice picks up *Vogue* magazine, which she has never in her life looked at. Never. But it's *good*, quite interesting, not the superficial waste of paper she always thought it was.

In a few minutes, here comes Pete back into the waiting room. He hands her a Snickers. Then Oreos. Then Skittles.

SIXTEEN

"BUT CAN YOU BELIEVE IT?" DOROTHY SAYS. "CAN YOU BElieve how he just made up that story about drinking beer with Walter? Who would ever think that in addition to everything else Pete Decker would turn out to be such a *mensch*! I wanted so much to tell him how wonderful it was, what he did. And now he's gone! Everyone's leaving, and I won't have had a chance to say one word to him!"

"Everyone is not leaving," Linda says. "And I'm sure Pete will be back. Why don't you just *relax*."

Well. Easy for Linda to say. She's on her fourth drink. Judy has had more than that. Dorothy has not had one bit of alcohol because she has to pay attention to what she's doing. If Pete does come back, he's likely to be upset. She'll need to have her wits about her. Oh, the nerve of that old man showing up and wrecking everything! Why in the world would Mary Alice Mayhew bring an *old man* to the reunion? Aren't they all old enough? Do they really need to be reminded of the wizened old creatures

they'll become in fewer years than any of them wants to admit? An old man in a wheelchair, no less! Say, that's a sexy thing to see! That'll put you in a great mood! Maybe they should have decorated with anti-embolism stockings, with colostomy bags!

She checks the entrance and then looks around the room yet again, to see if Pete and stupid Mary Alice have slipped back in without her noticing them. No. Well, the DJ is supposed to play for another hour. She supposes there is still time.

If Pete does come back tonight, Dorothy hopes Nora will be gone. Her date keeps yawning (without covering his mouth), and Nora has stopped chatting with everyone and is just sitting at the table stirring her drink with a swizzle stick, staring down into it as though it's a crystal ball. Dorothy wishes it were a crystal ball, and Nora would be seeing some gypsy wearing big hoop earrings and saying, *You will soon be leaving the room.* Dorothy needs time to get Pete to focus only on her; she doesn't need his eyeballs shifting around all over the place, trying to keep track of what Nora is doing. Can't he see that they're over? Dorothy can see it! Everyone can! Where is his pride? Spend a little time with Dorothy and he'll get his pride back, no problem!

Candy Sullivan has disappeared. And with Lester Hessenpfeffer! "Who'd a thunk it?" Judy said, when Dorothy remarked on their absence.

"Well, he is good-looking," Linda said. "And he's a vet. He probably makes a pile of dough."

Judy's nose wrinkled. "I know, but he's still . . ."

Linda shrugged and looked back toward where Candy and Lester had been sitting. "I don't know," she said, kind of sadly. And then, "I'm going to fix my face. You guys want to come?"

Judy did, but Dorothy stayed put, even though she could have used a little pee. It was important not to miss Pete if he came back. She needed to be the first one up to him so he wouldn't en-

counter any *other* distractions. She hoped the old man got admitted to the hospital and Mary Alice went home. Though even if she came back, she'd be no problem.

Dorothy had done a beautiful job of ignoring Pete when she first saw him, but he saw her, all right. *Saw* her. He couldn't help but see how nice she looked. No one could help but see that. Oh, that makeup person should win an Academy Award. At first, she was being all listless and kind of snotty, but then Dorothy confided in her about how this was her night to try to recapture an old flame, and boom! the girl went into high gear. She was a very young blond woman with three-inch-long black roots, wearing no makeup at all, which certainly gave Dorothy pause, you can just imagine. But it turned out she knew her stuff. Boy, did she. And she made Dorothy look like a million bucks, both Judy and Linda agreed.

"You look twenty years younger!" Judy had said, which was not true, of course. Maybe five years younger, though, especially if she remembered to keep her head held high.

And then hadn't Judy and Linda done just what she'd thought they'd do, and gotten made up themselves. But they hadn't looked as good as Dorothy. The makeup girl had to rush because she had other appointments coming: there was a formal that night at their old high school. Oh, the poignancy! Dorothy had wanted to take those young girls aside and give them a little talking-to. "Girls, don't do what I did. Listen to me. I was you once, going to dances at this very same school, full of hope and happiness, and then my life went straight to hell. Just watch out, girls. Just be careful. *Think* about things before you do them, will you promise me that?" She'd seen it just like in a movie, the girls all quiet and dewy-eyed, staring up at her, so grateful to her for taking the time. Though that probably wouldn't have happened. Probably what would have happened if they'd listened to her at all was that they'd have told her to fuck herself. Or sat there text-

ing each other the whole time she was talking, saying things like *Gag me w spn. Cn u belv ths fat cow?*

But anyway, because of those bratty girls, Judy and Linda hadn't gotten the full treatment, which included partial false lashes, and that was a pity, because what a difference *they* made. When Dorothy had gone up to her room to get ready, she'd hardly taken her eyes off herself, and she wasn't being vain, no she wasn't, she was just admiring craftsmanship, or art, or something. She'd decided not to wash the makeup off that night; she wanted to have the same face at the breakfast. She'd asked the makeup girl if there was something like hair spray for the face and the girl had said, "Oh, don't worry, unless you use a ton of cold cream, this stuff isn't going anywhere. It could even last a couple of days. I mean, don't *rub* it real hard or anything." Then Dorothy had gotten a little nervous, thinking of Pete and how he might inadvertently do that, he might even give her whisker burn. But he'd seemed clean-shaven, and anyway, he wouldn't be spending that much time on her face, Dorothy isn't that crazy about kissing, if the truth be told. She's never admitted it to anyone, but she could do without it. All that parrying and thrusting and saliva. Just get to it, is Dorothy's policy. She likes her nipples to be kissed first, that's what she likes, she'll show him. And then a straight shot to the nether regions. And she'll give *back,* of course. You don't get to be this old and not know a thing or two about a thing or two. As far as she's concerned, they can skip the old in-and-out. She never did care for that so much, either, and besides, now it kind of hurts. From what she can recall. If her *long-term memory* serves her well.

The DJ puts on Wilson Pickett's "In the Midnight Hour," and Dorothy's hips start undulating in her chair in spite of herself, moving back and forth in the time-honored rhythm. Oh, was she a sexy young thing the last time she danced to that! She feels a tapping on her shoulder and turns to sees Ben Small.

"Dorothy Shauman," he says.

"Ben Small." She smiles in what she hopes won't appear to be an artificial way, even though it is.

"May I have this dance?"

She starts to refuse, but what the heck. Ben wasn't so bad. She'll dance a bit, and still be able to watch for the whole reason she even came to this reunion.

She and Ben walk out to the dance floor and when Wilson sings, "and do *allll the things I told you,*" she and Ben sing along. He's not so bad. You'd never know he'd had such acne. He asks her something, and she stops dancing and steps up closer so she can hear him. She thinks he's asked her if she's married, and she looks at him more carefully. She decides she'll go out to dinner or a show with him, if he lives anywhere nearby. No sex, no. Not interested.

But what he asks is if Judy is married.

"Why don't you ask her yourself, if you're so interested?" Dorothy says, and walks off the dance floor.

She gets her purse and goes out into the hallway, blinking back tears. She stands there for a minute, trying to calm down, and then calls her daughter. "Nothing is working out!" she tells Hilly. "Pete isn't even here and no one is interested in me at all!"

"Oh, come on, Ma," her daughter says.

"No, it's terrible, Hilly! I shouldn't have come. This was such a waste of time and money!"

"Have you had a drink?" Hilly asks, and Dorothy says, "No! I have to stay sober!"

"Why?"

Dorothy stares out the large plate-glass window of the hotel into the darkness. "I don't know."

"I think you're just nervous," Hilly says. "Just get a drink and sit down and relax. You don't have to control everything, you know. You can't, anyway! Just sit down and have a drink and see

what happens. And try to *enjoy* what happens, even if it's not exactly what you planned. If you would just stop trying to *control* everything, I think you would find that your life is much easier."

"I guess."

"It's true, Ma. I had to learn that myself. You know what I did the other day? I told Mark he could pick out the cake totally without me. 'Surprise me,' I told him. And I was a nervous wreck because the cake is such a symbol, you know. Such a centerpiece! But he picked out the loveliest cake I ever saw. It's very simple and understated, botanic-inspired accents in the frosting, and groups of nasturtiums here and there. And you know what flavor it is? Orange! I would never have picked that, but I tasted it, and it's the most delicate, delicious thing! Now I'm thinking about letting him pick the bridesmaids' gifts. You see? Sometimes you just have to step back and get out of your own way, and things start coming to you."

"*Orange* cake?" Dorothy says.

"It's delicious," Hilly says. "And Ma? See? My cake is *not your decision*. Your job will be to eat it and enjoy it. Or not."

"Okay," Dorothy says.

"I'm just trying to help you."

"You did help, Hilly. Thank you. I'll call you tomorrow."

Dorothy snaps her phone shut and heads back to the ballroom. She walks quickly over to the bar. Hilly is right. Enough is enough. What if Pete doesn't come until the breakfast tomorrow? She tells the bartender she wants vodka, straight up and *cold*. When he hands her the glass and tells her that will be seven dollars, her perfectly colored and arched eyebrows go up.

"*Seven dollars?*"

"Yes, ma'am."

She holds up the glass to eye level. "Tell you what," she says. "You put some vodka in this glass, and I might *give* you seven dollars."

He hesitates, then adds a tiny bit more vodka to the glass. And she gives him seven dollars exactly. Some people tip no matter what. Not Dorothy. She tips according to how well she was *served*. Which is what tips are *for*. Which everyone seems to *forget*.

Back at her table, she takes out the mirror from her purse and inspects her face to see if tearing up smeared her eye makeup. No, thank God. She sees Linda on the other side of the room, blabbing away, apparently having a bang-up time. She crosses her legs, swings the top one in time to the music, drinks her vodka. She forces herself to keep a little smile on her face though she does not feel like smiling. She watches Ben Small and Judy dancing. For an artsy-fartsy type he certainly has no sense of style on the dance floor. Judy throws back her head and laughs, and Dorothy throws back her drink and then, teeth clenched, goes up to the bar for another.

After Dorothy sits back down at her table, Wendy Striker comes over and sits heavily beside her. "Remember me?" she says breathlessly, leaning in way too close to Dorothy. The woman is bombed out of her mind. Dorothy leans back a bit and offers a tight smile.

"*Do* you remember me?" Wendy asks.

"Well, of course I do," Dorothy says. "Wendy Striker. We were in Future Homemakers of America together. You and I teamed up for beef Stroganoff." Dorothy remembers that because Wendy had been such a slob. She'd gotten sour cream all over both of them and Dorothy's mom had gotten mad because she'd had to take Dorothy's skirt to the dry cleaner's.

"And *chorus*," Wendy says.

"And chorus, yes," Dorothy says, though she does not remember this.

"When you signed my yearbook, alls you wrote was 'Good luck to a nice kid.' I really wanted you to say more. Like, at *least,*

'Thanks for covering for me on our class trip.' I covered for you that time we went to Washington, D.C., and you snuck out with Pete Decker, remember? You could have said something about that."

"Sorry," Dorothy says. "I must have been in a hurry."

"Isz okay. I forgive you." Wendy thrusts her chest dramatically forward and then back, a kind of stretch, Dorothy supposes. A vulgar one. "Are you having a good time?" Wendy asks.

Dorothy shrugs.

Wendy peers into her face. "Is that . . . Are you wearing *false eyelashes*?"

Dorothy moves her chair back. *"No."*

"You are, too."

"So what?"

"So nothing. Jeez. Just asking. Don't have a cow." She laughs at herself, laughs and laughs, then abruptly stops. "So listen. *Are you having a good time? Is it what you expected?* This is your first reunion, right?" She gently burps. "Ecshuze me."

"Who told you it was my first one?"

"I *know*, because I've been to them *all*. But also Pam Pottsman. She told me. She tells everybody evvvvverything. What a fucking blabbermouth. But *is* it what you expected?"

"Not yet."

"Whattdya mean?" Wendy leans closer, savagely hikes up a bra strap. "What'd you think would happen? Huh? Did you think something would happen? Because oh. *Oh! I* did. That's what I thought, is that something would *finally* happen because this is the *last* one. Oh, my God, we're almost *dead*, all of us!" She sniffs, looks wistfully around the room, and some sort of whimpering sound escapes her. "Oh, we all got so old, we all look like *old* people." She turns back to Dorothy. "But *anyway*. I was getting ready in my room tonight? And I was just so *happy* thinking of all the things that could *happen* and you know what?

You know *what*? Not one damn thing has happened! I'm divorced," she adds, seemingly apropos of nothing.

"Hmm," Dorothy says. Where the hell are Judy and Linda?

"I'm divorced, so, I mean, anything *could* happen." She throws her arms up in the air. "I'm a free woman. YOO-HOO, BOYS! OVER HERE! I AM FREE!"

"I have to go," Dorothy says.

"Wait, wait, wait a minute," Wendy says, grabbing her arm. "I want to ask you something. Okay? I just really want to ask you something."

Dorothy raises an eyebrow.

Nothing.

"What did you want to ask me?"

Wendy lists to the left. "Huh?"

"I have to go," Dorothy says, and walks quickly away from the table.

"*Waaaaiiit!*" Wendy cries.

Dorothy keeps walking.

"*Doooorothy! Waaaaait!*"

Dorothy turns around and starts back to the table. *Hush!* she'll tell her. *Get hold of yourself, why don't you!* But then she sees that Wendy has found Dorothy's unfinished drink, and her attention is now taken up with something else. Look at her. Barefoot, her legs spread widely apart. Oh, it's awful the way some people behave!

She wanders over to the table where Nance and Buddy Dunsmore are sitting and plops herself down. "Hi," she says, miserably.

Buddy takes a quick look at her name tag and says, "Dorothy Shauman. Well. Hello."

Nance says nothing. She just holds her mouth in that well-well-well way. *Well, well, well; look what the cat dragged in.*

Dorothy regards the two of them. Nance and Buddy. Still going strong, she guesses.

"So how are you guys?" she says.

"We're just *fine*," Nance says. "Surprised?"

"Nance," Buddy says.

Nance turns to her husband. "What? Don't you remember what she did?"

Buddy smiles at Dorothy, then tells his wife, "It was a long time ago, hon."

Nance scratches at the top of her arm, says nothing.

Dorothy sighs. "Okay, you know what? I'm sorry. I am! Here it is, a formal apology: I'm *sorry. Really.* And I'll bet it has bothered me all these years a lot more than it has bothered you. Look at you! You're still together and you're happy!" She looks back and forth at their faces. "Aren't you?"

Buddy shrugs. "Yup."

"And your family is just perfect."

"We're not *perfect*," Nance says. She practically spits it out.

"Well, close enough," Dorothy says. "I heard about you guys. Pam Pottsman told me."

"Well. Pam *Pottsman*," Nance says, and now her voice seems to have softened a bit. Then she says, "Did you know Pam hit on the DJ?"

Dorothy turns around to see if she missed something attractive about the DJ. Absolutely not. He's a short little guy, exceedingly thin, with a beard he should never have tried to grow. It looks like a beard that some kid tried to color on his face with a crayon.

"She's three times his size!" Dorothy says.

Nance laughs. "I know. But I heard they're getting together after the dance is over. I'll bet they *hook up*."

"*What?*" Dorothy says.

"Some guys like large women," Buddy says. "For some guys, that's their thing."

"Well, good for them," Dorothy says bitterly. She stares into her lap.

"Dorothy?" Nance says. "How come you did that thing?"

"Aw, come on, Nance," Buddy says.

"No!" she says. "I want to know."

"Well, then I'm getting out of here for a while," Buddy says. "I'm going out to the parking lot and talk to the boys." When Nance starts to say something, he says, "What did I tell you? Don't worry, I won't. I told you I won't and I won't."

Dorothy watches him walk away. Then she asks Nance, "What won't he do?"

"Drugs," Nance says. "They're doing drugs out in the parking lot. The Lettermen's Club."

Dorothy's hand flies to her chest. The idea of doing drugs appalls her, but the thought of all the lettermen together, that kind of attracts her. Maybe she could go out there on some pretext or another. Just to see if anyone's there she might have forgotten about, now that that damn Pete still hasn't come back. She should have had a second choice in mind all along.

"What kind of drugs?" she asks.

Nance shrugs. "Pot for sure. Probably cocaine, too."

"Oh, my God," Dorothy says.

"Hey, Dorothy?" Nance says. "Can I give you some advice? *Don't tell.*"

Dorothy looks at her. "I *know.*"

"But why *did* you tell on us?" Nance asks.

"I thought it was wrong," Dorothy says. "I thought it was immoral. I guess I was kind of scared by it. I thought the others should know, in case they wanted to leave."

"Uh-huh. Know what I think?"

Dorothy sighs. "What?"

"I think you were jealous of us."

"You're right." She nods. "I still am. Now more than ever."

Nance waves to someone across the room and tells Dorothy, "I'm going over to talk to Betty Williams."

"Okay."

Nance grabs her purse. "You can come, too."

"That's all right."

"Oh, come *on*," Nance says, and Dorothy rises gratefully.

Following Nance across the room, she sees some people she remembers, and many she doesn't recognize at all. A group of women is standing around some guy demonstrating what looks like a yoga pose. Downward dog or whatever—Dorothy wonders if he teaches yoga. Judy and Linda are at the bar, talking to John Beckmeier, who was captain of the debate team. They would never have talked to him in high school, but they seem to be enjoying him now. They seem not to want to be with Dorothy, and she doesn't blame them; all she's talked about since they got here is Pete.

On the dance floor, two women are jitterbugging together in their bare feet, shrieking with laughter. A couple seated at a table in the shadows are kissing. She tries to see who it is and runs smack into a chair. Nance grabs her to keep her from falling, then links arms with her as they continue to walk. "Come on, you old tattletale," she says.

Dorothy can't look at her. She stares at the floor and holds back some strong feeling that could be laughter or could be tears, either one. Or both. It comes to her that all of the people in this room are dear to her. As if they all just survived a plane crash together or something. All the drunks and the show-offs and the nice kids and the mean ones. All the people she used to know and all the ones she never knew at all. And herself, too. She includes herself and her stingy little soul. And oh, what a feeling.

SEVENTEEN

Betty Williams is deeply engrossed in conversation with Pam Pottsman. But when she sees Nance and Dorothy coming over, she waves at them and points to the empty chairs at her table.

"Listen to Pam's great idea," Betty says, when they have seated themselves. "It's a really great idea. Tell them, Pammy."

Pam's face is flushed, her hair has fallen flat, her mascara is smeared, and the top of her bra is showing and it is not meant to be; no, that kind of Valkyric bra is not for display. But there is such excitement in her eyes that she looks lovely, Dorothy thinks. A happy person just looks good, no matter what. And a depressed person? Well, that's the opposite. You get some gorgeous woman who's all sad, and she doesn't look good. You don't want to be around her. It comes to Dorothy now that that's what "Pretty is as pretty does" means. She was always terrible at interpreting aphorisms. When she was in ninth grade, her English teacher, Mr. Hannigan, said, "'Fish and visitors smell in three

days.' Meaning? Dorothy?" She'd started when he called on her; she hadn't had her hand up, she'd been doodling daisies in the margins of her paper and hadn't been paying attention. "Pardon?" she'd said. And Mr. Hannigan had drawn himself up the way he always did if he noticed someone wasn't hanging on his every word and repeated coolly, " 'Fish and visitors smell in three days.' What does this mean?"

Dorothy had scootched her butt around a little in her chair and smiled at him. She'd had no *idea* what it meant. She remembers thinking, *Why do people* speak *that way? Why don't they just say what they* mean? *Why must their words wear little costumes?* But she wasn't going to say that, she wasn't going to delve into some completely unrelated subject like Wendy Peters, who one day raised her hand in history class and asked the teacher, "What is truth?" Imagine! But anyway, everyone had been staring at Dorothy that day, all the kids turned around and leering in that piranha-like way kids did when someone got in trouble. Dorothy had run the sentence through her head again: *Fish and visitors smell in three days.* Well, of course they did! And so she'd said, "Well, I think it's self-explanatory," which she thought sounded kind of smart. But Mr. Hannigan had sighed and called on Donna Whitby, that little National Honor Society, prissy nerd weirdo, and Donna had said, "It means 'Don't overstay your welcome,' " and then she had looked over at Dorothy and smirked. And Dorothy had looked down at her desk and thought, *So what. At least I have friends. And a figure.*

"Okay, so here's what I thought," Pam says. "I thought we would get a whole bunch of people to sit around the table and really open up. I'll ask certain questions, and they'll answer *really honestly* what their lives have really been like since we last saw each other."

Nance and Dorothy look askance at each other and Dorothy

gets a little thrill, thinking that she and Nance are now actually friends. Nance says, "Well, Pam, that's kind of a tall order, isn't it?"

"Yeah," Dorothy says. "Nobody's going to do that."

"Oh?" Pam says. "Well, I already asked four people, and they said yes and they're going to get more people. They're all coming back here. A whole bunch of them. And Betty and I were just coming up with the questions, and we've got some good ones."

"Nobody's going to sit in a *circle* and answer *questions*," Dorothy says, again.

"Well, your friends are," Pam says. "Linda and Judy."

"They are?"

"Yes."

"Who else?" Dorothy asks.

"Tom Gunderson, he's just getting another drink and then he's coming. President of the student council, in case you forgot. Lettered in four sports, in case you forgot. Really good-looking, still, in case you hadn't noticed. And *available*."

"I don't care about that," Dorothy says, but Betty has her number. Dorothy pulls her chair closer to the table. She's in. "So what are the questions?" she asks. She wants a jump on them so she's not caught off guard.

Pam holds the napkin close to her breast. "That's for me to know and you to find out. But if I were you, I'd get another drink."

"I've had enough," Dorothy says.

"No you haven't. Trust me, go and get a drink."

Dorothy asks Pam to save her place, and goes over to the bar. Annie Denato is ahead of her, ordering red wine. Annie Denato, class slut, but my goodness, hasn't she cleaned up! Dorothy heard two things about Annie: one, that she went to both medical school and law school; two, that she lives in New York City, on Park Avenue, thank you very much! Her streaked hair is in an

elegant chignon, she's wearing a pale blue shantung suit, and it fits her so perfectly Dorothy thinks it must have been tailor-made. Annie turns around and Dorothy sees that she is wearing diamond studs at least half a carat apiece and Dorothy doesn't think they could possibly be cubic zirconium, although later she will find out. "Dorothy?" Annie says, and Dorothy nods. "Hi, Annie."

"It's Anne now," she says, and then hugs Dorothy like they were old friends. And Dorothy hugs her back, God knows she's not going to hold a grudge or whatever after all this time! Though it's hard to escape memories of how Annie used to be. Hard not to think of her beneath the bleachers on the football field, humping away, everyone knew she did that.

"Know what I heard about you?" Dorothy says. "That you went to law school and medical school."

"True," Annie says.

"Why both?"

"Well, medicine is a symphony, and law is hip-hop. And I discovered I like hip-hop better than classical. Do you know what I mean?"

"Sure," Dorothy says, nodding, though she has no idea what Annie means. Who would?

"I use a lot of what I learned in medical school in my law practice," Annie says. "In my life, actually. But on a day-to-day basis, I prefer to practice law. How about you? What are you up to these days?"

"Oh, well," Dorothy says. "This and that. Not much. Nothing, actually."

"I'm going over to Pam Pottsman's Table o' Truth," Annie asks. "Are you coming?"

"I am," Dorothy says, and Annie waits for her while she gets another glass of wine. Finally, she's starting to have a good time! She doesn't even care if Pete ever comes back!

Well, yes she does, but not as much.

When Dorothy gets back, she sees that a sizable crowd has gathered. Three tables have been pushed together to make for a kind of round table, and many chairs are pushed up to it. Several people stand behind the chairs, too. *There must be twenty-five people here!* Dorothy thinks, and counts. *Well, twenty, but still.*

She claims her chair and looks around at the people. Tom Gunderson is across from her. Ron Rubin, the preacher's son, is on one side of her, and Marjorie Dunn is on the other. Tommy Metito is here, and he's still in terrific shape—he's taken off his suit jacket and tie, unbuttoned his shirt a few buttons down, and rolled up his sleeves. Yup, he's still in pretty good shape, even if his chest hairs are all white and wiry and stick-outish. He's wearing a gold necklace that Dorothy thinks is tacky—way too Tom Jones, but hey. Why not? Let the man be what the man wants to be! Here comes that soulful expansiveness she felt before.

Linda and Judy arrive, and sit in the last two chairs left at the table. Buddy is standing behind Nance, and now more people, drawn by the setup and the noise, curious about what's going on, have made their way over. "What's going on?" someone asks, and when they're told, some laugh loudly and others stand still, their expressions a mix of eagerness and apprehension.

Pam dings a spoon against the side of her wineglass and speaks loudly. "Everyone? Everyone?" A few people stop talking, but most people keep right on. Then Tom Gunderson stands up and claps his hands once, and everyone quiets down. Good old Tom. Dorothy remembers how he used to lean so earnestly on the lectern when he spoke at student assemblies. He began one speech by saying, "What does 'pep rally' really mean?"

"Thank you, Tom," Pam says. "Okay, everybody. Here's the deal. Betty and I were talking and it seems like we're all curious about certain things that don't exactly come up in general conversation. So we thought we'd just make it a kind of game. I'll

ask questions and anyone who wants to can answer. But if no one volunteers, I'll pick someone. And if that person won't answer the question, they have to buy a round for everyone. "

"Oh, fuck that, I'm out of here," a man says, and strides off angrily. It's someone Dorothy doesn't recognize, and then she hears someone say, "Well, Donnie Funderman, he'd never talk to anyone about anything. He never did. He was just always pissed off about everything. He got suspended about five thousand times, once for putting a cherry bomb down the toilet. He hated our school. He hated everybody *in* our school."

"Well, why'd he even come?" Judy asks, and no one answers.

Then, "Terrorist plot?" someone says, and everyone laughs, if ruefully.

"Well, the hell with Donnie Funderman," Pam says. "Let's start." She looks down at her list. "Okay. The first question is, What scared you about coming here tonight?"

"How I'd look to everybody!" Nance says immediately, and a number of people nod their heads, agreeing with her.

"Who'd not be here because they died," Ron Rubin says. "I guess everybody thinks about that, but it was on my mind particularly because *I* almost died not long ago. I wasn't going to tell anybody because it's not exactly . . . I mean, I thought I might get lucky tonight and I didn't want anybody thinking I'd keel over on them. In fact, just in case I do get lucky, I want everyone, especially Sally Harding, to know I'm *fine* now." He looks over at Sally and winks, and she smiles and winks back. "Six months ago," Ron says, "I had a stroke."

Steve Hoffman puts his hand on Ron's shoulder. "Whoa," he says. Then it gets very quiet.

"Aw, come on, didn't anybody *else* have a stroke?" Ron asks, and no one raises his or her hand.

"Heart attack?" he asks, almost gaily, and two hands go up, two men. "Okay, then!" Ron says. "Well, so, like I said, I had a

stroke. I was cleaning the leaves out of my gutters, up on a ladder, you know, and I got this really weird feeling. I came down the ladder, and the whole way down I was feeling more and more numb on one side. By the time I reached the ground, I was listing way over and my mouth was drooping and I thought, damn it, something's really wrong. And then I realized what was happening. I sat on the ground and called my ex-wife, who's a nurse. When she answered and I told her what was going on, she said, 'Call 911, you idiot!' and I said, 'No, I'd rather ride over with you.' We're still real good friends, and she only lives a couple of blocks away. I figured, if I'm going to die, I don't want to be with strangers. So she said she'd come, and I leaned against the house to wait. I looked up at the sky, and it was a real pretty blue with a kind of zigzag cloud I'd never seen before, and it occurred to me that every day of my life, there had been a different kind of sky overhead, and I was sorry I hadn't paid more attention. Then I saw the pack of cigarettes in my pocket and I thought, *Well, either I'm going to die or I'm going to quit smoking. Either way, I'm having these last two cigarettes.* So I smoked 'em, and then my wife came and we went to the hospital. On the way, I told her everything wrong in our marriage had been my fault. And she started crying and said cut it out or we'd get in an accident and both of us would die. 'I mean it,' I said, and she said, no, it was her fault, too, and she was sorry and she would always love me even if I was a ghost. But of course I didn't die. And after I got out of the hospital we got a little more estranged again. Still friends, but . . . you know. And here I am. Here I am with you guys again. And goddamn, I'm glad to be here! Sally, I'm really glad you're here, too."

"Well, *I've* had a hip replaced," she says, and everyone laughs.

But Dorothy has been deeply moved by Ron's story, and she gets out of her chair and goes over to him and puts her hands on

either side of his face and gives him a little kiss. He puts his hands over hers when she does this, and she is surprised and gratified by their warmth. "Ron Rubin," she says. And he says, "Dorothy Shauman," and smiles. "You're all right," he says, and she says thank you and goes back to her chair.

"Don't let's do health anymore," someone says. Dorothy agrees. She visited the memorial table, she saw those photos of classmates who are no longer with them. Vietnam. Disease. Accidents. There was a bouquet of flowers there, a black ribbon around the vase. Dorothy looked carefully at each photo, into the eyes of the unsuspecting young person. She looked at their collars and their ears and their shiny hair. *It's good we don't know our own futures,* she thought. *It's merciful.* A couple of other people came up to the table when Dorothy was there, and she moved away before they could say anything. There was nothing to say.

So yes, they should move on from this morose topic. Imagine if, when they were kids, they'd gone on and on over health concerns, their measles and mumps, their skinned knees and broken wrists and cavities. *Yeah, I was really worried about a staph infection with that skinned knee!* Or *Broken wrist, man alive, what a problem. I have to write with my left hand! I can't take a bath! Can't play volleyball! What will happen to me?* No. They did not complain when they were kids, with rare exception. They just went on with their temporary ailments, waiting to get right again. They got their casts signed and made it fun!

It's different now; Dorothy and her peers are on the other side of the incline. When something happens, they do not assume they'll get right again. They fear getting worse. And they wait for the next thing, and finally for the inevitable tap on the shoulder, that icy singling out.

When they were in their forties, Dorothy and Judy and Linda had made a vow never to talk about health problems the way

their mothers did. "Well, I just don't know *what* to do about my *gall*bladder," Judy had said that day, joking around. And now look. Just a week ago, she said that very same thing to Dorothy, and it wasn't funny at all. Dorothy thought, *Are you sure it's your gallbladder? Are you sure it's not your pancreas?* And then she started thinking about how she could not go on without Judy and Linda in her life, but at some point in the not-so-distant future, she'd have to. Or they'd have to go on without her. Unless they all died in a car wreck together, that actually might not be so bad. Bam! *Done.*

"Okay," Pam says. "Here comes the next question. Does anyone have any dirt on any of the teachers?"

"I screwed Miss Woodman in the art supply closet," Sam Noerper says, and a few people, including Dorothy, gasp.

Tommy Metito says, "I got her, too. Same place. A tube of oil paint came undone beneath her and she got cerulean blue all over her ass."

"Are you *kidding*?" Pam says.

Marjorie Dunn says, "I had sex with her, too."

"You so did not!" Linda says, and Marjorie laughs and says, "You're right. I didn't. But I did have sex with Mr. Garvis, that real young math teacher who came for the latter half of our senior year, but it was after graduation."

"But this is awful!" Dorothy says. "I had no idea!"

"Oh, come on," Buddy says. "Teachers used to flirt all the time. Remember how Mademoiselle Florin used to sit on the top of her desk and cross her legs and her skirt used to ride up real high?"

"*Noooo,*" Dorothy says.

"Well, she did it in our class," Buddy says. "Remember, guys?"

A few members of the Lettermen's Club look at each other and nod, grinning.

"Okay, *moving on*," Pam says. "Here's the next question. Did your life turn out to be anything like you thought it would be?"

Silence.

"Anybody?" Pam asks.

Jenny Freeman, who was always so quiet, always the great observer, speaks up now. "Not mine. All I ever wanted was to get married and have children. I thought it was a noble goal. But then the women's movement came along, and I felt compelled to work outside the house. It sounded great, you know, live up to your potential, everybody pitch in, it's going to be Equal City. Which, actually, it was not, and *is* not, but at the time I bought into it. When my second was two months old, I put her in day care and I got my real estate license and I got a job. I walked around in this horrible mustard-colored blazer, selling houses. Paid a fortune to get my face put on a bus stop bench. I sold a million houses, I swear, I made a lot of money. And I so regret doing it, because I don't feel like I ever got to know my daughter, not like I did my son. I had a red phone, it was a separate business line, and every time it rang, I'd stop whatever I was doing and talk to some client. I was afraid not to answer that goddamn phone, I might miss out! And the irony is, I did miss out. I've never been able to achieve the kind of relationship with my daughter that I have with my son."

"Oh well," Pam says. "That's girls, isn't it? Boys are just easier."

"No," Jenny says. "It's that I wasn't available to her. I can remember her trying to talk to me when she was growing up and I was always putting her off. The truth is, I was an awful mother."

"Oh, for God's sake," Judy says. "You set a good example for your daughter by having a successful career!"

"No, I didn't," Jenny says. "I was a fucking anxious wreck. I was always tired, always feeling so much pressure. I quit cook-

ing, which I really used to enjoy, especially baking, I used to love to bake. But after I started working, I used to have a *fit* if I got a notice to make something for a bake sale. Have you seen what bake sales have become, by the way? Nobody makes anything. It's all supermarket crap! Remember when everything used to be homemade? Remember the pies and the banana breads and the cookies, all tied up in ribbons? Remember the *cakewalks?*"

"Yeah," Judy says. "And remember when women used to medicate themselves in order to get through a day because they were so damn bored? You're being too hard on yourself."

"My daughter has been institutionalized three times for drugs. She's had four abortions. I can't . . . We don't really talk. She lives with a man I can't stand; I don't think he treats her right. I go to visit her and I want to be nonjudgmental and loving and try to repair our relationship but her apartment just reeks of cigarettes and dirty dishes and garbage overflowing from this big can they keep in the kitchen, and the cats are eating from it and . . ." She starts to cry and then laugh, saying, "Oh, I can't believe I said all this. I'm so embarrassed."

"Don't be," Karen Komall says, little Karen, who never measured more than four feet eleven and was regarded as a kind of pet for the student body. Everybody liked Karen, she was such a sweet girl. She ended up marrying her high school sweetheart, Tim Swift, who is one of the guys on the dead table. Vietnam. "I had a lot of problems with my son," she said. "A lot. It's hard to raise a son without a father. But he's okay now. It took a long time, but he's really got his life on track, now. If there's anything I've learned about life, it's that things always change. Which, for me, means that there's always hope. I'll give you my email—I'll be glad to talk to you about this anytime."

Jenny nods. "Thank you. I'm so . . . Thank you. Okay. Let's change the subject!"

Annie—Anne—Denato says, "Well, I have a question. What

did everyone hope to find, coming here tonight? And I'll answer first. I wanted a chance to show how much I've changed. I wanted you all to know how much you misjudged me."

"We did misjudge you," Nance says. "I for one am sorry. I knew you were smart, but you were . . ."

"I know," Anne says. "I had *reasons* for being that way. If you guys had had *any idea* of what went on in my house . . . My father did a number on me, okay? But I'm past it. I'm past all that stuff, I'm really happy now, I'm successful, and I wanted you all to *know* it. And yet, being here makes me feel like that girl in high school all over again.

"You know, when I told one of my colleagues I was coming to my fortieth high school reunion, he said, '*Don't go.*' We're good friends; he knows what life was like for me in high school. But anyway, he said so many people who go to reunions think that doing so can somehow change what happened to them. That the person you've become might erase the person you were then. But of course that doesn't happen. In some respects, this reunion has shown me that it's not that you can't go home again; it's that you can never leave." She swallows what's left of her drink and then offers a big smile. "Well, but here we all are, talking to each other in a way that's not bullshit. I say that counts for a lot. What about the rest of you? What did you want to find here?"

"Dorothy came for only one reason," Judy says, and Dorothy's eyes grow round and she says, "*Judy!*"

"I didn't say who," Judy says, but then Pam says, "Well, who is it?" and Judy says, "Pete Decker," and there it is, right out in the open for everyone to know.

"He's married, isn't he?" Ron asks, and Tom Gunderson says, "Getting divorced."

"Fair game then," Ron says, and winks at Dorothy.

"I'm going to the bathroom," Dorothy says, and Judy says, "Oh, Dorothy, sit down!"

"I have to pee!"

Pam picks up her purse. "Maybe we should all go, so none of us misses anything."

"If we all go, the momentum will be lost," Linda says.

"She's right," Judy says. And then, "Sit down, Dorothy."

"I'm not sitting down," Dorothy says, and Linda says, "Sit *down*!" so she does. Then she says, "Okay, I have a question. Who do you think is going to hook up tonight, besides Lester Hessenpfeffer and Candy Sullivan?"

"Lester and *Candy*?" Anne asks.

Dorothy nods gravely. "Somebody saw them on the elevator going up. They've been gone for a long time."

Susie Black says, "I don't think I'm going to hook up with anyone, but I did get kissed in the hallway. And you know who it was? It was Bill Anderson."

Bill Anderson! Dorothy thinks. He stayed for such a little while, she doesn't think he even finished his dinner. He was a wreck, nothing like his former self, Dorothy couldn't imagine what had happened to make him that way and wasn't inclined to ask. He was sort of scary, sitting alone at a table by the bar, staring off into space. Dorothy avoided him because he looked so sad and odd. It seemed like most people did. Susie had gained quite a bit of weight, but she still had a little left of what used to make her so cute. Still with the big blue eyes, the high cheekbones.

"It was the most extraordinary thing," she says. "The sweetest thing. We walked past each other in the hall—I was coming back from the bathroom and he was leaving, and we nodded at each other. Then he called my name, and I turned around, and he asked if I had a minute. Sure, I said. So he came up and stood real close and looked me right in the eyes for a long time. Then he told me he'd had a crush on me in high school, that he had loved me for years and he'd kept my picture in his helmet when he went to Vietnam. He said he'd wanted to ask me to the prom senior

year, but he was too scared. And you know, I sat alone on prom night. Well, not alone, I sat watching television with my parents, which was worse than sitting alone. I said, 'Oh, Bill, I would have gone with you,' and he said, 'You would?' and I said 'Yeah, I thought you were really cute!' and he said, 'You did?' and I said 'Yeah, in fact I had a crush on you.' Which I did, I liked how shy and mysterious Bill was, I liked that. And he was really cute, that black hair, those green eyes. Real tall, and he had a little dimple in his left cheek. He said, 'You had a crush on me?' and I said yeah, and he said, 'Huh. I wish you'd told me.' And I said, 'Me, too.' And then he put his finger under my chin just like in the movies and gave me the most gentle kiss. And I thought about how we were both pretty good-looking in high school and now we're both kind of wrecked, and here we were, sharing a smooch in the hallway under bad fluorescent lighting, and I thought we were more beautiful than we had ever been. You know?"

"Why don't you call him?" Betty says.

"I thought of that. I asked for his number and he said he'd rather not give it to me. He said he had a lot of problems; he wasn't really able to be with a woman. Wasn't able to be with anyone, really."

She shrugs, and Dorothy can see that she's close to tears. "It's too late. It really is. He was such a sweet guy, too. I knew him, and he was just so *sweet.*" She shakes her head. "Man oh man. There's just a million ways a life can go. Isn't there?"

EIGHTEEN

LESTER AND CANDY ARE LYING ON THEIR BACKS ON HER hotel bed. The lights in the room are out, but the drapes are open, revealing the bright moon and the many stars. Esther the bulldog lies between them at shoulder level, her head on her paws, her forehead wrinkled and worried looking. Lester and Candy are fully clothed, on top of the covers, and Candy is holding Lester's handkerchief pressed against her nose. After a moment, she says, "Okay, I think I'm done crying now. Sorry."

Lester looks over at her. "Oh, no; don't apologize. I'm honored! Truly. My wife used to say that to cry in front of someone was to offer them a compliment."

"She did?"

"Yes."

"What else did she used to say?"

He looks out at the night sky. "Well, she called stars silent commentators. Ancient, silent commentators."

"Huh. That's nice. What else?"

Lester's chest hurts now, but he says in as easy a tone as he

can muster, "Oh, she said a lot of things." He thinks about how, after the reconciliation that came after their first major argument, he told Kathleen he feared he'd lost her forever. And she said, "You know that song 'Till the End of Time'? Please review the lyrics, and then report back to me." But what he tells Candy is, "She used to say this all the time: 'If you can't beat 'em, beat 'em harder.'"

Candy laughs, and it makes Lester's spirits rise. Then she props herself up on one elbow and says, "I'm sorry. I've taken you away from the party."

"You didn't take me away. I wanted to come with you. For one thing, duty called. A dog with love handles is a dog that needs attention!"

"Oh, I was so scared she had a tumor. What a relief that she's only fat! I love fat!"

Lester rubs the top of Esther's head briskly. She licks him and snorts happily into his hand. Her tail is wagging so fast it's nearly a blur. "Don't you listen to her; you're gorgeous," Lester tells the dog. "Liz Taylor should have such beauty marks!" And then, to Candy, "You're gorgeous, too, by the way."

He sees her pull back slightly into herself, the automatic response of many pretty women who have been complimented too many times for reasons more suspect than sincere. "Oh, well, money helps," she tells him. "I'm on a first-name basis with more than a few plastic surgeons. I think I alone support many branches of the cosmetics industry."

"I didn't mean how you look, I meant how you *are*."

This seems to surprise her, and she starts crying again.

"Uh-oh," he says.

She waves her hand and blubbers, "It's just . . . Well! I guess a lot of things are hitting me all at once."

He could say the same. They had talked about so many things! From a random and seemingly weightless remark at a dinner table

to . . . this! He'd sat next to Candy Sullivan only to . . . well, to sit next to *Candy Sullivan.* To say a brief hello. And, if the truth be told, to have the opportunity to look at her close up—God, she was something. Then he'd intended to take a place at the nearly empty table where Ben Small was sitting. He was going to face the door so he could see when Mary Alice arrived, then wave her over to sit beside him—he had expected that, after their lovely after-noon, they might have dinner together. For starters.

But then he formed what felt like an immediate bond with the Homecoming Queen. "Candy Sullivan?" he said, and she turned around and looked up at him. He extended his hand and re-minded her of his name—he'd discovered that not all of the peo-ple there saw well enough anymore to read the name tags.

"Oh, *Lester*!" she said. "I know you. I remember you very well!"

She removed her purse from the empty seat beside her and he sat down and said, "So. The last time I saw you was the day be-fore you left to go to Boston for college, BU wasn't it?"

"It was! What a memory!"

"Well," he said. "What a goil. Everybody knew everything about you. That day, you were in line ahead of me at the Dairy Queen. Wearing . . . well, Candy, I think you would have to call them short shorts. And a white blouse, knotted at your waist. You were barefoot, and you had a daisy stuck between a couple of your toes. You were talking about how you were going to marry a neurosurgeon and have five children."

Her forehead wrinkled. "Did we talk that day?"

"Nah. I just overheard. You were surrounded by your usual friends and admirers. A guy couldn't wedge his way in with a . . . with a wedger."

Her eyes shifted briefly away from him. "Yes, well." She touched her right earring, her left. "And you were off to college, too. The University of Minnesota, right?"

Lester laid his hand over his heart. "I'm touched you remember."

She tilted her head and studied him. "I remember a lot about you, Lester Hessenpfeffer. I remember how smart you were, and how kind. How you were going to be a vet. How a lot of people were really awful to you. And how I never stood up for you when I could have."

He shrugged. "It didn't matter, really. I turned out fine. I'm happy! I'm a vet! So *did* you marry a neurosurgeon and have five children?"

"Not exactly," she said; and then her chin began to tremble, and she started telling him things that would have made him leaving her table rude, if not impossible. From the corner of his eye, he had seen Mary Alice come in, and he'd thought to give her some sort of sign—a finger held up in the air? A quick lift of his chin that would let her know he'd be right over? But then he'd noticed Pete Decker with her and thought, *Huh! Well, that's that.* Oh, he'd intended to validate his assumptions, not for nothing had he been trained in the scientific method. But as his talk with Candy grew more intimate, the idea of him pursuing a relationship with Mary Alice (sitting with *Pete Decker,* why was she sitting with *Pete Decker?*) became less and less urgent.

Dinner was delivered, and Candy sat staring at her plate. Then she began to cry into her filet mignon, tears suddenly spilling over and apparently taking her by surprise. "Oh!" she said, and quickly dabbed at her eyes with her napkin, her head down—embarrassed, he thought. "Gosh!" she said. The tears kept coming, and finally he gently took her arm and led her into the hall, where her crying turned into all-out sobbing. "Oh, for heaven's sake," she said. "I'm all right. Really. I'm so sorry. I'll just go up to my room. I'm fine."

"Well. No, you're not." He was frustrated by a sudden desire to do something for her without having any idea what that might

be. He imagined himself picking her up, swooping her into his arms, her white dress and her sparkly purse and the dinner napkin she still held clutched in her hand, and . . . what? Asking her if she'd like to take a truck ride with him to visit Elwood Masten's eleven golden retriever puppies, seven and a half weeks old and each one better looking than the next? Abandon their reunion dinner in favor of brown sugar meat loaf and carrot mashed potatoes and heavily buttered green beans and gooseberry pie at the Clean Plate Club? Which fortunately or unfortunately (depending on whether he was wearing his medical professional hat or his starving man hat) was right across the street from his clinic? Samson the mastiff had availed himself of half a sandwich made from that meat loaf when Lester had carelessly left his take-out lunch on top of the reception desk and Jeanine had turned her back, and that is probably why Samson never cowered in the waiting room anymore. No, Lester decided. He would give Candy her privacy.

He did punch the elevator button for her, though, and when the doors opened, the people who stepped off stared with blatant, nearly openmouthed curiosity. Lester stepped between them and Candy and thus ended up on the elevator with her. When they reached her floor, he walked her to her door. She hesitated, then said, "I wonder . . . would you come in and have a look at my dog? I'm sorry to take advantage of you this way. But I just noticed this awful swelling on both her sides, and I'm so worried that she—"

"I'd be happy to have a look," he said, and when she slid the key into the door, he couldn't help it; his heart sped up. And it wasn't *that* (although who could be a straight man with a functioning brain and not have the briefest of scenarios occur to him when a beautiful woman like Candy unlocks her hotel room to him?). But it wasn't that he wanted to have sex with Candy Sullivan. It was that he felt retroactively invited to sit at the Table.

He supposes some things never go away. Jeanine's mother lives in an old-age home where there's a Popular Table. "It's just like junior high, I swear," Jeanine had told him. "The royalty still saving seats for each other."

"Is your mother a member of the royalty?" Lester had asked.

"No," Jeanine had said, "and it drives her crazy. She says she doesn't care, but when I go to have a meal with her, all she does is watch them. Oh well, one of them will probably die soon, and then maybe she can move up the ladder."

After Lester examined Esther, he and Candy kept a respectful distance from each other, but then Candy slipped off her heels and stretched out on the bed and said, "Oh, boy, this feels good. Do you want lie down, Lester?" And he did. By that time, each knew that "lying down" was simply acknowledgment of presumed aches and pains and a reduced capacity for alcohol. If Candy weren't so sad, the situation might have been funny.

They talked about how Candy had been living a life more and more distant from what she had wanted it to be; how lately she had been having difficulty making simple decisions, and this made her feel she no longer knew herself at all. (Do *I like strawberries?* she'd asked herself at the supermarket recently and was literally unable to answer.) She said a weighty despair had insinuated itself into her life and now it was just the norm—every morning, she opened her eyes and searched the bedroom ceiling for long minutes at a time, looking for what was wrong. "What I finally decided," she said, "is that *everything* is." She talked, in halting tones, about how she feared her husband in ways too complicated to be fully acknowledged, and how she was ashamed of that fear, and didn't feel she had anyone she could talk to about it.

"Does he hit you?" Lester asked, a question that seemed balanced between obscene and necessary.

She hesitated, then said, "No. Not . . . like that. But if he did,

it wouldn't surprise me. Or even make me mad. I would just feel like it *belonged,* somehow." The elevator dinged out in the hall-way and she tensed, then looked quickly at the door as though waiting for a knock. Then she looked back at Lester and sighed. "You know, this diagnosis has been a kind of gift. It's making me look at things and *see* them."

She told him she had begun to think about what death really meant and what life really meant—nothing like death to make you think about life! She said a friend's baby had died at only eight months old from an overwhelming bacterial infection, and that she found consolation in remembering what that mother had put on her baby's gravestone: "A brief life, but oh so joyful." Candy said she intended to move toward joy, if only for the last several months of her life.

Lester talked about himself, too. It seemed that a certain type of intimate exchange could elicit more and more soulful admis-sions, especially if you'd had a few drinks and were experiencing the kind of jaunty surrealism a high school reunion can bring. Lester told Candy that he loved his little neighbor girl like a daughter, and that she had used his house for her last sleepover party because her mother had said never again. He said he had served seven little tomboys spaghetti and meatballs at the picnic table in his backyard, and then made ice cream sundaes, which he believed he was not alone in thinking were absolutely fantas-tic. He told her he'd recently offered Miranda another such party and she had refused him because of the unacceptable amount of time he'd spent hanging around the girls last time, thus prevent-ing them from talking. Which she hadn't wanted to tell him, but since he'd asked about doing it again . . . When Lester said he'd do better next time, Miranda said all right, how about two Sat-urdays from now, which by the way was the day he had promised to let her sit in on the day's surgeries, and he had readily agreed. Tacos, he was going to give those girls this time, and a repeat of

the sundaes. Then he was going to turn over the living room to them, and retire to his bedroom to read.

He described to Candy the impact his wife's and unborn child's deaths had had on him, not only right after they happened, but also the ripple effect of the ever-transforming but never quite resolving grief. "I guess I believe I owe it to her to keep on feeling the grief," he said.

"Hmm," Candy said. "I wonder. I wonder if you asked her if she wanted you to feel such pain, what she would say."

"She would want me to remember her," Lester said. "I know that."

"Yes, but in pain? How about another way? How about honoring the love you shared by loving someone again?"

"Well, funny you should say that," he said, and told Candy about how he was very attracted to Mary Alice Mayhew, of all people.

"What do you mean, 'of all people'?" Candy said, and Lester said nothing; he was embarrassed he'd put it that way. Talk about the pot calling the kettle black.

"She just didn't *try*," Candy said. "She was too smart to."

Lester nodded. "You're right. And you know, I had lunch with her today, and I noticed . . . She smells like *outside*."

"Well, that *alone*!" Candy said, smiling.

"But she's down there with Pete Decker. So I don't know. I guess I kind of blew it."

"Oh, come on," Candy said. And something about the way she looked at him made him believe he still had a chance after all.

They have just agreed to head back downstairs when they hear the tinny sound of salsa music, and Candy sighs. "My husband calling," she says. "I'll bet you a million dollars. I should never have turned the phone back on."

She pulls the cellphone out of her purse, looks at the caller ID, then puts it back in her purse without answering it. "Yup,"

she says. "That's who it is. Cooper Anthony Armstrong. My husband."

"Does this mean I have to pay you a million dollars?" Lester asks. "Do you take Visa?"

Candy shakes her head sadly. "See? This is how he is. I ask him to come with me and he says no. But now the whole time I'm here, he'll keep calling. This is how he always is, these mixed signals, and it's so confusing. I wonder why he doesn't ever just say *yes* to *any*thing I propose. Why doesn't he ever say, 'Sure, I'll go.' Just like that. It's as though he just likes to say no to me. Or *needs* to or something. Maybe it's something he learned.

"You know, at my father-in-law's wake, my mother-in-law was sitting in a corner by herself. She was sitting up so straight, her purse balanced on top of her knees, clutching a hankie. I went to sit by her and asked her how she was doing. She said, 'He never played cards with me.' I didn't know what she meant, of course, and I said something like, 'Oh?' And then she told me that she used to wait for her husband to come home every night, that was the highlight of her day. Half an hour before he was due, she changed into a dress and heels, put on lipstick and perfume, and combed her hair. Then she set the table—candles every night—and served him a nice dinner. Almost every night when they had finished eating, she would try to get him to spend some time with her. Just a card game, perhaps gin rummy, she would suggest. And he never did. She said when the kids were home, she could understand it; he was tired—well, so was she. But even after the kids left, all the years they were together without children, she would still make him dinner every night and she would still ask him for a little card game and he never did play with her. But here's the thing: he didn't say, 'I don't want to play cards.' Or 'I don't like to play cards.' He would say, 'Later,' and then never do it. *Why?*"

Lester has a few ideas about why, but he keeps them to him-

self. The question seems mostly rhetorical. Besides that, Candy's figuring things out for herself. And the process is new, still delicate. If he criticizes her husband, he suspects she'll find a way to defend him. Let silence be his only comment. He's known men like Candy's husband seems to be, and the kindest thing he can say about them is that he will never understand them, the way they deny themselves happiness and contentment because of a kind of stinginess and general obstinacy toward their wives, if not a weird sort of hatred. He thinks that such men feel there is a pattern of behavior that must be adhered to during courtship; after that, the onus is on the woman—and the woman alone—to please.

"I wish I had the courage to leave him," Candy says. "But then I'd be alone. It would be hard to deal with all that's going on if I were alone."

"I don't know," Lester says. "I think there's alone-alone; and then there's feeling alone when you're with someone, which is worse."

"You're right," she says. "You're absolutely right. Alone-alone is . . . clean. Isn't it?"

"I think it is."

"To be alone without longing, that's the thing."

"That is the thing."

"I have never in my life been alone. I have always had a man."

"Yes?"

"Yes. Since I was eleven years old. My God. Since I was *eleven*. That's when my boyfriend Billy Simpson would come over every day after school. Every day, and you know I would spend a good half hour getting ready for him. Instead of being outside and riding my bike or something, I would sit in front of my dresser mirror trying out different ribbons for my hair."

"Didn't your mom say anything?" Lester asks.

"Oh, sure. She told all her friends how wonderful it was that I had such a dedicated boyfriend so young. She was quite proud." She is quiet for a moment, and then she says gently, "Bless her heart. It was such a different time."

It is quiet for a while, and then Candy clears her throat and says, "Lester? In your professional opinion, do you think I'm going to die soon?"

He looks at her. "I'm a veterinarian."

"I know. But do you?"

"Well, I think . . . You know what? I think people get hung up on statistics. The reality is that, when it comes to the individual, it's zero or one hundred percent. And I'm struck, too, by the way that people assume a medical diagnosis is what's going to take them out of Dodge. I could go out for a walk tonight and get hit by a bus."

"Oh, I hope you don't," Candy says. "Then I'll never get my million dollars."

There is the sound of a door slamming, and then they hear a woman giggling on the other side of the wall. She giggles louder, whoops, and then there is the sound of the headboard banging against the wall in an unmistakable rhythm.

Candy's eyes grow wide and she whispers, "Do you think that's one of ours?"

"Someone from the reunion?"

She nods.

"God, I hope so," Lester says. "I hope it's Dorothy Shauman and John Niehauser." Lester hates to impugn the character of John this way, he was pretty a nice guy who had the misfortune to have been seen eating boogers in fourth grade and it followed him right up to the last year of high school, but Lester always liked him. He was a math genius, which put another nail in his high school coffin, and, as if that weren't enough, he liked to bring the newspaper to read at lunchtime while he drank coffee

from a plaid thermos. He was almost as big a nerd as Lester. But to pair Dorothy with someone so that they can put faces to the sounds of moaning and groaning is irresistible. He and Candy start laughing, just a little at first, and then long and loudly.

"Oh, *God*!" Candy finally says, her hand lying limp across her belly. "Whew!" She sits up and blows her nose and says, "All right. Let me fix my mascara and then we should go back down there. I've kept you here so long. I'm sorry."

"Hey, Candy. Would you do me a favor?"

"Stop apologizing?"

"Bingo."

"I know. One of the many habits I need to break."

"I'm *glad* we talked. I really am. I hope you know that."

"I'm glad, too. And now you've got to get down there and ask that sweet-smelling woman to dance."

Lester sits up, his face full of worry. "I am an awful dancer. Awful." He stares at his shoes, as though it's their fault.

Candy puts her hand on Lester's shoulder. "Here's what I know about Mary Alice Mayhew. She won't mind one bit."

"Yeah. I guess you're right."

"Ask her for a slow one."

"Slow's the ticket," Lester says, and Candy nods in a serious way like he's talking about all kinds of things, which he supposes he is.

When they get back to the dance, they see a large number of people sitting around a few tables that have been pushed together. "What's going on over there?" Candy asks, and Lester says, "Don't know. Let's go see." He scans the group quickly to see if Mary Alice is there. No. Nor does he see her anywhere else. Also missing: Pete Decker. *So.*

When Candy and Lester reach the table, there is a sudden silence. And then Pam Pottsman says, "Allllll right. Where have *you* two been?"

Lester drags two chairs over, and he and Candy squeeze in around the table. "We've been getting to know one another," he says, and the group says together, "*Ohhhhhhhh.*"

"And what are you guys doing?" Lester asks.

"We're telling the truth," Pam says. "Isn't that something?"

"About what?" Candy asks, and Buddy says, "Everything. We just finished horror stories about health a little while ago."

"Ah," Candy says, and it's all Lester can do not to reach over and take her hand. Then she says, "Here's something true. I just made a friend. Which I need. And always did need."

"Are you kidding?" Judy says. "*Everyone* was your friend in high school! And you had a date practically every night of the week!"

Candy nods, smiling. "Yeah, but you know what? The thing about *everybody* being your friend is that it can mean *no* one is.

"As for dating . . . Yes, I did date a lot. A *lot.* I took a kind of pride in it, too. I had a calendar hanging on my wall next to my desk, and I used to keep a tally at the bottom of the page, of how many dates per month I had. And I had a ritual I kind of enjoyed each time I got ready for a date. I'd wash and roll up my hair, and then dry it with one of those dryers you could put perfume in, remember those? I'd stand in front of the mirror putting my makeup on so carefully, trying this new thing or that. I'd debate for a long time about what outfit to wear. It was like a job, dating. It was what I did. I would go on all these dates, and when I came home, there would be my mother in her bathrobe, sitting at the kitchen table and smoking, waiting for me to tell her how everything went. I think she missed her own days of furious dating, and she would hang on every word I told her. But of course you don't talk to your mother like you would a girlfriend. You don't share certain things, you don't ask certain questions that you want to ask. I really needed girlfriends, and none of you ever really let me in."

"Why didn't you *ask* us?" Nance says.

"I couldn't," Candy says. "It was too embarrassing to admit how lonely I was. But I'll admit it now. I have lived a pretty lonely life, and I am ready for women friends!"

Linda puts her arm around Candy and says, "I'll be your friend."

"Can I . . . ? I want to say one more thing about health," Marjorie says, then adds quickly, "It's not a bad thing." She resettles herself in her chair and says, "I saw this picture in the paper the other day. It was bicyclists in a race, and the weather was awful, rain just pouring down. The riders looked so bedraggled and miserable, nothing like those cool Tour de France posters you see, where the bikers are in such impossibly good shape, and the day is perfect, and they're taking a turn with such grace and precision. I mean, they look like ballet dancers on wheels. The riders in the photo I saw were nothing like that. They were not in good shape, they had their heads down, and a lot of them were frowning, it seemed like they were gritting their teeth, just working so hard to get through the thing they'd signed up for, never thinking it would be like *this*. And I thought, that's what I am now. I'm a rider in the rain—out of shape, operating under less than optimal conditions, just trying to finish the race and not give up early. But I *like* myself better now. I like all of us better now. I think I had to get this old to understand some things I really needed to know. I needed to suffer some humiliation and to pick up a few battle scars. It's made me less shallow, and far more appreciative of *everything*. I've finally gained some perspective that lets me laugh about things that used to make me want to tear my hair out. Getting older is hard, you lose an awful lot. But I don't know, I think it's worth the trade. And, Candy? I'll be your friend, too. I always wanted to be your friend. Want to go shopping for rain gear?"

Lester's cellphone rings. He looks to see who it is, then answers quickly. It's Jeanine. More to the point, it's Samson.

NINETEEN

MARY ALICE STANDS WITH PETE AT THE ENTRANCE TO the ballroom. She doesn't see Lester anywhere, nor does she see Candy Sullivan. Well, there's *that* reunion story. For a moment, something seems to deflate inside her, but then she reminds herself of how pleasant an afternoon she and Lester had spent. There's always the breakfast, which he'd said he would definitely attend. "I'd never turn down breakfast," he said. "Even the *name* is right. And then if you add bacon, well . . ." He looked at her with some concern then, asking if she was a vegetarian, and she told him only in her ideal vision of self, which she never lived up to; and that she had recently seen a recipe that featured bacon crumbled on top of ice cream and thought it was brilliant.

She sees Pete scanning the crowd—looking for his wife, she supposes. She touches his arm and points in as unobtrusive a way as possible to where Nora is dancing with Fred. Mary Alice doesn't know Fred at all, and she doesn't really know Pete that much better, but the time she spent with him this evening has made her think his wife really should give him another chance. Mary Alice sees

him as an essentially kindhearted man a little derailed by his good looks and charm. But he has a generosity about him, a kind of *willingness* that, in Mary Alice's book, anyway, makes up for a lot.

She and Pete had put Einer to bed. "Drape my socks over my chair!" Einer ordered Pete. "I only wore them half a day!" Pete complied, aligning the socks with great care on the top of Einer's easy chair, the one he keeps stationed by the window. Pete also hung up Einer's suit jacket, pants, and shirt, and complimented him on his choice of fabrics. Before he left Einer's bedroom (Einer himself propped up on his pillows, as yet refusing to give in to the fatigue that was making both his mouth and his eyelids droop), Pete sat at the old man's bedside and shook his hand, thanking him for his friendship and counsel.

"That's all right," Einer said. "You ever make your way out here again, you know where to find me."

"I might take you up on that," Pete said.

When Pete stood to leave, Einer said, "Say, how about a little touch before you go? I've got some good scotch downstairs. Rita knows where it is, she likes a touch herself, every now and again. She thinks I don't know, but you have to get up early in the morning to fool this old bird."

Pete told Einer they'd have some on his next visit, and then he and Mary Alice made their way downstairs, where they waited at the kitchen table for Rita to come home. She arrived about fifteen minutes later. "Sorry," she said, "but boy, do I have a good excuse! Want to know what it is?"

"Tell me later," Mary Alice said, though there didn't seem to be too much mystery as to what had delayed her return.

On the drive back to the hotel, Pete told Mary Alice about his father, who was a philanderer of some note. "He didn't even try to hide it," Pete said. "His pockets were a treasure trove of evidence— he'd have matches from hotel bars, numbers written on scraps of paper; once, even, a tube of lipstick. My brother and I used to go

through his pockets to spare my mom—and to see if we could figure out if he'd seen the same woman twice. We also stole whatever change was in there and spent it on candy." When his father was home, which wasn't all that often, he had a heavy hand with his children, especially with Pete, because Pete had the balls to give him a little crap back. Pete admitted that he had cheated on his own wife and then left her but now realized his idiocy. "I know this sounds like bullshit," he said, "but I don't know who that *was,* the guy who did that. I feel like all of a sudden I'm starting to come to, to realize some things I should have known a long time ago." It was quiet in the car, and then Pete said, "You probably don't believe me when I say that, huh?" and Mary Alice said, "In fact, I do."

He said he had schemed to get Nora to come to the reunion, where he could see her alone and begin the process of getting her back. "I thought if I could just get some time with her," Pete said. "Whenever I come over to the house, she's itching the whole time for me to leave, I can tell. I wanted a chance to talk to her away from there. She doesn't really want a divorce; she's just hurt. And I don't blame her! I fucked up! But I figured if she came to this reunion, if she thought about how we used to be . . .

"And then that *clod* had to come with her. Mr. Personality. Let me tell you, that guy doesn't stand a chance in hell with Nora. He may be fine for now, something for her to do, a guy to take her places, you know; but believe me, I know my wife, and Fred Preston is not going to last much longer. He is on the way out. She's bored silly."

Well, not by the look of things. Fred and Nora are dancing to a slow song, and the look on Nora's face is anything but bored. *Deeply content* comes to mind.

Mary Alice can almost feel Pete's heart sink. She smiles at him, trying to think of something that will make him feel better, if only in the smallest way. But look at him, standing there with his hands in his pockets, his shoulders slumped, unable to turn

away from the thing that is causing him such pain. What words that she could offer would provide any solace? She feels so bad for him in his golf clothes, his shirt stained with blood and salad dressing, and now as well as with the lurid orange of a Cheeto he dropped on himself as they sat waiting for Einer in the ER.

"Pete?" she says softly.

He looks over at her, his face full of weariness. "Know what my kids would say about this situation?" he says, gesturing with his chin toward his wife and Fred.

"What?"

"'Game over,' that's what they'd say."

"Your kids wouldn't say that," she says, though of course she doesn't know Pete's children at all. "They'd say, 'Game on!'"

Mary Alice looks over at the couple again. Fred's still got Nora held up against him tightly, and now they both have their eyes closed.

"I was going to ask the DJ to play 'The Way You Look Tonight,'" Pete says, sadly. "That was our song."

Mary Alice puts her purse down at an empty table and reaches for Pete's hand. "Come on. Let's do that."

He hesitates for just a moment, then takes her hand and follows her to the DJ, who agrees to play that song right after this one finishes. Then Pete follows Mary Alice out onto the dance floor. "Okay, here's the plan," she says. "We dance with each other for a few seconds, and then we cut in on them. When the song ends, you keep hold of Nora for 'The Way You Look Tonight.'"

"What if she won't do it?"

"What have you got to lose?"

And so they position themselves next to Fred and Nora, dance a few steps, and then Mary Alice gives Pete the slightest of nods. He moves over and taps Fred on the shoulder. Fred opens his eyes, and when he sees it's Pete, opens them wider. He steps away from Nora, his hands in the air, as though he's being held up.

Pete holds his own hands up. "No worries, Fred; I'm just cutting in. Gentleman's prerogative."

Fred looks at Nora, who raises one shoulder: I *don't care.* But Mary Alice can see the concern in her face when she looks at her husband: his disheveled state, his obvious need.

Mary Alice taps Fred on the shoulder. "May I have the honor?" she asks, and Fred looks once again at Nora, then reluctantly takes Mary Alice into his arms.

"So you're Fred?" Mary Alice asks.

"Yes, that's right," he says. And automatically, mindlessly, he asks, "And you're . . ."

"I'm Jayne Mansfield," Mary Alice says.

"Uh-huh," he says, his eyes glued to Pete. The song ends, and, fortunately, the next one starts right away. Pete keeps hold of Nora, and she doesn't seem to mind. "*Someday,*" the Lettermen sing, "*when I'm awfully low, when the world is cold . . .*"

Fred dances stiffly, badly. Mary Alice tries to make conversation, but everything she says falls flat. Finally, "I live in a tree," she says.

"Is that right," Fred says, but then he looks at her. "Did you . . . What did you say?"

"I said, 'I live in a tree.' The very top branches. Lovely view."

He continues to stare at her, but before he can think of how to respond, the song ends. Mary Alice looks over at Pete and can tell instantly that their ploy did not exactly work. Nora is walking quickly back to Fred, shaking her head, and Pete is standing still, empty eyed.

"Last dance!'" the DJ says and starts playing another slow song, an instrumental that Mary Alice doesn't recognize. And now here come Dorothy Shauman and Pam Pottsman, from opposite sides of the room, headed straight for Pete Decker. Dorothy sees what Pam is doing and actually runs over and elbows her out of the way. "Wanna dance?" she asks breathlessly, and Pete takes her

in his arms like an automaton, then looks over the top of her head at Nora and Fred, holding hands and walking back to their table.

Pam stands beside Mary Alice, trying to catch her breath. She watches Pete and Dorothy dance, mindlessly anchoring a piece of hair that has fallen again from where it was pinned up. "Nuts," she says. Then, brightening, "Oh well, there's always breakfast."

Ben Small comes up to Mary Alice and shrugs. "How about it, toots?" She smiles and takes his hand. They dance right next to Pete and Dorothy. Neither she nor Ben talks, and Mary Alice is pretty sure it's so that they can better listen to Dorothy putting the moves on Pete. They hear her say, "I have wanted to dance with you all *night,* but I haven't had the *chance.* You look great, Pete! Which I'm sure you know. You look just great! Even in . . . those clothes."

Pete makes some sort of grunting sound.

"What are you driving now, Pete?"

"What?"

"What are you *driving* now?"

"Oh. A Nissan *Cube,*" he says, bitterly.

"Oh, I love those cars!" Dorothy says, and Pete says, "I was *kidding.* Jesus! I've got a Porsche. And a 'fifty-seven 'Vette."

"Oh, a vintage 'Vette!" Dorothy says. "Yes, that does sound more like you." She pulls him closer. "You know, I have to tell you, ever since I got the invitation to the reunion, I've been thinking about that time we had together, do you remember that *time* we had together? I do. I remember that time."

At last, Pete looks at her, and his face is full of misery. "Yeah, I remember," he says. "I think I got to second base." Now he smiles the smallest smile. "You were a cute girl."

"Well," she says, "we're a lot older now, aren't we? I mean, more mature and all. More *experienced.* But we're still kind of cute, aren't we?"

"Dorothy," Pete says. "Dorothy, Dorothy, Dorothy Shauman. Would you like me to bang your britches off? Is that it?"

And Dorothy giggles and says, "Yes, please."

Mary Alice squeezes her eyes shut and rests her head against Ben's shoulder. *Ah, Pete,* she's thinking.

The song ends and there is the sound of applause, and then the faint sounds of . . . *cheering?* Yes. In the corner of the ballroom, Judy and Linda are doing a cheer.

"I gotta see this," Pete says. "I always loved the cheerleaders." Mary Alice and Ben, Dorothy and Pete, they all move to where people have gathered around the two women.

Dorothy stands watching Pete smile at them, and then suddenly she's doing the cheer, too, her heels off, her dress held up to miniskirt level. Judy and Linda were cheerleaders, and Dorothy was always trying out, but she never made it. The truth is, she made a fool of herself every time she auditioned; she was no athlete, but she just kept trying. Now, she makes the moves as best she can, and along with her old friends chants the words to the Tony the Tiger cheer:

WE'VE got the boys on (clap!)
OUR team
They're grrrrreat! (clap clap!)
WE'VE got the spirit that
A great TEAM *needs, it's*
Grrrrreat! (clap clap!)

At the end of the cheer, the women leap into the air for a stag jump, but Dorothy slips and falls. Her friends rush over to her, and she says, "I'm fine, I'm fine," and looks anxiously into the crowd for Pete, who is no longer there. Mary Alice didn't see him go, but he is definitely not there.

Dorothy scrambles to her feet, yanks her dress down, and puts her heels back on. "Pete?" she calls. *"PETE?"*

A woman's voice calls back, "He's *gone,* Dorothy," with a

distinct note of satisfaction. Mary Alice turns to see who it was: Nora. And Dorothy bursts into tears.

Mary Alice turns to Ben and he shrugs, then says, "Pretty good Sturm und Drang, huh?" .

She smiles, shakes her head.

"You headed out?" Ben asks.

"I think so." She walks over to the table to retrieve her purse, and Ben goes with her.

"A bunch of us are going to the lobby bar for a nightcap," he says. "You want to come?"

"No, thanks," she says. "I'll be back for the breakfast, though."

"I'll see you then," Ben says and adds, "Did I tell you this? You look lovely, Mary Alice." She looks down at her dress, her shoes, this outfit she assembled with such care, and thanks him.

Mary Alice makes her way to the bathroom. She'll pee, then head on home. She thinks she has some leftover pizza in the refrigerator; she'll eat that. She's hungry, she realizes.

When she walks into the ladies' room, Mary Alice is met with a great cloud of smoke. Sitting on the floor, leaning against the wall, are Dorothy, Judy, and Linda. Dorothy is weeping into her hands while her friends puff on cigarettes and attempt to console her.

"Mary Alice!" both Judy and Linda say when they see her. She suspects she's a welcome diversion.

"Hey," she says, and she considers for a moment backing out of the room and using a bathroom elsewhere, or even waiting until she gets home.

But, "Sit down!" Judy says with an outsize, drunken generosity, mixed, Mary Alice suspects, with a kind of curiosity. Well, she's curious about them, too. Who are they now? For that matter, who were they then?

And so—why not? Mary Alice always did want to hang out in the bathroom with the popular girls, and even if these three

weren't *Candy Sullivan* popular, they'd held their own. She sits on the floor next to Judy.

"Cigarette?" Linda says, taking her pack out of her purse, and Mary Alice starts to decline—she's never smoked—but then she accepts a Marlboro, and Judy lights it for her.

She coughs immediately, and they all laugh, except for Dorothy, who continues to hold her face in her hands.

Judy rolls her eyes. "Hey, Dorothy," she says. "Look who's here! Mary Alice Mayhew!"

Nothing.

"Hi there, Dorothy," Mary Alice says. "How are you?"

And then, oh, terrible, she and Linda and Judy start laughing.

Now they hear Dorothy's muffled voice saying, "It's *not funny*!"

"Well, it *kind* of is," Linda says, in a tentative voice. "It's a *little* funny. If you could see that it's funny, then you wouldn't feel so bad." To Mary Alice, she says, "Take a smaller puff. And then hold it in your lungs just for a second. You have to get used to it. It burns a lot, at first."

Mary Alice tries again, successfully this time, although, good grief, she has no idea why people would want to go through this kind of thing. Still, "Can you teach me to French-inhale?" she asks, and Judy and Linda say together, "Absolutely!"

Dorothy takes her hands off her face, revealing scattered pink patches. "Fine. Don't pay any attention to me."

There is a lengthy silence, and then Linda says, "Well, yes, we are paying attention to you, Dorothy. We're giving you space. We're being respectful."

"Yeah," Judy says.

"If you're ready to talk, we're ready to listen," Mary Alice says.

"Oh, sure, Mary Alice *Mayhew*," Dorothy says. "My lifelong confidante." Then, "Oh, I'm *sorry*." She gives Mary Alice a quick once-over. "Huh! You look *nice*."

"Thank you." Mary Alice notices a false eyelash hanging perpendicular to Dorothy's eye, but now is probably not the time to tell her.

Dorothy reaches over and takes a cigarette from Linda's pack. "I gave these up years ago," she says. Judy lights the thing, and Dorothy takes in a deep drag and exhales slowly. "I might take it up again, though. Nothing else to do. Because I give up. I do. I just give up. I guess I'll never spend time with a man again. That's all over for me. I am D-U-N done."

"Hey, remember how we used to meet every day after math class and smoke in the bathroom just like this?" Judy says. "Remember that one time I told you guys I had a dream about a gigantic slide rule that Mr. Schultz was making me walk up and down? And then Miss Falk came in and busted us for smoking but she didn't turn us in to the principal because she was always trying to be our friend?"

"Well, of course I remember," Dorothy says. "I'm not senile. Yet." She honks her nose into some toilet tissue she has wadded in her hand.

"*Dorothy*," Linda says. "*Stop* it, now. You'll have another chance at breakfast. You'll see him then. And his wife won't be there. I saw her when everyone was leaving and she said she definitely wasn't coming tomorrow."

"Big deal," Dorothy says. "It won't matter. I made a fool of myself tonight. He was going to make *love* to me, he asked if I would like it if he made *love* to me and I said *yes* and then I had to try to do a *cheer*. A *cheer*! What was I *thinking*? Well, I know what I was thinking. I was thinking he'd think I was cute, like the old days, but all I did was pull up my dress too high and I'll bet he saw I was wearing Spanx and you know I have that one varicosity behind my knee, and *then* I had to go and fall *down*. God! It won't help if Nora's not at the breakfast. *Nothing* will help. He doesn't care about me. He never did! And I know why. It's be-

cause I'm a terrible person. I *am*! Even if I don't *want* to be, I just *am*!

"You know what I discovered tonight? Everyone is so much nicer than I thought. And it makes me so mad! Because I never knew that, I was always so poised to defend myself. And now it's too late. I was so mean and awful all the time, and now it is too late, the cows have come home to roost. I'll die a bitter old woman, alone. I'll be found weeks after the fact!"

"Yeah," Linda says. "And probably your stinky old corpse will be in a very unflattering position, too. They'll photograph you like that. They'll have to, for the police files."

"Wait," Judy says. "The *cows* have come home to roost?"

"You know what I mean," Dorothy says. She sniffs, wipes at her eyes. She's laughing a little, in spite of herself.

"Gosh," Linda says. "When you were fifteen and crying in the bathroom over some guy, did you ever think you'd be sixty years old and crying in the bathroom over some guy?"

"I'm not sixty yet!" Dorothy says.

"Oh, just say you are," Linda says. "I say I'm sixty-five because I love to hear people say how young I look."

"I do that, too!" Judy says.

"I know. I told you to."

"Oh yeah."

"My daughter hates me," Dorothy says.

"Oh, for Christ's sake," Judy says. "Will you *stop*? No woman's daughter likes her. But factoring that in, I'd say your daughter loves you very much."

"I'll bet my grandchildren will hate me, too. I'm not fun. I'm nervous and too critical. I have a bad way about me. If Hilly has kids, she'll never let me babysit."

Linda says, "I saw this show on TV? A dog that was missing for nine years reappeared! He was real cute. One of those shaggy guys. He just showed up, nine years later!"

"*And?*" Dorothy says.

"It just goes to show you," Linda says. "It's never too late. Except for dead people. Oh, wasn't it sad to see Patsy Sussman on the dead table? To die in a motorcycle accident right after graduation! All that studying for finals, and for what? She must have worked so hard, she always had a hard time keeping her grade point average up."

There is a long silence, and then Judy says, "Didn't she sort of have buck teeth?"

"What does that have to do with anything?" Dorothy snaps.

Judy shrugs. Then, quietly, she says, "I don't know."

"It's too late for the dead people *and* me," Dorothy says.

"Oh, that's an awful thing to say," Judy says.

"Why?" Dorothy says. "It's true. You know what I have in my life? Nothing."

"Dorothy?" Mary Alice says.

"What."

"Why would you insult your friends this way?"

"*What?*"

"I'm wondering why you would say you have nothing in your life, when your friends of so many years are sitting right beside you. I think it's insulting to them. Not that it's any of my business, really."

"Oh, it's your business," Judy says quickly. And to Dorothy, Judy says, "She's right. In a way, you're telling us we're losers."

"I am not!"

"Listen, Dorothy," Linda says. "We love you. All through high school, and all these years later, we *love* you."

"Though it wouldn't hurt for you to get some therapy," Judy says, and Linda says, "Judy!"

"What?" Judy says. "Let's just be honest here. You and I have talked about how she could use therapy. In a *loving way,* Dorothy! We want you to be happy, that's all."

"Oh, who's happy," Dorothy says.

A moment, and then Mary Alice raises her hand.

Dorothy looks at her. "Really?"

Mary Alice nods solemnly.

"Huh," Dorothy says.

Another woman comes into the bathroom, no one from the reunion. She wrinkles her nose, waves at the air, and says, "You are *not* supposed to *smoke* in here."

Mary Alice blows out a stream of smoke toward her and says, "Really?"

"Disgusting!" the woman says and exits the little room.

"We'll get you your black leather jacket and motorcycle boots in the morning," Linda says, and Mary Alice says, "Thank you. Please make sure there are zippers *everywhere*." And then, looking at her watch, "It already *is* morning."

"Let's go to sleep, now," Judy says, as though they are at a slumber party.

The women struggle to get up off the floor, and Mary Alice, who is first to stand, offers a hand to Dorothy.

"Thanks," Dorothy says. And then, "Mary Alice? Mary Alice Mayhew. Is it too late to say I'm sorry for the way I treated you in high school?"

"I never think it's too late for anything," Mary Alice says. "I have an appointment to try skydiving next week."

Dorothy straightens the shoulders of her dress, brushes off the back. She smiles, and Mary Alice sees in it the pretty, open-faced girl she used to be. "See you tomorrow," Dorothy says. "Want us to save you a seat at our table?"

"Sure. Thanks."

On the drive home, Mary Alice sings along with the radio. She hopes she'll be with Lester tomorrow, but if not, she's got friends who will keep a seat for her, no matter how late she gets there.

TWENTY

"WELL, HOW MUCH IS *THIS* GOING TO COST ME?" ALAN Heck asks Lester. His hands are on his hips and he's glowering at his dog, a small black collie mix named Lady with a white blaze down her nose. She'd be a good-looking dog if she were well cared for. As it is, her ribs protrude, her coat is dull and full of burrs, and Lester can tell from the smell that her right ear is probably infected.

"I'm not sure yet," Lester says, "I'll have to see how deep the cut is."

Alan shakes his head. "Fell right down the basement steps. How stupid is that?"

Lester doubts the dog did any such thing. One of his clients, Anna Pearson, lives next door to Alan Heck, and she told Lester he constantly abuses the dog.

"Aw, hell, put the damn thing to sleep," Alan says. "I suppose you're going to charge me for that, too."

Lester is tempted to punch the guy. He was up all night with Samson, and he is in no mood to deal with Alan Heck. He always

dreads seeing Alan, but this time is worse than usual. "I'll tell you what," he says. "You want to put her down? Why not just let us find her another home? If you do that, I'll treat her for free."

"Really?" Alan says. And then he makes some phony effort to show concern. "Hate to do it, of course," he says, furrowing his brow, shoving his hands in his pockets, and hunching his shoulders. "My wife loved the thing. But I just can't . . . I just can't keep it if it's going to keep costing me like this. There's always something, shots I'm supposed to get it and whatnot. And my business isn't what it used to be."

"I understand," Lester says. "A man's got to do what a man's got to do." He gives Alan a form to sign, releasing his rights to the dog.

Alan signs it without reading it, then hikes his pants up. "Okay! Well, so, that's that." He reaches down to pat the dog, and she lowers her head, her eyes rolled up in fear. "You be good," he tells her, and Lester nearly laughs out loud.

"See you around town, Doc."

"Right." After Alan leaves, Lester stands gently stroking the top of Lady's head and listening to Alan trying to joke with Jeanine, who ignores him, then tells him pointedly that she's busy.

"Whoa," Alan says. "That time of the month?"

Lester is gently lifting the dog off the table to bring her into the back when Jeanine bursts into the examining room. "If you ever let that man bring another animal in here, I'm going to have you put away."

"If I ever let that man bring another animal in here, I'll put myself away."

"Why did he even keep her after Rose died?" Jeanine asks, and when she looks at Lady, her eyes fill. "Oh, look at her. You can see every rib."

"Let's get her settled. I'm going to fix her up and then I'm going to find her a home that deserves her."

"He gave her up?" Jeanine says.

"Yeah."

"The bastard. I'll take her."

"You have four dogs, already."

"You only have one," she says hopefully, and Lester says,

"Jeanine."

It is Lester's policy, his desire, his need, to have only one dog at a time. He likes it that way. Jeanine knows this, but she regularly argues that dogs like it better when there is more than one. Together, they clean Lady up, put drops in her ears, temporarily dress an abrasion that runs long across her side, give her a dose of antibiotics, and then put her in a roomy cage with a soft blanket. "She'll probably need a few stitches," Lester says, "I can do it under local. You can help me. I doubt she'll put up much resistance. But let's feed her—and us—first." They give the dog food and water, and she immediately empties both dishes. Jeanine refills the water dish, and then she and Lester go into the staff break room for a bagel. Jeanine reaches out to touch Lester's arm. "You okay?"

"Yeah."

After they eat, Jeanine helps him put in the sutures Lady needs—the vet tech they most recently hired has called in sick. "She calls in sick way too often," Jeanine says. "You're going to have to fire her and find someone else."

Lester secures the dressing onto the dog's side. "I know. You do it."

"We'll have to find someone else, first," Jeanine says, and again Lester says, "I know. You do it."

As Lester predicted, the dog resists not at all. Nor does she attempt to go after her dressing, so they don't have to put a cone around her neck. Instead, they simply put her back in the cage, and she lies down and curls in a little ball in the far back corner. Lester stands watching her. At this point in his career, he's be-

come pretty good at shielding his heart, but this dog is getting to him. He remembers Alan's wife bringing her in as a puppy, how full of hope Rose had seemed, probably at the prospect of having something that would love her back.

"You must be exhausted," Jeanine tells Lester.

"You must be, too."

"I'm okay," she says. "I'll tell you, though—I can't believe Samson made it. That dog thinks he's a cat—nine lives."

Samson had been recovering well from his infection when he suffered another, unrelated problem: gastric volvulus, a sudden twisting of his stomach, rare and usually fatal. Luckily, Jeanine recognized what it was and called Lester immediately, and the dog went back into surgery. Now he is sleeping soundly, his "parents" beside him in lounge-type lawn chairs. They will not leave him until he comes home. Betty brought a picnic basket and a pile of library books, and Stan brought his transistor radio.

"All right, I'm going to bed," Lester tells Jeanine. "Call me if you need anything."

"You aren't going back to the reunion? Don't you have a breakfast?"

"Too much going on here," he says.

"I just called John Benning," Jeanine says. "He said he'd cover for you all day today. He's on the way. And he said he's glad to do it—you bailed him out lots of times."

"True," Lester says. "And he still owes me fifteen dollars from our last poker game."

"So, how *was* the reunion?" Jeanine says. "Did you have fun?"

"I did."

"Did you . . . meet anyone?"

"Sort of."

Jeanine is all business now. "Okay, you get back there. You go to that breakfast."

"Yeah, I don't know." He looks at his watch. "I'll be over pretty soon."

"Oh, no you don't," Jeanine says. "I know you. If you don't go back, you'll never see whoever you met again. That always happens whenever you meet anyone you're interested in. You just talk yourself right out of it. You let the whole thing drop!"

"Well, I don't know if there's a whole thing to drop, really. I met someone I kind of like, but I don't know if—"

"And that's exactly why you're going back."

"Jeanine, I'm too tired to drive. Really." Pete Decker, she was with.

"I'll call you a cab."

"I don't need a cab."

"Go and change. And *shave.*"

Lester goes into the back room once more to check on Lady. The dressing is fine, and the dog is lying still in her cage. She'll be here all day, with the exception of the times she'll be let out to pee. Lester pokes his fingers through the cage and gently scratches behind Lady's ear, and the dog looks up at him. Ah, what the hell. It's a nice day, not too hot, not too cold. "Want to go for a car ride?" he asks, and one ear moves. Lester opens the cage door and strokes the dog's back. "Want to come with me?" Her tail wags. He lifts her out of the cage and carries her into the waiting room. Jeanine is at the door, on her way out.

"Where are you going?" she says.

"You told me to shave."

Jeanine points to the dog, and Lester says, "She's coming."

"In a cab? Town Taxi is on the way."

"Jeanine, not for nothing did I go through training. I can go three days without sleep if I need to. Cancel the cab. I'm going to sleep for half an hour. Then I'm going to drink some more coffee. Then I'm going to the breakfast. Then I'm coming home to sleep for the rest of the day."

"All right, good," Jeanine says, and reaches out to pet Lady.

"I *could* have five dogs," she says wistfully, and Lester says, "Too late. We've bonded."

In fact, Lester sleeps for over an hour, and when he wakes up he sees that he has just enough time to get to the breakfast before it ends at noon. He leaves Lady sleeping on his bed while he quickly gets ready, then carries her downstairs to pee. He lays her on Mason's blanket in the front seat of the truck and lets Mason ride in the back, strapped into the harness he hates but will tolerate for the feel of the open air.

When Lester pulls into the parking lot, he narrowly misses hitting another car on its way out. Maybe he'd better drink a lot more coffee at the breakfast; he's more tired than he thought.

In the conference room where the breakfast is being held, Lester sees no sign of Mary Alice. She could be in the bathroom, he supposes, but he can't help feeling disappointed. What if he missed her altogether? He could call her, he knows now where she lives, but what he wanted to do at this breakfast was assure himself of a mutual attraction before he . . . Well, before he did anything.

He moves to the buffet table, which looks like it has been set upon by a pack of wolves. Bits of scrambled eggs are spilled onto the ripped paper tablecloth, none of the remaining pancakes are whole, and the syrup container sits in a sticky pool, with what must be a very happy fly directly in the middle of it. There's still a fair amount of bacon, and Lester lays a few strips on a plate, along with two slices of curled-up, overbuttered wheat toast. He has to tip the coffee urn to get out the last of what's there, and thinks the brand might most aptly be called Mississippi Mud.

"Not much good left here," he hears a voice say, and turns around to see Mike Massey, one of the star jocks in the old days, and someone who in the old days would never have deigned to speak to Lester.

"Nah, I got here too late, I guess," Lester says, and then no-

tices Mike's outfit: a golf shirt with stains, a cheap pair of khaki pants. It is very close to what Pete Decker wore last night and in fact is still wearing—there he is, sitting at a table with Candy Sullivan. Mary Alice is still nowhere in sight.

Mike notices Lester looking over at Pete and says, "Can you believe what Decker's wearing? There's five or six of us got together in a little show of solidarity. Went out to Kmart this morning and got ourselves some shitty-looking golf outfits." He shrugs. "Turned it into a goof, you know, so he wouldn't feel so bad." Mike shakes his head. "Poor guy's a wreck."

Lester nods. "Yeah, it's too bad." Pete doesn't look like a wreck now, however, sitting there with Candy, smiling. Has he moved on from Mary Alice, then? Is that why she's not here?

Lester gives the buffet table one more glance and sees a cheese Danish in decent shape in a metal bin at the end of the table. He points to it, saying to Mike, "I think I'll grab that pastry. Unless you want it."

Mike pats his stomach. "Nah, I got diabetes. Doc kept telling me to watch my weight, and I thought, *Yeah, yeah, mañana, you know?* And then damned if I didn't get it, just like he said I would. I can't have *any* fun anymore. My doctor is a sadist, man. He likes to tell me all the things I'm going to get. He was ecstatic when I had to go on high blood pressure pills. Hey, you're a doc, aren't you? What do those pharmaceutical companies do, cut you in or what?"

"I'm a veterinarian," Lester says.

"So's Don Summers. But he didn't come. Pulled out at the last minute—death in the family."

"That's too bad. Yeah, I was kind of looking forward to talking to him. That's one of the reasons I came."

A shaft of light suddenly broadens and fills the room with light, and Lester sees Candy shade her eyes against it, then stand and put on sunglasses. She's apparently leaving.

"Nice talking to you," Lester tells Mike.

"Well, hold on—*do* you get cut in with the pharmaceutical people? I've always wondered. I mean, for animal pills and shit?"

Lester looks at Mike and sighs. "No. Okay?"

Mike steps back, offended. "Yeah, okay, *Sorry.*"

Lester heads over to Candy and reaches her just as she's about to walk out the door. "Hey," he says. "Taking off?"

"Oh, Lester! There you are!"

"I got here late. Had an emergency. I've got two dogs with me."

"Where are they?"

"In my truck. I can't leave them for long, I think I'll take off now, too."

"Mary Alice just left a few minutes ago," Candy said. "We had a nice talk. I can see why you like her, Lester. I'm crazy about her. I asked her to come and visit me in Boston."

"Uh-huh, good for you." He keeps his face carefully neutral. He doesn't ask any questions about Mary Alice. He doesn't know, suddenly, if he *wants* to ask anything about her. On the drive over, with Lady curled up beside him and occasionally wagging her tail, apropos of nothing (though it *was* possible), he guessed, that she sensed she was now free from Alan Heck), Lester was thinking about what he'd say to Mary Alice when he saw her. Invite her to get together for dinner? Take in a show, a concert in the city? Oh, it was wearying, really, to even contemplate. He honestly didn't have time for a relationship, nor did he have the *need* for one, Jeanine's thoughts to the contrary notwithstanding. Good old Jeanine. He wants to give her another raise, but she says he has to wait at least six months because he just gave her a raise. She said, "Pretty soon, I'm going to be making more than you!" And he said, "You should!" Why not? His expenses are minuscule compared to

hers. He doesn't need much money. He doesn't *want* much
money. He was lucky to find a wife who felt that same way.

When he and his wife had just started dating, they'd been
talking one day about money because Kathleen's brother's wife
had just left him, saying he was never going to amount to anything, i.e., not provide her with the material things to which she
felt entitled. And Lester asked Kathleen how much a man would
need to have so that a woman like her would feel secure. They
were sitting in a booth at Sunday's, eating chicken-fried steak
with milk gravy and mashed potatoes and collard greens, which
they did on the first of the month, every month, and which he
continues to do. Kathleen had just untucked her napkin from
around her neck when he asked her this, saying she couldn't eat
one more bite, not one more, *nothing*, unless maybe he'd like to
share some lemon meringue pie. But when he asked her that
question about income, she settled back in the booth and looked
over at him, her arms crossed, her expression grave. And he
silently cursed himself, thinking he'd blown it now, he'd asked
too soon, and besides, the look on her face made him think she
was going to quote an amount that ultimately would be beyond
him. She was a direct and unfailingly honest person. She took in
a breath and pooched out her lips. "Hmmm. How much would
you need to have. Well, let's see." She searched the ceiling, as
though using it for her calculations. Then she said, "Don't you
have a bunch of lilacs on the hill behind your house?"

"I do," he said. "I have many lilacs. Acres. A small state, if
not a veritable *nation* of lilacs."

"Well, that's enough," she said. "That and this here chicken-
fried steak once a month."

He swallowed, then put his hands around his coffee cup and
gripped hard. "This is too soon, I know, but would you—"

"Yes," she said. "A *small* wedding. Amid the nation of lilacs."

Ah, who could come close to her? That's what Jeanine didn't understand. Besides, he was *busy.* He was perfectly content. He was a fifty-nine-year-old man who had grown at least a little set in his ways, and he didn't mind, he *liked* it. Why set himself up for a life of compromise—and make no mistake about it, a relationship was all about compromise—when what he really wanted now was something he'd solemnly declared to his mother as a seven-year-old: "I want to do whatever I want whenever I want to, forever." To which she'd responded, "Oh my. Good luck, honey."

Still, that pretty much *was* his life, now: he did whatever he wanted, whenever he wanted. His work was his passion: there wasn't a day he wasn't eager to get to the clinic. His free time was spent in ways he wanted to spend it, whether it was mountain climbing in Peru or bass fishing in Montana or sitting on the front porch with a glass of raspberry lemonade and doing nothing but watching the liftoff and descent of butterflies on his front yard bushes. The relationship he'd had with his wife was one that poets dream about, and he did not ever expect to have such a partnership, such a love, again. How much is one supposed to ask from life, anyway? He knows his own luck. He knows he's had more than his share.

When they reach his truck, Candy pets the dogs, especially Lady, especially after Lester tells Candy about the dog's circumstances. "But she's going to live with you now, right?" she says, and Lester says, "Yup. In *style.*"

Candy stands with her arms crossed, smiling at Lady. Then she sighs and says, "Well, I've got to go and get my own dog and then get a cab for the airport."

"Want a lift?" Lester asks. "I'd be glad to take you. Of course, you'd get dog hair all over your suit. Nice suit, by the way."

"I like dog hair," Candy says. "I'm tired of this suit. And I'd love a ride with you."

Lester walks the dogs while he waits for Candy to come back. After she does, he drives slowly, because he is enjoying her company.

When they arrive at the airport, Lester gets out of the truck to open Candy's door. He pulls a card from his wallet and gives it to her. "Let me know how you're doing, would you?"

She nods, and tears come to her eyes, but she is smiling. Her phone rings, and she ignores it. "I want to thank you," she says. "And I you."

She wheels her suitcase toward the terminal as he watches. Several other men watch, too. Candy Sullivan. He sighs.

He goes to the back of the truck and unhooks Mason from his harness so that he can move the dog into the front seat with Lady. After Mason hops in, he sees Lady and freezes. "It's going to be a little different around here," Lester tells the dog. "You might think at first that you won't like it, but you will."

TWENTY-ONE

"WELL, I TOLD YOU NOT TO GO," SARAH JANE, MARY Alice's sister, says. "Didn't I? I told you. All it did is make you sad. I absolutely *knew* that would happen!" She shakes her head. "Why would you possibly want to go back to be among people who were nothing but cruel to you? What good could possibly come of it?"

"I'm not sad!" Mary Alice tells her sister. "And a lot of good came from it! I don't know what you think you just heard, but what I *said* is that I had a really good time! Don't forget your purse when you go," she says, pointing to the little evening bag lying on the kitchen table.

"I *see* it. What, is this a hint? You want me to go now? Fine, I'll go."

"I don't want you to go, Sarah Jane, but as it happens, I have an appointment to get to."

"For what?"

"Just . . . a routine check. A Pap smear."

Sarah Jane narrows her eyes at her sister.

"It's true! I have an appointment in twenty minutes. Do you want to see the appointment card?" *Oh, please don't say yes.*

Sarah Jane puts the evening bag inside her larger purse.

"Well, call me later if you want. I hope you feel better."

"I'm fine!" Mary Alice watches her sister pull out of the driveway, scraping against the bushes as she always does, then attempting to straighten the car and scraping against them even more. She can see her sister's mouth moving, swearing, no doubt. And of course it is the bushes' fault, which translates to Mary Alice's fault.

She cleans up the lunch dishes and then goes up to her bed-room to lie down. It is Wednesday afternoon, chilly and gray, and she took off from work, a personal day. She never lies down in the middle of the day and so she admits at least to herself that perhaps her sister is a little bit right.

She puts her arms around David the pillow, closes her eyes, and reviews again the events of the reunion. She had enjoyed being around so many people, being so talkative for so long. She likes living alone, but the reunion sparked something inside her, brought forward a need she has long denied. Maybe she'll ask Marion to take English classes and she'll take Polish classes. Maybe that way they'll be able to advance their relationship to a more satisfying level of intimacy. Maybe she's ready for that. One needs, on occasion, to unpack one's heart, to share observations riskier than those about the weather.

She wishes things hadn't taken a nosedive with Lester. He saw her pulling out of the parking lot; he nearly crashed into her! He could have waved her over; they could have made some plans to get together. But he chose not to acknowledge her and instead drove on, intent, she supposed, on getting more time with Candy Sullivan. Clever of him to arrive just as everyone was leaving—that way, they could leave together. She wonders if they did leave together. Maybe she'll call Candy later and ask; she and Candy

had established a bit of a friendship that Mary Alice looks forward to deepening.

He drove a nice truck, Lester; it suited him. And had a glad-eyed dog in the back to boot. Mary Alice knows she shouldn't, but she envisions herself riding in that truck beside Lester, on the way to . . . oh, anywhere. A ball game, the Cincinnati Reds against the St. Louis Cardinals. A picnic in the fall, the leaves drifting down onto the plaid blanket, cocoa and marshmallows in a thermos. A driving trip to Texas, to see the tumbleweed. She knows she shouldn't do this, dip into such outlandish wishful thinking, but she does it anyway. She falls asleep holding David close up against her.

She is awakened by the phone ringing, and answers it like a teenage girl, hope in her throat. But it is not Lester. It is Marion, asking in his halting way if she would like to take a walk this evening. She turns onto her back and contemplates the ceiling. She thinks maybe she'll find a church that has Evensong. A surprise about her is that she has a lovely voice; let someone hear it.

"Marion?" she says. "I was thinking. Would you like to go into the city with me tonight? Would you like to drive to Cincinnati and have dinner there?"

A moment, and then he laughs and then "Ho! What would you think!"

She'll wear her reunion dress. It wouldn't be out of line. It might as well get used again, and even again.

She climbs out of bed and goes to look out the window.

"I'm not *sad*," she says, but look at how she presses her hand flat against the glass.

TWENTY-TWO

E INER LOOKS OUT THE WINDOW AT THE FINE MORNING, RE-
membering again the events of the reunion one week ago.
To think that he might not have gone! Why, it took years off him,
filled up his tank but good. When Rita comes up with his breakfast, he'll tell her to take the night off. He's going to invite Desiree
over for dinner. He'll order out Italian, and *he'll wait on her.*
She'll come, he knows she will, she gets a kick out of him. She's
told him that: *You old buzzard, you're a gas, do you know that?*
What a day! Not a cloud in the sky, the humidity lifted, the
birds singing. He knows he's developed a reputation for being a
cantankerous old man, but today his heart is light, and if he
could, he would stand on the rooftop and shout out glad tidings.
"Blessings on the world!" he would say. "Blessings to us all!"

No bodily aches and pains today, either, it's a miracle! He
breathes in deeply, and then, as he draws his head back in
through the window, he bangs it hard.

He cries out and puts his hand to the back of his head. He can
feel the goose egg starting to form already; it's going to be the size

of Toledo. Well, isn't that the way? Isn't that life? Right when you're on top of the world, something happens to take you down a notch. And vice versa, thank God.

He shuffles over the few steps to his chair and sits down. He presses again on the sore spot at the back of his head. He'll endure the pain a bit longer—enjoy it, even, in the odd way people do, before he calls down to Rita to bring him some ice.

He stares at his pill bottles. He supposes he should get busy on doling them out. He picks up the first bottle and suddenly feels a crushing sensation on the right side of his head, nowhere near the bump he just got. *Now what?* It feels like a terrible, terrible headache, and it keeps getting worse. "Wait," he whispers. "Wait a minute." He lets go of the pill bottle, pushes it away from himself, as though it were the cause of his pain. The pressure increases even more, and he opens his mouth to breathe. He leans back in the chair and regards the ceiling, notices for the first time a cobweb at one corner. He opens his mouth to call Rita, but cannot speak.

Desiree, he thinks. Then, in his mind's eye, he sees the yellow centers of the daisies he was just looking at, the ones that grow in his garden. His wife planted them there, she loved daisies, and he remembers her face now with a clarity he has not enjoyed for years.

His vision starts to fade, and then he is bombarded with memories: a dogfight in World War II, the ironed scent of his mother's apron, a bakery screen door, the flash of tadpoles in a stream, sleeping on the porch in summer, a painting he once dared to straighten on a museum wall, the fedora he wore for so many years. Now the pain seems to lessen, but he remains powerless to move, to speak. He blinks, struggles to stay alert, aware. *My name is Einer Olson. I live on . . .* What street does he live on? He must remember!

He counts in his mind to five; then, less ably, to ten. He tries

to recall one by one the people he saw at the reunion: *Think! Stay alive!* But it is unequivocally upon him, death; he knows it now, and suddenly he is not afraid. He relaxes; his hands loosen their grip on the arms of the chair, his face goes peaceful, and time seems to achieve a kind of elasticity that makes him feel he sees the future: someone over for Sunday dinner at his ex-wife's house and shaking the hand of her new husband. A woman moving the last of her things into her new house, a place full of light and flowers. A couple seated on a blanket in a park. A woman bending over her granddaughter and guiding her along, helping her learn to walk. And now, look: here are his tomatoes, they have ripened to perfection and they are sliced and laid out on a green platter and ready to be eaten, every one.

There is one more thing, he's got to do just one last thing, so important. He struggles to get up, then slumps to the side of the chair. Rita finds him there like that.

TWENTY-THREE

A T EIGHT-THIRTY ON A FRIDAY MORNING IN FEBRUARY, Candy Sullivan awakens in her condo and sees quarter-size flakes of snow drifting down. She moves to the window to look down at the Charles River, as she does every morning, to take comfort from its graceful progression forward. Today she has another checkup and she supposes it's natural for her to be nervous, yet there is a calmness at her center that makes her believe she will once again test negative.

"It happens, this kind of cure," Dr. Johnston told her. "It's rare, but it happens." And she knows it does; she knows she's not the only one. Still.

She'll shower and go to see her doctor, and then she'll meet with a group of women who have been diagnosed with ovarian cancer. She does this every Friday, goes to a small room at the hospital has provided and that she, with permission, had repainted. Rather than a bile-yellow color, it is now a soothing blue; and there is an oil painting on the wall of a field of lavender in late af-

ternoon sun—Candy decided it would be better here than in her bedroom. She sits in a circle of women holding Styrofoam cups of coffee, their purses on their laps, their coats over the backs of their chairs, everything that belongs to them kept close to them, because familiarity is comfort.

Usually, at first, the women are full of fear, or they display a false bravado. Sometimes they cry together; more often, they laugh. Candy's favorite story is one that a woman named Carolyn told: "So about an hour after I get home from being diagnosed, my best friend calls and says, 'Well, I am constipated as hell. I probably have cancer of the poop shoot, so I guess this is goodbye.' We used to joke around like that all the time. I take in a big breath and I look at the clock—I have no idea why, but I look at the clock, it says four forty-three—and I say, 'Ginny? I just found out I have ovarian cancer.' My mouth feels like I'm a puppet and someone else is making me talk, and I laugh. She says, 'That's not funny,' and I say, 'You're telling me?' She gets real quiet and then she says, 'For real?' and I say yes. And she bursts out crying and says all jerky, 'Boy, I guess that beats the hell out of c-c-constipation.'"

When a new person comes, Candy tells the story of how it was this disease that brought her to herself, that let her find the kind of peace and happiness she'd craved and despaired of ever finding. She says that the diagnosis let her recalculate the meaning of time and of relationships. Mostly, though, she listens. She understands the relief in being heard, the cure there is in that, at least.

After the group, she'll go to work at her part-time job at Winston Flowers; and then she'll join Don for dinner. She met Don Seaver a couple of months ago in the waiting room of Dr. Johnston's office. He's the exuberant Man Who Will Not Die, although he would be the first to admit he's getting closer, now. But, as he says, so is everyone else.

They enjoy each other, she and Don. She's so glad to be with someone so deeply appreciative of everything, such a cornball. He makes her laugh. He makes her cry, in the good way. They watch old movies together under his grandmother's quilt, they have long, searching conversations about everything from politics to the various meanings of the color red in art. They go to the Children's Museum to watch children; they go to flea markets and buy; they go to the Huntington Theatre to see plays or to the ballet or to the symphony and then to Rosie's bakery for dessert. Don's partner, Michael, died of AIDS many years ago, but Don loves him still, and so sometimes they go to Michael's grave and Candy sits a fair distance away on a bench while Don kneels at the headstone, his hand pressed against it.

Candy pulls her gloves on and steps out into the hall of her building. It's overly warm out there, as it always is, and she likes this. She likes almost everything, lately. The last time she talked to Mary Alice Mayhew, who has become a close friend, she remarked on her own optimism, and said it felt kind of silly admitting to it, almost embarrassing.

"It's not silly," Mary Alice said. "It feels great, doesn't it?"

And Candy said, "Yes. Yes, it does. It feels like I was wearing a big belt that was way too tight, and it has finally loosened. Loosened and fallen off! And I've looked down and said, 'Oh, I had a *belt* on.'" She laughed and said, "If *that* makes any sense."

And Mary Alice said, "Of course it does."

Candy asked how Lester was, and Mary Alice said, "Well, I moved in with him last week."

"Oh, my God," Candy said, and Mary Alice said, "I know."

"Oh, my God!" Candy said, and Mary Alice said, "I know."

"Will you come and visit soon?" Mary Alice asked, and Candy said, "Turn back the covers on the guest bed. I'll be there before you know it."

"Come for Valentine's Day," Mary Alice said. "And bring Don." Candy hesitated for just the briefest moment before she said okay.

It's cold outside, and a bit icy. Candy turns her collar up and walks slowly down the sidewalk. In every window she passes, there is so much to see.

Pete Decker hurries in the shower. He's late for dinner at his ex-wife's house. The whole family will be there, and it's been a while since he saw his children. He chooses a blue sweater to bring out his eyes, a nice pair of gray woolen slacks, loafers. He wouldn't be caught dead in galoshes. He applies some cologne Nora was always crazy about and races out the door.

When he arrives, he looks through the window and sees them all gathered at the dining room table: Nora, his sons and daughter, and Fred with his new wedding ring flashing like a semaphore. His chest starts to hurt in that familiar way and he reminds himself to do what his therapist, Suzanne Collins, always tells him to do: take a breath, then look to see if there isn't another side. And so he looks at the table and sees the place that's been left for him. She's right, there is always another way to look at things. She's good, Suzanne. Beautiful, too, a smoky brunette with legs from here to oh-my there. He told her that once, how beautiful she was, and she said, "Thank you. That's not what we're here for."

"Would you like it to be?" he asked, and she said nothing, only looked at him. He hates it when she doesn't say anything and just looks at him like that, and meanwhile the meter's running. She does that when he should know the answer, but couldn't she just *say* that?

Though he thinks this therapy finally might be working. Which it should be; he could have bought a small country for what he's paying her.

He rings the doorbell, rocks back and forth on his feet. And when Nora answers the door, he embraces her quickly, warmly, and then lets go.

"Who loves you?" Dorothy asks her granddaughter.

The toddler points to the exact center of Dorothy's chest.

"That's right!" Dorothy says. She lifts Jill from her crib and carries her down to the kitchen. "Grandma made you a sandwich," she says. "And after you eat it, guess who's coming over to play in the snow with us?"

"Ehwer!" the girl says, and Dorothy says quickly, "No, not Edward. Edward is all gone. Alll gone! Remember, Grandma said, BYE BYE, Edward! Remember? BYE BYE! Edward is all *gone!*"

The child leans around Dorothy to look at the sandwich cut into fours on her Elmo plate.

"It's *Ronnie* who's coming over," Dorothy says. "Remember Ronnie?"

A baleful glance.

"Well, you'll remember when you see him," Dorothy says. And then, more to herself than to her grandchild, she shrugs and says, almost happily, "Or not."

What a wise daughter Hilly is. She was absolutely right about getting out of your own way. As soon as Dorothy decided not to be in charge of getting a man into her life, didn't they start showing up like crazy! And at her age! She dated a man from her French conversation class. She dated one she met in the popcorn line at the movies and another one whom she met when she was having her car serviced, and he was, too. "Come here often?" he'd said, that was his pickup line. Oh, she'd liked that one, he was very witty and he had old-fashioned manners and knew things like how to help a woman out of her coat and back into it. But they sort of petered out after a couple of months. Nothing

seems to last for very long, but who cares? It's not really a man she's looking for. Turns out it never was. When Jill was born, Dorothy was the first one to hold her. Well, the first one after Hilly. Her daughter looked up at her and said, "Here, Mom, you want to hold her?" *That's* what she had been looking for, but she hadn't known it until that moment. She looked into that baby's eyes and made sure they had an understanding, and then she handed Jill to her grinning—and weeping—father.

"Diddle diddle dumpling!" Dorothy says to Jill, and her granddaughter slams down her sippy cup, says, "My son *John!*"

"Peas porridge hot!" Dorothy says, and Jill says, "My son *John!*"

Dorothy laughs and tucks one of Jill's golden curls behind her ear. She thinks of the afternoon hours before them. They'll read books. They'll rock baby dolls. They'll play grocery store. Also, Dorothy will offer Jill the new puzzle she bought for her the other day, she'll spread it out on the floor and remember *not to put it together herself.* Hilly has pointedly reminded Dorothy of this more than once. "Mom," she has said. "You have to let Jill do it. Let her make mistakes; let her get frustrated; that's how she'll learn." So Dorothy will do that. When she puts the puzzle pieces out, she'll remember to sit back and just watch, trusting that things will, in their own time and in their own way, come quite satisfactorily together.

ACKNOWLEDGMENTS

Many thanks to Erin Weiss at the Hartford Animal Clinic in Hartford, Wisconsin, who shared stories about animals and the practice of veterinary medicine with me, some of which were then fictionalized for use in this novel. Any mistakes are my own. Erin is a veterinarian par excellence, the one you really want when your pal is in trouble or just needs those pesky shots. If only she'd take my advice and serve as my doctor, too.

The usual gratitude is due to my longtime and beloved editor, Kate Medina, and to my agent, Suzanne Gluck, who is smart, upbeat, and really *fun*. Thanks also to the team at Random House, who take care of everything from cover design to copyediting to publicity to making sure I get a window seat on the airplane or a copy of the new Random House title I really need *right now*. I want to single out Avideh Bashirrad, Susan Brown, Gina Centrello, Sanyu Dillon, Barbara Fillon, Ashley Gratz-Collier, Kathleen McAuliffe, Beth Pearson, and Lindsey Schwoeri. And at

WME Entertainment: Claudia Ballard, Sarah Ceglarski, and Caroline Donofrio—I love you guys.

I spent a lot of time looking at high school yearbooks when I was writing this novel, and I want to offer a shout-out to Ed McGraw and Bill Cocos, who in their own ways kept trying to tell me that my high school wasn't so bad. They were right.

ABOUT THE AUTHOR

ELIZABETH BERG is the author of many bestselling novels, two collections of short stories, and two works of nonfiction. *Open House* was an Oprah's Book Club selection, *Durable Goods* and *Joy School* were selected as ALA Best Books of the Year, and *Talk Before Sleep* was short-listed for an Abby Award. She is a recipient of the New England Booksellers Award for her body of work. Her bestsellers include *Home Safe*, *The Year of Pleasures*, *The Day I Ate Whatever I Wanted*, and *Dream When You're Feeling Blue*. Berg has been honored by both the Boston Public Library and the Chicago Public Library and is a popular speaker at venues around the country. She lives in Chicago.